RESEARCH HANDBOOK ON JURISDICTION AND IMMUNITIES IN INTERNATIONAL LAW

RESEARCH HANDBOOKS IN INTERNATIONAL LAW

This highly original series offers a unique appraisal of the state-of-the-art of research and thinking in international law. Taking a thematic approach, each volume, edited by a prominent expert, covers a specific aspect of international law or examines the international legal dimension of a particular strand of the law. A wide range of sub-disciplines in the spheres of both public and private law are considered; from international environmental law to international criminal law, from international economic law to the law of international organisations, and from international commercial law to international human rights law. The *Research Handbooks* comprise carefully commissioned chapters from leading academics as well as those with an emerging reputation. Taking a genuinely international approach to the law, and addressing current and sometimes controversial legal issues, as well as affording a clear substantive analysis of the law, these *Handbooks* are designed to inform as well as to contribute to current debates.

Equally useful as reference tools or introductions to specific topics, issues and debates, the *Handbooks* will be used by academic researchers, post-graduate students, practicing lawyers and lawyers in policy circles.

Titles in this series include:

Research Handbook on International Law and Migration
Edited by Vincent Chetail and Céline Bauloz

Research Handbook on International Energy Law
Edited by Kim Talus

Research Handbook on International Law and Terrorism
Edited by Ben Saul

Research Handbook on the Law Treaties
Edited by Christian J. Tams, Antonios Tzanakopoulos and Andreas Zimmermann

Handbook of Space Law
Edited by Frans von der Dunk

Research Handbook on International Law and Cyberspace
Edited by Nicholas Tsagourias and Russell Buchan

Research Handbook on Transnational Labour Law
Edited by Adelle Blackett and Anne Trebilcock

Research Handbook on Jurisdiction and Immunities in International Law
Edited by Alexander Orakhelashvili

Research Handbook on Jurisdiction and Immunities in International Law

Edited by

Alexander Orakhelashvili

University of Birmingham, UK

RESEARCH HANDBOOKS IN INTERNATIONAL LAW

Edward Elgar PUBLISHING

Cheltenham, UK • Northampton, MA, USA

Published by
Edward Elgar Publishing Limited
The Lypiatts
15 Lansdown Road
Cheltenham
Glos GL50 2JA
UK

Edward Elgar Publishing, Inc.
William Pratt House
9 Dewey Court
Northampton
Massachusetts 01060
USA

A catalogue record for this book
is available from the British Library

Library of Congress Control Number: 2015943168

This book is available electronically in the **Elgar**online
Law subject collection
DOI 10.4337/9781783472185

MIX
Paper from
responsible sources
FSC® C013056

ISBN 978 1 78347 217 8 (cased)
ISBN 978 1 78347 218 5 (eBook)

Typeset by Columns Design XML Ltd, Reading
Printed and bound in Great Britain by TJ International Ltd, Padstow

Contents

Contributors

J. Craig Barker, Dean of the School of Law and Social Sciences, London South Bank University, England.

Robert Cryer, Professor of International and Criminal Law, University of Birmingham Law School, England.

Elizabeth Helen Franey, Legal Team Manager, International Jurisdiction, City of Westminster Magistrates' Court, London, England.

Richard Garnett, Professor of International Law, University of Melbourne, Australia.

François Larocque, Associate Professor, Faculty of Law, University of Ottawa, Canada.

Alexander Orakhelashvili, Lecturer, University of Birmingham, England.

Cedric Ryngaert, Professor of International Law, University of Utrecht, the Netherlands.

Aurel Sari, Senior Lecturer in International Law, University of Exeter, England; Director, Exeter Research Programme in International Law and Military Operations; Fellow, Allied Rapid Reaction Corps.

Yoshifumi Tanaka, Professor of the Law of the Sea, University of Copenhagen, Denmark.

Xiaodong Yang, Legal Officer, CTBTO Secretariat, Vienna, Austria.

Sienho Yee, Professor of International Law and Chief Expert at Wuhan University China Institute of Boundary and Ocean Studies and Institute of International Law, Wuhan, China; Member, Institut de droit international; Editor-in-Chief, *Chinese Journal of International Law*.

Preface

It is the basic truth that the assertion of, or the refusal to exercise state jurisdiction, for whatever reasons, is a matter of the domestic law of the state in the first place. However, the ultimate framework of the legality of national jurisdictions rests with the system of public international law which independently, and through the network of customary and conventional rules, suggests the criteria for the initial basis and ultimate legality of national jurisdictions, as well as determines the implications of the improper exercise of, or the improper failure to assert, the national jurisdiction. Much of the jurisdiction-related ground is a matter of private international law too, but public international law is the ultimate governing framework. Therefore, this *Research Handbook* presents the issues of state jurisdiction and state immunity from the overarching perspective of public international law in the first place, though also encompassing some issues of private international law and of national laws as they bear on those issues.

Several themes have dominated the discourse on state jurisdiction over the past two centuries. One issue is consular jurisdiction that European states exercised in non-European parts of the world on the basis of treaties concluded with non-European states and which extended, as Oppenheim described it, both to the cases arising as between expatriates, as well as to mixed cases involving native subjects (L. Oppenheim, *International Law* (2nd edn, 1912), vol. I, p. 498). Though advancing extra-territoriality, consular jurisdiction was essentially (in the background) the confirmation of the territorial supremacy of states and of the principle that the territorial jurisdiction of states is unlimited unless superseded, to the relevant extent, by a clear rule under conventional or customary international law. The early twentieth century saw the emphasis on the concurrence of state jurisdictions, culminating in the decision in the *Lotus* case rendered in 1927 by the Permanent Court of International Justice. The period after the Second World War saw the growth of inter-state agreements on the deployment of foreign armed forces on state territory, and on the allocation of jurisdictional competences accordingly. From the 1950s onwards, the assertion of extra-territorial jurisdiction by American courts in economic matters has generated jurisdictional controversies between the United States and the United

Kingdom, lasting over several decades. An even more extreme assertion of the American extra-territorial jurisdiction has taken place through the 1992 US Helms-Burton Act, as an instance of the use of extra-territorial jurisdiction as a tool for political pressure. And then, not to forget, there is a phenomenon of universal jurisdiction in civil and criminal proceedings, to be exercised over core international crimes and serious violations of human rights as well as of the laws of war.

In relation to immunities, the past century has witnessed the transition from the absolute to the restrictive doctrine of state immunity, and the growth of regulation of state immunity via national legislation as well as nascent international treaties. The growth of state involvement in commerce was then followed by the increasing potential of transnational human rights litigation which impacts the doctrine of immunity as it does in relation to the doctrine of jurisdiction. In relation to civil as well as criminal jurisdiction, the discussion of the immunity of states, as well as that of their individual officials, has acquired greater significance. Last but not least, more specialized areas such as the immunity of international organizations have been gaining in importance.

Each of these above developments has generated heavy discussions in the circles of scholars and of practitioners. There have been some great generalist analyses of jurisdiction and immunity by various prominent authors, such as Mann, Akehurst, Bowett, Jennings, Higgins and Crawford. But most of the time over the more recent decades (with very few exceptions such as the monograph by C. Ryngaert), the discussion of jurisdiction and immunities as a matter of public international law has been rather sectoral, restricted to a particular area such as antitrust or international crimes. What, however, is fascinating about state jurisdiction and state immunity is that, while they draw on important controversial aspects of the international legal system, they also relate to more fundamental categories of the international legal system, such as the doctrine of sovereignty, the doctrine of the sources of international law, and more broadly the relationship between legal reasoning and political ideologies. So far, there has been no comprehensive treatment of the matters of jurisdiction and immunities in a way that could benefit both the academic and practical elements of the legal profession.

Consequently, to remedy the gap created over the past few decades through the lack of comprehensive analysis of jurisdiction and immunity issues, this *Research Handbook* brings together a group of scholars who have distinguished themselves not only as recognized experts in the area of jurisdiction and immunities, but also through their scholarly and academic integrity, to provide impartial scholarly analysis of the underlying issues of jurisdiction and immunity, focusing on explaining and understanding the relevant legal issues as they are, without being affiliated to any agenda held in certain governmental or other quarters, or otherwise to any political ideology.

The overall result, we believe, is the most up-to-date, impartial and comprehensive work so far published examining these controversial issues. This *Research Handbook* is therefore a collective effort by a group of scholars with expertise in the areas of jurisdiction and immunities. What unites the individual contributions in the methodological sense is their reliance on the legal positivist method as the mainstream language for international legal discourse. At the same time, individual chapters allow the contributors also to offer their individual expertise to readers. Consequently, no attempt has been made to harmonize or unify the methods, opinions and approaches adopted by the various contributors. And this also reflects the idea behind such a *Research Handbook*, which is to provide a platform to assist in the conducting of research, rather than presenting a unified or harmonized perspective on the area of law dealt with here, which is especially inhospitable to preconceived attitudes and blanket solutions.

A. Orakhelashvili
Birmingham, 17 April 2015

1. State jurisdiction in international law: complexities of a basic concept

Alexander Orakhelashvili

1.1 MEANING OF STATE JURISDICTION

Jurisdiction is the principal tool of the assertion by states of their public and sovereign authority, possessing which distinguishes the state from the entities that operate under private law. Any exercise of public authority by the state, whether prosecuting a crime, expropriation of property, regulation of trade or taxation, or anything else, and whether lawful or unlawful under international law, involves the exercise of state jurisdiction. The exercise of state jurisdiction takes place in the context that rights may be acquired by individuals and other private entities outside the forum state's boundaries, which is a matter that could fall within the jurisdiction of more than one state. Similarly, the interest of individuals and corporations could also vary: some national legal systems could provide a better procedural standing, more effective remedies, or better access to the object of the relevant litigation, or otherwise confer advantages attractive to litigants and influence their choice as to in which legal system they should pursue litigation.

Under public international law, states are independent from, and unsubordinated to, each other. Absent special agreements, there is no centralized mechanism or arrangement for distributing jurisdictional entitlements among states, or determining their priority. Instead, jurisdictional relations operate, as it were, on an inter-state interactional plane. In the first place, there is an initial entitlement of, or claim by, the state to exercise jurisdiction over a particular person or matter. Then, there is an issue of whether that jurisdiction will be recognized as lawful, or otherwise accepted and accommodated, by other states, and accorded any effect within those states' territories, with or without inherently prejudicing the initial lawfulness of that exercise of jurisdiction. These factors are relevant not just in relation to controversial cases of the exercise of jurisdiction, but also in relation to most obvious and undisputed cases of state jurisdiction. This is so, if for no other reason, than because whichever kind of jurisdiction is asserted by the state, territorial or extra-territorial, the reach of that assertion is bound to be limited to the territory of that state.

There is no analytical or practical limit on the range of acts through which state jurisdiction can be introduced or asserted: any legislative, executive or judicial act of the state will in principle do. One way through which state jurisdiction can be asserted relates to national systems of private international law. Any national enactment of a 'conflict of law' rule in essence constitutes the relevant state's unilateral determination of the scope of its laws and, this way, inevitably constitutes an assertion of jurisdiction. According to Dicey, in this area an English court has to answer two questions, one regarding whether it has jurisdiction to determine the cases of the relevant kind; and, if the first question is answered in the affirmative, what law must be chosen to apply to those cases.[1]

International comity accounts for the development of some patterns in this area. On the one hand, comity could lead the forum state to recognize and apply foreign private laws, thereby in effect recognizing the competence of the foreign state to legislate with the extra-territorial effect. Curiously enough, the application of foreign laws in the conflict of law framework involves both the exercise of the territorial jurisdiction by the forum state, and the recognition by that state of (at times extra-territorial) jurisdiction of the state that authors the foreign rule in question.

On the other hand, as Savigny observed in the nineteenth century, no state can require the recognition of its laws beyond its own territory.[2] By and large English courts have taken the same approach. To illustrate, the UK House of Lords emphasized in *Government of India v Taylor* that foreign public and revenue laws would not be recognized or enforced in the English legal system.[3] What we see here is the obvious manifestation of a territorial jurisdiction of a state, perfectly lawful under international law on territoriality grounds, yet not given any effect by another state, without this inherently amounting to the United Kingdom taking the

---

[1] A.V. Dicey, *A Digest of the Law of England with Reference to the Conflict of Laws* (1896), pp. 1–2; see also A. Lowenfeld, 'The Limits of Jurisdiction to Prescribe' in A. Lowenfeld, *International Litigation and the Quest for Reasonableness* (1996), p. 15 at 16.

[2] Cited in M. Akehurst, 'The Doctrine of Jurisdiction in International Law' (1972–73) *BYIL* 219.

[3] *Government of India v Taylor* [1955] AC 451.

position that the particular assertion of foreign jurisdiction involving the operation of those public or revenue laws is unlawful under international law.

As a flipside, English courts will not enforce contracts that could lead to the violation of foreign law in the foreign state.[4] This is an implication of international comity.[5] The way comity works, and influences litigation outcomes, depends on what kind of prohibition has been enacted in the foreign jurisdiction and whether, then, English courts will consider obedience to that foreign prohibition to be dictated by comity.[6] The ultimate meaning and impact to be accorded to comity is thus dependent on its articulation and recognition in the forum state.

As Husserl suggests, 'Foreign law by itself is powerless to operate beyond the boundaries of its own territory – as is also the domestic law of the forum'.[7] Moreover, as Lorenzen has emphasized, the assertion of territoriality, for instance by subjecting contracts to the law of the place of their performance, essentially asserts that territorial law as extra-territorial.[8]

This demonstrates that jurisdiction is much more complex than its initial territorial basis from which state authority initially derives its existence, more interaction-focused and dynamic, more dependent on contexts premised on state choices and the reconciliation of those choices. 'Territoriality' as much as 'extra-territoriality' thus becomes a matter of degree and characterization. It is true, as Niboyet observes that, 'As territoriality involves the least sacrifice for each nation, it will be the

---

[4] *Regazzoni v KC Sethia (1944) Ltd* [1958] AC 301.

[5] See also *Driscoll* [1929] KB 470 at 510 (per Lawrence LJ): 'I am clearly of opinion that a partnership formed for the main purpose of deriving profit from the commission of a criminal offence in a foreign and friendly country is illegal, even although the parties have not succeeded in carrying out their enterprise, and no such criminal offence has in fact been committed … The ground upon which I rest my judgment that such a partnership is illegal is that its recognition by our Courts would furnish a just cause for complaint by the United States Government against our Government (of which the partners are subjects), and would be contrary to our obligation of international comity as now understood and recognized, and therefore would offend against our notions of public morality'.

[6] As was discussed in *Kleinwort* [1939] KB 678 at 688–9 (per Branson J).

[7] G. Husserl, 'Public Policy and *Ordre Public*' (1938) 25 *Virginia LR* 37 at 66.

[8] E.G. Lorenzen, 'Territoriality, Public Policy and the Conflict of Laws' (1924) 33 *Yale LJ* 736 at 743–4.

easiest principle on which to agree'.[9] Yet this is still subject to the principle that under public international law no state owes another state a duty to recognize the effect of its legislation – territorial or extra-territorial, public or private – in its own courts; and the approach which English courts have declared as embodied in *India v Taylor* is in principle (and subject to treaty obligations to the opposite effect) an option open to any state to elect, either through declining to recognize foreign law, or to use public policy or any comparable domestic doctrine to offset the relevance of that foreign law.

At the crossroads of public and private international law, we can identify the basic position that the laws of the state have no inherent force beyond that state's territory. A lawful exercise of territorial jurisdiction, premised on the exercise of core sovereign powers, could be denied the relevant transnational effect in another state, while jurisdiction that can in principle be contested could, at the end of the day, be given such effect via the route of private international law.

Therefore, the view that the private international law aspects of jurisdiction and applicable law are inherently determinative of the legality of state conduct as a matter of public international law could not be tenable. For any position taken as a matter of private international law is, in essence, a position unilaterally taken by the state. Such position cannot be regarded as self-judging as to its ultimate legality. To the contrary, public international law itself determines the ultimate legality and limit of private international law actions in the transnational field. Public international law is therefore a governing framework for private international law matters, not their mirror-image.

And in some cases, there may be public international law limits on the foreign state's jurisdiction and on the permissible ambit and reach of its laws. The forum state should treat it as subject to such limitation. This was made clear by the English Court of Appeal in *Al-Jedda*, where nationality laws of Iraq had to be applied in the United Kingdom subject to the requirements of international humanitarian law treaties binding on the United Kingdom.[10]

---

[9] J.-P. Niboyet, 'Territoriality and Universal Recognition of Rules of Conflict of Laws' (1942) 65 *Harvard LR* 582 at 586, 595.

[10] *Hilal Al-Jedda v Secretary of State for the Home Department* [2012] EWCA Civ 358, CA (Civ. Div.).

1.2 JURISDICTION IN THE CONTEXT OF PUBLIC INTERNATIONAL LAW

Some basic rules and standards of public international law as to the jurisdictional behaviour of states, especially in relation to the exercise of extra-territorial jurisdiction, raise issues as to those fundamental principles that govern the relations between states, especially the principle of non-intervention. For instance, Oppenheim, presumably illustrating a standard that could form the core of both comity and of international law on the matter, suggests that:

> Personal Supremacy [over nationals] does not give a boundless liberty of action … a State is prevented from requiring such acts from its citizens abroad as are forbidden to them by the Municipal Law of the land in which they reside, and from ordering them not to commit such acts as they are bound to commit according to the Municipal Law of the land in which they reside.[11]

But there also may be many matters that are not subject to strict prohibitions in the relevant foreign country – things and matters in relation to which the forum state may just be asserting its own jurisdiction extra-territorially. Does asserting such jurisdiction *per se* amount to the 'ordering' Oppenheim speaks about? To give an example, under the 1980 British Trading Interests Protection Act, enacted in response to the assertion by the US courts of extra-territorial jurisdiction in relation to economic matters, seen by the British government as excessive, could the United Kingdom be seen as wrongfully ordering its subjects and residents not to do certain things which they would be obliged to do in the United States, namely, comply with the US judicial decisions rendered within the US jurisdictional realm?

There might be a debate as to whether the 1980 Act was itself asserting the extra-territorial jurisdiction, and as to whether it did so rightfully as a reciprocal measure, and the outcome probably is that it was not an exercise of a far-reaching extra-territorial jurisdiction, instead complying with the territoriality and nationality jurisdiction requirements. Blocking orders were enforceable only in respect of the conduct within the UK

---

[11] L. Oppenheim, *International Law* (2nd edn, 1912), vol. I, p. 296; D. Bowett, 'Jurisdiction: Changing Pattern of Authority over Activities and Resources' (1982) 53 *BYIL* 1 at 7–8 also speaks of the law of the state of nationality requiring the individual to perform conduct illegal under the *loci delicti commissi*.

territory, or in relation to the conduct of UK citizens anywhere.[12] But even in that case, an example is furnished of one state obstructing the operation of another state's laws within the latter's realm, even without a far-reaching extra-territorial assertion of jurisdiction being expressly involved.

Section 6 of the 1980 Act included provisions on the recovery of 'non-compensatory' elements of US-awarded damages. They did not require proof of the UK jurisdiction over, or of the unlawfulness of the US jurisdiction in, the relevant matter. Instead they presumably infringed on the US jurisdiction exercised under its most traditional headings. The conclusion is advanced that the use of section 6 would have violated US sovereignty. But speaking more broadly, the economic sovereignty argument cuts both ways.[13] So also, presumably, would the non-intervention duty in relation to economic policies that the relevant state chooses to exercise be violated. Akehurst similarly observes that the state's economic policy may be expressed either in directing economic entities to do certain things or leaving them free to do as they think best. In either case, another state would break international law by requiring its nationals in the first state to act in a way thwarting that state's economic policies.[14] Again, such national freedom to direct private entities accordingly is available to any state.

Moreover, unless an obvious case is made as to the unlawfulness of the antecedent US extra-territorial jurisdiction to be exercised by US courts – which case would be difficult to make anyway – could it be a mere matter of appreciation as to whether the 1980 Act was trying to obstruct what was within the rights of US judicial authorities? Even in relation to 'ordering' British citizens to do or not to do certain things, that argument could (in conceptual and analytical terms) be sustainable, if the relevant British citizens had been placing themselves within the US jurisdiction through their presence and business.

And while in the absence of a treaty states are not obliged to enforce each other's economic policies or court judgments,[15] would it not be more analytically convenient to view this entire matter through the prism of parallel state autonomies, especially in terms of a state's own system of 'conflict of law', rather than through the prism that deals with the inherent lawfulness of foreign jurisdiction? Perhaps, then, the greatest

---

[12] A.V. Lowe, 'Blocking Extra-territorial Jurisdiction: The British Protection of Trading Interests Act, 1980' (1981) 75 *AJIL* 257 at 274–5.

[13] *Ibid.* 280.

[14] Akehurst, n. 2 above, 189.

[15] Lowe, n. 12 above, 276–7.

impact of the 1980 Act was to turn what was already open to the British government, as a matter of both international and domestic law, into a mandatory matter.

And then, as Sir Robert Jennings has illustrated, a more difficult question might arise 'in the much commoner situation where there is no direct collision between the local and the external laws, but where, nevertheless, the act which offended against the external law was perfectly lawful in the law of the place where it was done'. While in such cases the extra-territorial jurisdiction should not normally be exercised, Jennings suggests that this principle cannot operate as an absolute one. There may be cases where the state's laws are unreasonably lax in providing safeguards against the use of its territory for the fermenting of revolutionary disturbance among its neighbours. A neighbour state should be able to exercise extra-territorial jurisdiction in such cases.[16]

1.3 CONFLICTING JUSTIFICATIONS OF STATE JURISDICTION: SOVEREIGNTY-DRIVEN AND INTEREST-DRIVEN APPROACHES

According to authors such as Mann and Jennings, state jurisdiction is an extension of its sovereignty. Mann suggests that:

> International jurisdiction is an aspect or an ingredient or a consequence of sovereignty (or of territoriality or of the principle of non-intervention ... : laws extend so far as, but no further than the sovereignty of the State which puts them into force nor does any legislator normally intend to enact laws which apply to or cover persons, facts, events or conduct outside the limits of his State's sovereignty ... jurisdiction involves both the right to exercise it within the limits of the State's sovereignty and the duty to recognize the same right of other States.[17]

Jurisdiction involves 'a State's *right* to exercise certain of its powers ... like all attributes of sovereignty this liberty is subject to the overriding question of entitlement'.[18] Jurisdiction is generally associated with the

[16] R.Y. Jennings, 'Extra-territorial Jurisdiction and United States Antitrust Laws' (1957) 33 *BYIL* 146 at 151–2.

[17] F.A. Mann, 'The Doctrine of International Jurisdiction Revisited after Twenty Years' (1984) 186 *Recueil des Cours* 9 at 20.

[18] F.A. Mann, 'The Doctrine of Jurisdiction in International Law' (I-1964) 111 *RdC* 1 at 9 (emphasis in original); R. Jennings and A. Watts (eds), *Oppenheim's International Law* (9th edn, 1992), p. 456.

concept of sovereignty and a state's personal and territorial limits.[19] Furthermore, 'the connection between jurisdiction and sovereignty is, up to a point, obvious, inevitable and almost platitudinous, for to the extent of its sovereignty a State necessarily has jurisdiction'.[20] Bowett expresses a similar position.[21] All in all, 'the concept of territorial sovereignty has become a useful metaphor for a system of communication'.[22]

Under this approach, the principle of sovereignty could potentially be seen as a ready-made guide to enable us to assess the legality or propriety of any jurisdiction exercised by the state territorially or extra-territorially. The regulatory relevance of the concept of sovereignty is further suggested, for instance, 'by acknowledging that the right to control certain elements of economic activity is an essential component of sovereignty, it may be possible to identify a legal principle – "economic sovereignty" – to guide the resolution of jurisdictional disputes'.[23] Especially in the context of UK-US jurisdictional controversies regarding the exercise of extra-territorial jurisdiction, Lowe has also proposed to devise a more general theory of economic sovereignty that will support the superstructure of jurisdictional rules and relations.[24]

That there is an initial systemic link between the sovereignty of a state and its ability to exercise jurisdiction as cognisable by international law is undeniable. But how far the connection between these two elements could be taken, to assess the merit of specific exercises of jurisdiction, is less certain. To some extent, these matters constitute an issue of inter-state relations that is analytically antecedent to the issue of jurisdiction, which could reinforce as well as compromise various visions of territoriality. Thus, according to *Oppenheim*:

> a State can only require respect for its laws from such aliens as are permanently or transiently within its territory … No right for a State to extend its jurisdiction over acts of foreigners committed in foreign countries can be said to have grown up according to the Law of Nations.[25]

---

19 Mann, n. 18 1bove, 9; R.Y. Jennings, 'General Course of International Law' (II-1967) *RdC* 516.

20 Mann, n. 18 above, 22; Jennings and Watts, *Oppenheim*, n. 18 above, 457.

21 Bowett, n. 11 above, 1.

22 H.G. Maier, 'Jurisdictional Rules in Customary International Law' in K. Meessen (ed.), *Extraterritorial Jurisdiction in Theory and Practice* (London: Kluwer, 1996), p. 64 at 65.

23 A.V. Lowe, 'The Problems of Extraterritorial Jurisdiction: Economic Sovereignty and the Search for a Solution' (1985) 34 *ICLQ* 724.

24 Lowe, n. 12 above, 281–2.

25 Jennings and Watts, *Oppenheim*, n. 18 above, 204.

This thesis purports to impose a preconceived limit on the admissible exercise of state jurisdiction, and leaves the state of affairs uncertain in relation to the bulk of issues, such as subversive activities, or forging currency or other economic subversion.

Another extreme following of the territoriality cliché is proposed by Judge Moore, in his dissent in the *Lotus* case, to the effect that 'The principle of absolute and exclusive jurisdiction within the national territory applies to foreigners as well as to citizens or inhabitants of the country'.[26] The initial territorial sovereignty basis for the legitimation of jurisdiction thus becomes the ultimate limit of that jurisdiction. And it is bound to do so, if the initial legitimation advanced by Judge Moore is so strict and carved in stone. This makes clear that the sovereignty-driven view of jurisdiction does not account for the most obvious nationality-based instances of jurisdiction, and thus not only furnishes us with a preconceived cliché but also undermines the concurrence of various jurisdictions.

While it is true that any *exercise* of jurisdiction is an exercise of sovereign power, and that jurisdiction cannot be exercised without some public or sovereign powers being involved, this does not fully account for the *basis* on which the relevant exercise of jurisdiction rests, let alone for an ultimate limit, up to which the assertion or exercise of jurisdiction can be taken.

In fact, as Katzenbach observed, the sovereignty-centred approach does not sort these dilemmas, because the sovereign command is behind both the forum's rule and the foreign vested right.[27] The sovereignty of the state exercising jurisdiction in principle militates in favour of jurisdiction being taken as far as that state would like, while the other states' sovereignty would militate against the exercise of jurisdiction by the first state without those other states' consent.

For ascertaining the ambit of jurisdiction, territoriality is, at most, merely a conceptual starting-point, not the ultimate guide. For, as Brownlie has observed, states are entitled to enforce their interests on a basis other than territoriality, if a substantial connection is demonstrated with the relevant acts and events.[28]

---

26 *S/S Lotus (France v Turkey)* PCIJ Series A, No. 10, 28, Judge Moore, Dissenting Opinion, 69.

27 N. de B. Katzenbach, 'Conflicts on an Unruly Horse: Reciprocal Claims and Tolerances in Interstate and International Law' (1956) 65 *Yale LJ* 1087 at 1115.

28 I. Brownlie, *Principles of Public International Law* (OUP, 2008), p. 299.

It is right to say that the sovereign is territorially based and can enforce its laws only within its own boundaries (barring exceptions such as consular jurisdiction firmly consigned to textbooks of legal history). But it would be too presumptive to suggest that the state's entitlement to regulate the conduct of its nationals abroad, or even to prescribe rules as to its security and protection, is less sovereign than, say, prosecution of an act of theft perpetrated within that state's territorial boundaries.[29] Conversely, and while ordinarily states are supreme in their own territories, it is also the case that, as Akehurst observes, 'it is impossible to hold that *locus regit actum* is a mandatory rule', or that the application of *lex rei sitae* is a requirement under international law. Convenience and public international law requirements are not the same thing.[30]

The position that states can assert or exercise jurisdiction only in relation to matters and persons within their sovereign realm is unsustainable as a general theory of jurisdiction under public international law. It is not obvious at all that the boundary between national jurisdictions runs in the same place as the boundary between national sovereignties. It can be said with certainty that there can be no more than one sovereign over a particular territory. It could not be said with the similar certainty that any single person or matter should always and exclusively be subject to one single sovereign power. In other words, sovereignty does not do the same job in relation to the boundary between jurisdictions as it does in relation to the boundary between state territories. Territorial supremacy of the state does not determine any template for the ultimate reach of, or limitations on, that state's jurisdiction.

The confusion about the central importance of the territoriality approach is due to the failure to distinguish between the two things in the way in which they were distinguished by the Permanent Court of International Justice in the *Lotus* case. As the Court emphasized:

> the first and foremost restriction imposed by international law upon a State is that – failing the existence of a permissive rule to the contrary – it may not exercise its power in any form in the territory of another State. In this sense jurisdiction is certainly territorial; it cannot be exercised by a State outside its

---

[29] The magnitude of an interest is not always measured through its relation to territoriality. W.E. Hall points to the 'fact that maintenance of control over the men and ships of his mercantile marine is an object to a foreign sovereign of deeper importance than the assertion of jurisdiction on every occasion can be to the territorial authority', W.E. Hall, *A Treatise on Foreign Powers and Jurisdiction of the British Crown* (1894), p. 6; *ibid.* 12 reiterating the same to a broader extent.

[30] Akehurst, n. 2 above, 223–5.

> territory except by virtue of a permissive rule derived from international custom or from a convention.[31]

This has reinforced the understanding, expressed earlier on, that the exercise of the acts of sovereignty on the territory of another state is not the same as the exercise of jurisdiction in relation to acts that take place within that same state's territory.[32]

Once we conceptually and analytically separate the issue of jurisdiction as an entitlement to exercise sovereign authority in relation to a particular person or matter, from the issue of actually carrying out that sovereign authority within the territory of another state, the dilemma with the extra-territoriality of state jurisdiction becomes far less acute. Similarly, breaking out of the influence of the territoriality cliché, creating analytical difficulties for the operation of more than one extra-territorial category of jurisdiction, becomes far easier.

Conflicts of one state's jurisdiction with another state's territorial supremacy are no longer so inescapable either. For jurisdiction as such does not consist in *exercising authority* of the state abroad, nor *securing obedience* abroad to the same authority. It merely manifests the willingness of the state to exercise its own authority within its own sovereign realm, but in relation to certain acts and events that take place abroad.

Thus, territorial sovereignty is only one possible explanation for jurisdictional competence of states; it is also one that could lead to extreme results, as illustrated by the domestically developed perception that the UK Parliament, due to its sovereign legislative power, is subject to no territorial limits in terms of legislating and could take that power so far as to ban smoking in Paris or Vienna. The sovereignty-driven approach is therefore one that could provide some initial justification for the exercise of national jurisdiction, but also one that in practice requires a significant moderation, presumably by reference to validating and legitimating factors for jurisdiction other than the relevant state's sovereignty. Other reasons as to why the sovereignty-driven view is inconclusive, with its territoriality cliché, are that: (a) it does not provide enough allowance for the concurrence of competing jurisdictions; and (b) it does not give a clear and coherent view as to whether or why extra-territorial jurisdiction is permissible.

Another, complementary, explanation of state jurisdiction is the connection, link or nexus between the state and the relevant matter: the

---

[31] *Lotus*, n. 26 above, 19.

[32] E. Beckett, 'The Exercise of Criminal Jurisdiction over Foreigners' (1925) 6 *BYIL* 44.

connection that international law sees as manifesting the legitimate interest of the relevant state to be involved with the relevant matter. The initial question this prompts relates not to the abstract reach of the state's sovereignty, but to the legitimate connection of the state with the matter underlying that jurisdictional action. Consequently, the distinction between territorial and extra-territorial jurisdictions should not be seen as preconceived, nor do they require different degrees of proof.

To illustrate, as Akehurst observes, 'customary international law permits a State to levy taxes only if there is genuine connection between the State and the taxpayer',[33] not whenever the taxpayer is present or the relevant income is earned within the relevant state's domestic sovereign realm. Bowett concurs that, while the tax-related jurisdiction may appear to be based on the territorial principle, in reality it is not, because 'the obligations imposed often bear on the person whilst abroad'.[34]

With the interest-driven conception of state jurisdiction, the principal question is whether the state has what is ordinarily termed as a 'national interest' in the relevant matter (related to law-enforcement, economy or security); whether the assertion or non-assertion, exercise or non-exercise of a particular jurisdiction over the relevant person, event or affair makes that state better or worse off, causes benefit or burden, or brings advantage or disadvantage to it. These are issues only the state asserting jurisdiction could judge in the first place, as long as ultimate legal limits on the assertion of jurisdiction are observed.

Sir Eric Beckett admits that 'a state is the judge of what endangers its security or credit. It may choose to think that opium or gambling or atheistic literature is a menace to its safety, or speculation in its currency to its credit'.[35] Mann further specifies that 'the legally relevant point of contact will have to be defined as indicating the State which has a close, rather than the closest, connection with the facts, a genuine link, a sufficiently strong interest'.[36] And in this way jurisdiction comes across as a manifestation of public authority over something that can, one way or another, be said to be the business of the relevant state.

The legitimacy of state interest behind the assertion of state jurisdiction centres not on whether the state's law applies to the relevant matter in the first place, but whether international law allows, or eschews prohibiting, that state from making its own law applicable to that very same matter. In this sense, jurisdiction is not as free-standing an issue as

---

33 Akehurst, n. 2 above, 179.
34 Bowett, n. 11 above, 8–9.
35 Beckett, n. 32 above, 56.
36 Mann, n. 18 above, 46.

it sometimes appears to be. The assertion of jurisdiction may merely be a tool for giving effect to rights and entitlements the state may have, depending on the context. Sometimes a state cannot do X in the first place, but can do the same X as a reciprocity measure in response to a preceding internationally wrongful act. That could be anything ranging from the denial of justice in relation to the state's own nationals abroad to the expropriation of property. In that case, and within the limit allowed by international law to countermeasures,[37] jurisdiction could be asserted even if it otherwise would be wrongful under international law. Similarly, there are instances where the extra-territorial jurisdiction over particular foreign entities may be asserted in the context of economic boycott measures directed against the particular state.[38] In this case, it will in the first place be the boycott the legality of which has to be assessed, not jurisdiction. If the boycott is lawful, in the sense of not violating a particular rule of international law, so would the jurisdiction be that sustains it; if not, then not.

1.4 INITIAL ASSERTION AND ULTIMATE LEGALITY OF JURISDICTION

The initial decision to establish or exercise jurisdiction is always a matter of domestic law. The ultimate criteria as to whether that jurisdiction is established or exercised lawfully, are inevitably international. Thus, what is initially a question of national law then falls to be judged as a matter of international law, very much in the same way as the International Court of Justice suggested, in the *Nottebohm* case, in relation to the conferral of nationality to the individual.[39] An English court has similarly emphasized the need to ascertain 'To what extent can an English Court consistently with the general principles of international law that govern national jurisdictions exercise jurisdiction over the defendant domiciled abroad'.[40] This exercise could relate to the inherent characteristics in which jurisdiction is established or its particular applications, for instance, to distinguish between the assertion of jurisdiction through a statute and its application to particular facts.

[37] See Articles 49 to 54 drafted by the ILC, *Report of the International Law Commission on the Work of its Fifty-third Session* (2001), *Official Records of the General Assembly, Fifty-sixth Session, Supplement No. 10* (A/56/10).

[38] See, on this,1.10.3 below.

[39] *Nottebohm (Liechtenstein v Guatemala)* [1955] ICJ Reports 22.

[40] *Tallack v Tallack* [1927] P 211 at 219 (per Lord Merrivale).

While the assertion of jurisdiction may convey the legal conviction of the relevant state that it is lawful under international law, this is not as such determinative of its lawfulness. Similarly, abstention from the exercise of jurisdiction does not inherently amount to a legal conviction of the abstaining state that such jurisdiction is not available under international law, as the Permanent Court of International Justice has clarified in *Lotus*.[41] Nor are protests against the exercise of jurisdiction inevitably indications of illegality; protests assert illegality, they do not create or constitute it. A protesting state may be motivated by its own political and economic interests in the same way as the state asserting jurisdiction could be motivated. The legality of jurisdiction falls to be decided more on the basis of systemic considerations, such as the link or nexus factor, and the surrounding factor of concurrence.[42]

A state would, in principle, be liable for exercising its jurisdiction without the proper link to the matter, as well as for failing to establish or exercise jurisdiction as is, for instance, required by a treaty. As pointed out, 'an abuse or excess of jurisdiction over aliens is an infringement of the rights of their national states, against which, by virtue of the right which every state possesses to protect its citizens abroad, they are entitled to protest'.[43]

As Katzenbach suggests, in the area of the assertion and exercise of jurisdiction, 'each sovereign uses its power to effectuate what it conceives to be appropriate policy, and over a wide area there is agreement or, at least, tolerance'; the strongest case in this regard is presented by the ability to execute, and 'Legislative or judicial acts of state unaccompanied by an exercise of local power stand on a lesser footing in the international community'.[44] The factual effectiveness of the exercise of jurisdiction is no doubt an important practical consideration. Obviously, the development of the content of much of the private international law-related exercise of jurisdiction has been determined by the control national courts realize that they have over the relevant matter: in the sense of the domicile or presence of litigants, control of relevant assets. But the factual control of such matters is a merely factual precondition of jurisdiction, not a basis for entitlement to exercise it. As Akehurst clarifies, 'ineffectiveness is not the same as illegality'.[45]

---

41 *Lotus*, n. 26 above.
42 On which latter element see 1.5 below.
43 Beckett, n. 32 above, 45.
44 Katzenbach, n. 27 above, 1131–3.
45 Akehurst, n. 2 above, 181.

In the *Arrest Warrant* case (*DRC v Belgium*), President Guillaume asserted that the normal position in international law is that states can only exercise jurisdiction over a crime if, among other things, the accused is present in the territory of the state exercising jurisdiction.[46] However, the existence of universal jurisdiction as jurisdictional title is an issue qualitatively different from that of the exercise of universal jurisdiction *in absentia*. State jurisdiction never derives from a fact, but only from a legal ground. Nor can the scope of jurisdiction be reduced or trimmed down solely on the basis that a certain factual precondition is not there.

1.5 ESSENCE OF THE CONCURRENCE OF STATE JURISDICTIONS

The essence of concurrence is that the same person or matter could, at one time, be validly considered by international law as falling within the jurisdiction of more than one state. For instance, a war crimes suspect could be under the territoriality jurisdiction of one, nationality jurisdiction of another, and universality jurisdiction of all other states. Legally speaking, the exercise of each of these jurisdictions would be just as lawful as that of others; the other jurisdictions would not be abolished, but merely pre-empted.

Jurisdiction is not a thing, object or hard matter to be owned on any absolute or exclusive terms, but an entitlement which, in the decentralized legal system, is always relative to the parallel entitlements of other states. According to Jennings, various headings of jurisdiction – nationality, objective territoriality or security – are relative in that they represent different aspects of legitimate state interests.[47] The essence of the concurrence principle has been stated by the Permanent Court of Arbitration in the *Deserters of Casablanca* case, where the Tribunal stressed that 'the conflict of jurisdictions which has been mentioned cannot be decided by an absolute rule which would in a general manner accord the preference to either of the two concurrent jurisdictions'.[48] The doctrine of concurrence also dictates that no state will be able to exercise

---

[46] *Arrest Warrant (DRC v Belgium)* [2002] ICJ Reports 1, Separate Opinion, paras 16–17.

[47] Jennings, n 16. above 152.

[48] See *Deserters of Casablanca (France v Germany)*, Award, (1909) 3 AJIL 755; see, for discussion, Jennings and Watts, *Oppenheim*, n. 18 above, 502–4.

any exclusive jurisdiction over any matter unless so allocated under a particular conventional or customary rule of international law.[49]

The concurrence of jurisdictions is possible both under general international law and under particular treaty frameworks. Multilateral treaties can provide states with parallel jurisdiction under various headings. To illustrate, Article 5 of the Montreal Convention on Suppression of Unlawful Acts Against the Safety of Civil Aviation (1971), prescribes that states parties shall establish their jurisdiction over the relevant offences on various accounts of territoriality, nationality or presence within the state's territory.

The concurrence of two or more headings of jurisdiction exercisable in relation to the same person or subject matter means that, legally speaking, the basis of each of such jurisdictions is just as good as that of another. Akehurst takes an even more far-reaching view in favour of concurrence, in the sense that an individual may be subjected to jurisdiction under more than one national legal system, each of them requiring different kinds of conduct. But apart from extreme cases where one of those national laws are contrary to international law, which then would presumably be an issue of an internationally wrongful act relating to the content of legislation, rather than the legality of the jurisdictional heading through which that wrongful act is directed or perpetrated, Akehurst considers that there is no obvious way of resolving these conflicts of jurisdiction to legally prioritize one state's jurisdiction over that of another.[50] As Lowe has pointed out in relation to jurisdiction over antitrust matters, 'if jurisdiction were in truth concurrent, then neither State, as a matter of law, could be denied the right to exercise it in good faith'. There is also no obvious acceptance in international law of certain jurisdictions being more paramount than others when they are purported to be exercised in relation to the same matter.[51]

If, however, the British view in the 1960s was that, in antitrust matters, the jurisdiction of states being generally concurrent, the territorial jurisdiction claim should generally prevail to the exclusion of other

---

[49] Status of forces agreements regarding the presence of foreign armed forces on a state's territory provide the most conspicuous example of jurisdiction being allocated as between states as a way for one state to obtain absolute and exclusive jurisdiction over particular matters. On jurisdiction over foreign armed forces, see Aurel Sari, Chapter 11.

[50] Akehurst, n. 2 above, 167–8; and further elaboration on this issue at 207–8.

[51] Lowe, n. 12 above, 266.

claims,[52] then the view of this effectively taken was not of concurrent jurisdiction but of the priority jurisdiction available to one state, at times to the exclusion of another state's jurisdiction. The difficulty of this position would be that, while it accepts that the 'other' jurisdiction in principle exists and is lawful, the state's own jurisdiction should nonetheless be prioritized over it. It is hardly possible to find any intelligible support in state practice and *opinio juris* for such a complex, indeed cumbersome, position.

A conflict of jurisdictions does not inherently make any of conflicting jurisdictions illegal under international law. Instead, it is one of the essential implications of concurrence that national jurisdictions can and will be in mutual conflict from time to time.

1.6 CIVIL AND CRIMINAL JURISDICTION

It is common to speak of civil, criminal or administrative jurisdiction. The exercise of jurisdiction under most if not all of those headings is a matter of state choice,[53] rather than being based on categorical distinctions strictly required by international law.

There may be some situational differences between civil and criminal jurisdiction, but they are empirical rather than prescriptive. It is true that, in public and criminal law, the determining factors are shaped by interests that states hold in enforcing their law and constitution in relation to extra-territorial events. However, the dilemma of territoriality of the foreign state versus that of the forum state arises both in criminal law and civil law, for in both these areas national courts may have to assert the competence of their own sovereign versus that of other sovereigns. As Katzenbach observes, the territoriality of criminal law has been adamantly recognized due to its public order nature. However, states assert their right to prosecute crimes committed by their nationals abroad. This and other exceptions have resulted in the matters being relativised, because just like states admit the foreign element in civil litigation for the sake of justice and fairness in private relations, so are they interested in prosecuting crimes committed abroad, now also for the sake of upholding their own legal system, values and safety. And 'obviously as in the case of conflicts doctrine, the key to territoriality lies in defining the connecting link'.[54]

---

[52] Cf. *ibid.* 267.
[53] Cf. Bowett, n. 11 above, 1.
[54] Katzenbach, n. 27 above, 1139–43.

Either on a sovereignty-driven or a link-driven view of jurisdiction, any across-the-board projection of an inherent distinction between civil and criminal jurisdiction is unwarranted, either in terms of asserting jurisdiction in the first place, or determining its ultimate reach. Both types of jurisdiction, criminal or civil, presuppose the same sovereign authority, and both require the state to have a proper connection with, or interest in, the relevant matter. To illustrate, as Akehurst observes, whether the object of UK legislation is crime or tort, it may be lawful or unlawful under international law regardless of the criminal/civil distinction.[55] Overall, the legality of jurisdiction turns on the legitimacy of jurisdictional connection, regardless of the type of particular judicial proceedings, civil or criminal, through which jurisdiction is exercised.

In the United Kingdom, criminal jurisdiction is asserted mostly by statute.[56] Civil jurisdiction could derive from the statute, but the assertion of civil jurisdiction also takes place in the context of private international law. The House of Lords confirmed in *Atlantic Star* that there is a:

> general proposition that a foreign plaintiff, who can establish jurisdiction against a foreign defendant by any method recognised by English law, is entitled to pursue his action in the English courts if he genuinely thinks that that will be to his advantage and is not acting merely vexatiously. Neither the parties nor the subject matter of the action need have any connection with England. There may be proceedings on the same subject matter in a foreign court. It may be a far more appropriate forum. The defendant may have to suffer great expense and inconvenience in coming here. In the end the decisions of the English and foreign courts may conflict. But nevertheless the plaintiff has a right to obtain the decision of an English court.[57]

Then a careful description of the required balance follows in the House of Lords' judgment, in relation to a further issue of the stay of proceedings when national jurisdiction is purported to be used vexatiously, and the doctrine of *forum non conveniens* is accordingly discussed.

By claiming that its domestic conflict rule applies to a matter taking place abroad, the relevant state effectively claims jurisdiction over that very same matter in terms of public international law. According to Mann, English courts could assert jurisdiction if a contract is governed

---

[55] Akehurst, n. 2 above, 189.

[56] See 1.10.1 below.

[57] *Atlantic Star v Bona Spes* [1974] AC 436 at 453 (per Lord Reid); see for a similar approach P. North and J. Fawcett, *Cheshire and North's Private International Law* (14th edn, 2008), pp. 353–4.

by English law, even if there is no other domestic connection with the matter.[58] Broadly speaking, private international law rules, such as those on property abroad, also relate to the concurrence of various national jurisdictions as a matter of public international law.

1.7 PRESCRIPTIVE AND ENFORCEMENT JURISDICTION

Both Bowett and Brownlie say that a state has enforcement jurisdiction only to the extent needed to enforce its legislative jurisdiction.[59] But the question first to be asked is what test governs the legality of that legislative jurisdiction.

Mann suggests that 'The problem of enforcement jurisdiction arises when a State acts in foreign territory itself or at least takes measures which, though initiated in its own territory, are directed towards consummation, and require compliance, in the foreign State'.[60] The enforcement jurisdiction is generically a broad notion and can include various contexts right up to the state exercising physical force in the territory of another state to assert its rights, an extreme illustration of this being an extra-territorial abduction.[61] Generally speaking, then, the issue of enforcement jurisdiction is, analytically as well as practically, broader than the basic rationale underlying jurisdictional entitlements of states: to exercise sovereign powers in relation to a particular person or matter. In other words, the enforcement jurisdiction relates to the range of means the state can employ to give effect to jurisdiction that it is asserting on another, discrete, substantive ground, whether territorial or extra-territorial.

For instance, either the arrest of an individual within the state's own territory, or the abduction of an individual from the territory of a foreign state, could be an exercise of a kind of 'enforcement jurisdiction' while giving effect to the mainstream jurisdiction that the abducting state is lawfully or unlawfully asserting over that very same individual on the

---

[58] Mann, n. 17 above, 79.

[59] I. Brownlie, *Principles of Public International Law* (2008), p. 311; Bowett, n. 11 above, 1.

[60] Mann, n. 18 above, 128.

[61] *Ibid.* 129; see also F.A. Mann, 'Reflection on the Prosecution of Persons Abducted in Breach of International Law' in Y. Dinstein and M. Tabory (eds), *International Law at a Time of Perplexity: Essays in Honour of Shabtai Rosenne* (Dordrecht, 1989), p. 407.

basis of territoriality, extra-territoriality or even universality. Even despite the existence of that mainstream jurisdiction, states may have to decline its exercise because the custody over the relevant individual has been obtained through unlawful means.[62]

But this is not really an issue of a jurisdictional title, but of the consequent action that either respects or violates another state's sovereignty and territorial supremacy. Jurisdiction *per se*, whether 'prescriptive' or 'enforcement', is about whether, under international law, the state can act in relation to the relevant matter in the sense that there is a proper link between that state and that matter. The actual carrying out of this, whether by prescribing or by enforcing, obviously has to take place within that state's territory.

The issues arising and relevant across the above divide include matters relating to mutual legal assistance, provision of documents to assist litigation and extradition of suspects, as well as those relating to the reach and reciprocal recognition of judgments.[63] These matters are implications of the fact that, as Bowett observes, in certain cases the state may have prescriptive jurisdiction but not enforcement jurisdiction, because the accused over which the state establishes prescriptive jurisdiction may be outside its territory.[64]

These are the issues consequential upon the exercise of jurisdiction, but they do not inherently determine or preclude the lawfulness of the very existence or exercise of jurisdiction. Whether jurisdiction is exercised depends on the proper jurisdictional link. It is another issue whether the exercise of such jurisdiction is being assisted as a matter of national discretion to assist a lawful exercise of jurisdiction by another state, or opposed through the reaction to an internationally wrongful act which the excessive exercise of foreign jurisdiction may involve.

---

[62] See the decision of the House of Lords in *R v Horseferry Road Court, Ex p. Bennett* [1994] 1 AC 42; and the European Court of Human Rights in *Stocke v Germany*, ECHR Series A, No. 199; the only exception from this pattern relates to those who are being tried for the commission of core international crimes, see *Attorney-General of the Government of Israel v Adolf Eichmann* [1961] 36 ILR 5.

[63] See on this, Akehurst, n. 2 above, 210 at 232 ff.

[64] Bowett, n. 11 above, 1.

1.8 MERIT AND CONTINUING RELEVANCE OF *LOTUS*

The Permanent Court of International Justice in *Lotus* was dealing with the collision between French and Turkish vessels at sea, as a consequence of which the French officer was tried in Turkey. The challenge this situation presented to the Court was to rationalize jurisdictional principles not only in terms of their mainstream area of application but also, as it were, at their margins.

The Court had to address the ground that had already been debated in a substantial manner. A year before the Court handed down the *Lotus* judgment, Sir Eric Beckett wrote that:

> a rule or an exception to a rule of international law can only be made by the general consent of all members of the family of nations, and in such an apparent conflict of opinion the vital question is 'On whom is the burden of the proof? Who must show that the general consent of nations is on his side, he who asserts jurisdiction over aliens or he who denies it?' Framed in this way there seems to be only one possible answer: 'He who claims jurisdiction'. The opposite answer would involve the proposition, that … there was no limit by international law to a state's jurisdiction over aliens.[65]

Jennings, on the other hand, suggests in a later commentary that 'to ask on whom the burden of proof is to fall is little more than a way of begging the principal question'.[66] Straightforward as it was, Sir Eric Beckett's proposition was not taken up by the Permanent Court of International Justice. The PCIJ drew a key distinction between the exercise of jurisdiction in relation to a particular place and the exercise of sovereign authority within the same place. The Court held that:

> It is certainly true that … vessels on the high seas are subject to no authority except that of the State whose flag they fly. In virtue of the principle of the freedom of the seas, that is to say, the absence of any territorial sovereignty upon the high seas, no State may exercise any kind of jurisdiction over foreign vessels upon them. Thus, if a war vessel, happening to be at the spot where a collision occurs between a vessel flying its flag and a foreign vessel, were to send on board the latter an officer to make investigations or to take evidence, such an act would undoubtedly be contrary to international law. But

65 Beckett, n. 32 above, 50; *per contra* Akehurst, n. 2 above, 167.
66 Jennings, n. 16 above, 152.

> it by no means follows that a State can never in its own territory exercise jurisdiction over acts which have occurred on board a foreign ship on the high seas.[67]

According to the Court, 'This conclusion could only be overcome if it were shown that there was a rule of customary international law which, going further than the principle stated above, established the exclusive jurisdiction of the State whose flag was flown', and 'the existence of such a rule has not been conclusively proved'.[68] This was also due to broader considerations related to the system of international law, because:

> Far from laying down a general prohibition to the effect that States may not extend the application of their laws and the jurisdiction of their courts to persons, property and acts outside their territory, [international law as it stands at present] leaves them in this respect a wide measure of discretion which is only limited in certain cases by prohibitive rules; as regards other cases, every State remains free to adopt the principles which it regards as best and most suitable.[69]

The dissent by Lord Finlay required positive proof of the rule authorizing Turkey to exercise jurisdiction in such situation.[70] Later on, Article 11(1) of the 1958 Geneva Convention on the High Seas adopted a position different from *Lotus*,[71] but this provision merely constitutes a *lex specialis* against the background of the *Lotus* principle applying as part of the general law. More recently, in *R v Gul*, the UK Supreme Court adopted the approach that follows *Lotus*.[72]

In pragmatic terms, the principle stated in *Lotus* is useful as an organizing principle, because state practice often may be divided, unrepresentative or neutral, and thus be unable to provide a definite answer. This became clear when the issue of universal jurisdiction over core international crimes was discussed in the Joint Separate Opinion in the *Arrest Warrant* case:

---

67 *Lotus*, n. 26 above, 25.

68 *Ibid.* 25–6.

69 *Ibid.* 18–19.

70 *Ibid.*, Dissenting Opinion, 52.

71 Article 11 provides that, 'In the event of a collision or of any other incident of navigation concerning a ship on the high seas, involving the penal or disciplinary responsibility of the master or of any other person in the service of the ship, no penal or disciplinary proceedings may be instituted against such persons except before the judicial or administrative authorities either of the flag State or of the State of which such person is a national'.

72 *R v Gul* [2013] UKSC 64.

> none of the national case law to which we have referred happens to be based on the exercise of a universal jurisdiction properly so called, there is equally nothing in this case law which evidences an *opinio juris* on the illegality of such a jurisdiction. In short, national legislation and case law – that is, State practice – is neutral as to exercise of universal jurisdiction.[73]

This demonstrated the utility of having an organizing principle, when state practice cannot provide a definitive answer in terms of resolving conflicting presumptions. Moreover, the adoption of an approach contrary to the one set out in *Lotus* would lead to an extreme, and counter-factual, outcome that certain kinds of nationality jurisdiction, of the kind that France may have claimed in that case, are absolute and exclusive of the conflicting and concurrent jurisdictions of other states.

1.9 PARTICULAR HEADINGS OF JURISDICTION: TERRITORIALITY, NATIONALITY AND EXTRA-TERRITORIALITY

Being exercised under a particular (well-recognized and generally accepted) heading neither privileges the relevant jurisdiction, nor renders it dubious. However sound and obvious the particular jurisdictional heading may be, there is, more often than not, the possibility of the same matter concurrently falling within the jurisdiction of another state. Therefore, particular headings of jurisdiction should be viewed merely as analytical rationalizations of the genuine link between the state that asserts jurisdiction and the relevant person, matter or incident, not as by itself determinative of jurisdictional entitlements.

Many authors would agree that territorial jurisdiction is the most fundamental, obvious and undisputed instance of the state exercising its jurisdiction, because regulating state affairs within its territory is axiomatic. However, according to Bowett, the territoriality basis is used flexibly by states to support jurisdiction to protect the states' interests in resources located outside the territory of the state yet conceded under international law to be within the control of that state.[74]

The nationality jurisdiction is also among the obvious jurisdictional headings. It relates to prosecuting a state's national or a person who commits a crime against that national. On the other hand, the assertion of

---

[73] *Arrest Warrant*, n. 46 above, para. 45; and see para. 54 for reference to *Lotus*, in relation to the exercise of universal jurisdiction *in absentia*.

[74] Bowett, n. 11 above, 4–5.

jurisdiction over an individual due to the nationality link could prove just as controversial in practice, as could be the case with some other headings of extra-territorial jurisdiction. Accordingly, as Bowett suggested, 'the link of nationality may become no more than prima-facie evidence that the person's conduct is properly the concern of the State of nationality'.[75] The nationality link could indeed be used as a premise for politically motivated persecution of individuals.

Another aspect of the relevance of nationality jurisdiction could arise when the state's national is murdered or injured abroad. But even in such cases of obvious connection between the state and the crime (or indeed tort), controversies would not go away. The extra-territorial assertion of the nationality jurisdiction could be seen as politically controversial, aimed at frustrating the territorial jurisdiction of the state on whose territory the relevant incident has taken place. Whether that would be so would depend on the specific incidences of the particular case. Similarly, as Mcgarthy has demonstrated, the passive personality principle applicable, for instance, in the case of terrorist offences or used in some cases to protect the state's nationals present abroad, could cause political controversies and provoke claims of interference in another state's domestic affairs.[76]

The room for a conflict of interests is often there, anyway. To illustrate: the state of emigration may have an interest to cover departing nationals while the state of arrival has an interest to cover new domiciliaries.[77] Akehurst suggests an even broader position: that public international law would not prohibit states to apply the *lex fori* to determine the status of all individuals, whether or not having a connection to the relevant state.[78] A state may clash with a foreign state even if they try a foreign national on the basis of the crime committed within the forum's territory. Consequently, there is always some potential for aggravation and irritation in mutual relations of states, including in cases of the lawful assertion of state jurisdiction under its most mainstream and generally recognized headings.

It has been suggested that 'The Law of Nations does not recognize the assumption of jurisdiction for "protection"; there never has been any such general consent by the nations as would be required to make this doctrine

[75] *Ibid.* 8.

[76] And this has led some states to require executive consent before such jurisdiction is exercised. J.G. Mcgarthy, 'The Passive Personality Principle and Its Use in Combatting International Terrorism' (1989) 13 *Fordham JIL* 325.

[77] Akehurst, n. 2 above, 221.

[78] *Ibid.* 230.

a part of international law'.[79] On the other hand, Bowett suggests that there is no doubt of the validity of the protective principle, especially when a conduct that constitutes a crime is one that threatens the state's security. The protective principle justifies the criminalization, with extra-territorial effect, of espionage, sedition, counterfeiting of currency or attack against embassies or consulates abroad. Furthermore, 'there is little doubt, in this day and age, that a State's security is economic as well as political, so that the conduct posing a real threat to a State's economy could be subjected to the State's jurisdiction'.[80]

1.10 EXTRA-TERRITORIAL JURISDICTION

1.10.1 Criminal Jurisdiction of English Courts

In English criminal law, the process of criminalization, defining the ambit of particular crimes, also involves the assertion of territorial or extra-territorial jurisdiction. The initial approach has been, as the *Macleod* case suggested, that 'all crime is local' and criminal jurisdiction over it belongs to the territorial state.[81] However, as Sir Robert Jennings observed, the notion that all crime is local has never commanded a general assent of states and thus become part of international law.[82] It was stated in the early case of *Zollverein* that 'The laws of Great Britain affect her own subjects everywhere – foreigners only when within her own jurisdiction'.[83] As Lord Morris then observed in *Treacy*, 'the general principle of the common law of England is that the exercise of criminal jurisdiction does not extend to cover acts committed on land abroad'.[84]

A somewhat open-ended approach by Lord Morris in *Treacy* suggests that:

> Unless, therefore, there is some provision pointing to a different conclusion, a statute which makes some act (or omission) an offence will relate to some act (or omission) in the United Kingdom. Even where a statute creating a criminal offence is clearly expressed so as to cover acts committed outside the

[79] *Lotus*, n. 26 above, Dissenting Opinion of Lord Finlay, 56.
[80] Bowett, n. 11 above, 10–11.
[81] *Macleod* [1891] AC 455 at 458–9.
[82] Jennings, n. 16 above, 149.
[83] *Zollverein*, (1856) 166 ER 1038 at 1040.
[84] *Treacy v DPP* [1971] AC 537 at 552 (per Lord Morris).

> jurisdiction, it will, in the absence of further clear provision only be regarded as covering such acts when committed by British subjects.[85]

However:

> It would be open to Parliament to enact that if a British subject committed anywhere an act designated as blackmail he would commit an offence punishable in England. Such an enactment would, however, have to be in clear and express terms: specific provision would have to be made with regard to acts committed abroad.[86]

Thus, the notions of territoriality and extra-territoriality become relative even in cases where the criminalization is deemed to be primary territorial. Courts have some flexibility in construing jurisdiction by identifying where the crime has been committed either in terms of locus,[87] or of the relationship between the perpetrator and aider or abettor. Then, in *R v Oliphant*, also a more principled justification in favour of extra-territoriality of jurisdiction was offered by Lord Alverstone, dealing with the 'well-recognised rule of the criminal law that where an offence has been wholly committed abroad it cannot be tried in England' and with the argument that 'an act committed out of the jurisdiction, but having an effect within the jurisdiction, is triable in the place where it has that effect'.

According to Lord Diplock:

> It would be an unjustifiable interference with the sovereignty of other nations over the conduct of persons in their own territories if we were to punish persons for conduct which did not take place in the United Kingdom and had no harmful consequences there. But I see no reason in comity for requiring any wider limitation than that upon the exercise by Parliament of its legislative power in the field of criminal law.[88]

Lord Diplock further emphasized that:

> where the definition of any such offence contains a requirement that the described conduct of the accused should be followed by described consequences the implied exclusion is limited to cases where *neither* the conduct *nor* its harmful consequences took place in England or Wales.[89]

---

85 *Ibid.* 553.
86 *Ibid.* 552 (per Lord Morris).
87 *R v Oliphant* [1905] 2 KB 67 at 72–3.
88 *Treacy*, n. 84 above, 561.
89 *Ibid.* 564 (emphasis in original).

The separate reference to harmful consequences of the act, in addition to its perpetration, provides a boost for the extra-territorial jurisdiction on terms comparable to the effects doctrine.

The case of *Joyce*,[90] dealing with the pro-Nazi propaganda conducted from abroad by a person who had fraudulently acquired British citizenship, may be rather specific to be generalized in terms of jurisdictional reach of the English legal system. The reference there was made to the United Kingdom's continuing personal supremacy over Joyce while abroad,[91] and thus to the latter's continuing allegiance, even though his nationality in the first place had never been a straightforward matter. The real and major question is not whether Joyce could be prosecuted in England, but whether one could be prosecuted in England for the similar activities producing effect within the jurisdiction even if one has no nationality or comparable connection with the forum. To answer this question negatively would be to emasculate the forum's jurisdiction and render it impotent in dealing with precisely these kinds of dangerous activities. If you catch one and let ten others get away with it, solely because they are not the forum state's nationals, the whole rationale of criminalization becomes ethically dubious and practically ineffective. After all it was broadcasting, not nationality, that provided the initial and continuing rationale for prosecuting Joyce. Whoever's national Joyce was, the crime was inherently extra-territorial both in its design and effect, and in the longer run it may be counter-productive to pretend otherwise.

More recently, the purposive construction of a statute to secure its extra-territorial reach was adopted by the English Court of Appeal in *Hundal*, dealing with the counter-terrorist context:

> The question that arises is: does the fact that the activities and their involvement in the [relevant proscribed] organisation took place in Germany, where it was not proscribed, mean that they could not be guilty of the offence? If the position was that because an organisation carries on its activities in more than one country this meant that by joining the organisation in a country which is outside the jurisdiction of these courts, then the Terrorism Act would not apply to that organisation, this would enable a coach and horses to be driven through the objects of the legislation.[92]

Therefore, it looks rather odd that in the next paragraph of the judgment, the Court professes to disclaim the extra-territoriality of section 11(1) of

---

[90] *DPP v Joyce* [1946] AC 347.

[91] *Ibid.* 376 (per Lord Porter).

[92] *Hundal* [2004] EWCA Crim 389, paras 11–12.

the Terrorism Act 2000.[93] This looks like an attempt to square the circle. Even if the person would be prosecutable once on the British soil, they still would be prosecutable for what they did outside the United Kingdom. Under the 2000 Act, being physically in the United Kingdom is not an offence; being a member of the proscribed organization is.

The Terrorism Act 2006 subscribed to an even more far-reaching approach to extra-territoriality.[94] According to section 17(1):

> If (a) a person does anything outside the United Kingdom, and (b) his action, if done in a part of the United Kingdom, would constitute an offence falling within subsection (2), he shall be guilty in that part of the United Kingdom of the offence.

Such broad assertion of extra-territorial jurisdiction could hardly be rationalized if we adhere to the sovereignty-driven approach to jurisdiction, which approach would then result in a rather substantial presumption to be applied against the entitlement of the state to regulate extra-territorial matters in such a far-reaching manner. However, the United Kingdom's assertion of the extra-territorial jurisdiction would become more clearly understandable if we see it through the prism of the interest-driven approach to jurisdiction. This approach would enable us to rationalize this extra-territorial jurisdiction by reference to the interest of combatting terrorist activities which has motivated the UK Parliament to adopt such a statutory position on jurisdiction.

---

[93] The Court suggests that 'properly understood, the provisions of section 11 do not have extra-territorial effect. Properly understood, what is required is for there to be someone who is in this country, and therefore subject to its jurisdiction (as both the appellants were), who at the time that he is in this country is a member of the proscribed organisation. In order to establish that the person concerned is a member of the proscribed organisation, evidence can be given that the person joined the organisation from abroad or when abroad. That would not in itself make that person guilty of an offence. He would only be guilty of an offence when he was in this country. Either he would have to travel to this country in order to commit an offence after he became a member or he would already have had to be in this country and joined the local foreign branch of the proscribed organisation while in this country. But in any event the criminal law would apply to his activities because of his presence in this jurisdiction: his coming here as a member or his being a member in this country of the proscribed organisation', para. 13.

[94] As discussed in *Rangzieb Ahmed and Habib Ahmed v R* [2011] EWCA Crim 184, CA (Crim. Div.), 25 February 2011, para. 96 ff.

1.10.2 Effects Doctrine in the Jurisprudence of US and English Courts

Lowenfeld defines the effects-based jurisdiction as the 'jurisdiction to prescribe, on the basis of effects caused by the challenged activity in [the state's] territory, even when no part of the activity was carried out in its territory'; the effects must be 'direct, substantial, and foreseeable'.[95] Some, though insufficient, understanding of the extra-territorial effects doctrine was manifested in the early twentieth century. As Sir Eric Beckett observed by reference to a previous commentator:

> Wharton, an American writer, said in 1885, 'There is no civilized state that has not passed statutes making it a criminal offence for foreigners even in their own countries to forge its securities' – a statement which, though inaccurate, is strong evidence of his view of the legality of the jurisdiction claimed … Conspiracies against the life of the head of the state, revolutions fomented against the constitution, the circulation of forged currency notes through the post, are simple instances, not open to dispute.[96]

From here, one possibility would be to adopt a pedantic approach and require the existence of a positive rule of international law to validate the assertion and exercise of jurisdiction, in addition to the above example as to securities forgery, in relation to all other extra-territorial economic activities, whether currency forgery, antitrust or other economic threats. A more straightforward and down-to-earth approach would, however, be one that suggests that the widespread acceptance of the extra-territorial jurisdiction in relation to securities forgery is merely an implication of states admitting the legality of extra-territorial jurisdiction, whenever the proper link between the forum state and the matter covered by the relevant exercise of jurisdiction can be demonstrated.

According to Akehurst, whether the state will establish a civil or criminal jurisdiction over antitrust matters is its domestic legal choice, and the limits on civil and criminal jurisdiction in this case are the same.[97] Akehurst further suggests that a 'constituent element' of the act need not necessarily have occurred within the forum state's territory and that this applies both to civil and criminal jurisdiction.[98] The US Supreme

---

[95] A. Lowenfeld, 'Jurisdictional Issues Before National Courts: The *Insurance Antitrust* Case' in K. Meessen (ed.), *Extraterritorial Jurisdiction in Theory and Practice* (London: Kluwer, 1996), p. 6.

[96] Beckett, n. 32 above, 56.

[97] Akehurst, n. 2 above, 191–2.

[98] *Ibid.* 195–6.

Court decision in *Alcoa* sought to frame the effects doctrine in terms of the territoriality principle, referring to conduct outside the United States' borders 'that has consequences within its borders'.[99] Also, it was observed that:

> we are concerned only with whether Congress chose to attach liability to the conduct outside the United States of persons not in allegiance to it … Nevertheless, it is quite true that we are not to read general words, such as those in this Act, without regard to the limitations customarily observed by nations upon the exercise of their powers; limitations which generally correspond to those fixed by the 'Conflict of Laws'.[100]

The Court in *Alcoa* accepted the general interpretative relevance of international law and comity, yet adhered to a broader understanding of the effects jurisdiction.

A similarly expansive understanding of extra-territorial jurisdiction was upheld in *United States v ICI*. It was held not to be unlawful or an intrusion into a foreign sovereign's authority to direct a foreign company 'to remove the harmful effects on the trade of the United States'.[101] Later on, US courts began to introduce the balancing of interests test to further rationalize the nexus requirement with the relevant matter. To some extent, this amounted to a moderation. The Court of Appeals for the Ninth Circuit in *Timberlane* suggested:

> That American law covers some conduct beyond this nation's borders does not mean that it embraces all, however. Extraterritorial application is understandably a matter of concern for the other countries involved. Those nations have sometimes resented and protested, as excessive intrusions into their own spheres, broad assertions of authority by American courts … it is evident that at some point the interests of the United States are too weak and the foreign harmony incentive for restraint too strong to justify an extraterritorial assertion of jurisdiction.

It was further suggested that 'The effects test by itself is incomplete because it fails to consider other nations' interests'.[102] Not that the effects jurisdiction was unlawful; it was merely an initial criterion, to be complemented, as a matter of national judicial choice, by the balancing test to see how strong the relevant American interest was in comparison with other nations' interests to justify effect-based jurisdiction.

---

[99] *United States v Aluminium Company of America*, 4 F.Supp. 97 (1941).

[100] *United States v Alcoa*, 148 F.2d 416, 443 (1944).

[101] *United States v ICI*, 105 F.Supp. 215 (1952).

[102] *Timberlane Lumber Co. v Bank of America*, Ninth Circuit, 611–12 (1976).

The US court in *Laker Airways v Sabena* supported an even broader understanding of the effects jurisdiction, characterized as the 'territorial effects doctrine'. The court's approach was that:

> Even if invisible, the radiating consequences of anti-competitive activities cause economic injuries no less tangible than the harmful effects of assassins' bullets or thieves' telephonic impulses. Thus, legislation to protect domestic economic interests can legitimately reach conduct occurring outside the legislating territory intended to damage the protected interests within the territory. As long as the territorial effects are not so inconsequential as to exceed the bounds of reasonableness imposed by international law, prescriptive jurisdiction is legitimately exercised.[103]

If this reasoning is followed it seems that, on balance, the approaches of territoriality and of effects are not so much separate rules as interpretative rationalizations of the overall substantive connection test. Effects produced, from abroad, within the forum's territory can and do amount to such substantive connection. The court's approach was not dissimilar to the English court's above-mentioned references to extra-territoriality when 'harmful consequences' within the forum's territory could materialize from an act initially perpetrated abroad.

The *Sabena* case also conceived the entire matter within the framework of concurrence of jurisdictions as between courts of different states, observing that 'the parallel proceeding rule counsels against interference with a foreign court's exercise of concurrent jurisdiction'.[104] The court also articulated the reasons dictating that the effects doctrine can ultimately be more flexible, and less intrusive into foreign legal systems, than the nationality-based jurisdiction, for 'besides ignoring important domestic interests, the paramount nationality rule would generate more interference than it would resolve. Legislation based on nationality tends to encourage chauvinism and discrimination without enhancing international comity',[105] while the effects doctrine, at least in its American version, allows for a flexible balancing of interests. The overall premise for the US courts' jurisdiction was that 'No foreign court can supersede the right and obligation of the United States courts to decide whether Congress has created a remedy for those injured by trade practices adversely affecting United States interests'; and then, in the spirit reflecting the concurrence of the two jurisdictions, it was added that:

---

[103] *Laker Airways v Sabena*, 731 F.2d 909 (1984), at para. 43; and case review by M. Leigh in (1984) 78 *AJIL* 666.

[104] *Sabena*, n. 103 above, para. 72.

[105] *Ibid.* para. 103.

> Under the nationality base of jurisdiction, Britain can punish its corporations for walking through that courthouse door, but it cannot close the American door. Thus, although British courts can sanction their citizens for resorting to United States antitrust remedies, United States courts are not required to cut off the availability of the remedy.[106]

It seems, overall, that the US-style effects doctrine is not generically different from the versions of extra-territorial jurisdiction other states have used. After the evolving position in the US case law, Lowenfeld has concluded that 'it is now clear beyond doubt that the Supreme Court – majority and minority – understands that the reach of a nation's law is a subject of *international* law – public customary international law'.[107]

The interest-balancing exercise, as presumably required by comity, should be seen not as the mirror-image of the juridical lawfulness of the underlying exercise of the effects-based jurisdiction, but as one of the ways of making allowance for the options and possibilities that the concurrence framework as applicable to otherwise lawful exercises of extra-territorial jurisdiction allows the relevant states to take advantage of. The US courts' reliance on the reasonableness requirement as part of comity, and their consequently making that allowance for other nations' interests is, in essence, the unilateral moderation by US courts of the legality allowance available to this state under international law, instead of pressing the freedom available under that allowance to its extreme limits.

An early British reaction to the US antitrust jurisdiction came with the case of *British Nylon Spinners v ICI*,[108] where Lord Evershed MR responded to the US Court's position in the *ICI* case (above). The conceptual basis underlying Lord Evershed's approach was that:

> the right [involved in the case] may be described as their right under the contract, being an English contract made between English nationals and to be performed in England … That is a right … which is English in character and is subject to the jurisdiction of the English courts; and it seems to me that the plaintiffs have at least established a prima facie case for saying that it is not competent for the courts of the United States or of any other country to interfere with those rights or to make orders, observance of which by our courts would require that our courts should not exercise the jurisdiction which they have and which it is their duty to exercise in regard to those rights.[109]

106 *Ibid*. para. 101.
107 Lowenfeld, n. 95 above, 6 (emphasis in original).
108 *British Nylon Spinners v ICI* [1953] 1 Ch. 19.
109 *Ibid*. 26.

Lord Evershed further disagreed with the position of the US judge that 'it was not an intrusion on the authority of a foreign sovereign to make directions addressed to that foreign sovereign or to its courts or to nationals of that foreign Power effective to remove (as he said) "harmful effects on the trade" of the United States'.[110] Denning LJ was equally clear that 'The writ of the United States does not run in this country, and, if due regard is had to the comity of nations, it will not seek to run here'.[111]

It was precisely this reasoning that, on balance, leads to the conclusion that the jurisdictional attitude of the Court of Appeal has contradicted the thesis of the concurrence of British and US jurisdictions. The above observations demonstrate that the Court of Appeal opposed the very competence of US courts to exercise jurisdiction, even if it was clear that the relevant transactions had produced harmful effects within the United States, if the matter was in the first place governed by English law and litigated between British subjects.

Initially at least, then, what *British Nylon Spinners* contextually proves is that each forum is responsible for protecting its own trade and legal system and that, in the absence of some supra-national authority to distribute jurisdiction, British and US forums remain concurrently competent on the matter, each of them retaining their right not to give effect to another's prescriptions. It also bears repeating that the national assertion of jurisdiction takes place against the background of both *Lotus* and the concurrent nature of nearly all the jurisdiction that is available to states. The assertion of jurisdiction by one state does not inherently negate that of another state, but merely pre-empts its exercise.

As a matter of fact, English courts have encountered the situation where the exercise of foreign (US antitrust) jurisdiction was controversial, and was opposed by the executive branch of the British government,[112] partly on the grounds of its alleged unlawfulness, and Parliament had intervened through the adoption of the Protection of Trading Interests Act 1980. In *British Airways Board v Laker*, the issue was whether English courts could enjoin Laker from litigating its case against the British Airways before US courts.[113] The 1980 Act was raised in *Laker*, but without giving to the Act the inherent effect of offsetting US courts' jurisdiction to order threefold damages. English courts instead appear to

---

110 *Ibid.* 25.
111 *Ibid.* 28.
112 Lowe, n. 12 above, 257 at 267–72.
113 *BA Board v Laker* [1985] AC 58.

have located the matter, however controversial, within the context of the concurrence of British and US jurisdictions.

Similarly, it was asserted earlier before the House of Lords in *Westinghouse* that 'The assertion of extraterritorial jurisdiction in anti-trust matters represents an extension of the economic policy of one state which is likely to conflict with that of other states', and that the outcome that entailed was 'undesirable' for the business environment.[114] The relativity of this matter was then witnessed in Lord Wilberforce's observation that 'It is axiomatic that in anti-trust matters the policy of one state may be to defend what it is the policy of another state to attack'.[115] If so, then it is not really about considering the 'other' jurisdiction as inherently unlawful, but merely denying domestic effect to certain of its implications.

As a matter of international law, in antitrust cases containing foreign elements, concurrent jurisdiction is the rule rather than the exception. The interest balancing rule and the reasonableness requirement as such cannot be seen to be part of international law, because such an approach would aim (implausibly) at demonstrating the reasonableness of the action in a way acceptable to all states holding many different views.[116]

English courts have broadly subscribed to this approach. The High Court judgment in *Laker* disapproved:

> any submission that an antitrust action based in part, or even substantially, on acts committed outside the United States by English companies carrying on business in the United States in relation to the carrying on of that business constitutes such an invasion of sovereignty that a United Kingdom company engaged in a like business should be restrained from pursuing its claim … It is equally clear that invasion of sovereignty or extra-territoriality afford no ground. They too have been dealt with by Parliament, to some extent directly and to some extent by giving to the Secretary of State wide powers to act in case of need. The direct parliamentary intervention does not avail [the airlines]. The powers conferred by Parliament have not been exercised and a United Kingdom designated airline carrying on business in the United States by permission of the United States Government must prima facie comply with United States law or take the consequences.[117]

---

[114] *Westinghouse Electric Co.* [1978] AC 547 at 594; although it was also said that this jurisdiction was not in accordance with international law, *ibid.* 631 (per Viscount Dilhorne).

[115] *Westinghouse*, n. 114 above, 617.

[116] K.M. Meessen, 'Antitrust Jurisdiction under Customary International Law' (1984) 78 *AJIL* 783 at 801–2.

[117] *BA Board v Laker* [1984] QB 142 at 163–4 (per Parker J).

In the House of Lords in the *Laker* case, as Lord Diplock stated, their Lordships were:

> confronted in the civil actions with a case in which there is a single forum only that is of competent jurisdiction to determine the merits of the claim; and the single forum is a foreign court. For an English court to enjoin the claimant from having access to that foreign court is, in effect, to take upon itself a one-sided jurisdiction to determine the claim upon the merits *against* the claimant but also to prevent its being decided upon the merits *in his favour.* This poses a novel problem, different in kind from that involved where there are alternative fora in which a particular civil claim can be pursued: an English court and a court of some foreign country both of which are recognised under English rules of conflict of laws as having jurisdiction to entertain proceedings against a defendant for a remedy for acts or omissions which constitute an actionable wrong under the substantive law of both England and that foreign country.[118]

In *Westinghouse*, where the House of Lords has ruled that British authorities were not obliged to accede to the American letter rogatory addressed to the High Court, the terms of an international treaty, namely, the 1980 Convention on Taking Evidence Abroad, led English courts not to assist the exercise of US extra-territorial jurisdiction; but not to hold that anything determined in that jurisdiction was to be seen as inherently unlawful. In *Laker*, courts were asked to go much further than in *Westinghouse*, for in *Laker* a similar result offsetting the effect of the US extra-territorial jurisdiction was not necessarily obtainable on the basis of an international treaty. The difference between *Westinghouse* and *Laker* also was that, in the former case, English courts were requested to take positive action to assist the exercise of US extra-territorial jurisdiction; while in the latter case they were requested to issue injunctions against Laker not to take part in the US proceedings based on that jurisdiction. In neither case did they accede to the request. The overall conclusions in both cases did, by and large, avoid the legal condemnation of the US jurisdiction as such.

Thus, overall, the antitrust litigation saga before English courts did not amount to state practice that would adversely affect the legality of the US extra-territorial jurisdiction over non-nationals (and, given that in the English legal system law is what courts say it is, the position of the judiciary should be seen to carry greater weight). This litigation thus did

[118] *Laker*, n. 113 above, 80 (emphasis in original); Lord Diplock also agreed with Parker J of the High Court 'who held that it did not assist [the airlines] in their claims to injunctions', *ibid.* 85.

not inherently commit the United Kingdom against the extra-territorial jurisdiction in any manner. Even Lord Donaldson MR, who granted injunctions in the Court of Appeal in *Laker* (later on to be lifted by the House of Lords),[119] did not contradict the thesis that US courts did have the antitrust jurisdiction that they asserted pursuant to the US legislation.[120] It is therefore right to suggest, in relation to the British position regarding the US antitrust jurisdiction, that the view that:

> if jurisdiction were concurrent … the territorial claim should generally prevail to the exclusion of claims on other bases … is difficult to reconcile with the concept of concurrence, and it may be that no more than a principle of comity was being advanced here … rather than law.[121]

Another remark on what English courts have actually done is also pertinent:

> For a domestic court to take the position that considerations of relative national interests are irrelevant to the question whether legitimate authority to prescribe or enforce exists reinforces a perception that the court operates outside the international law formation process and should view itself as playing principally a political role in determining whether or not effective power should be exercised.[122]

This is accurate with one caveat: courts did not play a political role. They merely gave effect to the primary and secondary legislation to the extent that this covered ground in the case, and, for the rest, relied on the concurrence of jurisdictions of various states under international law.

By 1973, as Akehurst was reporting, there were hardly any examples of other states objecting to the exercise of US antitrust jurisdiction as such, but protests were mainly related to the far-reaching orders made at the end of the case. US courts had the authority to make such far-reaching orders.[123] The United Kingdom objected to US extra-territorial jurisdiction in matters of antitrust. This, however, was not a case of the inherent illegality of such jurisdiction but merely one due to the position

---

[119] Lord Diplock decided to 'allow Laker's appeals in both civil actions and discharge the injunctions granted by the Court of Appeal', *ibid.* 95; Lord Scarman also concluded that the airlines 'are not entitled to relief by way of injunction from an English court', *ibid.* 96.

[120] *Laker*, n. 117 above, 185–6.

[121] Lowe, n. 12 above, 267.

[122] H.G. Maier, 'Extraterritorial Jurisdiction at a Crossroads: An Intersection between Public and Private International Law' (1982) 76 *AJIL* 280 at 299.

[123] Akehurst, n. 2 above, 210.

of Britain as persistent objector, potentially generating, at the very most, the lack of opposability of such jurisdiction to the United Kingdom rather than its illegality as such.[124]

1.10.3 Some Controversial Uses of Extra-territorial Jurisdiction

While, as we have seen, the US judiciary has at times been willing to moderate accordingly, the legislative and executive branches of the US government on other occasions have shown the political willingness to press extra-territorial jurisdictional exercises to further extremes, and use them as tools of political and economic pressure on other countries, as witnessed both by the Soviet gas pipeline-related controversies and the Helms-Burton Act. The US measures, such as those adopted under the 1992 Helms-Burton Act, among other things aiming to isolate Cuba from international economic relations, have purported to reach much further than any previous US assertion of extra-territorial jurisdiction in antitrust matters. The most pertinent feature of the Act perhaps is that it enables American citizens to recover compensation from any person who knowingly sells, transfers or distributes, or uses in commercial activities, or otherwise profits from such use of, property that the Castro government confiscated from American citizens from 1 January 1959 onwards (section 4 of the Act). As Lowe states in examining the merit of those claims:

> The objectionable US jurisdictional claims here were not applications of the effects doctrine but were, rather, claims (1) to treat any company owned or controlled by US interests, whatever its nationality, as if it were a US company, and (2) to impress goods and technology originating in some sense in the United States with US nationality, so that transactions anywhere in the world involving them would be subject to US regulation.[125]

Another, earlier example was the attempt by the United States to impose an embargo on the supply by certain European companies of goods destined for use in the construction of the Soviet gas pipeline. The effect was to forbid the exportation to the USSR of specified oil and gas machinery in several different circumstances unless the permission of US authorities was first obtained. The *ratione personae* scope of those covered by these measures was rather broad including, under various

---

[124] Cf. Lowe, n. 12 above, 257 at 264.

[125] A.V. Lowe, 'US Extraterritorial Jurisdiction: The Helms-Burton and D'Amato Acts' (1997) 46 *ICLQ* 378.

headings, persons who were present within the United States or were considered by the United States to be subject to US jurisdiction.[126]

The European Community's reaction to such broad US measures was that:

> the so-called 'effects doctrine', under which conduct occurring outside the territory but causing direct, foreseeable and substantial effects – which are also constituent elements of a crime or tort – within the territory may be proscribed [has found less than general acceptance under international law]. … The 'effects doctrine' is not applicable. It cannot conceivably be argued that exports from the European Community to the U.S.S.R. for the Siberian gas pipeline have within the U.S.A. direct, foreseeable and substantial effects which are not merely undesirable, but which constitute an element of a crime or tort proscribed by U.S. law. It is more than likely that they have no direct effects on U.S. trade.[127]

It is possible to see the EC's approach here as a nuanced one, presumably eschewing definitive condemnation of the effects doctrine and attacking US measures as ones that could not be based on transparently demonstrable effects within the US territory. This position thus shows the understanding of the effects doctrine proper. The EC position is therefore a useful contribution to state practice, in the sense that it requires drawing a clear distinction between the effects jurisdiction proper and the use of extra-territorial jurisdiction for political purposes only.

This demonstrates that, for the purposes of the legality of the assertion of jurisdiction, extending state jurisdiction to foreign nationals active in foreign countries is not the same thing throughout, in terms of the legality as well as practicability of underlying jurisdictional measures. It also stands to reason that the ultimate legality of these pertinent US measures would turn on the legality of the underlying boycott, not inherently on the nature of jurisdiction that has been asserted.

In sum, the reactions and protests against particular exercises of state jurisdiction should be seen through the general prism of state practice as part of the process of the creation and development of customary

---

[126] As discussed in A.V. Lowe, 'Public International Law and the Conflict of Laws: The European Response to the United States Export Administration Regulations' (1984) 33 *ICLQ* 515 at 516–17; the jurisdiction seemed to have been asserted 'over US technology and its fruits wherever it or they might be', *ibid*. 517–18.

[127] Comments on the Amendments of 22 June 1982 to the Export Administration Regulations (1982) 21 ILM 891, paras 12–13. Sanctions imposed on European companies under the regulations were lifted in November 1982, see Lowe, n. 126 above, 519.

international law. Generally speaking, reactions and protests can have varying and diverse targets they react to, and the same applies to the object and means of the very measure of objection and protest. They could be against jurisdiction as such, its particular exercise, its reach, or merely be constrained to refusals to assist or support in any manner the exercise of the jurisdiction which is seen as unlawful, or otherwise objectionable or undesirable. Reciprocal measures may possess the character of countermeasures or reprisals, or be a mere retorsion. They may further be directed at foreign governments or entities, or at entities operating within the relevant state's domestic realm, whether national or foreign. This way, reciprocal measures of reaction may be ones relating to, and thus material for the legality of, jurisdiction as such, or ones relating to issues other than jurisdiction, such as enforcement of judgments and other issues of mutual inter-state legal cooperation. The precise scope of, and intention behind, the particular state reaction would then determine its precise contribution to state practice on these matters.

1.11 UNIVERSAL JURISDICTION: CIVIL AND CRIMINAL

1.11.1 General Relevance

From now on, our analysis will move on to one further particular heading of state jurisdiction which does not require the demonstration of any link to persons subjected to jurisdiction. This is universal jurisdiction over the perpetrators of core international crimes, such as torture, genocide, war crimes and crimes against humanity. Under customary international law, universal jurisdiction in relation to such proceedings is justified by reference to the community interest – separate from the interest individual states might have in the particular matters – in prosecuting relevant core international crime.

1.11.2 Universal Jurisdiction in Criminal Proceedings

Universal jurisdiction is exercised over the relevant crime in the absence of a connection point between that crime and the forum state. It is generally acknowledged that such universal jurisdiction currently exists over war crimes, crimes against humanity, torture and genocide. The 2005 Resolution of the Institute of International Law perceives universal jurisdiction as the primary tool for combating international crimes. As the

Preamble to the Resolution states, the primary responsibility for combating these crimes lies with individual states. The Preamble proceeds to affirm that 'universal jurisdiction is an additional effective means to prevent impunity for international crimes'. Article 1 of the Resolution states that 'Universal jurisdiction in criminal matters, as an additional ground of jurisdiction, means the competence of a State to prosecute alleged offenders and to punish them if convicted, irrespective of the place of commission of the crime and regardless of any link of active or passive nationality, or other grounds of jurisdiction recognized by international law'. Most significantly, Article 2 affirms that 'Universal jurisdiction is primarily based on customary international law'. The following articles specify the crimes to which universal jurisdiction applies.[128]

In England, the House of Lords in *Pinochet* clarified that universal jurisdiction is available in case of breaches of *jus cogens*, having demonstrated the clear link between the two notions.[129] The decision of the Australian Supreme Court in *Polyukovich* also suggests that universal jurisdiction 'is based on the notion that certain acts are so universally condemned that, regardless of the situs of the offence and the nationality of the offender or the victim, each state has jurisdiction to deal with perpetrators of those acts'.[130] Another Australian decision in *Nulyarimma* affirms that the customary *jus cogens* crime of genocide empowers all states to exercise jurisdiction over it. It was considered established that the crime of genocide 'has acquired the status of *jus cogens* or peremptory norm' and consequently 'States may exercise universal jurisdiction over such a crime'. This has been the legal position since at least 1948.[131] Finally, the International Criminal Tribunal for former Yugoslavia (ICTY) in *Furundzija* affirmed that perpetrators of torture could be held criminally responsible for torture, whether in a foreign state, or in their own state under a subsequent regime. It further specified, without referring to

---

[128] *Universal Criminal Jurisdiction with regard to the Crime of Genocide, Crimes Against Humanity and War Crimes* (International Law Institute Krakow Session, 2005).

[129] Crimes implicating breaches of *jus cogens* justify states in taking universal jurisdiction over them wherever committed, because offenders are common enemies of mankind and all nations have an equal interest in their apprehension and prosecution, per Lord Browne-Wilkinson, *Pinochet* [1999] 2 All ER 109; per Lord Millett, *ibid.* 177–8. See also Court of First Instance of Brussels (1999) 119 ILR 356–7.

[130] *Polyukhovich v Commonwealth* (1991) 91 ILR 118 (per Toohey J).

[131] *Nuliarimma* (1999) 165 ALR 621 at 632 (per Whitlam J); 641 (per Merkel J).

any territorial or nationality link to the crime, that 'one of the consequences of the *jus cogens* character bestowed by the international community upon the prohibition of torture is that every State is entitled to investigate, prosecute and punish or extradite individuals accused of torture, who are present in a territory under its jurisdiction'. The inherently universal character of the crime based on its peremptory status gives all states universal jurisdiction.[132]

In 2002, the conclusion that was reached by Judges Higgins, Kooijmans and Buergenthal in the *Arrest Warrant* case was therefore somewhat counter-factual, to the effect:

> That there is no established practice in which States exercise universal jurisdiction, properly so called, is undeniable ... This does not necessarily indicate, however, that such an exercise would be unlawful ... [For] a State is not required to legislate up to the full scope of the jurisdiction allowed by international law ... National legislation may be illuminating as to the issue of universal jurisdiction, but not conclusive as to its legality.[133]

As it happens, there was already a significant amount of practice at the time when the three judges wrote their Joint Separate Opinion. But more substantial is their main point, similar to the one made in *Lotus*, both in terms of the initial freedom to act in the exercise of jurisdiction in the absence of a prohibitive rule, and also in terms of how the court in *Lotus* declined to see the examples from state practice as an undeniable indication as to whether the relevant jurisdictional entitlement was or was not in place. The inconclusiveness of state practice is not an indication of a lack of jurisdictional entitlement of the state. Consequently, the universal jurisdiction over serious international crimes flows from grounds other than its recognition in individual situations in practice.

From the above analysis, it seems that there are three grounds that validate the existence and exercise of universal jurisdiction in international law. The first ground relates to the principles stated in *Lotus*. The second ground is the multiple recognition in conventional law which makes it possible for the customary rule against universal jurisdiction to materialize and gain effect. Examples could be furnished by reference to Articles 5 and 7 of the 1984 UN Convention Against Torture. Similar effect follows from Articles 49, 50, 129 and 146 of the 1949 Geneva Conventions which oblige states to search for and try persons accused of

---

[132] *Furundzija*, Case no. IT-95-17/I-T, ICTY, Judgment of 10 December 1998, paras 155–6.

[133] *Arrest Warrant*, n. 46 above, para. 45.

grave breaches of these Conventions. The same obligation is extended to breaches of Additional Protocol I under its Article 85. The Geneva Conventions impose on states parties obligations that require a more proactive action in terms of searching for offenders and establishing jurisdiction over them. The third ground for universal jurisdiction is *jus cogens*. These three grounds are not always mutually overlapping, but universal jurisdiction can be justified on each of those grounds separately.

The exercise of universal jurisdiction in practice has met support as well as a backlash. To illustrate, Belgium's amendment of its universal jurisdiction law, with more enhanced requirements as to the relevant person's presence on the Belgian territory,[134] was caused by completely non-legal factors, such as pressure from the US government, including the threat that Belgium would cease to be the host of the NATO headquarters. Also, the US pressure was based not on legal conviction but on practical concerns not to have its officials prosecuted in Belgium.

1.11.3 Two Related Points: The Presence of the Accused and the Duty to Prosecute

As we saw above, the dissent of Judge Guillaume in *Arrest Warrant* required the presence of the accused on the territory of the state before that state could try that person for core international crimes. This position was impliedly but effectively contradicted by the Court's majority in *Arrest Warrant* where, in the first place, the universal jurisdiction was not disputed by the respondent state even as it was exercised in the absence of the accused. Then, the International Court has at least implicitly recognized universal jurisdiction over serious international crimes, as it joined the parties in not disputing its existence; furthermore, the Court stated that one state can try another state's foreign minister after his/her retirement and did not specify that any territorial or nationality link was required either with the accused or the victim.[135] The Joint Separate Opinion has further endorsed this position in the sense that:

> National legislation, enacted to give effect to these treaties, quite naturally also may make mention of the necessity of the presence of the accused. These sensible realities are critical for the obligatory exercise of *aut dedere aut prosequi* jurisdiction, but cannot be interpreted *a contrario* so as to exclude a voluntary exercise of a universal jurisdiction.[136]

---

134 (2003) 42 ILM 1258.

135 *Arrest Warrant*, n. 46 above, para. 61.

136 *Ibid.*, Joint Separate Opinion, para. 57.

More generally, it cannot be asserted that the exercise of any extra-territorial jurisdiction, including the nationality-based jurisdiction, inherently requires the presence of the accused within the forum state's territory as a criterion validating that jurisdiction. There is no reason why that should be seen as a requirement specifically applicable to universal jurisdiction.

This discourse also raises the issue of the difference between the duty to prosecute core international crimes and the type of jurisdiction established, for that purpose, over the same crimes. A treaty imposing the duty to prosecute particular crimes may establish a completely new jurisdiction hitherto inapplicable to the relevant crime, or broaden an existing one under general international law, or actually reflect the pre-existing headings of jurisdiction and make them mandatory. It seems that the latter possibility is envisaged in the provisions of the 1984 Convention Against Torture (CAT) and the Geneva Conventions 1949, referred to above.

More broadly speaking, the duty to prosecute is not as much about establishing a particular jurisdictional entitlement as about turning its exercise into a duty. This could be in relation to any type of territorial or extra-territorial jurisdiction, universal or other. In addition, as the Joint Separate Opinion has also emphasized, the conventional duty to prosecute or extradite can require establishing jurisdiction with a view to extraditing or prosecuting: the aim is that the offender should be prosecuted within the spatial remit of the treaty-established jurisdictional network and that there should be no safe haven or impunity for the offender to benefit from. In the view of the three judges:

> The stated purpose of the provision was that the offences would not be left unpunished (the extradition provisions playing their role in this objective). It may immediately be noted that this is an early form of the *aut dedere aut prosequi* to be seen in later conventions. But the obligation to prosecute is primary, making it even stronger.[137]

137 *Ibid.* Joint Separate Opinion, 71 (para. 30).

1.11.4 Universal Jurisdiction in Civil Proceedings

Since the landmark judgment in *Filartiga*,[138] the US Alien Tort Statute (ATS)[139] has for decades been applied by US courts to violations of international law perpetrated outside the territory of the United States and committed by foreign citizens against foreign victims, provided that, in line with jurisprudence culminating with *Sosa*, the cause of action relied on a 'universal, definable and obligatory' norm of international law.[140] In more express terms, as to the normative basis of universal civil jurisdiction, was the Canadian Court of Appeal in *Bouzari*, which has recognized universal civil jurisdiction over the breaches of peremptory norms. Since by torturing Bouzari Iran had committed a breach of peremptory norms, it eliminated itself as a possible forum; the appellant was left without a forum and hence the application of the requirement that the tort must have a real and substantial connection with the forum was not easy.[141]

According to Article 14(1) of the CAT 1984, 'Each State Party shall ensure in its legal system that the victim of an act of torture obtains redress and has an enforceable right to fair and adequate compensation'. This clause includes no restriction *ratione loci*. Redress should be made available to any victim of torture, regardless of the locus of the act.[142]

In *Bouzari* before the Canadian Court of Appeal, and *Jones* before the UK House of Lords, this extra-territorial effect was not accepted, not because the relevant national courts denied the inherent potential of Article 14 to displace immunities, but because Article 14 was seen to

---

[138] *Filartiga v Pena-Irala*, US Court of Appeals, Second Circuit, (1980) 77 ILR 169.

[139] ATS s. 1791 provides that 'The district courts shall have original jurisdiction of any civil action by an alien for a tort only, committed in violation of the law of nations or a treaty of the United States'.

[140] *Sosa v Alvarez-Machain*, No. 03-339, 29 June 2004.

[141] *Bouzari v Islamic Republic of Iran*, Court of Appeal for Ontario, 30 June 2004, Docket: C38295, paras 36–8, per Goudge JA; although the court stated in para. 38 that it did not need to finally clarify this issue because the adjudication was refused on the basis of state immunity, which is an issue separate from the issues of jurisdiction.

[142] See for detailed analysis of Article 14 of the CAT, C.K. Hall, 'The Duty of States Parties to the Convention Against Torture to Provide Procedures Permitting Victims to Recover Reparations for Torture Committed Abroad' (2007) 18 *EJIL* 921.

relate only to torture committed within the forum state's territory.[143] But the UN Committee Against Torture has confirmed, in the aftermath of *Bouzari*, that the scope of Article 14 is not limited to torture committed within the forum state's territory.[144]

More recently, the Committee's General Comment No. 3 specified that 'the application of Article 14 is not limited to victims who were harmed in the territory of the State party or by or against nationals of the State party'.[145] The duty to implement Article 14 in line with General Comment No. 3 has been reiterated in relation to the United Kingdom specifically.[146]

National courts in *Bouzari* and *Jones* have, therefore, effectively engaged in a unilateral interpretation of Article 14, reading in a limitation that is not there. That the Committee's views are not inherently binding is, quite simply, immaterial. The Committee has been set up through the agreement of all states parties to the CAT and is, on that basis, in charge of implementing the Convention. Its views as to its content are supposed to be more authoritative than those of states parties put forward unilaterally. This is all the more obvious if all the Committee has done, in relation to both Canada and the United Kingdom, is to reaffirm the duty of both states to act in line with the plain and ordinary meaning of the obligation contained in Article 14.

1.11.5 Universal Civil Jurisdiction and the *Kiobel* Case

According to the Supreme Court in *Kiobel*,[147] the ATS that was at the forefront of the development of state practice regarding universal civil jurisdiction in this area, will only apply to whatever takes place within the United States, because in enacting the ATS, the Congress must be deemed to have so intended. The Court's principal point related to a presumption against extra-territoriality of legislative enactments. The

---

143 *Bouzari v Islamic Republic of Iran*, n. 141 above, paras 72–82 (per Goudge JA); *Jones v Saudi Arabia* [2006] UKHL 16, 14 June 2006, para. 20 (per Lord Bingham); para. 46 (per Lord Hoffmann).

144 UN Committee Against Torture, *Observations of the Report of Canada*, CAT/C/CO/34/CAN, paras 4(g) and 5(f).

145 UN Committee Against Torture, General Comment No. 3 (2012), para. 22.

146 Concluding Observations on the Fifth Periodic Report of the United Kingdom, adopted by the Committee at its 50th Session, 6–31 May 2013, para. 17.

147 *Kiobel v Royal Dutch Petroleum*, US Supreme Court, No. 10-4091, Judgment of 17 March 2013.

Supreme Court referred to two incidents in the late eighteenth century, before the adoption of the ATS, and involving foreign ambassadors, which allegedly reinforced such a restricted meaning of the ATS. While piracy was ordinarily understood to be within the scope of the ATS, it was singled out as a special category not affecting the otherwise applicable presumption against extra-territoriality.[148]

A further policy argument was to deny that 'the ATS was passed to make the United States a uniquely hospitable forum for the enforcement of international norms'.[149] Conversely, American citizens should be spared similar risks of being impleaded in foreign countries. The concurring opinion of Justice Breyer discussed alternatives to the majority's approach, enabling courts to assume a greater role in this process, such as the *forum non conveniens* doctrine or the balancing of underlying interests, including the relevance of the defendant's presence in the United States. Justice Breyer also warned against the United States becoming a safe haven for international criminals.[150]

The starting-point for the majority's approach to statutory interpretation was that 'when a statute gives no clear indication of an extraterritorial application, it has none', and 'when a statute provides for some extraterritorial application, the presumption against extraterritoriality operates to limit that provision to its terms'. This thesis is question-begging. If, as the Court accepts, 'a statute provides' for its own extra-territoriality, how can the Court's presumption against extra-territoriality limit its relevant provisions 'to its terms'? For, those 'terms' are the only means through which the Congress can manifest the intention for providing 'some extraterritorial application' of its enactments. Conversely, the common law presumption against extra-territoriality would have no independent value if it only 'operates to limit that [legislative] provision to its terms'.

As it happens, it was precisely the ambit of those very 'terms' that the Supreme Court's majority trimmed down through the use of the above-mentioned legislative presumption. As the majority argued:

> nothing in the text of the statute suggests that Congress intended causes of action recognized under it to have extraterritorial reach. The ATS covers actions by aliens for violations of the law of nations, but that does not imply extraterritorial reach – such violations affecting aliens can occur either within or outside the United States. Nor does the fact that the text reaches '*any* civil

---

148 *Ibid.* 5–14.

149 *Ibid.* 12.

150 *Ibid.*, Concurring Opinion, 7–15.

> action' suggest application to torts committed abroad; it is well established that generic terms like 'any' or 'every' do not rebut the presumption against extraterritoriality.[151]

The Court supported this approach by referring to *Amerada Hess*, where a clause in the Foreign Sovereign Immunities Act 1976 (FSIA) was construed as lacking extra-territorial application;[152] even though the relevant clause in the FSIA (section 1605(a)(5)) expressly refers to acts committed in the United States, while the ATS contains no similar limitation. Moreover, the ATS includes the words 'any' and 'every' in relation to the law of nations which is ordinarily concerned with issues arising from occurrences that take place abroad.

Subscribing in *Kiobel* to this blanket presumption, in principle superimposing it on all statutes, rather than applying each statute according to its ordinary meaning, is an entirely judicial choice. The Congressional intent was further compromised by reliance being placed on two pre-ATS incidents that happened before the Congress formed its legislative intention. Surely, for the purposes of statutory interpretation, the Congressional will must be seen as that of an institution which can form its intent independently of some antecedent occurrences and incidents, that intention then to be recorded on statute books accordingly.

On piracy in particular, the Court's argument was that 'pirates may well be a category unto themselves' and that:

> Applying US law to pirates, however, does not typically impose the sovereign will of the United States onto conduct occurring within the territorial jurisdiction of another sovereign, and therefore carries less direct foreign policy consequences.[153]

Here, the otherwise applicable presumption against extra-territoriality suddenly disappears. In reality, piracy is but one instance of the ATS extending to extra-territorial activities. It is, again, an entirely judicial choice to imply the presumption against extra-territoriality in respect of some provisions of the statute but not to others; and an approach that cannot make straightforward sense of what legislative intention Congress had in enacting the ATS. After all, if the Congress did not want the ATS to be extra-territorial and if the relevant presumption is so strong that not even the words 'any' and 'every' will rebut it, then that legislative

---

151 *Ibid.* 7.

152 *Argentine Republic v Amerada Hess Shipping Corp.*, 109 S.Ct. 683 (1989).

153 *Kiobel*, n. 147 above, 10.

intention must be respected and piracy too must be excluded from the ambit of the ATS.

The policy justification for construing the ATS so narrowly was that ATS litigation may involve a judicial interference into 'a delicate field of international relations', which must be affirmatively mandated by the Congress so 'that the Judiciary does not erroneously adopt an interpretation of US law that carries foreign policy consequences not clearly intended by the political branches'.[154] However, presupposing that US courts will erroneously interpret US law is a highly problematic approach: *jura novit curia*.

Similarly, the *Kiobel* point on whether 'other nations, also applying the law of nations, could hale our citizens into their courts for alleged violations of the law of nations occurring in the United States, or anywhere else in the world' is, quite simply, a matter of public international law entitlement of those other states to exercise their jurisdiction whenever the relevant link or nexus to the particular matter is present. The Supreme Court's presumption against extra-territoriality, a creature purely of US domestic law, and also hardly compatible with previous assertions of extra-territoriality in antitrust matters, could do precious little to upset that possibility. All in all, there is no such thing as a perfectly harmonious world in international relations and, even if there were one, the judiciary would not be best suited to determine exactly what it might look like.

1.12 CONCLUSIONS

The most important general conclusion to be drawn from the above analysis is that public international law provides states with a rather broad initial freedom to assert jurisdiction over a particular matter within the framework of concurrence, subject to any particular prohibitive rule of international law, or one that redistributes, *inter se*, the jurisdiction available under general international law. On the plane of general international law, the only visible restrictions are the requirement of a proper link, or nexus, with underlying events (with the exception of universal jurisdiction), and the prohibition of abuse or vexatious use of jurisdiction.

This chapter has proposed to view jurisdiction of states in terms of the overarching systemic framework under international law that determines

---

[154] *Ibid*. 4.

both the propriety and feasibility of the exercise of national jurisdiction. From there, we can have coherent answers as to right and wrong in jurisdictional controversies. Perhaps the most important lesson furnished by practice is that there is no feasible difference, in terms of general public international law, in terms of the assertion by states of civil and criminal jurisdiction; where there is criminal jurisdiction there is a civil one as well, as a matter of state entitlement at least; whether it is being exercised in practice does not prejudice the issue of whether it exists and could be exercised. It is state entitlement, and the connection between the state and the matter covered by jurisdiction, which matters for the existence of jurisdiction, not the particular type of judicial proceedings. That in some cases criminal and in other cases civil jurisdiction is regulated under various treaties, in a rather complex and detailed manner, is only an issue of special regulation that establishes a situational and empirical distinction from general international law, not a general position under it.

2. The concept of jurisdiction in international law*

Cedric Ryngaert

In this chapter, the concept of jurisdiction as exercised by states (or regional organizations such as the European Union) is analysed. Such jurisdiction is concerned with the reach of a state's law: what link, if any, is required for a state to apply its laws to situations and persons? Jurisdiction is an aspect of a state's sovereignty, as the right to prescribe and enforce laws is an essential component of statehood. In the classic Westphalian understanding, this right has been limited to a state's territory, a limitation that at the same time ensures that no state intervenes in another state's affairs (2.1). This idea is no longer strictly applied, if it ever was. Exceptions that allow for limited extra-territorial jurisdiction have been carved out, and, moreover, the territoriality principle has been construed rather liberally (2.2). To be true, some states employ a rather strict presumption that the legislature does not normally intend to apply its laws extra-territorially, but such a presumption does not limit the discretion of the legislature to do just that if it so desires (2.3).

The overlapping assertions that result from multiple states' invocation of permissive principles of jurisdiction may almost unavoidably result in international friction. This friction may be mitigated by a 'rule of reason', which instructs courts and regulators to balance the interests and connections of the case with the different states involved (2.4). This rule of reason has obvious drawbacks, notably the impropriety of unelected courts weighing political and economic interests, and the pro-forum bias which they may exude. Still, when transnational networks of judges and regulators are established, the ensuing mutual understanding may positively impact on the application of the rule of reason (2.5). It is further proposed in this chapter to infuse the rule of reason with a subsidiarity dimension: 'bystander' states should only exercise jurisdiction by default, in other words, where the state

* This chapter contains the main lines of argument featuring in the second edition of C. Ryngaert, *Jurisdiction in International Law* (Oxford University Press, 2015). The research resulting in this contribution has been funded by European Research Council Starting Grant 336230 (UNIJURIS) and the NWO VIDI innovational research scheme.

with the strongest nexus fails to assume its regulatory responsibilities to the detriment of the global interest (2.6).

2.1 NATURE OF JURISDICTION

In public international law, the concept of jurisdiction has traditionally had a strong link with the notion of sovereignty. Jurisdiction allows states to give effect to the sovereign independence which they are endowed with in a global system of formally equal states, through stating what the law is relating to persons or activities in which they have a legal interest. Sovereignty, however, not only serves as an enabling concept with respect to the exercise of jurisdiction, but also as a restraining device: it informs the adoption of international rules *restricting* the exercise of state jurisdiction. States may well adopt laws that govern matters that are not exclusively of domestic concern, and thereby impinge on other states' sovereignty. In essence, the laws of jurisdiction delimit the competences between states,[1] and thus serve as the basic 'traffic rules' of the international legal order.

When delimiting competences, the law of jurisdiction has mainly relied on the *territorial* dimension of sovereignty when devising permissive and prohibitive rules: a state's jurisdictional assertions that pertain to acts carried out *in its territory* are in principle lawful, while assertions that pertain to acts done *outside its territory* are suspect, and even presumptively unlawful. This emphasis on territoriality is a reflection of the persistent Westphalian bent of the international legal order: a system of territorially delimited nation-states that have full and exclusive sovereignty over their own territory, and no sovereignty over other states' territory. The centrality of territoriality in the law of jurisdiction, however, need not be a logical necessity. Ultimately, territoriality is historically contingent. It only rose to prominence in the seventeenth century owing to the centralization of administrative power within the state, as well as the rise of the science of

[1] F.A. Mann, 'The Doctrine of Jurisdiction in International Law' (1964) 111 *RCADI* 1 at 15 (stating that '[j]urisdiction ... is concerned with what has been described as one of the fundamental functions of public international law, *viz.* the function of regulating and delimiting the respective competences of States'.). Also A.F. Lowenfeld, 'International Litigation and the Quest for Reasonableness' (1994-I) 245 *RCADI* 9 at 29 ('I believe that while we will not here address the cosmic issues of war and peace, of nuclear weapons and terrorist assaults, we will deal with legitimate and serious concerns of private persons and of States, and surely of lawyers, embraced within what Story calls the comity of nations').

cartography that allowed for more certain borders to be drawn.[2] In pre-modern times, sovereignty was conceived of in a more tribal or community sense: people were subject to the laws of the community or tribe to which they belonged, rather than those of the territory on which they resided at a given moment.[3] Community-based conceptions of jurisdiction have recently made a normative return in the literature, especially in the work of Paul Schiff Berman, who has drawn attention to individuals' identification with transnational communities rather than with territorially-bound states, and who on that ground advocated an overhaul of the obsolete territory-based jurisdictional scheme.[4] While it is true that the steady increase in global communication, and especially the explosion of the Internet, has allowed spatially remote individuals to connect, and has restricted the role of the state, it remains no less true, however, that states have not surrendered just yet. States continue to consider territoriality as the most straightforward and certain way of delimiting competences between them.[5] As a result, jurisdictional analyses remain centred on territorial connections, even where such connections become increasingly artificial, for example, in the case of essentially non-territorial cyberspace,[6] or global climate change.[7]

---

[2] See notably R.T. Ford, 'Law's Territory (A History of Jurisdiction)' (1999) 97 *Mich. L Rev.* 843.

[3] S. Kassan, 'Extraterritorial Jurisdiction in the Ancient World' (1935) 29 *Am. J Int'l L* 237 at 240.

[4] See, for example, P.S. Berman, 'Global Legal Pluralism' (2007) 80 *Cal. L Rev.* 1155.

[5] See H.L. Buxbaum, 'Territory, Territoriality, and the Resolution of Jurisdictional Conflict' (2009) 57 *Am. J Comp. L* 631.

[6] Convention on Cybercrime, Council of Europe, 185 European Treaty Series (23 November 2001) ('Cybercrime Convention') sets forth territoriality as the main jurisdictional principle (see Article 22(1) of the Cybercrime Convention, which states that 'Each Party shall adopt such legislative and other measures as may be necessary to establish jurisdiction over any offence … when the offence is committed: a. in its territory') and several EU legal instruments addressing Internet-based criminality cite the constituent elements approach (see, for example, Council Framework Decision 2004/68/JHA, art. 8(1)(a); Council Framework Decision 2008/913/JHA, art. 9(1)(a); Council Framework Decision 2005/222/JHA, art. 10(1)(a), basing jurisdiction on the commission of the offence 'in whole or in part' on the territory of an EU Member State). Territoriality is also relied on in various shapes and colors in domestic criminal laws (see for an early survey: B.J. Koops and S.W. Brenner (eds), *Cybercrime and Jurisdiction: A Global Survey* (2006); S.W. Brenner, 'Approaches to Cybercrime Jurisdiction' (2004) 4 *J High Tech. L* 1 and for a later survey, A. Klip, 'International Criminal Law Information Society and Penal Law General Report' (2014) 85 *Revue Internationale de Droit Pénal* 381). Just a few states provide for

Given its roots in the Westphalian international legal system, the law of jurisdiction forms part of the traditional 'negative' international law of state co-existence, which mainly contains 'do not' obligations, or prohibitions, aimed at defending the sovereignty of all states, whether or not strong or powerful. For the law of jurisdiction, this means that states are in principle not allowed to assert jurisdiction over affairs which are in the domain of other states – typically acts that take place extra-territorially – as such would violate the sacrosanct principles on non-intervention and the sovereign equality of states.[8] In more recent times, however, the 'positive' dimension of jurisdiction has come to the fore somewhat more, reflecting the evolution of international law towards a law of cooperation rather than just co-existence between states. A positive understanding of jurisdiction implies that states may sometimes be *obliged to* exercise jurisdiction (rather than just being allowed to, let alone being precluded from doing so), especially in respect of values dear to the international community. Thus, a number of Conventions provide for a state's obligation to establish its criminal jurisdiction over the presumed offender of a particularly grave crime (for example, a war crime, an act of torture or an act of terrorism), provided that this person is present on the territory, and

---

technology-specific jurisdiction, see, for example, UK Computer Misuse Act 1990, ss. 4–5 (requiring a 'significant link with domestic jurisdiction'); 18 U.S.C. s. 1030(e)(2)(b) (US Computer Fraud and Abuse Act) (basing jurisdiction on the use of a computer, even if located outside the United States, 'in a manner that affects interstate or foreign commerce or communication of the United States'), applied in *United States v Ivanov*, 175 F.Supp.2d 367, 367–70 (D. Conn. 2001); US Patriot Act (basing jurisdiction on the involvement of an access device relevant for entities in the United States); Danish Penal Code, art. 9a (establishing jurisdiction over an online criminal act that has a relation to Denmark).

[7] C-366/10 *Air Transport Association of America and others v Secretary of State for Energy and Climate Change (ATA)*, Judgment of 21 December 2011, [2012] OJ C49/7, 18 February 2012, para. 151 ('In general, the European Union may require all undertakings wishing to provide services within its territory to comply with certain standards laid down by EU law. Accordingly, it may require airlines to participate in measures of EU law on environmental protection and climate change – in this case the EU emissions trading scheme – whenever they take off from or land at an aerodrome within the territory of the European Union').

[8] R.L. Muse, 'A Public International Law Critique of the Extraterritorial Jurisdiction of the Helms-Burton Act (Cuban Liberty and Democratic Solidarity (Libertad) Act of 1996)' (1996–97) 30 *Geo. Wash. J Int'l L and Econ.* 207 at 241–2; A. Bianchi, 'Extraterritoriality and Export Controls: Some Remarks on the Alleged Antinomy Between European and U.S. Approaches' (1992) 35 *GYIL* 366.

the state does not extradite him (the *aut dedere aut judicare* clause).[9] In the field of international human rights law, the concept of jurisdiction has similarly acquired an obligatory dimension, in that states that are contracting parties to human rights treaties are *required* to secure the rights to individuals falling within their jurisdiction,[10] even if these individuals find themselves outside their territory.[11]

2.2 FORMS OF JURISDICTION: PRESCRIPTIVE, ENFORCEMENT, ADJUDICATORY AND FUNCTIONAL

In the law of jurisdiction, most attention has been devoted to 'prescriptive' or 'legislative' jurisdiction. Such jurisdiction refers to the power of a state 'to make its law applicable to the activities, relations, or status of persons, or the interests of persons in things, whether by legislation, by executive act or order, by administrative rule or regulation, or by

[9] See, for example, Article 4(b) of the Convention on Offences Committed on Board Aircraft, Tokyo, 14 September 1963, 220 UNTS 10106; Article 6(2)(b) of the Convention for the Suppression of Unlawful Acts Against the Safety of Maritime Navigation, Rome, 10 March 1988, 222 UNTS 29004; Article 5(1)(c) of the Convention Against Torture and Other Cruel, Inhuman or Degrading Treatment or Punishment, New York, 10 December 1984, 1465 UNTS 85. See also ICJ, *Questions Concerning the Obligation to Prosecute or Extradite (Belgium v Senegal),* Judgment of 20 July 2012, paras 92–5.

[10] See, for example, Article 2(1) of the International Covenant on Civil and Political Rights (ICCPR), New York, 16 December 1966; Article 3 of the Convention for the Protection of Human Rights and Fundamental Freedoms (ECHR), Rome, 4 November 1950.

[11] Courts have indeed held that states have extra-territorial human rights obligations towards individuals who find themselves within the states' power or control, see *Al-Skeini and others v United Kingdom,* Application No. 55721/07, ECtHR, Judgment of 7 July 2011, para. 135; *Banković and others v Belgium and others,* Application No. 52207/99, ECtHR, Judgment of 12 December 2001, para. 71; *Loizidou v Turkey,* Application No. 15318/89, Preliminary Objections, ECtHR, Judgment of 23 March 1995, para. 62. See on state agent control: *Ilascu and others v Moldova and Russia,* Application No. 48787/99, ECtHR, Judgment of 8 July 2004, paras 392–4; *Xhavara and others v Italy and Albania,* Application No. 39473/98, ECtHR, Judgment of 11 January 2001; *Medvedyev v France,* Application No. 3394/03, ECtHR, Judgment of 10 July 2008, para. 50, and Grand Chamber, Judgment of 29 March 2010, paras 62–7; *Öcalan v Turkey*, Application No. 46221/99, ECtHR, Judgment of 12 May 2005, para. 91.

determination by a court'.[12] Under the principle espoused by the Permanent Court of International Justice in the 1927 *Lotus* case, states are in principle free to exercise prescriptive jurisdiction over a given situation as they please, unless a prohibitive rule to the contrary could be identified.[13] After *Lotus*, however, starting with the Harvard Research on International Law's 'Draft Convention on Jurisdiction with respect to Crime',[14] it appears that the international community has embraced a more restrictive approach, by requiring that the asserting state rely on a permissive principle for the exercise of jurisdiction to be lawful.[15] In this chapter, we will primarily focus on prescriptive jurisdiction, although in this section the related forms of jurisdiction known as 'enforcement', 'adjudicatory' and 'functional' jurisdiction will be clarified.

The most uncontested permissive principle of prescriptive jurisdiction, in light of the Westphalian underpinnings of the law of jurisdiction, may appear to be the territoriality principle. Pursuant to this principle, acts carried out in a state's territory fall within that state's jurisdiction. On closer inspection, however, territoriality is not as simple in application as it might seem, as crimes or other acts over which a state may desire to exercise jurisdiction may straddle borders: the act may be initiated in one state ('subjective territoriality'), but be completed, or cause effects in another ('objective territoriality'). The criminal law's classic approach to dealing with transboundary crime is to allow the exercise of jurisdiction by a state as soon as one of the constitutive elements of the crime has taken place in its territory.[16] This may seem to be straightforward enough, but where crime has become de-territorialized, such as in

---

12 Restatement (Third) of US Foreign Relations Law, s. 401(a).

13 *SS Lotus* (1927) PCIJ Reports, Series A, No. 10, 18–19.

14 Harvard Research on International Law, 'Draft Convention on Jurisdiction with respect to Crime' (1935) 29 *Am. J Int'l L* 439.

15 C.A. Bradley, 'Universal Jurisdiction and U.S. Law' (2001) *U Chi. Legal F* 323 (characterizing this as 'the conventional view'); also *Arrest Warrant (Democratic Republic of Congo v Belgium)* [2002] ICJ Rep. 3, Separate Opinion of Guillaume, para. 4 ('Under the law as classically formulated, a State normally has jurisdiction over an offence committed abroad only if the offender, or at the very least the victim, has the nationality of that State or if the crime threatens its internal or external security. Ordinarily, States are without jurisdiction over crimes committed abroad as between foreigners.').

16 What constitutes a constitutive element of a crime is essentially a matter of domestic law. See at length C. Ryngaert, 'Territorial Jurisdiction over Cross-Frontier Offences: Revisiting a Classic Problem of International Criminal Law' (2009) 9 *Int'l Crim. L Rev.* 187.

cyberspace, the use of the constitutive elements-based territoriality principle becomes particularly challenging.[17] Territoriality has also been relied on outside the criminal law, notably in competition law, where objective territoriality came to be known as the 'effects doctrine'.[18] The requirements of the territoriality principle have also been considered to be met where foreign airlines were obliged to surrender emissions allowances in respect of non-territorial air mileage on the ground that the relevant aircraft departed from, or landed at a territorial airport.[19] These liberal interpretations of territoriality in economic and environmental law

---

[17] Under the territoriality principle as applied to cybercrime, the odds of there being more than one *locus delicti* are high (criminal content may be accessed in multiple jurisdictions), and accordingly, the risk of jurisdictional conflict looms large. This is further compounded by the fact that cybercrime is rarely a single crime, but rather a conglomerate of criminal acts that are all more or less related to each other. In addition, as long as cybercrime is underregulated, the exercise of Internet jurisdiction may possibly raise *human rights* rather than jurisdictional concerns: individuals may not have expected to be subjected to foreign legislation and law enforcement, especially when they have not specifically *directed* content at users located in the foreign state, and when the production of such content was lawful under the law of their home state (see A. Klip, 'International Criminal Law Information Society and Penal Law General Report' (2014) 85 *Revue Internationale de Droit Pénal* 381). Indeed, a person cannot be expected to know the laws of all states, and it does not appear as acceptable that in practice he will be subjected to the strictest applicable law, or will have to modify the content he offers depending on the place where it is downloaded. See in this regard P.S. Berman, 'A Pluralist Approach to International Law' (2007) 32 *Yale J Int'l L* 301 at 317 (submitting that 'though geographical tracking software might seem to solve the problem by allowing websites to offer different content to different users, such a solution is probably illusory, because it would still require the sites to analyze the laws of all jurisdictions to determine what material to filter for which users').

[18] In US antitrust law, this 'effects doctrine' has been accepted as early as 1945, see *United States v Aluminium Corp. of America*, 148 F.2d 416 (2d Cir. 1945). The EU (then EC) followed suit in 1988, when the European Court of Justice adopted the 'implementation doctrine' in competition law, pursuant to which foreign anticompetitive practices that are implemented in the EU, notably through direct sales, are subject to EU territorial jurisdiction. See Joined Cases 89, 104, 114, 116, 117 and 125 to 129/85 *A. Ahlstrom Osakeyhtio v Commission* [1988] ECR 5193 ('Wood Pulp').

[19] See Directive 2008/101/EC of the European Parliament and of the Council of 19 November 2008 amending Directive 2003/87/EC so as to include aviation activities in the scheme for greenhouse gas emission allowance trading within the Community [2009] OJ L8/3, upheld in C-366/10 *Air Transport Association of America and others v Secretary of State for Energy and Climate Change (ATA)*, Judgment of 21 December 2011 [2012] OJ C49/7, 18 February 2012.

have given rise to substantial international tension. Foreign nations adopted 'blocking laws' to prohibit their corporations from complying with discovery requests concerning alleged 'extra-territorial' anti-competitive acts,[20] and threatened with legal action at the World Trade Organization.[21]

Apart from territoriality, the law of prescriptive jurisdiction features a number of principles that allow states to exercise jurisdiction on an extra-territorial basis, especially in the criminal law. These principles are usually premised on a link with the asserting state, notably nationality (the active and passive personality principles, which tie jurisdiction to the nationality of the perpetrator or respectively the victim), or political independence (the protective or security principle). The universality principle, in contrast, premises jurisdiction on the nature (gravity) of the crime rather than on a particular nexus with a state, although in practice universal jurisdiction is often only exercised when the alleged perpetrator is present on the state's territory.[22]

Where a state imposes its laws, possibly extra-territorially, logically it also wants to have these laws enforced. *Enforcement jurisdiction* then refers to a state's jurisdiction 'to enforce or compel compliance or to punish noncompliance with its laws or regulations, whether through the courts or by use of executive, administrative, police, or other nonjudicial action'.[23] The rules of enforcement jurisdiction are far stricter than the rules of prescriptive jurisdiction. As the Court held in the *Lotus* case, states are not entitled to enforce their laws outside their territory, 'except by virtue of a permissive rule derived from international custom or from

---

[20] See K.A. Knapp, 'Enforcement of U.S. Electronic Discovery Law against Foreign Companies: Should U.S. Courts Give Effect to the EU Data Protection Directive?' (2010) 10 *Rich. J Global L and Bus.* 113 at 123.

[21] Note that the World Trade Organization's dispute settlement mechanism has been reluctant to support territorial extension-based unilateral trade measures that purport to regulate conditions in other states. GATT and WTO Panels and the Appellate Body have long attempted to skirt the vexing jurisdictional issue, deciding cases before them narrowly, notably by finding that there was a sufficient nexus between the regulator and the object of regulation. See, for example, *United States – Import Prohibition of Certain Shrimp and Shrimp Products*, Appellate Body Report, WT/DS58/AB/R, 12 October 1998, where the Appellate Body found that a US import ban on shrimp harvested in ways that killed sea turtles was adequately based on a US nexus, as sea turtles traversed waters subject to US jurisdiction.

[22] See on universal criminal jurisdiction L. Reydams, *Universal Jurisdiction* (2003).

[23] Restatement (Third) of US Foreign Relations Law, s. 401(c).

a convention',[24] even where they have jurisdiction to prescribe their laws extra-territorially. Accordingly, enforcement can only happen through territorial measures, for example, by arresting a person who is voluntarily present on the territory, or by seizing property of the defendant located in the territory. Often, international cooperation will be required, for example, to bring about the presence of the presumed perpetrator by means of extradition, or to have a domestic court order enforced against assets located abroad. Such cooperation is not always forthcoming, which explains why states have sometimes resorted to extra-territorial enforcement measures, arguably in violation of international law.[25] It is not fully settled yet whether the prohibition of extra-territorial enforcement also applies to technological remote searches on computer networks located abroad.[26]

The jurisdiction exercised by the judiciary is typically denoted by the terms 'adjudicative' or 'adjudicatory' jurisdiction, which refer to a state's jurisdiction 'to subject persons or things to the process of its courts or administrative tribunals, whether in civil or in criminal proceedings, whether or not the state is a party to the proceedings'.[27] Adjudicative jurisdiction thus refers to the jurisdiction of the courts rather than to the reach of a state's laws, and pertains to the defendant's anticipation of being hauled before the courts of the state in question. As prescriptive and adjudicative jurisdiction do not coincide, states may have legitimate prescriptive jurisdiction over a situation on the basis of a permissive

---

[24] *Lotus*, n. 13 above, 18–19. A general permissive rule of extra-territorial enforcement jurisdiction may possibly be the rule which entitles the parties in an international armed conflict to wage war in the other party's or parties' territory.

[25] For example, Adolf Eichmann was kidnapped in Argentina by Israeli secret agents, without the consent of the territorial state, and charged with 'crimes against the Jewish people' and 'crimes against humanity' under the Nazis and Nazi Collaborators (Punishment) Law of 1 August 1950, but such actions have usually met with considerable protest by other states.

[26] Remote searches carried out by a state with respect to information held on websites, computers or servers located outside its territory are not contested where the information is publicly accessible (see Article 32 of the Cybercrime Convention 2001), the territorial state allows such searches, or the information-holder gives its consent. Some states, however, also carry out remote searches on foreign servers without relying on mutual legal assistance, or without seeking the consent of the territorial state (see, for example, Belgian Code of Criminal Procedure, art. 88*ter*, allowing an investigating judge to order the copying of data located abroad provided that the territorial state is informed). Such action appears to be in tension with the *Lotus*-based prohibition on extra-territorial enforcement jurisdiction.

[27] Restatement (Third) of US Foreign Relations Law, s. 401(b).

principle, but lack adjudicative jurisdiction, for example, because the defendant has no contacts with the state, or because the parties to a private contract have chosen another adjudicative forum. The principles of adjudicatory jurisdiction have been well-developed in the conflict of laws (private international law). In Europe, in civil and commercial matters, adjudicatory jurisdiction is mainly tied to the place of domicile or residence of the defendant.[28] The United States, for its part, historically had more liberal rules of adjudicatory jurisdiction. 'Minimum contacts' of the defendant with the forum sufficed for a finding of personal jurisdiction,[29] and even 'tag' jurisdiction, on the basis of the defendant's transitory presence in the forum, was accepted.[30] More recently, however, the US Supreme Court has required that the defendant be essentially 'at home' in the forum state,[31] thereby narrowing the gap with Europe.

'Functional jurisdiction', finally, is a term that is mostly used in the law of the sea, where, in essence, it refers to coastal states' limited jurisdiction over the activities in 'their' maritime zones (the territorial sea, the contiguous zone, the exclusive economic zone and the continental shelf),[32] and, to a limited extent, to any state's jurisdiction over certain activities on the high seas, such as piracy and the trade in slaves.[33] Such jurisdiction is in the first place geared towards protecting coastal states' own legitimate interests,[34] although exceptionally also towards

---

[28] Regulation (EU) 1215/2012 of the European Parliament and of the Council of 12 December 2012 on jurisdiction and the recognition and enforcement of judgments in civil and commercial matters (recast) [2012] OJ L351/1.

[29] *International Shoe Co. v Washington*, 326 U.S. 310, 316 (1945).

[30] *Burnham v Superior Court*, 495 U.S. 604 (1990).

[31] *Goodyear Dunlop Tires Operations v Brown* 131 S. Ct 2846, 2851 (2011) (holding that general jurisdiction exists over foreign corporations 'when their affiliations with the State are so "continuous and systematic" as to render them essentially at home in the forum State') and at 2856 (adding that 'continuous activity of some sort within a state … is not enough to support the demand that the corporation be amenable to suits unrelated to that activity').

[32] See for the detailed legal regimes United Nations Convention on the Law of the Sea (UNCLOS), Montego Bay, 10 December 1982.

[33] UNCLOS, Arts 99–107.

[34] See, for example, in respect of pollution UNCLOS, Art. 220 (allowing a coastal state, when a vessel is voluntarily within its port, to 'institute proceedings in respect of any violation of its laws and regulations adopted in accordance with this Convention or applicable international rules and standards for the prevention, reduction and control of pollution from vessels when the violation has occurred within the territorial sea or the exclusive economic zone of that State').

protecting common concerns.[35] It involves both a prescriptive and an enforcement component, which, however, do not necessarily coincide, for example, the coastal state may adopt laws and regulations relating to innocent passage through the territorial sea in respect of a considerable number of activities,[36] but it may only enforce those laws there (whether criminally or civilly) in limited circumstances.[37]

2.3 PRESUMPTION AGAINST EXTRA-TERRITORIALITY

The international law of jurisdiction is mainly developed through and applied by domestic courts and regulators, with little guidance having been given by international courts. In some jurisdictions, the international law of jurisdiction has played a rather limited role in circumscribing the reach *ratione loci* of domestic laws. This is especially so in the United States, where courts hardly rely on international norms of prescriptive jurisdiction, but rather on the presumption against extra-territoriality. This presumption is a canon of statutory construction pursuant to which Congress normally intends to regulate domestically. It can only be rebutted by a clear Congressional statement to the contrary.[38] Like the international law of jurisdiction, the presumption appears to be equally

---

[35] Apart from states' jurisdiction to tackle piracy and the slave trade, also the exercise of port state jurisdiction, in other words, jurisdiction exercised by the state in whose port a foreign-flagged vessel docks, with a view to tackling global governance challenges relating to fisheries, pollution, dumping, and employment conditions may be cited. See, for example, in respect of dumping UNCLOS, Art. 218. See more generally E.J. Molenaar, 'Port State Jurisdiction' (2014) *Max Planck Encyclopedia of Public International Law*, mpepil.com.

[36] UNCLOS, Art. 21(1).

[37] *Ibid.* Arts 27–28.

[38] *Foley Bros, Inc. v Filardo*, 336 U.S. 281, 285 (1949); *De Atucha v Commodity Exchange, Inc.*, 608 F.Supp. 510, 519 (D.C.N.Y. 1985) ('the laws of any jurisdiction apply only to activities within its borders unless there is some indication to the contrary'); *EEOC v Arabian American Oil Co. (Aramco)*, 499 U.S. 244, 251 (1991) ('The intent of Congress as to the extraterritorial application of the statute must be deduced by inference from boilerplate language which can be found in any number of congressional Acts, none of which have ever been held to apply overseas'); *Hartford Fire Insurance Co. v California*, 509 U.S. 764, 814 (1993) (Scalia J, dissenting); *Kollias v D & G Marine Maintenance*, 29 F.3d 67, 70 (2d Cir. 1994); *New York Central R.R. v Chisholm*, 268 U.S. 29, 31 (1925) ('Legislation is presumptively territorial and confined to limits over which the law-making power has jurisdiction'); *Morrison v National*

geared toward protecting, in the words of the US Supreme Court, 'against unintended clashes between [US] laws and those of other nations which could result in international discord'.[39] In reality, however, the presumption is mainly a matter of judicial deference to the foreign policy prerogatives of the political branches,[40] as Congress rather than the judiciary 'is likely to have superior informational and technical expertise on how to make [a] determination' whether a statute should have extra-territorial application.[41] This implies that the presumption is informed by constitutional law considerations regarding the separation of powers between the judiciary, on the one hand, and the legislature, on the other hand. In practice, the presumption has not been applied very consistently, with US courts sometimes conjuring up Congressional intent where in reality such intent was doubtful. This has made the outcome of particular cases difficult to predict. The doctrine has not failed to criticize this state of affairs, and some authors have advanced an increasing role for international law principles of jurisdiction in determining the reach of US law,[42] so far to little practical effect, however. In recent years, a rather strict interpretation of the presumption against extra-territoriality has led the US Supreme Court to hold, in *Kiobel*, that the Alien Tort Statute,[43] a statute that on its face allows foreigners to file civil claims against other foreigners in US federal court, only applies to cases that 'touch and concern' the United States,[44] and to hold, in

Australia Bank Ltd, 561 U.S. 247, 248 (2010) ('[w]hen a statute gives no clear indication of an extraterritorial application, it has none').

39 *EEOC v Arabian American Oil Co. (Aramco)*, 499 U.S. 244, 248 (1991) (Congress later overruled the Supreme Court by adopting 42 U.S.C. s. 2000(e) (Supp. V 1993); *Kiobel v Royal Dutch Petroleum Co.*, 133 S. Ct 1659, 1668–9 (2013) (submitting that recognizing a 'cause of action for conduct occurring in the territory of another sovereign', may result in 'diplomatic strife').

40 See also *Kiobel*, n 39 above, 1664 (warning, in the context of the presumption against extra-territoriality, of the 'danger of unwarranted judicial interference in the conduct of foreign policy').

41 J.G. Ku, 'Kiobel and the Surprising Death of Universal Jurisdiction under the Alien Tort Statute' (2013) 107 *Am. J Int'l L* 835, 840.

42 A.J. Colangelo, 'A Unified Approach to Extraterritoriality' (2011) 97 *Va. L Rev.* 1019 at 1108; J.H. Knox, 'A Presumption Against Extrajurisdictionality' (2010) 104 *Am. J Int'l L* 351 at 372–3.

43 28 U.S.C. s. 1350.

44 *Kiobel*, n 39 above, 1669 ('[E]ven where the claims touch and concern the territory of the United States, they must do so with sufficient force to displace the presumption against extraterritorial application', and holding that, in the case, the corporate presence of the defendants in the United States did not suffice to displace the presumption).

Morrison, that the US Exchange Act did not apply to foreign securities fraud where the link with the United States was only tenuous (thereby apparently overruling some long-standing contrary Circuit practice).[45]

2.4 JURISDICTIONAL REASONABLENESS

As can be collected from the overview of permissive principles of prescriptive jurisdiction, states can invoke a variety of jurisdictional grounds to address one and the same situation. Moreover, a multitude of states can potentially claim jurisdiction on the basis of the perceived transboundary effects of just one act. Inevitably, this may give rise to international friction. Unfortunately, international law has not (yet) come up with a rule that could resolve conflicts arising from overlapping, *prima facie* lawful jurisdictional claims. There is no rule giving priority to the 'most interested' or 'affected' state, although it may appear logical to give the territorial state (given the territorial anchoring of the law of jurisdiction) first right of way.[46] But even if such a rule were to be accepted, the question arises what state precisely qualifies as the territorial state. In transnational competition law, is it the state where participants entered into the price-fixing cartel, or is it the state where the adverse effects are felt? And what if the cartel is global in nature, involving a number of international participants and causing effects worldwide, such as the worldwide *Vitamins* cartel which led to the

---

[45] Morrison v National Australia Bank, 561 U.S. 247 (2010). See on earlier (contrary) practice at length G. Schuster, 'Extraterritoriality of Securities Laws: An Economic Analysis of Jurisdictional Conflicts' (1994) 26 *Law and Pol'y Int'l Bus.* 165.

[46] See arguing pro: for example, F.A. Mann, 'The Doctrine of Jurisdiction in International Law' (1964) 111 *RCADI* 1 at 90; J.H. Beale, 'The Jurisdiction of a Sovereign State' (1923) 36 *Harv. L Rev.* 241 at 252; G. Fitzmaurice, 'The General Principles of International Law' (1957-II) 92 *RCADI* 1 at 212; A.V. Lowe, 'Blocking Extraterritorial Jurisdiction: The British Protection of Trading Interests Act, 1980' (1981) 75 *AJIL* 257; G.R. Watson, 'The Passive Personality Principle' (1993) 28 *Tex. Int'l LJ* 1 at 17; *Bankovic and others v Belgium and 16 Other Contracting States*, Application No. 52207/99, ECtHR, 12 December 2001, para. 60 ('[A] State's competence to exercise jurisdiction over its own nationals abroad is subordinate to that State's and other States' territorial competence'); *Laker Airways Ltd v Sabena*, 731 F.2d 909, 935–6 (D.C. Cir. 1984) ('The purported principle of paramount nationality is entirely unknown in national and international law. Territoriality, not nationality, is the customary and preferred base of jurisdiction').

Empagran litigation in US courts?[47] Similarly, as regards Internet activity, a panoply of states could claim territorial contacts and thus jurisdiction, for example, on the basis of where the server is located, where the content is viewed, where the content is uploaded, where the content is deliberately directed to, where effects are felt, etc.[48]

In light of the potential for overlapping and possibly clashing jurisdictional assertions, a meta-rule of jurisdictional restraint or reasonableness may seem to be appropriate.[49] The drafters of the influential section 403 of the Restatement (Third) of US Foreign Relations Law (1987) have even taken the view that use of the jurisdictional 'rule of reason' is required by international law. This rule of reason implies that, while a jurisdictional assertion based on one of the permissive principles is presumptively valid, it will only be lawful if is exercised *reasonably*, i.e., after state courts and regulators have balanced the different interests involved in a transnational situation before establishing their jurisdiction, and (quite probably) applying their own law.[50] Ultimately, the rule of

---

47 In *E. Hoffmann-La Roche, Ltd v Empagran S.A.*, 124 S. Ct. 2359 (2004), several companies that were purchasing and reselling vitamins sued several vitamin manufacturers for illegal attempts to raise prices, both within the United States and in foreign countries. The manufacturers asked the district judge to dismiss several of the vitamin purchasers from the case because they only did business in other countries and, the manufacturers argued, could therefore not bring claims under the US Foreign Trade Antitrust Improvements Act of 1982 (FTAIA/Sherman Act). The purchasers countered that the foreign price-fixing attempts were linked to the domestic attempts and could therefore be heard under the exception to the FTAIA. The Supreme Court unanimously ruled that where anticompetitive behaviour, such as a price-fixing agreement, 'significantly and adversely affects both customers outside the United States and customers within the United States, but the adverse foreign effect is independent of any adverse domestic effect', plaintiffs who allege that they have been injured by the 'foreign effect' cannot invoke the jurisdiction of US antitrust laws or courts.

48 P.S. Berman, 'Globalization of Jurisdiction' (2002) 151 *U Pa. L Rev.* 311 at 447–58 (identifying eight possible tests).

49 H.G. Maier, 'Jurisdictional Rules in Customary International Law' in K.M. Meessen (ed.), *Extraterritorial Jurisdiction in Theory and Practice* (1996), pp. 64, 69 (arguing in favour of 'an accommodation process operating outside the limits of formal international law … described by the principle of international comity'); A. Bianchi, 'Reply to Professor Maier' in *ibid.* 74, 84 (arguing that solutions are developed 'by resorting to an equitable balance of equally legitimate claims').

50 The rule of reason has its roots in the US antitrust case law of the 1970s, which cushioned the unrestrained application of the effects doctrine. See *Timberlane Lumber Co. v Bank of America, NT and SA*, 549 F.2d 597, 605–8

reason aims at identifying the state with the strongest connection, in terms of contacts or interests, with the situation. While the rule of reason has been hailed as a 'shift from a focus on power to a focus on interests' as regards extra-territorial jurisdiction,[51] in practice, a rule of reason is difficult to objectively apply. Not only may reasonableness be in the eye of the beholder, and accordingly give rise to pro-forum bias, one may also wonder whether non-elected judges and administrative authorities are well-placed to conduct an interest-balancing test that involves considerations of political economy and may impinge on the political branches' prerogative to conduct foreign relations.

Given the political sensitivities of the rule of reason, applying a presumption that the political branches do not normally regulate extra-territorially, unless they have evinced a clear intent to do so, may appear to be the more attractive option. Nevertheless, as indicated above, the application of the presumption has been beset by problems as well, with some courts guessing what the intent of the legislature could have been in the absence of clear guidance in the statute's *travaux préparatoires*. Moreover, the presumption only applies to the judiciary. It does not solve jurisdictional conflicts where the political branches *did* intend to have a statute applied extra-territorially, irrespective of the international friction such application could engender.

2.5 HEEDING OTHER STATES' CONCERNS

Since the propriety of a jurisdictional assertion is determined by the state itself, with little to no international supervision, it is almost inevitable that the exercise of jurisdiction is prone to subjective, and even parochial interpretations. Still, as thanks to the rise of information and communication technology, regulators and courts have increasing contacts with their counterparts in other states through governmental networks,[52] it

(9th Cir. 1976)*; Mannington Mills, Inc. v Congoleum Corp.*, 595 F.2d 1287, 1292 (3d Cir. 1979).

[51] A.-M. Slaughter, 'Liberal International Relations Theory and International Economic Law' (1995) 10 *Am. U J Int'l L and Pol'y* 717 at 735–6 (arguing that '[f]rom a Liberal perspective, this focus on interests is likely to be more fruitful than a straightforward assertion of power at resolving the underlying conflict', while emphasizing the need to untie the rule of reason from territory and physical power).

[52] On government networks in particular A.M. Slaughter, 'Governing the Global Economy through Government Networks' in M. Byers (ed.), *The Role of Law in International Politics* (2000), p. 177.

may not be wishful thinking to submit that the emergence of this 'global administrative space'[53] may result in greater understanding of all affected states' legitimate concerns. In the field of antitrust law, the institutionalized contacts and dialogues, setting out duties of consultation,[54] information-sharing, positive comity[55] and conditional reciprocity[56] between transatlantic regulators, have surely contributed to the decrease of regulatory conflicts, although the substantive convergence of antitrust laws may also be an explanatory factor.

Where procedurally possible, states may also wish to file *amicus curiae* briefs with foreign courts to have their jurisdictional views heard. While exact causality cannot be established, these views may well influence the final determination made by the court hearing a transnational dispute. In the *Vitamins* litigation (2004), for instance, the US

---

[53] N. Krisch and B. Kingsbury, 'Global Governance and Global Administrative Law in the International Legal Order' (2006) 17 *Eur. J Int'l L* 1 (defining a 'global administrative space' as 'a space in which the strict dichotomy between domestic and international levels has largely broken down, in which administrative functions are performed in often complex interplays between officials and institutions on different levels, and in which regulation may be highly effective despite its predominantly non-binding forms').

[54] See, for example, OECD, Recommendation of the Council concerning Co-operation between Member Countries on Anticompetitive Practices affecting International Trade, C(95)130/FINAL (27 July 1995), para. 5(a) ('A Member country which considers that one or more enterprises situated in one or more other Member countries are or have been engaged in anticompetitive practices of whatever origin that are substantially and adversely affecting its interests, may request consultation with such other Member country or countries recognising that entering into such consultations is without prejudice to any action under its competition law and to the full freedom of ultimate decision of the Member countries concerned.').

[55] Article 6 of the 1998 Comity Agreement between the United States and the European Union. Whereas negative comity refers to the regulating state refraining from exercising jurisdiction because another state's interests may be more important (in other words, the traditional comity concept of jurisdictional restraint), positive comity refers to the competition authorities of a requesting party 'requesting the competition authorities of a requested party to investigate and, if warranted, to remedy anticompetitive activities in accordance with the requested party's competition laws'.

[56] Cf. the exemptions from the Sarbanes-Oxley Act granted by the SEC and the PCAOB, and the exemptions to be granted under the EC Statutory Audit Directive. Commonality (full harmonization) in the field of capital markets law has actually been deemed illusory by one of its main advocates, who instead believed that only reciprocity would be feasible. H. Kronke, 'Capital Markets and Conflict of Laws' (2000) 286 *RCADI* 245 at 378.

Supreme Court averred that it is to be assumed that the US Congress takes 'the legitimate sovereign interests of other nations into account'[57] when assessing the reach of US law, and avoids extending this reach when this would create a 'serious risk of interference with a foreign nation's ability independently to regulate its own commercial affairs'.[58] Apparently influenced by a number of *amicus curiae* briefs filed by foreign governments, the Court went on to decline jurisdiction over an antitrust claim alleging separable foreign harm. This is a far cry from the *Hartford Fire Insurance* case (1993), in which the same court had held that foreign policies and laws should not be heeded by US courts when giving extra-territorial application to US antitrust law, unless the foreign state compelled conduct which US law prohibited (or *vice versa*).[59]

Similarly, in the *Kiobel* litigation (2013), the US Supreme Court, while formally relying on the Congressional presumption against extra-territoriality, may well have been influenced by the *amicus* briefs filed by the European Commission and a number of foreign states, when holding that the Alien Tort Statute was not meant to apply to 'foreign-cubed' claims (claims filed by a foreign plaintiff against a foreign defendant for acts committed abroad) which do not 'touch and concern' the United States.[60] Indeed, the Commission, while not casting doubt on the legality of the exercise of universal tort jurisdiction as such, had reminded the

---

[57] *F. Hoffman-La Roche Ltd and others v Empagran S.A. and others*, 124 S. Ct. 2359, 2366 (2004).

[58] *Ibid.* 2367. Subsequent courts have accordingly held that US antitrust law does not reach antitrust claims for several harms caused by wholly foreign transactions. See notably *Empagran v F. Hoffmann-La Roche,* 417 F.3d 1267, 1270–1 (D.C. Cir. 2005); *In re DRAM Antitrust Litigation*, 546 F.3d 981 (9th Cir. 2008); *In re Monosodium Glutamate Antitrust Litigation*, 477 F.3d 535, 538 (8th Cir. 2007).

[59] *Hartford Fire Insurance Co. v California*, 509 U.S. 764 (1993). Holding otherwise might amount to breaching public international law restraints on the exercise of jurisdiction.

[60] *Kiobel*, n. 39 above, 1669 ('[E]ven where the claims touch and concern the territory of the United States, they must do so with sufficient force to displace the presumption against extraterritorial application', and holding that, in the case, the corporate presence of the defendants in the United States did not suffice to displace the presumption). Note that the US government did *not* argue in favour of applying the presumption to the Alien Tort Statute. See Supplemental Brief for the United States as *Amicus Curiae* in Partial Support of Affirmance, at 19–20, *Kiobel*, n. 39 above, (No. 10-1491), 19–20, available at www.americanbar.org/content/dam/aba/publications/supreme_court_preview/briefs/10-1491_affirmance amcuusa.authcheckdam.pdf.

Court to exercise this jurisdiction reasonably.[61] And in a more strongly worded brief, the United Kingdom and the Netherlands argued that the exercise of universal civil jurisdiction risks trampling on a foreign nation's prerogative to 'regulate its own commercial affairs',[62] and could adversely affect 'much needed direct foreign investment' in host countries.[63]

2.6 SUBSIDIARITY IN THE LAW OF JURISDICTION

In a variation on the jurisdictional rule of reason, it is suggested here that states, after hearing the views of other states, and arguably also foreign persons and businesses potentially subject to extra-territorial regulation, should refrain from exercising jurisdiction when another state is, in light of its contacts with the situation, better placed to bring its laws to bear, *unless* the latter state's failure to do so harms the *global interest*, and multilateral regulation and supervision are absent. In that case, it is advisable that a 'bystander' state, i.e., a state with a more tenuous nexus, could, and perhaps even should exercise *subsidiary* jurisdiction as a sort of 'trustee of mankind'.

---

[61] Supplemental Brief of the European Commission on behalf of the European Union as *Amicus Curiae* in Support of Neither Party, *Kiobel*, n. 39 above, (No. 10-1491), 33, available at www.sdshhlaw.com/pdfs/European%20Commission%20on%20Behalf%20of%20the%20European%20Union%20(Revised).pdf. ('[The] internationally recognized justifications for universal jurisdiction, although typically articulated in a criminal context, also contemplate and support a civil component where limited, as here, to the circumstances that would give rise to universal criminal jurisdiction') and at 22 (stating that, 'as far as the European Commission is aware, not a single State appears to have objected to the United States' exercise of jurisdiction over the extraterritorial ATS claim brought in *Filartiga* [the seminal ATS case], by an alien against an alien, for the universally condemned crime of official torture, which has occurred in a foreign country'). At 26 *et seq.*, the brief addresses the substantive and procedural limitations imposed by international law on the exercise of universal civil jurisdiction.

[62] Supplemental Brief of the Governments of the Kingdom of the Netherlands and the United Kingdom of Great Britain and Northern Ireland as *Amici Curiae* in Support of Neither Party, *Kiobel*, n. 39 above, (No. 10-1491), 31, available at www.americanbar.org/content/dam/aba/publications/supreme_court_preview/briefs/10-1491_neutralamcunetherlands-uk-greatbritain-andirelandgovs.authcheckdam.pdf.

[63] *Ibid.* 26.

This dynamic of subsidiarity is already at work in discrete fields of the law. In the field of international crimes, for instance, subsidiarity has been modelled on the International Criminal Court's complementarity principle, by virtue of which the ICC and *mutatis mutandis* bystander states can exercise jurisdiction if the state with the stronger connection (normally the territorial state or the state of nationality) fails to genuinely investigate or prosecute the case.[64] Prosecutorial application of subsidiarity is required by law in Belgium,[65] Spain[66] and Switzerland.[67] Subsidiarity is applied as a prudential doctrine by courts in Austria,[68] and as guiding the exercise of prosecutorial discretion in Germany,[69] the United

[64] See Rome Statute of the International Criminal Court, Art. 17. *In extenso* C. Ryngaert, 'Applying the Rome Statute's Complementarity Principle: Drawing Lessons from the Prosecution of Core Crimes by States Acting under the Universality Principle' (2008) *Criminal Law Forum* 153.

[65] Article 12*bis* of the Preliminary Title of the Belgian Code of Criminal Procedure (PTCCP) requires, *inter alia*, that the Belgian federal prosecutor inquire as to the quality of the proceedings that could be brought in an alternative jurisdiction.

[66] Fundamental Law of the Judiciary, art. 23(4) (requiring that Spanish prosecutors inquire whether no proceedings have been initiated in another competent country, leading to an investigation and effective prosecution of the offence). See for applications A.N. Madrid, Sala de lo Penal, Apelacio no. 31/2009, Auto, No. 1/09, 9 July 2009 (dismissing a case brought against seven Israeli officials allegedly involved in the killing of Hamas commander Shehadeh); J.C.I. No. 6, A.N. Madrid, Diligencias previas 134/2009, Auto, 4 May 2009 (judge deciding to send an international rogatory commission to the United States in a case brought against six former Bush administration officials in respect of abuses committed in Guantánamo, with a view to informing his application of the subsidiarity principle). See on the former case also S. Weill, 'The Targeted Killing of Salah Shehadeh from Gaza to Madrid' (2009) 7 *J Int'l Crim. Just.* 617, and on the latter case K. Ambos, 'Prosecuting Guantánamo in Europe: Can and Shall the Masterminds of the "Torture Memos" be Held Criminally Responsible on the Basis of Universal Jurisdiction?' (2009) 42 *Case Western Re. J Int'l L* 405.

[67] Amended Criminal Code, art. 264m(2)(a) (providing that a case can be dismissed where an authority of another state is investigating and/or prosecuting the alleged crime(s) and where the suspect can be extradited to such authority).

[68] Oberster Gerichtshof (OGH) [Supreme Court] 13 July 1994, No. 150s99/94, affirmed; Landesgericht Salzburg (LG Salzburg) [trial court] 31 May 1995, No. 150s99/94.

[69] Decision of the Federal Prosecutor of Germany, 2 October 2005, JZ 311.

Kingdom,[70] Denmark,[71] Norway[72] and Sweden.[73] While it is too early to state that the application of the subsidiarity principle is required by (international) law, it clearly serves as a restraining device, allowing for the exercise of jurisdiction only where the most interested state unduly fails to live up to its responsibilities. Also, in transnational tort litigation regarding gross human rights violations, subsidiarity, through a variety of domestic tort techniques, such as the exhaustion of local remedies requirement,[74] or *forum non conveniens*,[75] has come to play an important

---

[70] It has been reported by the Crown Prosecution Service (CPS) 'that there is a clear preference within the CPS for prosecutions in the territorial state', for example with respect to Rwandan genocide suspects, and that '[a]ccordingly, the CPS seeks to ensure the extradition to Rwanda of genocide suspects currently residing in the UK, despite jurisdiction over the genocide'. Crown Prosecution Service, Response to FIDH/REDRESS questionnaire, n. 1307; REDRESS/FIDH, *Extraterritorial Jurisdiction in the European Union: A Study of the Laws and Practice in the 27 Member States of the European Union* (December 2010), p. 262, n. 1307, referring to Correspondence on file with REDRESS. In a note submitted to the United Nations, the United Kingdom acknowledged that restraints may be called for in the view of competing jurisdictional claims with respect to atrocity cases. See United Kingdom of Great Britain and Northern Ireland, 'Scope and Application of the Principle of Universal Jurisdiction', Note submitted to the Office of Legal Affairs pursuant to UN General Assembly Resolution 65/33 of 6 December 2010 (15 April 2011).

[71] REDRESS/FIDH, n. 70 above (Danish Ministry of Justice stating that '[i]n cases of concurrent jurisdiction, the legitimate interest of Denmark in exercising jurisdiction may be balanced against the interest of other states in retaining (exclusive) jurisdiction on the basis of Section 12 of the Criminal Code').

[72] Submission by the Permanent Mission of Norway to the United Nations on the issue of Universal Jurisdiction, 7 May 2009, p. 5, available at www.un.org/en/ga/sixth/65/ScopeAppUniJuri_StatesComments/Norway.pdf (stating that a Norwegian prosecutor, when exercising universal jurisdiction, is required to assess whether the alternative jurisdiction has a 'properly functioning legal system').

[73] REDRESS/FIDH, n. 70 above, 246, n. 1225, referring to FIDH/REDRESS, MoJ/MFA Questionnaire ('The ability or willingness of the state where the alleged crimes were committed to investigate and prosecute the crimes is taken into account in the practical handling of a case').

[74] *Sarei v Rio Tinto, PLC*, 671 F.3d 736 (9th Cir. 2011) (en banc), *vacated,* 133 S. Ct. 1995 (2013); *Sarei v Rio Tinto, PLC*, 550 F.3d 822, 825–6 (9th Cir. 2008) (en banc); Torture Victim Protection Act, Pub. L No. 102-256, 106 Stat. 73 (12 March 1992), s. 2(b) ('A court shall decline to hear a claim under this section if the claimant has not exhausted adequate and available remedies in the place in which the conduct giving rise to the claim occurred').

[75] See *Spiliada Maritime Corp. v Cansulex Ltd* [1987] AC 460, HL; *Connelly v RTZ Corp.* [1998] 1 AC 854, HL; *Lubbe v Cape PLC* [2000] 4 All ER 268, HL;

restraining role. Exceptionally, considerations of subsidiarity may also *expand* rather than restrain the jurisdictional basis for transnational tort litigation, notably where 'forum of necessity'-based techniques allow states to affirmatively exercise jurisdiction when justice so demands, especially when the victim does not have reasonable access to another (territorial) forum, and the alleged violations are of sufficient gravity.[76]

In economic law, especially antitrust law, the jurisdictional subsidiarity principle appears to have taken the form of an economic principle that allows for the exercise of extra-territorial jurisdiction when such would increase global welfare, in the face of inaction of states with stronger links, for example, states condoning or even encouraging export cartels or corrupt practices.[77] Such an approach suggests that the international community has a shared interest in efficient and fair economic regulation – an approach which, given the wide discrepancies of national economic laws, may be open to criticism.[78] Before the US Supreme Court, the

---

Bil'in (Village Council) v Green Park Int'l Inc., No. 500-17-044030-0, Can. Montreal Sup. Ct, 7 July 2008, paras 326–7 (holding that the plaintiffs engaged in 'inappropriate forum' shopping and chose a Québec forum to 'avoid … the necessity… of proving [their case in Israel]… thus ensuring for themselves a juridical advantage based on a merely superficial connection of the Action with Québec'); *Bil'in (Village Council) v Green Park Int'l Inc.* [2010] CA 1455, Can. Que., para. 86 (observing that '[i]t requires a great deal of imagination to claim that the action has a serious connection with Quebec').

[76] The European Commission's *amicus* brief in *Kiobel* indicates that at least ten EU Member States can exercise such jurisdiction. Supplemental Brief of the European Commission on behalf of the European Union as *Amicus Curiae* in Support of Neither Party, *Kiobel*, n. 39 above, (No. 10-1491), 24, n. 66; *El-Hojouj v Unnamed Libyan Officials*, Case No. 400882/HAZA11-2252 (ECLI:NL:RBSGR:2012:BV9748) (Neth.), Arrondissementsrechtbank Den Haag [District Court of The Hague], 21 March 2012 (applicant claimed to have suffered damages following unlawful imprisonment in Libya for allegedly infecting children with HIV/AIDS); *Anvil Mining Ltd v Canadian Ass'n Against Impunity* [2012] CA 117, Can. Que., paras 96–103.

[77] As Guzman has observed, this law and economics method searches for rules that 'permit transactions to take place when the total impact on welfare is positive, and prevent transactions from taking place when the total impact on welfare is negative'. A.T. Guzman, 'Choice of Law: New Foundations' (2002) 90 *Geo. LJ* 883 at 896. Condoning export cartels may increase the welfare of the territorial state or certain segments of the territorial state, but will normally decrease overall welfare.

[78] See in favour, and rather convincingly, H.L. Buxbaum, 'National Jurisdiction and Global Business Networks' (2010) 17 *Ind. J Global Legal Stud.* 165 ('[I]s it always a pretense to suggest that we have a shared community of policy, interest and value, particularly in the area of economic regulation? In a world in

jurisdictional law and economics argument has possibly most strongly been made by leading economists Joseph Stiglitz and Peter Orszag in their *amicus* brief in the aforementioned *Vitamins* (*Empagran*) litigation, where they set out to convince the Court to take account of global deterrence arguments in US antitrust litigation, and thus to provide a remedy for antitrust harm suffered in foreign transactions.[79] The Court rejected this argument, however, declining to exercise jurisdiction over separate foreign antitrust harm, on the ground that the non-economic principle of non-intervention in the affairs of foreign states carried more weight.[80] This reasoning left foreign plaintiffs in the cold, as they could not recover their damages anywhere, their local courts being inaccessible.[81] From a global efficiency and fairness perspective, this outcome may not be satisfactory. But then, economic fairness is just one jurisdictional parameter, sovereignty and legitimate expectations are others. The Supreme Court's judgment bears testimony to the abiding relevance of territoriality, the limited jurisdictional power flowing from it, and states' reluctance to use their administrative resources to address problems that are ultimately not theirs. The US Supreme Court's judgments in *Kiobel* and *Morrison* have to be seen in the same light: it is not the duty of the United States, as a 'city upon a hill', to stamp out the 'universal evil' of securities fraud,[82] or to be the '*custos morum* of the whole world',[83]

---

which the ongoing incidence of securities fraud is seen to jeopardize the value of billions of dollars in pension funds, in which the activities of price-fixing cartels not only harm consumers worldwide but threaten the economic growth of developing countries. In which national laws, self-regulation and nonbinding codes combined are still perceived as inadequate to stem the misconduct of multinational enterprises?').

[79] Brief of *Amici Curiae* Economists J.E. Stiglitz and P.R. Orszag in Support of Respondents, *F. Hoffmann-LaRoche Ltd v Empagran S.A.*, 542 U.S. 155 (2004) (No. 03-724).

[80] *F. Hoffmann-LaRoche Ltd v Empagran S.A.*, 542 U.S. 155, 159–65 (2004); Buxbaum, n. 78 above, 175 ('[T]he court retreated into its "natural" space of engagement. It did not really engage the substance of the plaintiffs' argument regarding global under-deterrence').

[81] R. Michaels, 'Global Problems in Domestic Courts' in S. Muller, S. Zouridis, M. Frishman and L. Kistemaker (eds), *The Law of the Future and the Future of the Law* (2011).

[82] See in this respect J.D. Kelly, 'Let There be Fraud (Abroad): A Proposal for a New U.S. Jurisprudence with regard to the Extraterritorial Application of the Anti-Fraud Provisions of the 1933 and 1934 Securities Acts' (1997) 28 *Law and Pol'y Int'l Bus.* 477 at 491.

[83] *Kiobel*, n. 39 above, 1668.

offering a forum to any victim of human rights violations committed by foreigners against other foreigners.[84]

It is pointed out, however, that where states have already taken the lead to tackle global governance challenges via domestic regulatory measures, they may have an incentive to geographically extend their domestic regulation so as to level the international playing field.[85] Such territorial extension deprives foreign competitors of the competitive edge they have *vis-à-vis* domestic businesses that results from lax foreign regulation. The long jurisdictional arm of the US Foreign Corrupt Practices Act and its vigorous enforcement, for instance, can be explained by the United States' desire to protect the overseas competitiveness of US firms whose business opportunities could be undermined by the strict anti-corruption rules to which they are subjected under US law, also in their foreign operations.[86] Along similar lines, the European Union has extended its aviation legislation to foreign airlines so as to protect the business opportunities of EU-based airlines already subject to EU law.[87] Such legislative extension, however, is not just informed by the desire to protect national or regional trade interests, but also to further global public goods in ways that territorially limited domestic regulation cannot. In climate policy, this phenomenon is known as 'carbon leakage', i.e., an increase in emissions in a state with lax environmental regulation when production moves there because of strict regulation in another state. By

---

[84] Note that the US political branches have at times taken this duty upon themselves. See recently, for example, President Obama's authorization to use force to so as to protect the Yazidi religious minority in Iraq from attacks committed by the Islamic State in 2014. On 7 August 2014 the President announced that he authorized two operations in Iraq: targeted airstrikes to protect American personnel, and a humanitarian effort to help save thousands of Iraqi civilians trapped on Mount Sinjar, in order to 'prevent a potential act of genocide'. See White House, Statement by the President, 7 August 2014, available at www.whitehouse.gov/the-press-office/2014/08/07/statement-president.

[85] See on territorial extension of EU law J. Scott, 'Extraterritoriality and Territorial Extension in EU Law' (2014) 62 *Am. J Comp. L* 87.

[86] J. Wouters, C. Ryngaert and A.S. Cloots, 'The International Legal Framework Against Corruption: Achievements and Challenges' (2013) 14 *Melb. J Int'l L* 205.

[87] See Recital 16 in the Preamble to Directive 2008/101/EC of the European Parliament and of the Council of 19 November 2008 amending Directive 2003/87/EC so as to include aviation activities in the scheme for greenhouse gas emission allowance trading within the Community [2009] OJ L8/3 ('In order to avoid distortions of competition and improve environmental effectiveness, emissions from all flights arriving at and departing from Community aerodromes should be included from 2012').

the same token, firms incorporated in a state with lax anti-corruption legislation may take the place of firms incorporated in a state with strict legislation, as a result of which corruption overall does not decrease. To counter this phenomenon, states may be inclined to extend their territorial regulation. The cause may be noble and the technique understandable, but such jurisdictional extension may nevertheless be in tension with the classic rules of jurisdiction, which allow for the exercise of universal jurisdiction only for grave international crimes. Still, states may well be able to find some territorial nexus to justify their assertions.[88] Also the fact that a multilateral solution to address the global governance problem has failed to materialize may increase the legitimacy of the assertion.[89] Such an assertion then becomes an exercise of subsidiary jurisdiction in the face of a collective action problem.

---

[88] As far as climate change legislation is concerned, the EU has found a way around the problem of universality by relying on territorial links constituted by foreign aircraft departing from, or landing at EU airports. See C-366/10 *Air Transport Association of America and others v Secretary of State for Energy and Climate Change (ATA)*, Judgment of 21 December 2011 [2012] OJ C49/7, 18 February 2012, para. 125 (arguing that the extension of the Aviation Directive is in keeping with the public international law principle of territoriality). Accordingly, the Aviation Directive does *not* have universal application, in that it would subject *all* flights to EU law. The United States, for its part, when enforcing its anticorruption legislation (FCPA), has similarly relied on a broad interpretation of territoriality. The FCPA applies to 'any person' acting within US territory, notably if it causes, directly or through agents, an act in furtherance of the corrupt payment to take place within the territory of the United States (FCPA, ss. 78dd-1, 78dd-2, 78dd-3). This provision has allowed the Department of Justice and the Securities and Exchange Commission to bring corruption proceedings against foreign persons whose bribery acts may have had only a tenuous connection with the United States, for example routing payment through US bank accounts or sending an email to a US company (see, for example, *United States v Technip S.A. (Plea Agreement)* (SD Tex, No 4:10-CR-00439, 28 June 2010). The US enforcement agencies could thus bring claims against foreign issuers in respect of the bribery of foreign officials without any nexus with the United States, except their listing of stock on a US exchange (FCPA, s. 78dd-1(g)), and (in respect of foreign bribery) against foreign persons whose stock is not even listed in the United States, on the sole basis that some act furthering bribery has a link with the United States (FCPA, s. 78dd-2(i)).

[89] See Recital 9 in the Preamble to Directive 2008/101/EC of the European Parliament and of the Council of 19 November 2008 amending Directive 2003/87/EC so as to include aviation activities in the scheme for greenhouse gas emission allowance trading within the Community [2009] OJ L8/3.

2.7 CONCLUDING OBSERVATIONS

One may be tempted to believe that many jurisdictional problems will lose their salience as soon as transnational or global governance problems are adequately dealt with at a multilateral level, for example, when an international competition law regime is established, or when the International Civil Aviation Organization reaches agreement on aviation emissions caps, thereby obviating the need for unilateral, extra-territorial state action. At a theoretical level, that may well be true. In practice, however, individual states will continue to play the leading role in global governance in the face of the elusiveness of relevant multilateral agreements and centralized institutions.[90] Even in respect of international crimes, the existing, permanent International Criminal Court can only deal with a small number of atrocity cases.

Accordingly, the unilateral exercise of jurisdiction by states, or regional organizations, will be there to stay, to 'recast global problems in local terms' in Buxbaum's words.[91] One cannot deny that such unilateralism may well lead to abuse by economically and politically powerful states,[92] who may tend to limit foreign operators' market access in their own national rather than global interest.[93] In addition, it could lead to regulatory chaos where numerous states start to exercise jurisdiction over one and the same situation, thereby increasing transaction costs for transnational operators. Therefore, a rule of reason may be called for, requiring states to defer to other states that have a stronger regulatory

---

[90] J.A. Meyer, 'Dual Illegality and Geoambiguous Law: A New Rule for Extraterritorial Application of US Law' (2010) 95 *Minn. L Rev.* 110 at 123 (observing that 'nation-state governments will retain for the foreseeable future an essential and primary role in world governance'); G. Shaffer, 'International Law and Global Public Goods in a Legal Pluralist World' (2012) 23 *Eur. J Int'l L* 669 at 675 (noting that 'we lack legitimate, centralized institutions with general taxing and regulatory powers').

[91] Buxbaum, n. 78 above, 167 (borrowing the concept of 'scale' from political geography as an analytical tool 'in examining how global economic misconduct is situated before the courts of one particular country').

[92] It has been shown that extra-territoriality has been mainly used by the United States, and less frequently by other states, because '[t]he size of the U.S. economy and its high (in absolute terms) level of integration into global markets … give its courts unparalleled enforcement power across numerous issues' (T. Putnam, 'Courts Without Borders: Domestic Sources of US Extraterritoriality in the Regulatory Sphere' (2009) *Int'l Org.* 459 at 483).

[93] This is indeed one of the dangers of the territorial extension of economic law. See 2.6 above.

interest in, or nexus to, the situation. It has been argued in this chapter, however, that such deference should not be unconditional. It should hinge on the ability and willingness of the most interested state to genuinely address the situation in ways that serve the interest of the international community (even if such ways are not exactly those that the extra-territorially regulating state had in mind).[94] Failure to discharge this burden may legitimately yield to the exercise of subsidiary jurisdiction by bystander states.

---

[94] The latter implies that states may want to recognize other states' standards that provide equivalent protection. This process of mutual recognition has been usefully characterized as a mechanism of managing 'hybridity that the movement across territorial borders inevitably creates'. Berman, n. 4 above, 1224.

3. Universal jurisdiction: concept, logic and reality

*Sienho Yee**

3.1 CONCEPT AND LOGIC OF UNIVERSAL JURISDICTION

1. The perceived abuse in recent years in the resort to universal jurisdiction, particularly over African officials, caused the Group of African States to request in February 2009 the inclusion of an additional item on the 'Abuse of the principle of universal jurisdiction' in the agenda of the 63rd session of the United Nations General Assembly (UNGA). The request was accepted and universal jurisdiction has been a subject of heated discussion in the UNGA since that time. Debates were conducted on this topic in the autumn of 2009. The UNGA then asked governments to submit observations and information on state practice. Again debates were held on the topic in the autumn of 2010. Further information has been sought and further work has been scheduled for 2011.[1]

2. The comments and statements made by governments show that there is great confusion on the concept, the scope and application of universal jurisdiction. In order for us to properly understand universal jurisdiction, it will be helpful for us to recap the understanding of jurisdiction in general. Usually jurisdiction has three dimensions: prescriptive, adjudicative and

* First published in (2011) 10 Chinese Journal of International Law 503–30. The preparation of this article formed part of the work of Research Project No. 08&ZD055 of the China Social Sciences Foundation. The comments of William Schabas and the reviewers of the *Chinese JIL* on a draft are much appreciated. All opinions are personal. The article was completed on 12 September 2011. The websites cited were current as of this date unless otherwise noted. A postscript note commenting on subsequent developments is found at the end of this chapter.

[1] For the Request and the Explanatory Memorandum, see A/63/237 (3 February 2009) and Annex ('African Union Memo'). For summaries of development and documentation, see UN Sixth Committee, www.un.org/en/ga/sixth/64/UnivJur.shtml; www.un.org/en/ ga/sixth/65/ScopeAppUniJuri.shtml.

enforcement. It is said that national criminal jurisdiction[2] is normally justified on several grounds: territoriality, nationality, passive personality or protection of national vital interests. Sometimes the effects of an act upon a state are also assimilated to some of these principles. Sometimes a treaty may be considered an independent justification for the assertion of jurisdiction; whether a treaty without incorporating the normal links such as territoriality is a sufficient justification is a controversial question. Each justification for jurisdiction may inform its exercise and thus leads to a different type of jurisdiction. The different justifications enumerated above thus give rise to different types of jurisdiction generally characterized as territorial, nationality, passive personality and protective jurisdiction.

3. Given these considerations and given the fact that there is no internationally codified definition of universal jurisdiction at present, many proposed definitions and commentaries seem to have defined universal jurisdiction by an 'absence' of the normal jurisdictional links to the national legal system attempting to exercise jurisdiction. For example, the Institut de droit international (IDI) in its 2005 Resolution on universal jurisdiction, paragraph 1, stated:

> Universal jurisdiction in criminal matters, as an additional ground of jurisdiction, means the competence of a State to prosecute alleged offenders and to punish them if convicted, irrespective of the place of commission of the crime and regardless of any link of active or passive nationality, or other grounds of jurisdiction recognized by international law.[3]

In the view of the IDI Rapporteur of the project, 'It was [the] absence of link between the crime and the prosecuting State that captured the essence of universal jurisdiction'.[4] Similarly, the AU-EU Expert Report on this topic stated:

> Universal criminal jurisdiction is the assertion by one state of its jurisdiction over crimes allegedly committed in the territory of another state by nationals of another state against nationals of another state where the crime alleged poses no direct threat to the vital interests of the state asserting jurisdiction. In other words, universal jurisdiction amounts to the claim by a state to

---

[2] This chapter deals only with universal criminal jurisdiction.

[3] Institut de droit international (IDI), Resolution on universal criminal jurisdiction with regard to the crime of genocide, crimes against humanity and war crimes, para. 1, adopted in Krakow, 2005 (available at www.idi-iil.org/idiF/resolutionsF/2005_kra_03_fr.pdf).

[4] Christian Tomuschat, Rapporteur of the IDI Commission on Universal Criminal Jurisdiction, as quoted in IDI, (2006) 71(II) *Annuaire de l'Institut de droit international* 257; see also *ibid.* 261.

> prosecute crimes in circumstances where none of the traditional links of territoriality, nationality, passive personality or the protective principle exists at the time of the commission of the alleged offence.[5]

4. Behind the 'absence' façade, however, rests the basis for such an assertion of jurisdiction, normally formulated this way: the alleged crime is an attack on the fundamental values of the international community as a whole (in other words, a violation of *jus cogens* or a species of law that is very close to that genus however described, such as *erga omnes* obligations), so that the crime is a matter of universal concern, considered as such by the international community as a whole, and that every state in the world has an interest in prosecuting the perpetrator.[6] Another instrumental reasoning, which may apply with greater force to some situations than in others, is that the exercise of universal jurisdiction is *necessary* in order to ensure that certain crimes be punished. For example, piracy, normally committed on the high seas, may go unpunished if universal jurisdiction does not exist. As such, these crimes are also of universal concern, perhaps of a slightly different kind. So understood, it would seem better to characterize universal jurisdiction as 'universal concern jurisdiction',[7] in some contrast to other forms of jurisdiction such as 'territoriality jurisdiction', 'nationality jurisdiction' and 'national interests protection jurisdiction'. These terms would make immediately apparent the justification behind each assertion of jurisdiction. A definition of universal jurisdiction or universal concern jurisdiction should be the exercise of national jurisdiction, based on universal

---

[5] *AU-EU Expert Report*, para. 8, available at http://ec.europa.eu/development/icenter/repository/troika_ua_ue_rapport_competence_universelle_EN.pdf.

[6] See generally Restatement of the Law, Third, Foreign Relations Law of the United States, s. 404 and the associated comments and notes; IDI Resolution, n. 3 above; and the IDI deliberations, IDI, n. 4 above, 199–284; International Association of Penal Law (AIDP), XVIIII Congress in 2009, Resolution on Universal Jurisdiction, available at www.penal.org/?page=mainaidp&id_rubrique=24&id_article=95.

[7] See Restatement Third, n. 6 above, s. 404 ('A state has jurisdiction to define and prescribe punishment for certain offenses recognized by the community of nations as of universal concern, such as piracy, slave trade, attacks on or hijacking of aircraft, genocide, war crimes, and perhaps certain acts of terrorism, even where none of the bases of jurisdiction indicated §402 is present').

concern, over crimes that attack the fundamental values of international society.[8]

5. The logic of universal concern jurisdiction is easy to understand. Universal concern as a motivating force for national action was propounded by the International Court of Justice in the celebrated *Barcelona Traction* case in 1970.[9] That case was about diplomatic protection, and the Court's celebrated dictum therefore cannot be claimed as direct precedent or immediate support for universal jurisdiction.[10] But that dictum on this point is unmistakably of general applicability and can be considered the elaboration of the *ultimate* rationale for universal jurisdiction. There the Court said:

> 33. When a State admits into its territory foreign investments or foreign nationals, whether natural or juristic persons, it is bound to extend to them the protection of the law and assumes obligations concerning the treatment to be afforded them. These obligations, however, are neither absolute nor unqualified. In particular, an essential distinction should be drawn between the obligations of a State towards the international community as a whole, and those arising vis-à-vis another State in the field of diplomatic protection. By their very nature the former are the concern of all States. In view of the importance of the rights involved, all States can be held to have a legal interest in their protection; they are obligations *erga omnes*.
>
> 34. Such obligations derive, for example, in contemporary international law, from the outlawing of acts of aggression, and of genocide, as also from the principles and rules concerning the basic rights of the human person, including protection from slavery and racial discrimination. Some of the corresponding rights of protection have entered into the body of general international law (*Reservations to the Convention on the Prevention and Punishment of the Crime of Genocide, Advisory Opinion*, I.C.J. Reports 1951, p. 23); others are conferred by international instruments of a universal or quasi-universal character.

6. Intended to implement this idea,[11] Article 48 ('Invocation of responsibility by a State other than an injured State') of the International Law Commission's Articles on State Responsibility, adopted in 2001, states:

---

[8] See *ibid*.

[9] Case concerning the Barcelona Traction, Light and Power Company, Ltd, Second Phase, Judgment [1970] ICJ Reports 3.

[10] See Rosalyn Higgins, Problems and Process: International Law and How We Use It (1994), pp. 57–8.

[11] ILC Draft Articles on State Responsibility, art. 48, commentary, para.(8), in ILC Report, A/56/10 (2001), p. 321.

> 1. Any State other than an injured State is entitled to invoke the responsibility of another State in accordance with paragraph 2 if: … (a) The obligation breached is owed to a group of States including that State, and is established for the protection of a collective interest of the group; or … (b) The obligation breached is owed to the international community as a whole.[12]

7. Thus, as a general proposition, there are certain matters in the world that are of universal concern, and this universal concern is sufficient to justify certain action on the part of states. Applied to our inquiry in this chapter, this rationale alone, or this rationale plus another factor, potentially would justify a state's exercise of universal jurisdiction. However, universal jurisdiction is not a necessary corollary of universal concern, even when that concern assumes *jus cogens* proportions.[13] The sole fact of the violation of a rule that attains the *jus cogens* status does not give rise to the jurisdiction of the International Court of Justice or another international tribunal, as the Court ruled in *Democratic Republic of the Congo v Rwanda*;[14] nor do violations of *erga omnes* rights or obligations alone, as the Court has also ruled in *East Timor*.[15] Consent alone founds international jurisdiction or the jurisdiction of international courts and tribunals. Although the justification of the exercise of jurisdiction by a national legal order, our inquiry here, was not in issue in either case, the same conclusion may be drawn that the violation of a norm having *jus cogens* or *erga omnes* character does not in itself give rise to universal jurisdiction for the national legal systems. Whether the potential of universal concern in justifying the exercise of national jurisdiction has been realized, or the extent to which it has been, would depend on what crimes would be considered by states generally as crimes of universal concern and whether this universal concern has in fact been also considered by states as sufficient to justify an exercise of such jurisdiction. The answers to these questions will depend on the reality of the international law formation process. This is an issue that needs to be assessed according to the normal sources of law exercise under Article 38 of the Statute of the International Court of Justice (ICJ). That exercise will be attempted in Section 3.2 below. For now, let us briefly consider

---

[12] *Ibid.* 56.

[13] See Paolo Picone, 'The Distinction between *Jus Cogens* and Obligations *Erga Omnes*' in Enzo Cannizzaro (ed.), *The Law of Treaties Beyond the Vienna Convention* (2011), pp. 411, 421–2; but see generally Alexander Orakhelashvili, *Peremptory Norms in International Law* (2006).

[14] Armed Activities on the Territory of the Congo (New Application: 2002) (Democratic Republic of the Congo v Rwanda) [2006] ICJ Reports 3, para. 64.

[15] *East Timor (Portugal v Australia)* [1995] ICJ Reports 102, para. 29.

some general issues that may frame such an evaluation and help us to understand what may have factored into that reality.

8. As the term 'universal jurisdiction' has been used by various people to indicate various things in varying degrees of density or looseness, it will be helpful to offer some clarifications on the typology of situations that may constitute universal jurisdiction, properly so-called, or resemble it. To make things clear, the following characterizations, in the order of strength of 'universalness', can be used:

(1) 'Pure universal concern jurisdiction'. This form of jurisdiction would be an assertion of jurisdiction based solely on the universal concern character of the crime, without more. This would be the 'pure universal jurisdiction' or 'true universal jurisdiction'. If considered legitimate, this form of jurisdiction would entitle, as far as the jurisdictional requirement is concerned, the prosecuting state to the extradition of the suspect from a foreign state, if other conditions are met.[16] Sometimes 'universal jurisdiction *in absentia*' is used to describe this type of jurisdiction but this term can be confused with 'trial *in absentia*' and is not preferred here. Included in this form of jurisdiction are: (i) a state unilaterally asserting pure universal jurisdiction; and (ii) hypothetically a treaty allowing states parties to assert pure universal jurisdiction over nationals of non-parties for crimes occurring on territories of a third party. In the latter situation, the treaty regime as a whole does not have greater authority in relation to a third state than a particular state party to it, and the treaty granting jurisdiction to the parties to the regime does not add anything to our assessment.

(2) 'Universal concern plus presence jurisdiction'. This is illustrated by a state unilaterally asserting jurisdiction over a non-national who is present in that state for crimes of universal concern that have occurred in a foreign state. This is not universal jurisdiction properly so called, as the presence of the suspect may justify this form of jurisdiction as 'territorial', to some extent, or 'nationality' when the presence of the suspect is prolonged so as to assimilate it to nationality. When the presence of the suspect is fleeting (such as a weekend visit) or brief (such as a medical visit), such an exercise of jurisdiction gives rise to different characterizations: some call it universal jurisdiction, while others claim that this is jurisdiction

---

16 Cf. AIDP, n. 6 above, para. II(2); but see IDI Resolution, n. 3 above, para.3(b).

with some connection. If the absence of a link between the crime and the prosecuting state is the essence of universal jurisdiction, then a fleeting presence of the suspect in the prosecuting state may not disqualify the assertion of jurisdiction as that of universal jurisdiction. However, to the extent that the law about a state asserting jurisdiction based on brief presence is made clear, notice would have been given to any potential suspect. If he or she still comes to that state, voluntarily making that connection, such an exercise of jurisdiction can be considered 'non-universal', definitely not 'pure universal concern jurisdiction'.

(3) 'Universal concern plus treaty and presence jurisdiction'. This situation is similar to Situation 2, with the added obligation or right from a treaty to assert jurisdiction on that basis. An illustration would be a treaty allowing parties to exercise jurisdiction over a national of a third state, if present in the prosecuting state, for crimes of universal concern that have occurred in a third state.

(4) 'Universal concern plus treaty, presence and intra-regime territoriality or nationality jurisdiction'. This is similar to and narrower than Situation 3, with the added requirement that the suspect or the crime must be related to a party to the treaty setting up the regime in terms of territoriality, nationality or victim nationality. An illustration of an intra-regime nationality link would be a treaty allowing party A to the treaty to prosecute suspect B, a national of party C to the treaty, who is present in A, for crimes of universal concern that have occurred in state D, a non-party to the treaty. An illustration of an intra-regime territoriality link would be a treaty allowing party A to the treaty to prosecute suspect B, a national of a third state (non-party to the treaty), who is present on the territory of party A, for crimes which allegedly took place on the territory of party C to the treaty.

Among these situations, only the first situation is pure or true universal jurisdiction. The second situation moves away from pure and true universal jurisdiction but is closer to it than the other situations. Situations 3 and 4 are not universal jurisdiction in the true sense. The role of universal concern in justifying the exercise of jurisdiction in Situations 2 to 4 is, strictly speaking, redundant. Indeed, if presence triggers a treaty-based obligation to exercise jurisdiction, that jurisdiction can be, as described by the Joint Separate Opinion of Judges Higgins, Kooijmans and Buergenthal in *Arrest Warrant*,[17] 'really an obligatory territorial jurisdiction over persons'. If we were to call these situations 'universal jurisdiction', 'universal jurisdiction' would be purchased at the price of diluting and cheapening the concept; we would be playing a game of words.

9. Secondly, various factors may inform the international law-making process relating to universal jurisdiction, and these result in the reality of the extent of acceptance of it. First of all, universal jurisdiction can be rationalized as a system jurisdiction, for the protection of the interests of the international system including the protection of human rights and the fight against impunity, while employing the national legal systems, *faute de mieux*, to perform that task because of the lack of a central government in what we often call the 'international community'. In a way, the national legal systems can be considered to be in a situation of 'dédoublement fonctionnel'.[18] As a result, states hoping to protect the interests of the international system and to contribute to its maintenance and promotion should have incentives to promote the establishment and the application of the principle of universal jurisdiction. Furthermore, relating to this systemic consideration, universal criminal jurisdiction would seem to be necessary to implement or enforce *jus cogens*, another important systemic factor. Otherwise, that concept would be toothless. Those states that have recognized the idea of *jus cogens* probably may also have incentives to be friendly to the idea of universal jurisdiction.

10. On the other hand, the exercise of universal jurisdiction may infringe, or at least detract from, the principle of sovereignty and sovereign equality and is easily subjected to political abuse including discrimination as manifested in selective prosecution, thus destabilizing international relations. Because of this, this form of jurisdiction has been described as 'dangerous' by none other than Henry Kissinger.[19] Of course, any exercise of universal jurisdiction will most likely favor the big and powerful states.[20] If, as claimed by some states and Judge *ad hoc* van den Wyngaert in *Arrest Warrant*, the question is 'about what international law requires or allows States to do as "agents" of the

---

[17] Joint Separate Opinion of Judges Higgins, Kooijmans and Buergenthal [2002] ICJ Reports 74–5, para. 41.

[18] A term from Georges Scelle. See Antonio Cassese, 'Remarks on Scelle's Theory of "Role Splitting" (dédoublement fonctionnel) in International Law' (1990) 1 *EJIL* 210.

[19] Henry Kissinger, 'The Pitfalls of Universal Jurisdiction', *Foreign Affairs* (July–August 2001).

[20] As pointed out by Shahabuddeen, in IDI, n. 4 above, 228.

international community when they are confronted with complaints of victims of' heinous crimes,[21] one may immediately question whether such agents should be self-appointed by a particular state itself. This concern assumes a greater proportion if the *Lotus* dictum is allowed to prevail.[22] Furthermore, the political nature of universal jurisdiction is on full display when the attempt to exercise universal jurisdiction by states may indeed to be tradable, as in the case of Belgium which decided in 2003 to scuttle its strong universal jurisdiction authorization when threatened by the prospect of the NATO Headquarters moving away.[23] Also, the attempt can be shamed away at least to some extent, as, on my view, in the case of Spain which in 2009 dismantled its own strong universal jurisdiction authorization when Judge Garzon began to dig into Spain's old dirty laundry resulting from the Spanish Civil War.[24]

11. Obviously a regime of universal jurisdiction would present severe challenges to national reconciliation efforts such as those made in post-Apartheid South Africa or in some Latin American states. As stated by Kissinger:[25]

> It is an important principle that those who commit war crimes or systematically violate human rights should be held accountable. But the consolidation of

---

[21] Arrest Warrant, diss. op., ICJ Reports 2002, 141, para. 5.

[22] See paras 44–9 below.

[23] Act on Grave Breaches of International Humanitarian Law, 5 August 2003. As reported by none other than the person who did the threatening, Donald Rumsfeld, *Known and Unknown: A Memoir* (2011), pp. 596–8. Rumsfeld reported a 'frank and full exchange' with Mr Andre Flabaut, Belgium's Minister of Defense, in which Rumsfeld made clear that NATO could move its headquarters again as it did from France when the host was hostile and that American support for the building of a new NATO headquarters 'would evaporate instantly absent a prompt shift in the Belgium government's position'. *Ibid*. 598. Rumsfeld seemed to relish this: 'The difference in style between a Chicago-born American and member of the European diplomatic corps was on full display in that conversation. From his demeanor I could tell he fully understood my point. Within two months of that conversation, the Belgian government repealed their law'. *Ibid*. 598.

[24] See Jaclyn Belczyk, 'Spain Parliament passes law limiting reach of universal jurisdiction statute', 16 October 2009, available at http://jurist.law.pitt.edu/paperchase/2009/10/spain-parliament-passes-law-limiting.php; Daniel Woolls and Baltasar Garzon, 'Spanish Super Judge, suspended over alleged abuse', *AP News*, 14 May 2010, available at www.huffingtonpost.com/2010/05/14/baltasar-garzon-spanish-s_n_576872.html; Scott Horton, 'The Poet, the Judge, and the Falangists', available at http://harpers.org/archive/2010/04/hbc-90006895.

[25] Kissinger, n. 19 above.

law, domestic peace, and representative government in a nation struggling to come to terms with a brutal past has a claim as well. The instinct to punish must be related, as in every constitutional democratic political structure, to a system of checks and balances that includes other elements critical to the survival and expansion of democracy.

12. These factors, and others[26] not discussed here, no doubt have left their imprint in the international law formation process, resulting in the current state of affairs that we will examine in the following pages.

3.2 REALITY OF UNIVERSAL JURISDICTION IN INTERNATIONAL LAW

13. Reasonable as the idea of universal jurisdiction sounds, persuasive as its logic appears, one must not forget the teaching that 'The life of the law has not been logic: it has been experience'.[27] The experience and reality of international relations are such that universal jurisdiction over crimes other than piracy has not been established as a matter of international law.

14. An examination of the status of universal jurisdiction in international law is hampered by a lack of clear statement in the relevant primary official materials and a lack of dispassionate and rigorous analyses of them. Over-exaggerated statements expressing support for universal jurisdiction are often found in the works of various writers. Closer examination, however, may lead to differing conclusions.[28] Despite various difficulties, such an examination will be attempted in the

---

[26] See generally Luc Reydams, *The Rise and Fall of Universal Jurisdiction*, Leuven Centre for Global Governance Studies, Working Paper No. 37 (January 2010), available at http://ghum.kuleuven.be/ggs/publications/working_papers/new_series/wp31-40/wp37.pdf; papers by George Fletcher, Louise Arbour, Antonio Cassese and Georges Abi-Saab, in (2003) 1 *J Int'l Criminal Justice* 580.

[27] O.W. Holmes, *The Common Law* (1886), p. 1.

[28] See generally Reydams, n. 26 above; Luc Reydams, Universal Jurisdiction: International and Municipal Legal Perspectives (2003); William Schabas, 'Foreword' in Universal Jurisdiction: International and Municipal Legal Perspectives (2003); Zdzislaw Galicki, ILC Special Rapporteur, Fourth Report on the Obligation to Extradite or Prosecute (aut dedere aut judicare), A/CN.4/648 (31 May 2011), available at http://daccess-dds-ny.un.org/doc/UNDOC/GEN/N11/358/84/PDF/N1135884.pdf. For an optimistic assessment of the status of universal jurisdiction in international law, see V.D. Degan and Vesna Baric Punda, 'Universal Jurisdiction: An Option or a Legal Obligation for States' (2010) 13 International Law Review of Wuhan University 66.

following pages under the framework of Article 38 of the ICJ Statute, primarily under paragraph 1(a) and (b), in terms of treaty practice and customary international law. Since there is no dispute about the lawfulness of universal jurisdiction over piracy under international law, I will not deal with piracy in this chapter.

3.2.1 Treaty Practice

15. There are numerous treaties dealing with jurisdiction over crimes of universal concern, presenting a formidable task to any conscientious scholars. Literature also abounds regarding how these treaties should be classified and evaluated.[29] The task is made more difficult by the controversy surrounding what constitutes universal jurisdiction, properly so called. I will first recap the current discussion of the treaty practice with some commentary of my own and then attempt to sort through these treaties by giving my typological summary of them.

3.2.1.1 Current evaluation of treaty practice

16. The first and most eligible modern crime for pure universal jurisdiction is probably genocide. I believe I need not spill any more ink to prove the universal concern character of the crime of genocide. Yet, universal jurisdiction over this crime was expressly debated and rejected twice: first when the UNGA drafted and adopted Resolution 96(I) of 1946 and again when it drafted and adopted the Convention for the Prevention and Punishment of the Crime of Genocide ('Genocide Convention') of 1948.[30] The resultant Article VI of the Convention relies on the traditional territorial jurisdiction and on a yet to be established international court.

17. Those who claim to have found the existence of universal jurisdiction usually seize upon, as their evidence, the various 'extradite or prosecute' provisions in a large number of treaties and assert that these embody the existence of universal jurisdiction. This claim is not supported by a close examination of the treaty practice: although the universal concern character of the crimes dealt with may have motivated the conclusion of these treaties (a point few would disagree with), the exercise of jurisdiction may be justified on other grounds. 'Extradite or prosecute' is a means of exercising jurisdiction; it is not jurisdiction

[29] See Galicki, n. 28 above; Reydams, n. 28 above.

[30] See William Schabas, *Genocide in International Law: The Crime of Crimes* (2nd edn, 2009), pp. 49–116 at 411–16.

itself.[31] The ways and means of exercising jurisdiction should not be conflated with jurisdiction itself. The 'extradite or prosecute' obligation may apply jurisdiction that has been justified on any basis, whether territoriality, nationality, national vital interests or even universal concern. Thus the adoption of this means of exercise of jurisdiction does not necessarily lead to the finding of a particular kind or basis of jurisdiction itself, but of all the possible kinds utilized.

18. The pivotal point is to identify which kind of jurisdiction the means ('extradite or prosecute') is utilized to implement. Such an effort reveals no treaty expressly using 'extradite or prosecute' to implement pure universal jurisdiction, and thus no *express* treaty practice support for the idea of pure universal jurisdiction. Having chided the majority for not addressing the issue of jurisdiction and upon an examination of several important treaties, Judges Higgins, Kooijmans and Buergenthal concluded in their Joint Separate Opinion in *Arrest Warrant*:[32]

> 41. The parties to these treaties agreed both to grounds of jurisdiction and as to the obligation to take the measures necessary to establish such jurisdiction. The specified grounds relied on links of nationality of the offender, or the ship or aircraft concerned, or of the victim. See, for example, Hague Convention, Article 4(l); Tokyo Convention, Article 3(l); Hostages Convention, Article 5; Torture Convention, Article 5. These may properly be described as treaty-based broad extraterritorial jurisdiction. But in addition to these were the parallel provisions whereby a State party in whose jurisdiction the alleged perpetrator of such offences is found shall prosecute him or extradite him. By the loose use of language the latter has come to be referred to as 'universal jurisdiction', though this is really an obligatory territorial jurisdiction over persons, albeit in relation to acts committed elsewhere.

19. Whether the situation where a suspect's mere presence in the prosecuting state which refuses to extradite him or her, whose disputed acts had no link to that state, justifies the exercise of jurisdiction, is merely what was described by Judge Higgins *et al.*, or is in fact universal jurisdiction or a conditional form of universal jurisdiction, appears to be unsettled. This 'mere presence' subsequent to the alleged crime situation is apparently what was contemplated in the provisions of on the repression of 'grave breaches' of the Geneva Conventions of 1949

---

31 For another formulation of this difference see *AU-EU Expert Report*, n. 5 above, para. 11.

32 Joint Separate Opinion, n. 17 above, 74–5, para. 41.

(Articles 49 (I);[33] 50 (II); 129 (III); 146 (IV); 85 (AP(I)). The ICRC in various statements apparently considered this regime to be one of universal jurisdiction.[34] The ICRC Study on the status of the customary international humanitarian law also seems to believe so.[35] Expressed in another context[36] or in other ways,[37] some governments also seem to treat this situation as 'universal jurisdiction'.

20. This view apparently also receives the endorsement of the IDI. During the debate on the universal jurisdiction project, the IDI Rapporteur put emphasis on the lack of a link between the crime and the

---

33 Those Articles state in relevant part: 'The High Contracting Parties undertake to enact any legislation necessary to provide effective penal sanctions for persons committing, or ordering to be committed, any of the grave breaches of the present Convention defined in the following Article. Each High Contracting Party shall be under the obligation to search for persons alleged to have committed, or to have ordered to be committed, such grave breaches, and shall bring such persons, regardless of their nationality, before its own courts. It may also, if it prefers, and in accordance with the provisions of its own legislation, hand such persons over for trial to another High Contracting Party concerned, provided such High Contracting Party has made out a *prima facie* case'. The term 'search for' can be properly interpreted as 'search for persons said to be present on its territory'. See Jean S. Pictet's commentary, *Convention (I) for the Amelioration of the Condition of the Wounded and Sick in Armed Forces in the Field, Geneva, 12 August 1949* (1952), pp. 365–6, available at www.icrc.org/ihl.nsf/COM/365-570060?OpenDocument.

34 Statement by the ICRC representative in the Sixth Committee, A/C.6/65/SR.12 (15 October 2010), p. 6, para. 42; ICRC Official Statement, 27-08-2003, on the 'First Meeting of Experts of States Parties to the Biological and Toxin Weapons Convention, Geneva, 18–29 August 2003', available at www.icrc.org/web/eng/siteeng0.nsf/htmlall/5qkdpf ('It should be recalled that States are already required to exercise universal jurisdiction in respect of "grave breaches" [of] the 1949 Geneva Conventions and their Additional Protocol I of 1977, which refer to acts committed in situations of armed conflict against protected persons such as wilful killing, torture or inhuman treatment including biological experiments, and making the civilian population or individual civilians the object of attack. Use of biological weapons amounting to such "grave breaches" would thus require the assertion of universal jurisdiction.').

35 See Jean-Marie Henckaerts and Louise Doswald-Beck (eds), *Customary International Humanitarian Law*, vol. I, Rule 157 and the associated support in vol. II.

36 See views of governments as characterized in E/CN.4/1983/63, paras 22 and 23, on the proposed Convention Against Torture.

37 See generally the views of the UK government, as quoted in Ian Brownlie, *Principles of Public International Law* (7th edn, 2008), pp. 305–6.

prosecuting state as the criterion for finding universal jurisdiction.[38] Such 'mere presence' was apparently not considered to furnish such a link. The final text of the 2005 IDI Resolution in paragraph 2 states:

> Universal jurisdiction is primarily based on customary international law. It can also be established under a multilateral treaty in the relations between the contracting parties, in particular by virtue of clauses which provide that a State party in the territory of which an alleged offender is found shall either extradite or try that person.[39]

The second sentence was adopted despite the objections of some members, including Higgins and Abi-Saab.[40]

21. Furthermore, some treaties require that the alleged crimes have significant links to *some* parties to a particular treaty, such as territoriality or nationality; these links to the regime as a whole definitely disqualify the 'mere presence' situation as an exercise of truly universal jurisdiction. This would be 'universal concern plus treaty, presence and intra-regime territoriality or nationality jurisdiction' as highlighted above. Such a situation is a quintessential intra-regime cooperative affair, in the sense that at least one party to the regime can legitimately exercise jurisdiction based on a traditional criterion, and the prosecuting state party is simply performing the function of that other party in its stead, for whatever reason (such as its inability or unwillingness to do so). The regime in essence allows the parties to share their traditional jurisdictional powers, or permits one party to exercise the jurisdictional authority of another party. The Geneva Conventions use broadly worded language ('regardless of their nationality') to describe the 'extradite or prosecute' obligation, but the application of those Conventions may (though this is not clear) require that the alleged crime was committed on the territory of one of the parties to the Conventions, thus requiring a first level connection (such as nationality, territoriality, victim nationality or vital interests) with at least one party to the applicable Convention. In any event, subsequent treaties, such as the Convention Against Torture and Other Cruel, Inhuman or Degrading Treatment or Punishment of 1984, made it clearer that the 'mere presence' of a suspect in the territory of one of the parties is of a secondary nature; the crime or the suspect must have a first level link such as territoriality or nationality with one of the parties to the Convention for the suspect to be subject to some kind of process. This is

38 IDI, n. 4 above, 257, 261 (Rapporteur).

39 IDI Resolution, n. 3 above.

40 IDI, n. 4 above, 209–10 (Abi-Saab); 257 (Higgins).

at least one plausible reading of Article 5 of the Convention Against Torture, which states:

> Article 5
>
> 1. Each State Party shall take such measures as may be necessary to establish its jurisdiction over the offences referred to in article 4 in the following cases:
>
> (a) When the offences are committed in any territory under its jurisdiction or on board a ship or aircraft registered in that State;
> (b) When the alleged offender is a national of that State;
> (c) When the victim is a national of that State if that State considers it appropriate.
>
> 2. Each State Party shall likewise take such measures as may be necessary to establish its jurisdiction over such offences in cases where the alleged offender is present in any territory under its jurisdiction and it does not extradite him pursuant to article 8 to any of the States mentioned in paragraph 1 of this article.
>
> 3. This Convention does not exclude any criminal jurisdiction exercised in accordance with internal law.

Paragraph 1 of this Article provides for the obligation to establish jurisdiction based on territoriality, nationality or victim nationality. Paragraph 2 provides for the obligation to prosecute if the suspect is not extradited to 'any of the States mentioned in paragraph 1 of this article'. One reading of this provision would be that for paragraph 2 to apply, paragraph 1 must have been potentially applicable but the requested state is not willing to extradite the suspect; that is to say, the suspect (or the suspected crime) must have first level links to a state party ('any State mentioned in paragraph 1', which deals with states parties only) – territoriality, nationality or victim nationality – to establish that potential applicability. So read, Article 5(2) does not deal with matters outside the province of the regime.

22. A further and clearer illustration of this regime is the Rome Statute of the International Criminal Court, which in Article 12 provides for the ICC (which can be considered a cooperative of the states parties) to take jurisdiction based on territoriality links between the crime and a state party or nationality link between the suspect and a state party.

23. One may argue that there can be an alternative and broader reading of Article 49 of Geneva Convention (I) and the corresponding Articles in the other Geneva Conventions, as well as Article 5(2) of the Convention Against Torture. This alternative reading would not require first level links between the suspect (and the suspected crime) and a state party for the 'extradite or prosecute' obligation to be triggered. Indeed, Article 49

of Geneva Convention (I) is so broadly written that it may be susceptible of the alternative reading. Further, one can imagine a reading of Article 5(2) of the Convention Against Torture this way: that paragraph 2 is triggered whenever a suspect is not extradited to any state party, irrespective of the reasons for that. Under this reading, whether or not paragraph 1 is potentially applicable is immaterial, although if it is not applicable, it will be because the suspect is a national of a third state accused of a crime occurring on the territory of a third state against a national of a third state and is not extradited to any state party. However, this reading would seem to render part of the language of Article 5(2) redundant or unnaturally formulated. If such an alternative reading is accepted, this situation would be the 'universal concern plus treaty and presence jurisdiction' as highlighted above.

24. Other examples of this situation include Article 4(2) of the 1970 Hague Convention for the Suppression of Unlawful Seizure of Aircraft[41] and Article V of the Apartheid Convention.[42] Both can be read as

---

[41] See Joint Separate Opinion [2002] ICJ Reports 73, para. 35; President Guillaume, Separate Opinion, in his separate opinion, ibid. 38, para. 7. There President Guillaume emphasized the obligation to establish jurisdiction so that 'the obligation to prosecute was no longer conditional on the existence of jurisdiction, but rather jurisdiction itself had to be established in order to make prosecution possible', and he seemed to call this 'compulsory, albeit subsidiary, universal jurisdiction'. He took as the forerunner Article 4(2) of the Hague Convention for the Suppression of Unlawful Seizure of Aircraft of 1970. One may agree with this emphasis if the obligation to establish jurisdiction cannot be considered a logical extension of, or as included in, the term 'extradite or prosecute'. To prosecute implies the existence of the wherewithal to do so, in other words, the establishment of jurisdiction. In any event, a general promise to take effective measures to repress crimes would have included such an obligation. This is the understanding of the broadly worded Article 49, especially paragraph 1, of the Geneva Convention (I) of 1949 and the corresponding Articles in the other Geneva Conventions. Furthermore, Article 4(2) of the Hague Convention for the Suppression of Unlawful Seizure of Aircraft of 1970 expressly requires the presence of the suspect on the territory of the Contracting State, while Article 49 of the Geneva Convention has been construed as requiring the same. That is to say, potentially the 1970 Hague Convention may not be the first on the requirement to establish jurisdiction.

[42] Apartheid Convention, Art. V, which states: 'Persons charged with the acts enumerated in article II of the present Convention may be tried by a competent tribunal of any State Party to the Convention which may acquire jurisdiction over the person of the accused or by an international penal tribunal having jurisdiction with respect to those States Parties which shall have accepted its jurisdiction'. 'Acquire jurisdiction over the person of the accused' apparently

authorizing the exercise of jurisdiction over a suspect, a national of a third state, who is present in the prosecuting state party to the applicable Convention for crimes that have occurred in a third state. We cannot be certain that this reading is correct; there does not appear to be any record of these provisions being applied this way either administratively or judicially.

25. However, even this 'universal concern plus treaty and presence jurisdiction' is not true or pure universal jurisdiction, as a treaty permission or obligation to exercise jurisdiction and the presence of the suspect are required. Only when a treaty claims to give the parties thereto jurisdiction over crimes and suspects having no link with any of the parties to the treaty would one see pure universal jurisdiction. For example, if the 1970 Hague Convention would authorize jurisdiction over a national of a third party to the Convention who is not yet present in the prosecuting state party to the Convention for crimes occurring in a third state, that would present a 'pure universal concern jurisdiction' scenario. However, no such treaty is readily found, although I have not done exhaustive research on this. The judges in the *Arrest Warrant* case (especially those who issued opinions on the issue of universal jurisdiction) and the various scholars who have done thorough research on universal jurisdiction have not reported one, either.

26. The phrasing of some treaty provisions may give rise to the impression or the argument that the treaty somehow impliedly recognizes universal jurisdiction. For example, the Second Protocol to the Hague Convention for the Protection of Cultural Property in the Event of Armed Conflict (1999),[43] in Article 16(2)(a), states that the Protocol 'does not preclude … the exercise of jurisdiction under national and international law that may be applicable, or affect the exercise of jurisdiction under customary international law'. The ICRC experts on customary international humanitarian law were of the view that:

---

means his presence. This Convention is quite special both in terms of the circumstances of adoption and the political climate prevailing then. See comment by John Dugard, http://untreaty.un.org/cod/avl/pdf/ha/cspca/cspca_e.pdf, at 2 ('The Apartheid Convention allows State parties to prosecute non-nationals for a crime committed in the territory of a non-State party where the accused is physically within the jurisdiction of a State party (arts. 4 and 5) … No one was prosecuted for the crime of apartheid while apartheid lasted in South Africa. And no one has since been prosecuted for the crime.'). But cf. Reydams, n. 26 above, 18, who seemed to characterize the Apartheid Convention, Art. V, as granting universal jurisdiction.

[43] See http://portal.unesco.org/en/ev.php-URL_ID=15207&URL_DO=DO_TOPIC &URL_SECTION=201.html.

> The Second Protocol to the Hague Convention for the Protection of Cultural Property states that it does not affect 'the exercise of jurisdiction under customary international law', which was intended by delegates at the negotiation of the Protocol to refer to the right of States to vest universal jurisdiction in their national courts for war crimes.[44]

The experts did not present evidence from drafting history.

27. It is better not to read this provision this way; it is better to read it as a provision preventing an *a contrario* interpretation of Article 16 that it prohibits other forms of exercises of jurisdiction not spelled out in the Article. It would be a jump to read it as supporting a particular form of exercise such as universal jurisdiction. Such a meaning would have required affirmative support in the text of the treaty itself. This better interpretation is supported by the similar interpretation generally given to Article 5(3) of the Convention Against Torture.[45]

3.2.1.2 Summary of treaty practice

28. The messy treaty practice and scholarly treatment do not afford us much confidence when we attempt to distill any rules of customary international law from it. The universal concern character of the crimes under consideration may have motivated the conclusion of a substantial number of treaties, but whatever we would like to say about these treaties, it will be advisable for us to remember that a treaty right or obligation is only applicable to the parties thereto and is subject to a variety of conditions specific to that treaty.[46] Nevertheless, data do show that there is no instance of 'pure universal concern jurisdiction' being authorized in any treaty. Some treaties authorize or can be interpreted as authorizing 'universal concern plus treaty and presence jurisdiction'. Even more treaties authorize 'universal concern plus treaty, presence and intra-regime territoriality or nationality jurisdiction'. But neither of the latter two types can be properly called 'universal jurisdiction'.

3.2.2 Customary International Law

29. Turning to the customary international law status of universal jurisdiction, one is of course reminded of the requirements as stated in

---

[44] Henckaerts and Doswald-Beck, n. 35 above, vol. I, p. 605, n. 198.

[45] See Joint Separate Opinion, n. 17 above, paras 34, 38.

[46] See Statement of China, Observations, para. 6 (Chinese original available at www.un.org/en/ga/sixth/65/ScopeAppUniJuri_StatesComments/China.pdf; English translation by the UN available at www.un.org/en/ga/sixth/65/ScopeApp UniJuri_ StatesComments/China_E.pdf).

Article 38(1)(b) of the ICJ Statute for the finding of such a rule: customary international law is evidenced by a general state practice accepted as law (in other words, *opinio juris*).

30. In this regard, one is struck by the lack of evidence of clear exercise of 'pure universal concern' jurisdiction and the seemingly broad support for 'universal jurisdiction', loosely described, as evidenced in the various declarations and statements. If the latter were to be taken at face value, there appears to be *opinio juris* for the concept of 'universal jurisdiction', loosely used, over genocide, crimes against humanity and serious war crimes. For example, as early as in 1971, a General Assembly Resolution was broadly worded so as to be consistent with the idea of universal jurisdiction. There, the GA '*affirms* that refusal by States of cooperation in the arrest, extradition, trial and punishment of persons guilty of war crimes and crimes against humanity is contrary to the purposes and principles of the Charter of the United Nations and to generally recognized norms of international law'.[47] Many Western states have made statements supporting the concept of universal jurisdiction.[48] The African Union stated, in a memorandum annexed to the request for the inclusion of universal jurisdiction in the agenda of the 63rd session of the UNGA, that 'The principle of universal jurisdiction is well established in international law' and that 'The African Union respects this principle, which is enshrined in article 4(h) of the Constitutive Act' but that it was concerned about the uncertain scope and application of the principle and the abuse of it.[49] The American Law Institute, a national institute of legal experts, found that universal jurisdiction existed under customary international law over several crimes as early as 1986.[50] The IDI, a world academy of international law experts, also gave its support to the concept or principle of universal jurisdiction in 2005.[51]

31. In any event, data on state conduct asserting universal jurisdiction do not reveal sufficient evidence establishing true universal jurisdiction, other than in cases of piracy. This is more or less the conclusion of the

---

[47] UNGA Res. 2840 (1971).

[48] For further info, see *AU-EU Expert Report*, n. 5 above; Henckaerts and Doswald-Beck, n. 35 above.

[49] A/63/237, Annex (Explanatory Memorandum), para. 1. The States of the Non-aligned Movement seemed to hold a more ambiguous attitude. See A/C.6/64/SR.12 (25 November 2009), paras 20–1; A/C.6/65/SR.10 (13 October 2010), paras 55–6.

[50] Restatement Third, n. 6 above, s. 404 and the comments and notes thereto. The text is reproduced at n. 7 above.

[51] IDI Resolution, n. 3 above.

Western judges, including Judges Higgins, Kooijmans, Buergenthal and President Guillaume in *Arrest Warrant* (2002). The Joint Separate Opinion by Higgins, Kooijmans and Buergenthal in *Arrest Warrant* endorsed[52] the opinion of the authors of *Oppenheim's International Law* that:

> While no general rule of positive international law can as yet be asserted which gives rise to states' right to punish foreign nationals for crimes against humanity in the same way as they are, for instance, entitled to punish acts of piracy, there are clear indications pointing to the gradual evolution of a significant principle of international law to that effect. (9th edn, 1992, p. 998)

Subsequent development has not strengthened the status of universal jurisdiction; rather, it has weakened it, as discussed below (see especially paragraph 34). In a sense, the fortune of universal jurisdiction peaked in 2002 when *Arrest Warrant* was decided.

32. Although some states such as the United Kingdom[53] have asserted universal jurisdiction over war crimes in their military law or regulations in the form of manuals, this assertion does not appear to have attracted general following among states, or have extended to other crimes or to other prosecuting contexts. Indeed, the United Kingdom's military manual even has difficulty persuading its own legislature to implement that idea by statute,[54] and a 'clever' solution was found to implement the Rome Statute of the International Criminal Court. The ICRC Study seems to have a broader view of the exercise of 'universal jurisdiction' over war crimes.[55] A critical analysis of the data presented may not bear out its assessment.

33. The German legislations, including the Code of Crimes Against Humanity Law, in a complicated way have been considered by one commentator to allow for the possibility of pure universal jurisdiction,[56] with various conditions. This possibility remains a possibility even now, as no such prosecution has been made.

---

52 Joint Separate Opinion, n. 17 above, para. 52.

53 *British Manual of Military Law* (1956), vol. III, para. 637, as quoted in Higgins, n. 10 above, 59–60; see discussion of *ibid.* 56–61; Ian Brownlie, *Principles of Public International Law* (7th edn, 2008), pp. 305–6; UK Ministry of Defence, *The Manual of the Law of Armed Conflict* (2004), para. 16.30.

54 See Ian Brownlie, *Principles of Public International Law* (7th edn, 2008), pp. 305–6; Higgins, n. 10 above, 59–61.

55 See Henckaerts and Doswald-Beck, n. 35 above, Rule 157 and associated materials.

56 See the description and analysis of this law in Luc Reydams, *Universal Jurisdiction* (2003), pp. 141–7.

34. The limited support from national legislation for true universal jurisdiction has recently been further diminished. In 2003 and 2009, respectively, Belgium[57] and Spain,[58] the only two states (as commonly believed) that once had clear statutes asserting pure universal jurisdiction and have in fact attempted to exercise that jurisdiction (Germany is not one because of the ambiguities in its legislation and its record of non-exercise), have now modified their statutes to condition the exercise of jurisdiction on various links with the forum state.

35. The limited cases from the Western states regarding the attempt to exercise or the actual exercise of universal jurisdiction have been described as showing the courts had 'largely been cautious so far as reliance on universal jurisdiction is concerned'.[59] Alternatively, this situation was described in 2010 by Reydams[60] as follows:

> All in all some two dozen individuals have been tried by courts in Austria, Canada, Germany, Denmark, Belgium, the United Kingdom, the Netherlands, Finland, France, Spain, and Switzerland for 'war crimes' committed abroad. Without exception the defendants had taken up permanent residence in the forum state – as refugee, exile, fugitive, or immigrant – and resisted being 'sent back to the countries in which their abominable deeds were done'. In most cases the other states concerned acquiesced in or even supported prosecution. Not to overlook also is the fact that the majority of these cases concerned atrocities committed in the former Yugoslavia and in Rwanda; the

---

[57] Act on Grave Breaches of International Humanitarian Law (Belgium), 5 August 2003. See Luc Reydams, 'Belgium Reneges on Universality: 5 August 2003 Act on Grave Breaches of International Humanitarian Law' (2003) 1 *J Int'l Criminal Justice* 679.

[58] Ley Orgánica 1/2009, de 3 de noviembre complementaria de la Ley de reforma de la legislación procesal para la implantación de la nueva Oficina judicial, por la que se modifica la Ley Orgánica 6/1985, de 1 de julio, del Poder Judicial, available at http://noticias.juridicas.com/base_datos/Admin/lo1-2009.html (Spain). The essence of this new law, as stated by the representative of Spain in the UNGA, A/C.6/65/SR.11 (13 October 2010), p. 4, para. 21, is: 'judges could only prosecute perpetrators of serious crimes committed anywhere in the world when no other international or third-country court had initiated proceedings against them and when they were present in Spanish territory or when the victim was a Spanish national'.

[59] See the analysis in the Joint Separate Opinion, n. 17 above, para. 21.

[60] Reydams, n. 26 above, 22 (internal footnotes omitted). See also the description of state judicial practice in The Scope and Application of the Principle of Universal Jurisdiction: Report of the Secretary-General Prepared on the Basis of Comments and Observations of Governments, A/65/181 (29 July 2010), paras 55–65, 94–107, available at http://daccess-dds-ny.un.org/doc/UNDOC/GE N/N10/467/52/PDF/N1046752.pdf?OpenElement.

> prosecutor of the ad hoc international criminal tribunals for these countries and the UN Security Council had encouraged all states to search for and try suspects on their territory (cf. the obligations under the Geneva Conventions). Finally, extradition often was impossible, if not legally then practically.

In addition, the rare examples of express assertion of universal jurisdiction from Israel (*Eichmann*)[61] and the United States (*Demjanjuk*,[62] recognizing Israel's universal jurisdiction as a basis for extradition) have their value reduced by the special circumstances surrounding these prosecutions of perpetrators from the Nazi era and further by Israel's threats against the use of universal jurisdiction against its own officials, and the claim of the United States that other states 'should not even think about'[63] prosecuting its nationals.

36. Finally, it should be noted that no African state has ever exercised universal jurisdiction.[64]

37. But the IDI seems to believe that universal jurisdiction exists under customary international law but it finds it to be conditional on the 'presence' of the suspect, as described below.[65] One may find the IDI Resolution extraordinary, as it was passed in 2005 against the background of the *Arrest Warrant* Judgment arresting the over-enthusiasm for universal jurisdiction[66] and Belgium, the captain of universal jurisdiction,

---

61 *Attorney General of Israel v Eichmann*, 36 ILR (Supreme Court of Israel, 1962).

62 *In re Demjanjuk*, 603 F.Supp. 1468 (N.D. Ohio), affirmed, 776 F.2d 571 (6th Cir. 1985), cert. denied, 457 U.S. 1016 (1986).

63 Reydams, n. 26 above, 22.

64 *AU-EU Expert Report*, n. 5 above, paras 19, 26, 40.

65 IDI Resolution, n. 3 above.

66 After the Congo reformulated its claims, the ICJ did not rule in *Arrest Warrant* on the lawfulness of universal jurisdiction; rather, it held that it was unable to find any customary international law exception to the immunity from foreign national jurisdiction and the inviolability that an incumbent Foreign Minister enjoys, even where that Foreign Minister is accused of having committed war crimes or crimes against humanity. On the effect of *Arrest Warrant*, see Alain Pellet, 'Shaping the Future of International Law: The Role of the World Court in Law-making' in Mahnoush H. Arsanjani *et al.* (eds), *Looking to the Future: Essays on International Law in Honor of W. Michael Reisman* (2011), pp. 1065, 1080 ('the ICJ's Judgment in *Arrest Warrant Case* shows that the Court can also slow down and maybe go as far as durably jeopardizing highly desirable evolutions in the law in force'); Antonio Cassese in (2003) 1 *J Int'l Criminal Justice* 589. On immunities (not discussed in this chapter), see, for example, the reports of the ILC Special Rapporteur Roman Anatolevich Kolodkin and other materials, available at http://untreaty.un.org/ilc/guide/4_2.htm.

abandoning ship by modifying pure universal jurisdiction out of its statute in 2003.[67] That is to say, the trend in favor of pure universal jurisdiction, if at all, was reversing. In any event, the IDI Resolution did not arrest the reversing trend as yet, and in 2009 Spain did what Belgium did in 2003.[68]

38. It will be better for us to analyse these cases one by one, but the conscientious judges and scholars have done so and given conflicting assessments of the record. This alone reflects the uncertain state of universal jurisdiction in international law.

39. This state of affairs appears to be susceptible of several interpretations. First of all, the lack of actual exercise of pure universal jurisdiction may be considered to be evidence showing that the nice-sounding support for the concept is really political, rather than evidencing *opinio juris*.

40. The support of the African Union, as stated in its 2009 memorandum, for this concept is further weakened by its expressed reliance on Article 4(h) of its Constitutive Act,[69] which, the African Union statement claims, 'enshrine[s]'[70] the principle of universal jurisdiction. That Article recognizes 'the right of the Union to intervene in a Member State pursuant to a decision of the Assembly in respect of grave circumstances, namely: war crimes, genocide and crimes against humanity'. This Article in fact enshrines an intra-regime collective political action mechanism: it grants the right to the Union to take action in relevant situations, not to any individual state to take action; the action authorized is political collective enforcement action, not judicial enforcement action. It does not say anything about the Union's right to exercise universal jurisdiction, a much lesser extent than that of an individual state to exercise universal jurisdiction. These factors may not have received attention when the statement of the African Union states was formulated.

41. The exchange of views by states so far after the inclusion of universal jurisdiction on the agenda of the UNGA does not strengthen the status of universal jurisdiction. The number of states that have submitted statements to the UNGA is not substantial, only 44 in total, about 25 per cent of the membership of the United Nations.[71] Nor has this exchange

---

[67] See n. 57 above.

[68] See n. 58 above.

[69] Text accompany n. 49 above.

[70] African Union Memo, n. 1 above, para. 1.

[71] The statements are available at www.un.org/en/ga/sixth/65/ScopeAppUniJuri.shtml. For a summary by these statements, see *Report of the Secretary-General*, n. 60 above. In 2010 China submitted a statement (Statement

clarified much, as broad and loose language seems to continue to prevail. If anything, this exercise seems to lessen the meager support for the concept. Several states have noted that 'the scope and application of universal jurisdiction remained very much a matter of political and legal debate'.[72] Some states, such as Thailand,[73] have made clear statements arguing against universal jurisdiction over crimes other than piracy and/or slavery. Even the African Union, which clearly expressed support for the 'principle' of universal jurisdiction in 2009, seemed to have retreated in 2010 from its earlier position. The statement made on behalf the African Group of States before the Sixth Committee in October 2010 said:

> There was as yet no generally accepted definition of universal jurisdiction and no agreement on which crimes, other than piracy and slavery, it should cover or on the conditions under which it would apply. If few States had responded with information about their practice on universal jurisdiction, it was because the principle hardly existed in most domestic jurisdictions.[74]

Furthermore, rather than reiterating that the Constitutive Act of the African Union 'enshrined' the principle of universal jurisdiction, the statement now said that 'the Constitutive Act of the African Union accorded the Union the power to intervene in the affairs of its member States in situations of genocide, war crimes and crimes against humanity'.[75]

42. Secondly, the thin record of actual exercise is evidence that there is no positive rule of customary international law yet in favor of pure universal jurisdiction other than that over piracy.[76] Indeed, there is not even sufficient evidence to prove a customary international law rule permitting the exercise of 'universal concern plus presence' jurisdiction.

43. Finally, another interpretation, as put forward in the Joint Separate Opinion of Judge Higgins *et al.* in *Arrest Warrant*, is that this only shows

---

of China, n. 46 above). See also ZHU Lijiang, 'Chinese Practice in Public International Law: 2009' (2010) 9 *Chinese JIL* 607 at 647, para. 73.

[72] See, for example, Statement of Malaysia, A/C.6/65/SR.12 (15 October 2010), p. 5, para. 26.

[73] See, for example, Statement of Thailand, A/C.6/65/SR.11 (13 October 2010), p. 3, para. 12 ('With the exception of piracy, there was no general consensus among States as to which crimes were subject to universal jurisdiction under customary international law'); Statement of Sudan, A/C.6/65/SR.12 (15 October 2010), p. 4, para. 20; Statement of China, n. 46 above.

[74] A/C.6/65/SR.10 (13 October 2010), para. 60, available at http://daccess-ods.un.org/access.nsf/ Get?Open&DS=A/C.6/65/SR.10&Lang=E.

[75] *Ibid.* para. 61.

[76] See Statement of China, n. 46 above, Observations, paras 4–5.

that states have not '[legislated] to the full scope of the jurisdiction allowed by international law' and that:

> while none of the national case law to which [the judges] have referred happens to be based on the exercise of a universal jurisdiction properly so called, there is equally nothing in this case law which evidences an *opinio juris* on the illegality of such a jurisdiction. In short, national legislation and case law – that is, State practice – is neutral as to exercise of universal jurisdiction.[77]

3.3 POSSIBLE APPLICATION OF THE LOTUS DICTUM

44. Concluding thus, the Joint Separate Opinion by Judge Higgins *et al.* in *Arrest Warrant* argued in essence that the matter then turns not on whether the exercise of true or pure universal jurisdiction is supported by positive international law, but whether such an exercise is precluded by any prohibitive rule, in application of the *Lotus* dictum which militates in favor of state freedom. Finding no such prohibitive rule, these judges concluded that a state may exercise pure universal jurisdiction (or 'universal jurisdiction *in absentia*').[78]

45. President Guillaume, on the other hand, directly challenged the very dictum itself, at least in its application to the area of criminal jurisdiction. He said in his Separate Opinion in *Arrest Warrant*:[79]

> 14. This argument is hardly persuasive. Indeed the Permanent Court itself, having laid down the general principle cited by Belgium, then asked itself 'whether the foregoing considerations really apply as regards criminal jurisdiction'. It held that either this might be the case, or alternatively, that: 'the exclusively territorial character of law relating to this domain constitutes a principle which, except as otherwise expressly provided, would, *ipso facto,* prevent States from extending the criminal jurisdiction of their courts beyond their frontiers'. In the particular case before it, the Permanent Court took the view that it was unnecessary to decide the point. Given that the case involved

---

[77] Joint Separate Opinion, n. 17 above, para. 45. The UK explanation is found in Higgins, n. 10 above, 59–61.

[78] See Joint Separate Opinion, n. 17 above, paras 49–54, etc.

[79] President Guillaume, Separate Opinion in *Arrest Warrant* [2002] ICJ Reports 35 at 43. For further criticisms of the *Lotus* dictum, see Judge Simma, *Declaration in Accordance with International Law of the Unilateral Declaration of Independence in respect of Kosovo* (Request for Advisory Opinion) [2010] ICJ Reports 403, available at www.icj-cij.org/docket/files/141/1599 3.pdf; Sienho Yee, 'Notes on the International Court of Justice (Part 4): The Kosovo Advisory Opinion' (2010) 9 *Chinese JIL* 763, paras 22–6.

> the collision of a French vessel with a Turkish vessel, the Court confined itself to noting that the effects of the offence in question had made themselves felt on Turkish territory, and that consequently a criminal prosecution might 'be justified from the point of view of this so-called territorial principle'.
>
> 15. The absence of a decision by the Permanent Court on the point was understandable in 1927, given the sparse treaty law at that time. The situation is different today, it seems to me – totally different. The adoption of the United Nations Charter proclaiming the sovereign equality of States, and the appearance on the international scene of new States, born of decolonization, have strengthened the territorial principle. International criminal law has itself undergone considerable development and constitutes today an impressive legal *corpus*. It recognizes in many situations the possibility, or indeed the obligation, for a State other than that on whose territory the offence was committed to confer jurisdiction on its courts to prosecute the authors of certain crimes where they are present on its territory. International criminal courts have been created. But at no time has it been envisaged that jurisdiction should be conferred upon the courts of every State in the world to prosecute such crimes, whoever their authors and victims and irrespective of the place where the offender is to be found. To do this would, moreover, risk creating total judicial chaos. It would also be to encourage the arbitrary for the benefit of the powerful, purportedly acting as agent for an ill-defined 'international community'. Contrary to what is advocated by certain publicists, such a development would represent not an advance in the law but a step backward.

46. There is much force in President Guillaume's view. The *Lotus* dictum was indeed unnecessary in that case and its vitality results from the uncritical recitation to and following of it.

47. To some extent, the debate seems to be about which default rule is the proper one. When the decision was adopted by the Permanent Court of International Justice, states still adhered to the old rule of a right to use force to settle international disputes. It was probably natural that state freedom was considered paramount and therefore given priority. That apparently was the default rule behind the application of the *Lotus* dictum. In any event, developments since the date of the decision in 1927 militate against following it any longer. Since the first renunciation of the use of force as an instrument of national policy in the Kellogg-Briand Pact of Paris of 1928 and the restatement of this position in Article 2(4) of the UN Charter, state freedom is now subordinated to the territorial integrity and political independence of states. This is now the grand default rule for the entire international legal system. In the words of President Guillaume, these new developments have strengthened the territorial principle. The *Lotus* dictum therefore can be considered outdated at least as far as criminal jurisdiction is concerned. This is also

the view of some IDI members[80] expressed during the deliberations leading to the adoption of the 2005 Resolution on the topic. Indeed, in some areas states have by treaty positively reversed the holding of the PCIJ in *Lotus* regarding criminal jurisdiction.[81]

48. Rejecting the *Lotus* dictum in this context, China expressly stated in its statement submitted to the UNGA in 2010 on universal jurisdiction:

> Jurisdiction is an important element of State sovereignty. Under the principle of sovereign equality of States, the establishment and exercise of [jurisdiction] by one State may not impair the sovereignty of other States. Therefore the establishment of a State's [jurisdiction] should have as a prerequisite the existence of valid and adequate connections between that country and the cases involved, and should be limited to a reasonable scope.[82]

49. One cannot but await further development on this point with great interest. Before the *Lotus* dictum is defeated in this area, conceivably the states may prevent its application by making objections to universal jurisdiction, because the basis for its application, according to the Joint Separate Opinion in *Arrest Warrant*, is the fact that there is nothing that evinces an *opinio juris* on the illegality of universal jurisdiction. A state's silent non-support alone for universal jurisdiction will not necessarily prevent it from being applied to the nationals of that state, as the effect of the application of the *Lotus* dictum is such that it may permit a state's exercise of jurisdiction not authorized, but not prohibited either, by international law. This means that making clear objections has its benefits, while 'diplomatic' ambiguity or silence may have its perils as far as the application of the *Lotus* dictum is concerned.

3.4 POSSIBLE LIMITATIONS ON THE EXERCISE OF UNIVERSAL JURISDICTION IF PERMITTED

50. From the above analysis, we can see that universal jurisdiction may be a positive tool in the efforts to vindicate the fundamental values of the international community, to promote and protect human rights and to

---

[80] See IDI, n. 4 above, 245 (Rapporteur); 258 (Frowein).

[81] See for example, 1952 Brussels Convention for the Unification of Certain Rules relating to Penal Jurisdiction in Matters of Collision or Other Incidents of Navigation, Art. 1; UNCLOS, Art. 97.

[82] Statement of China, n. 46 above, Observations, para. 1. The English translation by the UN mistakenly translates 'guanxiaquan' into 'sovereignty'. 'Jurisdiction' is used here instead.

fight impunity. Its negative side is that the exercise of universal jurisdiction is at least in tension with the principle of sovereignty and sovereign equality and is easily subjected to political abuse, including discrimination as manifested in selective prosecution, thus destabilizing international relations.[83] If one were to assume, *arguendo*, that this doctrine or principle could be used for whatever reason and to attempt to reap the benefits of the tool while reducing its side effects, one can imagine that the exercise of universal jurisdiction may be placed under a variety of conditions, or indeed that such conditions should be made part of the 'definition' of universal jurisdiction, such as: (i) limiting that exercise to the most heinous crimes such as, in addition to piracy, slavery, genocide, crimes against humanity and serious war crimes; (ii) giving priority to the territorial state; (iii) applying the clean-hands doctrine;[84] (iv) requiring a decision of the highest state authority to trigger the exercise; (v) respecting applicable immunities of officials and states; (vi) possible approval of an international screening mechanism; and (vii) the presence of the suspect. These are not discussed herein, except that I will make some comments on the presence requirement or condition.

51. It seems that there is broad support for the point that there is no customary international law rule allowing the exercise of universal jurisdiction without the presence of the suspect.[85] There is insufficient support for the view that the presence of the suspect would legitimize the exercise of 'universal jurisdiction', absent support from a treaty. Furthermore, there is disagreement on the temporal point at which the presence requirement is triggered, if the exercise of universal jurisdiction is permitted for some reason. It seems that for Judge Higgins *et al.* in the *Arrest Warrant* case, who would still rely on the *Lotus* dictum, this finding about the role of presence in itself does not show that the presence of the suspect is thereby required for the exercise of universal jurisdiction; for a state to exercise universal jurisdiction, there need only be no prohibitive rule against it. The existence of such a presence requirement in the various treaty provisions on extradite or prosecute (in their view, '*Definitionally, this envisages presence on the territory*') is no ground for reaching an *a contrario* conclusion so that presence is

---

[83] See Kissinger, n. 19 above.

[84] See Sienho Yee, 'The *Tu Quoque* Argument as a Defence to International Crimes, Prosecution, or Punishment' (2004) 3 *Chinese JIL* 87.

[85] See Statement of Israel, A/C.6/65/SR.12 (15 October 2010), p. 3, para. 9 ('many States agreed that the accused should be present in the territory of the forum State').

required.[86] For these judges, 'If it is said that a person must be within the jurisdiction at the time of the trial itself, that may be a prudent guarantee for the right of fair trial but has little to do with bases of jurisdiction recognized under international law'.[87] One cannot but note that this view, reducing the presence requirement to the mere procedural requirement of a prudent guarantee for a fair trial, is far-reaching and extraordinary, against the trend in international criminal law shunning trials *in absentia*. Indeed, this trend may evince a certain attitude about or view of the world we live in, rather than a mere quest for a fairer trial. The far-reaching effect of the procedural view of the presence requirement will be greater still – perhaps exponentially so – when it is coupled with the application of the *Lotus* dictum, which the Joint Separate Opinion in *Arrest Warrant* argued for, because both are biased in favor of the freedom of the prosecuting state.[88]

52. According to the IDI and others, the trigger point appears earlier. The IDI Resolution, in paragraph 3(b), states:

> Apart from acts of investigation and requests for extradition, the exercise of universal jurisdiction requires the presence of the alleged offender in the territory of the prosecuting State or on board a vessel flying its flag or an aircraft which is registered under its laws, or other lawful forms of control over the alleged offender.

According to the Rapporteur, this paragraph:

> rejected the theory of absolute universal jurisdiction, insisting on the presence of the alleged perpetrator on the territory of the prosecuting State. However, it did allow any State to undertake acts of investigation which per se did not harm the individual, unlike the issue of an arrest warrant. Likewise, States should be free to request extradition, although there was no obligation for the requested State to comply with such request.[89]

While this approach is reasonable to some extent, there are still three major problems. The first is this: if the requested state is where the suspect holds an official position, it will probably not comply with an extradition request without a tough decision; if this requested state is one different from the suspect's home state (when the suspect/official travels

---

86 Joint Separate Opinion, n. 17 above, in particular para. 57 (emphasis in original).

87 Joint Separate Opinion, n. 17 above, para. 56.

88 This has the danger of leading to the maximum freedom of the prosecuting state, a sort of '*Lotus* maximum', see Yee, n. 79 above, 763, para. 26.

89 IDI, n. 4 above, 208 (the Rapporteur introducing the draft Resolution).

outside), different considerations may be entertained and the request for extradition may well be complied with.

53. The second is that existing judicial assistance or extradition treaties may indeed mandate extradition because under at least some of these treaties the requested state may be required to surrender a suspect if the requesting state has made out a prima facie case in terms of jurisdiction and evidence and pure universal jurisdiction may be considered sufficient to satisfy that jurisdictional requirement. How to reconcile the IDI Rapporteur's view that the requested state is under no obligation (resulting from the universal jurisdiction law itself) to comply with such a request and the requested state's obligation to comply under other species of law becomes a most important question. In other words, should there be, in the context of universal jurisdiction, an exception from the general obligation arising from other species of law to comply with requests?

54. Thirdly, in some countries the initiation of an investigation may result in compulsory judicial processes other than arrest and extradition. This lesser form of compulsory judicial processes can still present serious problems. However, arguing for conditioning the starting of an investigation on the presence of the suspect may be too much and will likely be rejected by many states. Perhaps a compromise position could be to condition the issuance of any compulsory judicial process on the presence of the suspect on the territory of the prosecuting state.

55. This discussion should raise a red flag to any cautious government that the relationship between the possible exercise of universal jurisdiction and all the judicial and police assistance treaties and the implications of the presence requirement on this relationship are a subject calling out for urgent examination. It may wish to attempt to modify these treaties to ensure a relaxed presence requirement will not present a problem for its conduct of international relations.

3.5 CONCLUDING REMARKS

56. True or pure universal jurisdiction is jurisdiction solely based on the universal concern character of the crime in issue. The concept and logic of universal jurisdiction is understandable, as each state has an interest in matters of universal concern. Universal jurisdiction can be a powerful instrument for the international system to protect its interests and to protect human rights and fight against impunity. However, the exercise of universal jurisdiction by one state may infringe the sovereignty and sovereign equality of another state and can be abused, thus destabilizing international relations.

57. These pros and cons, and others not discussed here, have influenced the international law formation process in such a way that so far only universal jurisdiction over piracy has been accepted in international law. There is insufficient support to show that 'pure universal concern jurisdiction' exists in international law over other crimes as yet. The evidence of state practice on 'universal concern plus presence' jurisdiction is not yet substantial so as to afford the finding of a customary international law rule in its favor. Treaty practice providing for 'universal concern plus treaty, presence and intra-regime territoriality or nationality jurisdiction' or 'universal concern plus treaty and presence jurisdiction' is limited to the particular treaty regime only. In the light of this state of affairs, the possible application of the *Lotus* dictum and the presence requirement, especially the weak, procedural view of it, can be of significance and deserves attention.

58. The movement for 'pure universal jurisdiction' has been 'trending down' since the conspicuous silence of the ICJ on the legitimacy of that jurisdiction in the *Arrest Warrant* case in 2002, when the Joint Separate Opinion of Judge Higgins *et al.* found some evolutionary trend toward universal jurisdiction.[90] The subsequent downtrend may have been in no small measure due to the cautious Judgment in that case. That Judgment can be said to have, in an ingenious way, helped to inject some calming elements back into international relations.[91] With Belgium and Spain now having abandoned pure universal jurisdiction by narrowing down their statutes, the universal jurisdiction movement appears to be a moving train without its locomotive.

POSTSCRIPT

59. This chapter, based on the author's 2011 article, was motivated by the fact that the debates on universal jurisdiction in the UNGA since 2009 had revealed great confusion on the concept, and its scope and application. This chapter attempts to present what I consider to be the proper understanding of universal jurisdiction and argues that whether such universal jurisdiction exists over a particular crime depends on a normal law-making or law-formation process, rather than on any *a priori* logical extension of any substantive norm. It calls for a more rigorous assessment of state practice in this regard.

---

[90] Joint Separate Opinion, n. 17 above, paras 45–52.

[91] For a stronger assessment of the influence of the *Arrest Warrant* Judgment, see Pellet, n. 66 above.

60. The subsequent developments since the original publication of this paper appear to have strengthened support for my positions, as well as the observation of a 'trending down' of pure universal jurisdiction. The ICJ Judgment of 3 February 2012 in *Germany v Italy*[92] confirms (in a substantial way, though not specifically) that universal jurisdiction does not follow from the nature of the primary act but depends on a normal law-making or law-formation process. The UNGA debates have yet to clear up the confusion; indeed in a Resolution adopted on 10 December 2014 the UNGA still proclaimed that it 'recognize[ed] the diversity of views expressed by States and the need for further consideration towards a better understanding of the scope and application of universal jurisdiction'.[93] The draft Resolution was adopted earlier in the Sixth Committee without a vote.[94] Furthermore, the '*opinio academico*' has been receptive to the positions I expressed. A Russian translation of this paper appeared in *Russian Juridical Journal* in 2012.[95] Then an important organization invited me to a closed-door consultation meeting with a small number of experts in the field, apparently concerned about the force of my arguments. In April 2013, the American Society of International Law invited me to present this paper in its annual meeting under the title 'A Call for a More Rigorous Assessment of Universal Jurisdiction'.[96]

61. As far as the 'trending-down' is concerned, Spain has continued it by legislation.[97] This trend is such that one commentator has now titled his article as 'Universal Jurisdiction is Not Disappearing: The Shift from "Global Enforcer" to "No Safe Haven" Universal Jurisdiction',[98] when

---

92 Jurisdictional Immunities of the State (Germany v Italy: Greece intervening), Judgment [2012] *ICJ Reports* 99.

93 A/Res/69/124, 10 December 2014, available at http://daccess-dds-ny.un.org/doc/UNDOC/GEN/N14/688/29/PDF/N1468829.pdf?OpenElement.

94 See a summary of the consideration during the 69th Session of the UNGA, available at www.un.org/en/ga/sixth/69/universal_jurisdiction.shtml.

95 Сиенхо Йии (Вухан, Китай) Универсальная юрисдикция: понятие, теория и практика, (2012) 4 РОССИЙСКИЙ ЮРИДИЧЕСКИЙ ЖУРНАЛ [*Russian Juridical Journal*] 7.

96 Sienho Yee, 'A Call for a More Rigorous Assessment of Universal Jurisdiction' (2013) 107 *ASIL Proceedings* 242.

97 See Ashifa Kassam, Spain regressing on human rights, says judge who pursued Pinochet, *The Guardian*, 14 Feb. 2014, available at http://www.theguardian.com/world/2014/feb/14/spain-human-rights-judge-baltasar-garzon.

98 Maximo Langer, Universal Jurisdiction is Not Disappearing: The Shift from 'Global Enforcer' to 'No Safe Haven' Universal Jurisdiction, (2015) 13 *J. Int'l Crim. Justice* 245–56.

championing universal jurisdiction. He observed that 'under the "global enforcer" universal jurisdiction conception, states may exercise jurisdiction because they have a role in preventing and punishing core international crimes committed anywhere in the world. Under the "no safe haven" universal jurisdiction conception, states may exercise universal jurisdiction to avoid becoming a refuge for participants in core international crimes.'[99] Thus he was apparently content with the 'universal concern plus presence jurisdiction', as discussed above in paragraph 8(2) and elsewhere in this chapter. As I argue, this form of jurisdiction is not truly universal jurisdiction; the connection with the forum state is a sufficient basis for jurisdiction. Even so, as argued above, there is no sufficient state practice to support it as a customary international law rule yet.

62. It is interesting to note that the ICJ in its Judgment of 20 July 2012 in *Questions relating to the Obligation to Prosecute or Extradite (Belgium v Senegal)*[100] was apparently not content with the force of the Torture Convention itself – which alone was in issue and which was sufficient for decision in the case – and felt the need to also invoke the power of the idea of universal jurisdiction, and it did so without any explanation of its meaning or supporting analysis for the existence of universal jurisdiction over the crime at issue. In paragraphs 74, 75, 84, 91, 118, the Court simply spilled out the phrase 'universal jurisdiction', despite the fact that in 2002 the Joint Separate Opinion in *Arrest Warrant* used the Torture Convention as an example of non-universal jurisdiction and criticized referring to that as 'universal jurisdiction' as 'loose use of the language'.[101] As a result, we do not know which version of the idea of universal jurisdiction the Court had in mind in this case and, thus, the Court's use of this term in such a manner may be confusing and misleading, and of course unnecessarily so in the light of the *obiter dicta* character of such use.

63. In any event, all the world can ask of the relevant decision-makers is for them to properly follow the law-making or law-formation exercise in this regard, and all the conscientious decision-makers can do, and

---

[99] Ibid., 249.

[100] [2012] ICJ Reports 422.

[101] Joint Separate Opinion, above n. 17, para. 41.

should do, is to conduct such an exercise conscientiously and rigorously.[102] What remains rests with the states as the primary law-makers in the international community.

[102] See, Sienho Yee, Report on the ILC Project on 'Identification of Customary International Law', (2015) 14 *Chinese JIL* 375–98, especially paras. 27–8 (Comment C).

4. Jurisdiction of states and the law of the sea

Yoshifumi Tanaka

4.1 INTRODUCTION

One of the primary functions of international law concerns the spatial distribution of jurisdiction of states,[1] and the same applies to the law of the sea. The contemporary international law of the sea divides the ocean into multiple jurisdictional zones. In principle, the law of the sea provides rules concerning state jurisdiction according to these jurisdictional zones. Given that the oceans constitute approximately 70 per cent of our planet, the examination of state jurisdiction over marine spaces is of particular importance when considering spatial order in international law. Thus this chapter will seek to examine jurisdiction of states in the international law of the sea.

4.2 TYPOLOGY OF STATE JURISDICTION OVER MARINE SPACES

4.2.1 The Divided Oceans

Multiple jurisdictional zones in the law of the sea are a product of history. Traditionally the law was based on the dualism on the oceans, namely, the narrow territorial sea which is under the territorial sovereignty of the coastal state and the vast high seas which are governed by the principle of freedom of the sea. After the Second World War, the oceans were further divided into multiple jurisdictional zones. The decisive step toward the division of the oceans was taken by the Truman Proclamations on the Continental Shelf and Fisheries of 28 September

[1] G. Scelle, 'Obsession du territoire,' *Symbolae Verzijl* (The Hague, Nijhoff, 1958), p. 349. See also J.L. Brierly, *The Outlook for International Law* (Oxford, Clarendon Press, 1944), p. 9; C. Tomuschat, 'International Law: Ensuring the Survival of Mankind on the Eve of A New Century' (1999) 281 *RCADI* 57.

1945.[2] In the Proclamations, the United States regarded the natural resources of the subsoil and sea-bed of the continental shelf beneath the high seas but contiguous to the coasts of the United States as appertaining to the United States, subject to its jurisdiction and control. The United States also regarded it as proper to establish conservation zones in those areas of the high seas contiguous to the coasts of the United States wherein fishing activities have been or in the future may be developed and maintained on a substantial scale. The Truman Proclamations became a catalyst for the extension of national jurisdiction of the coastal state toward the high seas with a view to controlling offshore natural resources.

Against that background, on 24 February 1958, the First United Nations Conference on the Law of the Sea (UNCLOS I) was convened in Geneva. The Conference successfully adopted four Conventions and an Optional Protocol on dispute settlement:

- Convention on the Territorial Sea and the Contiguous Zone (TSC);[3]
- Convention on the High Seas;[4]
- Convention on Fishing and Conservation of the Living Resources of the High Seas;[5]
- Convention on the Continental Shelf;[6] and
- Optional Protocol of Signature Concerning the Compulsory Settlement of Disputes.[7]

As provided in Article 1 of the Convention on the High Seas, the 1958 Geneva Conventions divided the ocean into three basic categories: internal waters, territorial sea and high seas. Internal waters and the territorial sea are subject to the territorial sovereignty of the coastal state, whilst the high seas are governed by the freedom of the sea. It may be said that the traditional dualism in the oceans was codified in the Geneva

---

2 US Presidential Proclamation No. 2667 Policy of the United States with respect to the Natural Resources of the Subsoil and Sea Bed of the Continental Shelf; US Presidential Proclamation No. 2668 Policy of the United States with respect to Coastal Fisheries in Certain Areas of the High Seas, both reproduced in A.V. Lowe and S.A.G. Talmon, *Basic Documents on the Law of the Sea: the Legal Order of the Oceans* (Oxford, Hart Publishing, 2009), p. 19 *et seq.*

3 516 UNTS 205, entered into force 10 September 1964.

4 450 UNTS 11, entered into force 30 September 1962.

5 559 UNTS 285, entered into force 20 March 1966.

6 499 UNTS 311, entered into force 10 June 1964.

7 450 UNTS 170, entered into force 30 September 1962.

Conventions as *lex scripta*. Further, the legal institutions of the continental shelf and the contiguous zone were embodied in the Convention on the Continental Shelf and the Convention on the Territorial Sea and the Contiguous Zone, respectively. However, no rule was adopted with respect to the breadth of the territorial sea since international practice and claims were not uniform on this matter. In order to discuss the outer limit of the territorial sea as well as the fishery zone, the Second United Nations Conference on the Law of the Sea (UNCLOS II) was convened in Geneva in 1960. Yet the efforts to fix the maximum breadth of the territorial sea proved once again in vain.

Later, the existing rules of the law of the sea as a whole were to be reviewed at the Third United Nations Conference on the Law of the Sea (UNCLOS III, 1973–1982). On 30 April 1982, the Conference finally adopted the United Nations Convention on the Law of the Sea (LOSC).[8] Significant enough, states agreed on a maximum seaward limit of the territorial sea of 12 miles.[9] Further, the legal regimes governing the archipelagic waters, the 200 nautical miles exclusive economic zone (EEZ) and the Area, in other words, the seabed and ocean floor and subsoil thereof, beyond the limits of national jurisdiction,[10] were created under the Convention. As a consequence, under the LOSC, the ocean is divided into multiple jurisdictional zones: internal waters, territorial seas, the contiguous zone, the EEZ, archipelagic waters, the continental shelf, the high seas and the Area.[11]

On the basis of the national jurisdiction of the coastal state, marine spaces in the law of the sea can be divided into two main categories: marine spaces under national jurisdiction and spaces beyond national jurisdiction (see Figures 4.1 and 4.2). The former category contains internal waters, territorial seas, international straits, archipelagic waters, the contiguous zone, the EEZ and the continental shelf, whilst the latter contains the high seas and the Area. The marine spaces under national jurisdiction can be further divided into two sub-categories.

4.2.2 Territorial Sovereignty

The first sub-category concerns marine spaces under territorial sovereignty. This category of marine spaces contains internal waters, territorial

[8] 1833 UNTS 3, entered into force on 16 November 1994.

[9] LOSC, Art 3.

[10] LOSC, Art. 1(1)-(1).

[11] International straits where Part III of the LOSC is applied constitute the territorial sea.

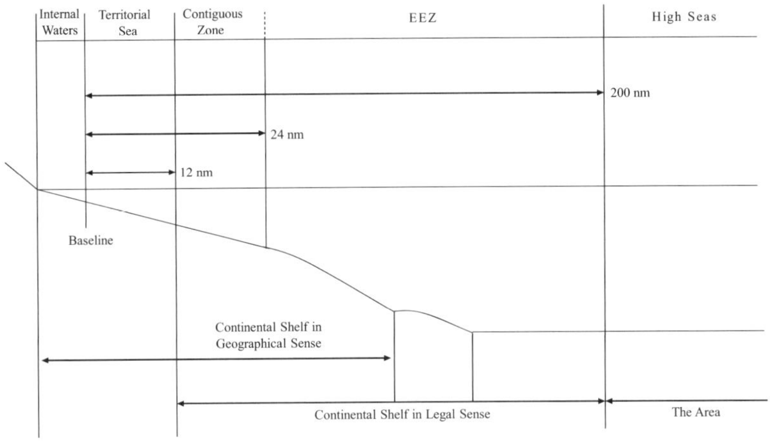

Source: Y. Tanaka, *The International Law of the Sea* (Cambridge, Cambridge University Press, 2012), p. 8.

Figure 4.1 The case where the outer edge of the continental shelf does not extend up to 200 nautical miles

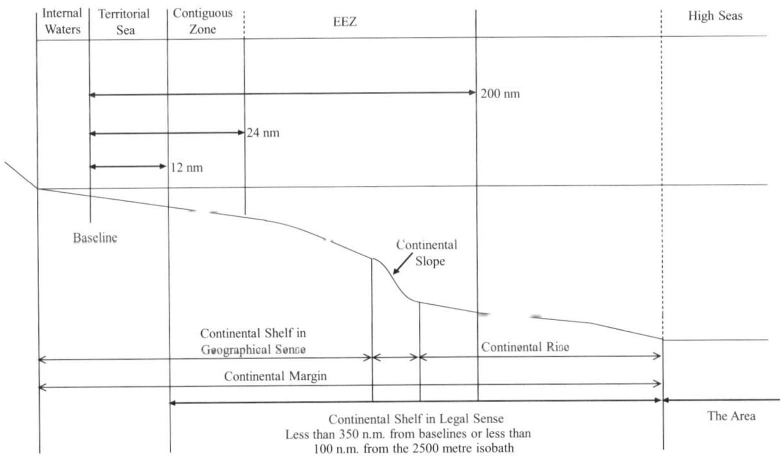

Source: Y. Tanaka, *The International Law of the Sea* (Cambridge, Cambridge University Press, 2012), p. 9.

Figure 4.2 The case where the outer edge of the continental margin extends beyond 200 nautical miles from the baselines

seas, international straits and archipelagic waters. Territorial sovereignty in international law is characterized by completeness and exclusiveness.[12] It denotes complete jurisdiction in the sense that it comprises three elements, unless international law provides otherwise:

(i) Territorial sovereignty comprises comprehensive jurisdiction, which includes both legislative and enforcement jurisdiction, over the state's territory.
(ii) The state exercises its jurisdiction over all matters within its territory. In other words, territorial sovereignty contains no limit *ratione materiae*.
(iii) The state exercises its jurisdiction over all people regardless of their nationalities. Territorial sovereignty thus contains no limit *ratione personae*.

At the same time, territorial sovereignty is exclusive in the sense that only the state in question may exercise jurisdiction over its territory.

In summary, in its territory, the state exercises legislative and enforcement jurisdiction over all matters and all people in an exclusive manner unless international law provides otherwise. It is important to note that territorial sovereignty is exercisable solely within the territory in question. In this sense, territorial sovereignty is spatial by nature. A jurisdiction that relates to a certain space and can be exercised solely within the space in question can be called 'spatial jurisdiction'. Territorial sovereignty is a typical example of spatial jurisdiction. In light of the comprehensive character of territorial sovereignty, one may call territorial sovereignty 'the complete spatial jurisdiction'.

4.2.3 Sovereign Rights

The second sub-category relates to marine spaces under sovereign rights. The EEZ and the continental shelf are included in this category.[13]

---

[12] By way of example, Article 1 of the 1944 Chicago Convention on International Civil Aviation explicitly stipulates that: 'The contracting States recognise that every State has complete and exclusive sovereignty over the airspace above its territory', 15 UNTS 295, entered into force 4 April 1947. See also Nguyen Quoc Dinh, P. Daillier, M. Forteau and A. Pellet, *Droit International Public* (8th edn, Paris, LGDJ, 2009), p. 527; P.-M. Dupuy and Y. Kerbrat, *Droit international public* (12th edn, Paris, Dalloz, 2014), p. 89; P. Reuter, *Droit international public* (Paris, PUF, 1993), pp. 188–92.

[13] LOSC, Arts 56(1) and 77(1).

Considering that the contiguous zone becomes part of the EEZ where it is established, it may not be unreasonable to put the contiguous zone into the same sub-category as the EEZ.[14] Sovereign rights of the coastal state over the EEZ and the continental shelf are limited to the matters defined by international law (limitation *ratione materiae*). In this regard, sovereign rights are distinguished from territorial sovereignty *per se*, which is comprehensive unless international law provides otherwise. Apart from this, however, sovereign rights have commonalities with territorial sovereignty:

(i) Sovereign rights concern a certain space and can be exercised solely within the space in question, that is to say, the EEZ as well as the continental shelf. In this sense, such rights are spatial by nature.

(ii) Concerning matters defined by law, the coastal state may exercise legislative and enforcement jurisdiction in the EEZ as well as the continental shelf.

(iii) The coastal state exercises its jurisdiction over all people regardless of their nationalities within the certain space in question. Thus, sovereign rights contain no limit *ratione personae*. In this respect, jurisdiction over the EEZ as well as the continental shelf should be distinguished from personal jurisdiction.

(iv) Sovereign rights are exclusive in the sense that no one may undertake the exploration and the exploitation of natural resources without the express consent of the coastal state.

What is of particular importance is that, in common with territorial sovereignty, the sovereign rights over the EEZ and the continental shelf are spatially limited by nature. As noted, the fact that jurisdiction can be exercised solely within the certain space is the essential element of spatial jurisdiction. Hence the sovereign rights over the EEZ and the continental shelf can be regarded as spatial jurisdiction, not as personal or any other type of jurisdiction.[15] Considering that sovereign rights are limited in their material scope, however, these rights should be called

---

[14] Where the EEZ is not claimed, however, the contiguous zone forms part of the high seas.

[15] J. Combacau, *Le droit international de la mer, Que sais-je?* (Paris, PUF, 1985), p. 21. Coastal state jurisdiction over the EEZ and the continental shelf is sometimes described as 'functional jurisdiction'. This is not an unreasonable view. However, every jurisdiction is functional in the sense that certain functions

limited spatial jurisdiction.[16] In summary, coastal states can exercise either territorial sovereignty (= complete spatial jurisdiction) or sovereign rights (= limited spatial jurisdiction) over marine spaces under national jurisdiction.

4.2.4 Other Rights and Jurisdiction of States

In addition to the spatial jurisdiction of coastal states, states exercise other types of rights and jurisdiction in the law of the sea. They include: the exclusive jurisdiction of the flag state; the right of hot pursuit; the right of visit; and the universal jurisdiction over suppression of piracy. These rights and jurisdiction will be discussed in 4.5 below.

4.3 MARINE SPACES UNDER TERRITORIAL SOVEREIGNTY

4.3.1 Internal Waters

4.3.1.1 Territorial sovereignty over the internal waters

Internal waters are 'those waters which lie landward of the baseline from which the territorial sea is measured'.[17] Under Article 2(1) of the LOSC,

---

are attributed to the jurisdiction. It appears that the functional nature is not an inherent feature of coastal state jurisdiction over the EEZ and the continental shelf.

[16] French writers call such jurisdiction 'la compétence territoriale limitée' or 'la compétence territoriale mineure'. See for example, C. Rousseau, *Droit international public: les compétences* (Paris, Sirey, 1977), vol. III, p. 8; S. Bastid, *Droit international public: principes fondamentaux Les Cours de droit 1969–1970* (Université de Paris), p. 804; Quoc Dinh *et al.*, n. 12 above, 536. In the United Kingdom, Brierly contrasts the fullest rights over territory, namely, territorial sovereignty with 'minor territorial rights'. A. Clapham, *Brierly's Law of Nations* (7th edn, Oxford, Oxford University Press, 2012), p. 182. Akehurst also argued that there are lesser rights over territory, that is to say, 'minor rights over territory'. P. Malanczuk, *Akehurst's Modern Introduction to International Law* (7th rev. edn, London and New York, Routledge, 1997), p. 158. In Japan, Kuwahara categorized marine spaces according to 'la compétence territoriale majeure' and 'la compétence territoriale mineure': T. Kuwahara, *Introduction to International Law of the Sea* (in Japanese) (Tokyo, Shinzansya, 2002), pp. 18–22. In essence, limited spatial jurisdiction is equivalent to 'minor territorial rights' or 'la compétence territoriale limitée'.

[17] LOSC, Art 8(1). Specifically internal waters in a legal sense embrace: (i) parts of the sea along the coast down to the low-water mark; (ii) ports and

'[t]he sovereignty of a coastal State extends, beyond its land territory and internal waters and, in the case of an archipelagic State, its archipelagic waters, to an adjacent belt of sea, described as the territorial sea'. Thus every coastal state enjoys full sovereignty over its internal waters. Unlike the territorial sea, the right of innocent passage does not apply to internal waters. The exception to this rule is that where the internal waters have been newly enclosed by a straight baseline, the right of innocent passage shall exist in those waters.[18] As ports are under the territorial sovereignty of the coastal state, that state may regulate foreign vessels' entry to its ports.[19] Therefore, apart from vessels in distress, there is no right of entry into ports of foreign states in customary international law.[20] In practice, however, it can be presumed that normally the ports of the coastal state are open to merchant vessels unless otherwise provided.

4.3.1.2 Criminal jurisdiction of the coastal state in internal waters

Normally the civil jurisdiction of the coastal state is not exercised in connection with disputes of a private nature arising between members of the crew. The exercise of the criminal jurisdiction of the coastal state leaves some room for discussions. In this regard, international lawyers have been accustomed to contrast the Anglo-American position with the French position.[21] According to the Anglo-American position, the coastal state has complete jurisdiction over foreign vessels in its ports. As a matter of comity, however, the coastal state may refrain from exercising its jurisdiction over those vessels. This position was echoed by the US Supreme Court in the 1887 *Wildenhus* case.[22] According to the French

---

harbours; (iii) estuaries; (iv) landward waters from the closing line of bays; and (v) waters enclosed by straight baselines. Y. Tanaka, *The International Law of the Sea* 2nd edn (Cambridge, Cambridge University Press, 2015), p. 78.

[18] LOSC, Art. 8. See also Geneva Convention on the Territorial Sea and the Contiguous Zone, Art. 5(2).

[19] *Military and Paramilitary Activities in and against Nicaragua (Nicaragua v United States)* [1986] ICJ Reports 111, para. 213.

[20] This conclusion was echoed by the 1957 Amsterdam Resolution of the Institut de droit international. Institut de droit international, 'The Distinction Between the *Régime* of the Territorial Sea and the *Régime* of Internal Waters', Session of Amsterdam, 24 September 1957, Part II. The French text is authoritative.

[21] L. Lucchini and M. Voelckel, *Droit de la mer* (Paris, Pedone, 1990), vol. I, pp. 157–9; I. Brownlie, *Principles of Public International Law* (7th edn, Oxford, Oxford University Press, 2008), p. 319.

[22] 120 U.S. 1, 11 (1887). The judgment was reproduced in K.R. Simmonds, *Cases on the Law of the Sea* (Dobbs Ferry, New York, Oceana Publications,

position, the coastal state has in law no jurisdiction over purely internal affairs on foreign vessels in its ports. This position derived from the opinion of the French Conseil d'Etat in the *Sally* and *Newton* cases in 1806.[23] As Gidel rightly observed, however, the opinion of the Conseil d'Etat of 1806 did not completely deny the territorial jurisdiction of the coastal state over offences committed on board foreign ships in French ports.[24] In fact, a French court, in the 1859 *Tempest* case, held that homicide of a fellow crew member compromised the peace of the port, and therefore brought the ship under local jurisdiction.[25] Therefore, it may be said that the points of difference between the two positions are minimal.

In modern practice, the scope of criminal jurisdiction of the coastal state over foreign merchant ships is provided by specific consular conventions.[26] Recent state practice seems to suggest that the coastal state does not exercise criminal jurisdiction over matters involving solely the internal discipline of the ship. However, the coastal state will exercise criminal jurisdiction in the following cases:

(i) when an offence caused on board the ship affects or is likely to affect the peace and order or the tranquillity of the port or on land, or its interests are engaged;
(ii) when its intervention is requested by the captain, or the consul of the flag state of the vessel;
(iii) when a non-crew member is involved;
(iv) when an offence caused on board the ship is of a serious character, usually punishable by a sentence of imprisonment for more than a few years; and

---

1977), vol. II, pp. 406–11 at 409. This position is also confirmed in *Restatement of the Law Third: The Foreign Relations Law of the United States* (American Law Institute Publishers, 1990), vol. II, para. 512, Reporter's Note 5, p. 42. The delegation of Great Britain explained its position at the 1930 Hague Conference. S. Rosenne (ed.), *League of Nations Conference for the Codification of International Law* (New York, Oceana, [1930] 1975), vol. II, p. 317.

23 The *Sally* and the *Newton* cases were reproduced in Simmonds, n. 22 above, vol. I, 77–8. France explained its position at the 1930 Hague Conference. Rosenne, n. 22 above, 299–300.

24 G. Gidel, *Le droit international public de la mer*, vol. II, *Les eaux intérieures* (reprint, Paris, Douchemin, 1981), pp. 87 and 204–5.

25 The *Tempest* case was reproduced in Simmonds, n. 22 above, vol. I, 448–59.

26 M. Hayashi, 'Jurisdiction over Foreign Commercial Ships in Ports: A Gap in the Law of the Sea Codification' (2004) 18 *Ocean Yearbook* 505.

(v) when matters which do not concern solely the 'internal economy' of a foreign ship, such as pollution and pilotage, are involved.

It is solely the coastal state which may determine the existence of a situation as described above. It must be noted that unlike merchant ships, warships and other government ships operated for non-commercial purposes enjoy sovereign immunity.[27] Members of the crew ashore on duty or official mission are immune from the local jurisdiction, when committing breaches of local law. Members of the crew committing breaches of local law when ashore on leave and rejoining the ship are also immune from the local jurisdiction.

4.3.2 Territorial Sea

4.3.2.1 Territorial sovereignty over the territorial sea

The territorial sea is a marine space under the territorial sovereignty of the coastal state up to a limit not exceeding 12 nautical miles measured from baselines.[28] The coastal state exercises territorial sovereignty over the territorial seas. It follows that the coastal state can exercise complete legislative and enforcement jurisdiction over all matters and all people in an exclusive manner unless international law provides otherwise.[29] However, it is of particular importance to note that unlike sovereignty over the internal waters, coastal states' sovereignty over the territorial sea is restricted by the right of innocent passage for foreign vessels.[30] Unless passage of foreign ships are considered to be prejudicial to the peace, good order or security of the coastal state,[31] that state is obliged not to hamper the innocent passage of foreign ships.[32] No charge may be levied upon foreign ships by reason only of their passage through the territorial sea.[33] Notwithstanding this, the coastal state can exercise legislative and

27 TSC, Art. 22(2); LOSC, Art. 32. Warships are defined in LOSC, Art. 29.

28 LOSC, Art. 3.

29 *Ibid.* Art. 2(3).

30 *Ibid.* Art. 17. See also, Y. Tanaka, 'Navigational Rights and Freedoms' in D.R. Rothwell, Alex G. Oude Elferink, K. Scott and T. Stephens (eds), *The Oxford Handbook on the Law of the Sea* (Oxford, Oxford University Press, 2015) pp. 539–49.

31 LOSC, Art. 19.

32 *Ibid.* Art. 24(1). However, the coastal state is empowered to temporarily suspend the innocent passage of foreign vessels in accordance with *ibid.* Art. 25(3).

33 *Ibid.* Art. 26.

enforcement jurisdiction with regard to the regulation of innocent passage. In this regard, five points must be noted.

First, under Article 21(1) of the LOSC, the coastal state possesses the legislative jurisdiction relating to innocent passage through the territorial sea with respect to all or any of the following:

(a) the safety of navigation and the regulation of maritime traffic;
(b) the protection of navigational aids and facilities and other facilities or installations;
(c) the protection of cables and pipelines;
(d) the conservation of the living resources of the sea;
(e) the prevention of infringement of the fisheries laws and regulations of the coastal state;
(f) the preservation of the environment of the coastal state and the prevention, reduction and control of pollution thereof;
(g) marine scientific research and hydrographic surveys;
(h) the prevention of infringement of the customs, fiscal, immigration or sanitary laws and regulations of the coastal state.

However, such laws and regulations will not apply to the design, construction, manning or equipment of foreign ships unless they are giving effect to generally accepted international rules or standards.[34]

Second, the coastal state is entitled to require foreign ships exercising the right of innocent passage through its territorial sea to use such sea lanes and traffic separation schemes as it may designate or prescribe for the regulation of the passage of ships by virtue of Article 22(1) of the LOSC. At the same time, the coastal state is under the obligation to clearly indicate such sea lanes and traffic separation schemes on charts to which due publicity must be given.[35]

Third, the coastal state is entitled to take the necessary steps in its territorial sea to prevent passage which is not innocent under Article 25(1) of the LOSC. Whilst this provision does not specify the necessary steps, they could include requesting a delinquent ship to stop certain conduct, requesting a ship to leave the territorial sea, and the intervention

---

[34] *Ibid.* Art. 21(2).

[35] *Ibid.* Art. 22(4). This obligation follows from the *dictum* in the *Corfu Channel* judgment [1949] ICJ Reports 22; M.H. Nordquist *et al.*, *United Nations Convention on the Law of the Sea 1982: A Commentary* (‘*Virginia Commentaries*’) (Leiden, Nijhoff, 1993), vol. II, p. 226.

of state authorities to board and exclude the ship from its territorial sea.[36] Where there are clear grounds for believing that a vessel navigating in the territorial sea of a state has violated laws and regulations of that state during its passage therein, the coastal state may undertake physical inspection of the vessel relating to the violation, and may, where the evidence so warrants, institute proceedings, including detention of the vessel.[37]

Fourth, in the case of ships proceeding to internal waters or a call at a port facility outside internal waters, the coastal state has the right to take the necessary steps to prevent any breach of the conditions to which admission of those ships to internal waters or such a call is subject by virtue of Article 25(2).

Finally, the state practice is divided as to whether foreign warships can enjoy the right of innocent passage through the territorial sea.[38] In any case, the coastal state may require any warship to leave its territorial sea if the warship does not comply with the laws and regulations of the coastal state by virtue of Article 30 of the LOSC.

4.3.2.2 Criminal and civil jurisdiction of coastal states with regard to innocent passage through the territorial sea

As the territorial sea is under the territorial sovereignty of the coastal state, theoretically the coastal state may exercise criminal jurisdiction over foreign vessels passing through the territorial sea. Under Article 27(1) of the LOSC, however, the criminal jurisdiction of the coastal state 'should not' be exercised on board a foreign ship passing through the territorial sea, save only in the following cases:

(a) if the consequences of the crime extend to the coastal state;
(b) if the crime is of a kind to disturb the peace of the country or the good order of the territorial sea;
(c) if the assistance of the local authorities has been requested by the master of the ship or by a diplomatic agent or consular officer of the flag state; or
(d) if such measures are necessary for the suppression of illicit traffic in narcotic drugs or psychotropic substances.

[36] D. Rothwell and T. Stephens, *The International Law of the Sea* (Oxford, Hart Publishing 2010), p. 218.
[37] LOSC, Art. 220(2).
[38] Tanaka, n. 17 above, 89–93.

The phrase 'should not' seems to suggest that the exercise of criminal jurisdiction is not strictly prohibited in other cases. It would follow that the coastal state has discretion with regard to the exercise of criminal jurisdiction. The restriction of criminal jurisdiction under Article 27(1) of the LOSC does not apply to the case of inward/outward-bound navigation.[39] Where a crime has been committed before the ship entered the territorial sea and the ship is only passing through the territorial sea without entering internal waters, however, the coastal state may not exercise criminal jurisdiction over the ship under Article 27(5) of the LOSC. This is a mandatory prohibition on the exercise of the criminal jurisdiction of the coastal state in the territorial sea.

Likewise, Article 28 of the LOSC limits the exercise of civil jurisdiction of the coastal state in certain cases. Under Article 28(1), 'the coastal State should not stop or divert a foreign ship passing through the territorial sea for the purpose of exercising civil jurisdiction in relation to a person on board the ship'. The term 'should not' seems to suggest that the restriction of the civil jurisdiction is a matter of comity.[40] Under Article 28(2), the coastal state may not levy execution against or arrest the ship for the purpose of any civil proceedings, save only in respect of obligations or liabilities assumed or incurred by the ship itself in the course or for the purpose of its voyage through the waters of the coastal state. However, Article 28(2) is not applicable to inward/outward-bound navigation.[41]

4.3.3 International Straits

4.3.3.1 Territorial sovereignty over international straits

Part III of the LOSC is devoted to international straits. The legal regime governing international straits creates sensitive issues with regard to the reconciliation between jurisdiction of the coastal state and the freedom of navigation through straits. Under the LOSC, international straits can be divided into two main rubrics according to the applicability of Part III: (i) straits to which Part III applies (type I); and (ii) straits outside the scope of Part III (type II). Part III of the LOSC applies to international straits as the territorial sea. The straits under Part III of the LOSC contain two

---

39 LOSC, Art. 27(2).

40 D.P. O'Connell, *The International Law of the Sea* (I.A. Shearer (ed.), Oxford, Clarendon Press, 1984), vol. II, p. 874; Sir Gerald Fitzmaurice, 'Some Results of the Geneva Conference on the Law of the Sea: Part I The Territorial Sea and Contiguous Zone and Related Topics' (1959) 8 *ICLQ* 107.

41 LOSC, Art. 28(3).

types of straits: (i) straits to which the regime of transit passage applies (type I-A); and (ii) straits to which the right of non-suspensible innocent passage applies (type I-B).[42] Both types of straits are under the territorial sovereignty of the bordering state. However, the territorial sovereignty over straits under the category of type I-A is limited by the right of transit passage. By the same token, the territorial sovereignty over straits under the category of type I-B is compromised by the right of non-suspensible innocent passage.

4.3.3.2 Coastal state jurisdiction with regard to transit passage

The coastal state can exercise both legislative and enforcement jurisdiction with regard to the transit passage. Under Article 42(1) of the LOSC, it has a right to adopt laws and regulations relating to transit passage through straits.[43] However, the legislative jurisdiction of the coastal state is qualified by Article 42(2) in two respects. The first limitation is that the laws and regulations of the coastal state bordering international straits 'shall not discriminate in form or in fact among foreign ships'.[44] The second limitation is that the application of the laws and regulations shall not 'have the practical effect of denying, hampering or impairing the right of transit passage'.

In this regard, an issue arises as to whether, in the case of the violation of the municipal law of the state bordering straits, that state could terminate the right of transit passage unilaterally. The cumulative effect of Articles 38(1), 42(2) and 44 seems to suggest that states bordering straits are not allowed to prevent transit passage merely on grounds of breach of their municipal law.[45] In the case of a violation of the laws and regulations referred to in Article 42(1)(a) and (b), however, Article 233 of

---

42 *Ibid.* Art. 45(2).

43 States bordering straits are required to give due publicity to all such laws and regulations in accordance with LOSC, Art. 41(3). See also Tanaka, n. 30 above, 551–2.

44 This provision has parallels in *ibid.* Arts 24(1)(b), 25(3), 52(2) and 227. *Virginia Commentaries*, n. 35 above, vol. II, 376.

45 *Ibid.* 377. H. Caminos, 'The Legal Régime of Straits in the 1982 United nations Convention on the Law of the Sea' (1987) 205 *RCADI,* p. 147 and pp. 149–50; T. Treves, 'Navigation' in R.-J. Dupuy and D. Vignes (eds), *A Handbook on the New Law of the Sea*, Vol. 2 (Dordrecht, Nijhoff, 1991), pp. 967–8; H. Caminos and V.P. Cogliati-Bantz, *The Legal Régime of Straits: Contemporary Challenges and Solutions* (Cambridge, Cambridge University Press, 2014) p. 268. However, it is not suggested that the state bordering straits cannot exercise its enforcement jurisdiction if the ship should enter that state's ports.

the LOSC explicitly allows the state bordering a strait to exercise its enforcement jurisdiction.

The state bordering straits may designate sea lanes and prescribe traffic separation schemes for navigation in straits where necessary to promote the safe passage of ships in accordance with Article 41(1) of the LOSC. At the same time, coastal states bordering straits shall undertake the following duties in accordance with Article 44: (i) not to hamper transit passage; (ii) to give appropriate publicity to any danger to navigation or overflight within or over the strait of which they have knowledge; and (iii) not to suspend transit passage. Article 43 of the LOSC also requires user states and states bordering a strait to cooperate: '(a) in the establishment and maintenance in a strait of necessary navigational and safety aids or other improvements in aid of international navigation; and (b) for the prevention, reduction and control of pollution from ships'.

In relation to this, a contentious issue arises with regard to coastal state's jurisdiction concerning environmental protection of international straits. This issue creates particular sensitivity for the freedom of navigation. A case in point is the compulsory pilotage system adopted by Australia.[46] In 2006, Australia established a compulsory pilotage system for certain vessels in the Torres Strait and Great North East Channel in order to protect sensitive marine habitats. Yet Australia's compulsory pilotage system was protested by the United States and Singapore. Later, Australia changed its position and effectively exempted vessels from compulsory pilotage if they were not intending to call at an Australian port.[47] In any case the controversy relating to the compulsory pilotage system in the Torres Strait seems to signal a growing tension between the navigational interest of the user states and the environmental interest of states bordering an international strait.[48]

---

[46] Generally on this issue, see R.C. Beckman, 'PSSAs and Transit Passage: Australia's Pilotage System in the Torres Strait Challenges the IMO and UNCLOS' (2007) 38 *ODIL* 325.

[47] P. Dorling, 'Reef Safeguard Cut Back', *The Age*, 12 September 2011, available at www.theage.com.au/environment/conservation/reef-safeguard-cut-back-20110911-1k4b3.html; D.R. Rothwell, *Compulsory Pilotage and the Law of the Sea: Lessons Learned from the Torres Strait*, ANU College of Law Research Paper No. 12-06 (2012), p. 17, available at http://ssrn.com/abstract=2020781.

[48] See also T. Scovazzi, 'The Evolution of International Law of the Sea: New Issues, New Challenges' (2000) 286 *RCADI* 186; D.R. Rothwell, 'International Straits' in D.R. Rothwell, Alex G. Oude Elferink, K. Scott and T.

4.3.4 Archipelagic Waters

4.3.4.1 Territorial sovereignty over archipelagic waters

'Archipelagic waters' mean the waters enclosed by the archipelagic baselines drawn in accordance with Article 47 of the LOSC regardless of their depth or distance from the coast.[49] As clearly stated in Article 49(1) and (2) of the LOSC, archipelagic waters are under the territorial sovereignty of the archipelagic state. However, this sovereignty must be exercised subject to Part IV of the LOSC.[50] Specifically, the territorial sovereignty of the archipelagic state is qualified by rights of third states in four respects.

First, the archipelagic state is required to respect the traditional fishing rights of third states.[51] This provision was intended to meet the concerns of Malaysia with respect to prospective Indonesian archipelagic waters.[52]

Second, under Article 51(2) of the LOSC, the archipelagic state is under the obligation to respect existing submarine cables. This provision applies only to existing cables, and no mention is made of pipelines. It would seem to follow that the laying of new cables and pipelines depends on the consent of archipelagic states.

Third, under Article 47(6) of the LOSC, if a part of the archipelagic waters of an archipelagic state lies between two parts of an immediately adjacent neighbouring state, existing rights and all other legitimate interests which the latter state has traditionally exercised in such waters and all rights stipulated by agreement between those states will continue and be respected. This situation can be seen between the Malaysian mainland and Sarawak by the extension of Indonesia's archipelagic waters associated with the Kepulauan Anambas and Kepulauan Bunguran.[53]

Fourth, by establishing archipelagic waters, some important navigation channels, such as the Sunda and Lombok Straits, fall under the territorial sovereignty of the archipelagic state. If passage through archipelagic

---

Stephens (eds), *The Oxford Handbook on the Law of the Sea* (Oxford, Oxford University Press, 2015), pp. 129–30; Tanaka, n. 17 above, 108–9.

[49] LOSC, Art. 49(1).

[50] *Ibid.* Art. 49(3).

[51] *Ibid.* Art. 51(1).

[52] *Virginia Commentaries*, n. 35 above, vol. II, 452.

[53] United Nations Office for Ocean Affairs and the Law of the Sea (UNDOALOS), *The Law of the Sea: Baselines: An Examination of the Relevant Provisions of the United Nations Convention on the Law of the Sea* (New York, United Nations, 1989), pp. 37–8.

waters is not accepted, sea communication will be considerably disturbed. Hence there is a strong need to guarantee the freedom of navigation of foreign vessels in archipelagic waters. Part IV of the LOSC ensures the freedom of navigation through archipelagic waters by providing the right of innocent passage and that of archipelagic sea lanes passage. The territorial sovereignty of an archipelagic state is thus qualified by the rights of navigation of foreign ships in archipelagic waters.

4.3.4.2 Rights and obligations of archipelagic states over archipelagic sea lanes passage

All ships and aircraft can enjoy the right of archipelagic sea lanes passage through archipelagic waters.[54] Under Article 53(3) of the LOSC, archipelagic sea lanes passage means the exercise in accordance with this Convention of the rights of navigation and overflight in the normal mode solely for the purpose of continuous, expeditious and unobstructed transit between one part of the high seas or an EEZ and another part of the high seas or an EEZ. Since Article 44 of the LOSC applies *mutatis mutandis* to archipelagic sea lanes passage,[55] archipelagic states must not hamper archipelagic sea lanes passage and must give appropriate publicity to any danger to navigation or overflight within or over the strait of which they have knowledge. Further, there must be no suspension of archipelagic sea lanes passage.

On the other hand, an archipelagic state may adopt laws and regulations relating to the prevention of marine pollution in archipelagic waters in accordance with Articles 42(1) and 54 of the LOSC. Ships in archipelagic sea lanes passage are required to comply with generally accepted international regulations, procedures and practice for the prevention, reduction and control of pollution from ships.[56] Although Articles 220 and 233 of the LOSC give the coastal state additional enforcement jurisdiction regulating pollution from ships in the territorial sea and the straits, these provisions contain no reference to archipelagic waters. However, Article 233 refers to LOSC, Article 42 concerning laws and regulations of states bordering straits relating to transit passage; and Article 42 applies *mutatis mutandis* to archipelagic waters in accordance

---

[54] Tanaka, n. 30 above, 553–4.

[55] LOSC, Art. 54.

[56] *Ibid.* Arts 39(2)(b) and 54. See also Tanaka, n. 17 above, 118–19.

with LOSC, Article 54. Therefore, it can be argued that Article 233 is also applicable to archipelagic waters.[57]

4.4 MARINE SPACES UNDER SOVEREIGN RIGHTS

4.4.1 Contiguous Zone

The contiguous zone is a marine space contiguous to the territorial sea up to a limit not exceeding 24 nautical miles measured from baselines.[58] Under Article 33(1) of the LOSC, the coastal state may, in its contiguous zone, exercise the control necessary to:

(a) prevent infringement of its customs, fiscal, immigration or sanitary laws and regulations within its territory or territorial sea; and
(b) punish infringement of the above laws and regulations committed within its territory or territorial sea.[59]

Considering that an incoming vessel cannot commit an offence until it crosses the limit of the territorial sea, it would appear that head (b) of Article 33(1) can apply only to an outgoing ship. By contrast, head (a) can apply only to incoming ships because prevention cannot arise with regard to an outgoing ship in the contiguous zone. Further, under Article 303(2) of the LOSC, the coastal state may exercise control with regard to the protection of objects of an archaeological and historical nature found within the contiguous zone.

Although the contents of the 'control necessary to punish infringement' of municipal law of the coastal state in its contiguous zone remains less clear, the coastal state may undertake the hot pursuit of foreign ships within the contiguous zone under Article 111(1) of the LOSC.[60] Under

---

57 *Virginia Commentaries*, n. 35 above, vol. II, 187. See also, R.P.M. Lotilla, 'Navigational Rights in Archipelagic Waters: A Commentary from the Philippines' in D.R. Rothwell and S. Bateman (eds), *Navigational Rights and Freedoms and the New Law of the Sea* (The Hague, Nijhoff, 2000), p. 156.

58 LOSC, Art. 33(2).

59 Article 33(1) contains no reference to internal waters. However, it would be inconceivable that the drafters of this provision had an intention to exclude the internal waters from the scope of this provision since these waters are under the territorial sovereignty of the coastal state. Thus it appears to be reasonable to consider that internal waters are also included in the scope of 'its territory or territorial sea'.

60 The right of hot pursuit will be discussed in 4.5.1 below.

Article 111(6), (7) and (8), the coastal state has the right to stop a ship, the right to arrest the ship, and the right to escort the ship to a port. One can say, therefore, that the coastal state jurisdiction to punish the infringement of its municipal laws in the contiguous zone includes these rights.

Article 33(1) of the LOSC literally means that the coastal state may exercise only enforcement, not legislative, jurisdiction within its contiguous zone. It would follow that relevant laws and regulations of the coastal state are not extended to its contiguous zone; and that infringement of municipal laws of the coastal state within the zone is outside the scope of this provision.[61] However, some take a liberal interpretation, arguing that the coastal state may regulate the violation of its municipal law within the contiguous zone for some limited purposes. For instance, Oda argued that in the contiguous zone, the coastal state should be entitled to exercise its authority as exercisable in the territorial sea only for some limited purposes of customs or sanitary control.[62]

It is true that a strict reading of Article 33(1) does not allow coastal states to extend legislative jurisdiction to its contiguous zone. Notwithstanding this, the contiguous zone becomes part of the EEZ when the coastal state claims the zone. As will be seen next, in the EEZ, the coastal state may exercise both legislative and enforcement jurisdiction for limited matters provided by the law of the sea. Accordingly, claims to legislative jurisdiction in the zone will not cause a serious problem in reality.[63] If this is the case, as a matter of practice, it may not be

---

[61] Fitzmaurice, n. 40 above, 114.

[62] S. Oda, 'The Concept of the Contiguous Zone' (1962) 11 *ICLQ* 153. This view was echoed by O'Connell and Shearer. See O'Connell, n. 40 above, 1060; I.A. Shearer, 'Problems of Jurisdiction and Law Enforcement against Delinquent Vessels' (1986) 35 *ICLQ* 330.

[63] R.R. Churchill and A.V. Lowe, *Law of the Sea* (3rd edn, Manchester University Press, 1999), p. 138. Some states claim both legislative and enforcement jurisdiction over the contiguous zone. Examples include: India, the Territorial Waters, Continental Shelf, Exclusive Economic Zone and Other Maritime Zones Act 1976, s. 5(5); Pakistan, Territorial Waters and Maritime Zone Act 1976, s. 4(3); Sri Lanka, Maritime Zones Law, No. 22 of 1976, s. 4(2). For the text of these provisions, see UNDOALOS, *The Law of the Sea: National Legislation on the Territorial Sea, the Right of Innocent Passage and the Contiguous Zone* (New York, United Nations, 1995), pp. 160, 257, 354, respectively. Some states claim jurisdiction for the purpose of security within the contiguous zone. But these claims have been protested by the United States. See J.A. Roach and R.W. Smith, *United States Responses to Excessive Maritime Claims* (3rd edn, Leiden and Boston, Nijhoff, 2012), pp. 154–7.

unreasonable to extend the legislative jurisdiction of the coastal state over the contiguous zone for the limited purposes provided in Article 33.

4.4.2 Exclusive Economic Zone

4.4.2.1 Sovereign rights over the EEZ

The EEZ is an area beyond and adjacent to the territorial sea, not extending beyond 200 nautical miles from the baseline of the territorial sea.[64] In the EEZ, the coastal state has *sovereign rights* for the purpose of exploring and exploiting, conserving and managing the natural resources, whether living or non-living, of the waters superjacent to the sea-bed and of the sea-bed and its subsoil, and with regard to other activities for the economic exploitation and exploration of the zone, such as the production of energy from the water, currents and winds.[65] In this regard, it is of particular importance to note that the sovereign rights of the coastal state over the EEZ are essentially limited to economic exploration and exploitation (limitation *ratione materiae*). In this respect, as noted, sovereign rights are distinguished from territorial sovereignty, which is comprehensive unless international law provides otherwise. With respect to matters provided by the law, however, the coastal state exercises both legislative and enforcement jurisdiction in the EEZ. This is clear from LOSC, Article 73(1). Whilst this provision provides enforcement jurisdiction for the coastal state, the reference to 'the laws and regulations by it' seems to suggest that the state also has legislative jurisdiction. It is beyond serious doubt that the measures provided under Article 73(1) can be applied to foreign vessels within the EEZ. This is clear from Article 73(4) which explicitly refers to 'in cases of arrest or detention of foreign vessels'. Thus a coastal state jurisdiction within its EEZ contains no limit *ratione personae*.

Although Part V of the LOSC contains no provision with regard to the exclusiveness of the coastal state jurisdiction over the EEZ, Article 2(2) of the 1958 Geneva Convention on the Continental Shelf makes clear that: 'The rights referred to in paragraph 1 of this Article [sovereign rights] are exclusive in the sense that if the coastal State does not explore the continental shelf or exploit its natural resources, no one may undertake these activities, or make a claim to the continental shelf, without the express consent of the coastal State'. It may be argued that the sovereign rights in the EEZ are essentially exclusive in the sense that

---

[64] LOSC, Arts 55 and 57.

[65] *Ibid.* Art. 56(1)(a).

no one may undertake these activities or make a claim to the EEZ, *without the express consent of the coastal state*. It is true that third states have the right of access to natural resources in the EEZ.[66] Considering that the exercise of the right is conditional upon agreement with the coastal state, however, it does not challenge the exclusive nature of the coastal state's jurisdiction over the EEZ.[67]

In summary, unlike territorial sovereignty, the sovereign rights of the coastal state over the EEZ lack comprehensiveness of material scope. With respect to matters accepted by international law, however, the coastal state can exercise both legislative and enforcement jurisdiction over all people within the EEZ in an exclusive manner. The essential point is that the rights of the coastal state over the EEZ are spatial in the sense that they can be exercised solely within the particular space in question regardless of the nationality of persons or vessels. Thus the coastal state jurisdiction over the EEZ can be regarded as a spatial jurisdiction. Due to the lack of comprehensiveness of material scope, as already mentioned, this jurisdiction should be called a limited spatial jurisdiction.[68]

The *raison d'être* of the EEZ for the coastal state is to control natural resources. For this reason, sovereign rights which allow the coastal state to exercise exclusive jurisdiction over natural resources are of central importance. At the same time, it must be stressed that the coastal state is under the obligation to ensure that the maintenance of the living resources in the EEZ is not endangered by over-exploitation.[69] Considering that approximately 90 per cent of all commercially exploitable fish stocks are caught within 200 nautical miles,[70] the role of the coastal state in conservation of living resources in the EEZ is particularly important.

---

[66] *Ibid.* Arts 62(2), 69 and 70.

[67] B. Kwiatkowska, *The 200 Mile Exclusive Economic Zone in the New Law of the Sea* (Dordrecht, Nijhoff, 1989), p. 15.

[68] R.-J. Dupuy took the view that the coastal state enjoys 'power of a spatial type' in the EEZ. R.-J. Dupuy, 'The Sea under National Competence' in R.-J. Dupuy and D. Vignes (eds), *A Handbook on the New Law of the Sea*, Vol. 1 (Dordrecht, Nijhoff, 1991), p. 293. Combacau considered the coastal state's jurisdiction over the EEZ as territorial jurisdiction. Combacau, n. 15 above, 21. Bastid considered the continental shelf and the EEZ as maritime domain under limited territorial jurisdiction (*la compétence territoriale limitée*). Bastid, n. 16 above, 814–15.

[69] LOSC, Art. 61(2).

[70] Malanczuk, n. 16 above, 183; P.G.G. Davies and C. Redgwell, 'The International Legal Regulation of Straddling Fish Stocks' (1996) 67 *BYIL* 200; Churchill and Lowe, n. 63 above, 162.

However, any disputes relating to a state's sovereign rights concerning living resources in the EEZ or their exercise are exempted from the compulsory settlement procedure embodied in Part XV of the LOSC.[71] There is no review process by a third party to examine the validity of the conservation measures of the coastal state in its EEZ. Thus it may have to be accepted that the normativity of the obligation concerning the conservation of living resources in the EEZ remains modest.

4.4.2.2 Jurisdiction of coastal states over the EEZ

The coastal state possesses jurisdiction over matters other than sovereign rights concerning the exploration and exploitation of marine natural resources.[72]

First, under Article 60 of the LOSC, the coastal state has exclusive jurisdiction, including both legislative and enforcement jurisdiction, over installations and structures for economic purposes by virtue of Article 60. In this regard, an issue arises as to whether or not the coastal state also has the jurisdiction to authorize and to regulate the construction and use of installations and structures for non-economic purposes, such as military purposes. It appears that state practice is not uniform on this particular matter. When ratifying the LOSC, Brazil, Cape Verde and Uruguay made declarations claiming that the coastal state has the exclusive right to authorize and regulate the construction and use of all kinds of installations and structures, without exception, whatever their nature or purpose.[73] By contrast, when ratifying the LOSC, Germany, Italy, the Netherlands and the United Kingdom declared that the coastal state enjoys the right to authorize, construct, operate and use only those installations and structures which have economic purposes.[74] Whilst this remains a debatable issue, the preferable view appears to be that a dispute falls within the scope of Article 59 of the LOSC because the Convention does not explicitly attribute rights or jurisdiction in this matter to a coastal state or to other states.[75]

---

[71] LOSC, Art. 297(3)(a).

[72] *Ibid.* Art. 56(1)(b) and (c).

[73] Lowe and Talmon, n. 2 above, 915, 917 and 967.

[74] *Ibid.* 935, 941, 948–9 and 965.

[75] A.V. Lowe, 'Some Legal Problems Arising from the Use of the Seas for Military Purposes' (1986) 10 *Marine Policy* 180; R.R. Churchill, 'The Impact of State Practice on the Jurisdictional Framework Contained in the LOS Convention' in A.G. Oude Elferink (ed.), *Stability and Change in the Law of the Sea: The Role of the LOS Convention* (Leiden and Boston, Nijhoff, 2005), p. 136. It is

Second, under Article 56(1)(b)(ii) of the LOSC, the coastal state has jurisdiction with regard to marine scientific research in the EEZ. Specifically coastal states, in the exercise of their jurisdiction, have the right to regulate, authorize and conduct marine scientific research in their EEZ and on their continental shelf in accordance with the relevant provisions of the Convention under Article 246(1) of the LOSC. Marine scientific research in the EEZ and on the continental shelf is to be conducted with the consent of the coastal state in conformity with Article 246(2). In normal circumstances, coastal states are to grant their consent for marine scientific research projects by other states or competent international organizations, which are exclusively for peaceful purposes pursuant to Article 246(3). However, coastal states may in their discretion withhold their consent to the conduct of a marine scientific research in conformity with Article 246(5).

Third, under LOSC, Article 56(1)(b)(iii), in the EEZ, the coastal state has legislative and enforcement jurisdiction with regard to the protection and preservation of the marine environment. In this regard, Articles 210(1) and 211(5) of the LOSC provide legislative jurisdiction of the coastal state concerning the regulation of dumping and vessel-source pollution. Further, Articles 210(2) and 220 contain enforcement jurisdiction of the coastal state with regard to the regulation of dumping and ship-borne pollution.

The LOSC contains no provision with regard to the coastal state jurisdiction over archaeological and historical objects found within the EEZ beyond the contiguous zone. The protection of these objects would need to be assessed by the application of LOSC, Article 59.

4.4.2.3 Coastal state jurisdiction with regard to the regulation of bunkering in the EEZ

A particular issue which arises in this context concerns the legality of bunkering in an EEZ of a foreign state. The LOSC contains no explicit provision on this subject. This issue was, for the first time in the International Tribunal for the Law of the Sea (ITLOS) jurisprudence, raised in the 1999 *M/V Saiga (No. 2)* case between Saint Vincent and Grenadines and Guinea. The M/V *Saiga* was a tank vessel flying the flag of Saint Vincent and Grenadine. On 28 October 1997, the *Saiga*, awaiting the arrival of fishing vessels to which it was to supply gas oil, was arrested by Guinean authority in its EEZ on the ground that the *Saiga*

---

also to be noted that freedom to construct artificial islands and other installations is not included in Art. 58(1) and (2).

violated Law L/94/007 by importing gas oil into the customs radius of Guinea. Criminal proceedings were subsequently instituted by the Guinean authorities against the Master of the *Saiga*, and the Tribunal of First Instance in Conakry, Guinean capital, found the Master guilty as charged and imposed on him a fine. A central question in this case was whether or not Guinea was entitled to apply its customs law in its EEZ. In this regard, ITLOS held that whilst the coastal state has jurisdiction to apply customs laws and regulations in respect of artificial islands, installations and structures in the EEZ pursuant to Article 60(2) of the LOSC, the Convention does not empower a coastal state to apply its customs laws in respect of any other parts of the EEZ not mentioned in that provision.[76]

A similar dispute was raised in the 2014 *M/V Virginia G* case between Panama and Guinea-Bissau. On 20 August 2009, the M/V *Virginia G*, an oil tanker flying the flag of Panama, supplied gas oil to fishing vessels flying the flag of Mauritania in the EEZ of Guinea-Bissau. On 21 August 2009, the M/V *Virginia G* was arrested by the authority of Guinea-Bissau and the tanker, along with its gear, equipment and products on board, was confiscated. Panama thus instituted arbitral proceedings against Guinea-Bissau pursuant to Annex VII to the LOSC in a dispute concerning the M/V *Virginia G*. Later the dispute was transferred to ITLOS. The principal question to be addressed by ITLOS was whether Guinea-Bissau, in the exercise of its sovereign rights in respect of the conservation and management of natural resources in its EEZ, has the competence to regulate bunkering of foreign vessels fishing in this zone. In this regard, ITLOS took the view that the regulation by a coastal state of bunkering of foreign vessels fishing in its EEZ is among those measures which the coastal state may take in its EEZ to conserve and manage its living resources under LSOC, Article 56 read together with Article 62(4).[77] According to ITLOS, the coastal state's jurisdiction over bunkering of foreign vessels fishing in its EEZ derives from the sovereign rights of that state to explore, exploit, conserve and manage natural resources. At the same time, ITLOS added that the coastal state does not have such competence with regard to other bunkering activities, unless otherwise determined in accordance with the LOSC.[78]

76 *M/V Saiga (No. 2)* (1999) 38 ILM 1351, para. 127.

77 *M/V Virginia G*, Case No. 19, ITLOS, Judgment of 14 April 2014, pp. 61–4, paras 208–17 (electronic text accessed in June 2015).

78 *Ibid.* 65, paras 222–3.

4.4.3 Continental Shelf

4.4.3.1 Sovereign rights over the continental shelf

The continental shelf of a coastal state comprises the sea-bed and subsoil of the submarine areas that extend beyond its territorial sea throughout the natural prolongation of its land territory to the outer edge of the continental margin, or to a distance of 200 nautical miles from the baselines.[79] Under Article 77(1) of the LOSC, the coastal state exercises sovereign rights over the continental shelf for the purpose of exploring and exploiting its natural resources.[80] Unlike the sovereign rights over the EEZ, the sovereign rights of the coastal state over the continental shelf are inherent rights, and do not depend on occupation, effective or notional, or on any express proclamation. In this sense, a continental shelf exists *ipso facto* and *ab initio*.[81] Apart from this point, the sovereign rights over the continental shelf contain commonalities with that over the EEZ.

First, the sovereign rights of the coastal state relate to the exploration and exploitation of natural resources on the continental shelf. Non-natural resources are not included in the ambit of sovereign rights of the coastal state even if they are found on the continental shelf. For instance, wrecks lying on the shelf do not fall within the ambit of the sovereign rights over the continental shelf.[82] The sovereign rights over the continental shelf are thus characterized by the lack of comprehensiveness of material scope. On this point, the sovereign rights are distinguished from territorial sovereignty.

The natural resources on the continental shelf basically consist of the mineral and other non-living resources of the sea-bed and subsoil. However, exceptionally sedentary species are also included in natural resources on the continental shelf. Under Article 77(4), the sedentary species are organisms which, at the harvestable stage, either are immobile on or under the sea-bed or are unable to move except in constant physical contact with the sea-bed or the subsoil. Examples include oysters, clams

---

[79] LOSC, Art. 76(1).

[80] It must be noted that the exercise of the rights of the coastal state over the continental shelf must not infringe or result in any unjustifiable interference with navigation and other rights and freedoms of other states as provided for in LOSC, Art. 78(2).

[81] [1969] ICJ Reports 22, para. 19.

[82] Churchill and Lowe, n. 63 above, 152.

and abalone. Yet it is open to debate whether crab and lobster fall within the category of sedentary species.[83]

Second, although there is no provision like Article 73(1), there seems to be a general sense that the sovereign rights include legislative and enforcement jurisdiction to explore and exploit natural resources on the continental shelf. In fact, under Article 111(2) of the LOSC, the right of hot pursuit will apply *mutatis mutandis* to violations in the EEZ or on the continental shelf, including safety zones around continental shelf installations, of the laws and regulations of the coastal state applicable in accordance with this Convention to the EEZ or the continental shelf. This provision appears to suggest that the coastal state has legislative and enforcement jurisdiction with respect to the continental shelf.

Third, the sovereign rights of the coastal state are exercisable over all people or vessels regardless of their nationalities. Thus there is no limit concerning personal scope.

Lastly, the rights are exclusive in the sense that if the coastal state does not explore the continental shelf or exploit its natural resources, no one may undertake these activities without the express consent of the coastal state.[84]

Overall sovereign rights of the coastal state over the continental shelf are limited to certain matters provided by international law. With respect to matters provided by international law, however, the coastal state may exercise legislative and enforcement jurisdiction over all peoples regardless of their nationalities in an exclusive manner. In essence, rights over the continental shelf are spatial in the sense that they can be exercised solely within the particular space in question regardless of the nationality of persons or vessels. Hence, like the EEZ, the sovereign rights of the coastal state over the continental shelf can be regarded as a limited spatial jurisdiction.

4.4.3.2 Coastal state jurisdiction over the continental shelf

In addition to these sovereign rights for the purpose of the exploration and exploitation of natural resources on the continental shelf, the coastal state can exercise jurisdiction with regard to artificial islands, marine scientific research, dumping and other purposes.

First, under Article 80 of the LOSC, Article 60 concerning the coastal state's jurisdiction over artificial islands is applied *mutatis mutandis* to

83 *Ibid.* 151.

84 LOSC, Art. 77(2); Geneva Convention on the Continental Shelf, Art. 2(2). The ICJ echoed this view: [1969] ICJ Reports 22, para. 19.

the continental shelf. It follows that on the continental shelf, the coastal state has exclusive rights to construct and to authorize and regulate the construction, operation and use of: (a) artificial islands; (b) installations and structures for the purposes provided for in Article 56 and other economic purposes; and (c) installations and structures which may interfere with the exercise of the rights of the coastal state in the EEZ. The coastal state also has exclusive jurisdiction over such artificial islands, installations and structures, including jurisdiction with regard to customs, fiscal, health, safety and immigration laws and regulations.

Second, on the continental shelf, the coastal state has jurisdiction with regard to marine scientific research in accordance with Articles 56(1)(b)(ii) and 246(1) of the LOSC. Under Article 246(2), marine scientific research in the EEZ and on the continental shelf must be conducted with the consent of the coastal state.[85]

Third, under Article 210(5) of the LOSC, the coastal state has the right to permit, regulate and control dumping on the continental shelf. At the same time, the coastal state has enforcement jurisdiction with respect to pollution by dumping on the continental shelf.

Finally, the coastal state 'shall have the exclusive rights to authorize and regulate drilling on the continental shelf for all purposes' by virtue of LOSC, Article 81. The phrase, 'for all purposes', seems to suggest that the exclusive rights of the coastal state concerning drilling on the continental shelf are not limited to the purposes of exploration and exploitation of natural resources.

4.4.3.3 Coastal state jurisdiction over the superjacent waters of the continental shelf

Under LOSC, Article 78(1), the rights of the coastal state over the continental shelf do not affect the legal status of the superjacent waters or of the airspace above those waters.[86] It follows that where the coastal state has not claimed an EEZ, the superjacent waters above the continental shelf remain the high seas. Where the coastal state has established an EEZ, the superjacent waters above the continental shelf beyond 200 nautical miles are always the high seas under the LOSC. Hence all states enjoy the freedoms of navigation and fishing in the superjacent waters of the continental shelf and the freedom of overflight in the airspace above those waters. In practice, however, it appears that freedoms of third states

---

[85] However, with regard to the continental shelf beyond 200 nautical miles, the discretion of the coastal state is limited by LOSC, Art. 246(6).

[86] See also 1958 Convention on the Continental Shelf, Art. 3.

may be qualified by the coastal state in the superjacent water of the continental shelf beyond 200 nautical miles in some respects.

First, the coastal state has exclusive jurisdiction over the construction of artificial islands as well as installations and structures on the continental shelf beyond 200 nautical miles by virtue of LOSC, Article 80. In practice, artificial islands and other installations are constructed in superjacent waters above the continental shelf. It would seem to follow that freedom to construct artificial islands may be qualified by the coastal state jurisdiction, even though literally the superjacent waters of the continental shelf beyond 200 nautical miles are the high seas.

Second, in practice, coastal states explore and exploit natural resources on the continental shelf from the superjacent waters above the continental shelf. Accordingly, it appears inescapable that the coastal state exercises its jurisdiction in the superjacent waters above the continental shelf for the purpose of the exploration and exploitation of natural resources.[87] As noted, Article 111(2) of the LOSC provides the right of hot pursuit in respect of violations on the continental shelf, including safety zones around continental shelf installations, of the laws and regulations of the coastal state applicable to the continental shelf. In practice, safety zones are established on the superjacent waters of the continental shelf. It would seem to follow that the coastal state jurisdiction relating to the exploration and exploitation of the continental shelf is to be exercised at least in safety zones on the superjacent waters of the shelf.

Third, under LOSC, Article 78(2), the exercise of the coastal state's rights over the continental shelf must not infringe or result in any unjustifiable interference with navigation. The language of this provision seems to imply that the coastal state may interfere in a justifiable manner with navigation in the exercise of its sovereign rights over the continental shelf.[88]

Fourth, as noted, the coastal state has jurisdiction with regard to marine scientific research *on* the continental shelf under LOSC, Articles 56(1)(b)(ii) and 246(1), and such research on the continental shelf is to be conducted with the consent of the coastal state pursuant to Article 246(2). On the other hand, LOSC, Article 257 provides that all states have the right to conduct marine scientific research *in* the water column beyond the limits of the EEZ 'in conformity with this Convention'. A question arises whether the complete freedom of marine scientific

---

[87] S. Oda, 'Proposals for Revising the Convention on the Continental Shelf' in S. Oda, *Fifty Years of the Law of the Sea: With a Special Section on the International Court of Justice* (The Hague, Nijhoff, 2003), p. 275.

[88] Treves, n. 45 above, 891.

research applies to superjacent waters of the continental shelf. According to a literal interpretation, consent under Article 246(2) seems to be required only for research physically taking place on the sea floor. Considering that normally marine scientific research is carried out from the superjacent waters or airspace above the continental shelf, however, it appears to be naïve to consider that coastal states will not exercise their jurisdiction to regulate marine scientific research there.[89]

In summary, it appears that at least in some respects, the freedom of the high seas may be qualified by coastal state jurisdiction in the superjacent waters above the continental shelf beyond 200 nautical miles. The jurisdiction of coastal states over the superjacent waters above the continental shelf may also be at issue in conservation of marine biological diversity beyond areas of national jurisdiction.[90]

4.5 MARINE SPACES BEYOND NATIONAL JURISDICTION

4.5.1 High Seas

4.5.1.1 Exclusive jurisdiction of the flag state

Under Article 86 of the LOSC, the high seas are defined as 'all parts of the sea which are not included in the EEZ, in the territorial sea or in the internal waters of a State, or in the archipelagic waters of an archipelagic State'. The high seas are governed by the principle of freedom. However, it is not suggested that there is no legal order on the high seas. The order on the high seas is essentially ensured by the principle of the exclusive

---

[89] Y. Takei, *Filling Regulatory Gaps in High Seas Fisheries: Discrete High Seas Fish Stocks, Deep-sea Fisheries and Vulnerable Marine Ecosystems* (Leiden, Nijhoff, 2013), p. 45.

[90] In the open-ended working group to study issues relating to the conservation and sustainable use of marine biological diversity beyond areas of national jurisdiction, some delegations stated that, in conformity with the LOSC, 'the coastal State was fully entitled to adopt any conservation and management measures it deemed necessary to protect its sedentary species on the continental shelf. Those may include the possibility of imposing restrictive measures on fishing activities in the high seas over its continental shelf, including on fishing practices that were deemed to have a negative impact on sedentary species'. United Nations General Assembly, *Report of the Ad Hoc Open-ended Informal Working Group to Study Issues Relating to the Conservation and Sustainable Use of Marine Biological Diversity Beyond Areas of National Jurisdiction*, A/61/65 (20 March 2006), p. 7, para. 22. See also Takei, n. 89 above, 45–7.

jurisdiction of the flag state, in other words, the state which has granted a ship the right to sail under its flag.[91]

The principle of the exclusive jurisdiction of the flag state is well established in customary international law and is embodied in LOSC, Article 92(1). The flag state jurisdiction comprises both legislative and enforcement jurisdiction over its ships on the high seas. The flag state exercises enforcement jurisdiction over all peoples within its ships flying its flag regardless of their nationalities. In this regard, ITLOS stated that: '[T]he ship, every thing on it, and every person involved or interested in its operations are treated as an entity linked to the flag State. The nationalities of these persons are not relevant'.[92] The flag state is entitled to make claims against other states in case of damage to its ship or injury to the seamen manning it, regardless of their nationality.[93]

The legal basis of the principle of the exclusive jurisdiction of the flag state was sometimes explained by the theory of the territoriality of the ship. According to this theory, a ship is considered as a 'floating island' or a 'detached part of the territory' of the state to which it belongs.[94] Nonetheless, the theory of the territoriality of the ship is contrary to the fact that, in certain circumstances, merchant vessels are subject to the right of visit by foreign warships, and vessels within internal waters and the territorial seas are in principle under the territorial sovereignty of the coastal state.[95] Hence the theory of the territoriality of the ship is obsolete and indefensible. The principle of the exclusive jurisdiction of the flag state should be considered as a corollary of the freedom of the high seas and the requirement of the submission of the high seas to law.[96] As the high seas are not subject to any national jurisdiction and there is no centralized authority governing the high seas, legal order on the high seas is to be ensured primarily by the flag state.

The principle of the exclusive jurisdiction of the flag state plays a dual role. First, this principle prevents any interference by other states with vessels flying its flag on the high seas. In so doing, the principle of the

---

[91] Generally on flag state jurisdiction, see R.A. Barnes, 'Flag States' in D.R. Rothwell, Alex G. Oude Elferink, K. Scott and T. Stephens (eds), *The Oxford Handbook on the Law of the Sea* (Oxford, Oxford University Press, 2015), pp. 304–24.

[92] *M/V Saiga (No. 2)* n. 76 above, para. 106.

[93] *Restatement of the Law Third*, n. 22 above, vol. II, s. 502, Comment (h), p. 21.

[94] *SS Lotus*, PCIJ, 1928 Series A, No. 10, p. 25.

[95] *Ibid.*, Dissenting Opinion of Lord Finlay, at 53.

[96] See also Gidel, n. 24 above, 225.

exclusive jurisdiction of the flag state ensures the freedom of activity of vessels on the high seas. Second, under this principle, the flag state has responsibility to ensure compliance with national and international laws concerning activities of ships flying its flag on the high seas.[97]

A particular issue that may arise in this context concerns the extent of flag state jurisdiction in the situation where vessels flying the flags of different states have collided on the high seas. In this regard, the most often cited instance is the 1928 *Lotus* case. On 2 August 1926, the French mail steamer *Lotus* collided with a Turkish vessel *Boz-Kourt* on the high seas. As a result of the collision, the Turkish vessel sank and eight Turkish nationals on board lost their lives. Upon the arrival of the *Lotus* in Constantinople, the Turkish authorities instituted criminal proceedings against, among others, Lieutenant Demons, a French officer of the watch on board the *Lotus* at the time of the collision. On 15 September 1926, the Criminal Court sentenced Lieutenant Demons to 80 days' imprisonment and a fine of 22 pounds. The action of the Turkish judicial authorities gave rise to a dispute between France and Turkey and, by a special agreement signed at Geneva on 12 October 1926, the two governments submitted the case to the Permanent Court of International Justice (PCIJ).

In this case, the PCIJ ruled that 'there is no rule of international law prohibiting the State to which the ship on which the effects of the offence have taken place belongs from regarding the offence as having been committed in its territory and prosecuting, accordingly, the delinquent'.[98] The Court thus held, by the President's casting vote, that Turkey had not acted in conflict with the principle of international law, contrary to Article 15 of the Convention of Lausanne of 24 July 1923.[99]

Nonetheless, the *Lotus* judgment was much criticized because penal proceedings before foreign courts in the event of collision on the high seas may constitute an intolerable interference with international navigation.[100] As a consequence, the 1952 Brussels Convention for the Unification of Certain Rules relating to Penal Jurisdiction provided for the exclusive jurisdiction of the flag state or of the state of nationality of an offender in the event of a collision or any other incident of navigation

---

[97] The obligations of the flag state are specified in LOSC, Art. 94 in some detail.

[98] *Lotus*, n. 94 above, 25.

[99] *Ibid.* 32.

[100] ILC, *Report to the General Assembly Covering its Work of the Eighth Session, Articles concerning the Law of the Sea with Commentaries*, Art. 35(1) in (1956-II) *YILC* 281.

concerning a sea-going ship.[101] This rule was echoed in Article 11 of the Geneva Convention on the High Seas and Article 97 of the LOSC. Furthermore, LOSC, Article 98(1)(c) places a clear obligation upon every state to require the master of a ship flying its flag, after a collision, to render assistance to the other ship, its crew and its passengers.

The flag state has the primary responsibility to ensure compliance with rules relating to conservation of marine species on the high seas by vessels flying its flag.[102] In reality, however, a serious concern has been voiced with regard to problems with the flag of convenience. The flag of convenience states allow shipowners to evade national taxation and to avoid the qualifications required of the crews of their ships, whilst these states receive a registry fee and an annual fee. It is problematic that the effective implementation of the flag state's jurisdiction over fishing vessels is undermined by the practice of flag of convenience states, which often lack the will and the capability to properly regulate fishing activities by vessels flying its flag. Fishing vessels can also easily evade the regulation of the flag state by the simple expedient of re-flagging to another state.[103] In order to address this problem, various treaties and non-binding instruments attempt to strengthen the flag state's responsibility, such as the 1993 Agreement to Promote Compliance with International Conservation and Management Measures.[104] Yet some doubts could be expressed regarding whether flags of convenience states will ratify the Food and Agriculture Organization (FAO) Compliance Agreement or other relevant treaties in the near future.[105] Hence it may have to be accepted that the flag state's responsibility alone is inadequate to properly conserve marine living resources.[106]

---

[101] 439 UNTS 234, Arts 1 and 3.

[102] The LOSC contains provisions concerning general obligations which are to be met by the flag State in all maritime areas regulated by the Convention. See LOSC, Articles 91, 92, and 94 as well as 192 and 193; *Request for an advisory opinion submitted by the Sub-Regional Fisheries Commission (SRFC)(hereafter 2015 ITLOS Advisory Opinion)*, Case No. 21, Advisory Opinion of 2 April 2015, p. 32, para. 111 (electronic text accessed in July 2015), available at www.itlos.org/.

[103] P. Birnie, A. Boyle and C. Redgwell, *International Law and the Environment* (3rd edn, Oxford, Oxford University Press, 2008), p. 743.

[104] FAO Compliance Agreement, Preamble, para. 10 (1994) 33 ILM 968, entered into force on 24 April 2003.

[105] As at June 2015, the number of parties to the FAO Compliance Agreement was 40.

[106] In this regard, the role of non-flag states, including port states, is increasingly important. Tanaka, n. 17 above, 244–50.

4.5.1.2 Exceptions to the exclusive jurisdiction of the flag state (1): right of hot pursuit

The principle of the exclusive jurisdiction of the flag state applies to warships as well as ships used only on government non-commercial service without any exception. This is clear from Articles 95 and 96 of the LOSC.[107] On the other hand, private ships are subject to two types of exception: the right of hot pursuit and the right of visit.

The right of hot pursuit which may be undertaken by the competent authorities of the coastal state seeks to safeguard the interests of coastal states. In this regard, Article 111 of the LOSC specifies six conditions to exercise the right.

First, the hot pursuit must be undertaken by warships or military aircraft, or other ships or aircraft clearly marked and identifiable as being on government service and authorized to that effect.[108]

Second, the hot pursuit of a foreign ship may be undertaken when the competent authorities of the coastal state have good reason to believe that the ship has violated the laws and regulations of that state. If the foreign ship is within a contiguous zone, the pursuit may only be undertaken if there has been a violation of the rights for the protection of which the zone was established, that is to say, customs, fiscal, immigration or sanitary laws.[109]

Third, in essence, hot pursuit is a temporary extension of the coastal state's jurisdiction onto the high seas. Accordingly, the pursuit must be commenced when the foreign ship or one of its boats is within the internal waters, the archipelagic waters, the territorial sea or the contiguous zone of the pursuing state.[110] The right of hot pursuit is to apply *mutatis mutandis* to violations of the laws and regulations of the coastal state in the EEZ or on the continental shelf, including safety zones around continental shelf installations.[111]

Fourth, the pursuit may only be commenced after a visual or auditory signal to stop has been given at a distance which enables it to be seen or heard by the foreign ship.[112] In this connection, the use of radio signals was at issue in *R v Mills and other* in 1995. In light of the development of modern technology, Judge Devonshire at Croydon Crown Court ruled

---

[107] Ships owned by a government may be regarded as private ships if such ships are involved in commercial activities.
[108] LOSC, Art. 111(5).
[109] *Ibid*. Art. 111(1).
[110] *Ibid*. Art. 111(1) and (4).
[111] *Ibid*. Art. 111(2).
[112] *Ibid*. Art. 111(4).

that the transmission of the radio signals complied with the preconditions of the Convention on the High Seas concerning the right of hot pursuit.[113]

Fifth, the pursuit must be hot and continuous. The aircraft giving the order to stop must itself actively pursue the ship until a ship or another aircraft of the coastal state arrives to take over the pursuit, unless the aircraft is itself able to arrest the ship pursuant to Article 111(6)(b).[114] It is also recognized that hot pursuit can be transferred between ships, although there is no explicit provision on this particular matter.[115]

Finally, the right of hot pursuit ceases as soon as the ship pursued enters the territorial sea of its own state or of a third state,[116] since pursuit in the territorial sea of another state would violate the territorial sovereignty of that state. It would follow that hot pursuit may continue in the EEZ of a third state. Where the hot pursuit was unjustified, compensation will be paid for any loss or damage that may have been sustained thereby.[117] According to ITLOS, the conditions for the exercise of the right of hot pursuit under this provision are cumulative and each of them has to be satisfied for the pursuit to be legitimate under the LOSC.[118]

4.5.1.3 Exceptions to the exclusive jurisdiction of the flag state (2): right of visit

As provided in LOSC, Article 110(1), states are allowed to exercise the right of visit in certain circumstances. Article 110(1) distinguishes two cases where the foreign warship or the military aircraft may exercise the right of visit.

The first is the case where acts of interference derive from powers conferred by specific treaties. In those cases, only the states parties to relevant Conventions are entitled to exercise the right of visit on vessels flying the flag of other states parties. In fact, some fishery treaties allow a state party to board and inspect vessels of other parties on the high seas.[119]

---

[113] W.C. Gilmore, 'Hot Pursuit: The Case of *R v Mills and Others*' (1995) 44 *ICLQ* 957.

[114] LOSC, Art. 111(6)(b).

[115] (1956) 2 *YILC* 285, para. 2(c). In fact, in the *I'm Alone* case between Canada and the United States, two United States coastguard vessels were involved in the hot pursuit: (1933) 3 *RIAA* 1609.

[116] LOSC, Art. 111(3).

[117] *Ibid.* Art. 111(8).

[118] *M/V Saiga (No. 2)*, n. 76 above, 1354, para. 146.

[119] See for instance, Article 21(1) of the Agreement for the Implementation of the Provisions of the United Nations Convention on the Law of the Sea of 10 December 1982 Relating to the Conservation and Management of Straddling

The second case relates to the right of visit with respect to activities of foreign vessels enumerated in Article 110(1). In this case, the warship or military aircraft may send a boat under the command of an officer to the suspected ship in order to verify the ship's right to fly its flag. If suspicion remains after the documents have been checked, it may proceed to a further examination on board the ship pursuant to Article 110(2). If the suspicions prove to be unfounded, however, it must be compensated for any loss or damage that may have been sustained in accordance with Article 110(3).[120] The exceptions listed in Article 110(1) are:

(a) the ship is engaged in piracy;
(b) the ship is engaged in the slave trade;
(c) the ship is engaged in unauthorized broadcasting and the flag state of the warship has jurisdiction under Article 109;
(d) the ship is without nationality; or
(e) though flying a foreign flag or refusing to show its flag, the ship is, in reality, of the same nationality as the warship.

The scope of the right of visit varies according to each item. As we shall discuss in the next section, states can exercise universal jurisdiction to seize a pirate ship or aircraft and arrest suspected pirates. In other cases, as will be explained below, the scope of the right of visit is more limited.

(i) A warship or a military aircraft which encounters on the high seas a foreign ship which is suspected to be engaged in the slave trade can board it. In this case, it is generally considered that enforcement jurisdiction beyond the right of visit is limited to the flag state.[121]

(ii) On the high seas, a state having jurisdiction under Article 109(3) of the LOSC is empowered to arrest any person or ship engaged in unauthorized broadcasting and seize the broadcasting apparatus.[122] Under Article 109(3), states which have jurisdiction on this matter are:

Fish Stocks and Highly Migratory Fish Stocks. 2167 UNTS 3. Entered into force 11 December 2001.

[120] Under LOSC, Art. 110(4), provisions under Art. 110(1), (2) and (3) apply *mutatis mutandis* to military aircraft.

[121] Churchill and Lowe, n. 63 above, 212; T. Treves, 'High Seas' in R. Wolfrum (ed.), *Max Planck Encyclopaedia of Public International Law* (Oxford, Oxford University Press, 2008–2011), p. 4, para. 19; available at www.mpepil.com.

[122] LOSC, Art. 109(4).

(a) the flag state of the ship;
(b) the state of registry of the installation;
(c) the state of which the person is a national;
(d) any state where the transmissions can be received; or
(e) any state where authorized radio communication is suffering interference.

(iii) Under LOSC, Article 110(1) and (2), a warship or a military aircraft is empowered to visit and verify the ship's right to fly its flag where there is a reasonable ground to suspect that the ship is without nationality. Although the LOSC is silent on the legal consequences of being a stateless vessel, it can be said at least that unlike in the case of piracy, the LOSC does not provide universal jurisdiction over a stateless vessel.

(iv) Concerning ships with suspicious nationality, a warship or a military aircraft may visit and verify the ship's right to fly its flag where there is a reasonable ground for suspecting that a ship, though flying a foreign flag or refusing to show its flag, is of the same nationality as the warship in reality.[123] It is recognized that warships of every state may seize, and bring to a port of their own for punishment, any foreign vessel sailing under the same flag as the inspecting warship without any authorization.[124]

4.5.1.4 Universal jurisdiction over piracy

As pirates[125] are treated as outlaws, they are denied the protection of the flag state and any state may capture and punish them.[126] Under LOSC, Article 105, on the high seas, or in any other place outside the jurisdiction of any state, every state may seize a pirate ship or aircraft, or a ship or aircraft taken by piracy and under the control of pirates, and arrest the persons and seize the property on board. The courts of the state which carried out the seizure may decide upon the penalties to be imposed, and may also determine the action to be taken with regard to the ships, aircraft or property, subject to the rights of third parties acting

---

[123] *Ibid.* Art. 110(1)(e).

[124] Sir Robert Jennings and Sir Arthur Watts (eds), *Oppenheim's International Law*, vol. I, *Peace* (9th edn, Harlow, Longman, 1992), p. 737.

[125] For a definition of piracy, see LOSC, Art. 101. For a recent study of the piracy provisions, see R. Churchill, 'The Piracy Provisions of the UN Convention on the Law of the Sea: Fit for Purpose?' in P. Koutrakos and A. Skordas (eds), *The Law and Practice of Piracy at Sea: European and International Perspective* (Oxford, Hart Publishing, 2014), pp. 9–32.

[126] *Lotus*, n. 94 above, Dissenting Opinion of Mr Moore, at 70.

in good faith. The seizure of piracy is the oldest and the most well-attested example of universal jurisdiction.[127] In this respect, the UN Security Council, in its Resolution of 11 April 2011, explicitly recognized that 'piracy is a crime subject to universal jurisdiction'.[128] In this regard, two comments can be made.

First, in dealing with piracy suspects, states cannot be released from obligations arising under applicable human rights treaties, such as the Convention Against Torture, the European Convention on Human Rights and the International Covenant on Civil and Political Rights. The human rights obligations that may be at issue include: (i) the right to be brought promptly before a judge; (ii) *non refoulement*; (iii) fair trial guarantees; and (iv) the right to an effective remedy.[129] Hence careful consideration should be given to the protection of the human rights of piracy suspects.

Second, the language of Article 105 suggests that the power to seize and prosecute a pirate ship or aircraft is facultative, not an obligation. Accordingly, there is no guarantee that action against pirates will be effectively taken.[130] In fact, it is not uncommon that seizing states are reluctant to prosecute pirates owing to the lack of domestic legislation, legal complexities in criminal proceedings, and the expense involved.[131]

---

[127] M.D. Evans, 'The Law of the Sea' in M.D. Evans (ed.), *International Law* (4th edn, Oxford, Oxford University Press, 2014), p. 666; M. Shaw, *International Law* (7th edn, Cambridge, Cambridge University Press, 2014), p. 285; *Restatement of the Law Third*, n. 22 above, vol. 1, s. 404, pp. 254–5.

[128] UN Security Council Resolution 1976 (2011), S/RES/1976 (2011), 11 April 2011, para. 14. See also Separate Opinion of Judge Guillaume in *Arrest Warrant of 11 April 2000* [2001] ICJ Reports 37, para. 5. See also Joint Separate Opinion of Judges Higgins, Kooijmans and Buergenthal, *ibid.*, 81, paras 60–61.

[129] D. Guilfoyle, 'Counter-Piracy Law Enforcement and Human Rights' (2010) 59 *ICLQ* 141 (in particular 152–67). See also S.P. Bodini, 'Fighting Maritime Piracy under the European Convention on Human Rights' (2011) 22 *EJIL* 829–48; A. Petrig, 'Piracy' in D.R. Rothwell, Alex G. Oude Elferink, K. Scott and T. Stephens (eds), *The Oxford Handbook on the Law of the Sea* (Oxford, Oxford University Press, 2015), pp. 857–8.

[130] T. Treves, 'Piracy, Law of the Sea, and Use of Force: Developments off the Coast of Somalia' (2009) 20 *EJIL* 402. In the period from 1998 to 2009, the incidence of universal jurisdiction over piracies was just under 1.5 per cent of reported cases: E. Kontorovich and S. Art, 'An Empirical Examination of Universal Jurisdiction of Piracy' (2010) 44 *AJIL* 444.

[131] UN Doc. S/PV. 6046 (16 December 2008), p. 28 (Denmark). See also Treves, n. 130 above, 408–10; M.D. Fink and R.J. Galvin, 'Combating Pirates off the Coast of Somalia: Current Legal Challenges' (2009) 56 *NILR* 389. In Singapore, the Comité Maritime International adopted the 'Model National Law on Acts of Piracy or Maritime Violence' in 2001.

State practice shows that piracy suspects are being transferred for trial to relevant states. Whilst Somali piracy suspects are standing trial in various countries, including Somalia (Puntland), France, Yemen, the Netherlands, Japan, the Republic of Korea and the United States, Kenya seems to remain the preferable venue of choice.[132] In relation to this, the Kenyan government concluded agreements on prosecuting suspected pirates with the United Kingdom, the United States, the EU, Canada, China and Denmark in 2009. Although the government of Kenya withdrew from those agreements in March 2010, it continues to accept piracy suspects for prosecution on a case-by-case basis.[133] In 2010, the Kenyan government, with the aid of international funds, opened a special court to try piracy suspects operating from Somalia in the Gulf of Aden.[134]

Third, the factual situation has proven that the individual exercise of universal jurisdiction alone is less effective to suppress piracy. Thus various attempts are made to promote international cooperation in the suppression of piracy. In particular, counter-piracy operations through international institutions, such as the IMO, NATO, the EU and the United Nations, and operations through regional treaties merit particular notice.[135]

4.5.2 The Area

As declared in LOSC, Article 136, the Area and its resources are the common heritage of mankind. All rights in the resources of the Area are vested in mankind as a whole, on whose behalf the Authority is to act.[136] Under LOSC, Article 153(1), activities in the Area will be organized, carried out and controlled by the Authority on behalf of mankind as a

---

132 Guilfoyle, n. 129 above, 142.

133 UN Security Council, *Report of the Secretary-General on Specialised Anti-piracy Courts in Somalia and Other States in the Region*, S/2012/50 (20 January 2012), p. 22, para. 78. See also J.T. Gathii, 'Kenya's Piracy Prosecutions' (2010) 104 *AJIL* 416; Paul Musili Wambua, 'The Jurisdictional Challenges to the Prosecution of Piracy Cases in Kenya: Mixed Fortunes for a Perfect Model in the Global War Against Piracy' (2012) 11 *WMU Journal of Maritime Affairs* 95.

134 D. Akande, 'Anti-Piracy Court Opens in Kenya', *EJIL: Talk*, 28 June 2010, available at www.ejiltalk.org/anti-piracy-court-opens-in-kenya/.

135 Tanaka, n. 17 above, 382–6.

136 LOSC, Art. 137(2).

whole. Thus no state can exercise territorial sovereignty or sovereignty rights over the Area and its natural resources.[137]

Under the so called 'parallel system', activities in the Area are carried out by the Enterprise, an operational organ of the Authority, and other commercial operators.[138] These operators include states parties to the LOSC, state enterprises, and natural or juridical persons which possess the nationality of states parties or are effectively controlled by them or their nationals, as provided for in Article 153, who can carry out activities in the Area. It follows that states and state enterprises can explore and exploit natural resources in the Area under the supervision of the Authority. At the same time, states must undertake obligations with respect to the sponsorship of the activities in the Area.

According to the Seabed Disputes Chamber of ITLOS, obligations of sponsoring states can be divided into two principal categories: 'responsibility to ensure' and 'direct obligations under the LOSC and other relevant instruments'. 'Responsibility to ensure' aims to establish a mechanism through which the rules of the LOSC concerning activities in the Area become effective for sponsored contractors which find their legal basis in domestic law. This obligation may be characterized as an obligation 'of conduct', not 'of result', and as an obligation of 'due diligence'.[139] 'Direct obligations' include:[140]

(i) the obligation to assist the Authority in the exercise of control over activities in the Area;
(ii) the obligation to apply a precautionary approach;
(iii) the obligation to apply best environmental practices;
(iv) the obligation to take measures to ensure the provision of guarantees in the event of an emergency order by the Authority for protection of the marine environment;
(v) the obligation to ensure the availability of recourse for compensation in respect of damage caused by pollution; and
(vi) the obligation to conduct environmental impact assessment.

---

[137] Under LOSC, Art. 133(a), 'resources' means all solid, liquid or gaseous mineral resources in situ in the Area at or beneath the sea-bed, including polymetallic nodules.

[138] *Ibid.* Art. 153(2).

[139] Responsibilities and Obligations of States Sponsoring Persons and Entities with respect to Activities in the Area, List of Cases No. 17, 1 February 2011, pp. 40–41, paras 107–10, available at www.itlos.org/.

[140] *Ibid.* 44, paras 121–2.

Furthermore, a sponsoring state must take necessary and appropriate measures in order to fulfil its responsibility under the LOSC, in particular Article 134, Annex III, and the 1994 Agreement.[141] The existence of such laws, regulations and administrative measures is a necessary requirement for compliance with the obligation of due diligence of the sponsoring state and for its exemption from liability. Such measures should also be in force at all times that a contract with the Authority is in force and should be kept under review so as to ensure that they meet current standards and that the contractor meets its obligations effectively without detriment to the common heritage of mankind.

4.6 CONCLUSIONS

The above consideration shows that multiple jurisdictions of states exist in the international law of the sea. The coastal state can exercise territorial sovereignty (= complete spatial jurisdiction) over internal waters, territorial seas, archipelagic waters, whilst it can exercise sovereign rights (= limited spatial jurisdiction) over the contiguous zone, the EEZ and the continental shelf. Apart from internal waters, however, territorial sovereignty of the coastal state over marine spaces is qualified by multiple navigational rights, in other words, the right of innocent passage, the right of non-suspensible innocent passage, the right of transit passage, and the right of archipelagic sea lane passage. In so doing, the law of the sea reconciles territorial sovereignty with the freedom of navigation. Further, the exclusive jurisdiction of the flag state provides a foundation for maintaining a legal order on the high seas. However, the exclusive jurisdiction of the flag state is subject to two exceptions. One is the right of hot pursuit which seeks to safeguard the interests of the coastal state, and the other is the right of visit which aims to protect common interests of the international community.

Whilst the legal order in the oceans is maintained by the exercise of jurisdictions of states according to multiple jurisdictional zones, it cannot pass unnoticed that this system contains some limitations particularly in marine environmental protection, including conservation of marine living resources and biological diversity. For instance, several species, such as straddling and highly migratory species, do not respect man-made limits and maritime delimitation lines. Marine ecosystems may also straddle

---

[141] 1994 Agreement relating to the Implementation of Part XI of the United Nations Convention on the Law of the Sea, 1836 UNTS 42. Entered into force 28 July 1996.

maritime limits and boundaries. Hence a clear-cut distinction between marine spaces under the coastal state's jurisdiction and marine spaces beyond national jurisdiction is not always suitable for conservation of marine living resources and biological diversity.[142] Further, presently conservation of marine biological diversity beyond national jurisdiction is becoming a matter of more pressing concerns. Although, as explained earlier, the legal order on the high seas is maintained primarily by the principle of the exclusive jurisdiction of the flag state, it is apparent that individual exercise of the flag state jurisdiction alone is inadequate to preserve biological diversity on the high seas. Considering that international cooperation between states is a prerequisite to effectively protect the marine environment, including marine living resources and marine biological diversity, the establishment of more institutionalized mechanisms for securing international cooperation should be an important issue in the future development of the international law of the sea.

[142] Scovazzi, n. 48 above, 131. D. Freestone, 'The Conservation of Marine Ecosystems under International Law' in C. Redgwell and M. Bowman (eds), *International Law and the Conservation of Biological Diversity* (The Hague, Kluwer, 1996), pp. 94 and 102; E.A. Kirk, 'Maritime Zones and the Ecosystem Approach: A Mismatch?' (1999) 8 *Review of European Community and International Environmental Law* 68.

5. State immunity from jurisdiction between law, comity and ideology

Alexander Orakhelashvili

5.1 BASIC CONCEPT OF STATE IMMUNITY AND KEY DISTINCTIONS

The immunity of foreign states and their officials from the national jurisdiction is a matter closely connected to the matter of state jurisdiction. In empirical terms, any grant of immunity involves declining to exercise national jurisdiction, while any denial of immunity results in the assertion of jurisdiction. However, this purely empirical focus is liable to obscure the more fundamental distinction between jurisdiction and immunities, in the sense that the issue of jurisdiction is antecedent to that of immunities. As the International Court of Justice specified in the *Arrest Warrant* case, 'it is only where a State has jurisdiction under international law in relation to a particular matter that there can be any question of immunities in regard to the exercise of that jurisdiction'.[1]

Sometimes such terminology is used confusingly. In *Littrell*, focusing on state immunity, Lord Hoffmann suggested that:

> If the case had concerned an assault within the [UK-stationed] base by one American serviceman on another, I think that under customary international law the English courts would have declined both civil and criminal jurisdiction.[2]

While semantically 'declining jurisdiction' sounds as if it encompassed both jurisdictional and immunity matters, normatively speaking the two matters are different. If it was a matter of declining jurisdiction purely and simply, then it could be done either out of grace towards the sending state and its jurisdiction; or on the basis of an agreement with that sending state that allocates jurisdiction accordingly; or (rather implausibly) by pretending that the US base territory in the United Kingdom is, to all intents and purposes, part of the US territory, so that the United

[1] *Arrest Warrant (DRC v Belgium)* [2002] ICJ Reports 19, para. 46.
[2] *Littrell v United States* [1995] 1 WLR 182.

Kingdom must decline jurisdiction in relation to whatever goes on in the base without requiring any further legal reason for doing so.[3] The mere presence of an army base on the foreign territory does not entail any such magic consequences in terms of shifting jurisdiction from one state to another.

In relation to that army base example, the jurisdictional question is whether the forum state's jurisdiction is ousted by some rule whereby the forum state has agreed, either via customary international law, or a bilateral treaty, or via statute, to the effect that it will not try the relevant offences and that such offences are within the sending state's exclusive jurisdiction, in derogation from the concurrence of jurisdiction principle that would otherwise apply.

In relation to immunities, the question only arises once the above first question is answered in the negative, the putative outcome being that the host state's territorial jurisdiction subsists, and the query then relates to the identity of the defendant and the nature of the act they perform, *not* as to how far the host state could take its jurisdictional authority as such. International law, depending on the substantive content of its specific rules, may either direct the relevant state not to exercise jurisdiction as such in the relevant situation; or it may direct it to grant immunity to defendants when otherwise they would fall within its jurisdiction.

State immunity has to be distinguished from some more specialized areas of immunities that are subject to special regulation. These are diplomatic immunity and that of special missions, as discussed by the English High Court in *Khurts Bat*.[4] The difference between state immunity and such other areas as diplomatic immunity is that these other areas are codified under generally accepted treaties. Furthermore, diplomatic agents obtain immunity from national jurisdiction not merely on the basis of their designation as diplomatic agents by their sending states, but also on the basis of an additional agreement to be granted by the receiving states. This requirement is made clear in Article 4 of the 1961 Vienna Convention on Diplomatic Relations.

However, state immunity in relation to both states and their officials operates without such additional legitimation. State immunity is about the immunity of the entire state and of all its officials, admitting no

---

[3] *Per contra* L. Oppenheim, *International Law* (2nd edn, 1912), vol. I, p. 50; but while upholding the view that 'in camp' offences are exempted from the local state territorial jurisdiction, Oppenheim does not provide positive legal evidence, instead stating that this is the view prevailing among writers.

[4] *Khurts Bat v Mongolia* [2011] EWCH 2029 (Admin), High Court, 29 July 2011.

reasonable room for the analogy with those other, more specialized areas. A broad and blanket restriction on state jurisdiction, involved with state immunity, requires serious and convincing evidence to be substantiated. What this is really about is the issue of correspondence of the positive legal right of one state to demand to be granted immunity before another state's national courts, and the positive legal obligation of the forum state to grant such immunity.[5] Needless to say, when a legal position along those lines is advocated, it should also be addressed whether that legal position is reflected in the relevant sources of international law.

Furthermore, the relevance of state immunity is quite narrow in the sense that it is supposed to protect the rights and interests of the state when that state, or its officials, are directly impleaded before foreign courts. In *Belhaj*, the English Court of Appeal refused to apply the doctrine of state immunity in relation to the foreign state where that foreign state was not party to the proceedings, yet it was claimed that the adjudication would adversely affect its rights and interests.[6] Another case decided by the High Court, *Yunus Rahmatullah*, similarly rejected the relevance of the doctrine of 'indirect impleading'.[7] In this regard, the issue of state immunity before *national courts* bears no relation to the approach adopted by the International Court of Justice in *Monetary Gold*, that an *international court* should not adjudicate on the conduct of a state which is not party to its proceedings.[8] It would be unsound to try and transpose this approach to a domestic plane where courts operate under completely different jurisdictional premises.

Last but not least, the immunity of a state from foreign jurisdiction is different from immunity from execution;[9] the latter being not about protecting the sovereign authority of the state, but about protecting particular items and properties from the execution proceedings. Jurisdictional immunity prevents adjudication over who is right and who is wrong in the relevant matter. The immunity from execution is thus of consequential importance, and protects only the particular assets and

[5] See, in general, on jurisprudential aspects of correspondence between legal rights and legal obligations, W. Hohfeld, *Fundamental Legal Conceptions as Applied in Judicial Reasoning* (1917).

[6] *Belhaj v Straw* [2014] EWCA Civ 1394, CA, 30 October 2014, para. 43 ff.

[7] *Yunus Rahmatullah* [2014] EWHC 3486 (QB), para. 45 ff.

[8] *Monetary Gold* [1954] ICJ Reports 32; and see *Rahmatullah*, n. 7 above, paras 77–8.

[9] On which see Xiaodong Yang, Chapter 12.

property from seizure or attachment, once that initial issue of right and wrong has been judicially determined.

Again, the proper distinction between all these concepts and categories is crucial for at least two reasons. Justification and rationale is different for each of them; and so is the normative position under the sources of international law.

5.2 JUSTIFICATION OF STATE IMMUNITY

One conceptual justification for state immunity, especially in relation to serious violations of human rights and humanitarian law norms, is the thesis that national courts should not assume such jurisdiction as will entail adjudication over the conduct of another state without its consent.[10] But this view is not generally shared. In fact, the very fact of state immunity not being absolute testifies precisely to the opposite effect.

Moreover, a different view is expressed by Jennings and Watts, to the effect that, 'there is no obvious impairment of the rights of equality, or independence, or dignity of a State if it is subjected to ordinary judicial processes within the territory of a foreign State'.[11] Earlier than that, Sir Hersch Lauterpacht has observed that foreign state immunity is an inheritance of the sovereign's position in relation to its subjects as *legibus solutus* and its consequent immunity before its own courts. The imperatives of the rule of law, according to Lauterpacht, rather than issues relating to the expansion of state activities to gradually encompass private and commercial matters, have been paramount in terms of restricting the scope of foreign state immunity.[12] On the same side of the doctrinal equation, Crawford refers to 'The simple assertion, *par in parem non habet jurisdictionem,* which is said to underlie the principle of jurisdictional immunity', further querying as to 'Why should not a forum State assume jurisdiction to do justice in a matter occurring within its boundaries and governed by its law?'.[13] Higgins has similarly warned

[10] H. Fox, 'State Immunity and the International Crime of Torture' (2006) *EHRLR* 142 at 144.

[11] R. Jennings and A. Watts (eds), *Oppenheim's International Law* (9th edn, 1992), p. 342.

[12] H. Lauterpacht, 'The Problem of Jurisdictional Immunities of Foreign States' (1951) *BYIL* 232 at 236; Lauterpacht's point was also seconded by Lord Clyde, *Holland v Lampen-Wolfe* [2000] 3 All ER 845, 1579–80.

[13] J. Crawford, 'International Law and Foreign Sovereigns: Distinguishing Immune Transactions' (1983) *BYIL* 75 at 77.

that 'It is very easy to elevate sovereign immunity into a superior principle of international law and to lose sight of the essential reality that it is an exception to the normal doctrine of jurisdiction'.[14]

The view presenting state immunity as an inherently superior value compared to other competing values, such as the territorial jurisdiction and sovereignty of forum states, their policy choices, or values related to justice and accountability in general, is therefore fallacious. The various stated rationales of state immunity are at times legal and at times political or ideological. Therefore, being on a sound methodological ground is not of second-rate importance. It is one thing to argue that, in certain circumstances, the grant of immunity to a foreign state is politically and ideologically desirable, or takes place on empirical terms. It is quite another thing to argue that the same grant of immunity is required or allowed by national or international law. There may, thus, be legal outcomes that may or may not be compatible with the political or ideological agenda or preferences held in certain quarters.

5.3 SCOPE OF STATE IMMUNITY

The above considerations dictate that a careful approach needs to be taken before asserting that state immunity is regulated by international law in a particular manner and entailing particular consequences. In a relatively early contribution, Crawford suggested that:

> there is virtually universal agreement that a State is entitled to immunity with respect at least to some transactions. This agreement might perhaps be illusory, in that the formulae used to embody this 'hard core' of immune transactions may turn out on analysis to be empty of content or devoid of meaning. But the point is that one cannot simply assume either possibility.[15]

It is the ordinary pattern of the operation of the doctrine of sources of international law that the existence of a customary rule of international law on a relevant matter will not be readily assumed in the absence of a consistent, representative and durable state practice indicating the existence of the customary rule on that very matter. To illustrate, the

---

[14] R. Higgins, 'Certain Unresolved Aspects of the Law of State Immunity' (1982) 29 *NILR* 265 at 271.

[15] J. Crawford, 'International Law and Foreign Sovereigns: Distinguishing Immune Transactions' (1983) *BYIL* 75 at 78.

International Court of Justice declined to find the existence of a customary rule on continental shelf delimitation in the *North Sea* case,[16] or of one on nuclear deterrence in the *Nuclear Weapons* Advisory Opinion.[17] The customary rule coextensive with the prohibition of the use of force under the Charter of the United Nations was identified in the *Nicaragua* case only on the basis of representative and written evidence that all member states of the United Nations were committed to the relevant rule as part of international law.[18]

On the other hand, state immunity could hardly be seen as meeting such strict requirements. Accordingly, some part of judicial practice on state immunity tends to assume too readily that immunities are affirmatively regulated by customary international law, without proving this point through the sufficient analysis of state practice. The European Court of Human Rights in *Al-Adsani v United Kingdom* referred to the 'generally recognized rules of public international law on State immunity',[19] without illustrating the ways in which those rules acquired that 'generally recognized' character. Nor did the UK House of Lords examine state practice in *Jones v Saudi Arabia*, confining itself instead to the assertion that state immunity is a requirement under customary international law.[20]

In *Arrest Warrant (DRC v Belgium)*, the International Court of Justice (ICJ) identified the 'firmly established' rule on immunity of an incumbent Foreign Minister from two national court decisions, one of which (the *Pinochet* decision of the UK House of Lords) related to a former head of state not an incumbent Foreign Minister; and the second one (the *Ghaddafi* decision of the French Cour de Cassation) related to the immunity of a serving head of state, whose immunity was actually held to be subjected to some exceptions, even if those were not dealt with in the instant case.[21]

The ICJ's analysis of state immunity in *Germany v Italy* focused on three separate, albeit somewhat interdependent, questions: torts committed within the forum's territory; acts committed by armed forces; and the

---

16 *North Sea Continental Shelf* [1969] ICJ Reports 3.

17 *Legality of the Use of Nuclear Weapons*, Advisory Opinion [1996] ICJ Reports 227.

18 *Military and Paramilitary Activities In and Against Nicaragua, Merits* [1986] ICJ Reports 14.

19 *Al-Adsani v United Kingdom* (2002) 34 EHRR 11 at 289, para. 56.

20 *Jones v Saudi Arabia* [2006] UKHL 16, 14 June 2006.

21 *Arrest Warrant of 11 April 2000, Merits* [2002] ICJ Report 3s, General List No. 121, 14 February 2002, paras 51–4.

scope of acts *jure imperii*. When focusing on the practice related to acts of armed forces, the Court's inference was that these attract immunity as far as they are *jure imperii*.[22] Having essentially acknowledged the two-tiered nature of the problem – acts of armed forces *and* their performance as part of sovereign authority – the Court did not really address the second aspect, relying instead on the Italian concession that the relevant war crimes were committed as an exercise of sovereign authority.

When confronted with the reality that most national practice denies immunity for territorial torts, either generally or in conjunction with the acts of armed forces, the Court simply pleaded its lack of awareness that those statutory provisions had been applied by national courts to that effect; and then recast the issue of tort immunity into that of armed forces immunity.[23] This was a rather curious way of excluding from the Court's focus a practice that stood in the way of the desired outcome.

The Court then turned to another (rather limited) part of practice that dealt with the conduct of armed forces during an armed conflict.[24] What makes this odd is the inference, on the basis of judicial decisions adopted in a small number of states, that the conduct performed during an armed conflict provides, under customary international law, a separate basis, distinct from the territorial tort issue, on which immunities can be accorded or denied; and that anything armed forces do during an armed conflict is immune.[25] But, if the context of the occurrence of the act, not the nature of the act, were crucial, then anything committed during an armed conflict (or for that matter in prisons or other official facilities) would be a sovereign act and attract immunity. We call this the absolute immunity doctrine.

One would ordinarily expect that the more complex and nuanced the putative rule, the greater amount of evidence should be required from the relevant court to prove how that rule was created in that precise form to bind states, and thus the heavier the burden to prove its customary law status. Courts that uphold state immunity for serious violations of human

22 *Jurisdictional Immunities of the State (Germany v Italy: Greece Intervening)* [2012] ICJ Reports 3, Judgment of 3 February 2012, para. 72.

23 *Ibid.* paras 70–77.

24 *Ibid.* paras 73–4.

25 Moreover, even if the ICJ's approach to acts committed in war is that they are *ipso jure* immune, that would still not affect the position that the bulk of cases not dealing with acts committed in an armed conflict should still be excluded from immunity. Thus, the reasoning in *Germany v Italy* cannot be a direct legitimation of *Al-Adsani* or *Jones*.

rights and humanitarian law, as well as for core international crimes, have so far not properly discharged the applicable burden of proof, and have not demonstrated the basis on which the relevant states would be entitled to immunity in the first place.

5.4 ABSOLUTE AND RESTRICTIVE DOCTRINES OF STATE IMMUNITY

As Max Weber has emphasized, sovereign authority of a state is not a matter of fact and power, but law and prescription; authority is not the same as power, but a legitimate power.[26] Any entity could have power, but only the state could have public authority. Sir Hersch Lauterpacht was an early advocate of the narrower view of state immunity, constraining its scope to acts of sovereign authority proper. Examples were the nationalization of property or the denial of justice through the national judicial process. There were some elements in Lauterpacht's vision relating to contract and tort that should attract immunity,[27] though it is dubious by now whether the sovereign power of states encompasses any of those matters within any national jurisdiction.

It is important to understand the essence of both absolute and restrictive doctrines before we can properly understand the nature of the process of evolution that resulted in the replacement by the restrictive of the absolute doctrine of immunity. The absolute immunity doctrine, that was deemed to be in force for a long time right up to the mid-twentieth century, enabled states and their officials to evade foreign proceedings merely on the basis of their identity. Lord Wright suggested in the *Cristina* case in the UK House of Lords that, pursuant to the absolute immunity rule the state:

> renounces *pro tanto* the competence of its Courts to exercise their jurisdiction even over matters occurring within its territorial limits, though to do so is prima facie an integral part of sovereignty. The rule may be said to be based on the principle 'par in parem non habet imperium', no State can claim jurisdiction over another sovereign State … Or it may be taken to flow from reciprocity, each sovereign State within the community of nations accepting

---

[26] Cf. A Heywood, *Political Theory* (Palgrave, 2004), p. 130.
[27] Lauterpacht, n. 12 above, 237–8.

> some subtraction from its full sovereignty in return for similar concessions on the side of the others.[28]

Each state was thus expected to give as much as it would receive. The rule that went by the identity of the defendant rather than the nature of the act made this easier. The *par in parem* rule, denying jurisdiction of an equal over an equal, was therefore an essential premise for the absolute immunity rule.

The transition from the absolute to the restrictive immunity doctrine was never by way of admitting exceptions to absolute immunity while preserving the rest of that immunity on residual terms. This transition was, instead, a matter of a complete redefinition of the rationale and scope of the principles on the basis of which one state could expect another state not to exercise national jurisdiction over its conduct.

The key element of the transition from the absolute to the restrictive doctrine has been a modification of key questions to be asked. The maxim *par in parem non habet imperium* would now apply not just by virtue of the state being a sovereign entity, but would protect it from foreign adjudication only if, in addition to that, the act impleaded before the foreign court was an exercise of sovereignty.[29]

National courts, especially English courts, have identified both absolute and restrictive doctrines with public international law which is, by way of its direct incorporation doctrine, applied by national courts in England. The pronouncement in *Duke of Brunswick* in the nineteenth century was that there was no obvious law to apply to the immunity of foreign sovereigns. As clarified, 'there is no English law applicable to the present subject, unless it can be derived from the law of nations, which, when ascertained, is to be deemed part of the common law of England'. When moving to the law of nations proper, the court stated that:

> In a case where there is no precedent – no positive law – no evidence of the common consent of nations – no usage which can be relied on – where reasons important and plausible are arrayed in opposition to each other – and where no clear and decided preponderance is to be found, it seems reasonable to endeavour to borrow for our guidance such light, however feeble and uncertain, as may be afforded by analogous cases, from whence have been

---

[28] *Cristina* [1938] AC 485 at 502–3; Lord Maugham also approved 'insisting as a condition of immunity on the adherence of other foreign governments to the same rule as to immunity', *ibid.* 518.

[29] As was clear in Lord Wilberforce's reasoning in *I Congreso* [1983] 1 AC 268, HL, as followed by Lord Cooke in *Holland v Lampen-Wolfe*, n. 12 above, 1579.

> derived rules adopted with great, though not perfect uniformity, by all nations.[30]

The roots of restrictive doctrine were then identified by Lord Philimmore in *Charkieh* thus:

> No principle of international law, and no decided case, and no dictum of jurists of which I am aware, has gone so far as to authorize a sovereign to assume the character of a trader, when it is for his benefit; and when he incurs an obligation to a private subject to throw off, if I may so speak, his disguise, and appear as a sovereign, claiming for his own benefit, and to the injury of a private person, for the first time, all the attributes of his character; while it would be easy to accumulate authorities for the contrary position.[31]

It is often said that French and Belgian courts were the first to start distancing themselves from the absolute immunity doctrine. Then, the 1952 Tate Letter announced the shift of the US position from the absolute to the restrictive immunity. This move was driven by the requirements of international commerce and the increasing assumption by states of private and commercial tasks.[32] Yet, around the same period, English courts continued to adhere to the absolute immunity doctrine. A first indication of the opposite was given by Lord Denning in *Rahimotola v Nizam of Hyderabad*,[33] even though other judges were less enthusiastic to endorse this position.

On balance, it would be right to say that the restrictive doctrine as we know it emerged in that shape from the 1950s and 1960s onwards through the practice of national courts which faced the actual task of identifying the exact nature of particular acts dealt with in the litigation. An early endorsement of the restrictive doctrine of state immunity, as we know it today, came from the Austrian Supreme Court in *Holubek v United States*, to the effect that immunity should not attach to acts performed by state organs if these are acts of private law 'as can also be performed by private persons'.[34]

Judicial endorsement of the restrictive doctrine was also given in *Empire of Iran* by the German Constitutional Court, suggesting that the distinction between sovereign and non-sovereign acts does not depend

---

[30] *Duke of Brunswick v King of Hanover* (1844) 49 ER 724 at 741–2.

[31] *Charkieh* [1872–75] 4 LR 59 at 99–100.

[32] I. Sinclair, 'The European Convention on State Immunity' (1973) 22 *ICLQ* 254 at 262–3.

[33] *Rahimtoola v Nizam of Hyderabad* [1958] AC 379.

[34] *Holubek v United States* (1961) 40 ILR 73, Austrian Supreme Court.

'on whether the State has acted commercially. Commercial activities of States are not different in their nature from other non-sovereign State activities'. What mattered was the nature of the transaction rather than its underlying motive and policy, whether the state acted in the exercise of its sovereign authority or in a private capacity in the same way that any private person could act.[35]

The UK House of Lords in *I Congreso* held that the conduct of a state is not a sovereign act and attracts no immunity, if it is an act which could be performed by any private actor, and a state invokes no governmental authority, even if all that situation had to do with a highly contingent political context.[36] On this view, the category of *acta iure imperi* would only encompass a narrow category of acts inherent to the sovereign authority of a state.[37] In *Trendtex*,[38] Lord Denning endorsed a similar approach. In the US jurisdiction, the same approach was adopted in the *Victory Transport* case.[39] In *Ortiz*, Lord Denning saw this narrowly defined restrictive doctrine to be so obviously a part of international law[40] that he did not hesitate to apply it to other, non-immunity, matters dealing with transnational litigation involving foreign states before English courts.

The further application of the restrictive doctrine by English courts, such as in *Lampen-Wolfe* and *Littrell*,[41] cases concerned with the activities of foreign armed forces, has followed the *Congreso* approach, and focused on the nature of the relevant act in the underlying context, rather than it having been performed by armed forces as such, in determining whether immunity should be accorded. By and large, then, various jurisdictions have been uniform in applying that pattern of the restrictive doctrine. Its basic essence is that an act which anyone can perform is not one that is unique to state authority (*jure imperii*).

Given such position, the sovereign/non-sovereign distinction applies as a matter of common law that incorporates public international law (which

---

[35] *Empire of Iran* (1963) 45 ILR 57 at 80, Bundesverfassungsgericht, 30 April 1963.

[36] *Congreso*, n. 29 above.

[37] R. Higgins, *Problems and Process* (Oxford, Oxford University Press, 1994), p. 84.

[38] *Trendtex Trading v Bank of Nigeria* [1977] 1 QB 529, 552–3.

[39] *Victory Transport Inc. v Comisaria General*, 336 F.2d 354 (1964) at para. 10.

[40] *Attorney-General of New Zealand v Ortiz* [1984] AC 1 at 20–21.

[41] *Holland v Lampen-Wolfe*, n. 12 above, 845–6; *Littrell v United States*, n. 2 above.

is different from the general rule/particular exceptions statutory approach under the State Immunity Act (SIA) 1978). As Lord Clyde suggests in *Lampen-Wolfe*, it is the nature of individual acts that matters, not preconceived categories within which to fit those particular acts:

> particular facts [must be considered] against the whole context in which they have occurred. There is little if anything to be gained by trying to fit the case into a particular precedent or to devise categories of situations which may or may not fall on the one side of the line or the other. It is the nature and character of the activity on which the claim is based which has to be studied, rather than the motive or purpose of it. The solution will turn upon an assessment of the particular facts. The line between sovereign and non-sovereign state activities may sometimes be clear, but in other cases may well be difficult to draw.

Nevertheless, as His Lordship observes, 'Difficult as the distinction may be at common law, we have to do the best we can to apply it'.[42]

Presumably there can be no exhaustive list of *jure imperii* acts. A list of sovereign activities was included in the Resolution of the Institute of International Law adopted at the proposal of the Special Rapporteur Ian Brownlie.[43] But such lists cannot be exhaustive. On balance, there can only be a transparent criterion that helps to determine which acts fall within and which acts are out of the scope of state immunity. As Sir Ian Sinclair suggested, 'the concept of *acta jure imperii* is not really capable of precise delimitation, and a certain amount of freedom must be left to the courts to develop the necessary criteria'.[44]

As Mann suggests, 'an activity may be in the exercise of sovereign authority even if it is unlawful. Property taken by force may be taken by way of sovereign authority'.[45] Along those lines, there may be some instances of the genuine exercise of sovereign power which may be characterized as such in law, such as expropriation of property; malicious prosecution and handling the documents of public importance in that process; taxation, even if discriminatory and used as pretext to impact the market dynamics or frustrate the operation of contracts or transactions of a particular kind; or the introduction of minimum wage as a regulatory measure. Even if some of those acts may entail, *in casu*, an internationally wrongful act and be actionable before international courts and

---

42 *Holland v Lampen-Wolfe*, n. 12 above, 1580.

43 *Contemporary Problems Concerning the Immunity of States in relation to Questions of Jurisdiction and Enforcement*, IDI Basel Session, 1991, Art, 2(3).

44 Sinclair, n. 32 above, 278.

45 F.A. Mann, 'The State Immunity Act 1978' (1980) 51 *BYIL* 43 at 53.

tribunals, they may still attract immunity before national courts. This is so for the sole reason that all these above-mentioned acts are ones that the state can perform and private entities cannot, because private entities do not have sovereign public authority needed for the performance of those acts. On the other hand, acts that are not subsumable within the proper scope of sovereign authority do not, under the restrictive doctrine, attract any immunity.

In the eyes of public international law, the state performing private law activities is, for the purposes of immunities, on the same footing as any private person, not as if the nature of those private law activities was to be thereby suddenly transformed into public law activities. Commerce is but one instance of activities in which the state could engage without using its sovereign powers and authority. The sovereign/non-sovereign divide, or the public/private law divide does not coincide with the commercial/non-commercial divide. Similarly, while trading is not a sovereign activity, nor is monopolizing trade; press and media are not such an activity either, nor is their monopolization within the state arm. What, more broadly, needs to be understood is that not every matter the state takes up is a uniquely public state affair; not every state activity is a public law activity; and also that not every public interest or national interest is invariably pursued through the exercise of public and sovereign powers uniquely available to the state.

When we move to judicial practice that grants or approves the grant of immunity to states for serious violations of human rights and humanitarian law, the common feature of this part of practice is that all pertinent cases confirming immunity to the state in civil proceedings fail to focus on the requirements under the restrictive doctrine. The European Court of Human Rights (ECtHR) decision in *Al-Adsani* did not utter a single word regarding the (non-)sovereign nature of torture, as the restrictive doctrine as detailed above would require it to do.[46] The House of Lords in *Jones* did not focus on the restrictive doctrine either, instead asserting that once the relevant acts were attributable to Saudi Arabia under the law of state responsibility, these acts attracted immunity as well;[47] much as there is some link between attributing an act to the state and according to it immunity for it. The *Germany v Italy* judgment did not examine the restrictive doctrine in any detail, and instead relied on the Italian concession that German war crimes were sovereign acts. When

46 *Al-Adsani v United Kingdom*, n. 19 above.

47 *Jones*, n. 20 above, paras 11–12 (per Lord Bingham); 76 (per Lord Hoffmann).

focusing on the acts of armed forces, the International Court of Justice (ICJ) focused on the identity of the perpetrator, not the nature of acts, and essentially accorded immunity to Germany on the basis of the (now outdated) absolute immunity doctrine.[48] In *Jones v United Kingdom*, the Fourth Chamber of the ECtHR did not provide any more substantiated explanation of the rationale and basis of state immunity than its simple derivation from the sovereignty of states.[49] This case has provided yet another endorsement of the doctrine of absolute state immunity in relation to human rights violations.

5.5 NORMATIVE STATUS OF STATE IMMUNITY IN THE BALANCE

Before we claim that a particular version of state immunity doctrine is recognized as part of customary international law, we must be careful to identify the precise scope of the endorsed putative rule. There are three candidate doctrines that differ from the old absolute immunity in the sense that they specify that the state should be immune for some acts and not others. First, there is the approach adopted by national statutes on state immunity, such as the UK SIA 1978 and the US Foreign Sovereign Immunities Act (FSIA) 1976, stating the pattern that the immunity is available to the foreign state before national courts under a general rule of immunity, unless the case falls within one of the exceptions that the statute provides in relation to that general rule. But this pattern is, *per se*, not representative of the general practice of states, because the overall number of states that have adopted state immunity legislation is rather modest.

Secondly, there is the restrictive doctrine proper, focusing on the exact nature of the act complained of in the relevant litigation. Each act falls to be assessed on its merits, and there are no presumptions warranted as to whether the relevant act is covered by any general rule or an exception to such general rule.

Thirdly, there is a purpose-related approach, mostly practised by French courts.[50] This approach is liable in practice to come quite close to the absolute doctrine, because the public purpose behind any (including

[48] *Jurisdictional Immunities of the State (Germany v Italy: Greece Intervening)*, n. 22 above.

[49] *Jones and others v United Kingdom*, Application Nos. 34356/06 and 40528/06, Fourth Section, 14 January 2014, para. 188.

[50] Sinclair, n. 32 above, 264–5.

commercial or other private) transaction could render that transaction immune.

These are three competing and mutually incompatible approaches to state immunity. Much as they have all made some impact in practice, they also have adversely affected each other's potential to provide a template for the formation of customary law on state immunity, because practice in support of any of these three patterns is inevitably practice that is opposed to other patterns. Quite simply, a general rule on the scope of immunity cannot feasibly be agreed upon by states in such situation.

Therefore, it is more than likely that the doctrine of state immunity does not, in any shape, have the force of binding law. There is reluctance among states to subscribe to the customary law nature of state immunity in the shape that has been endorsed in *Germany v Italy*. The United States does not subscribe to such version of the 'restrictive' theory as has been expounded in *Al-Adsani*, *Jones* and *Germany v Italy*. The US Congress has repeatedly amended the FSIA 1976 to enable the victims of terrorist attacks to recover damages from the relevant states;[51] and more recently Canada followed suit after the ICJ delivered its judgment in *Germany v Italy*.[52] More broadly, US courts have emphasised that 'the grant of immunity is a privilege which the United States may withhold from any claimant'.[53] On the other hand, China still adheres to the doctrine of absolute immunity, as was demonstrated in a recent litigation.[54]

On balance, it seems (the *Al-Adsani* and *Jones* claims to the contrary notwithstanding) that Lord Denning's point that 'there is no consensus whatever' as to the customary law status of immunities still stands.[55] It is much more plausible to view state immunity requirements as part of

---

51 See for an overview R. Bettauer, 'Germany Sues Italy at the International Court of Justice on Foreign Sovereign Immunity: Legal Underpinnings and Implications for US Law', *ASIL Insight*, 19 November 2009.

52 See the amendments to the Canadian State Immunity Act (RSC 1985, c. S-18), 13 March 2012.

53 *Lafontant v Aristide* (1994) 103 ILR 586; see also *United States v Noriega* (1991) 99 ILR 162, to the effect that the United States does not consider itself bound under international law to accord immunity to foreign states and their agents. See, to the same effect, the judgment of the US Supreme Court in *Republic of Austria v Altmann*, 541 U.S. 677 (2004).

54 *Democratic Republic of the Congo v FG Hemisphere Associates*, Hong Kong Court of Final Appeal, 8 June 2011.

55 *Trendtex* [1977] 1 QB 552.

international comity, not international law. This view has also been endorsed by the US Supreme Court in *Altmann*.[56]

The UK courts' self-referential assertion as to the customary law status of state immunity rests on a dubious ground, for two reasons. First, the current position of UK courts contradicts the position taken by UK courts at earlier stages when they denied the customary law status of immunities. Secondly, other jurisdictions, such as the United States, take the view that state immunity is not part of customary international law.

There is, by now, a visible trend that courts which accord state immunity for serious human rights violations adopt a highly selective approach in relation to state practice. They prioritize that state practice which accords with the predetermined goal to accord state immunity. They either overlook, or remain silent on, or explain away as exceptional, such state practice as does not accord with that predetermined goal. The reasoning provided by courts that uphold state immunity for serious human rights violations, even if capable of providing ideological comfort to those who consider that state immunity should be available for serious violations of human rights and humanitarian law norms, is incapable of reinforcing their legal argument.

5.6 NEED FOR A HUMAN RIGHTS EXCEPTION TO STATE IMMUNITY?

The discourse of a human rights exception to the otherwise applicable general rule on state immunity being needed is initially inspired by instances of national litigation where attempts were made to persuade national courts to read into national statutes on state immunity exceptions that suggest that the relevant statute does not immunize human rights violations. There were no such exceptions stated in the relevant statutes, and relevant courts, mostly in common law jurisdictions, have declined to admit such without being directed accordingly by the national legislator.[57] But national courts in such cases do not operate against the background of the restrictive doctrine which is accepted on the international plane. They instead operate on a general immunity-particular exceptions pattern. The fact that an exception needed to be identified, and

---

[56] *Austria v Altmann*, n. 53 above.

[57] See the following British and American cases: *Siderman de Blake v Argentina* (1992) 103 ILR 455; *Princz v Federal Republic of Germany* (1994) 33 ILM 1483; *Smith and others v Libyan Arab Jamahiriya* (1997) 36 ILM 100; *Al-Adsani v Kuwait* (1996) 107 ILR 536.

was not so identified, at the national level is not by itself sufficient to validate the position that, under international law, a similar requirement applies that a human rights exception should be identified within the existing general rule of state immunity.

Writers discuss the possibility of a discrete human rights exception to state immunity as a matter of its propriety and desirability.[58] But views like these command no authority apart from their approval by a particular writer. What really matters is that, in terms of state practice and international law, under the restrictive doctrine, human rights violations cannot be considered as acts of sovereignty, but they are private acts that can be committed by the state as well as by private entities. Therefore, it is a methodologically false approach to specifically require the existence of a separate and discrete human rights exception in relation to acts that the restrictive doctrine already considers not to be immune. And again, it bears repeating that the fact that such position may not be acceptable on ideological grounds in certain quarters does not by itself evidence that such position is incompatible with the state of positive international law.

5.7 STATE IMMUNITY AND OFFICIAL IMMUNITY

Before national courts, state immunity issues arise not only when the state as such is impleaded, but also when officials of the state are parties to proceedings. Obviously, not all officials are in the same position. Some high-ranking officials – heads of state or government or Foreign Ministers – could enjoy the immunity *ratione personae*, which is broader in scope, but limited in time for the period when the relevant person holds the relevant high office. Other officials could in principle enjoy *ratione materiae* immunities regardless of such time limit. Yet this latter immunity only covers such acts as the relevant official has perpetrated in the exercise of the relevant state's public and sovereign authority.

UK SIA 1978, section 14(1) immunizes the conduct of 'a head of [a foreign] State in his public capacity'. However, the SIA 1978 does not directly extend to the immunity of state officials *ratione materiae*. The restrictive doctrine of immunities, as part of international law and of English common law, accordingly applies to the immunity claims raised to the benefit of both the state and of its officials. The only reason why the relevant official should benefit from the immunity is that the state would enjoy immunity for the pertinent act in the first place.

---

[58] See, for example, I. Wuerth, 'Reassessing Pinochet's Legacy' (2012) 106 *American Journal of International Law* 731.

The *Propend* case before an English court concerned a police superintendent who took possession of documents that were seized when private premises were searched under a search warrant. The position of this particular official not being covered by SIA 1978, the restrictive doctrine was applied to the underlying facts, and it was concluded that the matter was an exercise of public powers uniquely available to the state, not to private entities.[59]

Given that state officials would enjoy immunity as being agents of the state and not in a personal capacity, the requirement of ascertaining the scope of their immunity is to extend to them only such immunity as the state would enjoy itself, and deny immunity in relation to acts that they have committed in the service, or using the resources or facilities of, the state when the relevant act is not an exercise of sovereign and public authority. Thus, not every act carried out by a state official is an expression of the state's sovereign authority. In other words, the state itself would not be enjoying immunity for those acts as ones *jure imperii* and nor should its officials. There is, quite simply, no other intelligible test cognizable under law or comity. To immunize the official's conduct just because it has been perpetrated as part of its official tasks, or using state facilities, would be to re-introduce, in relation to officials, the absolute immunity doctrine through the backdoor: the official would be able to stand up and demand immunity for anything they did when using or abusing their official position, whether or not the relevant act was an expression of the relevant state's sovereign authority.

What needs to be properly understood is that immunities are determined by the nature of the acts in relation to which immunities are claimed, not by the context in which these acts were perpetrated or by the nature of the facilities that were used to perpetrate them. It is always the nature of the particular act that attracts immunity, not its context or purpose.

Of particular importance is here Article 1 of the 1984 UN Convention Against Torture (CAT) which defines torture, specifically for its own purposes, as:

> any act by which severe pain or suffering, whether physical or mental, is intentionally inflicted on a person … by or at the instigation of or with the consent or acquiescence of a public official or other person acting in an official capacity.

---

[59] *Propend Finance Pty Ltd and others v Sing and another*, QBENI 96/0556/E, CA (Civ. Div.), 17 April 1997.

The question raised in jurisprudence is whether such definition has any bearing on whether torture could be a sovereign act protected by immunity. Lord Browne-Wilkinson suggested in *Pinochet* that the CAT applied to Pinochet's activities precisely because he had acted as a public official, namely, as head of state.[60] Lord Millett, however, observed that 'The official or governmental nature of the act, which forms the basis of the immunity, is an essential ingredient of the offence [under the CAT]. No rational system of criminal justice can allow an immunity which is co-extensive with the offence'.[61]

It seems that, under either of these approaches, Article 1 hardly touches upon the issue of immunities. Article 1 mentions the 'act', 'public official' and 'official capacity' as separate categories. The meaning of one cannot pre-empt or predetermine that of another. The fact that Pinochet acted as a public official does not answer the question as to the nature of his acts. Capacity means 'ability or power to do something' and 'a specified role or position'.[62] The adjective 'official' means 'relating to an authority' and 'permitted or done by a person or group in a position of authority'.[63] Therefore, for the purposes of the CAT, 'official capacity' should be understood as the use of that potential, resource or facility that the fact of being public official uniquely enables one to possess or use. 'Official capacity' can at most mean acts committed 'while in office' or 'when on duty'. The nature of the 'act' perpetrated in that 'capacity' remains a separate issue. Even if a public official acting in an official capacity is a requirement for the application of the CAT to the particular act of torture, this is immaterial for state immunity. Immunities focus on the nature of particular acts, not on what 'capacity' has been used to perpetrate them. Therefore, the reasoning by Lord Hoffmann in *Jones v Saudi Arabia* that if torture was 'official enough' to fall within Article 1 of the CAT, then it was 'official enough' to attract immunity,[64] should be considered as flawed. For, would a breach of contract or another act relating to commercial relations by the official while in office also be 'official enough'? If so, what would remain of the restrictive doctrine?

More recently, the UN International Law Commission (ILC) has taken up the topic of the immunity of foreign states from foreign criminal jurisdiction. In its 2001 Draft Articles on the Responsibility of States for Internationally Wrongful Acts, Article 2(e), the ILC suggests that '"State

---

60 *Pinochet* [2000] 1 AC 200.
61 *Ibid.* 277.
62 *Compact OED* (3rd edn, 2005), p. 139.
63 *Ibid.* 703.
64 *Jones*, n. 20 above, para. 83.

official" means any individual who represents the State or who exercises State functions'. Article 5 of the Draft specifies that 'State officials acting as such enjoy immunity *ratione materiae* from the exercise of foreign criminal jurisdiction'. The commentary further specifies that:

> Although various terms, such as 'prerogatives of public power', 'public functions', 'sovereign authority', 'governmental authority' or 'inherent functions of the State' have been suggested in order to reflect this idea, the Commission has chosen the term 'State functions' as being the most suitable at the current stage of work.[65]

As can be seen, the ILC has opted for a rather general and vague criterion expressed by the words 'as such', instead of following the sovereign authority test that has been accepted in jurisprudence over several decades. It is dubious whether the ILC's approach on this matter is reflective of the applicable international law. At any rate, the approach taken in the text of Draft Article 5 shows no verifiable reflection of the merit of the restrictive doctrine and its sovereign authority requirements.

The Joint Separate Opinion of Judges Higgins, Kooijmans and Buergenthal in the *Arrest Warrant* case had earlier addressed this issue and concluded that:

> it is generally recognized that in the case of such [serious international] crimes, which are often committed by high officials who make use of the power invested in the State, immunity is never substantive and thus cannot exculpate the offender from personal criminal responsibility.[66]

Consequently, the three judges observed that:

> The nature of such crimes and the circumstances under which they are committed, usually by making use of the State apparatus, makes it less than easy to find a convincing argument for shielding the alleged perpetrator by granting him or her immunity from criminal process.[67]

Unlike the ILC's vague and open-ended above-mentioned criterion, the three judges' reasoning provides for a clear distinction between the factual use of state apparatus, resources or facilities, and the use of state authority or entitlement. The former involves material factors, while the latter emphasizes the concept of state authority in its legal and normative context.

---

65 ILC Report, UN Doc. A/69/10 (2014), pp. 231–6.

66 *Arrest Warrant*, n. 1 above, Joint Separate Opinion, para. 74.

67 *Ibid.* para. 79.

The three judges concluded that:

> serious international crimes cannot be regarded as official acts because they are neither normal State functions nor functions that a State alone (in contrast to an individual) can perform. This view is underscored by the increasing realization that State-related motives are not the proper test for determining what constitutes public state acts.[68]

This approach properly applies the restrictive doctrine of state immunity to the immunity of state officials for international crimes. The use of the restrictive doctrine under international law in the criminal case of *Pinochet* crucially determined the scope of sovereign functions and that they do not include international crimes.[69] It may be tempting to conclude that, after the threat of jurisprudence culminating with the ICJ's judgment in *Germany v Italy*, civil cases are different. Nevertheless, the 2009 Naples Institut de Droit International (IDI) Resolution upheld the lifting of immunity in civil proceedings for conduct that constitutes international crime (Article III). This Resolution was not addressed or discussed by the ICJ in *Germany v Italy*. Nor was the issue properly addressed that the sovereign or non-sovereign nature of the pertinent act as a matter of the restrictive doctrine of immunity is a pre-proceeding issue applicable to civil and criminal immunities alike. Needless to say, the restrictive doctrine has the same content in relation to both criminal and civil proceedings. The contention that an act is or is not sovereign and public in its nature depending on the nature of judicial proceedings in which the nature of that very same act is being discussed, would be absurd.

Moving to the immunity of high state officials *ratione personae*, such as heads of state, heads of government and Foreign Ministers, we can see that they enjoy more comprehensive immunity but one that is limited for the duration of their office. Once these officials cease to be in office, the immunity *ratione personae* no longer protects them.

The reasons stated by the ICJ in *Arrest Warrant* for according immunities *ratione personae* to the incumbent Foreign Minister of the DRC are arguably instructive:

> In the performance of these functions, he or she is frequently required to travel internationally, and thus must be in a position freely to do so whenever the need should arise. He or she must also be in constant communication with the Government, and with its diplomatic missions around the world, and be

---

68 *Ibid.* para. 85.

69 *Pinochet*, n. 60 above, 200.

> capable at any time of communicating with representatives of other States. The Court further observes that a Minister for Foreign Affairs, responsible for the conduct of his or her State's relations with all other States, occupies a position such that, like the Head of State or the Head of Government, he or she is recognized under international law as representative of the State solely by virtue of his or her office.[70]

This reasoning could be debated or challenged. But what it inevitably does is to endorse a narrower version of immunities *ratione personae*, by identifying the small group of high-level officials that are covered by such immunities. The Court's criteria are so narrow and strict that it is not easy to extend the immunity these criteria define to other members of a national government.

5.8 STATE IMMUNITY AND THE HIERARCHY OF NORMS IN INTERNATIONAL LAW

5.8.1 General Relevance of Normative Hierarchy

For national courts the real question, according to international law, and contrary to the approach taken in *Jones v Saudi Arabia*, or *Germany v Italy*, is not whether by denying or granting immunity to a foreign state international law is complied with or violated. The above analysis has already demonstrated that the grant of state immunity to foreign states cannot be seen as a requirement positively imposed on states under general international law.

The real question instead is whether, by granting immunity to foreign states, national courts engage the forum state into the violation of a competing rule or principle of international law that may require from that state that proceedings go ahead and, if need be, remedies be granted to the aggrieved individual or other private entity. Curiously enough, the issue of the hierarchy between norms acquires a pressing importance from the viewpoint of those who insist that state immunity is affirmatively regulated under customary international law and that its scope is broad enough to encompass and protect acts that involve serious violations of human rights and humanitarian law norms. To illustrate, in the *Al-Malki* case, Arden LJ spoke in terms of normative hierarchy, suggesting the correctness 'of upholding a well-established rule of international

---

[70] *Arrest Warrant*, n. 1 above, 22, para. 53.

law unless it is required to yield to *another rule of international law*'.[71] It now remains to see whether, were state immunity among the requirements applicable under customary international law, it would be compatible with the relevant other rules of international law.

5.8.2 State Immunity and the Right of Individuals to Access to a Court (Article 6 ECHR)

Article 6 of the European Convention on Human Rights (ECHR), as it stands, guarantees access to court to 'everyone', which would prima facie include persons suing sovereign states, and thus at least potentially conflicts with state immunity.[72] True, the right of access to court is not absolute and may be regulated by a state to meet certain needs of society, but this must never injure the substance of the right itself or cause its total absence, nor conflict with other Convention rights.[73] On the other hand, the class of exception to the scope of Article 6, which has just been discussed, is substantially different from the exception to the same provision on state immunity grounds. For immunity does not require restricting the operation of Article 6 rights because the beneficiary of those rights has the restricted ability to exercise those rights. Instead, immunity-based limitations relate to the importation, within the scope of Article 6, of some utilitarian calculus according to which the relations between the forum state and the state whose conduct is being impleaded before the forum state's courts, are more important and paramount that the enjoyment by individuals of their Article 6 rights on straightforward terms. The outcome then is the deprivation of Article 6 rights to a particular discrete category of individuals, or in relation to a particular class of cases in a total manner.

It is difficult to deny the existence of a normative conflict between the two rules that require mutually exclusive things: one (Article 6 ECHR) requiring the grant of access to a court to the individual and the continuation of judicial process, and the other (state immunity) requiring

---

[71] *Reyes and Suryadi v Al-Malki and Al-Malki* [2015] EWCA Civ 32, para. 63 (emphasis in original).

[72] Lord Millett would preserve immunity in the face of Article 6, *Holland v Lampen-Wolfe,* n. 12 above, 847–8, but Lord Cooke would deny immunity in the face of Article 6, unless a clear *jure imperii* act is involved, *ibid.* 838.

[73] *Golder v United Kingdom,* ECHR Ser. A, No. 18, Judgment of 21 February 1975; *Winterwerp v The Netherlands,* ECHR Ser. A, No. 33, Judgment of 24 October 1979. These decisions emphasize that this right may be limited so as not to benefit minors and persons of unsound mind.

directly the opposite, namely, the denial of such access to the court. The conflict between norms here is not marginal or incidental but relates to the core of both conflicting norms.

The justification for granting state immunity in *Al-Adsani v United Kingdom* was that:

> measures taken by a High Contracting Party which reflect generally recognised rules of public international law on State immunity cannot in principle be regarded as imposing a disproportionate restriction on the right of access to a court as embodied in Article 6§1.

This was because the ECHR had to be interpreted in line with other principles of international law pursuant to Article 31(3)(c) of the 1969 Vienna Convention on the Law of Treaties (VCLT).[74] No further discussion was undertaken as to the precise nature of the acts of torture in the light of the restrictive doctrine of state immunity.

In a rather curious contrast, the two other judgments of the ECtHR, delivered on the same day as *Al-Adsani* – the judgments in *Fogarty v United Kingdom* and *McElhinney v Ireland* – have adopted a more nuanced interest-balancing approach. Unlike *Al-Adsani*, these two cases have provided a discussion of the sovereign nature of the relevant acts before the Court moved on to justify the grant of state immunity to relevant states. The contrast between the two approaches has been vividly illustrated by the dissent of Judge Loucaides in *Al-Adsani*:

> Any form of blanket immunity, whether based on international law or national law, which is applied by a court in order to block completely the judicial determination of a civil right without balancing the competing interests, namely those connected with the particular immunity and those relating to the nature of the specific claim which is the subject matter of the relevant proceedings, is a disproportionate limitation on Article 6§1 of the Convention and for that reason it amounts to a violation of that Article. The courts should be in a position to weigh the competing interests in favour of upholding an immunity or allowing a judicial determination of a civil right, after looking into the subject matter of the proceedings.

Consequently, the learned judge has concluded that immunities are 'incompatible with Article 6§1 in all those cases where their application is automatic without a balancing of the competing interests'.[75] This is also similar to what the Italian Constitutional Court has observed

---

[74] *Al-Adsani*, n. 19 above, para. 56.

[75] *Ibid.* Dissenting Opinion, 301.

regarding the conflict between the right to access to a court and state immunity, in the aftermath of the ICJ's decision in *Germany v Italy*.[76]

In a contribution soon after *Al-Adsani* was decided by the ECtHR, Lloyd Jones presented the relationship between state immunity and Article 6 ECHR as a hierarchy of norms issue, and proposed resolving the conflict of norms in favour of immunities, suggesting that:

> The supervening effect of the various immunities arising in international law is to deny to that State the power to adjudicate in certain proceedings. Article 6 does not confer on Contracting States adjudicative powers that they are denied by international law. Indeed, even if it did so among States parties to the European Convention on Human Rights, this could not confer on a Contracting State a power of adjudication over a non-Contracting State.[77]

This has mirrored the view expressed by Lord Millett, who suggested in *Lampen-Wolfe* that state immunity is a creature of customary international law, not a self-imposed restriction on the jurisdiction of the courts which a state chooses to adopt, but a limitation imposed from without upon the sovereignty of a state; and that 'The United Kingdom cannot, by its own act of acceding to the Convention and without the consent of the United States, obtain a power of adjudication over the United States which international law denies it'.[78] Furthermore, Lloyd Jones presented the three above cases, decided in 2002, as if decided on similar grounds.[79]

This approach carries with it some question-begging assumptions: first, that immunities are firmly recognized as part of customary international law with the effect of adversely affecting the territorial jurisdiction of states (which the above analysis has already demonstrated is not the case); and secondly, the ECHR as a treaty cannot operate as *lex specialis* and displace whatever the customary international law allegedly requires

---

[76] Judgment No. 238, Italian Constitutional Court, 22 October 2014, para. 5 (the Constitutional Court observes here that 'the absolute sacrifice of the right of judicial protection of fundamental rights – one of the supreme principles of the Italian legal order, enshrined in the combination of Articles 2 and 24 of the Republican Constitution – resulting from the immunity from Italian jurisdiction granted to the foreign State, cannot be justified and accepted insofar as immunity protects the unlawful exercise of governmental powers of the foreign State, as in the case of acts considered war crimes and crimes against humanity, in breach of inviolable human rights').

[77] D. Lloyd Jones, 'Article 6 ECHR and Immunities Arising in Public International Law' (2003) 52 *ICLQ* 463 at 470.

[78] *Holland v Lampen-Wolfe*, n. 12 above, 1588.

[79] Lloyd Jones, n. 77 above, 468.

from states to do. The third problem Lloyd Jones' reasoning raises relates to the objective nature of ECHR obligations, which is their generally recognized and undisputed quality, in the sense that the scope of ECHR obligations which are owed both by states parties to each other on a bilateral plane, and also to individuals as such, objectively and regardless of their nationality,[80] cannot be affected by considerations of whether the state party's jurisdiction in compliance with the ECHR provisions is exercised over the non-party state or their agent or official.

Lord Hope in *Lampen-Wolfe* had adopted a somewhat narrower perspective on the role of immunities in this area, and he 'would hold that Article 6 of the Convention does not preclude a state from granting immunity to a foreign state in accordance with its international law obligations in respect of acts which can properly be characterised as *jure imperii*'.[81] This narrows down the room for conflict between the two rules, in the sense that the properly sovereign nature of the underlying act must first be ascertained to be within the narrower category of *jure imperii* acts (as was done in *Fogarty* and *McElhinney* but not in *Al-Adsani v United Kingdom*), and then some limits on the operation of Article 6 could come into play. It could then become easier to demonstrate that such limited state immunity imposes restrictions on Article 6 rights but not in a disproportionate manner.

The ECtHR has itself treated this matter as one of hierarchy of norms, in terms of the relationship between conflicting treaty and customary rules. However, and especially in *Al-Adsani v United Kingdom*, the Court effectively denies the *lex specialis* nature of the ECHR, requiring it to be interpreted in accordance what it sees as the general international law on state immunity (so-called harmonious interpretation). This approach to treaty interpretation would presuppose that the law-making capacity of states parties to the treaty trumping immunities is lesser than that used to agree on a putative customary rule that confers immunities.

This interpretative exercise also rests on a dubious normative basis, being not reflected in the law of interpretation of treaties as codified in VCLT, Articles 31 and 32.[82] Not less importantly, also, the ECtHR itself operates the interpretative approach, in relation to various other areas to which it applies the European Convention on Human Rights, to the effect that wherever the ECHR is in conflict with other treaties, the former

---

80 *Austria v Italy* (1961) 4 YB ECHR 136.

81 *Holland v Lampen-Wolfe*, n. 12 above, 1578.

82 For a detailed analysis see A. Orakhelashvili, *The Interpretation of Acts and Rules in Public International Law* (Oxford, Oxford University Press, 2008), ch. 10.

should prevail and operate regardless of the requirements under the latter.[83] It is difficult to reconcile the *Al-Adsani* approach to the interpretation of the ECHR with the one used by the ECtHR in relation to several such other areas.

As one way of resolving these dilemmas, Lloyd Jones has suggested that:

> It seems that Article 6 may *in future* be applied in a way which allows a margin of appreciation to States to act *on their own view of the extent of their obligations* in international law, at least within the area of reasonably tenable views, and to permit limitations on access to their courts by reference to the criteria of legitimate aim and proportionate response.[84]

Lloyd Jones thus essentially portrays the ECtHR's approach as premised on two factors. One is the judicial redefinition of the scope of treaty obligations which, in reality, is beyond the statutory gift of the Strasbourg Court. The second factor is to allow individual states parties the power to unilaterally auto-determine the scope of their international obligations. This is, quite simply, not language that could be sustained in relation to any issue of treaty interpretation, or in the reasoning of any international tribunal. Auto-interpretation is inimical to the international legal reasoning.

5.8.3 State Immunity and *Jus Cogens*

The general doctrine of *jus cogens*, consisting in its primacy over inconsistent acts and rules, was initially determined in the 1969 VCLT, and then extended to non-treaty acts, states of affairs and transactions. As Crawford has emphasized, it is difficult to justify the position that *jus cogens* rules are sacrosanct in one context and freely prescriptible in

---

83 See, for the confirmation of this approach, *M & Co. v Federal Republic of Germany*, Application No. 13258/87 (1990) 33 YB ECHR 51, ECtHR, 9 February 1990; *Waite and Kennedy v Germany*, Application No. 26083/94, ECtHR, 18 February 1999, para. 67; *Matthews v United Kingdom*, Application No. 24833/94, ECtHR, 18 February 1999, paras 26–35; *Bosphorus Hava Yollari Turizm v Ireland*, Application No. 45036/98, ECtHR, 30 June 2005, paras 155–6; *Soering v United Kingdom*, Application No. 14038/88, ECtHR, Judgment of 7 July 1989; *Al-Saadoon and Mufdhi v United Kingdom*, Application No. 61498/08, Fourth Chamber, Judgment of 2 March 2010; *Capital Bank v Bulgaria*, Application No. 49429/99, ECtHR, 24 November 2005, paras 38, 43, 110–11.

84 Lloyd Jones, n. 77 above, 470 (emphasis added).

another.[85] Even under the law of treaties, non-derogability is rationalized not just through the initial disapproval of it under VCLT, Article 53 which determines that treaties contrary to *jus cogens* are void, but also via the network of consequential rules under VCLT, Articles 44, 45 and 71 of the same Convention. Non-treaty areas mirror the same approach.

In relation to state recognition and more broadly state responsibility, from the 1960s onwards, Sir Robert Jennings, John Dugard and later on the ILC itself, have adopted the same consequential approach: the issues of recognition, waiver and acquiescence in relation to situations produced by the original breach of *jus cogens* are dealt with in the same consequential perspective both in treaty and non-treaty areas.[86] Most notably, Article 41 of the ILC's 2001 Draft Articles focuses on situations created by the breach of peremptory norms and requires abstaining from any conduct that may lead to recognizing that situation as lawful.[87]

There is enough practical evidence of *jus cogens* applying and censoring unilateral acts or conduct of states accordingly. The International Tribunal for the former Yugoslavia (ICTY), as well as the Special Court for Sierra-Leone, have concluded that amnesties granted to offenders in violation of *jus cogens* have no effect in international law.[88] In *A v Secretary of State*, following *Furundzija*, the UK House of Lords affirmed that the peremptory status of the prohibition of torture 'requires member states to do more than eschew the practice of torture'.[89] A similar approach was applied by the House of Lords in *Kuwait Air Corp.*,

---

85 J. Crawford, *Creation of States* (1979), p. 82.

86 R.Y. Jennings, *Nullity and Effectiveness in International Law*, Cambridge Essays in International Law (1965), p. 74; J. Dugard, *Recognition and the United Nations* (Cambridge, Cambridge University Press, 1987).

87 See for the text and commentary, *Report of the International Law Commission on the Work of its Fifty-third Session* (2001), Official Records of the General Assembly, Fifty-sixth session, Supplement No. 10 (A/56/10).

88 *Furundzija*, Case No. IT-95-17/I-T, ICTY, Judgment of 10 December 1998, para. 155; *Prosecutor v Morris Kallon and Brimma Bazzy Kamara*, Case Nos SCSL-2004-15-AR72(E) and SCSL-2004-16-AR72(E), Special Court for Sierra-Leone, Decision on Challenge to Jurisdiction: Lomé Accord Amnesty, 13 March 2004, para. 71.

89 *A (FC) and others (FC) v Secretary of State for the Home Department* [2005] UKHL 71, HL, 8 December 2005.

in relation to the act of state doctrine.[90] More recent English cases of *Belhaj* and *Youssef* have endorsed the same approach.[91]

The proponents of the narrow or restrictive view on *jus cogens* propagate the difference between the original prohibitions under *jus cogens* rules and the enforcement of those prohibitions, and contend that the relevant unlawful act remains unlawful on a general plane, but is excused in relation to a particular case or particular class of cases.[92] But this very approach is, contrary to the initial design of those who advance this thesis, precisely a confirmation that a derogation from *jus cogens* is being envisaged. For there is only one feature of a rule being a *legal rule* as opposed to being a moral or ethical one: the ability to produce a binding effect in relation to its subject matter and legal consequences when violated. It is the very essence of a derogation that a norm remains generally in force, but in relation to particular specified situations it does not apply as a legal rule. That a norm has not been abolished in a wholesale manner is not a proof that it has not been derogated from. Derogation from *jus cogens* is not about a rule that purports to abolish the relevant *jus cogens* rule and make the act outlawed under it lawful across the board, but about a rule that abolishes the normativity of that *jus cogens* rule, preventing it from operating as a legal rule and replacing the legal consequences that rule prescribes by those prescribed under another rule, in this case one requiring the grant of immunity to a foreign state.

Although in various areas the consequential effect of *jus cogens* is plainly recognized, there are some vehement statements in academic writings that, in relation to immunities of states and their officials from foreign jurisdiction, a specific *jus cogens* exception to immunities has not

---

90 *Kuwait Airways Corp. v Iraqi Airways Co.* [2002] 2 AC 883, HL, 16 May 2002, paras 114, 117.

91 *Belhaj v Straw* [2014] EWCA Civ 1394, CA, 30 October 2014, para. 116; *R (Youssef) v Secretary of State for Foreign and Commonwealth Affairs* [2013] EWCA Civ 1302, paras 54–5.

92 See H. Fox, *The Law of State Immunity* (2001), pp. 524–5; H. Aust, *Complicity and the Law of State Responsibility* (2011), pp. 39–40; S. Sivakumaran, 'Impact on the Structure of Treaty Obligations' in M. Scheinin and M. Kamminga, *The Impact of Human Rights Law on General International Law* (2009), p. 133 at 149; T. Rensmann, 'Impact on the Immunity of States and their Officials' in M. Scheinin and M. Kamminga, *The Impact of Human Rights Law on General International Law* (2009), p. 151 at 164–5; J. Vidmar, 'Rethinking *Jus Cogens* after *Germany v Italy*: Back to Article 53?' (2013) 60 *Netherlands International Law Review* 1.

crystallized in state practice,[93] which was also the ICJ's principal point in *Germany v Italy*, upholding the plea of state immunity for war crimes committed by the Third Reich.[94] This is, however, the analytically and methodologically false question to ask, for once the overall non-derogability of peremptory norms is acknowledged, it makes little sense to require another, additional, rule of positive law to the effect that the rule generally possessing non-derogable status should apply as non-derogable in relation to the particular area of immunities. In addition, that the non-derogability of the rule should be additionally recognized through those very same rules to which the non-derogability of *jus cogens* is supposed to apply and censure is a plainly absurd position to take.

The UK House of Lords in *Pinochet* recognized the effect of *jus cogens* in relation to immunities in criminal proceedings.[95] Courts granting immunity for torture in civil proceedings try to distinguish between civil and criminal proceedings, suggesting that while immunity can be denied in criminal proceedings, civil cases are arguably different.[96] This may be true empirically in terms of *national law* in the United Kingdom where there is statutory regulation in relation to the immunity in civil proceedings (SIA 1978) not making the allowance for the effect of *jus cogens* cases, but not in relation to criminal proceedings. But that is hardly indicative of what the position under *international law* is; here the matter is solely one of normative conflict and non-derogability. If *jus cogens* prevails over immunities in criminal cases, it does inevitably have the same procedural effect in relation to civil cases as well. There is no reason to assert that criminal and civil cases are to be treated differently.

The ICJ in *Germany v Italy* can further be shown to have admitted the derogation from *jus cogens* as it has attempted to present the scope of Draft Article 41 as narrower than it in fact is.[97] Contrary to what the Court professes, Article 41 requires the non-recognition of situations created after the breach of a peremptory norm. In this case the impunity created through the grant of immunity, the lack of any other remedy for victims, and the consequent practical denial of the capacity of the

---

93 See, generally, references in n. 92 above.

94 *Jurisdictional Immunities of the State (Germany v Italy: Greece Intervening)*, n. 22 above.

95 *Pinochet*, n. 60 above, 242.

96 *Al-Adsani v United Kingdom*, n. 19 above; *Jones v Saudi Arabia*, n. 20 above; *Khurts Bat v Mongolia*, n. 4 above, para. 74.

97 *Jurisdictional Immunities of the State (Germany v Italy: Greece Intervening)*, n. 22 above, paras 92–102.

relevant rules of *jus cogens* to operate, clearly amounts to a situation produced and persisting after the initial violation.

A full-fledged derogation from *jus cogens* is, therefore, clearly involved. The judicial and academic opinion to the opposite effect is misleading. Those who tell us that immunities do not derogate from *jus cogens* essentially tell us that they do not abolish *jus cogens* rules. We know that much already. The issue here relates, however, to derogation from *jus cogens* which is not about the abolition of the relevant rule, but about preventing the relevant norm operating in relation to underlying facts.

After *Germany v Italy*, which case is regarded by some as a definitive statement of the legal position on this matter, there have been further cases that confirm the lack of immunity for breaches of *jus cogens*, notably in Swiss and US courts.[98] On an empirical plane, state practice on this matter is divided, while the ICJ's approach purports to be plain and straightforward. In *Jones v United Kingdom*, while upholding state immunity for torture, the ECtHR deliberately eschewed taking on state practice head on, and expressly stated that:

> it is not necessary for the court to examine all of these developments in detail since the recent judgment of the International Court of Justice in *Germany v Italy* … – which must be considered by this court as authoritative as regards the content of customary international law – clearly establishes that, by February 2012, no *jus cogens* exception to state immunity had yet crystallised.[99]

One wonders here what the basis of the ECtHR's decision on immunities is: customary international law or a law made in the ICJ's judicial decision on the basis qualitatively different from state consent? Is the law the Strasbourg Court projects one agreed as between states or one created by courts in the process of adjudication? This is a basic issue relating to the doctrine of the sources of international law, inevitably impacting the correctness of the relevant courts' approaches.

The ECtHR declined according probative weight to the US case of *Samantar* as an instance of state practice on the matter, as it was still pending before the US Supreme Court. But the day before *Jones v United Kingdom* was decided by the ECtHR in 2014, the Supreme Court decided

---

[98] *A v Attorney-General of Switzerland*, Case No. BB.2011.140, Judgment of 25 July 2012, paras 5.3.5 and 5.4.3; *Bashe Abdi Yousuf v Mohamed Ali Samantar*, Application No. 11-1479, ECtHR, 2 November 2012, at 23.

[99] *Jones and others v United Kingdom*, n. 49 above, para. 198.

not to grant certiorari in this case,[100] with the implication that the Court of Appeals decision remained in force as a valid instance of state practice. On the whole, the ECtHR has not properly confronted the dissenting state practice. For this reason, its analysis proves nothing as to the state of customary law, or the reach of the general doctrine of *jus cogens*.

All these factors and developments require a recognition of the position that the substance-effect dichotomy in relation to *jus cogens*, as portrayed in immunity cases, is anomalous if compared with the overall relevance of non-derogability in other areas within which *jus cogens* operates. Once the consequential effect of *jus cogens* is there, immunities should give way. It could not sensibly be contended that there are consequential effects of *jus cogens* in relation to some derogations but not others, nor is any court competent to introduce such qualification, which is entirely a law-making issue and depends on inter-state agreement rather than on judicial input and innovation.

5.9 CONCLUSIONS: INITIAL RATIONALE AND CURRENT BALANCE

The above analysis has demonstrated that, the further the reach of state immunity is pressed, the less coherent the justification for its underlying rationale as well as its normative status, and the greater the moral dilemma the grant of immunity to the state produces. The initial development of the doctrine of state immunity in relation to individual rights and private law relations was driven by its limited scope and the requirement that regard had to be had to the competing interests affected by immunity decisions. As Sir Robert Phillimore observed in *Parlement Belge*, the individual's rights should not to be taken away without pressing legal reason:

> If the Crown had power without the authority of parliament by this treaty to order that the *Parlement Belge* should be entitled to all the privileges of a ship of war, then … the right of the subject, but for this order unquestionable, to recover damages for the injuries done to him by her is extinguished.[101]

---

[100] See www.scotusblog.com/case-files/cases/samantar-v-yousuf-2/ (petition denied on 13 January 2014).

[101] *Parlement Belge* (1879) 4 PD 129 at 154.

The same dilemma underlies the reasoning of Sir Hersch Lauterpacht, that the restrictive doctrine as understood narrowly, and the discourse regarding the impact of Article 6 ECHR, point to the imperative not to exempt the individual from the ordinary legal process to a greater extent than is pressingly needed. This spirit has also found its expression in the ICJ's decision in *Arrest Warrant*, to the effect that immunity is not the same as impunity, and that the immunity *ratione personae* of the incumbent Foreign Minister was endorsed on the condition that he could feasibly be prosecuted in several other contexts.[102]

This imperative has not been honoured in cases that involved the grant of immunity to a foreign state for serious human rights violations. In *Al-Adsani v United Kingdom*, the grant of immunity to Kuwait was approved against the background that the UK government did not afford the claimant diplomatic protection against Kuwait, and then argued before the ECtHR that the proper way of obtaining remedies was diplomatic representation.[103]

Lords Bingham and Hoffmann suggested in *Jones v Saudi Arabia* that state immunity does not really contradict the *jus cogens* prohibition of torture but merely diverts its enforcement to other fora.[104] But no such other fora were identified. The ICJ in *Germany v Italy* backtracked even on this nominal endorsement of the requirement that alternative remedies should be available, and held that it did not matter that no alternative remedies were available to victims, because 'The Court [could] find no basis in the State practice from which customary international law is derived that international law makes the entitlement of a State to immunity dependent upon the existence of effective alternative means of securing redress'.[105]

The equation between immunity and impunity was thus effectively endorsed. This is presumably due to a utilitarian prioritization of certain interests over others, avoiding irritation in inter-state relations being perceived as a 'greater good' than helping the victims. It is only natural that such a blanket assertion of the doctrine of state immunity in *Germany v Italy* was contradicted by the Italian Constitutional Court.[106]

---

[102] *Arrest Warrant*, n. 1 above, para. 61.

[103] *Al-Adsani v United Kingdom*, n. 19 above, 280, 288, paras 19, 50–51.

[104] *Jones v Saudi Arabia*, n. 20 above, paras 24 and 44 (both referring to H. Fox).

[105] *Jurisdictional Immunities of the State (Germany v Italy: Greece Intervening)*, n. 22 above, paras 92–102.

[106] Judgment No. 238, Italian Constitutional Court, 22 October 2014, para. 5 (the Constitutional Court 'declares the unconstitutionality of Article 1 of Law

This broadly validates the point this author has made previously, to the effect that the decision in *Germany v Italy* was *ultra vires* for its misapplication of underlying sources of international law, and that it would be for the Italian authorities to choose, not their legal obligation, to comply with the ICJ's decision.[107] On balance, the grant of immunity which secures impunity for underlying crimes should not carry the day.

No. 848 of 17 August 1957 (Execution of the United Nations Charter, signed in San Francisco on 26 June 1945), so far as it concerns the execution of Article 94 of the United Nations Charter, exclusively to the extent that it obliges the Italian judge to comply with the Judgment of the ICJ of 3 February 2012, which requires that Italian courts deny their jurisdiction in case of acts of a foreign State constituting war crimes and crimes against humanity, in breach of inviolable human rights').

[107] See A. Orakhelashvili, '*Jurisdictional Immunities of the State (Germany v Italy)*, Case Review' (2012) *American Journal of International Law* 609.

6. Shared foundations and conceptual differentiation in immunities from jurisdiction

J. Craig Barker

6.1 INTRODUCTION

The issue of immunities from jurisdiction is one of the most controversial in contemporary international law. The reasons for this are many and varied. They include, for example, the increasing expansion of the extra-territorial reach of domestic civil and criminal jurisdiction,[1] as well as advances in new and expanding areas of international law, such as human rights and international criminal law, in the context of which the law relating to immunities from jurisdiction is increasingly challenged.[2] Unfortunately, much of the current controversy concerning immunities from jurisdiction derives from misunderstandings, accidental or deliberate, about the nature and purpose of immunities from jurisdiction.

There is a clear tendency, particularly in the academic literature and in some judicial dicta, to conflate the various forms of immunity into one single concept, and then, in some cases, to denigrate the notion of immunity as out-dated, state-centric and distorted. Some of this criticism of the concept of immunities is undoubtedly valid and worthy of further analysis and critique. The idea that immunities from jurisdiction, which are, by their very nature positivist constructs, are themselves somehow immune from challenge should be rejected. Nevertheless, if the challenge is merely an attempt to sweep aside all forms of immunity from

[1] The importance of the link between immunity and jurisdiction is self-evident. As Judges Higgins, Kooijmans and Buergenthal made clear in their Joint Separate Opinion in the *Arrest Warrant* case: '"Immunity" and "jurisdiction" are inextricably linked'. *Arrest Warrant of 11 April 2000 (Democratic Republic of the Congo v Belgium)* [2002] ICJ Reports 63 at 64.

[2] For a discussion of this controversy see J.C. Barker, 'Negotiating the Complex Interface Between State Immunity and Human Rights: An Analysis of the International Court of Justice Decision in *Germany v Italy*' (2013) 15(4) *International Community Law Review* 415.

jurisdiction in pursuit of a 'greater' agenda of human rights and human dignity, then that process itself might have some very considerable and problematic unintended consequences.

The purpose of this chapter is to seek to clarify and explain the conceptual and theoretical differences between the many different forms of immunity and to argue for a much more nuanced and specific understanding of immunities from jurisdiction in international law. It is suggested that part of the problem in distinguishing between the different types of immunity is the rather obtuse and unhelpful use of Latin maxims that serve simply to obfuscate the various concepts. Accordingly, this chapter will eschew these maxims and seek to distinguish between various forms of immunity based on their history, necessity and importance. Ultimately, it will be argued that it is only through analysing the shared foundations and conceptual differentiation of immunities from jurisdiction that we can advance multifaceted solutions to what is the complex problem of understanding immunities from jurisdiction.

6.2 PERSONAL IMMUNITY OF STATE REPRESENTATIVES SERVING ABROAD

6.2.1 Diplomatic Agents

It is well-known and generally accepted that the first form of immunity from jurisdiction developed during ancient times in relation to the treatment of envoys or messengers. There is considerable evidence, particularly during the time of the Ancient Greeks and Ancient Romans,[3] that representatives from 'others' when travelling to or arriving in a foreign territory, were accorded a form of inviolability insofar as they were not subject to interference to their person or to their mission.[4]

---

[3] On Greek and Roman diplomacy see, generally, Coleman Phillipson, *The International Law and Custom of Ancient Greece and Rome* (London, MacMillan & Co. Ltd, 1911); D.J. Hill, *A History of Diplomacy in the International Development of Europe* (London, Longman, Green & Co., 1905); H. Nicolson, *Diplomacy* (2nd edn, Oxford, Oxford University Press, 1949); H. Nicolson, *The Evolution of Diplomatic Method* (London, Constable Co. Ltd, 1949); E. Young, 'The Development of the Law of Diplomatic Relations' (1964) 40 *British Yearbook of International Law* 14.

[4] According to *Satow's Guide to Diplomatic Practice* (6th edn, 2009), paras 8.11, 8.14 and 9.3, 'Personal inviolability is of the privileges and immunities of missions and diplomats, the oldest established and most universally recognised'. The principle, which is now guaranteed under Vienna Convention on Diplomatic

Whether or not this inviolability amounted to diplomatic immunity is moot, and depends essentially upon the level of development of the jurisdiction from which the envoy or messenger could have been said to be immune. The original justification for the granting of such inviolability was simple necessity, backed up by a form of religious sanctity.[5]

As diplomatic relations developed, so too did the sophistication of diplomatic law. Through the relative professionalism of the Byzantine diplomatic method,[6] to the austerity of the 'international' relations of the Pope,[7] diplomatic inviolability came to be more and more firmly established. By the time of the establishment of permanent diplomatic relations in the middle of the fifteenth century, the necessity of providing more developed rules of diplomatic law, including rules concerning the immunity from local jurisdiction of ambassadors and their retinue, was gradually addressed, primarily by writers and theorists. Initially, the writers of the period drew on Roman Law doctrines and practices, these doctrines and practices having themselves been influenced by notions of Natural Law.[8] However, by the time Grotius published his *De Jure Belli Ac Pacis* in 1625, the so-called classical writers had begun to study contemporary state practice as the basis of diplomatic law, instead of relying on an extension of Roman Law doctrines which provided insufficient explanation of the diplomatic relations between different states.[9]

Relations 1961, Art. 29, 500 UNTS 95, 'has two distinct aspects in modern international law. The first is immunity from any legal process or action by the law enforcement officers of the receiving State. The second aspect … is the duty of protection laid on the receiving State'. *Ibid.*

5 J.C. Barker, 'The Theory and Practice of Diplomatic Law in the Renaissance and Classical Periods' (1995) 6 *Diplomacy and Statecraft* 593 at 595.

6 See Nicolson, *Diplomacy,* n. 3 above, 10 and Nicolson, *Evolution,* n. 3 above, 26.

7 See D. Behrens 'Origins of the Office of English Resident Ambassador in Rome' (1934) 49 *English Historical Review* 640.

8 As this author has previously noted: 'Most important among the early treatises on diplomatic law were Ayrault's impressively titled *L'ordre, formalite et instruction judiciaire dont les anciens Grecs et Romains ont usee et accusations publiques (sinon qu'ils ayent commence a l'execution) confers au stil et usage de nostre France* (1576), Gentilis' *De Legationibus Libri Tres* (1585), and Hotman's *L'Ambassadeur* (1603).

9 Of the many excellent treatises on the subject of diplomacy written after this point, the most notable include Wicquefort's *L'Ambassadeur et ses fonctions* (1681), Cornelius Van Bynkershoek's *De Foro Legatorum* (1721) and Vattel's *Le Droit des Gens* (1750). See Barker, n. 5 above, 598.

Three apparently competing theoretical explanations emerged during this period as the juridical explanation for the granting of immunity to ambassadors.[10] The earliest, and arguably most important, of these was the so-called 'representative character' theory. In fact, this theory consisted of a range of theories that 'ultimately traces immunity to the sovereignty of the State [or sovereign] which sends the agent'.[11] A second theory of diplomatic immunity that emerged in the early period of permanent diplomatic relations was the 'exterritoriality' theory. This theory considered ambassadors to be outside not only the jurisdiction of the receiving state but actually physically resident outside its territory. Ambassadors pursued their daily activities as if in a bubble of their own state's territory and jurisdiction. The genesis of the theory is disputed and is often ascribed to a mistranslation of the words of Grotius by later writers.[12] Additionally, the theory has always been described as a fiction,[13] and gave rise to some absurd situations.[14] The theory was gradually discredited to the extent that it was abandoned as a basis of diplomatic immunity around the turn of the twentieth century,[15] and was not considered during the negotiation of the Vienna Convention on Diplomatic Relations 1961. In spite of this, the theory remains popular as a descriptive explanation for diplomatic law, particularly in the popular

---

[10] During this early period of the establishment of diplomatic relations, the classical writers generally referred only to the position of ambassadors and their households.

[11] M. Ogdon, *Juridical Bases of Diplomatic Immunity* (John Byrne & Co., 1936), p. 105.

[12] See J.C. Barker, *The Abuse of Diplomatic Privileges and Immunities: A Necessary Evil* (Ashgate, 1996), pp. 36–40.

[13] See Grotius, *De Jure Belli ac Pacis* (1625), vol. II, Bk II, ch. XVIII, p. 443.

[14] The understanding that ambassadors were considered as resident in their home state gave rise to the so-called *franchise du quartier,* as a result of which whole areas of the world's major capital cities were considered to be outside local jurisdiction and, as a consequence became dens for outlaws and criminals. According to Anderson, for example, 'By the eighteenth century, the position in Rome had become so impossible … that the papal police had to be equipped with special maps to show them which streets they were permitted to pass through'. M.S. Anderson, *The Rise of Modern Diplomacy* (Longman, 1993), p. 56.

[15] See *Report of the Special Rapporteur to the Sub-Committee on Diplomatic Immunities to the Committee of Experts for the Progressive Codification of International Law*, League of Nations Doc. C.45.M.22.1926, (1926) 20 ILM 153 (Supp.) which noted that 'It is perfectly clear that exterritoriality is a fiction which has no foundation in either law or in fact'.

media. A third theory of 'functional necessity' updated and formalized the reliance on the necessity of diplomatic intercourse that had characterized the early according of diplomatic inviolability. Although not initially considered as the primary justification for the granting of diplomatic immunity, all of the classical writers referred, to a greater or lesser extent, to the protection of the diplomatic function. Arguably the greatest emphasis on the necessity of the diplomatic function was placed by Vattel who argued that: 'ambassadors and other public ministers are necessary instruments in the maintenance of that general society of nations and of that mutual intercourse between them'.[16]

The juridical basis of diplomatic law today is quite clearly based on functional necessity. Thus, the Preamble to the Vienna Convention on Diplomatic Relations (VCDR) 1961 notes that 'the purpose of [diplomatic] privileges and immunities is not to benefit individuals but to ensure the efficient performance of the functions of diplomatic missions'.[17] Functional necessity is not an absolute concept and depends on 'degrees of necessity'. On the other hand, the immunity of a diplomat cannot be limited strictly to the performance of diplomatic function. Rather, as Ogdon puts it, functional immunity 'demands the immunity necessary to permit the agent to perform the *bona fide* diplomatic functions in complete freedom, independence and security'.[18]

In particular, it must be remembered that ambassadors, and other diplomatic agents, and their families are not occasional visitors to the jurisdiction of other states. Their primary function is to live in the territory of the receiving state; to represent the sending state, protecting its interests and those of its nationals; to negotiate on behalf of the sending state, interacting on a daily basis with officials, but also with the ordinary population of the receiving state with the view to the promotion of friendly relations.[19] The importance of the 'representative character' of diplomatic agents is acknowledged in the Preamble to the Vienna Convention which describes diplomatic agents 'as representing States'. This is not simply a throwaway phrase but is, rather, a reminder of the important role that diplomatic agents play in the conduct of international relations. The immersion of diplomatic personnel within the jurisdiction of the receiving state is complete and their immunity is part of a broader,

---

16 Vattel, n. 9 above, Bk IV, ch. VII, 376.

17 Preamble to the Vienna Convention on Diplomatic Relations 1961, para. 4.

18 Ogdon, n. 11 above, 177.

19 On the functions of the diplomatic mission see VCDR 1961, Art. 3. See also E. Denza, *Diplomatic Law: Commentary on the Vienna Convention on Diplomatic Relations* (3rd edn, Oxford University Press, 2008), ch. 3.

self-contained regime of privileges and immunities that serve not only to facilitate diplomatic relations but also to provide protection for these individuals from the activities of the receiving state and from its populace, who will often not share the same legal, political or religious interests and beliefs.[20] Accordingly, attempts to reduce or limit diplomatic immunity should be considered only with serious forethought and due and careful consideration of the possible consequences not only for international relations but also for the individuals whose lives may be adversely affected.

6.2.2 Consular Officials

The origins of consular relations can be traced back almost as far as those of diplomatic agents, if not further. It has been pointed out, for example, that the Ancient Roman office of *preator peregrinus* can be considered as the forerunner of modern consulates.[21] It is unlikely, however, that holders of these offices were entitled to any form of immunity or even inviolability.[22] Nevertheless, as trading relations developed over the ensuing centuries, the practice of granting capitulations emerged. Capitulations were agreements between nations conferring rights and privileges on foreign subjects trading in one another's territories.[23] In some cases, these capitulations effectively rendered the recipients outside the jurisdiction of the local territory. As a result, certain trading posts acquired a degree of autonomy and the right to appoint special magistrates or judges known as 'consuls', whose competence came to comprise 'all civil and criminal jurisdiction over, and protection of, the privileges, rights and property of their countrymen'.[24]

---

[20] On the importance of diplomatic law as the basis for the protection of diplomatic personnel, see J.C. Barker, *The Protection of Diplomatic Personnel* (Ashgate, 2006). See also the decision of the International Court of Justice in *United States Diplomatic and Consular Staff in Tehran* [1980] ICJ Reports 3.

[21] *Report on Consular Intercourse and Immunities by Mr J. Zourek, Special Rapporteur to the International Law Commission*, UN Doc. A/CN.4/108 (1957) II *Yearbook of the International Law Commission* 73.

[22] *Ibid.*

[23] See John P. Grant and J. Craig Barker, *Encyclopaedic Dictionary of International Law* (3rd edn, Oxford University Press, 2009), p. 79.

[24] R. Jennings and A. Watts (eds), *Oppenheim's International Law* (9th edn, 1992), vol. I, p. 1132. It should be noted that capitulations did not exist between European states and ultimately came to be linked with colonialism and discrimination between Western and other states who were required to grant capitulations in order to secure trading rights and privileges.

As international trade continued to grow, sovereigns increasingly took control of appointing consuls and increasingly relied on them to undertake the business of the state, particularly in far-flung territories. However, as Zourek makes clear, 'to do so, they had to be vested with sufficient authority, hence the need for the consul judge to become a real public minister. So the State took over the right to send consuls, who ceased to represent the traders, and became official State representatives performing certain diplomatic functions and enjoying corresponding privileges and immunities'.[25] This period of development was rather short-lived. Numerous factors contributed to what became a significant diminution of the powers of consuls. The extra-territoriality of foreign citizens was increasingly recognized as incompatible with the sovereignty of the host state and many of the judicial powers previously enjoyed by consuls were 'returned' to the host state. In addition, the growth and spread of permanent diplomatic missions in the sixteenth and seventeenth centuries resulted in the removal from consuls of diplomatic powers, although the 'representative character' of consuls remained disputed until at least the nineteenth century.[26] The functions of consuls were therefore somewhat radically reduced to those functions, fulfilment of which might well have been the original rationale for the emergence of the institution, that is, 'the task of looking after the interest of the State and its citizens, *particularly in trade, industry and shipping*'.[27]

There was some dispute among the classical writers about the extent of the privileges and immunities of consuls. Wicquefort and Bynkershoek, for example, were unwilling to accord to them any privileges and immunities. However, Vattel took a more balanced approach. Writing in *Les Droits des Gens* in 1758, Vattel identified consuls as 'persons sent by a Nation to the chief commercial towns, and especially the ports, of foreign countries, with a commission to watch over the rights and privileges of their Nation, and to settle differences that may arise between its merchants'.[28] Crucially, for Vattel, the exchange of consuls was a sovereign or governmental matter. Thus, he noted that 'a Nation which wishes to send [a consul] must obtain the right to do so in its treaty of commerce'. Furthermore, the consul, 'being entrusted with the affairs of

---

25 Zourek, n. 21 above, 74.

26 *Ibid.* 75.

27 See below, emphasis in original.

28 E. de Vattel, *The Law of Nations or the Principles of Natural Law applied to the Conduct and to the Affairs of Nations and of Sovereigns*, reproduced in J.B. Scott (ed.), *Classics of International Law* (Washington, 1916), p. 4.

his sovereign and receiving orders from him, remains subject to him and accountable to him for what he does'.

The modern juridical basis for the granting of consular privileges and immunities is clearly stated in paragraph 5 of the Preamble to the 1963 Vienna Convention on Consular Relations as being 'to ensure the efficient performance of functions by consular posts'. However, once again, reference back to representative character is apparent from the final phrase of that paragraph which notes that those functions are fulfilled 'on behalf of their respective States'. Crucially, it should be remembered that consular officials, like their diplomatic cousins, are not itinerant visitors to foreign states but, rather, live and work there acting on behalf of their sending states. It is this final element, as much as any other, that requires the granting of a significant degree of privileges and immunities.

6.3 PERSONAL IMMUNITY OF STATE REPRESENTATIVES NOT SERVING ABROAD

6.3.1 Heads of State and High-ranking State Officials

While the immunity of diplomats and, to a lesser extent, that of consular officials can be traced back at least to the time of the ancients, the same cannot be said of the immunity of foreign sovereigns or, indeed, of the immunity of foreign states,[29] which are of much more recent origin. This is partly due to the fact that the use of envoys limited the need for leaders personally to undertake missions abroad. In cases where leaders chose personally to negotiate with their counterparts, considerations of treatment and safety would have been foremost in their deliberations and negotiations when deciding to travel. Moreover, at least until the latter Middle Ages, the lack of equality between sovereigns meant that there was no need to consider questions of sovereign immunity. It is certainly the case that during the period when Christendom was considered to be a Commonwealth, individual leaders would be subject to the overriding authority of the Pope. Most importantly, however, the notion of sovereignty was yet to fully emerge.

The Peace of Westphalia 1648, which brought an end to the Thirty Years War, resulted in a new legal and political order, the cornerstone of which was territorial sovereignty. Writing in 1651, Thomas Hobbes laid

[29] On state, or sovereign, immunity, see further below.

the foundations of this new order in his acclaimed work *Leviathan*. Insofar as Hobbes's sovereign was not subject to external interference, the possibilities for international law were limited. On the other hand, the work of earlier writers remained influential. With regard to sovereignty, writers such as Gentili argued that human society was united. Drawing on the work of Plato and Baldus he argued that the restraints on private citizens should apply equally to sovereigns. Specifically, according to Gentili, 'as a private citizen conducts himself with reference to another private citizen, so ought it to be between one sovereign and another'.[30] Similarly, Grotius believed in the society of states and argued that the sovereignty of kings did not permit them to ignore the law of nature, divine law, nor, indeed the law of nations.[31] In relation to the specific question of the position of foreign sovereigns vis-à-vis one another, both Gentili and Grotius undertook an extensive discussion of their roles both at home and abroad. However, nowhere did they consider directly the question of their immunity, nor even their inviolability. However, other contemporary writers, including, most notably, Richard Zouche, did consider the question and concluded that sovereigns who were found in the territory of another were subject to the jurisdiction of the territorial courts in the same way that private citizens would be.[32] This opinion would seem to fit with the idea that sovereigns had exclusive control over the territory of their state and would not seem to contradict any of the views put forward by Gentili or Grotius. On the other hand, another of the classical writers, Cornelius van Bynkershoek, 'could not see at all why a prince in the dominions of another cannot exercise the rights of sovereignty'.[33] Bynkershoek linked his argument in favour of the immunity of sovereigns directly to the immunity of ambassadors. According to Bynkershoek:

> [I]f ambassadors, who represent the prince, are not subject either in the matter of contracts or of crimes to the jurisdiction of him in whose country they are serving as ambassadors ... are we to come to the opposite conclusion in the case of the prince? Shall we decline to accept in the case of the prince, who is himself present and happens to be transacting his business in person, a situation which reason and the consent of all nations has accepted in the case

30 Robert Gentilis, *De Jure Belli Libri Tres* (1585), Bk I, ch. XV, p. 68.
31 Grotius, *De Jure Belli ac Pacis*, n. 13 above, 121.
32 Zouche, *De Jure Feciali Inter Gentes* (1650), Part II, section 2, question 6.
33 *Ibid.*

> of ambassadors solely because they represent the prince and are the interpreters of his message? Is not his inviolability greater than that of his ambassadors?[34]

In fact, as *Oppenheim* points out, there are many reasons for the granting of immunity to foreign sovereigns, or, as *Oppenheim* refers to them, heads of state:

> The basis for the special treatment accorded to Heads of State is variously ascribed, inter alia, to the dignity which is a recognised quality of States as international persons …; the respect due to them as representatives of sovereign States; their personal character as sovereigns (in the case of monarchs); the equality and independence of sovereigns and sovereign States and the principle *par in parem non habet imperium*; the incompetence of municipal law in an essentially international relationship; the practical need to ensure the free exercise by him of his functions as the highest organ of the State; the requirements of satisfactory international intercourse; the implied licence of the State being visited; and the dictates of international comity and courtesy. At one time or another each of these considerations has to a greater or lesser degree played its part, in conjunction in particular countries with purely domestic considerations, such as the English doctrine that the Crown could not be sued in its own courts.[35]

Given that the origins and juridical foundations of the immunity of heads of state is so contested, it is perhaps not surprising that there is no international treaty dealing with the issue. However, it appears that customary international law now provides for the immunity of both heads of state and other senior state officials.[36] This immunity is commensurate with that of diplomatic agents.[37] The essence of the modern conception of such immunity, as with diplomatic and consular immunity, embraces concepts of functional necessity and representative character. As was made clear by the Institute of International Law in 2001, in its non-binding Resolution on the immunities of heads of state and of governments, 'immunities are granted to a Head of State or a Head of Government, as a representative of that State and not in his or her personal interest, because this is necessary for the exercise of his or her

---

[34] *Ibid.* 18.

[35] Jennings and Watts, *Oppenheim*, n. 24 above, 1034.

[36] See the Opinion of the ICJ in *Arrest Warrant of 11 April 2000 (DRC v Belgium)* [2002] ICJ Rep. 3, para. 51.

[37] *Ibid.* See also A. Watts, 'The Legal Position in International Law of Heads of State, Heads of Government and Foreign Ministers' (1994) 247 *Hague Recueil* 9 at 52–3.

functions and the fulfilment of his or her responsibilities in an independent and efficient manner'.[38] Crucially, and perhaps somewhat confusingly given what has been said above about diplomats and consular officials living in the territory of the receiving state, the immunity of heads of state and senior officials applies while they remain in post *erga omnes* at all times, wherever they may be located.[39] The position of former heads of state and senior officials was addressed in the *Pinochet* litigation and relates more directly to state immunity and will be addressed as such in the following sections.

6.4 IMMUNITY OF THE STATE

Historically there was no comparable juridical foundation for the immunity of the state as was apparent in relation to diplomatic and consular agents, nor even to the more limited and controversial justification for the immunity of the sovereign. The case of *The Schooner Exchange v McFaddon*,[40] which is often held up as the starting point for the development of the concept of sovereign (or state) immunity, evidences this lack of juridical foundation rather well.

The circumstances of *The Schooner Exchange* are well known and will not be further rehearsed here. Suffice to say that the vessel in question had belonged to two private citizens of the United States and was seized on the high seas by French forces and later refitted as a French warship. When the vessel was forced to put into an American port during a storm, the vessel was seized, arrested and detained in pursuance of an action raised by the libellants, including Mr McFaddon. On 4 October 1811, a District judge dismissed the libel, with costs, on the ground that 'a public armed vessel of a foreign sovereign, in amity with our government, is not subject to the ordinary judicial tribunals of the country, so far as regards the question of title, by which such sovereign claims to hold the vessel'. The Circuit Court reversed this decision on 28 October 1811, although the basis of this reversal is not clear. The matter was appealed by the District Attorney to the United States Supreme Court.

Before the Supreme Court, Mr Dallas noted that the vessel had arrived in the United States in distress and that no agreement to submit to the

---

[38] Immunities from Jurisdiction and Execution of Heads of State and of Government in International Law, Preamble, para. 3, reproduced in (2000–01) 69 *Institute of International Law YB* 743.

[39] Watts, n. 37 above, 53.

[40] 11 U.S. 116 (1812).

jurisdiction of the United States could be presumed. Furthermore, there was, according to Dallas, 'no implied waiver of the peculiar immunities of a public vessel'.[41] Dallas was also concerned that to allow one individual to raise a claim against a sovereign state would cause considerable difficulty in the future: 'The peace of our ports and harbours would be at the mercy of the individuals. It would be impossible to carry it into practice. The sentence of the Court could not be executed. It is beautiful in theory to exclaim '*fiat justicia – ruat coelum*' but justice is to be administered with a due regard to the law of nations and to the rights of other sovereigns'.[42] Dallas accepted that the private acts of a sovereign in a foreign state fell within the jurisdiction of the courts of that state and noted specifically that 'if a sovereign descend from the throne and becomes a merchant, he submits to the laws of the country. If he contracts private debts, his private funds are liable … the distinction is between his private acts, and his acts as sovereign, and between his private and public property'. Ultimately, Dallas accepted that the vessel had been seized by France but that this had been done by virtue of the sovereign prerogative. According to Dallas, 'whenever the act is done by a sovereign in his sovereign character, it becomes a matter of negotiation, or of reprisals, or of war, according to its importance'.[43] In other words, the exercise of the sovereign prerogative caused the matter to become a dispute between sovereign states and no longer a dispute between individual citizens of the United States and the government of France. As a result, Dallas argued, the seizure of the vessel and its subsequent operation by a French naval officer, could not come within the jurisdiction of the United States.[44]

On behalf of the libellants it was argued that the possibility of a flood of claims against states was 'remote and improbable' given that they would have to be supported by sufficient evidence. More importantly, the libellants saw significant dangers in not allowing their claim to proceed. In words that have echoed down the two centuries since they were

---

41 *Ibid.*

42 *Ibid.*

43 *Ibid.* 122.

44 'There is … no municipal law, nor any practical construction by the executive, the legislative or the judicial department of our government, which authorizes the jurisdiction now claimed; we can only have recourse to the law of nations to try the validity of that claim. The law requires the consent of the sovereign, whether express or implied, before it can be subject to foreign jurisdiction. There is no express assent of a foreign sovereign to the jurisdiction over his prerogative.'

uttered, the libellants called upon the Supreme Court to 'consider the inconveniences on the other side. Your own citizens plundered. Your national rights violated. Your courts deaf to the complaints of the injured. Your government not redressing their wrongs but giving sanction to their spoliators'.[45] Ultimately, the libellants argued forcibly for the territorial operation of the law. Citing Vattel, the libellants argued that anything within a country was exclusively within the authority of the territorial sovereign and his courts. While acknowledging some limited exceptions to this principle in the case of the person of the sovereign as well as ambassadorial immunity and the immunity of armed forces, they failed to see an established exception in the case of sovereign property. Thus, they asserted that: 'The exemption of the sovereign himself, his ambassador and his armies, depends upon particular reasons which do not apply to his property, nor to his ships of war'.[46]

The judgment of the court was delivered by Chief Justice Marshall. Marshall's starting point was that 'the jurisdiction of a nation within its own territory is necessarily exclusive and absolute. It is susceptible of no limitation not imposed by itself ... all exceptions, therefore, to the full and complete power of a nation within its own territories, must be traced up to the consent of the nation itself'.[47] On the other hand, according to Marshall, with respect to the relations between sovereign states, the world was 'composed of distinct sovereignties, possessing equal rights and equal independence, whose mutual benefit is promoted by intercourse with each other, and by an interchange of those good offices which humanity dictates and its wants require, all sovereigns have consented to a relaxation, in practice, in cases under certain peculiar circumstances, of that absolute and complete jurisdiction within their respective territories which sovereignty confers'. Marshall continued:

> This full and absolute territorial jurisdiction being alike the attribute of every sovereign and being incapable of conferring extra-territorial power, would not seem to contemplate foreign sovereigns nor their sovereign rights as its objects. One sovereign being in no respect amenable to another; and being bound by obligations of the highest character not to degrade the dignity of his nation by placing himself, or its sovereign rights within the jurisdiction of another, can be supposed to enter a foreign territory only under an express licence, or in the confidence that the immunities belonging to his independent

---

45 *Ibid.* 128.
46 *Ibid.*
47 *Ibid.* 136.

> sovereign station, thought not expressly stipulated, are reserved by implication, and will be extended to him.[48]

For Marshall, the existence of these exceptions to jurisdiction were caused by the implied waiver by the territorial sovereign of his complete and exclusive territorial jurisdiction and applied in three specific cases. The first of these is 'the exemption of the person of the sovereign from arrest or detention within a foreign territory'.[49] In explaining the reason for the exemption, Marshall referred directly to the fact that 'a foreign sovereign is not understood as intending to subject himself to a jurisdiction incompatible with his dignity, and the dignity of his nation'. As well as suggesting complete immunity from jurisdiction, this passage asserts the essence of the immunity of the sovereign as being the concept of dignity.

The second exception to complete and absolute territorial jurisdiction 'standing on the same principles as the first' is, according to Marshall, 'the immunity, which all civilized nations allow to foreign ministers'. Here the assertion is of immunity from jurisdiction as well as inviolability. Marshall is unclear as to the rationale for the immunity of Foreign Ministers which derive either from his representative character or from the fiction of extra-territoriality, although he asserts that it is something to which sovereigns have consented. This consent is again closely linked to the dignity of the sending sovereign: 'The assent of the sovereign to the very important and extensive exemptions from territorial jurisdiction which are admitted to attach to foreign ministers, is implied from the considerations that, without such exemption, every sovereign would hazard his own dignity by employing a public minister abroad'.[50]

A third exception applied in the case of the troops of a foreign prince whom a sovereign will allow to pass through his dominions. In such cases, according to Marshall, the free passage of an army would be defeated if the sending sovereign did not retain its exclusive command: 'The grant of a free passage therefore implies a waiver of all jurisdiction over the foreign troops during their passage and permits the foreign general to use that discipline, and to inflict those punishments which the government of his army may require'.[51] According to Marshall, this

---

48 *Ibid.* 137.
49 *Ibid.* 137.
50 *Ibid.* 138–9.
51 *Ibid.* 140.

exemption would apply equally to public warships insofar as it 'constitutes a part of the military force of her nation'.[52] Marshall continued:

> [The sovereign] has many and powerful motives for preventing those objects from being defeated by the interference of a foreign state. Such interference cannot take place without affecting his power and his dignity. The implied license therefore under which such vessel enters a friendly port, may reasonably be construed, and it seems to the Court ought to be construed, as containing an exemption from the jurisdiction of the sovereign within whose territory she claims the rites of hospitality.[53]

Marshall did not seek to draw a clear distinction between the private and public acts of a sovereign, although he did accept that 'a prince, by acquiring private property in a foreign country, may possibly be considered as subjecting that property to the territorial jurisdiction; he may be considered as so far laying down the prince, and assuming the character of a private individual'. More important for Marshall, was the character of the vessel in question as a public warship and it was that character which, by analogy with the immunity of foreign armed forces, secured the exemption of the vessel from the jurisdiction of the United States in the case in question.

A careful analysis of *The Schooner Exchange* highlights the limitations of the case as a precedent for anything other than the immunity of a public warship from the jurisdiction of a foreign court. Nevertheless, Marshall's dictum has come to be regarded by many as the starting point for state immunity generally. It is certainly the case that the decision was cited with approval in many subsequent cases, particularly in common law jurisdictions, leading to the establishment of the so-called absolute theory of state immunity.[54] In the US case of *Berizzi Brothers Co. v Steamship Pesaro*,[55] the US Supreme Court argued that:

> When, for the purpose of advancing the trade of its people or providing revenue for its treasury, a government acquires, mans and operates ships in the carrying on of trade, they are public ships in the same sense that warships are. We know of no international usage which requires the maintenance and advancement of the economic welfare of a people in time of peace as any less a public purpose than the maintenance and training of a naval force.

---

[52] *Ibid.* 144.

[53] *Ibid.* 144.

[54] In the United Kingdom see, for example, *The Parlement Belge* [1880] 5 PD 197; *The Porto Alexandre* [1920] P 30; and *Cheung (Chung Chi) v R* [1939] AC 160.

[55] 271 U.S. 562 (1926).

The effect of such a statement is effectively to ensure that any act by a government can be considered as public and so entitled to attract immunity. This was not a foundation on which the theory of absolute state immunity could easily rest and the development of the restrictive doctrine of state immunity depended not on an abandonment of this distinction but, rather, on a gradual reassessment of the all-encompassing notion that any act carried out by a government constituted a public act.

The false juridical foundations of state immunity were identified and deconstructed by Sir Hersch Lauterpacht, in a seminal article published in 1951.[56] Drawing to some extent on the dictum of Chief Justice Marshall in *The Schooner Exchange,* Lauterpacht noted that the doctrine of state immunity was apparently built upon the concepts of independence, equality, sovereignty and dignity. However, he convincingly argued that these concepts do not provide an adequate basis, individually or together, for the maintenance of state immunity. In relation to independence and equality, he argued that:

> It is not easy to see why the principles of independence and equality should preclude the courts of a state from exercising jurisdiction over another state and its property so long as the state exercising jurisdiction merely applies its ordinary law, including its rules of private international law, and so long as it applies it in an unobjectionable manner not open to the reproach of denial of justice or of the disregard of the legislative and administrative sovereignty of the foreign state.[57]

In relation to the concept of sovereignty, he noted that:

> No legitimate claim of sovereignty is violated if the courts of a state assume jurisdiction over a foreign state with regard to contracts concluded or torts committed in the territory of the state assuming jurisdiction. On the contrary, the sovereignty, the independence and the equality of the latter are denied if the foreign state claims as a matter of right – as a matter of international law – to be above the law of the state within the territory of which it has engaged in legal transactions or committed acts entailing legal consequences according to the law of that state.[58]

Lauterpacht reserved his greatest criticism for the concept of dignity, which he described as an anarchic survival that would not be derogated from by subjecting the state to the normal operations of the law with

---

[56] Sir Hersch Lauterpacht, 'The Problem of Jurisdictional Immunities of Foreign States' 28 *British Yearbook of International Law 220 (1951) 220.*

[57] *Ibid*, 229.

[58] *Ibid*, 229.

regard to contracts it has concluded or torts it has committed. He considered that 'the dignity of foreign states is no more impaired by their being subjected to the law, impartially applied, of a foreign country than it is by submission to their own law'.[59]

It is worth noting further that Lauterpacht did not see any benefit in the development of the distinction between acts *jure gestionis* and acts *jure imperii*, declaring that 'it is doubtful whether that distinction can accurately or profitably be accepted as the basis of future law'.[60] Nevertheless, he did accept that it was possible and desirable to salvage from it that element which appears to be sound and practical. As a result of his analysis, Lauterpacht proposed the abandonment of the doctrine of state immunity, subject to specified safeguards and exceptions. One of these, it should be noted, was that immunity should remain 'in respect of executive and administrative acts of the foreign state within its territory'. He continued: 'no action should lie with regard to torts committed by foreign states and their organs in their own territory. This must be left either to judicial remedies within that foreign state or to appropriate diplomatic action in accordance with the accepted practice of diplomatic protection of citizens abroad'.

Lauterpacht's analysis foreshadowed and likely influenced the development of the restrictive theory of state immunity, at least in the United Kingdom. In the United States, the so-called Tate Letter of 19 May 1952[61] signalled a shift in US policy away from absolute state immunity to the restrictive theory which disallowed state immunity for commercial acts. In the United Kingdom, it took until the mid-1970s for the restrictive theory finally to crystallize, mainly as the result of a judicial onslaught against absolute state immunity, led primarily by Lord Denning.[62] Finally, through a series of cases, beginning in 1976, the United Kingdom finally adopted the restrictive theory of state immunity. The importance of these developments for the purposes of this chapter is not to rehearse again the development of the restrictive theory *per se*, but, rather, to emphasize that there is no inherent conceptual reason why state immunity should not be challenged and, where appropriate, set aside. This should be contrasted, it is submitted, with the position regarding

---

59 *Ibid*, 231.

60 *Ibid*, 227.

61 26 State Dept. Bull. 984 (1952), (1953) 47 AJIL 93.

62 See, for example, *Rahimtoola v Nizam of Hyderabad* [1958] AC 379; *Thai-Europe Tapioca Service Ltd v Government of Pakistan, Directorate of Agricultural Supplies* [1975] 1 WLR 1485; *The Philippine Admiral* [1977] AC 373; *Trendtex Trading Corp. v Central Bank of Nigeria* [1977] QB 529.

diplomatic and other forms of personal immunity explored above which, while sharing common foundations with state immunity, are conceptually very different.

The academics and practitioners who sought, successfully, to challenge the absolute theory of state immunity in the middle of the twentieth century did so, at both an international and domestic level, by arguing that the customary international law of state immunity had changed to reflect a more restrictive approach.[63] This understanding of the state of customary international law on the question of state immunity was supported by the European Convention on State Immunity 1972, and the statutory reform, particularly in Anglo-American jurisdictions, where adherence to the absolute rule had been most strict.[64] The effect of this process of solidifying customary international law around the restrictive theory, however, was to freeze the restrictive theory at a particular stage in time and in relation to an understanding of the restrictive theory that was enmeshed in the vagaries of Cold War politics. This was made particularly problematic by the methodology of the relevant instruments, which was to crystallize the concept of state immunity, subject to a very limited number of exceptions, most of which related to commercial matters, reflecting the contemporary understanding of the restrictive theory of state immunity.

That same limited analysis of the restrictive theory of state immunity has now itself been codified in the 2004 United Nations Convention on the Jurisdictional Immunities of States and Their Property. The Convention adopts the methodology of confirming state immunity subject to a few specific exceptions. During the negotiation of the Convention, some states and a number of human rights organizations pressed for the inclusion in the Convention of an exception for serious human rights abuses, or at the very least, the addition of an Optional Protocol permitting the removal of state immunity in relation to such activities. Not only was this rejected but certain states argued for a restriction on the restrictive theory advocating a return to absolute immunity. It is not because of the concern for the granting of immunity in the case of human

---

[63] This was perhaps most apparent in the dictum of Lord Denning in *Trendtex* in which he opined that: 'If this court today is satisfied that the rule of international law on a subject has changed from what it was 50 or 60 years ago, it can give effect to that change – and apply the change in our English law – without waiting for the House of Lords to do it'. *Ibid.* 554.

[64] Reference may be made specifically to the Foreign Sovereign Immunities Act 1976 in the United States and to the State Immunity Act 1978 in the United Kingdom.

rights abuses that adherence to the Convention is low. It is rather because, in the view of many states, the Convention allows for the removal of immunity in too many cases.

So it is left to individuals and organizations to continue to challenge the law of state immunity in domestic, regional and international courts. Some such challenges have had limited success. General Augusto Pinochet, for example, was found not to have immunity from the criminal jurisdiction for acts of torture committed in Chile during his dictatorship, but this was a case of head of state immunity as opposed to state immunity, and was dependent on his being a former head of state and on the fact that torture committed abroad had been specifically criminalized in English law as an 'official' crime, thereby removing any coexistent immunity.

For the most part, such challenges have, ultimately, been unsuccessful. What can be gleaned from the jurisprudence is that state immunity in many states is limited only by the specific exceptions developed in the 1970s and codified in the relevant legislation. Furthermore, state immunity pursues a legitimate international purpose and is not a breach of the right to a fair trial in the context of Article 6 of the European Convention on Human Rights, although it may breach European Union law. State immunity is not trumped in the situation of an alleged breach of a *jus cogens* norm, primarily on the grounds that state immunity is a procedural question that must be addressed before consideration can be given to the substantive issues. Finally, state immunity is a principle that is closely guarded by states and state officials. The impact of the development of the restrictive theory of state immunity, the codification of the concept in the 2004 Convention and the effect of recent high-level decisions of international courts, has been to solidify the principle in both domestic and international law.

That having been said and bearing in mind this author's earlier assertion that there is no juridical foundation to state immunity and no inherent reason why state immunity cannot be further restricted, if not entirely done away with, the question is raised as to how this might be done. Conceptual challenges will continue, for example, along the lines of the challenging Dissenting Opinion of Judge Cinçado Trindade in the *Jurisdictional Immunities of the State* case before the ICJ. Challenges to state immunity will also continue to occur in domestic courts. However, it is asserted here that what is required is a significant policy change by governments and work should be undertaken to facilitate direct changes in the law, both domestic and international.

6.5 SHARED FOUNDATIONS AND CONCEPTUAL DIFFERENTIATION: CONCLUSIONS

The purpose of the chapter has been, in part, to provide an overview of the historical development of, and conceptual framework for, immunities from jurisdiction as a general category of public international law. The aim has been to facilitate better understanding of the application and importance of the different types of immunity from jurisdiction.

In addition the chapter has sought to highlight the conceptual differentiation between various different types of immunity, particularly the personal immunity of diplomats, consuls and high-ranking state officials, the restriction of which, it has been argued, should be approached carefully and cautiously. The justification of, and conceptual framework for, state immunity, on the other hand, is more brittle, although, perhaps ironically, the legal doctrine supporting the concept is arguably stronger than in relation to personal immunity. It is possible robustly to challenge the concept of state immunity. It has been suggested that the best way to do that is to focus on challenging states to change their policy focus, rather than directly to challenge the established legal doctrine that supports state immunity.

7. Immunity from the criminal jurisdiction of national courts

*Elizabeth Helen Franey**

7.1 INTRODUCTION

International law recognizes that state immunity confers, upon certain individuals, immunity from the criminal jurisdiction of the domestic courts of states of which they are not nationals. Immunity from criminal jurisdiction means that a person cannot be prosecuted, cannot be summonsed and cannot be required to answer questions. Such a person, who is immune from criminal jurisdiction, is also inviolable, which means s/he cannot be arrested and a warrant cannot be issued for his/her arrest. There are two types of immunity from criminal jurisdiction of other states, immunity *ratione personae*, immunity conferred because of the position a person holds in a state; and immunity *ratione materiae*, immunity conferred because of conduct undertaken on behalf of a state.

State immunity is an aspect of the sovereignty of a state. It protects the rights and interests of the state. It belongs to the state, not the individual. A state entitled to immunity may waive the immunity of an individual and say that immunity will not apply. Such immunity is only accorded to officials who represent a sovereign state, not a constituent part of a state.[1]

State immunity from the criminal jurisdiction of foreign states is a matter of customary international law which is created largely by the consent of states. Customary international law is described as 'international custom, as evidence of a general practice accepted as law'.[2] This means that 'State practice, including that of States whose interests are specially affected, should be both extensive and virtually uniform', which

* This chapter is based on the author's thesis, and book, *Immunity, Individuals and International Law: Which Individuals are Immune from the Jurisdiction of National Courts under International Law?* (LAP Lambert Academic Publishing, 2011), available at theses.lse.sc.uk/309/1/Franey.

[1] See, for example, *R (on the application of Diepreye Solomon Peter Alamieyeseigha) v Crown Prosecution Service* [2005] EWHC 2740 (Admin), (2005) 145 ILR 619.

[2] Statute of the International Court of Justice, Art. 38(b).

practice has 'occurred in such a way as to show a general recognition that a rule of law or obligation is involved'[3] (this is known as *opinio juris*). In other words, the relevant questions are: How were the actions carried out? Does the practice of states show that the actions are considered to be legally binding? Is there a general consensus that the practice is a matter of law? Custom therefore is deduced from the practice and behaviour of states and state agents. It is an area of law which responds as states react to changes in international society. All states may take part in its formulation. If a state is not directly affected it may still take part in the formulation of the law, or try to change the law, by stating whether it agrees that a certain practice is lawful or not.

Customary international law is part of the common law of England and Wales and does not have to be incorporated by an Act of Parliament. English law accepts that customary international law changes as time changes.[4]

State immunity is upheld by both national courts and international tribunals. In 1999, when Spain requested the extradition of Senator Pinochet, the former head of state of Chile, for offences including torture, the House of Lords in *Pinochet (No. 3)*[5] confirmed that a serving head of state cannot be subjected to the criminal process of a foreign state for any purpose and could not be extradited for any offences and held that Senator Pinochet had continuing immunity for offences of murder and conspiracy to murder. In 2003, the International Court of Justice (ICJ) in the *Arrest Warrant* case[6] in considering the issue of a warrant of arrest for the incumbent Foreign Minister of the Democratic Republic of Congo for offences constituting grave breaches of the Geneva Conventions and crimes against humanity said that the immunity which protects high state officials, heads of state and heads of government, also extends to Foreign Ministers.

The International Law Commission (ILC) included the topic of immunity of state officials from foreign criminal jurisdiction in its

---

3 *North Sea Continental Shelf Cases* [1969] ICJ Rep. 3, para. 74.

4 *Re Piracy Jure Gentium* [1934] AC 586, per Lord Sankey LC at 592: 'International law was not crystallised in the seventeenth century, but is a living and expanding code'; *Trendtex Trading Corp. v Central Bank of Nigeria* [1977] QB 529, per Lord Denning at 554H: 'International Law knows no rule of stare decisis'.

5 *R v Bow Street Metropolitan Stipendiary Magistrate and others, ex parte Pinochet Ugarte (No. 3)* [2000] 1 AC 147.

6 *Case concerning the Arrest Warrant of 11 April 2000 (Democratic Republic of Congo v Belgium)* (2002) 128 ILR 1, ICJ, 14 February 2002.

programme of work in 2006 and in 2007 appointed Mr Roman A. Kolodkin as Special Rapporteur, who was replaced by Ms Concepcion Escobar Hernandez in 2012. In 2011, the General Assembly of the United Nations requested the ILC to give priority to this topic.[7] In 2013, the Drafting Committee of the ILC adopted three Draft Articles pertaining to the immunity of state officials from the criminal jurisdiction of another state.[8]

Immunity is an exception to a state's jurisdiction,[9] it is not a defence to a criminal charge. Immunity from criminal jurisdiction and individual responsibility are separate concepts. Jurisdictional immunity is procedural in nature, whereas criminal responsibility is a question of substantive law. Jurisdictional immunity may bar prosecution for a certain period or for certain offences but it does not exonerate the person to whom it applies from all criminal responsibility.[10]

Immunity from criminal prosecution exists and is a matter of importance to the international community but the extent of the protection afforded to individuals by immunity from criminal jurisdiction is not entirely clear.

7.2 WHY DOES STATE IMMUNITY EXTEND TO CRIMINAL JURISDICTION?

A state can be liable under civil law, but it cannot be prosecuted,[11] whereas criminal liability is the liability of an individual for his own unlawful actions. Why should anyone not be criminally responsible? What is the justification for immunity from prosecution? Immunity is criticized for promoting impunity and allowing a class of persons to be unaccountable for their actions,[12] so why do states uphold the concept? It

---

7 GAR 66/98 of 9 December 2011, para. 8.

8 A/cn.4/L.814,

9 *Arrest Warrant*, n. 6 above, para. 59.

10 *Ibid.*para. 60.

11 Robert Jennings and Arthur Watts (eds), 'Introduction' in *Oppenheim's International Law*, vol. 1, Peace (9th edn, 1992), Part 1 (pp. 533–4) provides that a state may bear criminal responsibility for egregious violations of international law and refers to (1976) 2 *ILC YB* 361. There is at present no international convention agreeing that states should be prosecuted for crimes. There is no law in England which provides a procedure whereby a state may be prosecuted.

12 Redress Trust, *Immunity v Accountability* (December 2005), available at www.redress.org/publications/StateImmunity.pdf. The Preamble to the Rome Statute for the International Criminal Court states that the states parties are

is only when the rationale for state immunity is clear, and its purpose understood, that intelligible arguments can be made regarding the extent of immunity.

The foundation for the principle is to be found in the concept of monarchy, and the idea of the sovereign. Historically, the head of state, usually a monarch, and the state were seen as synonymous; and the immunity of the state was that of the monarch;[13] the sovereign was the embodiment of the state.[14] As such he was above the law, as he was the person from whom the law emanated; his dignity was that of the state; an affront to the state was also an affront to the sovereign, and likewise an action which offended a sovereign caused offence to the state.[15] Such a head of state has always been immune from the jurisdiction of the domestic courts of other states.[16]

The judgment in *The Schooner Exchange v McFaddon*[17] in 1812 discusses the relationship between sovereigns, and their envoys, the predecessors of present day diplomats. It was held in this case (which is still cited) that:[18]

> One sovereign being in no respect amenable to another, and being bound by obligations of the highest character not to degrade the dignity of his nation, by placing himself or its sovereign rights within the jurisdiction of another, can be supposed to enter a foreign territory only under an express licence, or in the confidence that the immunities belonging to his independent sovereign station, though not expressly stipulated, are reserved by implication, and will

---

determined to put an end to impunity for the perpetrators of atrocities and thus contribute to the prevention of such crimes.

13 See Sir Arthur Watts, 'The Legal Position in International Law of Heads of State, Heads of Government and Foreign Ministers' (1994) 247 *Receuil des Cours de l'Academie de droit international de la Haye* 9, Part IV 'Protection, Privileges and Immunities', (1) General, where he discusses the relationship between a sovereign and his state. He says 'In many respects the state could almost be seen as the property of the ruler, and it was to a considerable degree the ruler's personal attributes of sovereignty which gave his state the quality of being a sovereign state, rather than the other way round'.

14 W.B. Lawrence (ed.), *Wheaton's Elements of International Law* (6th edn, 1855), p. 35: 'Wherever, indeed, the absolute or unlimited monarchical form of government prevails in any state, the person of the prince is necessarily identified with the state itself'.

15 Watts, n. 13 above, 35.

16 See Watts, n. 13 above, 54.

17 7 Cranch 116 (1812), US Supreme Court.

18 Lord Millett in *Pinochet (No. 3)*, n. 5 above, 271 described this as a seminal judgment. It is quoted in *Aziz v Aziz and others* [2007] EWCA Civ 712.

> be extended to him. This perfect equality and absolute independence of sovereigns, and this common interest impelling them to mutual intercourse, and an interchange of good offices with each other, have given rise to a class of cases in which every sovereign is understood to waive the exercise of a part of that complete exclusive territorial jurisdiction, which has been stated to be the attribute of every nation.

Sovereigns had absolute jurisdiction over their territory, and needed to interact with each other for the purposes of trade, and to resolve disputes. Such interaction requires different rules; as sovereigns have to show respect for each other in their international dealings.

The concept of equal sovereigns, who have dignity[19] and must be treated with respect, has continued to the present, but with the emphasis upon dignity as an aspect of the sovereignty of the state rather than an attribute of monarchy.[20]

All states are equal in international law, they are equal members of the international community, and consequently no state can claim jurisdiction over another state. This is expressed in the rule, *par in parem non habet imperium*, an equal has no authority over an equal; that is, one sovereign state is not subject to the jurisdiction of another state. This is one of the basic principles of modern international law under which all states are considered equal.[21] Even though states are different they have equal rights and duties and are equal members of the international community. Sovereign equality includes the principle that one state shall not interfere with the internal matters of another state.[22]

Heads of state are granted special status and treatment, including immunity *ratione personae* because they represent the persona of independent equal sovereign states. The head of government is also granted immunity *ratione personae*, but this is not because he is a sovereign. He is representing a sovereign state which is the equal of other sovereign states.

The Foreign Minister is also granted immunity *ratione personae*. This immunity is granted not for personal benefit but to ensure the effective

---

19 *Case concerning Certain Questions of Mutual Assistance in Criminal Matters (Djibouti v France)* (2008) 148 ILR 1, ICJ.

20 In *Aziz v Aziz*, n. 18 above, the publication of details of the personal life of the Sultan of Brunei was not an attack on his state's dignity.

21 United Nations Charter, Art. 2.1 and further elaborated in the Declaration on Principles of International Law concerning Friendly Relations and Co-operation among States in accordance with the United Nations, GA Res. 2625 (XXV) (1970).

22 United Nations Charter, Art. 2.

performance of functions on behalf of the state. In 2002, the ICJ in the *Arrest Warrant* case[23] decided that the immunity *ratione personae* accorded to a serving Minister for Foreign Affairs had to be determined on the basis of the functional justification for immunity. The court considered the role of the Foreign Minister: that he is in charge of the government's diplomatic activities and generally acts as its representative; ambassadors and other diplomatic agents carry out their duties under his/her authority; and he/she has full powers to act on behalf of the state[24] and that needed to be able to travel and communicate freely to be able to fulfil his/her role.

The court justified the immunity conferred upon the Foreign Minister by reference to his position, not just to ensure he could perform his functions. The immunity is justified by the special status of a Foreign Minister in international society, which is acknowledged in international law, and the power the Foreign Minister has. It is conferred to protect the Foreign Minister from the actions of other states, to enable him to perform his functions as one of the pre-eminent members of his state. It is about the power of a state and who represents that power; and the decision of the court was that a Foreign Minister is completely immune and inviolable from the criminal jurisdiction of other states.

This functional justification for immunity is that it enables officials to perform their duties. But this justification does not make sense when an official has left office as there are no functions to perform. In any event, how can it be the function of an official, whether or not he is entitled to immunity, to commit crimes?

Immunity *ratione materiae* prevents the immunity of a state being circumvented by taking action against the state's agents or officials. This principle has been articulated and developed in civil cases. Originally it was customary international law that a state could not be sued in the domestic courts of a foreign state. During the twentieth century states became involved in trade, entered into contracts and state officials began to use motor vehicles. Customary international law developed in response to these changes. State immunity changed and allowed a state to be sued in contract and tort for acts which a private individual could perform; that is for *acta jure gestionis*, acts of a private nature, whereas *acta jure imperii*, acts which are of a governmental or sovereign nature, continue to be immune. This is called the restrictive doctrine. These restrictions upon immunity for commercial matters, and for some torts, are now part

---

23 *Arrest Warrant*, n. 6 above, para. 54.

24 Vienna Convention on the Law of Treaties 1969, Art. 7(2)(a).

of conventional[25] and customary international law and have been incorporated into the law of the United Kingdom[26] and other states.[27] These are expressed in the form that states are immune, except as provided.

The principle that state agents cannot be sued if the state itself cannot be sued continues to apply to *acta jure imperii*. It is perceived to be unfair, and there have been a number of attempts to overturn the principle in order to sue individuals, but it has been consistently upheld in a number of jurisdictions in recent years, even for the most serious of allegations.[28] Neither a state nor state officials can be held civilly liable before the courts of foreign states, even for very serious criminal offences such as kidnapping and perverting the course of justice, or for breaches of peremptory norms such as torture, if such conduct is *acta jure imperii*. The state is immune, and that immunity cannot be circumvented by pursuing the state officials. The official is immune only if the state is immune, and this rationale means that the immunity continues to apply to officials after they have left office.

The reason given for this immunity is that the conduct itself carries the immunity, and the officials are not individually responsible for what they do. They are the agents or servants of the state and do what their state requires of them. They do their duty, and are therefore not responsible. The state is responsible, and to make the official responsible when the state is immune would be to circumvent that immunity. Conversely, it is the duty of the state to protect its officials who are acting in the interests of the state. This model of the responsibility of state officials portrays the state as an entity which is bigger than the individuals who make it up. On the international plane the state is responsible, but individuals are not.

This justification does not fit easily in relation to criminal proceedings, as criminal conduct is committed by individuals, and criminal responsibility is that of the individual who committed the criminal conduct. To

---

25 European Convention on State Immunity 1972.

26 State Immunity Act 1978 (UK).

27 Foreign States Immunity Act 1976 (US) (1976) ILM 15 1388; State Immunity Act 1982 (Canada) (1982) ILM 21 798; Foreign States Immunities Act 1985 (Australia) (1986) ILM 25 715.

28 *Church of Scientology* case (1978) 65 ILR 193 (Germany); *Herbage v Meese and others* [1990] ILR 101 (US); *Jaffe v Miller and others* [1994] ILR 556 (Canada); *Al-Adsani v Government of Kuwait and others* (1996) 107 ILR 536 (UK) and (2001) 34 EHRR 273 (ECHR); *Propend Finance Pty and others v Sing and others*, CA (Civ. Div.), 17 April 1997, *The Times*, 2 May 1997 (Transcript: Smith Bernal) (UK); *Jones v Ministry of the Interior England* [2005] QB 699, 129 ILR 629, HL (UK).

say that the conduct was committed in the exercise of duty would be mitigation, not a defence, in criminal courts.

In civil cases there can be only one liability, and one entitlement for compensation, and therefore if the state is immune, the responsible officials must also be immune. The same is not true of criminal proceedings. The fact that a state is civilly responsible does not relieve an individual of criminal responsibility, which has been recognized in international law since the affirmation of the Nuremberg Principles by the UN General Assembly in 1946.[29]

The justification for the continuing immunity is that to prosecute the functionary would be to question the conduct of the state, and thereby circumvent the sovereign immunity of a state. The immunity of the state would be illusory if an individual could be held responsible when a state cannot. This makes sense in civil proceedings as any liability would be that of the state. But criminal proceedings are different, a state cannot be prosecuted, and individuals are responsible for their own criminal conduct; that is why an act is classed as criminal. A state in proscribing certain conduct as criminal is stating that an individual is to be punished for such actions.[30]

Immunity is one of the mechanisms used by modern sovereign states to facilitate friendly relations between states, and to prevent disputes. States need to work together, and to do so they need to work through people such as ministers and diplomats. Such persons would be hampered in their functions if they could not feel safe in a foreign jurisdiction, or whilst travelling. Modern sovereign states are independent and equal. Their internal arrangements are not to be scrutinized by other states, and their policy and public administration are not subject to interference from foreign courts. The concept of the dignity of a state and of its agents is one of the ways in which states maintain appropriate standards in their dealings with each other. International law requires that

---

[29] GAR 95(I).

[30] In *Khurts Bat v Investigating Judge of the German Federal Court* [2011] EWHC 2029 (Admin), (2011) 147 ILR 633, Lord Justice Moses approves this distinction stating (at para. 74) 'As Dr Elizabeth Franey points out in *Immunity, Individuals and International Law* (LAP, Lambert, 2011) p. 204, there is an essential distinction between civil and criminal liability. It does not follow that because there is immunity from civil suit, an individual, acting as an official on behalf of his State, is immune from criminal liability'.

states settle their disputes by peaceful means, and to do this requires international mechanisms for the orderly management of disputes.[31]

Judges Higgins, Kooijmans and Buergenthal in their Joint Separate Opinion in the *Arrest Warrant* case made this point stating (at paragraph 75):

> immunities are granted to high State officials to guarantee the proper functioning of the network of mutual inter-State relations, which is of paramount importance for a well-ordered and harmonious international system.[32]

If one state considers that an official act by another state is illegal, that is an international dispute, which should be dealt with on the international plane. The municipal law of one state, which is created by that state, is not competent to adjudicate upon the official decisions of another state, as that state is equal to and independent from the first state. For the courts of one state to decide whether another state's official acts are illegal or not is to introduce international politics into national courts. One function of international law is to manage disputes in an orderly manner, and state immunity assists by removing some disputes from the national to the international plane.

The justifications for immunity *ratione personae* and immunity *ratione materiae* are not identical. A person who is entitled to immunity *ratione personae* is completely immune during the time he is in office. This is to protect his person, as a representative of his state, and to enable him to perform his functions, whilst he is in office. Immunity *ratione personae* protects the state by protecting individual high state officials whilst in office. Immunity *ratione materiae* protects a state by protecting conduct performed on behalf of a state from interference from, and the scrutiny of, another state. Any protection thereby afforded to an individual is incidental. The purpose of immunity *ratione materiae* is to protect a state and state business from interference by other states. It protects state sovereignty and sovereign acts by preventing them being examined and questioned in the courts of other states. The different justifications for the

31 'The object of international law, in this as in other matters, is not to work injustice, not to prevent the enforcement of a just demand, but to substitute negotiations between governments, though they may be dilatory and the issue distant and uncertain, for the ordinary use of courts of justice in cases where such use would lessen the dignity or embarrass the functions of the representatives of a foreign state.' *The Charkieh (No. 1)* (1873) LR 4 A&E 59 at 97.

32 *Arrest Warrant*, n. 6 above, Joint Separate Opinion of Judges Higgins, Kooijmans and Buergenthal.

two kinds of immunity results in the immunity conferred on individuals being different.

7.3 IMMUNITY *RATIONE PERSONAE*

Immunity *ratione personae*, which is also called status immunity, is immunity from the jurisdiction of other states conferred on an individual because of the position the person holds in a state. Immunity *ratione personae* is absolute whilst the person is in office but ends when the office ends. The person entitled to immunity *ratione personae* is completely immune from the jurisdiction of other states, both civil and criminal for actions which are performed in an official capacity, and for those performed in a private capacity, including actions which amount to international crimes, regardless of whether the actions concerned were performed before the person concerned assumed office or when in office.[33]

Immunity *ratione personae* is accorded to those persons holding the highest positions within a state. There are three office holders who are entitled to immunity *ratione personae*: the head of state, the head of government and the Foreign Minister. The immunity of heads of state and heads of government is a long accepted principle of customary international law, but the position of Foreign Ministers was not so certain. Despite the fact that the Foreign Minister is obviously at the heart of diplomatic and international relations, there was doubt about his immunity *ratione personae*, which was resolved by the ICJ in the *Arrest Warrant* case in 2002.[34] The Court held (at paragraph 51 of its judgment): 'the Court would observe at the outset that in international law it is firmly established that … certain holders of high-ranking office in a State, such as the Head of State, Head of Government and Minister for Foreign Affairs, enjoy immunities from jurisdiction in other States, both civil and criminal'. This crystallized customary international law and from this time the immunity *ratione personae* of the Foreign Minister, alongside that of the head of state and head of government, has been clear.

These three office holders hold full powers and need no further accreditation to represent a state for the purposes of adopting or authenticating the text of a treaty.[35] Statements made by these office

---

[33] *Arrest Wa*rrant, n. 6 above, para. 55.

[34] *Ibid.*

[35] See Vienna Convention on the Law of Treaties 1969, Art. 7.

holders, on behalf of their government, are binding upon their state.[36] They are also internationally protected persons;[37] if a crime were committed against any of them it would constitute a threat to the maintenance of normal international relations.

Such persons are completely immune from the jurisdiction of other states and inviolate whilst in office. A warrant should not be issued for the arrest of a high state official even if it is not intended to be executed until he has left office. The warrant should not be issued, rather than withdrawn when immunity is claimed. A state should consider immunity *ratione personae* of its own motion and should not wait for such immunity to be claimed.[38]

This immunity is afforded to an individual as a representative of the state. It is not the title which confers immunity, but the position which is held. A head of state can be either a monarch or a president or may be called by a different title. The head of state may be an individual or a group of people, and may or may not have political power. International law does not prescribe what sort of head a state should have, but howsoever constituted, that entity represents the state itself. To be entitled to immunity as a head of state the person afforded such immunity must be the representative of the sovereignty of the state.[39] The head of state is

---

36 *Case concerning the Legal Status of Eastern Greenland (Denmark v Norway)*, (1933) PCIJ (ser. A/B) N. 53 (April 5). A recorded and minuted declaration made by Mr Ihlen, the Norwegian Foreign Minister, on 22 July 1919 informing the Danish Minister that the Norwegian government would not make any difficulties in the settlement of the recognition of Danish sovereignty over Eastern Greenland was binding upon Norway.

37 Convention on Crimes Against Internationally Protected Persons 1973, Art. 1.

38 *Arrest Warrant*, n. 6 above, para. 60, in which the court stated that the issuance of the warrant was a breach of an international obligation. See also Roman A. Kolodkin, Special Rapporteur, *ILC Third Report on Immunity of State Officials from Foreign Criminal Jurisdiction*, A/CN.4/646 (2011), para. 61(e): 'When a foreign Head of State, Head of Government or minister for foreign affairs is concerned, the State exercising criminal jurisdiction itself must consider the question of the immunity of the person concerned and determine its position regarding its further action within the framework of international law. In this case, it is appropriate perhaps to ask the official's State only about a waiver of immunity. Accordingly, the official's State in this case does not bear the burden of raising the issue of immunity with the authorities of the State exercising criminal jurisdiction'.

39 See *United States v Noriega*, 746 F.Supp. 506 (1990), where the US courts refused to grant Manuel Noriega immunity as head of state on the grounds he had never been constitutional head of Panama; *Re Honecker* (1984) 80 ILR

a state official, but a very special one. He is the prime representative of the state. A head of state holds that position wherever he is, and at all times. As Oppenheim says: 'The highest organ of the state, representing it, within and without its borders, in the totality of its relations, is the Head of State'.[40]

The head of government is the second high state official granted immunity *ratione personae* by virtue of his office. Not all heads of state are also head of government, although some, such as the President of the United States are both head of state and head of government. In the United Kingdom, the Queen is the head of state, and as such she has a constitutional role; and the Prime Minister is the head of government. Other states use other titles for their head of government; again it is the role that matters, not the title. The head of government is completely immune from the jurisdiction of other states and inviolable whilst he is in office.

The third high state official entitled to immunity because of his position is the Foreign Minister. He can act internationally on behalf of his state. He is the head of the Ministry for Foreign Affairs, the department of a state which communicates with other states, and he is in charge of his state's ambassadors and consuls. Under Article 10 of the Vienna Convention on Diplomatic Relations, the Ministry of Foreign Affairs has to be notified of the appointment of members of diplomatic missions, their arrival and departure; and by Article 41.2, unless states agree otherwise, all official diplomatic business is conducted with the Foreign Ministry of the receiving state. The immunity of the Foreign Minister is now an established tenet of customary international law.

The ICJ in the *Arrest Warrant* case (at paragraph 51 of the judgment) said that there is a 'firmly established rule of customary international law that certain holders of high ranking office in a State, such as the head of State, head of government and minister for foreign affairs, enjoy immunities from the jurisdiction of other States, both civil and criminal'. By using the term 'such as', the ICJ was not limiting the high state officials entitled to immunity to those three offices, rather those three offices are quoted as examples of those to whom such immunity is granted.

365, where the courts of the then Federal Republic of Germany (West Germany) held that the Chairman of the Council of State of the German Democratic Republic (East Germany) was entitled to immunity from prosecution; *Re Gaddafi* (2001) 125 ILR 490, in which the French courts granted Colonel Gaddafi, President of the Command Council of the Revolution of Libya, immunity; *Re Robert Mugabe*, Bow Street Magistrates Court, 14 January 2004 (unreported).

[40] Jennings and Watts, *Oppenheim*, n. 11 above, 1033 n. 17.

This could mean that the functions of these three high state officials may be undertaken by other officials or that other ministers of state are entitled to immunity.[41]

In *Khurts Bat v Secretary of State for Foreign Affairs*,[42] the High Court considered whether the Head of the Office of National Security of Mongolia was entitled to immunity *ratione personae*. Lord Justice Moses (at paragraph 59 of the judgment) said that the wording of the ICJ in the *Arrest Warrant* case:

> demonstrates that the paradigm of those entitled to such immunity is a Head of State or Head of Government. The words 'such as', whilst indicating that the list is not limited to those they identify, also carries with it the implication that in order to fall within that narrow circle it must be possible to attach to the individual in question a similar status.

The field of international relations changes, and the numbers of ministers of state and other state officials who are responsible for some aspect of international relations are increasing.[43] But ministers, other than Foreign Ministers, do not play a role which is primarily concerned with foreign affairs. Although some aspects of their responsibility may have an element of international relations, it is not their first concern. They do not represent their state at all times in the international arena. They do not need to travel freely in the way that a Foreign Minister does, as any delegations will be planned in advance with the agreement of the territory visited. A Foreign Minister has to be able to react to international

---

41 A Defence Minister and a Minister of Commerce were afforded immunity by District Judges in Courts of First Instance in 2004 and 2005: *Re Mofaz* (2004) 128 ILR 709 and *Re Bo Xilai* (2005) 129 ILR 713. In 2008, a Central African Republic minister resident in London was not afforded immunity: *Duris v Durbar*, City of Westminster Magistrates Court, 7 November 2008 (unreported).

42 *Khurts Bat*, n. 30 above.

43 In *Case concerning Armed Activities on the Territory of the Congo (Democratic Republic of the Congo v Rwanda)* (2006) 145 ILM 562, ICJ, the Court, in considering whether a statement made by the Rwandan Minster of Justice was binding upon Rwanda, noted that in modern international relations, other persons representing a state, in specific fields, may be authorized by that state to bind it by their statements in respect of matters falling within their purview. The ICJ gave the example of holders of technical ministerial portfolios exercising powers in their field of competence in the area of foreign relations, and then said this was true 'even of certain officials'.

incidents as and when they develop, but this is not the case with other ministers.[44]

In 2013, the ILC adopted Draft Articles on the Immunity of State Officials from Foreign Criminal Jurisdiction. Paragraph 2 of Draft Article 3 relates to persons enjoying immunity *ratione personae*: 'Heads of State, Heads of Government and Ministers for Foreign Affairs enjoy immunity *ratione personae* from the exercise of foreign criminal jurisdiction'. It is respectfully suggested that the adoption of this Draft Article by such an august body crystallizes customary international law on this point. The future conduct of states and the development of customary international law will be influenced by this statement restricting state immunity to the head of state, head of government and Foreign Minister.

7.4 SPECIAL MISSIONS

Being a member of a special mission provides individuals with immunity from foreign jurisdiction as a matter of customary international law. A special mission is temporary mission sent by one state to another state with the consent of the latter state. The Convention on Special Missions was adopted by the General Assembly on 8 December 1969,[45] and it entered into force on 21 June 1985. The United Kingdom signed the Convention on 17 December 1970, and therefore should give effect to it even though it has not ratified it.

The convention is now considered to be declaratory of customary international law having been quoted with approval both in the *Pinochet* case, and in the *Arrest Warrant* case, as providing 'useful guidance on certain aspects of the question of immunities'.[46]

A special mission is sent by one state with consent to another state for the purpose of dealing with the second state on specific questions, or of performing, in relation to that second state, a specific task, and must not

---

[44] In *Case concerning Certain Questions of Mutual Assistance in Criminal Matters (Djibouti v France)*, n. 19 above, the ICJ stated that the Djibouti procureur general and Head of National Security were not immune from the criminal jurisdiction of France and could be summonsed to give evidence as persons implicated in an offence; and on 17 June 2003, the ICJ refused a request for provisional measures in *Case concerning Criminal Proceedings in France (Republic of the Congo v France)* [2003] ICJ Reports 102, where a warrant was issued in France for the arrest of the Inspector General of the Congolese Armed Forces, General Norbert Dabira.

[45] GA Res. 2530 (XXIV).

[46] *Arrest Warrant*, n. 6 above, para. 52.

have the character of a mission responsible for maintaining general diplomatic relations between states.[47] The mission must be of a temporary nature; it cannot be a permanent specialized mission, such as a trade mission.

The prior consent of the receiving state is required regarding all aspects of a special mission.[48] The functions of the mission are determined by mutual consent; the receiving state has to be informed of the size and composition of the special mission, and in particular the names and designations of the persons the sending state intends to appoint. The Foreign Ministry of the receiving state has to be informed of all arrangements made for the mission. The receiving state may decline to accept a special mission of an unreasonable size, and may, without giving reasons, decline to accept any person as a member of the mission, or may notify the sending state that a representative of the mission is *persona non grata*.

The members of a special mission are present on the territory of the receiving state, with the consent of that state, for the purpose of the mission. Whilst they are there, Article 29 of the Convention provides that they are inviolable, and are not liable to any form of arrest or detention, and Article 31 provides that they are immune from the jurisdiction of the receiving state.

Whether a person is a member of a special mission is a fact, and if the proceedings were in England, such facts come within the category that is within the knowledge of the Foreign and Commonwealth Office (FCO), and a certificate[49] can be issued. For examples of cases where such

---

[47] The Draft Articles provide that the term 'special mission' cannot be considered to include missions sent by political movements to establish contact with a particular state, or missions sent by states to establish contact with a political movement. A mission sent by the opposition party to establish contact with the government of another state, or missions sent by a local politician, such as the Mayor of London, would not come within the definition as they are not sent by a state.

[48] See *Tabatabai* (1983) 80 ILR 389 and *Syrian National Immunity* (1998) 127 ILR 88.

[49] The Foreign and Commonwealth Office may issue conclusive certificates or statements of fact which are conclusive evidence in English courts. This practice is accepted at common law. Diplomatic Privileges Act 1964, s. 4, provides that such a certificate is conclusive evidence of any fact relating to whether a person is entitled to any diplomatic privilege or immunity. State Immunity Act 1978, s. 21, provides that such a certificate is conclusive evidence of whether a country is a state, whether any territory is a constituent territory of a federal state, and as to the person or persons to be regarded as head or

certificates have been issued see *R v Governor of Pentonville Prison, ex parte Teja*[50] and *Khurts Bat v Investigating Judge of the German Federal Court.*[51] In the *Khurts Bat* case, the High Court explained that the consequences of the fact that the United Kingdom did not recognize the visit as a special mission is exclusively a matter for the court. Whether or not the UK government chose to consent to Khurts Bat's visit as a special mission was exclusively a matter for the government and not for the court.

7.5 CONTINUING IMMUNITY: IMMUNITY *RATIONE MATERIAE*

Some officials who have immunity *ratione personae* will continue to have immunity *ratione materiae* after they leave office in respect of official conduct. That is, they will have continuing immunity attaching to conduct they performed whilst they held office and were entitled to immunity *ratione personae*.[52] It is also known as subject matter immunity, or immunity for official acts, and is not time limited. Such an immunity probably has to be claimed by the state on behalf of its officials, rather than considered by the state exercising jurisdiction of its own motion.[53]

The ICJ in the *Arrest Warrant* case (in paragraph 61) outlined four situations in which an incumbent or former Foreign Minister would not enjoy immunity, and the third exception was that once the person ceased to hold office a court of a foreign state could prosecute him for acts committed before or after he took office, and for acts committed during

---

government of a state. On 6 October 2011, the Director of Public Prosecution, relying on a certificate that Tzipi Livni, the Israeli opposition leader, was visiting London as part of a special mission, refused to agree to the issue of a warrant for her arrest for alleged war crimes.

[50] [1971] 2 QB 274.

[51] *Khurts Bat*, n. 30 above.

[52] Vienna Convention on Diplomatic Relations 1961, Art. 39.2; Vienna Convention on Consular Relations 1963, Art. 43; Convention on Special Missions 1969, Art. 43.2.

[53] *Case concerning Certain Questions of Mutual Assistance in Criminal Matters (Djibouti v France)*, n. 19 above. See also Kolodkin, n. 38 above: 'The state exercising jurisdiction is not obligated to raise and consider the issue of immunity *proprio motu*'.

his time in office in a private capacity.[54] This is defining the immunity by what it does not include, as opposed to what it does cover. This exclusionary description must mean that the continuing immunity is for actions performed during the time that the office is held, and for actions that are part of his official functions in whatever office is held. Thus a person entitled to immunity *ratione personae* can only be prosecuted for illegal private actions performed when in office, after they have left office.

This is recognized by the ILC Draft Articles on Immunity of State Officials from Foreign Criminal Jurisdiction. Draft Article 4 states that heads of state, heads of government and Ministers for Foreign Affairs enjoy immunity *ratione personae* only during their term of office; such immunity covers all acts performed, whether in a private or official capacity prior to or during their term of office; and the cessation of immunity *ratione personae* is without prejudice to the application of the rules of international law concerning immunity *ratione materiae*.

Does immunity *ratione materiae* also apply to officials of the state who have never been entitled to immunity *ratione personae*? Is an ordinary official immune from prosecution if they commit a crime on official business? If the purpose of immunity *ratione materiae* is to protect the state, then logically it should apply to all state officials carrying out state affairs.

Writers have asserted that state officials have continuing immunity *ratione materiae*. Lady Fox wrote:

> Broadly it would seem that, with the exception of certain international crimes, immunity continues for acts performed in the course of official functions. Criminal proceedings may be brought against the official on vacating office but the position in classical law is to declare such criminal liability of officials to be restricted to private acts and acts committed outside the course of their official functions.[55]

All seven judges in *Pinochet (No. 3)* were agreed that all state officials, even minor officials, have continuing immunity from prosecution, immunity *ratione materiae*, for acts performed in the exercise of their official functions; that is, for *acta jure imperii*. They were agreed that such immunity is enjoyed by state officials for all official conduct, except for Lord Phillips who thought that there was an exception in the case of

---

[54] The other exceptions are that there is no immunity in the minister's own country; there is no immunity if the state which they represent decides to waive that immunity; and there is no immunity before certain international tribunals.

[55] *Law of State Immunity* (2nd edn, 2008), p. 94.

criminal jurisdiction in relation to international crimes, and Lord Millett in relations to crimes in the forum state. The House of Lords did not examine state practice before coming to the conclusion that all state officials, regardless of their status, cannot be prosecuted in a foreign state for their actions if those actions are attributable to the state.

This is not the only case where the assertion that all state officials are immune in respect of official conduct has been accepted. This assertion was also accepted without a full analysis in *Blaškić Subpeona Duces Tecum*[56] before the Appeal Chamber of the International Criminal Tribunal for the former Yugoslavia (ICTY), where that court considered the individual liability of individuals, in the context of whether the Tribunal had the power to issue binding orders to state officials.

The Appeal Chamber (at paragraph 38 of the judgment) dismissed the possibility of the ICTY addressing subpoenas to state officials acting in their official capacity, saying that such officials are mere instruments of a state, and their official position can only be attributed to the state. They cannot be the subject of sanctions, or penalties, for conduct that is not private, but undertaken on behalf of a state. State officials cannot suffer the consequences of wrongful acts which are not attributable to them personally, but rather to the state on whose behalf they act; the Tribunal said such officials enjoy what is called 'functional immunity'. The Appeals Chamber stated that 'This is a well-established rule of customary international law going back to the eighteenth and nineteenth centuries restated many times since'.

The judgment refers, as examples, to the *Governor Collot* case in 1797,[57] the *McLeod* case in 1837,[58] the *Rainbow Warrior* case in 1985[59] and *Eichmann* in 1961.[60]

This author in Chapter 4 of her thesis and book[61] examined these authorities carefully and found that they do not support the assertion that state officials are entitled to immunity *ratione materiae* for criminal

---

[56] *Prosecutor v Tihomir Blaškić*, ICTY Appeals Chamber, Judgment of 29 October 1997 on the request of the Republic of Croatia for review of the decision of the Trial Chamber II of 18 July 1997, available at www.un.org/icty/blaskic/appeal/decision-e/71029JT3.html.

[57] J.B. Moore, *A Digest of International Law* (1906), vol. II, p. 23.

[58] British and Foreign State Papers, vol. 29, p. 1139.

[59] (1985) 74 ILR 241.

[60] *Attorney-General of the Government of Israel v Eichmann* (1961) 36 ILR 5, District Court of Jerusalem.

[61] *Immunity, Individuals and International Law: Which Individuals are Immune from the Jurisdiction of National Courts under International Law?* (LAP Lambert Academic Publishing), available at theses.lse.sc.uk/309/1/Franey.

conduct performed on behalf of a state. The *Governor Collot* case is a very old civil case, and is therefore not on point. *McLeod* concerned an incident in December 1837, when Canada was a British Colony. There was a rebellion and a ship, *The Caroline*, crewed by US citizens, assisted the rebel forces. British forces boarded *The Caroline*, and towed the ship into the river from where it descended Niagara Falls. Two people died, Amos Durfee and a cabin boy, little Billy, who was shot whilst trying to leave the ship. Alexander McLeod, a Canadian Deputy Sheriff, whilst in New York, boasted of taking part in the destruction of *The Caroline*. He was arrested and committed for trial. The British Minister, Mr Fox, wrote to the US Secretary of State, Mr Forsyth, asserting that the United States' national courts did not have jurisdiction to try individuals for involvement in *The Caroline* incident. Mr Forsyth replied that the Federal Executive had no power to intervene with the jurisdiction of the tribunals of the State of New York. In 1841, there was a change of administration in Washington and Mr Fox wrote to Mr Webster, who had replaced Mr Forsyth, demanding the release of Alexander McLeod, stating that:

> when a foreign power has redress to demand for a wrong done to it by any State of the Union, it is to the Federal Government, and not to the separate State, that such power must look for redress of that wrong. And such foreign Power cannot admit the plea that the separate State is an independent body over which the Federal Government has no control.[62]

Mr Webster wrote to the US Attorney-General, sending a copy to Mr Fox, stating:

> That an individual forming part of a public force, and acting under the authority of his Government, is not to be held answerable, as a private trespasser or malefactor, is a principle of public law sanctioned by the usages of all civilized nations, and which the Government of the United States has no inclination to dispute. But whether the process be criminal or civil, the fact of having acted under public authority, and in obedience to the orders of lawful superiors must be regarded as a valid defence; otherwise, individuals would be holden responsible for injuries resulting from the acts of Government, and even from the operations of public war.[63]

The British and US governments were not agreed about what should happen, and had different views on the process. The British position was that McLeod should not be tried, not that he should be acquitted, whereas

---

[62] Note of 12 March 1841, British and Foreign State Papers, vol. 29, p. 1126.

[63] *Ibid.* 1139.

the position of the US government was that he should be released by judicial process. The Supreme Court of New York refused leave to enter the *nolle prosequi*, and rejected an application for a writ of *habeas corpus*. It was proposed that there should be an appeal to the Federal Court, but Alexander McLeod demanded a trial, as he wanted no further delay. At the trial there was no evidence to show that he had been present at the destruction of *The Caroline*, and he was acquitted in October 1841, having been held in custody for almost a year.

The *McLeod*[64] case as an example of state practice is confusing. The US Department of State said one thing, the New York State officials did another, and the national government had no control over the federal officials. It is an old case from 1837, over 170 years ago, and international law has developed since that time. The restrictive doctrine has been accepted, statutes and conventions have been agreed, and the law relating to international crimes and individual responsibility has been formulated. The facts of this case were oversimplified in the *Blaškić* judgment in the ICTY. The attack, which involved British forces entering the territory of the United States, and attacking the ship without concern for civilians or property, would now be described as an armed attack. The death of little Billy, the cabin boy who was trying to leave the boat, would be wilful killing, as would probably be that of Amos Durfee, and therefore grave breaches of the Geneva Conventions. The destruction of the ship would probably also be a grave breach, as it was extensive destruction, and difficult therefore to justify as military necessity. It is not here being argued that the British soldiers involved in the expedition to destroy *The Caroline* should have been prosecuted. What is being suggested is that the facts of this case and the law applicable thereto are time specific. Customary international law changes to reflect the needs of the international community. It is only if state practice and *opinio juris* show that states continue to hold to the same tenets, that the law in the mid-nineteenth century can be quoted as the law now. The international community, and the consensus regarding international law, has changed so fundamentally since those events that the agreement of the British and US governments as to the law at that time indicates what the law was understood to be at that time, but further investigation is required before it can be stated to be the law now.

---

[64] The facts and the quotes regarding this case are taken from the excellent article R.Y. Jennings, 'The Caroline and McLeod Cases' (1938) 32 *AJIL* 82.

The *Rainbow Warrior* case[65] involved French agents committing very serious criminal offences on New Zealand territory. A boat, the *Rainbow Warrior* owned and operated by Greenpeace, an international organization concerned with conservation and environmental matters, was blown up, without warning, using explosives, and a person was killed. The operation was pre-planned and carried out by agents of the Directorate General of External Security (DGSE), part of the French Ministry of Defence. The government of France subsequently admitted responsibility and two French agents, Major Mafart and Captain Prieur, pleaded guilty to manslaughter and causing wilful damage by explosions and were sentenced to substantial periods of imprisonment.[66] New Zealand requested restitution. The French said that no settlement was possible without the release of the agents who had been acting under orders, whereas the New Zealand government did not consider that this exempted the agents from personal responsibility for their criminal acts. The two states agreed to refer all outstanding disputes between them regarding the *Rainbow Warrior* affair to the UN Secretary General, and to accept his ruling as binding.[67] The Secretary General ordered that the prisoners should be transferred to French military custody, and that they should be incarcerated for three years. France breached the agreement and on 30 April 1990 the arbitration tribunal declared that France had committed a violation of its international obligations towards New Zealand.[68]

The ICTY in *Blaškić* reported France as saying the imprisonment of the agents was not justified. That is correct, but the state practice to be noted from this case is much more complicated than that. New Zealand never accepted that the French agents were not individually responsible; neither did the UN Secretary General. France did not assert that the French agents should not be prosecuted. France only asserted that the agents should not be punished in arbitration proceedings before the UN Secretary General, after they had been convicted and sentenced. Taken at its highest France's position was that the French agents should not be punished, not that they were not responsible, and not that they should not be prosecuted.

New Zealand prosecuted and it demonstrated *opinio juris* in declaring that it had the right to prosecute. This view was reinforced by the UN Secretary General who accepted that New Zealand had the right to

65 (1985) 74 ILR 241.

66 *R v Mafart and Prieur* (1985) 74 ILR 241.

67 (1985) 74 ILR 256.

68 (1990) 82 ILR 499.

prosecute and punish the French officers. The UN Secretary General is an international person whose actions are of international significance, and in this instance his assertions in this arbitration are evidence of customary international law.

The *Rainbow Warrior* case does not support the proposition that state officials have immunity from prosecution for criminal offences. It is state practice which demonstrates that state officials have individual criminal liability for offences which they commit on the territory of another state, at the behest of their state and whilst on duty. France did not intervene in the trial to assert immunity. New Zealand asserted jurisdiction and prosecuted, sentenced and imprisoned the agents. The fact that they were acting as state agents was considered to be mitigation of sentence. The UN Secretary General rejected the submission that the French officials were not individually responsible. The International Tribunal declared that France was in breach of its obligations towards New Zealand in not keeping the officers in custody as required.

The final case cited in the *Blaškić* case is that of Adolf Eichmann, who was tried in Israel, accused of crimes against humanity during the Second World War. Eichmann argued that the crimes were committed within the framework of the anti-Jewish decrees of the Nazi regime, and that he was acting in accordance with law, and that by the Act of State doctrine the court was precluded from looking behind those laws. The Act of State doctrine is that there are certain actions taken by a state, in its own territory, which a foreign court is not capable of adjudicating upon, and this includes foreign legislation. The *Eichmann* case decided that this doctrine was limited when applied to international crimes, as these were acts against the law of nations, for which there is individual responsibility. This has been followed in English courts, and there is a residual power which is to be exercised with 'caution and the greatest circumspection' to disregard a foreign law provision when to do otherwise would be an affront to basic principles of justice and fairness.[69] This is not a case about immunity.

On examination, these cases cited by the ICTY in the *Blaškić* case, to support the proposition that functional immunity for all state officials is a well established rule of customary international law, do not support that proposition in criminal prosecutions.

---

[69] *Oppenheimer v Cattermole* [1976] AC 249, HL; *Kuwait Airways v Iraqi Airways Co.* [2002] UKHL 19, HL, per Lord Nicholls at para. 18.

This author undertook research into state practice to identify what conduct is official and imparts immunity.[70] Diplomats and consular officials have continuing immunity for official conduct,[71] and the small number of cases reported where such officials have been accused of criminal conduct and those where states have claimed, requested or waived immunity were analysed to assist in understanding what conduct is performed in the exercise of functions. Further, this author undertook extensive research into state practice from reports of cases where states arrested, prosecuted or issued warrants of the arrest of the agents of other states using the following criteria: the person arrested must clearly be a state actor, as opposed to a terrorist or a secessionist, or a person acting alone, or as part of a group for ideological reasons; the person must be a foreign national acting on behalf of a state, in what can only be described as state activity, in a second state.[72] The assertion of the state where the conduct took place that the activity was on behalf of another state was taken as sufficient. The understanding of the prosecuting state is of importance: Does the state prosecuting assert that the criminal conduct alleged was performed by and on behalf of a foreign state, and that there is the right to prosecute? The denial of the allegation by the foreign state does not affect the assertion of the right to prosecute. The person must have been arrested, charged and usually tried and sentenced. There is clearly no duty upon states to try foreign nationals who commit offences on their territory, and often states expel persons involved in undesirable conduct. The fact that they are not tried does not mean that states cannot try them; there are many reasons why a state may not wish to try a particular person such as lack of evidence, political embarrassment, or public interest immunity considerations. The cases identified and analysed included prosecutions for terrorism, terrorism by disguised members of armed forces, assassination, kidnapping, passport offences, trespassing and collecting information.

The analysis concluded that the cases show that state officials do not have immunity *ratione materiae* for criminal charges in respect of acts committed on the territory of the forum state, or the territory of a third state, unless that immunity is accorded by a special regime such as that

[70] *Immunity, Individuals and International Law*, n. 61 above, ch. 4.

[71] Vienna Convention on Diplomatic Relations 1961, Art. 39.2; Vienna Convention on Consular Relations, Art. 43.

[72] Cases involving the drug trade or other criminal activity, and cases where missionaries or other religious figures were involved, were not included as the motivations of all involved are mixed, and cases where it is unclear on whose behalf a person is acting were also omitted from the analysis.

afforded diplomats and consuls, or by consent such as that accorded to special missions, or by ad hoc agreement. Only those state agents who have had immunity *ratione personae* are entitled to immunity for offences committed on the territory of a foreign state. State practice shows that agents are not only held responsible for what can be considered serious crimes of violence, such as murder, planting bombs and kidnapping, but they are also routinely arrested and prosecuted for trespassing and collecting information. State practice shows that states demonstrate *opinio juris* by arresting, charging and prosecuting the agents of other states, and by not objecting to their own agents being prosecuted. States demonstrate a responsibility towards their agents, and make great efforts to get their agents returned, they make representations and arrange exchanges, but they never assert immunity.

There is continuing immunity for those who have been entitled to immunity *ratione personae* for conduct performed in the exercise of their functions. This extends to conduct which is connected to functions such as parking offences, but it does not encompass serious crimes of violence such as bombing or kidnapping even if committed on behalf of the sending state. Other officials, not entitled to immunity *ratione personae* do not have immunity from prosecution for any offences on the territory of the receiving state.

This analysis was cited with approval in *Bat v Investigating Judge of the German Federal Court.*[73] Khurts Bat, the Head of the Mongolian Office of National Security, was arrested in the United Kingdom as his extradition was sought by Germany for an offence of kidnapping. It was alleged that Khurts Bat and other members of the Mongolian Secret Service kidnapped a Mongolian national in France and removed him to Germany and then Mongolia where the national was wanted on charges of involvement in the assassination of a Mongolian government minister.

The High Court held that Khurts Bat's did not benefit from immunity *ratione materiae*. There is an essential distinction between civil and criminal liability. State practice shows that an official of one state was not entitled to immunity for a criminal act performed on the territory of another state, especially where the second state had not consented to the presence of that official or to his engaging in conduct of that kind.

Roman Kolodkin, the first Special Rapporteur to the ILC in his second *Report on Immunity of State Officials* concluded (at paragraph 94):

> State officials enjoy immunity *ratione materiae* from foreign criminal jurisdiction, ie immunity in respect of acts performed in an official capacity, since

---

[73] *Khurts Bat*, n. 30 above.

> these are acts of the State which they serve … A situation where criminal jurisdiction is exercised by a State in whose territory an alleged crime has taken place, and this State has not given its consent to the performance in its territory of the activity which led to the crime and to the presence in its territory of the foreign official who committed this alleged crime, stands also in this regard as a special case. It would appear that in such a situation there are sufficient grounds to talk of the absence of immunity.

The consent of the receiving state, not only to the discharge of the function, but to the presence of the foreign official in its territory, is crucial. Lord Justice Moses said (at paragraph 99) that he was persuaded 'by the full and cogent analysis of Dr Franey, supported by Special Rapporteur Koldkin, that the appellant does not enjoy immunity by reason of his conduct as an official of the Government of Mongolia from prosecution in Germany' and concluded that there is no customary international law affording Khurts Bat immunity *ratione materiae.* Offences committed on the territory of an official's own state are another question. Most crimes committed on the territory of one state are not justiciable on the territory of another state, as there would have to be extra-territorial jurisdiction to prosecute. One area where states have agreed to assert such jurisdiction is in relation to international crimes, such as genocide, war crimes, crimes against humanity and torture. In an effort to prevent the perpetrators of such crimes being able to evade justice states have signed conventions agreeing to prosecute such persons.

7.6 INTERNATIONAL CRIMES AND IMMUNITY

Is there a conflict in international law between the immunity enjoyed by high state officials for conduct which constitutes international crimes, and the individual responsibility which attaches to those offences? Have the two areas of international law developed separately and without reference to each other to the extent that they are incompatible? The purpose of this immunity is to protect the state and enable the individual to perform his or her functions. The purpose of individual responsibility for international crimes is to prevent the creation of safe havens for those committing such crimes, and thus to act as a deterrent to future offenders. If immunity provides protection from prosecution for an international crime such as genocide or torture, for which there is a duty to prosecute, then there are two conflicting obligations under international law. Does the immunity enjoyed by high state officials for conduct which constitutes international crimes conflict with the concept of individual responsibility, and the duty to prosecute? Have the two areas of law developed separately to the extent that they are incompatible?

This conflict was at the heart of the *Pinochet* case. Pinochet was accused of using murder and torture to overthrow and defeat his political opponents, and then to maintain his power in Chile. To this end he used the institutions of his government: the police and the military. Spain asked for his extradition, and the extradition crime was official torture; that is torture as defined in the torture convention, torture 'inflicted by or at the instigation of or with the consent or acquiescence of a public official or other person acting in an official capacity'. The definition of the crime of torture requires that the offence be committed as an action of the state, by a state official, and the governmental nature of the allegations raised the question of immunity from prosecution.

Professor Campbell McLachlan observed the independent development of the two areas of international law relating to immunity and human rights when he wrote:

> As those involved in the *Pinochet* litigation discovered, these two bodies of law had developed largely independently. Their potential incompatibility had not been resolved, despite the fact that many international conventions had been concluded during the latter half of the 20th Century, which provided for national court jurisdiction over international crimes.[74]

After the Second World War, the United Nations was created; the ILC and International Committee of the Red Cross (ICRC) developed international law to protect individuals from the excesses of government and for the protection of the victims of armed conflict. The resultant Conventions were designed to be multilateral treaties entered into by all states. The Conventions all take basically the same approach. A crime is stated to be of international concern; the crime is defined; individual responsibility is confirmed; the jurisdiction to be asserted is described; and the obligation to prosecute asserted. Within this framework the Conventions became progressively more sophisticated.

The General Assembly of the United Nations adopted the Universal Declaration of Human Rights in 1946[75] and the International Covenant on Civil and Political Rights in 1966.[76] These Resolutions recognized the

---

[74] C. McLachlan, 'After Baghdad: Conflict or Coherence in International Law' (2003) 1 *NZJPIL* 25.

[75] GAR 217A (III), 10 December 1946, which recognized 'the inherent dignity and the equal and inalienable rights of all members of the human family is the foundation of freedom, justice and peace in the world'.

[76] GAR 2200 (XXI).

rights to life and the prohibition on torture which are now part of customary international law.

In 1946, the General Assembly declared that genocide is a crime under international law and that punishment of individuals for the crime is a matter of international concern,[77] and in 1948 adopted the Genocide Convention1948.[78] The Convention confirms that genocide is a crime, defines the offence, and provides that anyone committing the offence of genocide shall be punished regardless of their status. The Convention specifically refers to constitutionally responsible rulers, public officials and private individuals being punishable. It then goes on to provide for jurisdiction based on territory, or by an international penal tribunal, even though there was no international criminal tribunal at that time. The General Assembly invited the ILC to study the possibility of establishing an international court for the trial of persons charged with genocide, but there was not to be one for over 40 years.

The Genocide Convention does not refer to the immunity of individuals. The specific reference to the punishability of constitutionally responsible rulers, and public officials, implies that they are not entitled to immunity for the crime of genocide, but the treaty does not address immunity directly. Immunity was not an issue because the jurisdictional Article provides only for trial before the territorial court, where immunity would not be an issue if the alleged perpetrator was a citizen of that state, or before an international criminal tribunal where a state would consent to jurisdiction before surrendering its citizens.

There is a requirement in the Convention to extradite an offender in accordance with the laws and treaties in force, and genocide is not to be considered as a political crime for the purposes of extradition, but there was no consideration of immunity in the context of extradition. There is no responsibility to prosecute. Although the prohibition on genocide became *jus cogens*, the prosecution and punishment of those committing the crime of genocide was wishful thinking, as those in power who commit genocide did not give up their power and submit to prosecution.

On 12 August 1949, the text of the four Geneva Conventions was agreed. The Conventions deal with the wounded and sick in armed forces in the field; the wounded, sick and shipwrecked in armed forces at sea; prisoners of war; and civilians. The four Conventions have common principles and Articles, and created the concept of grave breaches of the

---

77 GAR 96 (I), 11 December 1946.
78 GAR 260 (III), 2 December 1948.

provisions of the Conventions, such breaches to be punishable by all states parties.

Each of the Conventions defines grave breaches by reference to particular acts 'if committed against persons or property protected by the Convention'. The states parties undertake to enact legislation necessary to provide effective penal sanctions for persons committing, or ordering to be committed, any of the grave breaches. Each state party is under an obligation to search for persons alleged to have committed, or to have ordered to be committed, such grave breaches, and to bring such persons, regardless of their nationality, before its own courts. Such state party may, if it prefers, in accordance with the provisions of its own legislation, hand such persons over for trial to another state party, provided there is a prima facie case. There are also safeguards relating to fair trial.

These four Conventions created a scheme for the location, prosecution and punishment of war criminals. There is jurisdiction without a connection with territory or nationality, and there is an obligation to search for and prosecute persons present on a state's territory. The primary obligation is to prosecute, but a person may be extradited instead, if a requesting state can prove a prima facie case. Immunity is not referred to. All the alleged perpetrators would be state officials, in that they would be members of the armed forces.

In 1975, the General Assembly adopted the Declaration on the Protection of All Persons from Being Subjected to Torture and Other Cruel, Inhuman or Degrading Treatment or Punishment.[79] In 1985, the Convention Against Torture and Other Cruel, Inhuman or Degrading Treatment or Punishment was opened. Torture is defined as an offence which can only be committed in an official capacity.[80] The official character of the torture, the prohibition against which is *jus cogens*, is a fundamental element of the offence.

The aim of the Torture Convention is to create a system where no state is complicit in torture, and no torturer can evade justice. All states parties are required to take effective legislative, administrative, judicial or other

---

[79] GAR 3452, 9 December 1975.

[80] Torture Convention, Art. 1 defines torture as 'any act by which severe pain or suffering, whether physical or mental, is intentionally inflicted on a person for such purposes as obtaining from him or a third person information or a confession, punishing him for an act he or a third person has committed or is suspected of having committed, or intimidating or coercing him or a third person, or for any reason based on discrimination of any kind, when such pain or suffering is inflicted by or at the instigation of or with the consent or acquiescence of a public official or other person acting in an official capacity'.

measures to prevent acts of torture in any territory under their jurisdiction. No exceptional circumstances whatsoever are allowed; war or the threat of war, internal political instability or any other public emergency, are not to be invoked as a justification of torture, nor can an order from a superior officer or a public authority be invoked as a justification of torture. No one is to be extradited, deported or returned by one state to another state where there are substantial grounds for believing that the person would be in danger of being subjected to torture. Each state party must ensure that all acts of torture are offences under its criminal law, including attempt, complicity or participation in torture. All states parties agree to make these offences punishable by appropriate penalties which take into account their grave nature.

Each state party must establish its jurisdiction[81] when the offences are committed in any territory under its jurisdiction,[82] and where the alleged offender is a national of that state. If the victim is a national of the state then the state may take jurisdiction.

If an alleged offender is present in any territory under the jurisdiction of a state and the state does not extradite him, then the state must establish its jurisdiction, and submit the case to its competent authorities for the purpose of prosecution. Any decision regarding prosecution is to be taken in the same manner as in the case of any ordinary offence, of a serious nature, under the law of that state. The standards of evidence required for prosecution and conviction are in no way less stringent than those for other cases, and there are provisions for taking an alleged offender into custody, and guarantees as to fair trial.

States must take jurisdiction on the basis of territory, and of the nationality of the offender, and jurisdiction may be taken on the basis of the nationality of the alleged victim. These are the traditional agreed bases of jurisdiction. Jurisdiction also has to be taken on the basis of the presence of the offender on state territory; if the offender is not extradited, then he is to be prosecuted if there is sufficient evidence. This gives precedence to the territorial state, or state of nationality, but is designed not to allow a perpetrator to escape because there is a bar to his extradition. The immunity of an alleged offender is not considered at all.

The concept of individual responsibility for international crimes was articulated in Article 7 of the Charter of the International Military Tribunal for the trial of war criminals at Nuremburg, which provided that 'The official position of defendants, whether as heads of state or

---

81 *Ibid.* Art. 5.

82 This includes on board a ship or aircraft.

responsible officials in government departments, shall not be considered as freeing them from responsibility or mitigating punishment'.[83] The Tribunal emphasized this in its judgment, saying that immunity could not apply:

> The principle of international law which, under certain circumstances, protects the representatives of a state cannot be applied to acts condemned as criminal by international law. The authors of these acts cannot shelter themselves behind their official position to be freed from punishment.[84]

The Tribunal also stated that 'Crimes against international law are committed by men, not by abstract entities, and only by punishing individuals who commit such crimes can the provisions of international law be enforced'.

The General Assembly[85] unanimously affirmed the principles of international law recognized by the Charter of the Nuremburg Tribunal and the judgment of the Tribunal, and in 1950 accepted the Principles as formulated by the ILC.[86] Nuremberg Principle I provides that any person who commits an act which constitutes a crime under international law is responsible therefore and liable to punishment, and Nuremberg Principle III provides that the fact that a person acted as head of state or responsible government official does not relieve him of responsibility under international law.[87]

The (ICTY) and the International Criminal Tribunal for Rwanda (ICTR) were created by the Security Council under Chapter VII of the UN Charter in 1993 and 1994, with the power to prosecute persons for the most serious violations of international humanitarian law.[88] The Security Council did not purport to legislate: the International Tribunals

---

[83] London, 8 August 1945, 82 UNTS 278, Art. 7: 'The official position of defendants, whether as Heads of State or responsible officials in Government Departments, shall not be considered as freeing them from responsibility or mitigating punishment'.

[84] *The Trial of German Major War Criminals: Proceedings of the International Military Tribunal Sitting at Nuremberg in Germany* (London, HMSO, 1950), Pt 22.

[85] GAR 95(1), 11 December 1946.

[86] GAR 488 (V), 12 December 1950.

[87] Principles of International Law Recognised in the Charter of the Nuremberg Tribunal and in the Judgment of the Tribunal 1950, reproduced in (1950) II *Yearbook of the ILC* para. 97.

[88] SCR 827 (1993) and SCR 955 (1994).

apply existing international law.[89] Article 7 of the ICTY Statute and Article 6 of the ICTR Statute both provide for individual responsibility. The fact that an accused person acted pursuant to an order of a government or of a superior does not relieve him of criminal responsibility, but may be considered in mitigation of punishment if the International Tribunal determines that justice so requires. Article 27 of the Statute of the International Criminal Court (ICC) provides for individual responsibility. The official position of any person, including any head of state or government, does not exempt them from criminal responsibility nor does it mitigate punishment.

The creation of these International Tribunals, and the specific provisions in their Statutes that heads of state and government officials are not exempt from responsibility and can be tried by the Tribunals, rather than demonstrating that there is no state immunity for these acts, implies that there is such immunity. This immunity has been specifically excluded by these Statutes, and this is one of the reasons that the International Tribunals and the ICC have been established.

The first case in which the interaction of the duty to extradite, individual responsibility and immunity was considered was that of *Pinochet*, and the English courts struggled to reconcile the conflicting principles.

Pinochet was a former head of the state of Chile who was arrested in England because his extradition was requested by Spain for offences including torture. As a former head of state, customary international law required that he be granted immunity *ratione materiae*, that is, immunity for alleged criminal offences committed in his public capacity whilst he was head of state. He was accused, *inter alia*, of official torture in Chile, his own state, but the Torture Convention makes no mention of state immunity, despite the fact that jurisdiction is given to the national courts of other states.

It was submitted on behalf of Pinochet that as a former head of state he did not have immunity in respect of personal or private acts, but that he continued to enjoy immunity in respect of public acts performed by him as head of state, that is, in respect of the exercise by him of sovereign power in that capacity, and that the conduct alleged against him related not to his private or personal conduct, but to his conduct when exercising

[89] *Report of the UN Secretary General 3 May 1993 on the Legal Basis for the Establishment of the ICTY*, S/25704, para. 29, as requested in SCR 808 (1993), para. 2.

sovereign power as head of state of the Republic of Chile. The allegations were that he used the apparatus of the state to torture and murder. The proceedings were complicated, with the basis upon which Pinochet's extradition was requested changing, and there were three decisions by the House of Lords.[90]

On 25 November 1998, the House of Lords[91] gave judgment and found that Pinochet was not immune, but it was a close call with two of the five judges finding that he was entitled to immunity. All of the Law Lords were agreed that the crucial question was whether the acts alleged were done by Pinochet in the exercise of his functions as head of state. On 15 January 1998, the House of Lords[92] set aside the judgment of the 25 November 1998 on the grounds that the court was not properly constituted, and on the 24 March 1999, the House of Lords,[93] comprising seven different judges, gave a second and final judgment as to whether Pinochet was entitled to immunity from the criminal jurisdiction of the English courts.

The court considered whether Pinochet was entitled to immunity as an ex-head of state performing the conduct in the exercise of his official functions. Any date at which he lost immunity became of great importance, as the number of offences for which he could potentially be extradited were different depending upon which date was decided. In this context the dates upon which the countries ratified the Torture Convention became significant; Spain ratified the convention on 21 October 1987, Chile ratified on 30 October 1988, and the United Kingdom on 8 December 1988.

All seven of the judges gave separate reasons for their decision regarding whether Pinochet lost his immunity, and if he did the date at which he lost it. Six of the judges agreed that he was not immune, but the dates at which the immunity was lost differed. Lord Goff disagreed, and said that Pinochet was entitled to immunity for torture and conspiracy to torture; the fact that no mention was made of state immunity in the Convention was decisive – had it been intended to exclude state immunity, then the Torture Convention would have provided for that.

---

[90] For a detailed explanation of the case and an analysis of the decisions see the author's thesis and book, *Immunity, Individuals and International Law*, n. 61 above.

[91] *R v Bow Street Metropolitan Stipendiary Magistrate and others, ex parte Pinochet Ugarte (Amnesty International and others intervening)* [2000] 1 AC 61.

[92] *R v Bow Street Metropolitan Stipendiary Magistrate and others, ex parte Pinochet Ugarte (No. 2)* [2000] 1 AC 119.

[93] Pinochet (No. 3), n. 5 above.

Lord Browne-Wilkinson (at 204H to 206A) found that Pinochet lost his immunity on 8 December 1988, the date when all three states involved had ratified the Torture Convention. He reasoned that it cannot be an official function in international law to do something which international law criminalizes. It is an essential feature of the international crime of torture that it is committed by a state official. If immunity *ratione personae* applied then no case could be brought outside the forum state without a waiver by that state.

Lord Hope (at 247G, 262D and 263E) decided that immunity was lost on 30 October 1988. He said that there was no express waiver, nor an implied term in the Torture Convention, but that the obligations which were recognized by customary international law, in the case of allegations of systematic torture, by the date when Chile ratified the Convention, were so strong as to override any objection by it on the ground of immunity *ratione materiae*.

Lord Hutton (at 251C) stated that the prohibition of torture had acquired the status of *jus cogens*, and having regard to the provisions of the Torture Convention, acts of torture after 29 September 1988 were not a function of a head of state, and therefore Pinochet was not immune after 29 September 1988.

Lord Saville found that Pinochet's immunity ceased at 8 December 1988 as the terms of the Torture Convention expressly state that a former head of state, who allegedly resorts to torture for state purposes, falls within the terms of the Convention, and should be dealt with in accordance with them; and (at 267F) he found that the express and unequivocal terms of the Convention were a clear and unambiguous waiver of immunity.

Lord Millett found that Pinochet was not entitled to immunity for offences of torture, and conspiracy to torture; he stated (at 277A–278B) that the definition of torture is entirely inconsistent with the existence of a plea of immunity *ratione materiae*. The official or governmental nature of the act, which forms the basis of the immunity, is an essential ingredient of the offence, and that no rational system of criminal justice can allow an immunity which is coextensive with the offence.

Lord Phillips (at 290F) stated that Pinochet was not entitled to immunity for the offences of torture, and conspiracy to torture, as the Torture Convention is incompatible with immunity *ratione materiae*. In his view immunity *ratione materiae* cannot coexist with international crimes, and extra-territorial jurisdiction in relation to them, as the exercise of extra-territorial jurisdiction overrides the principle that one state will not intervene in the internal affairs of another.

All of the judges were struggling to reconcile the two strands of international law.

In conclusion the court found by six to one, Lord Millett dissenting, that torture was not an extradition crime until 29 September 1988, when torture became a crime under UK law; and secondly by six to one, Lord Goff dissenting, that Pinochet was not entitled to immunity for torture and conspiracy to torture. There were different decisions as to the date when immunity was lost. Three of the judges, Lord Browne-Wilkinson, Lord Hope and Lord Saville, found that it was when all three states involved had ratified the Torture Convention, that is, 8 December 1988. Lord Hutton found it was 19 September 1988 when torture became an offence in the United Kingdom; and two judges, Lord Phillips and Lord Millett, found that he was not entitled to immunity for the international crime of torture. Therefore the majority decided the date was 8 December 1988, and Pinochet was found to have lost his immunity as of that date.[94]

In 2006, the House of Lords again considered the question of state immunity in *Jones v Ministry of Interior*.[95] The House of Lords was considering whether state immunity applies to civil claims for torture committed by state officials abroad and decided unanimously that state immunity does apply to such claims and that the English courts have no jurisdiction to hear them. In coming to its conclusion, the House of Lords considered what was decided in the *Pinochet* case regarding immunity from prosecution for official torture. Lord Bingham (at paragraph 19 of the judgment) said that the essential ratio in the *Pinochet* case was that international law could not without absurdity require a state to prosecute and, at the same time, require immunity to be granted to those properly charged. Lord Hoffman (at paragraph 81) stated that the reason why General Pinochet did not enjoy immunity *ratione materiae* was because 'by necessary implication, international law had removed the immunity'.

The judges in all the *Pinochet* judgments and in the *Jones* case struggled to make sense of the system of criminal responsibility and accountability introduced by the Torture Convention, when no mention was specifically made regarding immunity. The only way to implement the Torture Convention, without allowing those most responsible for the most serious crimes to escape the regime, was to find that the Torture

---

[94] The extradition proceedings then continued. The Secretary of State did not order Senator Pinochet's extradition on the grounds of ill health. On 2 March 2000, Senator Pinochet returned to Chile.

[95] *Jones v Ministry of Interior Al-Mamlaka Al-Arabiya AS Sauduya (Kingdom of Saudi Arabia) and others* [2006] UKHL 26, 129 ILR 629, HL.

Convention removed immunity *ratione materiae*. This was reading something into the Convention which was not really there, and led to criticism of the extradition proceedings. There was no wholehearted approval of the *Pinochet* case, and that was because the Torture Convention does not address the issue.

On 14 February 2003, the ICJ in the *Arrest Warrant* case confirmed that serving heads of state, heads of government and Foreign Ministers are entitled to immunity *ratione personae*, including immunity from prosecution for international crimes, including official torture.

The Court held (at paragraph 59) that the rules governing the jurisdiction of national courts must be carefully distinguished from those governing jurisdictional immunities, as jurisdiction does not imply absence of immunity, while absence of immunity does not imply jurisdiction, and stated that an obligation under an international convention to extend criminal jurisdiction in no way affects immunities under international law:

> the rules governing the jurisdiction of national courts must be carefully distinguished from those governing jurisdictional immunities, as jurisdiction does not imply absence of immunity, while absence of immunity does not imply jurisdiction.

The Court emphasized (at paragraph 60) that immunity does not mean impunity and that immunity from criminal jurisdiction and individual criminal responsibility are quite separate concepts. The Court said that jurisdictional immunity is procedural in nature, whereas criminal responsibility is a question of substantive law. Jurisdictional immunity may well bar prosecution for a certain period or for certain offences, but it cannot exonerate the person to whom it applies from all criminal responsibility.

The Court (at paragraph 61) explained four ways in which a person who has immunity *ratione personae* may be prosecuted:

(1) Such persons enjoy no criminal immunity under international law in their own countries, and may thus be tried by those countries' courts in accordance with the relevant rules of domestic law.
(2) They will cease to enjoy immunity from foreign jurisdiction if the state which they represent or have represented decides to waive that immunity.
(3) After a person ceases to hold office, he or she will no longer enjoy all of the immunities accorded by international law in other states. Provided that it has jurisdiction under international law, a court of

one state may try the former official of another state in respect of acts committed prior or subsequent to his or her period of office, as well as in respect of acts committed during that period of office in a private capacity.

(4) An incumbent or former official may be subject to criminal proceedings before certain international criminal courts, where they have jurisdiction.

The probability of high state officials who commit such serious offences being tried in these circumstances is not high. Their own country is usually the one they are oppressing, and therefore there will be no national prosecution. Such a person will not surrender power; he is likely to grant an amnesty to himself before abdicating. He will not waive immunity, or voluntarily surrender to an international tribunal. Those who are capable of committing genocide, war crimes, crimes against humanity and torture, will not be concerned by the fact that, even though they cannot be tried, they have criminal responsibility.

This exception that a former high state official can be tried for actions committed, whilst in office in a private capacity, returns to the central question in the *Pinochet* case. Is torture by a state official an official action, is it *acta jure imperii* and therefore immune? Is the act, by its nature and not its purpose, a governmental act? Pinochet instigated torture to preserve his regime, is that not a governmental act? It is not the action of a human rights compliant government, but he was using the apparatus of the state to protect the government. As Lord Millett (at 268) said in *Pinochet (No. 3)*, this exception to immunity is not *acta jure gestionis*, rather it is 'a parallel and in some respects opposite development'.

The explanation of when a former high state official can be prosecuted was not necessary for the ICJ's decision in the *Arrest Warrant* case, and has been criticized. Hazel Fox[96] has stated that 'there is some questioning of this ruling which may be described as obiter dicta, since the facts on which the judgment was based concerned a minister while serving in office'. Steffen Wirth[97] has argued that the assertion that Foreign Ministers are immune for official acts, even when they are no longer in office, is *obiter dictum*, and also that it is not well reasoned, and difficult to reconcile with the existing law of state immunity. He went on:

---

[96] 'State Immunity and the International Crime of Torture' (2006) 2 *EHRLR* 142.

[97] 'Immunity for Core Crimes? The ICJ's Judgment in the Congo v Belgium Case' (2002) 13 *EURJIL* 877.

> the Court hardly adduces any evidence for the existence of the rule which it asserts, and, what is more, there is a gap in its reasoning: whereas all arguments made by the Court in discussing the merits of the case relate only to incumbent Ministers of Foreign Affairs, the conclusion drawn in paragraph 61 of the decision then includes former Ministers of Foreign Affairs.

He has argued that once a high state official leaves office he should be protected only by immunity *ratione materiae*, which should be interpreted as providing no protection against prosecution for international crimes.

Andrea Bianchi[98] has also argued that no immunity should be granted with regard to prosecutions for international crimes, contending that:

> the very notion of crimes of international law is inconsistent with the application of jurisdictional immunities … particularly as regards those crimes which by their very nature either presuppose or require state action. If immunity were granted to state officials … prosecution of such crimes would be impossible and the overall effectiveness of international criminal law irremediably undermined.

In their Joint Separate Opinion in the *Arrest Warrant* case,[99] Judges Higgins, Kooijmans and Buergenthal (at paragraph 85) quote Andrea Bianchi and note that it is claimed in the literature that serious international crimes cannot be regarded as official acts because they are not normal state functions nor functions that a state alone, in contrast to an individual, can perform, but this has not been followed by state practice. There have not been prosecutions by national courts of ex-high state officials of other states for international crimes. This also has not been followed by the House of Lords in *Jones v Ministry of the Interior*[100] and it is at odds with the principles of state responsibility. A state will incur responsibility in international law if one of its officials is acting under apparent authority even if the official exceeds his authority or contravenes his instructions: the question is whether he was acting with apparent authority.[101] If so, the state will be responsible for his actions,

[98] 'Denying State Immunity to Violators of Human Rights' (1994) 46 *Austrian Journal of Public and International Law* 227; 'Immunity Versus Human Rights: The Pinochet Case' (1999) 10 *EJIL* 237 at 277–8.

[99] *Arrest Warrant*, n. 6 above.

[100] [2007] 1 AC 270.

[101] Articles on the Responsibility of States for Internationally Wrongful Acts, with commentaries, reproduced in (2001) II *Yearbook of the ILC* 31, para. 77, commentary to Art. 7 para. (8).

which are therefore official, albeit internationally wrongful, actions. Actions do not cease to be official because they are illegal.

A decision of the ICJ has no binding force except between the parties and in respect of that particular case,[102] but the ICJ was explaining customary international law in the *Arrest Warrant* case and these are influential pronouncements. The ICJ appears to be saying that the decision of the House of Lords in *Pinochet (No. 3)* was incorrect.[103]

Campbell McLachlan[104] has suggested that 'it would be preferable if international law were to admit of an exception to state immunity for the prosecution of individuals for international crimes, that such an exception develop as an independent head'. But he says '[w]hether such an exception is in truth developing as part of international law's "living and expanding code" is debateable', and '[a]lthough the ICJ's judgment should properly be limited to the specific issue, as to serving foreign ministers, which it decided, the conservatism at the core of the decision is bound to have a chill effect on national judicial activism on related immunity issues, and thus inhibit the further development of state practice'.

In the *Pinochet* case, the House of Lords decided that international law has to make sense and be internally consistent. The Torture Convention requires states to extradite or prosecute persons on their territory accused of crimes of torture, and the definition of the offence of torture requires that the person accused of the offence will have immunity *ratione materiae*, as the offence will have been committed as an official act. The House of Lords decided that the only coherent decision was that Pinochet was not immune, and that states parties to the Torture Convention must have meant that immunity did not apply. The House of Lords decided that immunity continues for the offences of murder and conspiracy to murder. It was not the seriousness of the offences, nor the abuses of human rights, which removed the immunity, but the absurdity which would prevail if Pinochet was found to be immune. As Lord Browne-Wilkinson (at 205E) said 'the whole elaborate structure of universal jurisdiction over torture committed by officials is rendered abortive'. The complicated reasons given by the judges for their decision, and the fact that no really sensible *ratio* can be deduced from the case, shows the difficulty which the judges had in making their decision, and what the judges did was to interpret the Torture Convention by reading into it a provision which was not there.

---

[102] Statute of the ICJ 1945, Art. 59.

[103] *Arrest Warrant*, n. 6 above, para. 59.

[104] 'Pinochet Revisited' (2002) 51(4) *ICLQ* 959.

The *Pinochet* case was about a former head of state and immunity *ratione materiae*, whereas the *Arrest Warrant* case before the ICJ was about the immunity of a serving Foreign Minister, that is, immunity *ratione personae*. The ICJ stated clearly that treaty provisions regarding jurisdiction cannot change the immunity of an individual under customary international law. This statement was unnecessary for the decision the Court came to, but it is a brave national court which would issue a warrant when the ICJ says that immunity prevails.

The ICJ also said that one way in which a person with immunity can be brought to justice is before an international tribunal. The International Tribunals have been successful in arresting and prosecuting individuals, and the International Criminal Court has been created since the *Pinochet* case. The principle of complementarity in the ICC Statute gives precedence to states with traditional bases of jurisdiction, territory and nationality, and only allows for prosecution if those states are unwilling or unable to prosecute.

As Lord Browne-Wilkinson said in *Pinochet (No. 3)* (at 190F):

> It may well be thought that the trial of Senator Pinochet in Spain for offences all of which related to the state of Chile and most of which occurred in Chile is not calculated to achieve the best justice.

Criminal offences should be prosecuted in a state with a proper connection to the offence, and if that is not possible because a person is so powerful, then it is submitted that the venue should be an international criminal tribunal, and not the domestic courts of another state.

7.7 INTERNATIONAL CRIMINAL COURT

There have been developments in this area of international law since the *Pinochet* case. The ICTY and the ICTR have demonstrated that international tribunals are an effective way to deal with alleged war criminals, internationalized domestic tribunals have been established in Sierra Leone, East Timor and Cambodia to assist national courts deal with the prosecution of those responsible for atrocities, and the International Criminal Court (ICC) has been created by treaty.

The ICC Statute[105] was adopted on 17 July 1998 and entered into force on 1 July 2002. In the Preamble, the states parties recognize that grave crimes threaten the peace, security and well-being of the world, and

[105] 2187 UNTS 3.

affirm that the most serious crimes of concern to the international community as a whole must not go unpunished, and that their effective prosecution must be ensured by taking measures at the national level, and by enhancing international cooperation. They say they are determined to put an end to impunity, and thus contribute to the prevention of such crimes. The ICC is complementary to national criminal jurisdictions. Finally, the states parties are resolved to guarantee lasting respect for, and the enforcement of, international justice.

The Court has jurisdiction over 'the most serious crimes of concern to the international community as a whole', that is, genocide, crimes against humanity and war crimes. It also has jurisdiction over the crime of aggression, once it is defined. Its jurisdiction is limited to crimes occurring after the Statute came into force on 1 July 2002. A state on becoming a party to the Statute accepts the jurisdiction of the Court. The primary jurisdiction of the ICC is by consent. States parties may refer a situation to the prosecutor for investigation on the basis of territory or nationality, or the prosecutor may initiate an investigation in those circumstances. A state which is not a party to the Statute may, by declaration, accept the exercise of jurisdiction of the Court, with respect to a specific crime.

The Court also has a non-consensual jurisdiction under Articles 13 to 15 of the Statute, whereby the Security Council acting under Chapter VII of the UN Charter may refer a situation, in which one or more crimes appear to have been committed, to the prosecutor.[106]

The complementarity principle is given effect by acknowledging that the domestic jurisdiction of a state takes precedence unless that state is unable or unwilling to prosecute.

The Statute of the ICC expressly considers immunity, not just in relation to the capacity of the Court, but also in relation to national courts. Persons who are wanted by the Court will be arrested, and appear before a national court, before being transferred to the ICC. The provisions relating to immunity are carefully considered.

A person who commits a crime within the jurisdiction of the ICC is individually responsible and liable for punishment,[107] and official capacity is irrelevant as the Statute applies equally to all persons without any distinction based on official capacity. In particular, official capacity as a head of state or government, a member of a government or parliament, an

---

[106] SCR 1593, 31 March 2005, referred the situation in Darfur, Sudan since 1 July 2001 to the Prosecutor of the ICC.

[107] Statute of the ICC, Art. 25.2.

elected representative or a government official does not exempt a person from criminal responsibility under the Statute. Immunities or special procedural rules which may attach to the official capacity of a person, whether under national or international law, do not bar the Court from exercising its jurisdiction over such a person.[108]

This applies to a person who is before the ICC accused of a crime, but if a person is before a national court, arrested on a warrant issued by the ICC, then:

(1) the Court may not proceed with a request for surrender or assistance which would require the requested state to act inconsistently with its obligations under international law with respect to the state or diplomatic immunity of a person or property of a third state, unless the Court can first obtain the cooperation of that third state for the waiver of the immunity;
(2) the Court may not proceed with a request for surrender which would require the requested state to act inconsistently with its obligations under international agreements pursuant to which the consent of a sending state is required to surrender a person of that state to the Court, unless the Court can first obtain the cooperation of the sending state for the giving of consent for the surrender.[109]

This provision acknowledges that states and national courts have an obligation under international law to recognize state and diplomatic immunity. The Article provides that the ICC may not proceed with a request which would require the requested state to act inconsistently with its obligations under international law. This implies that these obligations are a matter for the ICC to decide. It is submitted that this is too narrow a construction of the Article. International law is binding upon both the requested state and the ICC, both are required to abide by it. The requested state cannot surrender a person who is entitled to immunity, and the ICC cannot proceed with the request.

The English legislation deals with this by providing that such a decision be taken by the Secretary of State not the courts. International Criminal Court Act 2001, section 23, headed 'Provisions as to State or Diplomatic Immunity', provides that any state or diplomatic immunity attaching to a person by reason of a connection with a state party to the ICC Statute does not prevent proceedings. This includes immunity under

108 *Ibid.* Art. 27.
109 *Ibid.* Art. 98.

customary international law. Where immunity attaches to any person by reason of a connection with a state which is not a party to the ICC Statute, then if the ICC has obtained a waiver of that immunity in relation to a request for that person's surrender to the ICC, that waiver is treated as extending to the proceedings in the United Kingdom in connection with that request. A certificate by the Secretary of State that a state is or is not a state party, or that there has been a waiver, is conclusive. The Secretary of State may in any particular case after consultation with the ICC and the state concerned direct that proceedings, which would be prevented by state or diplomatic immunity if the state was not a party to the ICC, or a waiver, shall not be taken.

If the request is for the surrender of a person who has immunity because of a connection with a state not a party to the ICC, then the power under section 1 of the United Nations Act 1946 to make Orders in Council may be used. This power is to give immediate effect by Order in Council to UN Security Council Resolutions not involving the use of armed force. Orders in Council made under this section 'shall be laid before Parliament forthwith'. The procedure has been considered in *A and others v HM Treasury*,[110] in which the Court of Appeal decided that the fact that the Order in Council must be laid before Parliament, even though there is no procedure to enable Parliament to scrutinize or amend it, meant that it was not possible to challenge the lawfulness of the Orders on the ground they were *ultra vires*, as an individual Member could seek to initiate a debate if he or she felt that an Order was unsatisfactory. Sir Anthony Clarke MR said 'the likelihood of Parliamentary scrutiny seems more theoretical than real'.

The International Criminal Court Act 2001 therefore takes any decision regarding the immunity of an individual out of the hands of the national court.

7.8 CONCLUSION

State immunity is a principle of international law based upon the consent of states.

There are two different immunities which attach to individuals because they are state officials: immunity *ratione personae* and immunity *ratione materiae*. Immunity *ratione personae* is described as being immunity conferred because of the position held by an official in a state, or the

---

[110] [2008] EWCA Civ 1187.

immunity granted because of the official's status. Immunity *ratione materiae* is accorded because of the activity undertaken by a state official, the immunity attaching to official acts. Although both of these immunities are accorded to individuals because they are state officials, and the immunity is that of the state inasmuch as it is the state that can waive the immunity, they are not the same. Immunity *ratione materiae* is simply an expression of the immunity of the state – if the state is not immune then neither is the official; whereas immunity *ratione personae* has a separate existence to the immunity of the state. A person is entitled to immunity *ratione personae* whether or not the state would be entitled to claim immunity in civil proceedings for the actions of the state official.

Immunity *ratione personae* protects the person of the most important state officials. Since the ILC adopted Draft Article 3 on the Immunity of State Officials from Foreign Criminal Jurisdiction, the indication is that international law is developing and immunity *ratione personae* is restricted to the head of state, head of government and Foreign Minister. It is an immunity afforded only to those officials of the highest status. It protects the dignity of the state by protecting the office held by the official, who is inviolable. It means that high state officials can go freely about their state business, enabling such officials to perform their functions without interference, or fear of interference, from other states. This immunity is all encompassing. It applies to all actions of the individual, whether in their own state, the forum state or a third state, both before and after taking office, and it includes all civil and criminal proceedings, including those alleging the most serious of international crimes. A foreign state has to accord a person entitled to immunity *ratione personae* of its own motion and not wait for it to be claimed.

There are also special regimes which give state officials immunity *ratione personae* for limited agreed periods of time. Diplomatic immunity, consular immunity and the immunity accorded to the members of special missions are all based upon the consent of states and are well established in international law. These regimes all accord immunity to specific state officials for particular periods of time by agreement between both states involved. The purpose of the immunity conferred under these regimes is to enable state officials to perform particular tasks or undertake specific roles on behalf of their state. This immunity *ratione personae* is all encompassing for the time agreed, usually the time the officials are present on the territory of the receiving state. An official who benefits from this immunity has an obligation to abide by the laws of the receiving state, and if he does not do so the sanction available to the receiving state is to expel the official.

The immunity accorded to members of special missions can cover visits by state officials for state business. This regime has the advantage of being agreed in advance, so that the sending and receiving states know the purpose of the special mission, and know who has immunity, and for how long.

What is less clear is whether there is continuing immunity *ratione materiae* accorded to those who have had immunity *ratione personae* once that immunity comes to an end; and also, whether there is immunity from prosecution for officials who perform official actions. Immunity *ratione materiae* is immunity attaching to conduct undertaken on behalf of a state and it is described as being for *acta jure imperii*, actions of an official nature.

The concept that the immunity of the state also covers the official has been developed in civil proceedings. The rationale for this immunity in civil cases is that if an individual is sued, then the state is sued by proxy, and the immunity of the state is thereby undermined. To allow the individual to be sued when the state is immune would be to circumvent the immunity provided to the state. There is only one entitlement in civil proceedings to compensation, and the responsibility is that of the state. If the conduct of an official is attributable to the state and the state is in international law responsible, then the state may claim immunity unless an established exception to immunity applies, and in these circumstances the state may also claim immunity for the individual state official. In a civil context, if a state is entitled to and claims immunity regarding conduct by its officials, then this immunity extends to all officials and ex-officials for this conduct, provided they were acting in an official capacity. Acting in an official capacity means the same here as it does in the context of the law of state responsibility.[111] So if a state claims immunity for its officials that state is accepting responsibility for their actions.[112]

The entitlement of individuals to immunity in civil cases is different to the entitlement to immunity in criminal cases. The responsibility of the individual and the state is not co-terminus when criminality is alleged, as a person who commits a crime is individually responsible for that crime, and can be punished. Individual responsibility for crimes under international law has been a principle of international law since the acceptance of the Nuremburg Principles after the Second World War. Individual

---

[111] ILC Draft Articles on the Responsibility of States for Internationally Wrongful Acts 2001, Arts 4 and 7; *Case concerning Certain Questions of Mutual Assistance in Criminal Matters (Djibouti v France*, n. 19 above, para. 196.

[112] *Jones v Ministry of the Interior*, n. 100 above, para. 12.

criminal responsibility is separate from and additional to any responsibility of the state. Associated with the concept of individual responsibility for offences are the ideas of the punishment and prevention of crime. A person who is responsible for a crime should be punished, and the possibility of prosecution and punishment should thereby act as a deterrent to others. There is nothing inconsistent in saying that the state is immune in respect of a particular act, but that an individual official can be prosecuted and punished for it.

The concept of immunity *ratione materiae* covering criminal liability was raised by the arrest of Pinochet, and in *Pinochet (No. 3)* the judges in the House of Lords were all agreed that all state officials are entitled to continuing immunity *ratione materiae*, but this premise was accepted without proper analysis or argument. There have been statements in cases such as *McLeod*[113] and *Blaškić*,[114] that officials should not be punished for acting on behalf of their state, but analysis shows these statements are not supported by state practice. The analysis of those cases, and the other cases referred to in the *Blaškić* judgment, do not support that conclusion. The analysis of state practice shows that states regularly prosecute state officials for actions performed on behalf of their states.

The place where the criminal conduct occurs has a bearing on whether immunity *ratione materiae* attaches to that conduct. The evidence of state practice analysed demonstrates that states have regularly prosecuted and punished officials of foreign states for acts committed on the territory of the forum state. This includes not only serious offences such as terrorism, assassination and kidnapping, but also less serious matters such as collecting information and trespassing. There is a marked contrast between the treatment of officials who have immunity *ratione personae*, such as diplomats, who are expelled, and other officials who are prosecuted, and often severely punished, for the same conduct. The analysis of state practice shows that only those state officials who are present on the territory of a foreign state with the consent of the second state and have immunity *ratione personae* are entitled to immunity *ratione materiae* from prosecution after they have left the territory or cease to hold office. They have immunity *ratione personae* for an agreed period, and thereafter they have continuing immunity *ratione materiae* for conduct legitimately performed in the exercise of their functions. This immunity extends to conduct which is connected to their functions but does not cover serious crimes of violence, even if committed on behalf of

113 British and Foreign State Papers, vol. 29, p. 1139.
114 *Prosecutor v Tihomir Blaškić*, n. 56 above.

the sending state. In the criminal context, acting in an official capacity does not include acts of violence on the territory of a foreign state. An official present on the territory of another state who does not have immunity *ratione personae* does not have immunity from prosecution for any offences committed on that territory.

The analysis of state practice demonstrates that immunity does not attach to conduct alone, for a person to have continuing immunity *ratione materiae* from prosecution for offences committed on the territory of a foreign state they must initially have had immunity *ratione personae*. The forum state must have agreed to the official being present on its territory, and agreed to the purpose of the visit. Those officials present on the territory of a foreign state, with the consent of that state, who have immunity *ratione personae*, have continuing immunity *ratione materiae* only for official conduct, *acta jure imperii*, with the proviso that the conduct must be part of the legitimate functions of the official. This does not extend to acts of violence.

There is the question regarding the extent of immunity for offences committed by an official on the territory of his own state in the exercise of his official functions. For the most part states do not have jurisdiction to prosecute crimes committed on the territory of another state and therefore the question does not arise. States have signed conventions undertaking to assert extra-territorial jurisdiction in relation to international crimes, and agreeing to extradite or prosecute alleged offenders present on their territory. Most states are party to the four Geneva Conventions 1949 and the Torture Convention 1984. These Conventions both require states parties to assume jurisdiction over alleged offenders present on their territory. All states parties have a duty to extradite a person alleged to have committed any offence as defined in the Conventions or to submit the case to its competent authorities for the purpose of prosecution. Grave breaches of the Geneva Conventions are most likely to be committed by soldiers and other state officials and the definition of torture in the Torture Convention requires that the offence is committed by officials acting under the guise of official authority. Therefore these offences are almost certain to be committed by persons acting in an official capacity. There is a tension between the principle of immunity and the obligation under international law to prosecute these crimes.

The ICJ in the *Arrest Warrant* case (at paragraph 61 of its judgment) said that after a person ceases to hold office a court of one state may try the former official of another state in respect of acts committed during that period of office in a private capacity. This was the central question in *Pinochet*: Is torture an offence that has to be committed by a state official, an 'official act' in the sense that it carries immunity *ratione materiae*?

One way to reconcile these two decisions is to say, as the judges did in the *Pinochet* case, that official torture committed by a state official as defined in the Torture Convention cannot be an act which carries with it immunity *ratione materiae*. This would mean that the terms 'official act' and 'acts committed in a private capacity' have different meanings in different contexts. In civil proceedings, an official act means an act for which a state may claim immunity, an act for which it is in international law responsible. In criminal proceedings, an official act cannot include conduct prohibited by international law. This is saying that official torture does not carry immunity *ratione materiae* because it is official.

The ICJ also stated (at paragraph 59 of its judgment) that a treaty provision regarding jurisdiction cannot change the immunity of an individual under international law. It said that rules governing the jurisdiction of national courts must be carefully distinguished from those governing jurisdictional immunities, and that jurisdiction does not imply the absence of immunity while the absence of immunity does not imply jurisdiction. This is all very well, but if there is no jurisdiction for official torture, the Torture Convention is rendered meaningless. The ICJ continued that the obligations of prosecution or extradition imposed by Conventions for the prevention and punishment of serious crimes require states to extend their criminal jurisdiction, but that such extension of jurisdiction in no way affects immunities under customary international law, including the immunity of high state officials. The ICJ stated that those immunities remain opposable before the courts of foreign states even where those courts exercise such a jurisdiction under those Conventions.

The statements of the ICJ about the immunity of former state officials were not necessary for the decision of the Court, and they have been criticized. The *Arrest Warrant* case was about the immunity *ratione personae* of high state officials, whereas the *Pinochet* case was about immunity *ratione materiae* to be afforded to former high state officials for offences, and therefore the two cases are distinguishable. But the statements of the ICJ in the *Arrest Warrant* case are powerful and clear declarations of that Court's understanding of customary international law. Any national court issuing a warrant for the arrest of a former high state official of a foreign state for torture or grave breaches of the Geneva Conventions engages the responsibility of the state, and must expect the issuance of such a warrant to be challenged in higher courts and on the international plane.

The ICJ suggested that another exception to the immunity of former high state officials would be prosecution before an international criminal tribunal which has jurisdiction. The principle of complementarity in the ICC Statute gives precedence to prosecution by states with traditional bases of jurisdiction, territory and nationality, and only allows for prosecution before the ICC if those states are unwilling or unable to prosecute. It is submitted that the Statute of the ICC provides a coherent hierarchy and a clear decision-making process for deciding where the trials of former high state officials for international crimes should be held.

8. The UK State Immunity Act 1978: history, scope and relation to international law

Alexander Orakhelashvili

8.1 GENERAL NATURE AND RELEVANCE AND HISTORY OF ADOPTION OF SIA 1978

Ordinarily, the national courts' practice can be seen as part of state practice in terms of the formation of customary international law on the relevant matter of public international law. However, the terms of reference to be used by national courts may be determinative of the actual extent to which their jurisprudence will contribute to that state practice. To illustrate, at times, the cases decided by English and US courts on the basis of national legislation on state immunity, such as the State Immunity Act (SIA) 1978 in the United Kingdom and the Foreign Sovereign Immunities Act (FSIA) 1976 in the United States, are prevented from applying the restrictive doctrine on state immunity, because the latter doctrine, as embodied in the common law that incorporates international law, has been displaced, in relation to those national jurisdictions, by the statute that prescribes that a general immunity persists unless a specific exception from it is identified.[1] The practice of national courts that applies a national statute conflicting with the pre-existing common law, and thus with international law, has far lesser potential to contribute to state practice in terms of the creation of customary rules of international law.

What options are available to English courts for dealing with the above dilemma, and to what extent are they supposed to take part in resolving it? According to F.A. Mann, the SIA 1978 is a remedial statute, given that it makes a 'new provision' on the issues of state immunity in the UK legal system.[2] At the same time, there is no fixed general typology of

[1] As reflected in the argument put forward by J. Crawford, 'A Foreign State Immunities Act for Australia?' (1983) *Australian YIL* 71 at 105–6.

[2] F.A. Mann, 'The State Immunity Act 1978' (1980) 51 *BYIL* 43; the Act's long title is as follows: 'An Act to make new provision with respect to

statutes in English law, nor is there any imperative reason to assume that the equation as between the legislative intention and common law should be different for some statutes than for others. For, as the House of Lords stated a century ago in *R v Halliday*, all statutes are to be interpreted in the same way.[3]

When the 1978 Act was being enacted and deliberated upon in Parliament, Lord Wilberforce and Lord Denning expressed some misgivings about it. Both their Lordships spoke against universalizing the regional regime of the 1972 European Convention on State Immunity and making it applicable to all states.[4] Lord Denning went further and suggested that the state immunity Bill had to be put on hold because (a) it did not reflect international law as it then stood (along with the distinction between the restrictive doctrine and statutory tests that the SIA 1978 now provides); and (b) it aimed at conserving the legal position which was in a constant state of development.[5]

As we have already seen,[6] the common law standard that incorporates general international law requires the application of the restrictive, or functional, approach to immunities under which the acts that constitute the proper exercises of governmental authority do attract immunity and the ones that do not fall within such category do not. The 1978 Act eschews such classification and instead turns to the 'general rule versus specific exceptions' approach, under which all that does not fall within the specified statutory exceptions, and whatever the underlying nature of the relevant act or transaction, whether in essence sovereign or private, will attract immunity under the residual general statutory rule of immunity. Results could, then, be substantially different depending on which of these two approaches is taken in practice.

The initial purpose behind the adoption of the SIA 1978 presumably was to incorporate the approach under the 1972 European Convention on State Immunity (ECSI), though it should be emphasized that the text of

---

proceedings in the United Kingdom by or against other States; to provide for the effect of judgments given against the United Kingdom in the courts of States parties to the European Convention on State Immunity; to make new provision with respect to the immunities and privileges of heads of State; and for connected purposes'.

[3] *R (at the prosecution of Arthur Zadig) v Halliday* [1917] AC 260.

[4] It will be noted that ECSI has only eight states parties and thus it was not applicable to the major controversies focused upon in this chapter.

[5] See, generally, *Hansard* (HL) vol. 388 cols 51–78, 17 January 1978; and vol. 949 cols 405–20, 3 May 1978 (interventions by Lords Wilberforce and Denning).

[6] See Chapter 5.

the SIA 1978 does not expressly allude to the immunity provisions of the 1972 Convention (while its Preamble does allude to ECSI provisions regarding the execution of judgments). In the light of the absolute and restrictive doctrines of state immunity, the difference was also addressed by Lord Diplock in *Alcom*, to the effect that:

> although comprehensive, the Act in its approach to these two aspects of the jurisdiction exercised by courts of law does not adopt the straightforward dichotomy between *acta jure imperii* and *acta jure gestionis* that had become familiar doctrine in public international law, except that it comes close to doing so in section 14(2) in relation to the immunity conferred upon 'separate entities that are emanations of the state'. Instead, as respects foreign states themselves the Act starts by restating in statutory form in section 1(1) the general principle of absolute sovereign immunity, but makes the principle subject to wide-ranging exceptions for which the subsequent sections in Part I of the Act (sections 2 to 17) provide.[7]

As one commentary also emphasises, 'The English statute opens with a restatement of the absolute rule and then proceeds to abolish that rule, for most practical purposes, by the exceptions which follow'. The affirmation of the absolute immunity rule is also reinforced in section 14 by the need to clarify whether the particular entity is a 'foreign State'.[8]

An Act making 'new provision' on state immunity in the English legal system could arguably be seen as displacing the restrictive doctrine that previously was part of common law via international law. Such literal approach seems to have prevailed in some previous cases before English courts, to the effect that the 1978 Act was deemed to be a 'comprehensive code' on state immunity, precluding domestic courts from addressing the distinction between sovereign and non-sovereign acts as comity and international law may require to be taken into account.[9]

But this is not the only approach featuring in the reasoning of English courts. As the UK House of Lords stated in *Lampen-Wolfe*, 'The immunity which is accorded by English law to foreign states in civil proceedings is the subject of two separate regimes. The first is that laid down by Part 1 of the State Immunity Act 1978 … [the] second regime is

---

[7] *Alcom v Colombia* [1984] AC 580 at 600.

[8] S. Bird, 'The State Immunity Act of 1978: An English Update' (1979) 13 *International Lawyer* 619 at 626.

[9] See the following British and US cases: *Siderman de Blake v Argentina* (1992) 103 ILR 455; *Princz v Federal Republic of Germany* (1994) 33 ILM 1483; *Smith and others v Libyan Arab Jamahiriya* (1997) 36 ILM 100; *Al-Adsani v Kuwait* (1996) 107 ILR 536.

that under the common law. It applies to all cases that fall outside the scope of Part I of the Act'.[10] Thus, under this approach, while it makes a 'new provision' on immunity, there is no imperative reason to consider the SIA 1978 as a comprehensive regulation of foreign state immunities in English law. It does leave some cases to be decided by reference to the common law. Therefore, the suggestion that the SIA 1978 makes some previous English case law merely of historical importance[11] should be seen as ill-founded.

8.2 STATUTORY EXCEPTIONS TO IMMUNITY AND THEIR INTERPRETATION

Generally, the issue of interpreting the statutory rules that provide for exceptions from other, more general statutory rules, has been a matter of significant debate.[12] F.A. Mann's view is that the exceptions the SIA 1978 admits to the residual general state immunity should not be narrowly construed, even if it is a general rule of statutory interpretation that when there is any doubt the general rule rather than the exception applies, and the exception does not derogate from the general principle to an extent greater than its words strictly require.[13] Higgins has spoken in similar terms, to the effect that 'as the exceptions increase in scope, the truth is that we begin to *think* in other terms. We begin to think of immunity as not normally being allowed unless – exceptionally – the acts are *acta jure imperii*'. This issue was important, 'because in any marginal case issues about the burden of proof will arise'.[14]

Mann has thus contrasted the conflicting approaches to the interpretation of the SIA 1978, suggesting that 'it would be unjustifiable to subject sections 2 to 11 of the Act to a narrow construction on the ground that they contain exceptions to the principle laid down in section I [of the Act]'. Furthermore:

---

[10] *Holland v Lampen-Wolfe* [2000] 3 All ER 845, 1575–6 (per Lord Hope).

[11] As contended by M. Dixon, R. McCorquodale and S. Williams, *Cases and Materials on International Law* (2nd edn, Oxford, Oxford University Press 2009), p. 318.

[12] See, for example, G. Williams, 'The Logic of "Exceptions"' (1988) 47 *CLJ* 261.

[13] Mann, n. 2 above, 50.

[14] R. Higgins, 'Certain Unresolved Aspects of the Law of State Immunity' (1982) 29 *NILR* 265 at 270–71 (emphasis in original).

> In England it has frequently been a technique of statutory interpretation to say that an exception does not derogate from the principle to a greater extent than the words used strictly require, that, in other words, in case of doubt the principle rather than the exception should be held to apply. But this is not invariably so and should certainly not be so in the present case. What the legislator described as exceptions represents a very broad sector of State activity. Its limits should be so drawn as to fit the legislative purpose behind each provision rather than the drafting technique that the legislator followed. The so-called exceptions are a far-reaching group of provisions which are not subordinate, but equal, to and on the same level as the so-called principle. Hence the rule usually applicable to the construction of exceptions does not fit.[15]

What Mann's approach does is to enhance the role of judicial interpretation and reduce the reliance on the will of Parliament: the ascertainment of 'legislative purpose' behind the Act is a judicial task, while the relevance of 'the drafting technique'[16] should be seen to refer to the role and will of the Parliament. On this approach, courts should be having a greater freedom to select between the application of the general immunity rule or of specific exceptions to it, on balance one being not more or less important than the other. In a way, both the general residual immunity and specific exceptions to it have been willed and intended by the legislator. Both are supported by the text of the statute the ascertainment of the meaning of which is exclusively a judicial affair. There is, presumably, no inherent hierarchy between the two kinds of legal prescriptions.

Mann's position could also possibly be seen as a statement of the agenda to re-introduce the pre-SIA restrictive doctrine through the back-door. While, on overall terms, courts have to operate subject to the duty of judicial obedience to statutes, the very subject matter of the statute could be used here to revert the judicial reasoning of the courts to the common law standards again. In this way we may achieve a two-stage relevance of the common law in relation to the area regulated by the statute: first in relation to issues that the SIA 1978 has expressly left to the common law to regulate; and then with regard to issues in relation to which English courts can use common law principles and approaches to influence the content of particular provisions of the SIA 1978.

---

[15] Mann, n. 2 above, 50.

[16] A 'convoluted style of draftsmanship', as Lord Diplock described it in relation to the SIA 1978 in *Alcom*, n. 7 above, 600.

All this demonstrates that there is a legal and judicial possibility that, at least in relation to litigation involving states that are not parties to ECSI, the SIA 1978 can be treated as sort of codifying statute that reflects the existing common law,[17] rather than universalizes an effectively sub-regional legal framework of ECSI that applies to eight states only. The SIA 1978's content could then be applied in a way somewhat reflective of the restrictive doctrine as accepted under comity or customary international law and, correspondingly, under the pre-SIA common law in England. One example of this approach is provided by *NML v Argentina*, which essentially approved this vision by interpreting the 'commercial exception' under SIA 1978, section 3 in the light of the broader context of the restrictive immunity doctrine.[18] In this way, the common law may provide a background that could inform the meaning of statutory provisions to make them operate as part of the broader legal context.

The Court of Appeal in *Benkharbouche* struck a somewhat stricter note, arguably endorsing the more limited role for the judiciary in applying statutory exceptions to state immunity; in that particular case, those dealing with employment matters and those reserved for a separate legal regulation (SIA 1978, sections 4 and 16). The Court of Appeal in this case approached the matter in terms of the constitutional distribution of authority as between the courts and the Parliament. The court accordingly said that:

> the Parliamentary intent expressed in the SIA was to confer immunity subject to specific exceptions. In his view the Act was framed so as to create a careful, detailed and clear pattern which balances considerations known to the legislature. He considered that if a court or tribunal were to alter the width of a provision limiting an exception to immunity (section 4(2)) or of a clear statement that section 4 does not apply to particular people (section 16) there would be a danger of its affecting the overall balance struck by the legislature whilst lacking Parliament's panoramic vision across the whole of the landscape.[19]

The approach that courts should not re-draw or re-define the balance of interests embodied in legislative decisions of the Parliament has been

---

[17] Cf. on the relevant classification of statutes, F. Bennion, *Statutory Interpretation* (London, Butterworths, 1997), pp. 465–6 (section 212).

[18] *NML v Argentina* [2011] UKSC 31, SC, 6 July 2011, para. 39 (per Lord Phillips).

[19] *Benkharbouche v Embassy of the Republic of Sudan* [2015] EWCA Civ 33, CA, 5 February 2015, para. 67.

recognized in English law for a long time, and is a matter of allocation of the authority between the political and judicial branches of government, the ability to make judgments on particular issues of policy or law being reserved to each of these branches.[20] But curiously enough, the relationship between preserving the legislatively specified balance of interests, and the ascertainment of the meaning of provisions arguably sustaining that balance of interests, may at times be circular rather than strictly isolated. The Court of Appeal's pronouncement is, therefore, not a definite argument against what has been expounded by F.A. Mann, and later on by the Supreme Court in *NML*, in relation to the ways of understanding the scope and meaning of statutory exceptions under the SIA 1978. Furthermore, the Court of Appeal's somewhat stricter approach should also be seen part of the wider legal background in the English legal system which, in modern times, includes the possibility (used in *Benkharbouche*) of declaring the particular provision of the SIA 1978 incompatible with the Human Rights Act 1998.[21]

8.3 SOME ASPECTS OF THE STRUCTURE AND SUBSTANCE OF SIA 1978

8.3.1 Appearance, Non-appearance and Counter-claims

Section 1(b) of the 1978 Act states that, 'A court shall give effect to the immunity conferred by this section even though the state does not appear in the proceedings in question'. The non-appearance by the foreign state does not compromise the possibility of the immunity being granted to it, and there is no straightforward requirement that the state positively claims immunity. Furthermore, by virtue of section 2(6), 'A submission in respect of any proceedings extends to any appeal but not to any counter-claim unless it arises out of the same legal relationship or facts as the claim'. The foreign state is thus exposed to counter claims from the litigation adversary to a limited extent.

That seems to be somewhat different from ECSI, Article 3(1) which does not expressly privilege counter-claims in this way.[22] However,

[20] For a prominent discussion of these issues see *Duport Steels Ltd v Sirs* [1980] 1 WLR 142.

[21] See further below.

[22] '1. A Contracting State cannot claim immunity from the jurisdiction of a court of another Contracting State if, before claiming immunity, it takes any step in the proceedings relating to the merits. However, if the State satisfies the Court

ECSI, Article 1(3) suggests that 'A Contracting State which makes a counterclaim in proceedings before a court of another Contracting State submits to the jurisdiction of the courts of that State with respect not only to the counterclaim but also to the principal claim'. To compare further, Article 9(3) of the 2004 UN Convention on Jurisdictional Immunities suggests, in a reverse manner, that 'A State making a counterclaim in a proceeding instituted against it before a court of another State cannot invoke immunity from the jurisdiction of the court in respect of the principal claim'.

8.3.2 Meaning of 'Commercial Transactions' and 'Commercial Purposes'

Section 3 of the 1978 Act states, in its relevant parts, that:

> (1) A State is not immune as respects proceedings relating to:
> (a) a commercial transaction entered into by the State; or
> (b) an obligation of the State which by virtue of a contract (whether a commercial transaction or not) fails to be performed wholly or partly in the United Kingdom. …
> (3) In this section 'commercial transaction' means:
> (a) any contract for the supply of goods or services;
> (b) any loan or other transaction for the provision of finance and any guarantee or indemnity in respect of any such transaction or of any other financial obligation; and
> (c) any other transaction or activity (whether of a commercial, industrial, financial, professional or other similar character) into which a State enters or in which it engages otherwise than in the exercise of sovereign authority.

The meaning of SIA 1978, section 3(3)(c) and its reference to activities 'into which a State enters or in which it engages otherwise than in the exercise of sovereign authority'[23] raises most pertinent questions, both from the viewpoint of statutory interpretation and the restrictive doctrine of immunities as a common law issue. On one reading, the exception which section 3(3)(c) provides could appear to be quite narrow, if the words 'other similar character' are seen to cover acts and transactions belonging to the commercial genus.

---

that it could not have acquired knowledge of facts on which a claim to immunity can be based until after it has taken such a step, it can claim immunity based on these facts if it does so at the earliest possible moment.'

23 See also, for analysis, *Alcom*, n. 7 above, 603 (per Lord Diplock).

Also, the words 'otherwise than in the exercise of sovereign authority' in section 3 are somewhat baffling, for they imply that such purely private and commercial activities could also be entered into, in the exercise of the state's sovereign authority, thereby contradicting the distinction between public and private acts, as part of the restrictive doctrine, from *Charkieh* onwards.[24] As Bird also aptly clarifies, 'there will always be a gray area where states may seek immunity on the basis that they are exercising sovereign authority, and it may be a weakness that the statute does not give more guidance'.[25]

Thus, the statute certainly provides ground for tempting foreign states litigating before English courts to advance the sovereign authority argument where it does not belong, claiming that the pertinent commercial act is an exercise of state sovereignty, that is, in essence a private act is a public act. However, the answer will always have to be sought in the restrictive theory as recognized on the international plane: it should always be about the particular act complained of, not its purpose or context, which would determine whether the exercise of sovereign authority is involved.

The solution adopted here by the SIA 1978 in the United Kingdom is not in principle incompatible with the one adopted by the US FSIA 1976, section 1603(d), stating the position that 'The commercial character of an activity shall be determined by reference to the nature of the course of conduct or particular transaction or act, rather than by reference to its purpose'. As Mann has emphasized in relation to SIA 1978, section 3, a commercial transaction 'is determined by its objective nature rather than its possibly subjective purpose'.[26]

The Lord Chancellor's statement in *Hansard* could be instructive to understand the precise remit of 'commercial transactions':

> That wide definition of 'commercial transaction' will mean that the clause will cover practically all the cases where a State can be said to be acting *jure gestionis*, that is to say, in the same manner as a private person. Subsections 3(a) and (b) are intended to remove possible doubt from the classes of transactions of common occurrence which can be argued to fall into either class – sovereign or non-sovereign – and about which, indeed, the courts of different countries have come to different conclusions.[27]

---

24 See, on this, Chapter 5.

25 Bird, n. 8 above, 630.

26 Mann, n. 2 above, 58.

27 *Hansard*, vol. 389, cols 1491–540, 16 March 1978.

A 'commercial transaction' under SIA 1978, section 3 could, then, possibly mean a non-sovereign act, even if not performed for commercial purposes, as long as it is a transaction that could be performed by a private entity as well as by the state. Not every act or transaction that has no inherent or prevailing commercial purpose could be deemed to have been performed through the use of the foreign state's sovereign authority (again, that authority and its scope being a matter for the common law, not for the statute, to determine). This reading appears even more plausible given that, whenever the SIA 1978 emphasizes the 'commercial purposes' of the subject matter in relation to which immunity may or may not be claimed, as in section 10 on admiralty proceedings, it expressly uses that very term.

Mann has subscribed to such broader reading of the commercial activities exception in a passage worth quoting at length:

> It is submitted that the definition is such as to render it possible to sue a foreign State in respect of a tort other than those mentioned in sections 5 to 7 which has been committed in England … The only activity which cannot in any circumstances be a commercial transaction is one exercised by virtue of sovereign authority – a phrase which, it is submitted, only qualifies the word 'activity', not the words 'any other transaction' … Section 3 comprises torts wherever committed, provided the English court has (territorial) jurisdiction in respect of the claim or counter-claim. A tort committed abroad may yet have been committed in England if the damage has occurred here. Furthermore, the fact that certain torts are specifically mentioned does not necessitate the conclusion that other torts are not caught by the wide terms of section 3.[28]

Thus, the relevant provisions of the SIA 1978 could possibly be seen as importing back the restrictive doctrine of immunities into the realm of statutory law, and also possibly opening the extra-territorial torts litigation route before English courts. This option has not received any intensive attention in judicial practice, and may even be based on a reading of the statutory language that is ideologically unacceptable in some quarters. But these factors do not disqualify such reading of SIA 1978, section 3 from being one that could well be sustained on the basis of the use of statutory interpretation methods to ascertain what Parliament intended when enacting the 1978 Act.

The Court of Appeal in *Svenska Petroleum* stated the initial policy as to the flexibility of the interpretative approach applicable to SIA 1978, section 3, to the effect that:

---

[28] Mann, n. 2 above, 52–3.

> the expression 'relating to' is capable of bearing a broader or narrower meaning as the context requires. Section 3 is one of a group of sections dealing with the courts' adjudicative jurisdiction and it is natural, therefore, to interpret the phrase in that context as being directed to the subject matter of the proceedings themselves rather than the source of the legal relationship which has given rise to them.[29]

A further clarification was provided by Lord Phillips in *NML* at the Supreme Court, suggesting that:

> I can see no justification for giving section 3(1)(a) a narrow interpretation on the basis that it is desirable to restrict the circumstances in which it operates to those where the commercial transaction has a link with the United Kingdom. The restrictive doctrine of sovereign immunity does not restrict the exemption from immunity to commercial transactions that are in some way linked to the jurisdiction of the forum.[30]

Thus, not only the narrow scope of general residual immunity and the broad scope of the exception from that immunity is endorsed, but Lord Phillips also dis-applies the interpretative presumption, applicable otherwise, that where the statute does not expressly point to the opposite, it must be deemed to apply only to things, persons and matters within the UK jurisdiction. On those grounds, Lord Mance was 'unable to agree with Lord Phillips on … the scope of section 3 of the State Immunity Act 1978 … [and did] not consider that the drafters of that Act or Parliament contemplated that section 3(1)(a) of the 1978 Act had in mind that it would or should apply to a foreign judgment against a foreign state'.[31]

The dilemma in their Lordships' approach to section 3 is not just about the reach of state immunity in relation to commercial transactions, but raises some deeper issues of UK constitutional law as to how the legislative intention of Parliament should be ascertained, and more importantly what, if any, the territorial limits on the exercise of Parliament's legislative supremacy are.

Traditionally, English courts have approached the territorial reach of English statutes as a matter of statutory interpretation, in terms of whether and to what extent the legislator has intended that its prescriptions should apply to events, acts or persons abroad. In some cases,

---

[29] *Svenska Petroleum v Government of Lithuania* [2006] EWCA Civ 1529, para. 137.

[30] *NML v Argentina*, n. 18 above, para. 39.

[31] *Ibid.* para. 88.

courts have also treated this matter as one of the *vires* of Parliament.[32] Here in *NML v Argentina*, Lord Phillips is prioritizing the literal meaning of the statutory text to apply it to anything wherever that literal meaning takes it. Lord Mance, on the other hand, prioritizes the extra-statutory, common law, presumption against the extra-territoriality of statutes. Now, given the complex history of this matter, it cannot safely be said that UK constitutional law categorically prioritizes the relevance of one of these approaches over the other. Instead, the interpretative flexibility available to English courts at common law makes it possible to arrive at statutory interpretation results that are compatible, rather than at variance, with public international law. This issue also runs into the presumption that Parliament must have intended to legislate in accordance with international law, unless the text of the statute mandatorily suggests that it is otherwise.

SIA 1978, section 10(2), which relates to admiralty proceedings, raises an important issue of distinguishing the nature and purpose of commercial transactions from each other. The standard provided for ascertaining the scope of immunities is here expressly related to the purpose of transactions. As section 10(2) provides:

> A State is not immune as respects:
>
> (a) an action in rem against a ship belonging to that State; or
> (b) an action in personam for enforcing a claim in connection with such a ship, if, at the time when the cause of action arose, the ship was in use or intended for use for commercial purposes.

Section 10(4)(a) then provides that:

> A State is not immune as respects:
>
> (a) an action in rem against a cargo belonging to that State if both the cargo and the ship carrying it were, at the time when the cause of action arose, in use or intended for use for commercial purposes.

Note that here the SIA 1978 adopts the purpose-driven approach to determine whether immunity accrues to the ship or the cargo (unlike the approach taken in section 3 on commercial transactions, as discussed above). As Mann comments in relation to the ambit of immunities under section 10:

---

[32] See, for example, the earlier case of *Le Louis* (1817) 2 *Dodson* 210, 15 December 1817, which shows the long history of this constitutional dilemma.

> A warship which happens to be used for carrying motor cars for civilian use cannot be immune, but if a trading ship carries ammunition for military purposes both the ship and the cargo are immune, at least if there is no commercial cargo on board. Cement carried in a trading ship may be immune: the result depends on the purpose for which it will be used. If the consignee intends to sell the cement to the military administration, but is not contractually bound to do so, the non-commercial purpose does not in a legally relevant sense exist … Shoes for the army (to revert to an often-discussed example) are cargo for a non-commercial purpose, but if they are consigned to a private merchant who only hopes to sell them to the army, the purpose remains commercial. If the consignee is the State itself and intends to use the cargo for the business of a State monopoly such as a tobacco or alcohol monopoly, this is a commercial purpose, though the consignee may regard it as a public purpose. Conversely, if there exists in England a monopoly for the production and sale of certain goods (as at present is not the case) this would not prove that similar goods carried in a foreign ship are not intended for commercial purposes: a State monopoly as such is not by any means a non-commercial venture.[33]

As can be seen, the determination of the purposes of the relevant act or transaction is bound to provide a shape of immunities available to foreign states which is different from that which it would have when the relevant transaction is evaluated in terms of its inherent nature and the involvement of the sovereign authority element. It could be the case that the SIA 1978 adopts this purpose-driven approach to make it specifically applicable to the *in rem* proceedings with which section 10 is concerned.

8.3.3 Territorial Torts

Section 5 of the 1978 Act provides that:

> A State is not immune as respects proceedings in respect of:
>
> (a) death or personal injury; or
> (b) damage to or loss of tangible property,
>
> caused by an act or omission in the United Kingdom.

But what is 'an act or omission in the United Kingdom'? More importantly, is the territorial connection issue to be determined as a matter of private international law,[34] or merely as a matter of statutory interpretation of the letter of section 5? The issue of where a conduct or

---

33 Mann, n. 2 above, 58.

34 For discussion of which see R. Higgins, 'Certain Unresolved Aspects of the Law of State Immunity' (1982) 29 *NILR* 265 at 272.

activity spreading over the borders of various states would stand in relation to the scope of section 5 could raise controversies in terms of construing the scope of section 5. To illustrate, in *Al-Adsani v United Kingdom*, the situation was encountered that, while the initial act of torturing Al-Adsani had taken place in Kuwait, there was a follow-up to this torture that actually occurred within the United Kingdom. When, afterwards, Al-Adsani was in the United Kingdom, he also suffered psychological damage and was diagnosed as suffering from a severe form of post-traumatic stress disorder, aggravated by the fact that, once in England, he received threats warning him not to take action or give publicity to his plight.[35]

Now, the issue of whether the original torture and the subsequent harassment (both having contributed to the post-traumatic stress disorder Al-Adsani was suffering from) should be regarded as a single event deemed, for the purposes of the relevant litigation, to have occurred entirely in the United Kingdom, or entirely in Kuwait, or whether they could be split to hold those who committed torts accountable for what they did in the United Kingdom while leaving them immune in relation to acts having taken place abroad, is in essence a policy choice relating to the statutory interpretation of section 5. There is nothing in the text of the SIA 1978, or in general principles of statutory interpretation, to force English courts to adopt a blanket approach, to the effect that the totality of the underlying facts should be deemed to have occurred outside the United Kingdom, in Kuwait. Some factors (at least) that contributed to Al-Adsani's condition did take place in the United Kingdom. It remains to conclude that the court in *Al-Adsani* made its own policy choice in a rather arbitrary manner, to entirely exclude Al-Adsani's situation, including its UK-based elements, from the scope of section 5.

8.3.4 Issues that SIA 1978 Does Not Cover: Immunity of Foreign Armed Forces

SIA 1978, section 16(2), provides that the Act 'does not apply to proceedings relating to anything done by or in relation to the armed forces of a State while present in the United Kingdom'. Accordingly, the House of Lords has observed in *Lampen-Wolfe* that 'Section 16(2) applies, and the question of immunity must be determined according to the common law'.[36] It was also held in *Littrell* that the 1978 Act was

[35] *Al-Adsani v United Kingdom* (2002) 34 EHRR 11 at 289.

[36] *Lampen-Wolfe*, n. 10 above, 1577.

immaterial in the relevant proceedings involving foreign armed forces.[37] The case thus fell to be decided on the basis of the restrictive doctrine as part of common law.

The residual role of common law thus again resurfaces in this area, and further exposes the potential which the common law has in construing the meaning and scope of the exception to statutory immunities under section 16(2), in the sense that the meaning of terms included in that section will, as a matter of judicial construction, determine the scope of immunities available to the foreign state under that section.

To illustrate, Lord Hope in *Lampen-Wolfe* suggested that:

> the expression 'armed forces' in section 16(2) cannot be regarded as meaning only military personnel or servicemen and women who handle weapons and equipment and are in uniform. Regard must be had to the fact that it is a matter for each state to decide how best to organise its own armed forces and related services. We are concerned in this case with events that took place on a military base on which the United States of America maintains units of its armed forces by arrangement with her Majesty's Government. The organization and support of armed forces on a military base overseas is a complex exercise.[38]

This is yet another instance of the interpretative flexibility being available to English courts when construing the exceptions to general state immunity as stated in the SIA 1978. The statute does not define what the armed forces and their activities are: courts do, as a matter of common law. What also matters is that, once the non-applicability of the SIA 1978 pursuant to its section 16(2) is ascertained, the matter falls to be decided according to the narrower restrictive doctrine of immunity as part of common law, which Lord Cooke in *Lampen-Wolfe* again thought was that endorsed in Lord Wilberforce's judgment in *I Congreso*.[39]

8.3.5 'Separate Entities' under SIA 1978, Section 14(2)

SIA 1978, section 14(2) provides that:

> The immunities and privileges conferred by this Part of this Act apply to any foreign or commonwealth State other than the United Kingdom; and references to a State include references to:

---

37 *Littrell v United States* [1995] 1 WLR 87 (per Rose LJ).

38 *Lampen-Wolfe*, n. 10 above, 1576.

39 *Ibid.* 1578–9; see also per Lord Clyde at 1579; and see *Littrell*, n. 37 above, 92 (per Hoffmann LJ); see further Chapter 5.

> (a) the sovereign or other head of that State in his public capacity;
> (b) the government of that State; and
> (c) any department of that government,
>
> but not to any entity (hereafter referred to as a 'separate entity') which is distinct from the executive organs of the government of the State and capable of suing or being sued.

The discussion of the issue of what could validly be considered as such a 'separate entity' was taking place well before the SIA 1978 was adopted, in the context of the general doctrine of restrictive immunity that focuses on the sovereign or non-sovereign nature of the underlying act.

One area where restrictive doctrine and the ensuing sovereign authority test can be used even within domestic statutory frameworks relates to 'separate entities' under SIA 1978, section 14(2), which prescribes that the entity affiliated with the governmental apparatus of the foreign state is immune only if 'the proceedings relate to anything done by it in the exercise of sovereign authority'. This was confirmed in *Kuwait Air Co.*, where Lord Goff emphasized that 'it is not enough that the entity should have acted on the directions of the state, because such an act need not possess the character of a governmental act. To attract immunity under section 14(2), therefore, what is done by the separate entity must be something which possesses that character'.[40] Thus, section 14(2) requires first identifying the identity of the organ and then applying the restrictive doctrine to its action.

The issue was addressed before the SIA 1978 came into force in the *Trendtex* case, where Shaw LJ and Stephenson LJ refused to consider the Central Bank of Nigeria as an organ of the Nigerian state, as the relevant legislative amendments that threw light on the Bank's status fell short of revealing legislative intention to that effect.[41] A similar philosophy underlies the pronouncements in *Rolimpex* that the entity in question was not part of the Polish state since, even if it 'bought and sold for the State', it retained a considerable freedom in relation to day-to-day commercial activities.[42] To some extent, then, the very status of a 'separate legal entity', as *Trendtex* had it, will depend on the nature of its tasks and the degree of its affiliation with the sovereign functions of the state. In *Rolimpex* the entity in question was confirmed in that status to enable it to claim substantive defence against non-compliance with

40 *Kuwait Air Co.* [1995] 1 WLR 1147 at 1160 (per Lord Goff).
41 *Trendtex* [1977] 1 QB 565 at 573.
42 *Czarnikow Ltd v Rolimpex* [1979] AC 351 at 364 (per Lord Wilberforce); 367 (per Viscount Dilhorne).

contractual obligations due to government intervention beyond their control, an issue unrelated to immunities. But the underlying test of state public authority remained the same for both areas of law; in both cases the core issue was – and was answered in the negative – whether the entity in question was acting as part of the state and exercising its sovereign functions. Capitalizing on previous jurisprudence, Lord Goff concluded in *Kuwait Air Co.* that 'in the absence of such [governmental] character, the mere fact that the purpose or motive of the act was to serve the purposes of the state will not be sufficient to enable the separate entity to claim immunity under section 14(2) of the Act'.[43]

As for the governing law on this issue, it was emphasized in *Trendtex* that:

> the constitution and powers of a Nigerian corporation must be viewed in the light of the domestic law of Nigeria. But its status in the international scene falls to be decided by the law of the country in which an issue as to its status is raised. In civilised states that law will derive from those principles of international law which have been generally accepted among such states.[44]

It is therefore affirmed that the domestic forum must, whenever possible, select international law as the law determining the (non-)sovereign status of the entity. As Shaw LJ observed, even if the Bank was a sub-serving agent for government departments, that was not sufficient to make it part of the government.[45] Domestic law provided the initial point of reference, while international law assessed the nature of the relevant domestic legal arrangements, and ultimately determined where sovereign authority lies. The entire discourse, then, took place within the context of the restrictive doctrine of immunities, focusing on the exact nature of underlying acts, as part of the common law and international law.

8.4 RELATIONSHIP OF SIA 1978 TO INTERNATIONAL LAW

Perhaps the most important thing to understand about the SIA 1978 is that this Act is a source of UK domestic law, not of international law. It represents the legal position the UK Parliament has chosen to make domestically applicable in the English legal system. It does not determine

---

43 *Kuwait Air Co.*, n. 40 above, 1160.

44 *Trendtex*, n. 41 above, 575 (per Shaw LJ).

45 *Ibid.* 575.

what states legally owe each other on an international plane, or what they owe to individuals as a matter of international law.

In *I Congreso*, the UK House of Lords was asked to consider that the SIA 1978, which was not directly applicable because of its non-retroactivity, embodied applicable international law. Lord Wilberforce refused, considering that 'to argue from the terms of a statute to establish what international law provides is to stand the accepted argument on its head', and added that 'if one State chooses to lay down by enactment certain limits, that is by itself no evidence that those limits are generally accepted by States. And particularly enacted limits may be (or presumed to be) not inconsistent with general international law – the latter being in a state of uncertainty – without affording evidence what that law is'.[46] Similarly, the Irish Supreme Court in *McElhinney* remarked that 'statutes are evidence of domestic law in the individual States and not evidence of international law generally'.[47]

The principal question here is whether particular provisions of SIA 1978 are in accordance with or in violation of international law. No sensible objection could be advanced to the fact that, while domestically an expression of legislative supremacy of the Parliament, internationally the SIA 1978, as a domestic statute, is a mere fact which will either be seen as compliant with or violative of international law. Domestic laws are merely facts in the eyes of international law, and their legality falls to be assessed accordingly.[48]

The European Court of Human Rights (ECtHR) held in *Al-Adsani v United Kingdom* that the SIA 1978 was compatible with Article 6 of the European Convention on Human Rights (ECHR), on margin of appreciation grounds, in the sense that the grant of immunity to Kuwait was not a disproportionate restriction of Al-Adsani's rights under Article 6 of the Convention. Before the ECtHR's judgment in *Al-Adsani*, however, English courts had ordinarily said that the requirements under the SIA 1978 and international law may be different, rather than that the former is compliant with the latter; and that national courts apply the SIA 1978

---

46 *I Congreso* [1983] 1 AC 260, HL.

47 *McElhinney* (1995) 104 ILR 691 at 701, Irish Supreme Court, 15 December 1995.

48 See *Certain German Interests in Polish Upper Silesia*, PCIJ Series A, No. 7, 19; see also *United States – Import Prohibition of Certain Shrimp and Shrimp Products*, AB-1998-4, Report of the WTO Appellate Body, WT/DS58/AB/R, 12 October 1998, para. 138.

because they are domestically bound to do so, even regardless of the requirements of international law.[49]

One understanding of the doctrine of legislative sovereignty of the UK Parliament is that, even if violating international law, the Parliament arguably has the power to legislate in such a way. As Dicey wrote, no judge would listen to a counsel arguing that an Act of Parliament should be declared void because it does not comply with international law.[50] But then, the consequences under international law would be serious, as the firm adherence to the Diceyan approach would essentially constitute an admission of the United Kingdom's liability for misapplying the scope of the doctrine of state immunity as international law either recognizes or tolerates as a matter of comity. Policy-wise, this would amount to using the domestic constitutional framework to domestically entrench and continuingly validate violations of international law. The alternative, again, lies with the proper use of statutory interpretation methods to avoid such extreme results.

The use of the presumption that domestic legislation in the United Kingdom does not intend to contradict international law may require the taking of the position that, to the extent that ECSI represents a *lex specialis* in relation to general international law (or comity), the legislator may be presumed to be implementing ECSI domestically, via the SIA 1978, on those *lex specialis* conditions, that is, in relation to states parties to ECSI and to their mutual relations (and also subject to their Article 24 declarations).[51] But applying the SIA 1978 beyond that scope, to states not parties to the Convention, is no longer warranted by the interpretative presumption that statutes should be interpreted as compliant with international treaties.

In terms of the further dynamics of comity and general international law, the SIA 1978 has experienced no dynamic developments comparable to the Flatow amendment of the US FSIA 1976 and similar amendments of the Canadian state immunity legislation.[52] On that account, the SIA 1978 could be seen as the United Kingdom's contribution to state practice on state immunity on an international plane even less than might be the case with state immunity statutes operative in other common law jurisdictions.

Last but not least, it is a commonplace that in the UK legal system, the adoption of the Human Rights Act 1998 has provided a halfway house

---

49 See n. 9 above, in relation to both English and US judicial practice.

50 A.V. Dicey, *The Law of the Constitution* (8th edn, 1915), pp. 64–5.

51 On which see Chapter 9.

52 On which see Chapter 5.

between the two options, one of which is the application of domestic statutes in violation of international human rights, and the other is the review of such statutes by courts if they are found incompatible with those human rights. The 1998 Act provides for the possibility, in its section 4, for a declaration of incompatibility to be made when another Act of Parliament offends against the requirements of the Human Rights Act 1998. Such declaration of incompatibility was indeed made in *Benkarbouche*, where the Court of Appeal pronounced SIA 1978, sections 4 and 16 to be incompatible with ECHR, Article 6.[53]

8.5 CONCLUSION

There is, on its face, no correspondence between the legal position stated in the SIA 1978, on the one hand, and the restrictive doctrine as arguably part of general international law, or any treaty on state immunity whether in force or not, on the other. The statutory interpretation process provides the potential for such a flexible construction of the 1978 Act anyway. By and large, the way in which the SIA 1978 is applied in English courts validates F.A. Mann's early observations as to the interpretative flexibility available to courts in a common law jurisdiction to construe and apply SIA provisions, including ones that provide exceptions from the generally applicable residual statutory immunity. The result may not always be that divergent from the restrictive doctrine of immunities as may be applied under comity or general international law, and thus under the English common law. This approach would be an alternative to the 'dualist' isolationism which is shown in the *Al-Adsani* approach to treating the SIA 1978 as a 'comprehensive code'. On balance, Mann's view could better characterize the scope of the SIA 1978, to the effect that:

> it is only a residual immunity which a foreign State can claim in relatively few cases. The denial of immunity is so far-reaching that it is more appropriate to treat the 'exceptions' as distinct categories. Accordingly it is submitted that what may be described as the usual rules about proving exceptions should not be applicable.[54]

The full potential that the SIA 1978 has due to the possibility of ascertaining the true meaning, by way of statutory interpretation, of the

---

53 *Benkharbouche*, n. 19 above, para. 68.
54 Mann, n. 2 above, 62.

exceptions it provides in relation to the general and residual immunity rule, has not been properly exploited as yet. The nature of the statutory interpretation process, and its broad flexibility, advises against viewing the relationship between a domestic statute, such as the SIA 1978, and the relevant international legal requirements, as one between two compartmentalized and mutually isolated areas. The SIA 1978 is inherently designed to deal with the matters arising under international law and Parliament, as well as courts, have been aware of this from the outset of the pertinent legislative process. The relationship between the two sources of English law should instead be seen in a more dynamic, mutually reinforcing perspective.

Otherwise, the domestic courts' potential to impact the development of international law would be compromised, as follows from Mann's and Crawford's above-mentioned points. Mann's further remark, one to be understood with the broad national and international legal context in mind, is that:

> There can be no question of foreign legal developments being a source of English law governing the interpretation of an English statute. Yet where the English statute intends to codify the law in a manner consistent with international law, comparative material will have persuasive authority of varying strength in construing terms that are now accepted to be common to most countries and expressive of the present state of international law.[55]

The SIA 1978 should be viewed as an element of the dilemma that several national legal systems face. The options are either to protect and conserve the domestic utilitarian policy choices that are arguably dictated by the 'greater good' entailed by the exclusion of litigation with foreign elements domestically, or the preservation of better relations with states that engage in serious human rights violations internationally, or to resort to the use of statutory interpretative methods that make the 1978 Act operate as one element that might contribute to the United Kingdom having greater influence on the development of state practice internationally. Whatever policy preference one would adopt, either as a scholar or as a practitioner, it should be obvious, from any analytical or ideological point of view, that domestic isolationism and international contribution are highly unlikely, indeed practically impossible, to cohabit in the same juridical space.

---

[55] *Ibid.* 49–50.

9. Treaties on state immunity: the 1972 and 2004 Conventions

Alexander Orakhelashvili

9.1 INTRODUCTION

Treaties on the subject matter of state immunity purport to introduce discrete legal frameworks to bind their states parties to a particular legal approach on this subject matter. Yet, the low participation of states in these treaties is a matter that cannot be overlooked. The 1972 European Convention on State Immunity is in force as between eight states only;[1] while the 2004 UN Convention on Jurisdictional Immunities of States and Their Property is not in force yet, and it is uncertain when it will be.[2]

An issue different from the normative content and status of these instruments is the political and ideological suitability of these instruments in terms of a particular vision of state immunity, especially for granting immunity to states for serious human rights violations. The proper understanding of the structure and content of these two treaties may be of assistance towards enhancing our understanding as to whether these instruments legally assist that political and ideological agenda or merely provide a political cover to do certain things in a certain manner. This could help to clarify the question as to whether and to what extent international lawyers' minds should be so strongly preoccupied with these instruments.

The enthusiasm about both Conventions has been quite widespread. The 1972 Convention has been repeatedly used in judicial practice. Similarly, the adoption of the 2004 UN Convention was met with significant initial enthusiasm, hailing the 2004 Convention as an important document and a 'great achievement'.[3] It was argued that the UN

[1] European Convention on State Immunity, 1972, ETS No 074 (Basle, 16. V. 1972).

[2] United Nations Convention on Jurisdictional Immunities of States and Their Property, adopted on 2 December 2004, opened for ratification on 17 January 2005; for the text and ratification status see https://treaties.un.org.

[3] J. Foakes, *State Immunity: The United Nations Convention and its Effect*, Chatham House ILP BP 05/01 (May 2005), para. 42.

Convention would provide strong grounds for viewing state immunity as part of international law rather than comity.[4] Gerhard Hafner was similarly enthusiastic about the 2004 Convention, suggesting that '[o]ne may conclude that the new convention reflects the generally accepted state of affairs regarding state immunity'. And, 'once the Convention enters into force, it will create a common basis for recognizing restrictions on state immunity'.[5]

9.2 CONTENT OF THE TWO TREATIES AND THEIR DIVERGENCE FROM THE RESTRICTIVE DOCTRINE OF STATE IMMUNITY

9.2.1 1972 Convention: Limited Framework and its Dual Regime

One thing to be borne in mind is that when the 1972 Convention was being drafted, the transition from the absolute to the restrictive doctrine of immunity was not conclusively accepted in all relevant quarters. The whole structure of the 1972 Convention casts some doubt on a possible assumption that this Convention may serve as evidence of general (or customary) international law binding states even in the absence of the Convention. The substantive provisions of the Basle Convention (Articles 1 to 14) are framed in such a way not as recognizing the existence of state immunity in certain cases or obliging (or even empowering) states to grant immunity to other states in such cases, but merely as proscribing a grant of immunity to the extent of their applicability. Article 15 of the Convention states that, subject to the provisions embodied in the previous Articles, a state party may claim immunity in the courts of another state party. By and large, the 2004 Convention replicates the pattern followed by the 1972 Convention, in the sense that it states the general rule of state immunity, applying when the relevant case does not fall within one of the Convention-specified exceptions from that general immunity. Both Conventions, thus, diverge from such requirements of state immunity as may be applicable under comity and general international law, namely, the restrictive doctrine of immunity properly so-called.

---

4 H. Fox, 'In Defence of State Immunity: Why the UN Convention on State Immunity is Important' (2006) 55 *ILCQ* 399 at 405.

5 G. Hafner, 'Accountability and Immunity: The United Nations Convention on Jurisdictional Immunity of States and Their Property and the Accountability of States' (2005) 99 *ASIL Proceedings* 237 at 242.

As judge ad hoc Gaja has stated in *Germany v Italy*, the 1972 Convention:

> is clearly of limited significance for the purpose of ascertaining the existing rules of general international law on State immunity. It received only eight ratifications, all by States from a defined geographical area (Austria, Belgium, Cyprus, Germany, Luxembourg, Netherlands, Switzerland and United Kingdom). Moreover, it does not attempt to state general rules, but only considers the immunity of a Contracting State from the jurisdiction of other Contracting States.[6]

These factors do cast important doubts on views that present the 1972 Convention as an incidence of generally applicable law on immunities.

Lord Millett in *Lampen-Wolfe* spoke of the 1972 Convention as reflective of the immunities that accrue to states under general international law, suggesting that the position stated under the state immunity doctrine:

> operates to prevent the official and governmental acts of one state from being called into question in proceedings before the courts of another. The existence of the doctrine is confirmed by the European Convention on State Immunity (1972) (Cmnd. 5081), the relevant provisions of which are generally regarded as reflecting customary international law.[7]

A rather far-reaching point here is in effect made, that the 1972 Convention is, in its relevant parts at least, an instance of codification of the restrictive doctrine of immunities, focusing on the sovereign nature of the relevant acts that should attract immunity, which arguably has the force of law under general, or customary, international law.

However, as is the case with most of the written law on immunities, national or international, the correspondence between the legal position stated in such written instruments, and the one under comity or general international law, cannot be taken for granted. The dilemmas along those lines were already clear when the 1972 Convention was being drafted by its states parties. As Sir Ian Sinclair explained in relation to the 1972 Convention in a passage worth quoting at length:

> There appeared to be three possible solutions: (a) to assimilate the foreign State to the position of the State of the forum before its own courts; (b) to

[6] *Jurisdictional Immunities of the State (Germany v Italy: Greece Intervening)* [2012] ICJ Reports 310, ICJ, Judgment of 3 February 2012, Dissenting Opinion.

[7] *Holland v Lampen-Wolfe* [2000] 3 All ER 845, 1583.

> establish a list (illustrative or exhaustive) of acts *jure gestionis* and of acts *jure imperii*; (c) to maintain, in general, the immunity of the foreign State, except for certain defined categories of activities in relation to which the State would not enjoy immunity. In the event, it was felt that solution (a) was unsatisfactory, since it would leave the foreign State in a different legal position vis-à-vis each State seeking to exercise jurisdiction over it. The second solution was soon discarded, in view of the difficulty of defining sufficiently clearly the content of acts *jure gestionis* and acts *jure imperii*. The third solution is accordingly, with some variations, the one which is reflected in the Convention; Articles 1 to 14 contain a catalogue of cases in which immunity cannot be claimed and Article 15 embodies the residual rule of absolute immunity.[8]

This clearly confirms that the structural arrangement of the rights and obligations under the 1972 Convention, and effectively also under the 2004 Convention, substantially diverges from the restrictive doctrine of state immunity which we may be familiar with under comity and international law.

Ways to resolve the dilemma within the English legal system have been suggested. As Lord Phillips pointed out in *NML v Argentina*, the State Immunity Act (SIA) 1978 was enacted to give domestic effect to the 1972 European Convention on State Immunity (ECSI). However, '[t]he ECSI does not give effect to the restrictive doctrine of sovereign immunity'.[9] There is also some evidence that the authors of the ECSI have themselves realized the difference between the immunities regime under ECSI and under general international law. ECSI, Article 24(1) provides that:

> any State may, when signing this Convention or depositing its instrument of ratification, acceptance or accession, or at any later date, by notification addressed to the Secretary General of the Council of Europe, declare that, in cases not falling within Articles 1 to 13, its courts shall be entitled to entertain proceedings against another Contracting State to the extent that its courts are entitled to entertain proceedings against States not party to the present Convention. Such a declaration shall be without prejudice to the immunity from jurisdiction which foreign States enjoy in respect of acts performed in the exercise of sovereign authority (*acta jure imperii*).

---

[8] I. Sinclair, 'The European Convention on State Immunity' (1973) 22 *ICLQ* 254 at 267.

[9] *NML v Argentina* [2011] UKSC 31, 6 July 2011, para. 37 (per Lord Phillips).

As Lord Goff also observed in *Kuwait Air Co.*, the overall impact of ECSI, Article 24, which enables states parties to declare accordingly, entails the 'inapplicability in English law of the principle of sovereign immunity in cases in which the sovereign was not acting *jure imperii*'.[10]

The initial divergence between ECSI and general international law regimes has therefore been realized from the outset by its states parties. As Sir Ian Sinclair observed, 'In so far as the Convention rules on immunity are consistent with the current trend in international law towards the restrictive rule of immunity, it should be possible to apply these rules *erga omnes*'.[11] Therefore, as far as not restating the otherwise applicable international law, the regime that the 1972 Convention creates is not really opposable to non-parties and constitutes no law applicable in relation to such non-party states.

Thus, as we have seen, the 1972 Convention itself acknowledges that the version of state immunity doctrine it endorses does not in all aspects coincide with the distinction that is known as a matter of comity or international law as between *acta jure imperii* and *acta jure gestionis*. The states parties are enabled to make a declaration under Article 24, whereby they declare their intention to dis-apply the terms of the 1972 Convention and adopt the approach that comity and general international law prescribe or tolerate.

The government of Luxembourg has, for instance, made the declaration that:

> In accordance with Article 24 of the Convention, the Courts of Luxembourg are entitled, in cases falling outside Articles 1 to 13 of the Convention, to entertain proceedings against another Contracting State to the extent to which its Courts are entitled to entertain such proceedings against States not Party to the Convention.

Similar declarations have been made by the Netherlands, Switzerland and the United Kingdom.[12] All these states are therefore legally precluded from advancing arguments based on ECSI 1972 in any litigation where the state not party to ECSI is claiming sovereign immunity. What this also shows is that, in practice, the relevance of the ECSI-specific regime of immunities is bound to be even less than that of the law applicable *inter se*, even as between the Convention's parties, and even less

---

[10] *Kuwait Air Co.* [1995] 1 WLR 1147 at 1158 (per Lord Goff).

[11] Sinclair, n. 8 above, 283.

[12] Texts of all these declarations are available at http://conventions.coe.int/.

representative of the general attitude to state immunity within the international system.

Due regard to these factors is required, so that foreign states are not accorded immunity where applicable international law does not require doing so or, alternatively, denied such immunities as may be due to be accorded on grounds other than those provided for under ECSI. In fact, ECSI, Article 24 effectively recognizes that the Convention regime is a special one that purports to derogate from the general international law that applies in relation to non-parties and would, but for the Convention regime, apply *inter se* as well. The possibility is thus provided to depart, for the purposes of the relevant case, from the 'general immunity versus specific exceptions' approach and revert to the fall-back position under general international law that focuses on sovereign and non-sovereign acts. As Sir Ian Sinclair has suggested, 'This optional regime was included because certain states already applying the rule of relative immunity were afraid that some acts *jure gestionis* might fall outside the catalogue of cases of non-immunity, thereby restricting the jurisdiction of their courts',[13] thus manifesting the understanding that the underlying regimes of immunity are dual. As the Explanatory Report to the 1972 Convention specifies, 'the regime applied by the courts of a state which has made the declaration will not be affected by the Convention, and can even continue to develop along its own lines'.[14]

This throws an adverse light on the merit of some instances of the use of the 1972 Convention in English courts. To illustrate, Lord Millet articulated the impact of the 1972 Convention regime on domestic legal proceedings in the United Kingdom as follows:

> In according immunity from suit before the English courts to foreign states the State Immunity Act 1978 and the common law give effect to the international obligations of the United Kingdom.[15]

This approach is rather question-begging. In that case (*Lampen Wolfe*), their Lordships took care not to subject the United States to UK jurisdiction pursuant to the requirements of the European Convention on Human Rights (ECHR), particularly in terms of the right of individuals of access to a court under ECHR, Article 6, on the grounds that the United States is not party to the ECHR. But, if the ECHR does not apply

---

13 Sinclair, n. 8 above, 268.

14 Explanatory Report to the European Convention on State Immunity, Basel, 16.V.1972, 19.

15 *Lampen-Wolfe*, n. 7 above, 1583.

to UK-US relations, it is unclear why and how the ECSI should so apply, because the United States is not party to the ECSI either. The problem in that case was somewhat mitigated by their Lordships' decision to deal with the matters arising in the case on the basis of the common law doctrine of restrictive immunity, not the SIA 1978. But methodological and normative problems remain, as was also clear in *Al-Adsani*, where the 1972 Convention was resorted to with a view to articulating the immunity of Kuwait before English courts[16] – a state which not only was not party to ECSI but was actually not even eligible to become one.

9.2.2 2004 Convention: Ratification Status and Declarations Made by States Parties

The 2004 Convention does not contain saving clauses comparable to those that are part of the 1972 Convention. Nevertheless, the continuing potential of the 2004 Convention to determine or impact the development of the law of state immunity, even if and after the Convention were to enter into force, is limited in practically the same manner as could be observed in relation to the 1972 Convention.

Article 30(1) of the 2004 Convention provides that 'The present Convention shall enter into force on the thirtieth day following the date of deposit of the thirtieth instrument of ratification, acceptance, approval or accession with the Secretary-General of the United Nations'. A significant number of reservations and interpretative declarations have been appended to the ratification statements made by the 16 states that have so far ratified the 2004 Convention. These reservations and declarations are rather broad in scope, and they have the potential of adversely affecting not only the possibility of the 2004 Convention's text being uniformly understood and applied in practice, but also its consequent ability to provide a generally applicable law.

In their declarations appended to the 2004 Convention, Finland and Sweden considered that 'the Convention does not apply to military activities, including the activities of armed forces during an armed conflict, as those terms are understood under international humanitarian law, and activities undertaken by military forces of a State in the exercise of their official functions'. Italy stated, on comparable though not identical terms, 'its understanding that the Convention does not apply to the activities of armed forces and their personnel, whether carried out

[16] *Al-Adsani v United Kingdom* (2002) 34 EHRR 11 at 289.

during an armed conflict as defined by international humanitarian law, or undertaken in the exercise of their official duties'.

The declarations which states parties have appended to the 2004 Convention emphasize that these states parties do not consider that the Convention can prevent such further developments in relation to human rights and humanitarian law matters as may occur in relation to state immunity. Finland and Norway considered that 'the Convention is without prejudice to any future international development in the protection of human rights'. In a more far-reaching manner:

> Switzerland considers that article 12 does not govern the question of pecuniary compensation for serious human rights violations which are alleged to be attributable to a State and are committed outside the State of the forum. Consequently, this Convention is without prejudice to developments in international law in this regard.[17]

These are, in essence, the attitudes expressed by states which effectively deny full-fledged normative potential to the 2004 Convention. If and when it enters into force, the 2004 Convention should, in theory, be able to operate as a normative instrument with such full-fledged force. However, the ever-persisting uncertainties as to its scope, raised within the International Law Commission (ILC) as well as among the limited number of states that have signed and ratified the 2004 Convention, demonstrates that the Convention's potential to have such full-fledged effect, ordinarily available to treaties, has been seriously compromised in practical terms.

All this is more than enough to demonstrate that the uniformity of application of the 2004 Convention at its face value is going to be problematic in practice. It is also material that, in the case of one state that has ratified the 2004 Convention, Italy, the Italian Constitutional Court has declared unconstitutional the law of Italy on the accession to this Convention.[18]

---

[17] All these texts of declarations can be found in the 2004 Convention entry available at https://treaties.un.org/.

[18] Judgment No. 238, Constitutional Court of Italy, 22 October 2014.

9.3 THE TWO CONVENTIONS AND THEIR RELATIONSHIP TO CUSTOMARY LAW

As we have seen, claims have been made that the 1972 and 2004 Conventions may be seen as representative of the state of the law of state immunity under general international law. These claims must be verified against the requirements of the formation of customary international law in its relationship to conventional law. The *North Sea Continental Shelf* case contains classical pronouncements as to the conditions subject to which the rules stated in a multilateral convention could be seen as part of customary international law. The International Court of Justice (ICJ) has stated that 'it is clear that only a very definite, very consistent course of conduct on the part of a State' could serve as evidence of the provisions of the relevant Convention being accepted as part of customary law. Such a strict requirement was due to the fact that the stakes are rather high in situations where a state may be subjected to rules laid down in a Convention which it has chosen not to become a party to. At the risk of being seen to be making too fine a point, the Court specified that:

> when a number of States, including the one whose conduct is invoked, and those invoking it, have drawn up a convention specifically providing for a particular method by which the intention to become bound by the régime of the convention is to be manifested, namely by the carrying out of certain prescribed formalities (ratification, accession), it is not lightly to be presumed that a State which has not carried out these formalities, though at all times fully able and entitled to do so, has nevertheless somehow become bound in another way.[19]

In a similar spirit, Lord Wilberforce in *I Congreso* refused to treat the ECSI 1972 and the 1926 Convention on the Immunity of State-owned Ships as evidence of customary law on state immunity, because in order to be capable of custom-generation, a Convention must 'bear a legislative character and there must be a wide general acceptance of it as law-making, before that condition is satisfied'.[20]

There is no rational consideration, admissible as part of international legal reasoning, that could militate in favour of viewing the 1972 and 2004 immunity Conventions as exempted from the above-mentioned pattern as to international law-making.

---

[19] *North Sea Continental Shelf* [1969] ICJ Reports 25.

[20] *I Congreso* [1983] 1 AC 260, HL.

The texts of both Conventions contain some indications as to how strong or weak the claim regarding the customary law status of the rules they embody would be. The 1972 Convention itself indicates in the Preamble that this instrument is not a codification of the generally applicable law. The position taken in its Preamble is rather reserved and tentative. The Preamble refers to the states parties:

> Taking into account the fact that there is in international law a tendency to restrict the cases in which a State may claim immunity before foreign courts; [and] Desiring to establish in their mutual relations common rules relating to the scope of the immunity of one State from the jurisdiction of the courts of another State, and designed to ensure compliance with judgments given against another State.

The 1972 Convention thus seems to assume that such general rules are absent outside the regime of that Convention, in other words, in general international law. For, if one declares that his intention is to 'establish' rules and not amend, codify or replace existing ones, one may assume that he considers that such rules do not exist.

UN General Assembly Resolution 59/38 of 2 December 2004, whereby the Assembly adopted the 2004 Convention and opened it for signature, reads 'Stressing the importance of uniformity and clarity in the law of jurisdictional immunities of States and their property, and emphasizing the role of a convention in this regard'. Uniformity and clarity in the law of immunities was, therefore, seen merely as an outcome yet to be attained.

Thus, whatever the intention and ambition driving the adoption of these two Conventions, the authors of these instruments had a proper understanding that these were instruments proposing particular legal positions anew, not re stating what already would have been a generally accepted legal position. In the same spirit, the English Court of Appeal emphasized that, 'in view of this limited [state] participation, it [the 2004 Convention] cannot be considered to be reflective of a rule of customary international law'.[21] This contradicts the approach that the House of Lords took in *Jones v Saudi Arabia*, without regard to the Convention's ratification status.[22]

---

21 *Belhaj v Straw* [2014] EWCA Civ 1394, CA, 30 October 2014, para. 47.
22 See 9.5 below.

9.4 SUBSTANTIVE REGULATION OF IMMUNITIES UNDER THE CONVENTIONS

9.4.1 Entities Benefitting from State Immunity

The 1972 Convention does not provide for the positive definition of a state. Its Article 27 states, nevertheless, that:

1. For the purposes of the present Convention, the expression 'Contracting State' shall not include any legal entity of a Contracting State which is distinct therefrom and is capable of suing or being sued, even if that entity has been entrusted with public functions.
2. Proceedings may be instituted against any entity referred to in paragraph 1 before the courts of another Contracting State in the same manner as against a private person; however, the courts may not entertain proceedings in respect of acts performed by the entity in the exercise of sovereign authority (*acta jure imperii*).
3. Proceedings may in any event be instituted against any such entity before those courts if, in corresponding circumstances, the courts would have had jurisdiction if the proceedings had been instituted against a Contracting State.

As the Explanatory Report to the 1972 Convention states, 'Paragraph 2 [in Article 27] is worded in such a way that where an entity is authorised to exercise public functions in the State of the forum an action may be brought against it provided the proceedings do not relate to acts performed by the entity in the exercise of sovereign authority (*acta iure imperii*)'.[23]

The 2004 Convention defined a state rather broadly in its Article 2, as including:

(i) the State and its various organs of government;
(ii) constituent units of a federal State or political subdivisions of the State, which are entitled to perform acts in the exercise of sovereign authority, and are acting in that capacity;
(iii) agencies or instrumentalities of the State or other entities, to the extent that they are entitled to perform and are actually performing acts in the exercise of sovereign authority of the State;
(iv) representatives of the State acting in that capacity.

Note that, with regard to political subdivisions and instrumentalities of the state, express reference is made to the exercise of sovereign authority,

---

[23] Explanatory Report, n. 14 above, 22.

while representatives of the state merely act 'in that capacity'. So state officials, rather broadly defined by the ILC at that time as 'all the natural persons who are authorized to represent the State in all its manifestations',[24] while in service, are possibly purported to be given a virtually absolute immunity coextensive with that of the state, as the Convention does not require ascertaining whether acts they perform 'in that capacity' are ones pertaining to the sovereign authority of the state.

One (rather curious in terms of the framework of the 2004 Convention itself) implication is that while the 'state' itself obtains absolute immunity subject to exceptions listed in the Convention, the agencies or instrumentalities of states are subjected to the same regime of immunity provided that they act in the exercise of sovereign authority, in other words, in essence when they fit within the requirements of the restrictive immunity doctrine.

Paragraphs (ii) and (iii) are worded in strikingly similar, albeit not identical, terms that emphasize the actual acting in the exercise of sovereign authority. Yet, the 1991 ILC Commentary suggests (only in relation to agencies or instrumentalities in what is now Article 2(b)(iii)) that 'Beyond or outside the sphere of acts performed by them in the exercise of the sovereign authority of the State, they do not enjoy any jurisdictional immunity'.[25] Then, paragraphs (ii) and (iii) are drafted differently from the pertinent clauses in Article 2 of the 1991 ILC Draft Articles on Jurisdictional Immunities of States and Their Property, to the effect that under the ILC's approach, political subdivisions, constituent units, agencies and instrumentalities were not placed on the same footing in terms of being subjected to a further requirement of acting in the exercise of sovereign authority,[26] while under the Convention they *are* placed on the same footing. This could mean that all these entities would have to be denied immunity unless they demonstrate that, over and above the 2004 Convention's requirements, they have been performing the relevant act in the exercise of the sovereign authority of the state – the very authority which the 2004 Convention does not purport to define (indeed, as we shall see below, it deviates from the restrictive doctrine that requires the scope of such sovereign authority to be ascertained in

24 [1991] *YB ILC* 18.

25 [1991] *YB ILC* 17.

26 Draft Article 2 referred to the '(ii) constituent units of a federal State; (iii) political subdivisions of the State which are entitled to perform acts in the exercise of the sovereign authority of the State; (iv) agencies or instrumentalities of the State and other entities, to the extent that they are entitled to perform acts in the exercise of the sovereign authority of the State'.

particular cases). Thus, the matter inevitably reverts to general international law and comity.

It may be that, in relation to agencies and instrumentalities, but possibly also in relation to constituent units and political subdivisions, the 2004 Convention may be purporting to adopt a solution similar to UK SIA 1978 section 14 and ECSI, Article 27, as cited above, which single out the role of 'separate entities' and emphasize the sovereign authority requirement before immunity is granted.

But the difference is that the SIA 1978 subjects those separate entities to the separate regime of immunities as well. They are not subjected to the 1978 Act general immunity/listed exceptions framework, but to the test of 'sovereign authority' under the residually applicable common law. The oddity of the regime proposed by the 2004 Convention in this respect is that it requires the agency or instrumentality under paragraph (iii) to be acting through sovereign authority, yet treats it as subjected to the framework of general immunity/listed exceptions, which is a substantially different regime not requiring an examination of whether the act in question was performed through the use of sovereign authority. So a rather absurd result obtains in the sense that the 2004 Convention, at one time, places the relevant entities outside its own scope and subjects them to its own provisions and framework.

9.4.2 General Concept of State Immunity

The 2004 Convention arguably distances itself from absolute immunity, but it is nevertheless premised on grounds other than the restrictive doctrine focusing on the extent of sovereign authority. The 1991 Draft Articles of the ILC, which are the birthplace of the 2004 Convention's rationale and framework, specify that the state enjoys immunity 'without the additional requirement that [officials] perform acts in the exercise of the sovereign authority of the State'.[27] The nature of the act is, therefore, irrelevant under the 2004 Convention regime. What matters is whether the relevant matter is covered by one of the exceptions to the immunity as fixed by the Convention.

Article 6 of the 2004 Convention provides that:

> 1. A State shall give effect to State immunity under article 5 by refraining from exercising jurisdiction in a proceeding before its courts against another State and to that end shall ensure that its courts determine on

---

27 [1991] YB ILC 16.

their own initiative that the immunity of that other State under article 5 is respected.

2. A proceeding before a court of a State shall be considered to have been instituted against another State if that other State:
   (a) is named as a party to that proceeding; or
   (b) is not named as a party to the proceeding but the proceeding in effect seeks to affect the property, rights, interests or activities of that other State.

Section 6(2) contains a rather broad formulation, especially the words 'interests or activities' of the foreign state. The ILC's approach on this issue was curious. On the one hand, the ILC said that this provision was about property and related to *in rem* interests, and:

> The words 'to bear the consequences of a determination by the court which may affect', in the last part of the sentence was also deleted, because it appeared to create too loose a relationship between the procedure and the consequences to which it gave rise for the State in question and could thus result in unduly broad interpretations of the paragraph.[28]

On the other hand, it is still the case that Article 6(2) of the 2004 Convention is drafted rather broadly and can, on its face and wording, encompass issues other than property and *in rem* actions, especially actions for damages subsumable within the category that the above-cited ILC Commentary considered should not be included, as it would have been an 'unduly broad interpretation'.

As the English Court of Appeal stated in *Belhaj*:

> It is significant that 'State' is defined in Article 2(1)(b)(iv) of the Convention as including 'representatives of the State acting in that capacity'. Accordingly, the purpose of Article 6(2)(b) cannot be to extend immunity to proceedings to which the representative of the state is a party.[29]

The High Court decision in *Rahmatullah* adopted a similar approach to reject the approach based on 'indirect impleading' of foreign states before English courts in the way the approach stated in Article 6(2) purported to reinforce it.[30]

---

28 Commentary to Article 6, paras 12–13.
29 *Belhaj v Straw*, n. 21 above, para. 46.
30 *Yunus Rahmatullah* [2014] EWHC 3486 (QB), para. 74 ff.

9.4.3 Commercial Transactions

Article 2(2) of the 2004 Convention provides that:

> In determining whether a contract or transaction is a 'commercial transaction' under paragraph 1(c), reference should be made primarily to the nature of the contract or transaction, but its purpose should also be taken into account if the parties to the contract or transaction have so agreed, or if, in the practice of the State of the forum, that purpose is relevant to determining the non-commercial character of the contract or transaction.

There is no reference to here to the involvement or lack of sovereign authority in the relevant transaction. Moreover, a further encouragement towards the absolute doctrine is made, by inserting in Article 2 the mutually contradictory requirements in the definition of commercial transaction regarding its nature as well as its purpose.

9.4.4 Territorial Torts

Article 11 of the 1972 Convention provides that:

> A Contracting State cannot claim immunity from the jurisdiction of a court of another Contracting State in proceedings which relate to redress for injury to the person or damage to tangible property, if the facts which occasioned the injury or damage occurred in the territory of the State of the forum, and if the author of the injury or damage was present in that territory at the time when those facts occurred.

Article 12 of the 2004 Convention provides that:

> Unless otherwise agreed between the States concerned, a State cannot invoke immunity from jurisdiction before a court of another State which is otherwise competent in a proceeding which relates to pecuniary compensation for death or injury to the person, or damage to or loss of tangible property, caused by an act or omission which is alleged to be attributable to the State, if the act or omission occurred in whole or in part in the territory of that other State and if the author of the act or omission was present in that territory at the time of the act or omission.

The ILC's treatment of this exception in what is now Article 12 was interesting. The Commission stated that:

> The exception contained in this article is therefore designed to provide relief or possibility of recourse to justice for individuals who suffer personal injury, death or physical damage to or loss of property caused by an act or omission

> which might be intentional, accidental or caused by negligence attributable to a foreign State … the scope of article 12 is wide enough to cover also intentional physical harm such as assault and battery, malicious damage to property, arson or even homicide, including political assassination.[31]

If that position had been applied in *Al-Adsani v United Kingdom*, Al-Adsani ought to have been able to succeed on the denial of Kuwait's immunity, as the acts done in relation to him met the requirement that 'the act or omission occurred in whole or in part in the territory of that other state'.

9.4.5 Issues Not Covered by Treaties on State Immunity: Armed Forces' Activities

Article 31 of the 1972 Convention provides that:

> Nothing in this Convention shall affect any immunities or privileges enjoyed by a Contracting State in respect of anything done or omitted to be done by, or in relation to, its armed forces when on the territory of another Contracting State.

A similar position is not expressly endorsed in the 2004 Convention, but there is a widespread understanding, based mainly on positions repeatedly stated by and within the ILC, that it does not apply to the activities of armed forces. The ICJ in *Germany v Italy* has also shared this understanding. The ICJ refers to the ILC Commentary suggesting that the 2004 Convention does not apply to activities in armed conflicts.[32] According to Gerhard Hafner, Chairman of the ILC Drafting Committee, 'The general understanding had always prevailed that [military activities and 'situations of armed conflicts'] were not' covered by the 2004 Convention.[33]

But this is a questionable approach to treaty interpretation. One wonders, moreover, whether the 'general understanding' as to the treaty's scope could be obtained in any way better than through focusing on its text. And the 2004 Convention's text does not convey such 'general understanding'. The 2004 Convention should be interpreted by what its text says in the first place. As Judge Gaja summed up this position, 'The exclusion suggested in the ILC commentary has not found its way either

---

31 See [1991] *YB ILC* 44; see also Judge Gaja in *Germany v Italy* [2012] ICJ Reports 313, to the same effect.

32 *Germany v Italy*, n. 31 above, para. 69.

33 A/C.6/59/SR.13, para. 36.

into the text of the UN Convention or into the understandings which represent an annex to the Convention'.[34]

On that account, the 2004 Convention should be seen as in principle extending to the armed forces' activities. It may be true that the ILC thought otherwise. But in what way does the text reflect this position – a position that would make a rather substantial difference in terms of the Convention's scope and thus on the calculus of rights and obligations of its states parties? Or, should we assume that the ILC's position should, as a matter of the doctrine of the sources of international law, be placed on the same normative level as the text of the 2004 Convention if and whenever it were to enter into force?

Doubts are further corroborated by those very same reservations by Nordic countries that the Court has expressly alluded to. The relevance of those statements is precisely opposite to what the Court ascribes to them. The Nordic states must be deemed to have entered those reservations precisely because they must have thought that without those reservations the text of the Convention would indeed have extended to the activities of armed forces. In fact, whether these statements are interpretative declarations or actually amount to reservations to the 2004 Convention, is not an issue to be resolved by reference to how the relevant state frames them. The issue instead falls to be determined by reference to the objective relationship between the text of the 2004 Convention and the relevant declaration made by the state party, as was confirmed in the *Belilos* judgment of the European Court of Human Rights (ECtHR).[35]

Now, the scope of that putative 'general understanding' as to the 2004 Convention, the normative status of which is rather dubious anyway, seems to be narrower than the broader, indeed nearly comprehensive, exclusion of the activities of foreign armed forces stationed within the forum state's territory from the scope of the 1972 Convention pursuant to latter's Article 31. This difference also has implications.

If the 2004 Convention were to enter into force and become binding on the United Kingdom, this would make a difference to the SIA 1978, section 16(2) of which exempts from the scope of the Act only those actions of foreign armed forces that take place within the United Kingdom; while the 2004 Convention does not follow this approach and would instead, under its Article 12, require the United Kingdom, not to extend section 16(2) of the 1978 Act to the actions of armed forces

---

[34] *Germany v Italy*, n. 31 above, 315.

[35] See *Belilos v Switzerland*, Application No. 10328/83, ECtHR, Judgment of 29 April 1988.

wherever they take place, but rather to apply the other provisions of the Act to armed forces' activities across the board. There is also another distinction between the 2004 Convention regime and the SIA 1978, in the sense that 'military activities' under the 2004 Convention are not really the same thing as the armed forces' activities which section 16(2) of the 1978 Act refers to. 'Military activities' refer to the substance of the relevant activities. They are therefore narrower than the broader range of activities which armed forces could undertake, even if the particular activity is not of military character. The UK courts' practice under section 16(2) confirms precisely this point.[36] And again, activities in 'armed conflicts' are different in scope from the previous two notions, in the sense of being limited to the duration of armed conflicts, yet arguably being broader than 'military activities' proper: consider activities of a commercial nature or torts of non-military character performed during the armed conflict.

Therefore, if the 2004 Convention were to enter into force in relation to the United Kingdom, it would be liable to create a conflict between the two instruments, for instance, by requiring the extending of the Convention's Article 12 (which according to the ILC and the ICJ is dis-applied from armed conflicts and military activities, not from all activities of armed forces) to such matters as are currently considered in the UK jurisdiction to arise under SIA 1978, section 16(2), rather than section 5 which deals with territorial torts.

9.5 USE OF THE TWO CONVENTIONS IN JUDICIAL PRACTICE

It is noteworthy and curious, at the same time, that both the 1972 and 2004 Conventions have found enthusiastic use in the practice of national and international courts, and that they have done so not even just as accessory elements in litigation, but as ones that reinforce, if not determine, the principal outcomes to be reached in the relevant case. To recall the *Al-Adsani v United Kingdom* decision, the ECtHR considered that the grant of immunity to Kuwait under the SIA 1978 was in accordance with the ECSI 1972.[37] This Convention had no relevance whatsoever for that case. It has been ratified by eight states only and it certainly cannot generate any obligation to grant immunity to Kuwait, a

[36] See generally Chapter 5; and this point also features in Finnish and Swedish declarations appended to the 2004 Convention.

[37] *Al-Adsani v United Kingdom*, n. 16 above, 280, 289–90, paras 22, 57–8.

state which not only is not a party to that treaty, but is not even eligible to become such.

The UK House of Lords in *Jones* suggested that the UN Immunity Convention, recently adopted by the UN General Assembly, but not yet ratified, is 'the most authoritative statement available in the current international understanding of the limits of State immunity in civil cases', and that none of its provisions admit the *jus cogens* exception to state immunity.[38] It is, however, unclear how a Convention which is not ratified nor in force, including non-ratification by the forum state, can be the 'most authoritative' statement of the legal position or any of its understandings. It could well be a statement of the intention of the body that adopted the Convention as to the future state of the law after the Convention enters into force. But before then, it cannot be taken as a source of law, even if it conceptually reinforces the judges' own perception as to the required legal position.

The ICJ in *Germany v Italy* pronounced that both the 1972 and 2004 Conventions were inapplicable to acts of armed forces. The 1972 Convention includes a saving clause on armed forces, while the 2004 Convention was understood to have been generally interpreted the same way through state practice. The Court also suggested that Article 12 of the 2004 Convention, denying immunity for territorial torts, does not represent customary law.[39] The Court's conclusion on this issue is inevitably, and counter-factually, premised on the assumption that the 2004 Convention as a whole is an embodiment of customary international law on state immunity.

The reason why, in any event, the rule stated in Article 12 of the 2004 Convention could not have a strong claim to customary law status, is solely that the state practice that matters for identifying any possible customary law in this area (that is, practice relating to immunities specifically and performed against the background of international, not national, law) does not take the locus of the act as the principal point of departure; it merely refers to a simple and straightforward distinction

---

38 *Jones v Saudi Arabia* [2006] UKHL 16, HL, 14 June 2006, para. 26 (per Lord Bingham); para. 47 (per Lord Hoffmann).

39 As indicated in *Germany v Italy*, n. 31 above, para. 64; in para. 70 'the Court concludes that the inclusion in the Convention of Article 12 cannot be taken as affording any support to the contention that customary international law denies State immunity in tort proceedings relating to acts occasioning death, personal injury or damage to property committed in the territory of the forum State by the armed forces and associated organs of another State in the context of an armed conflict'.

between acts that are unique to public authority and those that are not.[40] There is a possibility that general, or customary, international law does not specifically furnish a rule that exempts torts from the scope of immunity as long as they are committed within the relevant forum state's territorial realm. However, that position is not by itself sufficient to demonstrate that the same general international law positively considers war crimes as an exercise of sovereign authority of the state (*acta jure imperii*).

This is the angle through which Judge Gaja's observation that 'no court of any of the States which enacted legislation incorporating the "tort exception" has raised any question of consistency between the relevant legislation and general international law',[41] should be seen. A national legislative provision not expressly replicating the position under public international law cannot provide an outcome contrary to international law, even if it states a position that public international law does not, in so many words, expressly approve.

To illustrate, Ireland which has no national immunity statute, would grant immunity to foreign states for territorial torts, provided that the underlying tort involves the exercise of sovereign authority of the foreign state, and is properly an act *jure imperii*. This position has been stated by the Irish Supreme Court, remarking in *McElhinney* that 'statutes are evidence of domestic law in the individual States and not evidence of international law generally'.[42] Applying the same approach to the situation involved in *Germany v Italy*, and given that Italy does not operate state immunity legislation comparable to the UK SIA 1978 and its section 5, the outcome should have been that, whether or not the territorial tort 'exception' applied to German war crimes, Germany was not immune for those crimes because they did not amount to acts *jure imperii*.

Even if Article 12 of the 2004 Convention does not apply to armed forces and acts of the latter are supposedly governed by customary law, this should revert us to the restrictive doctrine that focuses on acts unique to state authority, *not* to the 'general immunity versus specific exceptions' approach. Cases on the immunity of armed forces clearly articulate a version of the restrictive doctrine, as is clear from *Littrell* and *Lampen-Wolfe*, decided directly on the basis of English common law which incorporates international law. The ICJ in *Germany v Italy* was

40 See generally Chapter 5.

41 *Germany v Italy*, n. 31 above, 310.

42 *McElhinney* (1995) 104 ILR 691 at 701, Irish Supreme Court, Decision of 15 December 1995.

also aware of Norwegian and Swedish positions regarding the scope of the 2004 Convention and used this as one of the justifications for dis-applying the territorial tort principle that Article 12 embodies.[43] But this does not quite represent the overall position of the Nordic states, which is a more pro-accountability one and might equally require denying immunity.[44] Nor, in the same problematic spirit, did the Court address the implications of the Swiss position and that of the ILC's Working Group that the 2004 Convention was not meant to apply to serious violations of human rights and breaches of *jus cogens*.[45]

A further problematic use, in a number of cases, of the 2004 Convention as an non-ratified treaty and one inapplicable *inter se*, was witnessed in the ECtHR's jurisprudence to determine whether the respondent state was bound to grant immunity in the particular case. The Court acknowledged that the 2004 Convention is not ratified, not in force and not binding law, yet went on to subject the states parties' conduct to that Convention's standards.[46]

---

[43] *Germany v Italy*, n. 31 above, para. 69.

[44] In fact, as the Norwegian government put it to the Sixth Committee in 2011 on behalf of the Five Nordic countries, developments including the adoption of the 1946 Nuremberg Principles have made it clear that 'no State official could have been in any doubt about his or her potential personal responsibility if participating in acts regarded by international law as crimes of concern to the international community as a whole'; and that these 'developments relating to international criminal justice [have] contributed significantly to the normative production and clarification of rules pertaining to the scope for invocation of immunities. Consequentially, international criminal justice has a bearing on the general state of the law of immunities, which ought to be recognized'. Ms Margit Tveiten, Deputy Director General, Nordic Statement delivered to the Sixth Committee of the General Assembly, 11 January 2011.

[45] Switzerland 'considers that article 12 does not govern the question of pecuniary compensation for serious human rights violations which are alleged to be attributable to a State and are committed outside the State of the forum. Consequently, this Convention is without prejudice to developments in international law in this regard'. The position of the ILC Working Group is that 'the Convention does not address questions concerning immunity arising from civil claims in relation to acts of a State in violation of human rights norms having the character of *jus cogens*, particularly the prohibition of torture'. *Immunity of State Officials*, Memorandum by the Secretariat, A/CN/4/596 (31 March 2008), pp. 31–2, para. 46.

[46] *Cudak v Lithuania*, Application No. 15869/02, ECtHR, 23 March 2010, para. 66 ('As to the 2004 Convention, Lithuania has admittedly not ratified it but did not vote against its adoption either'); *Sabeh El Leil v France*, Application No. 34869/05, ECtHR, 29 June 2011, para. 57; *Wallishauser v Austria*, Application

9.6 CONCLUSIONS

All the factors and elements discussed above confirm that the assumptions motivated out of enthusiasm for the 2004 Convention have not been borne out by practical developments. This Convention, similar to the 1972 Convention, was initially born with a handicap manifested through its limited applicability, low state participation, and the transparent absence of any uniform vision as to its content. The subsequent practice has demonstrated the lack of any uniform understanding of these two Conventions' provisions among states, and also a lack of their uniform use by international and national courts. The discourse in the ILC, ICJ and more broadly in state practice has done everything in its power to preclude us from having analytically safe premises even to begin coherent legal reasoning as to the identifiable calculus of rights and obligations under these two Conventions.

The repeated judicial use of these two Conventions should be seen not as following any international legal requirement, but as the product of judicial acceptance of the ideological agenda that state immunity principles should be used expansively, so that transnational human rights litigation faces obstacles and stalemate. Such ideology-driven use of the two Conventions, when legally speaking they should not be used, responds to the political priorities of the day. This phenomenon is further reflected in the position stated by the New Haven policy-oriented school in relation to non-ratified treaties, proposing to pretend that they have been ratified and are fully in force, whenever a particular political or ideological agenda may require such an outcome to be upheld.[47]

It is also noteworthy how majorities in courts that grant, or affirm the grant of, immunity to a foreign state for war crimes or other serious human rights violations want to have it both ways. When it comes to the absence of the specific human rights exception, the texts of the two Conventions are regarded as authoritative. When it comes to territorial tort, however, all of a sudden it is realized that the relevant provisions of

No. 156/04, ECtHR, 2012, para. 31; *Oleynikov v Russia*, Application No. 36703/04, ECtHR, 14 March 2013, para. 66 ('Russia has not ratified [the 2004 Convention] but has not opposed it: on the contrary, it signed the convention on 1 December 2006'). See also, in relation to the treaty ratification requirement, Vienna Convention on the Law of Treaties 1969, Art. 14.

[47] See generally, W.M. Reisman, 'Unratified Treaties and Other Unperfected Acts in International Law: Constitutional Functions' (2002) 35 *Vanderbilt Journal of Transnational Law* 729.

the two Conventions do not amount to the generally applicable law on state immunity.

The opportunist use of non-ratified or inapplicable treaties could have little practical limit when there is will to use them in such a manner. If it is possible for courts to use such treaties when they are not in force or are inapplicable to the relevant case, pretending that these treaties still provide the law applicable to the case, then it would be even more possible to use them if and when there is a limited *lex specialis*, pretending that this is evidence of the general law.

Even if coming in force through the gathering of the required 30 ratifications, the 2004 Convention would still not be a generally applicable legal instrument, but would only provide a framework applicable *inter se* between the limited number of ratifying states. The Convention will not take away political problems associated with domestic adjudication over the foreign state in *any* matter where significant financial and reputational costs are involved, including purely commercial matters. The rather convoluted treatment of the requirements under this Convention by the ICJ in *Germany v Italy*, and by the European Court of Human Rights is, in essence, a forewarning as to the potential state of affairs when the 2004 Convention sometimes is and at other times is not seen to embody general international law. In a world run by national interests of states, any *a priori* imposition of an immunity template, even if ideologically acceptable in certain quarters, has proved futile in the past, and is likely to do so in the future.

10. Foreign state immunity: a private international law analysis

Richard Garnett

In 1999, the present author proposed that the doctrine of foreign state immunity be abolished for claims against foreign states and be replaced by an approach that exclusively relied upon private international law principles of personal jurisdiction.[1] The basis of the argument was that, while the rationale of immunity was to protect foreign states from the domestic jurisdiction of other countries in certain circumstances, such an objective could be equally achieved by application of principles of private international law. The purpose of this chapter in the *Research Handbook* is to review the position after 15 years and to reassess the case for abandonment of foreign state immunity.

The origins of foreign state immunity lie in the sovereign equality of states in public international law, with the key idea being that it is incompatible with a state's sovereignty and dignity for it to be subject to adjudication by another state's courts. Such a principle formed the basis of the doctrine of absolute immunity, which provided that under no circumstances could a state be impleaded before the courts of another. Yet such a principle did not operate without qualification. There also existed in parallel another principle of public international law: the concept of territorial sovereignty. Pursuant to this idea, a state is considered to have exclusive and unqualified competence with regard to matters occurring within its territory, including the power to exercise its jurisdiction over acts and persons within its borders.[2] Consequently, the principle of territoriality is perhaps the most strongly accepted basis in public international law for the exercise of domestic jurisdiction by

[1] R Garnett, 'Should Foreign State Immunity be Abolished?' (1999) 20 *Australian Yearbook of International Law* 175.

[2] Judge Keith, in his separate Concurring Opinion in *Jurisdictional Immunities of the State (Germany v Italy)* [2012] ICJ Rep. 99, ICJ, 3 February 2012, noted the tension between these principles and suggested that the evolving law of state immunity is an attempt to reconcile them: at paras 2–3.

states[3] and in most national systems of private international law the idea of territorial nexus with the forum state is a guiding principle in the establishment of personal jurisdiction.

10.1 TERRITORIAL NEXUS

Hence, it has always been arguable that, at least for acts committed in the forum state, principles of public international law do not require the grant of immunity to foreign state defendants, given the strong territorial interests of the forum state. This territorial approach to the grant of immunity was strongly espoused by Lauterpacht who argued that a foreign state should only enjoy immunity where the claim concerned the legislative, executive or administrative acts of that state on its territory or a contract with no connection to the forum state.[4] It is important to note that Lauterpacht's view was expressed at a time when absolute immunity still likely represented the customary international law position. Since at least the 1970s, restrictive state immunity is now the customary law view, although there have been different versions of this principle. One approach, expressed in the legislation of common law countries, reflects the influence of Lauterpacht's notions of territoriality. For example, in the United States, a foreign state is not immune: (i) in an action based upon a commercial activity carried on in the United States; (ii) upon an act performed in the United States in connection with a commercial activity of a foreign state elsewhere; or (iii) upon an act outside the territory of the United States in connection with a commercial activity of the foreign state elsewhere that causes a direct effect in the United States.[5] Another key illustration of the influence of territoriality in state immunity laws is in the field of torts or civil wrongs: in the legislation of Australia, the United States, Canada and the United Kingdom, a foreign state is not immune in claims for personal injury or property damage where the harm was caused by an act of omission in the forum.[6] In the case of the United Kingdom and Australia, territorial linkage with the forum state is also the

[3] M. Shaw, *International Law* (6th edn, Cambridge University Press, 2008), pp. 652–3.

[4] H. Lauterpacht, 'The Problem of Jurisdictional Immunities of Foreign States' (1951) 28 *British Yearbook of International Law* 220.

[5] Foreign Sovereign Immunities Act (FSIA) 1976, s. 1605(a)(2) (US).

[6] FSIA 1976, s. 1605(a)(5) (US); State Immunity Act (SIA) 1978, s. 5 (UK); Foreign States Immunities Act (FSIA) 1985, s. 13 (Australia); State Immunity Act (SIA) 1985, s. 6 (Canada).

basis of the exceptions to immunity for claims in relation to intellectual property rights,[7] immovable property[8] and employment contracts.[9]

The focus on territorial connections in the current immunity legislation of common law countries has some similarities with those states' private international law principles of personal jurisdiction. For example, in Australia and the United Kingdom (for non-EEA domiciled defendants) service out of the jurisdiction is permissible in a tort or contract claim where the tort or contract has a specified territorial link to the forum.[10] While such connections are not identical to those specified in the immunity legislation, the key point is that both doctrines use territoriality as a criterion for establishing jurisdiction. Such commonality suggests that a move to exclusive adoption of a private international law model for civil litigation against foreign states may be less radical (at least in those states) than at first appears.

Yet, it must be acknowledged that many other states, particularly of the European civil law tradition, place little reliance on territorial nexus as the criterion for immunity determinations. Instead, focus is placed on the nature of the acts engaged in by the foreign state, with the state immune from jurisdiction for its public or sovereign acts but susceptible to adjudication for its private or commercial acts.[11] Such a distinction is also relevant in common law countries such as the United States, United Kingdom, Australia and Canada which provide an exception to immunity for commercial activity or transactions.[12] In many countries it is the protection of this uniquely sovereign interest and the consequent preservation of harmonious relations between forum and foreign state that is still cited as a major objective of foreign state immunity.[13]

---

[7] SIA 1978, s. 7 (UK); FSIA 1985, s. 15 (Australia).

[8] SIA 1978, s. 6 (UK); FSIA 1985, s. 14 (Australia).

[9] SIA 1978, s. 4 (UK); FSIA 1985, s. 12 (Australia).

[10] See for example, for Australia Uniform Civil Procedure Rules 2005 (NSW) Sch. 6 and for the United Kingdom Civil Procedure Rules, r. 6.36, Practice Direction 6B para. 3.1.

[11] See for example, *Dralle v Republic of Czechoslovakia* (1950) 17 ILR 155, Supreme Court of Austria; *Empire of Iran* (1963) 45 ILR 57, West German Supreme Constitutional Court. See generally H. Fox and P. Webb, *The Law of State Immunity* (3rd edn, Oxford University Press, 2014), pp. 150–59.

[12] FSIA 1976, s. 1605(a)(2) (US); SIA 1978, s. 3 (UK); FSIA 1985, s. 11 (Australia); SIA 1985, s. 5 (Canada).

[13] Note that the sovereign-private distinction formed the basis of the decision of the ICJ in *Germany v Italy* [2012] ICJ Rep. 99 where the court considered that the acts of armed forces during an armed conflict were immune as sovereign acts.

10.2 *FORUM NON CONVENIENS*

In the 1999 article[14] (and subsequent writing)[15] it was asserted that private international law principles of personal jurisdiction (at least in common law countries) could 'accommodate' the sovereign interest of foreign states through the medium of the doctrine of *forum non conveniens*. Such a principle allows a forum court to decline jurisdiction and stay or dismiss proceedings, even where the plaintiff has established a basis for long arm or extended jurisdiction over a foreign defendant. Such a principle is widely accepted in common law states with the defendant having the burden of proving that the local forum is either less appropriate[16] than another located abroad for resolution of the dispute or 'clearly inappropriate'.[17]

It was suggested that there would be scope for a foreign state to argue that a forum was inappropriate where, for example, the law governing the transaction was that of the foreign state, where the case involved events that almost wholly took place inside the foreign state's territory or where the claimant held the nationality of the foreign state. Similarly, a foreign state could contend that a local court should not exercise jurisdiction in a matter because to do so would unduly compromise its sovereignty or security interests, such as where the conduct of its diplomats or military forces are involved. Hence, many of the issues that underlie the protection of the foreign state in the immunity doctrine could be accommodated within the rubric of a *forum non conveniens* test, the difference being that while immunity imposes a blanket bar on adjudication, *forum non conveniens* is a discretionary principle that requires the court to weigh competing interests against each other in the decision to accept or decline jurisdiction. Whereas immunity is an 'all or nothing' determination, *forum non conveniens* is a more flexible and calibrated doctrine which gives forum courts scope to adjust jurisdictional decisions to the facts of the case. For example, it is a standard principle in all current *forum non conveniens* tests that the forum will only order a stay or dismissal of

---

[14] See n. 1 above.

[15] R. Garnett, 'State Immunity Triumphs in the European Court of Human Rights' (2002) 118 *Law Quarterly Review* 367; R. Garnett, 'Foreign States in Australian Courts' (2005) 29 *Melbourne University Law Review* 704.

[16] For the United Kingdom see *Spiliada Maritime Corp. v Cansulex Ltd* [1987] 1 AC 406; for the United States see *Gulf Oil Corp. v Gilbert*, 330 U.S. 501 (1947); and for Canada see *Club Resorts Ltd v Van Breda* [2012] 1 SCR 572; 2012 SCC 17.

[17] *Voth v Manildra Flour Mills Pty Ltd* (1990) 171 CLR 538.

proceedings where there is an available, alternative forum abroad for adjudication of the matter.[18]

Anglo-American jurisprudence reinforces this concept by requiring further that a stay or dismissal of forum proceedings will not be awarded where the plaintiff would suffer a loss of a 'juridical advantage' that is, where it will be 'denied justice' in the foreign court.[19] The combined effect of the alternative forum and juridical advantage requirements, therefore, is to secure access to justice for claimants. So in *Piper Aircraft v Reyno*,[20] the United States Supreme Court said that to be 'truly available' the alternative forum must provide a remedy that is roughly comparable to that of the initial forum, even if it is less generous to the plaintiff. If, however, the effect of dismissal of the suit in the forum would be to deprive the plaintiff of a remedy altogether, then this fact will weigh substantially against dismissal as the court may conclude that it would not be in the interests of justice.

A good example of the 'available alternative forum' criterion being used to deny a stay in litigation against a foreign state entity occurred in *Kuwait Airways v Iraqi Airways Co*.[21] There, an English court refused to stay a claim for conversion of aircraft seized by the Iraqi government following the invasion of Kuwait when it was clear that Iraq could not provide a forum in which the claimant's complaint would be heard justly. Also, in *Mohammed v Bank of Kuwait*,[22] the English Court of Appeal refused to stay a proceeding brought by an Iraqi citizen against his Kuwaiti employer for the reason that his personal safety would be in

---

[18] For Australia see *Oceanic Sunline Shipping v Fay* (1988) 162 CLR 197 at 247–8; for the United States see *El-Fadl v Central Bank of Jordan*, 75 F.3d 668 (D.C. Cir. 1996) and R. Felix and R. Whitten, *American Conflicts Law* (6th edn, Carolina Academic Press, 2011), p. 115; and for Canada see *Club Resorts Ltd v Van Breda* [2012] 1 SCR 572, para. 103 where it was said that the defendant must 'identify another forum that has appropriate connection under the conflicts rules and that should be allowed to dispose of the action'. For the United Kingdom see *Spiliada Maritime Corp. v Cansulex Ltd* [1987] 1 AC 406 at 474, *Cherney v Deripaska* [2009] EWCA Civ 849 and *Connelly v RTZ* [1998] AC 854.

[19] For Canada see *Club Resorts Ltd v Van Breda* [2012] 1 SCR 572, para. 111; for the United Kingdom see *Spiliada Maritime Corp. v Cansulex Ltd* [1987] 1 AC 406 at 482; for Australia see *Voth v Manildra Flour Mills Pty Ltd* (1990) 171 CLR 538 at 564–5; and for the United States see *Piper Aircraft v Reyno*, 454 U.S. 135, 254 n. 22 (1981).

[20] *Ibid*.

[21] (1992) 103 ILR 340, QB.

[22] [1996] 1 WLR 1483.

question if he travelled to Kuwait and also his inability to obtain adequate legal representation in that country.[23] In a similar vein, a Canadian court allowed a matter to proceed in the forum where it found that the plaintiff might suffer discrimination and hardship if his case (against a US company) were heard in the United States, due to his Iraqi heritage and the then-current US war in Iraq.[24]

Occasionally, the objection has been raised that it is inappropriate and unseemly for a forum court to review the 'ability or willingness of the courts of another country to accord justice to the plaintiff in the particular case'.[25] Yet Lord Collins, giving the advice of the Privy Council in *AK Investments v Kyrgyz Mobil Tel Ltd*[26] thought that such concerns should bow to the overriding need to ensure access to justice for claimants. Simply stated, there is no bar to the forum court considering whether the claimant would obtain justice in the foreign court in a *forum non conveniens* inquiry:

> The true position is that there is no rule that the English court … will not examine the question whether the foreign court system is corrupt or lacking in independence. The rule is that considerations of international comity will militate against such a finding in the absence of cogent evidence … [o]therwise the paradoxical result would follow that, the worse the system of justice in the foreign country, the less it would be permissible to make adverse findings on it.

In keeping with this desire to protect claimants from injustice in foreign proceedings, courts will often go further and require that the defendant submit to the jurisdiction of such courts in the foreign country or waive any obstacles to suit there as a condition of the order being granted.[27] While an undertaking by a foreign state defendant to submit to trial elsewhere may not completely assuage all the concerns of the claimant as to his or her likely receipt of a fair trial, a court would likely consider such an act as a demonstration of good faith on the part of the defendant state to have the matter adjudicated. Of course, if such trust in the foreign

---

23 See also, to the same effect, *Oppenheimer v Louis Rosenthal & Co. AG* [1937] 1 All ER 23 (claimant of Jewish faith not required to litigate in the courts of Nazi Germany).

24 *Samson v Hooks Industrial Inc.* 2003 CanLII 8549 (ONSC), Ontario Superior Court of Justice, 10 October 2003.

25 *Voth v Manildra Flour Mills Pty Ltd* (1990) 171 CLR 538 at 559.

26 [2012] 1 WLR 1804, para. 101.

27 *Vasquez v Bridgestone/Firestone Inc.*, 325 F.3d 665 (5th Cir. 2003); *Abbott v Owens-Corning Fiberglas Corp.*, 444 S.E.2d 285 (W Va. 1994).

state's willingness to open its courts to the claimant proved to be misplaced, the court could lift its stay order and allow the claimant to sue in the forum. By contrast, where the state immunity doctrine applies, foreign states feel under no such compulsion to offer an alternative forum for trial (or indeed make an offer to settle the litigation), given that, at least in torture cases, immunity will almost certainly be available. The foreign state defendant can therefore effectively extinguish a claimant's right to bring such an action in any forum by an immunity plea, since the threat of forum proceedings against it cannot be used as leverage.

Hence, *forum non conveniens* is a doctrine of great flexibility and utility in transnational litigation, including in actions against foreign states. By contrast, the problem with state immunity is that, given the disproportionately privileged position it confers on foreign states, such entities are under no pressure or obligation to make any commitment to an individual claimant that his or her grievance will be properly adjudicated elsewhere.[28] The parties are not treated with equality before the law.

10.3 JURISDICTION AND ARBITRATION CLAUSES

There is also scope in the civil jurisdiction rules of private international law for states to limit their jurisdictional exposure to foreign courts by including a jurisdiction (choice of court) or arbitration clause in a contract. In most common law countries[29] and also in Europe under the Brussels I Regulation (recast)[30] a forum court is normally required to stay or dismiss any proceedings brought in breach of a clause to litigate in a foreign country unless the clause is invalid or (in some cases) enforcement would be manifestly contrary to public policy. Similarly, Article II of the 1958 United Nations Convention on the Recognition and Enforcement of Foreign Arbitral Awards requires courts of a contracting state to decline jurisdiction when confronted with an agreement stipulating arbitration in a foreign state. Once again, therefore, existing private

---

[28] Garnett, n. 15 above, 372.

[29] For the United Kingdom see *The Eleftheria* [1970] P 94; for the United States see *Bremen v Zapata Off-Shore Co.*, 407 U.S. 1 (1972); for Australia see *Global Partners Fund v Babcock & Brown Ltd (in liq.)* (2010) 79 ACSR 383; and for Canada see *Momentous.ca Corp. v Canadian American Ass'n of Professional Baseball Ltd* 2012 SCC 9.

[30] Regulation (EU) 1215/2012, art. 25. See also the Convention on Choice of Court Agreements of 30 June 2005, Art. 6 (not yet in force).

international law principles of civil jurisdiction offer states substantial protection from adjudication by foreign courts by allowing them to determine the forum in advance.

At the same time, where a foreign state has consented in advance by contractual stipulation to the jurisdiction of the forum's courts, such a provision has been held not only to vest jurisdiction in the forum but also to 'waive' any immunity that the foreign state may have enjoyed.[31] This circumstance provides another example where rules of private international law and state immunity coincide to achieve a similar result, again suggesting that immunity is redundant.

10.4 ACTIONS AGAINST INDIVIDUALS

Further, there is some evidence of courts relying on private international law principles of civil jurisdiction instead of state immunity in the case where the defendants in question were individuals and not the foreign state itself.

The English Court of Appeal in *Jones v Saudi Arabia*[32] had endorsed a distinction between defendant states and defendant individual state agents in terms of immunity, saying that it would only be where such persons performed 'state conduct' under customary international law that they could claim immunity. The court also emphasized that the doctrine of *forum non conveniens* would still be available to such defendants seeking to resist jurisdiction, with the test providing sufficient flexibility to balance the sovereignty and security concerns of state agents against the claimant's right to recovery.[33] In essence, therefore, a private international law analysis was advocated and adopted in place of immunity.

This approach of the Court of Appeal was, however, rejected on appeal to the House of Lords who considered that state agents and states themselves should be treated alike for the purposes of application of the immunity rules.[34] The House of Lords dismissed the notion that private

---

[31] For the United States see FSIA 1976, s. 1605(a)(1); for Australia see FSIA 1985, s. 10; for Canada see SIA 1985, s. 4; and for the United Kingdom see SIA 1978, s. 2 and *NML Capital Ltd v Argentina* [2011] 2 AC 495.

[32] [2005] QB 699.

[33] *Ibid.* 750–1 (per Mance LJ).

[34] *Jones v Saudi Arabia* [2007] 1 AC 270; this decision has been followed in Australia in *Zhang v Zemin* [2010] NSWCA 255; in Canada in *Kazemi Estate v Islamic Republic of Iran* 2014 SCC 62; and in New Zealand in *Fang v Jiang* [2007] NZAR 420.

international law rules of civil jurisdiction could somehow operate as a substitute for state immunity, saying that immunity is not granted at the discretion of domestic courts but imposed 'from the outside' by public international law and so cannot be avoided by states.[35] State immunity, therefore, is not on the same level as other jurisdictional control strategies of the forum because it is sourced in public international law. One response to this argument is to say that if the principle of access to justice (of which *forum non conveniens* is arguably an illustration) also forms part of customary international law then the 'hierarchy of norms' analysis[36] breaks down as both state immunity and access to justice are concepts competing on the same plane. Indeed, US commentary tends to consider both immunity and *forum non conveniens* as 'transnational litigation avoidance doctrines' without prioritizing them by reference to their source, whether it be public or private international law.[37] The approach of US courts has also been to rely on both grounds of jurisdictional abstention interchangeably with no deference to one over the other.[38]

A second response to the House of Lords view is that the analysis fails to recognize that public international law rules themselves are often changed by domestic court practice; indeed this was the principal means by which the doctrine of absolute immunity evolved into restrictive immunity. Surely it is not beyond possibility that still further evolution could occur whereby state immunity is entirely displaced in favour of the sole regulation of claims against foreign states by principles of private international law. Interestingly, Judge Keith in *Germany v Italy* noted that the parameters of state immunity have altered over time 'and no doubt will continue to change in the direction of a narrowing of immunity'.[39]

Some support for this view comes from the United States where some courts have held that individual foreign state officials are not entitled to

---

[35] *Jones v Saudi Arabia*, n. 34 above, 298.

[36] For a further consideration of this idea see A. Orakhelashvili, 'State Immunity and Hierarchy of Norms: Why the House of Lords Got It Wrong' (2007) 18 *European Journal of International Law* 955.

[37] See for example, P. Bookman, 'Once and Future US Litigation' in P. Stephan (ed.), *Foreign Court Judgments and the United States Legal System* (Leiden, Koninklijke Brill NVE, 2014), p. 35 at 36.

[38] See for example, *Skanga Energy & Marine Ltd v Arevenca SA*, 875 F.Supp.2d 264 (SDNY 2012).

[39] *Germany v Italy* [2012] ICJ Rep. 99, Separate Opinion of Judge Keith, para. 3.

state immunity in respect of torture claims, either under the FSIA[40] or at common law.[41] The European Court of Human Rights (ECtHR) in *Jones v United Kingdom*[42] recently acknowledged that there was 'some emerging support in favour of a special rule or exception in public international law in cases concerning civil claims for torture lodged against foreign state officials'.[43] So, despite the House of Lords' emphatic rejection of this approach, there may still be scope for development in the future of a jurisprudence of claims against individual state officials that are determined not by state immunity but by principles of civil jurisdiction in private international law.

10.5 ECHR, IMMUNITY AND ACCESS TO JUSTICE

Since 1999, the arguments in favour of a private international law solution to the problem of litigation against foreign states have, if anything, become even more convincing. While historically the objects of private international law rules were to limit conflicts between the forum and foreign state and unfairness to defendants, such matters have now been joined by another 'counterbalancing concern', that is, to provide access to justice for claimants.[44] The principle of access to justice is enshrined in many international texts the most significant of which is Article 6(1) of the European Convention on Human Rights (ECHR). Article 6 provides that 'in the determination of his civil rights and obligations … everyone is entitled to a fair hearing … by (a) tribunal'. Article 6(1) must be examined both for its direct and indirect impact on state immunity.

In terms of direct impact there have been since 1999 a number of cases brought before the ECtHR in which member state court decisions to grant state immunity to foreign states have been challenged on the ground that they are inconsistent with a claimant's right to court access in Article 6(1). The approach adopted by the ECtHR has, however, been insufficiently protective of private rights to redress. It has simply found

---

40 *Xuncax v Gramajo*, 886 F.Supp. 162 (1995); *Cabiri v Assasie-Gyimah*, 921 F.Supp. 1184 (SDNY 1996).

41 *Yousuf v Samantar*, 699 F.3d 763 (4th Cir. 2012).

42 Applications Nos 34356/06 and 40528/06, 14 January 2014.

43 *Ibid.* para. 213.

44 A. Mills, *Rethinking Jurisdiction in International Law* (2014), p. 35, available at http://bybil.oxfordjournals.org/content/early/2014/10/31/bybil.bru003.full.pdf.

that where the grant of state immunity by the forum member state in a particular case is consistent with the principles of public international law, then there can be no breach of Article 6. In such a case, the limitation on court access imposed by state immunity 'pursues a legitimate aim' and has a 'reasonable relationship of proportionality between the means employed and the aims sought to be achieved'. In the clear majority of cases the ECtHR held that a member state's grant of state immunity was consistent with public international law and so there was no breach of Article 6.[45]

Two features of the ECtHR's approach show a denial of two key principles of the private international law methodology suggested above as appropriate for resolution of civil cases against foreign states. The first omission is a failure by the court to weigh the interests of the forum state (in granting immunity to the foreign state), on the one hand, against the claimant's right to redress, on the other. Such a gap is particularly puzzling since some type of balancing seems mandated by the Court's own articulation of the test for breach of Article 6: that there be 'a reasonable relationship of proportionality between the means employed and the aims sought to be achieved'. The reference to proportionality certainly suggests an accommodation or compromise between competing principles, not simply a finding that one principle (immunity) prevails in every case where public international law permits.[46] In taking such an approach, the court is effectively imposing an automatic blanket bar on adjudication of the matter.[47]

---

[45] See for example, *Al-Adsani v United Kingdom* (2002) 34 EHRR 273; *McElhinney v Ireland* (2002) 34 EHRR 322; and *Fogarty v United Kingdom* (2002) 34 EHRR 12. Cf. *Cudak v Lithuania* (2010) 51 EHRR 15, where the grant of immunity was found to be inconsistent with customary international law and so in breach of Article 6.

[46] *Al-Adsani v United Kingdom* (2002) 34 EHRR 273, para. 115 (Judge Loucaides); E. Voyiakis, 'Access to Court and State Immunity' (2003) 52 *International and Comparative Law Quarterly* 297 at 312; M. Gestri, 'Access to a Court and the Jurisdictional Immunities of States: What Scope for the Balancing of Interests Test?' (2010) 20 *Italian Yearbook of International Law* 91 at 92; C. Whytock, 'Foreign State Immunity and the Right to Court Access' (2013) 93 *Boston University Law Review* 2033 at 2081. Cf. M. Kloth, *Immunities and the Right of Access to Court under Article 6 of the European Convention on Human Rights* (Martinus Nijhoff, 2010), pp. 41, 201, who contends that the existing approach adopted by the ECtHR does achieve an adequate balancing of interests.

[47] Garnett, n. 15 above, at 371.

The second major omission in the ECtHR's approach is its general failure to recognize the significance of an alternative forum in which the claimant can obtain redress for his or her grievance. Such a gap seems particularly glaring given the express terms of Article 6(1), which requires access to a tribunal for adjudication of a claimant's complaint. Yet, according to the court, the only tribunal that is relevant for the purposes of Article 6(1) is the forum state before which the claim has been filed and if such court has barred access to its jurisdiction consistently with the principles of public international law, then no further inquiry is needed. A better approach, and one which is more consistent with the *forum non conveniens* doctrine in private international law above, would be for the ECtHR to hold a member state in compliance with Article 6(1) only where the claimant has available to it or has been offered a 'reasonable alternative means' of securing redress. Hence, if a forum state court were to grant immunity to the foreign state (even in accordance with principles of public international law) and decline to adjudicate the action, such conduct would only be consistent with Article 6(1) if evidence was provided that the claimant had an available forum elsewhere.

In practice such an outcome would be achieved by requiring the foreign state defendant, as a condition of immunity being granted from the litigation in the forum, to offer its own courts (or those of a third party state) as a good faith tribunal for resolution of the dispute.[48] Pursuant to this analysis, even if the foreign state undertook to submit the case to its own courts for adjudication, the forum court must still be persuaded that such courts would not deny the claimant justice in the sense that they would follow the rule of law, would not be plagued by bias or corruption and there would be no threat to the claimant's safety in travelling to the foreign state to pursue its action.[49] According to this view, therefore, the immunity inquiry would adopt a key feature of the doctrine of *forum non conveniens*.

As argued above, however, a simpler approach may be to replace state immunity altogether with a *forum non conveniens* test where the defendant's concerns for sovereignty and dignity could be more directly weighed against the claimant's right to justice and with the defendant being required to show, as a condition of stay or dismissal, that an alternative forum exists. Yet even if this 'fully fledged' approach is not

---

[48] M. Tomonori, 'Denying Foreign State Immunity on the Grounds of the Unavailability of Alternative Means' (2008) 71 *Modern Law Review* 734 at 745.

[49] Whytock, n. 46 above, 2061–2.

taken, the modified approach of making immunity subject to provision of an alternative forum should be adopted in future Article 6 cases.[50]

Interestingly, the ECtHR in the *McElhinney* case, showed some awareness of the concept of available alternative forum by noting that the claimant, in the circumstances of that case, could have brought an action in the Northern Ireland courts against the UK Secretary of State for Defence.[51] In both *Fogarty* and *Al-Adsani*, however, no reference was made to whether another forum was available; in *Al-Adsani* this is perhaps not surprising since the claim was for torture against the foreign state authorities who would hardly be keen to provide their courts as a venue for determination of such a complaint. Moreover, even if such a tribunal were offered there may often in practice be serious doubts as to its integrity and impartiality, particularly where in the foreign state in question the judiciary is not independent of the executive. More recently in *Jones v United Kingdom*,[52] the ECtHR, in again upholding a decision by the English courts to grant immunity in the context of torture allegations, once more specifically rejected the view that alternative means of redress was relevant to an Article 6 inquiry.

Finally, there is also a clear inconsistency here with the ECtHR's jurisprudence on Article 6 and the immunity of international organizations. In *Waite and Kennedy v Germany*,[53] the Court found that a member state may only grant immunity where there existed a reasonably available alternative dispute settlement mechanism. It is hard to understand why such a principle was not found to be equally compelling in the context of state immunity.[54]

The consequence must be, however, that where no available alternative forum is shown to exist (as is likely to be the case in situations of serious human rights abuses) then immunity cannot be granted by a forum

---

[50] By contrast, Whytock (*ibid.* 2082) would allow immunity to be claimed by a foreign state even where no access would be available to the foreign state's own courts, where there were 'compelling foreign relations reasons (as between the forum and foreign states) to grant immunity'. The greater the gravity of the wrongs alleged, the stronger the foreign relations justification required for retention of immunity. It is thought, however, that such concerns could be adequately addressed in a broad, discretionary *forum non conveniens* inquiry without the need to retain immunity as a separate concept.

[51] *McElhinney v Ireland* (2002) 34 EHRR 322, para. 39.

[52] Application Nos 34356/06 and 40528/06, 14 January 2014, para. 195.

[53] (1999) 116 ILR 121.

[54] C. Ryngaert, '*Jones v United Kingdom*: The European Court of Human Rights Restricts Individual Accountability for Torture' (2014) 30 *Utrecht Journal of International and European Law* 47 at 49.

member state of the ECHR consistent with Article 6(1). The action must be allowed to continue in the forum, which is precisely the same result that occurs in *forum non conveniens* cases where a defendant is unable to show an alternative forum in which the matter can be adjudicated.

10.6 ICJ DECISION IN *GERMANY v ITALY*

The International Court of Justice (ICJ) in *Germany v Italy*[55] also rejected any link between alternative means of redress and state immunity. The case concerned Germany's liability for war crimes that took place on Italian territory during the Second World War. Germany claimed immunity from the jurisdiction of the Italian courts, which was rejected and Germany then sought review in the ICJ, arguing that the refusal to grant immunity violated customary international law. One of Italy's arguments before the ICJ was that immunity should be denied in this case 'because all other attempts to secure compensation for the various groups of victims involved in the Italian proceedings had failed'.[56] The ICJ rejected the argument, saying that it could 'find no basis in … customary international law … that makes the entitlement of a state to immunity dependent upon the existence of effective alternative means of securing redress'.[57] Although there was no countervailing access to justice principle directly engaged in this case, unlike in the decisions on Article 6(1) of the ECHR, it is nevertheless disappointing that the ICJ showed no awareness at all of the right, particularly since it has itself been recognized as a principle of customary international law.[58]

In an interesting recent postscript to the *Germany v Italy* decision the Italian Constitutional Court, in a judgment of 22 October 2014,[59] found certain Italian legislative provisions that had been adopted to give effect to the ICJ decision to be in breach of the Italian Constitution and so

---

[55] [2012] ICJ Rep. 99.

[56] *Ibid.* para. 98.

[57] *Ibid.* para. 101.

[58] F. Francioni, 'The Right of Access to Justice under Customary International Law' in F. Francioni (ed.), *Access to Justice as a Human Right* (2007), p. 50. Judge Yusuf, in his Dissenting Opinion in *Germany v Italy* decried the Court's failure to recognize the link between immunity and the need for an effective remedy and its unwillingness to give weight to the issue of alternative means of redress: see n. 39 above, Dissenting Opinion, paras 7–10, 30.

[59] Judgment No. 238/2014.

invalid. The fundamental constitutional right in question was the individual's right of access to justice enshrined in article 24 of the Constitution. While the ICJ's determinations concerning state immunity for war crimes and crimes against humanity undoubtedly represented customary international law, such principles could nevertheless not be admitted in Italian domestic law since they would violate the fundamental norm of access to justice. Two facts were particularly compelling for the Italian court: first, Germany's acts were unquestionably unlawful; and second, the grant of immunity to the foreign state here would have left the individual victims with no alternative means of redress. In such circumstances, immunity must bow to the 'higher' right of access to justice. In effect, the Italian court employed 'a balancing exercise'[60] or a 'hierarchy of norms'[61] analysis between the rights to state immunity and access to justice, which was the very approach that had been eschewed by both the ICJ and the ECtHR.

10.7 JURISDICTION BY NECESSITY

So, the direct impact of the right of court access on state immunity has so far been limited, as seen in the ECtHR and ICJ jurisprudence, although there is a strong body of commentary advocating a greater role for the principle. The right of access to justice may, however, have had greater 'indirect' impact on state immunity. The indirect effect can arguably be seen in the recent emergence of a new category of civil jurisdiction under the private international rules of many countries. The doctrine has been called 'forum of necessity' or 'jurisdiction by necessity' and has some similarities with the principle of *forum non conveniens* in recognizing that a claimant who has suffered injury should be entitled to at least one forum in which its case will be adjudicated.

Hence, in an action against a foreign state defendant, if the defendant's courts or other avenues for redress are deemed unsuitable or futile for the claims, the forum state must exceptionally allow the matter to proceed. The key difference with *forum non conveniens*, however, is that the latter doctrine presupposes that the forum has initial jurisdiction to determine

---

[60] D. Roughton and A. Hoffmann, *Constitutional Rights Versus State Immunity: Implementation of an ICJ Decision on Sovereign Immunity Declared Unconstitutional* (2014), available at http://hsfnotes.com/publicinternationallaw/2014/11/11/constitutional-rights-vs-state-immunity-implementation-of-an-icj-decision-on-sovereign-immunity-declared-unconstitutional/.

[61] Orakhelashvili, n. 36 above.

the matter and is then being asked to decline such jurisdiction in its discretion, in deference to another tribunal situated abroad. Jurisdiction by necessity, by contrast, creates a new ground of jurisdiction in the forum where none previously existed. Jurisdiction by necessity therefore provides a much more far-reaching implementation of the principle of access to justice.

Jurisdiction by necessity is well established in most civil law countries and so provides a convenient point of unity and international consensus with common law countries and their doctrines of *forum non conveniens*. When considered together, jurisdiction by necessity and *forum non conveniens* arguably form a powerful private international law vehicle to challenge the historical dominance of foreign state interests underlying foreign state immunity. As will be seen below, jurisdiction by necessity, like *forum non conveniens*, only operates where the foreign state cannot or will not provide a forum in which the claimant's complaint may be adjudicated. To that extent, once again, the foreign state is not compelled to litigate in the forum and may avoid local jurisdiction by offering its courts as an alternative venue.

Jurisdiction by necessity, as noted above, is well established in many civil law countries and jurisdictions; for example, Argentina, Austria, Belgium, Costa Rica, Estonia, Finland, Germany, Iceland, Japan, Lithuania, Luxembourg, Mexico, the Netherlands, Poland, Portugal, Quebec, Romania, Russia, South Africa, Spain, Switzerland, Turkey and Uruguay have all adopted versions of the doctrine.[62] The Swiss provision is typical (article 3 of the Swiss Code of Private International Law):

> if the Code does not provide for jurisdiction in Switzerland or if proceedings abroad are impossible or cannot reasonably be required to be brought, the Swiss judicial … authorities at the place with which the facts are sufficiently connected shall have jurisdiction.

In an important study[63] the doctrine was described as 'a general principle of public international law' and is said to have three key elements in the practice of the majority of states: (a) the absence of jurisdiction in the

---

[62] C. Nwapi, 'Jurisdiction by Necessity and the Regulation of the Transnational Corporate Actor' (2014) 30 *Utrecht Journal of International and European Law* 24 at 31–2.

[63] A. Nuyts, *Study of Residual Jurisdiction: Review of the Member States' Rules Concerning the Residual Jurisdiction of Their Courts in Civil and Commercial Matters Pursuant to the Brussels I and II Regulations* (3 September 2007), available at http://ec.europa.eu/civiljustice/news/docs/study_residual_jurisdiction_en.pdf.

forum under existing national rules of personal jurisdiction; (b) the requirement of some connection with the forum; and (c) the impossibility of bringing the proceedings in the country whose courts have jurisdiction.[64]

The first criterion is self-explanatory but the second, the requirement of sufficient factual connection with the forum, requires some discussion. The common approach among states has been to demand that the claimant at least be a resident or national of the forum state before he or she can invoke the jurisdiction of necessity ground. A typical situation may be an individual fleeing to country B after suffering human rights abuse in country A; in such a case temporary subsequent residence in country B would suffice. Some sort of connection is required to prevent the creation of a universal civil jurisdiction, an outcome which would be inconsistent with traditional private international law principles of jurisdiction.[65]

The third criterion, that it is impossible to bring proceedings in the country whose courts would have jurisdiction, would cover both legal and practical impediments to justice. For example, it would include a case where the claimant would suffer threats to his or her person if forced to return to the country where the wrong was committed, where the foreign government would have immunity under its own law before its own courts[66] or the corruption and bias of such courts would mean that relief could not in practice be obtained.

There are also recent signs of jurisdiction by necessity being accepted in common law countries, in particular, Canada. Not only is the principle recognized in the provinces that have adopted the Uniform Court Jurisdiction and Proceedings Transfer Act 1994[67] (Yukon, Nova Scotia, British Columbia and Prince Edward Island) as well as Quebec,[68] it has also been adopted in the common law of Canada. The doctrine was first mentioned in a common law decision involving a claim for damages for torture against a foreign state, *Bouzari v Islamic Republic of Iran*.[69] The court there noted that the country of torture could hardly be an appropriate forum for a civil action based on torture by the son of the Iranian President and officers of the foreign state.[70] In practical terms, if the

64 Nwapi, n. 62 above, 33–9.
65 Mills, n. 44 above, 39.
66 Cf. *Garsec Pty Ltd v Sultan of Brunei* (2008) 250 ALR 682.
67 See s. 6.
68 Civil Code, art, 3135.
69 (2004) 71 OR (3d) 675.
70 *Ibid.* para. 36.

Canadian court did not assume jurisdiction, the claimant would be left with no place to sue – an obviously undesirable result.[71] Yet, almost ironically, the court then proceeded to dismiss the action by the doctrine of foreign state immunity, curiously ignoring the fact that the imposition of immunity would itself create the invidious result referred to above, namely, no forum of redress for the claimant.

So, while the recognition of jurisdiction by necessity principle was admirable in *Bouzari* it would have been even more valuable had the court identified the clear scope for inconsistency between the concept and the state immunity doctrine. Such conflict could instead be addressed by either making any grant of immunity conditional on the foreign state providing an alternative forum, or preferably, replacing immunity with the jurisdiction by necessity test to ensure that a claimant would always have access to at least one forum for the vindication of its rights. Note that in Canada there also exists the *forum non conveniens* principle[72] and so there would be scope for jurisdiction by necessity and *forum non conveniens* to be amalgamated, with a stay or dismissal only to be granted where an adequate alternative forum exists to the claimant.

The next reference to the doctrine of jurisdiction by necessity in Canadian common law jurisprudence occurred in the decision of the Ontario Court of Appeal in *Van Breda v Village Resorts Ltd*.[73] There, Sharpe JA noted that:

> the forum of necessity doctrine recognises that there will be exceptional cases where, despite the (non-compliance with forum rules of personal jurisdiction) the need to ensure access to justice will justify the assumption of jurisdiction … where there is no other forum in which the plaintiff can reasonably seek relief there is a residual discretion to assume jurisdiction.[74]

The court's reasoning on this point has been cited with approval by other Canadian provincial courts[75] and referred to without comment by the Supreme Court of Canada on appeal in *Club Resorts Ltd v Van Breda*.[76] The Ontario Court of Appeal very recently examined the principle again in *West Van Inc. v Daisley*,[77] where it noted that jurisdiction by necessity

---

71 *Ibid*. para. 37.

72 *Club Resorts Ltd v Van Breda* [2012] 1 SCR 572; 2012 SCC 17.

73 (2010) 98 OR (3d) 721.

74 *Ibid*. para. 100.

75 *Ayles v Arsenault* 2011 ABQB 493, paras 32–3; *Fewer v Ellis* 2011 NLCA 17, paras 45–6.

76 [2012] 1 SCR 572, paras 82, 100.

77 2014 ONCA 232.

applied where 'there is no other forum in which the plaintiff can reasonably seek relief'.[78] Significantly, for the purposes of this chapter, the court noted the following examples of situations in which the principle may operate: 'the breakdown of diplomatic or commercial relations with a foreign state, the need to protect a political refugee [and] the existence of a serious physical threat if the debate were to be taken before the foreign court'.[79]

The examples given in the above passage would seem perfectly apt in the situation where a claimant has been the victim of human rights abuse by foreign state officials in the state's own territory. Indeed it may again be asserted that a state (such as Canada)'s retention of the foreign state immunity doctrine, while at the same time recognizing jurisdiction by necessity, may in practice be a hollow and futile exercise for claimants. This conclusion flows from the fact that many of the cases in which no available alternative forum exists will be where there is a foreign state perpetrator whose own courts are either closed to claimants or not impartial. So, if the necessity principle is to be given realistic application then foreign state immunity must be abolished.

Interestingly, in a later stage of the *Bouzari* litigation, an Ontario court appeared to apply the necessity principle despite the defendants being presumably entitled to immunity. In *Bouzari v Bahremani*,[80] the court assumed jurisdiction on the basis of necessity in a civil action brought against the son of the Iranian President who had authorized the claimant's torture. The court found such jurisdiction to exist on the basis that the claimant was a Canadian resident and there was 'no reasonable basis upon which [he could] be required to commence the action in a foreign jurisdiction, particularly the state where torture took place, Iran'.[81] What is notable about this case is that no reference was made to the doctrine of state immunity. This omission may have been due to a number of reasons: first, because the defendant did not appear in the litigation and so did not raise any question of immunity; or second, because the son of the President was not an official of the foreign state and so not entitled to immunity (although this seems unlikely).

Whatever was the precise reason why immunity was not referred to, the result in the *Bouzari v Bahremani* litigation was that the jurisdiction by necessity rule operated, unobstructed, to provide a forum to a claimant

---

78 *Ibid*. para. 20.

79 *Ibid*. para. 40.

80 Judgment of 6 August 2011, unreported, extracted at http://cdn.theatlantic.com/static/mt/assets/international/Ontario%20Court%20Endorsement.pdf.

81 *Ibid*. para. 5.

where none elsewhere existed.[82] A better result, however, especially for claimants in the position of Bouzari, in terms of obtaining an enforceable money judgment, would have been to allow the claim to be brought directly against the *foreign state*, rather than simply the individual torturer. Such persons are often difficult to locate for service of process or otherwise impecunious. Jurisdiction by necessity should therefore have been used in the earlier stage of the *Bouzari* litigation[83] to overcome state immunity.

10.8 EVALUATION

Hence, the right to access or justice is now a major factor supporting the erosion or abandonment of foreign state immunity. The arguments in favour of abolition of immunity and its replacement with private international law principles of jurisdiction therefore seem even stronger than in 1999. Not only has the profile and influence of Article 6(1) of the ECHR been dramatically raised since then but also the doctrine of jurisdiction by necessity has become much more widely accepted. Vindication of private rights is now seen as a crucial objective and the fact that the defendant who caused the harm is a foreign state should not obscure or exclude this fact.

Yet, as noted in 1999, foreign states do have uniquely sovereign interests which must be respected by domestic courts of other countries. It is suggested here that such concerns of foreign states will be adequately protected by adoption of a joint jurisdiction by necessity/*forum non conveniens* test. Jurisdiction by necessity is required to ensure that claimants have access to the courts of the forum where the court's ordinary rules of jurisdiction are not satisfied and where no foreign court would be available. The principle of *forum non conveniens* provides a unique discretionary mechanism enabling the forum court to weigh and balance the foreign state's concerns regarding adjudication of its affairs by the forum court and any impact on relations between the forum and foreign state executives, against the individual claimant's right to redress, in the decision to accept or decline jurisdiction. Most important of all, both doctrines recognize that a foreign state should only be permitted to

---

[82] The claimant Bouzari would have risked 'rearrest or worse' if he had returned to Iran in order to pursue his legal claims: N. Novogrodsky, 'Immunity from Torture: Lessons from *Bouzari v Iran*' (2007) 18 *European Journal of International Law* 939 at 940.

[83] (2004) 71 OR (3d) 675.

avoid litigation in the forum where there is another tribunal available to the claimant.

This last point aims to encourage a foreign state defendant to offer its courts as a good faith venue for adjudication of allegations made against the state. If such a 'first stop' principle were to gather hold then immunity, even if not formally abolished, would likely become redundant as claimants would presumably be content to have their cases determined by the courts in the foreign state, assuming that they would receive a fair hearing and pursuing such proceedings would not otherwise be burdensome or oppressive to them.

While the ECtHR in its Article 6 immunity cases has not yet undertaken a proper balancing of immunity and claimant interests, nor recognized the relevance of an available alternative forum, it is hoped that the above developments in the domestic law of civil jurisdiction will inspire the Court to change course. Arguably, since both foreign state immunity and access to justice are customary international law principles, the needs of 'proportionality' suggest that a different approach to simply upholding immunity is required. So, to summarize, the case for exclusive regulation of litigation against foreign states by private international law principles of civil jurisdiction is strong.

The significance of the right to access to justice seems not to have been fully appreciated by some advocates for retention of foreign state immunity, such as Fox[84] and McLachlan.[85] Their argument for preserving immunity is that the doctrine performs the function of allocating jurisdiction between states' domestic courts in disputes concerning state activities and removing friction among states, particularly between the forum and foreign states. According to this argument, while states are equals before international tribunals such as the International Court of Justice, the position of the foreign state in domestic litigation is different since it involves one state exercising its power to adjudicate upon the acts of another, with the risk of conflict between sovereigns. Hence, the ordinary rules of civil jurisdiction from private international law are inappropriate and need modification and supplementation to reflect the foreign state's unique status and to minimize inter-state disputes. The rules of foreign state immunity perform this function.

The 'foreign relations purpose'[86] of state immunity is, with respect, less persuasive in a time of increased concern for the rights of the

84 Fox and Webb, n. 11 above, 1.

85 C. McLachlan, *Foreign Relations Law* (Cambridge University Press, 2014).

86 *Ibid.* 495.

individual, including the right of access to justice. As has been recently argued,[87] 'jurisdiction is no longer exclusively a right of states or even an obligation owed by states to each other but … is … a matter of individual right, that is an obligation owed to individuals'. Similarly, Judge Cançado-Trindade in his Dissenting Opinion[88] in *Germany v Italy*, described state immunity as a product of the 'myopia of a State-centric approach which could only behold inter-State relations and [has] unduly underestimated and irresponsibly neglected the position of the human person in international law'. In examining the rules of domestic jurisdiction of states it is therefore incomplete to focus solely on the interests of the forum state and the foreign state and to attempt to reconcile such interests or determine the appropriate 'allocation' of competence. Such an inquiry fails to give adequate weight to the claimant's right to redress, especially in times of greater mobility of persons and heightened interaction with foreign legal systems. Once the element of access to justice is added to the equation, then the scales tip even more strongly in favour of the elimination of foreign state immunity. Unlike immunity, which is a narrow and state-focused inquiry, a combined jurisdiction by necessity and *forum non conveniens* test is flexible enough to embrace both state and claimant interests and to allow weighing of such competing concerns in the decision to adjudicate. Yet, ultimately, it is hoped that rules of immunity will become redundant in the future as foreign states are required to provide a fair and impartial system of justice for claimants. If such a practice developed, there would be less incentive or need for claimants to seek out alternative forums for redress.

---

87 Mills, n. 44 above, 43.

88 *Germany v Italy*, n. 39 above, Dissenting Opinion, para. 181.

11. The status of armed forces in public international law: jurisdiction and immunity

*Aurel Sari**

11.1 INTRODUCTION

States have sent their armed forces into the territory of other states since the dawn of modern international law. Throughout much of this period, national forces have ventured abroad primarily in order to fight wars, occupy territory or transit through another country.[1] However, during the course of the twentieth century, the nature of foreign deployments has changed dramatically. With the onset of the Cold War, states for the first time stationed large numbers of troops on foreign territory on a semi-permanent basis in times of peace. Peace-keeping emerged as a key instrument of collective security, together with the growing involvement of international organizations in military operations. The responsibilities of national forces have become more diverse.[2] In addition to engaging in combat operations, the armed forces of many nations now regularly operate outside the traditional battlefield to pursue a broad variety of other missions, ranging from disaster relief to re-establishing the rule of law. The mobility of the military has increased too, enabling states to deploy their troops into distant lands at short notice. In the wake of these strategic developments, foreign military deployments have now become a common feature of contemporary international relations.

* All views are expressed in the author's personal capacity.

[1] For historical examples of military occupation and transit arrangements, see Raymond Robin, *Des Occupations Militaires en Dehors des Occupations de Guerre* (Dissertation, Paris, 1913) and Rainer von Rosenberg, *Soldatenwerbung und militärisches Durchzugsrecht im Zeitalter des Absolutismus: Eine rechtsgeschichtliche Untersuchung* (Dissertation, Frankfurt am Maine, 1973), pp. 145–60.

[2] See for example, Timothy Edmunds, 'What *are* Armed Forces For? The Changing Nature of Military Roles in Europe' (2006) 82 *International Affairs* 1059.

The presence of foreign troops in the territory of another state raises a range of legal questions. Foremost amongst these are questions of status: what jurisdictional privileges and immunities from local jurisdiction do foreign forces enjoy in another state? International law does not provide a straightforward answer to this question. The law applicable in this area is multifaceted. This is a major source of uncertainty and misunderstanding. For example, it is often assumed that 'in the absence of an international agreement defining their rights and responsibilities, the status of foreign military personnel travelling in or through a friendly country in peacetime is essentially that of foreign tourists'.[3] This is most emphatically not the case. Not only are national armed forces organs of the state to which they belong, they are also organs unlike any other. Their distinct function and nature was recognized by the Parliamentary Assembly of the Council of Europe in the following terms:

> The army is the institution which is responsible for protecting the state and defending the community. Combat is its *raison d'être*, the very purpose of its existence, and it is bound by the specific constraints of rules regarding unity, hierarchy, discipline and compliance with orders.[4]

As this passage underlines, national armed forces are a key component of the modern state, protecting it from internal and external foes and projecting its power beyond its borders. They guarantee its identity, integrity and continuity.[5] International law recognizes that, unlike tourists, the armed forces are entrusted with unique responsibilities and for this reason merit special legal treatment.

The purpose of the present chapter is to provide an overview of the rules of international law governing the exercise of jurisdiction over national armed forces present in the territory of another state. Section

---

[3] Paul J. Conderman, 'Status of Armed Forces on Foreign Territory Agreements (SOFA)' in R. Wolfrum (ed.), *The Max Planck Encyclopedia of Public International Law* (Oxford, Oxford University Press, February 2013), para. 2, available at opil.ouplaw.com/home/ORIL. This is not an isolated view among practitioners: see Thomas Desch, 'Military Forces Abroad', in *ibid.* para. 30; Dieter Fleck, 'Present and Future Challenges for the Status of Forces (*ius in praesentia*): A Commentary to Applicable Status Law Provisions' in Dieter Fleck (ed.), *The Handbook of the Law of Visiting Forces* (Oxford, Oxford University Press, 2001), p. 47. See also Steven J. Lepper, 'A Primer on Foreign Criminal Jurisdiction' (1994) 37 *Air Force Law Review* 169 at 171.

[4] Parliamentary Assembly of the Council of Europe, Human Rights of Members of the Armed Forces, Recommendation 1742, 11 April 2006, para. 1.

[5] Cf. Krystyna Marek, *Identity and Continuity of States in Public International Law* (Geneva, Librairie E. Droz, 1954), pp. 439–40.

11.2 offers a general introduction to the position of the armed forces in international law. Section 11.3 discusses the legal bases for the exercise of jurisdiction over military personnel present abroad, while 11.4 examines the jurisdictional immunities applicable to such forces and their members under general international law. Finally, 11.5 turns to the relevant aspects of status of forces agreements.

11.2 POSITION OF THE ARMED FORCES IN INTERNATIONAL LAW

No single regime or branch of international law regulates the activities of the armed forces in a comprehensive manner. This may be contrasted with other areas of international law, for example, the law of diplomatic relations. According to the International Court of Justice (ICJ), the rules of international law governing diplomatic intercourse constitute a 'self-contained regime' which lays down certain substantive standards of conduct and also certain rules addressing breaches of these standards.[6] Describing diplomatic law as a self-contained regime does not imply that it is independent from other branches of international law or that it regulates the conduct of diplomatic relations exhaustively.[7] Rather, it expresses the notion that special rules have emerged in international practice to govern the conduct of diplomacy and that these rules form a coherent and systematic whole in a manner which sets them apart from other areas of international law. However, no such self-contained regime has come into existence to govern the activities of the armed forces. The purpose of the present section is, first, to discuss the reasons for the absence of such a regime and its implications and, second, to offer an overview of the main doctrines and features of international practice relating to the status of foreign forces.

---

[6] *Case concerning the United States Diplomatic and Consular Staff in Tehran (United States v Iran)* [1980] ICJ Rep. 41, para. 86.

[7] See *Report of the Study Group on the Fragmentation of International Law*, finalized by Martti Koskenniemi, UN Doc. A/CN.4/L.682 (13 April 2006), pp. 65–101. See also Bruno Simma and Dirk Pulkowski, 'Of Planets and the Universe: Self-contained Regimes in International Law' (2006) 17 *European Journal of International Law* 483.

11.2.1 Presence and Status of Foreign Forces

In contemporary international relations, it is common for states to send their armed forces abroad into the territory of other states. The objectives pursued by such deployments vary. They range from the conduct of armed hostilities at one end to humanitarian assistance missions and training exercises at the other. Generally speaking, the principles which govern the legal status of foreign forces during their presence abroad reflect the nature and operational context of their mission. In this respect, it is helpful to distinguish questions relating to the legal basis of the presence of foreign troops from questions concerning their legal status during their stay abroad.[8] The two are distinct, albeit closely related, matters.

The presence of foreign forces is subject to one very simple principle: no state may deploy its armed forces into the territory of another state without a valid legal justification.[9] International law recognizes a number of such justifications. The territorial state may consent to the presence of foreign troops,[10] for example, by inviting them to assist it in

---

[8] Cf. Dieter Fleck, 'Introduction' in Dieter Fleck (ed.), *The Handbook of the Law of Visiting Forces* (Oxford, Oxford University Press, 2001), p. 3 at 7–8. See also Dieter Fleck, 'Legal Issues of Multinational Military Units: Tasks and Missions, Stationing Law, Command and Control' (2000) 75 *International Law Studies* 161 at 166–71.

[9] General Assembly Resolution 2131 (XX), Declaration on the Inadmissibility of Intervention in the Domestic Affairs of States and the Protection of Their Independence and Sovereignty, UN Doc. A/RES/20/2131 (21 December 1965), para. 1; General Assembly Resolution 2625 (XXV), Declaration on Principles of International Law concerning Friendly Relations and Co-operation among States in accordance with the Charter of the United Nations, UN Doc. A/RES/25/2625 (24 October 1970), third principle. See also *Case concerning Military and Paramilitary Activities in and against Nicaragua (Nicaragua v United States) (Merits)* [1986] ICJ Rep. 14, paras 202–9.

[10] Terry D. Gill, 'Military Intervention at the Invitation of a Government' in Dieter Fleck and Terry D. Gill (eds), *The Handbook of the International Law of Military Operations* (Oxford, Oxford University Press, 2010), p. 229. See also Théodore Christakis and Karine Mollard-Bannelier, 'Volenti non fit injuria? Les effets du consentement à l'intervention militaire' (2004) 50 *Annuaire Français de Droit International* 102. In relation to peace-keeping practice, see Nabil Elaraby, 'United Nations Peacekeeping by Consent: A Case Study of the Withdrawal of the United Nations Emergency Force' (1968) 1 *New York University Journal of International Law and Politics* 149; David Wippman, 'Military Intervention, Regional Organizations, and Host-State Consent' (1996–97) 7 *Duke Journal of Comparative and International Law* 209.

humanitarian relief efforts.[11] The deployment of troops into the territory of another state may be lawful in the exercise of the right of individual or collective self-defence.[12] A valid justification may also take the form of an authorization issued by the Security Council under Chapter VII of the UN Charter.[13] These legal justifications are not mutually exclusive, but may complement one another.[14] However, where foreign forces are deployed abroad without a valid legal basis, their presence is *prima facie* in breach of the principle of non-intervention and therefore unlawful as a matter of international law.[15] In some cases, extenuating circumstances may mitigate or even preclude the wrongfulness of their presence, for

---

11 See for example, Exchange of Notes Constituting an Agreement regarding the Status of US Military and Civilian Personnel of the Department of Defense present in Nicaragua in connection with the Disaster Relief/Assistance Effort and Mutually Agreed Follow-on Activities, KAV 5581 (25 November 1998).

12 Terry D. Gill, 'Legal Basis of the Right of Self-Defence under the UN Charter and Under Customary International Law' in Dieter Fleck and Terry D. Gill (eds), *The Handbook of the International Law of Military Operations* (Oxford, Oxford University Press, 2010), p. 187. Whether or not it is necessary to deploy forces into the territory of an aggressor state in self-defence depends whether or not the requirements of proportionality and necessity are met: see Judith Gail Gardam, *Necessity, Proportionality, and the Use of Force by States* (Cambridge, Cambridge University Press, 2004), pp. 162–7. The deployment of armed forces into the territory of another state without its consent in self-defence against an armed attack emanating from a non-state actor raises different legal questions. See Noam Lubell, *Extraterritorial Use of Force Against Non-State Actors* (Oxford, Oxford University Press, 2010), pp. 36–42; Ashely S. Deeks, '"Unwilling or Unable": Toward a Normative Framework for Extraterritorial Self-Defense' (2011–2012) 52 *Virginia Journal of International Law* 483.

13 See, for example, N.D. White and Özlem Ülgen, 'The Security Council and the Decentralised Military Option: Constitutionality and Function' (1997) 44 *Netherlands International Law Review* 378; Danesh Sarooshi, *The United Nations and the Development of Collective Security* (Oxford, Oxford University Press, 1999); Nils Blokker, 'Is the Authorization Authorized? Powers and Practice of the UN Security Council to Authorize the Use of Force by "Coalitions of the Able and Willing"' (2000) 11 *European Journal of International Law* 541. Generally, see A. Vaughan Lowe *et al.* (eds), *The United Nations Security Council and War: The Evolution of Thought and Practice since 1945* (Oxford, Oxford University Press, 2008).

14 See for example, Security Council Resolution 678, UN Doc. S/RES/678 (29 November 1990). See Christopher Greenwood, 'New World Order or Old? The Invasion of Kuwait and the Rule of Law' (1992) 55 *Modern Law Review* 153 at 163–9; Eugene V. Rostow, 'Until What? Enforcement Action or Collective Self-Defense?' (1991) 85 *American Journal of International Law* 506.

15 See nn. 9 and 10 above.

instance, where they intrude into the territory of another state by accident[16] or as a result of an emergency.[17] However, in the absence of such extenuating circumstances, the non-consensual presence of foreign forces will almost certainly violate the principle of non-intervention and, depending on the circumstances, may also contravene the prohibition on the use of force in international relations.[18]

The legal basis for the presence of foreign forces, or the absence of a valid legal basis, has major implications for their legal status. Where armed forces stay abroad at the invitation of the territorial sovereign, the states concerned tend to enter into agreements to define the legal position of the troops and to address various practical questions raised by their presence. Such agreements are known as status of forces agreements.[19] Where foreign forces are deployed abroad without the consent of the territorial state, the legal framework will be different. For a start, it is unlikely that a status of forces agreement will be negotiated, since the forces are present without the permission of the territorial sovereign and potentially against its will. The generally applicable rules of international law will therefore play a more prominent role. Moreover, if the foreign forces engage in hostilities, their legal status will also be governed by the law of armed conflict. It is worth emphasizing that the applicability of the law of armed conflict to foreign troops depends on whether or not they participate in hostilities, not whether their presence is consensual or non-consensual. For example, a state may invite another state to assist it in fighting a non-international armed conflict taking place on its territory. In such cases, the presence of foreign troops is consensual, but they are subject to the law of armed conflict nonetheless.[20] Similarly, it is

---

[16] A case in point is the accidental 'invasion' of Liechtenstein by 170 Swiss troops who got lost in a military exercise in 2007: see Peter Stamm, 'Switzerland invades Liechtenstein', *New York Times*, 13 March 2007.

[17] For example, the Hainan Island incident. See Eric Donnelly, 'The United States-China EP-3 Incident: Legality and Realpolitik' (2004) 9 *Journal of Conflict and Security Law* 25; Yann-Huei Song, 'The EP-3 Collision Incident, "International Law and Its Implications on the U.S.-China Relations"' (2001) 19 *Chinese (Taiwan) Yearbook of International Law and Affairs* 1.

[18] For example, if foreign forces are present in the territory of another state in material breach of the terms of their invitation. See General Assembly Resolution 3314 (XXIX), Definition of Aggression (12 December 1974), Art. 3(e).

[19] See section 11.5 below.

[20] For example, the International Security Assistance Force. See Françoise Hampson, 'International Law and the Classification of Conflicts' in Elizabeth

conceivable that foreign troops are present both without the permission of the territorial state and without engaging in hostile actions against it.[21]

Consequently, the two principal factors which determine the legal status of foreign armed forces in the territory of another state is the consensual or non-consensual nature of their presence and whether or not they participate in an armed conflict.

11.2.2 Absence of a Self-contained Regime

International law recognizes that the responsibilities entrusted to the armed forces raise unique considerations which warrant special treatment. For example, international law makes special provision for warships. The United Nations Convention on the Law of the Sea not only confirms that warships enjoy immunity from the jurisdiction of other states, but it also restricts the right of coastal states to take measures against any warships passing through their territorial waters which do not comply with the applicable national laws and regulations.[22] Special rules and considerations apply to the armed forces in other fields of international law too.[23] While the armed forces thus find themselves subject to various specialized rules and regimes across several branches of international law, so far these norms have not merged into a single, overarching legal regime regulating military activities in a comprehensive manner. It seems that the potential uses of military power are simply too

---

Wilmshurst (ed.), *International Law and the Classification of Conflicts* (Oxford, Oxford University Press, 2012), p. 242.

[21] See n. 17 above.

[22] United Nations Convention on the Law of the Sea, 10 December 1982, 1833 UNTS 3, Arts 30, 32 and 95. In addition, Art. 236 of the Convention also exempts warships from the application of its provisions regarding the protection and preservation of the marine environment. The controversy surrounding the right of innocent passage of warships in the territorial sea further underlines the existence of special considerations relating to warships. Generally, see Bernard H. Oxman, 'The Regime of Warships under the United Nations Convention on the Law of the Sea' (1984) 24 *Virginia Journal of International Law* 809.

[23] For example, the applicability of special considerations to the armed forces and their activities have been recognized in international human rights law: see *Engel and others v The Netherlands (No. 1)*, Application Nos 5100/71, 5101/71, 5102/71, 5354/72 and 5370/72 (1979) 1 EHRR 647, ECtHR, Judgment, 8 June 1976, para. 54; *Stoyanovi v Bulgaria*, Application No. 42980/04, ECtHR. Judgment, 9 November 2010, para. 61.

diverse, straddling too many disparate areas of practice and law, to allow the development of a single regulatory framework at the international level.

Neither the so-called *law of visiting forces* nor the emerging field of *international law of military operations* fills this space. The law of visiting forces is concerned with the rules governing the presence and legal status of armed forces stationed abroad in the context of military alliances.[24] It focuses heavily on status of forces agreements, rather than on general rules of international law, and excludes enforcement or combat operations from its scope. By contrast, the international law of military operations is concerned mainly with the rules governing active military deployments in third countries.[25] Its precise contours, in particular its relationship with the law of armed conflict, the rules governing the use of force and the law of peace operations, are somewhat unclear. At the present stage of their development, both disciplines are best conceived as distinct areas of study and legal practice, rather than as self-contained legal regimes. In any event, neither claims to cover the international legal aspects of military operations in a comprehensive manner.

In the absence of an overarching regime, the legal framework governing the activities of the armed forces in international law is multifaceted and fragmented.[26] The applicable rules derive from a variety of sources, including multilateral treaties,[27] rules of customary international law[28] and bilateral instruments.[29] They consist of general norms relevant to all state organs as well as specific norms which apply only to the armed

---

[24] Cf. Dieter Fleck (ed.), *The Handbook of the Law of Visiting Forces* (Oxford, Oxford University Press, 2001).

[25] Cf. Dieter Fleck and Terry D. Gill (eds), *The Handbook of the International Law of Military Operations* (Oxford, Oxford University Press, 2010).

[26] For an overview, see Marco Odello and Ryszard W. Piotrowicz, 'Legal Regimes Governing International Military Missions' in Marco Odello and Ryszard W. Piotrowicz (eds), *International Military Missions and International Law* (Leiden, Martinus Nijhoff, 2011), p. 25.

[27] See for example, the UN Charter and international human rights instruments, such as the International Covenant on Civil and Political Rights, 16 December 1966, 999 UNTS 171.

[28] For example, the principle of non-intervention and functional immunity (see 11.4.2 above).

[29] See for example, status of forces agreements, such as the Military Technical Agreement between the International Security Assistance Force (ISAF) and the Interim Administration of Afghanistan (Interim Administration), 4 January 2002 (2002) 41 ILM 1032.

forces or to certain military formations.[30] Some of these rules are relevant at all times, whereas others are applicable only in specific circumstances, such as during times of armed conflict.[31] As a consequence of these factors, the rules of international law governing military activities are complex and context specific. The same holds true for the rules regulating the exercise of jurisdiction over the armed forces. So far, no overarching regime of jurisdictional principles and immunities has emerged at the international level. Instead, the rules applicable in this area too remain complex and context specific. As Philippa Webb and Lady Hazel Fox observe:

> The deployment of armed forces on territory other than their national State raises a range of immunity issues and usually involves a mixture of legal sources. The legal situation may be confused by uncertainty as to customary international law, by the existence of special regimes (bilateral and multilateral) established in respect of visiting armed forces, and by ambiguity in the application to armed forces of national legislation on State immunity.[32]

To better appreciate the reasons for this state of affairs, it is useful to briefly consider the evolution of the main doctrines and aspects of international practice relating to the status of foreign armed forces.

11.2.3 The Schooner Exchange

The modern position concerning the legal status of friendly foreign forces was formulated in 1812 by the US Supreme Court in the case of *The Schooner Exchange*.[33] The judgment is widely regarded not only as a *locus classicus* for the principle of state immunity,[34] but also as the first

---

[30] See for example, the UN Convention on the Law of the Sea, n. 22 above, and status of forces agreements, such as Agreement between the Government of Australia and the Government of Malaysia concerning the Status of Forces, 3 February 1997, 2116 UNTS 318.

[31] For example, the extra-territorial applicability of international human rights instruments is limited to persons who fall within the jurisdiction of the contracting parties: see Karen da Costa, *The Extraterritorial Application of Selected Human Rights Treaties* (Leiden, Martinus Nijhoff, 2013).

[32] Hazel Fox and Philippa Webb, *The Law of State Immunity* (3rd edn, Oxford, Oxford University Press, 2013), p. 593.

[33] *The Schooner Exchange v McFaddon*, 11 U.S. 116 (Sup. Ct 1812).

[34] See for example, Xiaodong Yang, *State Immunity in International Law* (Cambridge, Cambridge University Press, 2012), p. 8.

ever judicial pronouncement on the law of visiting forces.[35] Delivering the Court's judgment, Chief Justice Marshall observed that the mutual intercourse between states has given rise to 'a class of cases in which every sovereign is understood to wave the exercise of a part of that complete exclusive territorial jurisdiction'.[36] According to Marshall, such a waiver of jurisdiction has generally been extended to the person of a foreign sovereign and to ambassadors on their travels abroad. In addition, it also extends to foreign troops passing through another country with the consent of the local government.[37]

Chief Justice Marshall's analysis of the legal position of such troops rests on a careful balance between the interests of the receiving state and the interests of the sending state. On the one hand, adopting the receiving state's point of view, Marshall distinguishes visiting forces from visiting warships on the basis that the former pose a greater threat to the receiving state's security than the latter. Visiting forces therefore may enter a foreign territory only if the territorial sovereign has consented to their presence in express terms, whereas in the case of warships this consent may be implied.[38] On the other hand, taking the sending state's perspective, Marshall suggests that one cannot presume that a sovereign state intends to subject a portion of its military might to the jurisdiction of a foreign nation whenever it sends its forces abroad. The territorial sovereign's consent to the presence of foreign military forces, be they troops or warships, must consequently imply their exemption from local jurisdiction.[39] According to Marshall, the immunity of visiting forces thus ultimately rests on a tacit agreement between the territorial sovereign and the sending state, whereby the former impliedly undertakes to waive its jurisdiction.[40] As long as this implied waiver can be presumed to remain in force, the territorial sovereign would be considered, by the common usage of states, as violating its good faith if it were to assume

---

[35] See for example, Bert A. Abrams, 'International Law and Friendly Foreign Forces' (1957) 32 *New York University Law Review* 351 at 353; George Stambuk, *American Military Forces Abroad: Their Impact on the Western State System* (Columbus, OH, Ohio State University Press, 1963), pp. 125–6.

[36] *The Schooner Exchange*, n. 33 above, pp. 136–7.

[37] *Ibid.* 139.

[38] *Ibid.* 140.

[39] *Ibid.* 140 and 143.

[40] Marshall seems to import the understanding of customary international law as a 'tacit agreement' from E. de Vattel, *The Law of Nations or the Principles of Natural Law: Applied to the Conduct and to the Affairs of Nations and of Sovereigns* (Washington, DC, Carnegie Institution of Washington, 1916), Book I, para. 25.

jurisdiction over those foreign troops without giving prior notice.[41] However, the territorial sovereign 'is capable of destroying' this implied promise of immunity by expressly subjecting foreign forces present within its territory to the jurisdiction of its tribunals.[42]

One of the most influential aspects of *The Schooner Exchange* is the justification offered by Chief Justice Marshall for the immunities of friendly foreign forces. According to Marshall, foreign troops must benefit from immunity by necessary implication because subjecting them to the jurisdiction of the receiving state would undermine their effectiveness as a military unit and defeat the purpose of their free passage. The jurisdictional immunities of visiting forces thus rests on a functional basis,[43] namely, considerations of military effectiveness and necessity.[44] In this, Marshall seemed to follow the opinion of Vattel, who suggested that:

> The grant of a right of passage includes the grant of whatever is naturally connected with the passage of troops, and of those things without which it could not take place; this includes the right … to exercise military discipline over the soldiers and officers.[45]

The justification offered by Marshall for the jurisdictional immunities of visiting forces has been adopted by the majority of writers in the nineteenth and twentieth centuries.[46] It has also been cited with approval

---

[41] As Marshall puts it at an earlier passage: '[a] nation would justly be considered as violating its faith, although that faith might not be expressly plighted, which should suddenly and without previous notice, exercise its territorial powers in a manner not consonant to the usages and received obligations of the civilized world': *The Schooner Exchange*, n. 33 above, 137.

[42] *Ibid.* 146 and 147. In this, Marshall follows Bynkershoek's *De Foro Legatorum*, Ch. XIX.

[43] The immunities of visiting forces are functional in the sense that their basic objective is to protect the ability of visiting forces to carry out their functions. See *Aziz v Aziz and others* [2007] EWCA Civ 712, paras 58–61, CA.

[44] Roland J. Stanger, *Criminal Jurisdiction over Visiting Armed Forces* (Washington, DC, US Government Printing Office, 1965), p. 83.

[45] Vattel, n. 40 above, Book III, para. 130.

[46] See for example, Travers Twiss, *The Law of Nations Considered as Independent Political Communities: On the Rights and Duties of Nations in Time of Peace* (2nd edn, Oxford, Clarendon Press, 1884), vol. I, p. 271; Charles Cheney Hyde, *International Law Chiefly as Interpreted and Applied by the United States* (Boston, NJ, Little, Brown, and Company, 1922), vol. I, p. 346; William Edward Hall and Pearce A. Higgins, *A Treatise on International Law* (8th edn, Oxford, Clarendon, 1924), pp. 250–51.

in numerous cases.[47] Other commentators, including Lassa Oppenheim writing in the first edition of his leading work on international law,[48] have discussed the jurisdictional privileges and immunities of visiting armed forces with reference to the concept of exterritoriality.[49] On this view, foreign troops are considered in law to remain outside the territory of the receiving state and thus beyond the reach of its legal authority. Faint echoes of this understanding of immunity can be found in the case law.[50] However, exterritoriality has never developed into a coherent theory rivalling the functional understanding of the jurisdictional immunities of visiting forces put forward by Chief Justice Marshall in *The Schooner Exchange*, which remains the dominant position today.

11.2.4 Scope of Immunity

Commentators have disagreed in their interpretations of *The Schooner Exchange* as regards the scope of the privileges and immunities enjoyed by friendly foreign forces. Some have hailed the judgment as the seminal precedent laying down the principle that visiting forces enjoy complete immunity from local jurisdiction under international law.[51] This doctrine of absolute immunity is sometimes known as the law of the flag

---

[47] See *Coleman v Tennessee*, 97 U.S. 509, 515–16 (Sup. Ct 1878); *Tucker v Alexandroff*, 183 U.S. 424, 433 (Sup. Ct 1902); *Hamilton v McClaughry*, 136 F.445, 448–9 (Cir. Ct, D. Kansas 1905); *Chung Chi Cheung* [1939] AC 160, Privy Council; *Reference Re Exemption of United States Forces from Proceedings in Canadian Criminal Courts* [1943] SCR 483, paras 78–80, Supreme Court of Canada; *United States v Weiman*, 11 CMR 216, 219 (CMA 1953).

[48] L. Oppenheim, *International Law: A Treatise*, *vol. I*, *Peace* (1st edn, London, Longmans Green and Co., 1905), p. 483.

[49] See for example, Rino Borin, 'L'Extraterritorialità delle Forze Armate' (1937) 16 *Rivista di Diritto Internazionale* 186; John H. Wigmore, 'The Extraterritoriality of the United States Armed Forces Abroad' (1943) 29 *American Bar Association Journal* 121.

[50] *In Re Gilbert* (1944) 13 AD 86, Supreme Federal Court of Brazil; *United States v Sinigar*, 20 CMR 46, 53 (CMA 1955).

[51] Henry Wheaton and Richard Henry Dana, *Elements of International Law* (Oxford, Clarendon Press, 1866), p. 128; John S. Myers and Sheldon Z. Kaplan, 'A Consideration of Penal Jurisdiction over Military Personnel, Particularly Discharged Personnel, Implicated in Criminal Acts Committed Overseas while Still in the Military Service' (1947) 35 *Georgetown Law Journal* 303 at 310. See also Archibald King, 'Jurisdiction over Friendly Foreign Armed Forces' (1942) 36 *American Journal of International Law* 539. King is often cited as a prominent proponent of the doctrine of absolute immunity. However, his position is in fact more nuanced.

principle.[52] Certainly, Chief Justice Marshall's ruling that the grant of free passage to foreign forces 'implies a waver of *all jurisdiction* over the troops during their passage' does seem to suggest that they are exempt from all forms of local jurisdiction.[53] Others, however, have pointed out that the judgment does not in fact recognize in so many words the complete immunity of individual members of a foreign force from local civil and criminal jurisdiction, but is concerned primarily with the exercise of disciplinary and supervisory jurisdiction over foreign contingents as a whole.[54] This suggests that the immunity of friendly foreign forces from local jurisdiction is not absolute, but that sending states and receiving states exercise their jurisdiction in different areas. This approach is known as the principle of concurrent jurisdiction.

Although neither position is without merit, on balance it seems that Marshall's reasoning, in particular his suggestion that the territorial sovereign may unilaterally revoke the presumption that it has exempted visiting forces from its jurisdiction, is not compatible with the law of the flag doctrine.[55] The US Supreme Court itself has declined to read *The Schooner Exchange* as a precedent for the proposition that international law confers complete immunity from local jurisdiction on foreign public ships.[56] In fact, few of the cases usually cited in support of the law of the flag doctrine actually lend much credence to the theory of absolute immunity.[57] Only a small number of judicial decisions endorse the

---

52 Conderman, n. 3 above, para. 31; Lepper, n. 3 above, 170–71; *Italy v Lozano*, No. 07/21 (2008) 91 Rivista di Diritto Internazionale 558, Judgment, 14 October 2007; *Lozano v Italy*, No. 31171/2008, ILDC 1085 (IT 2008) (2008) 91 Rivista di Diritto Internazionale 1223, Appeal Judgment, 24 July 2008.

53 *The Schooner Exchange*, n. 33 above, 140 (emphasis added).

54 G.P. Barton, 'Foreign Armed Forces: Immunity from Supervisory Jurisdiction' (1949) 26 *British Yearbook of International Law* 380 at 384–6; Murray L. Schwartz, 'International Law and the NATO Status of Forces Agreement' (1953) 53 *Columbia Law Review* 1091 at 1104–5.

55 *The Schooner Exchange*, n. 33 above, at 146.

56 *The Santissima Trinidad*, 20 U.S. 283, 352–4 (Sup. Ct 1822).

57 For example, it has been suggested that the Permanent Court of Arbitration has recognized the 'exclusive jurisdiction of the officers and military tribunals of a nation over its own troops in a friendly foreign country' (King, n. 51 above, 544) in *Casablanca Arbitration Award* (1961) 11 RIIA 119. Far from it: the case actually involved a conflict between a French claim to exercise jurisdiction in Morocco over deserters from the French Foreign Legion on the basis of the law of belligerent occupation, and a German claim to exercise jurisdiction over the same persons based on an earlier agreement with Morocco granting Germany exclusive jurisdiction over all German nationals in Morocco.

doctrine of complete immunity unequivocally.[58] These cases must be seen in the light of other decisions which expressly deny the existence of a rule of international law granting visiting armed forces absolute immunity from local jurisdiction. In *Wright v Cantrell*, for example, the Supreme Court of New South Wales concluded on the basis of a detailed review of state practice that the doctrine of absolute immunity is 'completely lacking' in general assent among states.[59] While the law of the flag doctrine certainly benefitted from support in the period before the Second World War, it never seems to have established itself as the dominant legal principle. The fact that it so clearly favours the interests of sending states, instead of balancing them against the competing interests of receiving states, seems to have prevented it from attracting more general support in state practice.

Occasionally, the law of the flag doctrine is portrayed as the traditional legal position which over time gradually gave way to the more progressive principle of concurrent jurisdiction.[60] This suggests that the principles governing the status of foreign armed forces have evolved in a linear fashion in a way that is reminiscent of the development of the law of state immunity from an absolute doctrine to a limited theory. This view rests on a double misunderstanding. First, the notion of a seamless evolution is not borne out by a more detailed historical analysis. As we have seen, the doctrine of the law of the flag never became the dominant principle governing the status of friendly foreign forces, but was merely one amongst several competing approaches. Second, and this is the more important point, the idea of progressive evolution wrongly assumes that a single principle is capable of defining the legal status of foreign forces regardless of their operational context and that one of the competing principles is therefore more appropriate than the other. This overlooks the fact that the status of the armed forces is not regulated in a uniform

---

[58] For example, *In Re AF* (1945) 12 AD 163, Tribunal Correctionelle of the Isle of Chios (Greece); *Dizon v Philippines-Ryukus Command* (1948) 81 Phil. 286, Supreme Court of the Philippines. See also *Chow Hung Ching v The King* (1948) 77 CLR 449, High Court of Australia, where Justice Dixon endorsed the theory of absolute immunity not as a matter of international law, but of common law alone.

[59] *Wright v Cantrell* (1943) 12 AD 133 at 140, Supreme Court of New South Wales (Australia);. See also *Manuel v Ministère Public* (1943) 12 AD 154, Cour d'Assises of Egypt.

[60] Conderman, n. 3 above, paras 31–2; Lepper, n. 3 above, 170–72; *Lozano v Italy*, n. 52 above, 1228–9.

manner under international law. Rather, international practice demonstrates that different legal arrangements are considered appropriate for different circumstances, ranging from the broad exemption of combat forces from the adjudicative and enforcement jurisdiction of their adversary during armed conflict at one end[61] to the sharing of jurisdiction by sending and receiving states in the context of military alliances at the other.[62]

11.2.5 Developments in International Practice since 1945

Since the end of the Second World War, international practice relating to the legal status of foreign armed forces has revolved around several pivots. Four of these are worth noting in this context. First, we have witnessed a proliferation of bilateral and multilateral status of forces agreements. Gradually, international agreements have become the primary source of international law in this area, while other sources have receded into the background. Domestic courts have increasingly decided cases involving visiting armed forces by applying the rules contained in the applicable international agreements and domestic legislative acts, rather than by having recourse to general principles or rules of customary international law. Many of the cases brought in the post-war period are thus concerned with the application and interpretation of the relevant treaty provisions and domestic norms, rather than the underlying principles of general international law.[63]

Second, with the emergence of peace-keeping and collective self-defence arrangements during the Cold War, international organizations have assumed an increasingly prominent role in the deployment of military personnel. Despite certain aborted attempts at direct recruitment,[64] no international organization currently recruits its own armed forces. Instead, they rely on personnel and contingents made available to them by their member states or third states. This significantly complicates the legal position of such forces. On the one hand, national armed

---

[61] See 11.4.3 above.

[62] See 11.5.1 above.

[63] See for example, *R v Birkenhead Borough Justices, ex parte Smith* [1954] 1 WLR 471, QBD; *H.K. Smallwood v Clark M. Clifford*, 286 F.Supp.97 (DDC 1968); *R v Peterson, ex parte Hartmann* [1969] 14 FLR 1, Supreme Court of Victoria (Australia).

[64] Treaty Establishing the European Defence Community, 27 May 1952 (Cmd. 9127, 1954). See Edward Fursdon, *The European Defence Community: A History* (London, Macmillan, 1980).

forces placed at the disposal of another state or international organization do not lose their character as organs of their state of origin.[65] States retain ultimate authority and control, known as 'full command', over their armed forces at all times.[66] As such, they never fully divest their military personnel of their national character. On the other hand, states frequently do transfer more limited powers of control over their national contingents to other states or to international organizations in the context of multinational operations.[67] In the case of peace-keeping operations established by the United Nations, national contingents are even incorporated into the institutional structure of the UN itself.[68] This means that national contingents deployed in multinational operations may enjoy a dual status and are subject to multiple layers of regulatory authority.

Third, by entering into similar status of forces agreements under similar circumstances on successive occasions, states and international organizations have built up a substantial body of practice relating to certain types of military deployments. Two types of arrangements stand out very clearly in international practice. Status of forces agreements concluded in the context of structured military cooperation between politically equal partners have frequently been modelled on the NATO Status of Forces Agreement (NATO SOFA) of 1951.[69] The jurisdictional arrangements of the NATO SOFA are based on the principle of reciprocity.[70] They attempt to balance the competing interests of sending states and receiving states in an equitable manner by putting into place a

---

[65] *Attorney-General v Nissan* [1970] AC 179 at 222, HL.

[66] Blaise Cathcart, 'Command and Control in Military Operations' in Terry D. Gill and Dieter Fleck (eds), *The Handbook of the International Law of Military Operations* (Oxford, Oxford University Press, 2010) p. 235 at 237.

[67] For command and control arrangements in peace-keeping operations, see Ray Murphy, 'Legal Framework of UN Forces and Issues of Command and Control of Canadian and Irish Forces' (1999) 4 *Journal of Conflict and Security Law* 41 at 48–55. For NATO practice and terminology, see Fleck, n. 8 above, 171–4.

[68] This has important implications in the field of international responsibility. See Aurel Sari, 'UN Peacekeeping Operations and Article 7 DARIO: The Missing Link' (2012) 9 *International Organizations Law Review* 77; Paolo Palchetti, 'The Allocation of Responsibility for Internationally Wrongful Acts Committed in the Course of Multinational Operations' (2013) 95 *International Review of the Red Cross* 727.

[69] Agreement between the Parties to the North Atlantic Treaty regarding the Status of Their Forces, 19 June 1951, 199 UNTS 67.

[70] Aurel Sari, 'The NATO SOFA at Sixty: Heading for Retirement or Has Life Just Begun?' (2012) *NATO Legal Gazette* 2 at 5–6.

system of concurrent jurisdiction over foreign forces.[71] By contrast, different arrangements apply to peace-keeping operations and similar active deployments. Given the more challenging legal and operational environment of such missions, status of forces agreements adopted for the purposes of peace operations are not based on the principle of complete reciprocity. Instead, they are weighed in favour of sending states and organizations. They typically confer more extensive privileges and immunities on foreign forces, as reflected in the terms of the UN Model Status of Forces Agreement (UN Model SOFA) of 1990.[72] As these two arrangements demonstrate, the legal status of foreign forces depends on the nature of their presence. Different legal considerations and principles apply in different circumstances.

Finally, the armed forces are subject to growing levels of accountability and legal review. Examples include cases arising in relation to military operations conducted in the territory of the former Yugoslavia,[73] allegations of widespread sexual exploitation and abuse by UN peacekeepers[74] and proceedings before domestic courts[75] and the ICJ[76] arising out of the acts of German armed forces during the Second World War. The spectacular growth of international criminal law has reinforced

---

71 NATO SOFA, Art. VII. See Paul J. Conderman, 'Jurisdiction' in Dieter Fleck (ed.), *The Handbook of the Law of Visiting Forces* (Oxford, Oxford University Press, 2001), p. 99.

72 *Model Status-of-Forces Agreement for Peace-keeping Operations: Report of the Secretary-General*, UN Doc. A/45/594 (9 October 1990).

73 See for example, *Nuhanović v Netherlands*, LJN:BR5388, ILDC 1742 (NL 2011), Netherlands Court of Appeal, Judgment, 5 July 2011; *Presidency of the Council of Ministers v Markovic and others*, ILDC 293 (IT 2002), (2002) 85 Rivista di Diritto Internazionale 799, Italian Court of Cassation, Preliminary Order on Jurisdiction, 8 February 2002; and *Bici v Ministry of Defence* [2004] EWHC 786, QB.

74 See *A Comprehensive Strategy to Eliminate Future Sexual Exploitation and Abuse in United Nations Peacekeeping Operations* (Zeid Report), UN Doc. A/59/710 (24 March 2005). For a detailed assessment, see Róisín Sarah Burke, *Sexual Exploitation and Abuse by UN Military Contingents: Moving Beyond the Current Status Quo and Responsibility under International Law* (Leiden, Brill, 2014).

75 See for example, *Ferrini v Germany*, No. 5044/04 (2004) 87 Rivista di Diritto Internazionale 540, 128 ILR 658, Italian Court of Cassation, Judgment, 6 November 2003 and *Perfecture of Voiotia v Federal Republic of Germany (Distomo Massacre)* (2000) 129 ILR 514, Greek Court of Cassation, Judgment, 4 May 2000.

76 *Jurisdictional Immunities of the State (Germany v Italy, Greece Intervening)* [2012] ICJ Rep. 99.

accountability at the level of the individual soldier, as the establishment of the International Criminal Court in order to 'put an end to impunity for perpetrators' of the most serious international crimes underlines.[77] The effect of this increased emphasis on accountability is twofold. First, it puts the onus on sending states and organizations to ensure that any exemptions that their forces enjoy from local jurisdiction do not stand in the way of holding them accountable for any misdeeds they may have committed. However, sending states and organizations continue to be reluctant to restrict or waive the immunities of their personnel, whilst at the same time they often lack the legal and practical means to exercise jurisdiction themselves.[78] Second, the scope of the immunities traditionally enjoyed by foreign armed forces is subject to growing scrutiny. For example, it has been suggested that the immunities conferred by the UN Model SOFA are excessive, because they are not limited to what is strictly necessary to enable a particular peace operation to function.[79] However, leaving local courts to determine the scope of the immunities enjoyed by foreign forces on a case-by-case basis is neither practical nor compatible with the underlying purpose of conferring immunities in the first place.[80] The growing emphasis on accountability therefore creates pressures which have not yet been resolved.

11.3 JURISDICTION OVER THE ARMED FORCES

The purpose of this section is to consider the application of the principles of the law of state jurisdiction to armed forces present abroad. The topic is of considerable interest for several reasons. States are normally expected to justify their assertion of jurisdiction with reference to a

---

[77] Rome Statute of the International Criminal Court, 17 July 1998, Preamble, 2187 UNTS 90.

[78] See for example. *Jaloud v The Netherlands*, Application No. 47708/08, ECtHR, Judgment, 20 November 2014, Joint Concurring Opinion of Judges Casadevall, Berro-Lefevre, Šikuta, Hirvelä, López Guerra, Sajó and Silvis, para. 6.

[79] Róisín Burke, 'Status of Forces Deployed on UN Peacekeeping Operations: Jurisdictional Immunity' (2011) 16 *Journal of Conflict and Security Law* 63 at 93.

[80] Aurel Sari, 'The Status of Foreign Armed Forces Deployed in Post-Conflict Environments: A Search for Basic Principles' in Carsten Stahn *et al.* (eds), *Jus Post Bellum: Mapping the Normative Foundations* (Oxford, Oxford University Press, 2014), p. 467 at 498–9.

permissive rule of international law.[81] It is therefore important to understand what permissive principles states may invoke in order to justify their exercise of authority over armed forces deployed abroad. An analysis of these principles reveals that, depending on the circumstances, international law entitles sending states, receiving states as well as third states to exercise jurisdiction over visiting forces and their members. This may lead to a conflict of jurisdiction in cases where more than one state enjoys the right to exercise its authority in relation to the same subject matter. While this conflict is mitigated by the existence of certain immunities from jurisdiction, it is important to appreciate that other principles of international law also impose limits on the exercise of jurisdiction and thus help to resolve such conflicts.

11.3.1 Principles of Jurisdiction

11.3.1.1 Territorial states

A state's capacity to exercise jurisdiction is commonly regarded as an aspect or manifestation of its sovereignty.[82] As Max Huber famously noted in his arbitral award in the *Island of Palmas* case, sovereignty entitles a state to exercise within its territory the functions of statehood to the exclusion of all other states.[83] Modern international law is based on the premise that sovereignty confers on every state the right to perform the functions of government within its territory, in particular by establishing and enforcing its own legal and political order. The territorial principle thus enables the state to exercise prescriptive, adjudicative and enforcement jurisdiction over all persons and objects located in its territory and over any activities and events taking place therein. For this reason, it furnishes the most fundamental and most comprehensive basis of jurisdiction in international law.

When foreign armed forces are present in its territory, the territorial principle entitles the receiving state, in principle, to subject the force and its individual members to its laws and legal processes in both criminal and civil matters. The authorities of the receiving state therefore may rely on the principle of territoriality as the primary legal basis to exercise their

---

81 Cedric Ryngaert, *Jurisdiction in International Law* (Oxford, Oxford University Press, 2008), p. 21.

82 See for example, F.A. Mann, 'The Doctrine of Jurisdiction in International Law' (1964) 111-I *Recueil des Cours* 1 at 16; cf. Franklin Berman, 'Jurisdiction: The State' in Patrick Capps *et al.* (eds), *Asserting Jurisdiction: International and European Legal Perspectives* (Oxford, Hart, 2003), p. 3 at 3–4.

83 *Island of Palmas* (1928) 2 RIAA 829 at 838, PCA.

jurisdiction over visiting forces. This point is well established in international practice. As far as prescriptive jurisdiction is concerned, it is a common feature of status of forces agreements to stipulate in express terms that foreign forces are bound to respect the law of the territorial state.[84] As far as enforcement jurisdiction is concerned, status of forces agreements clearly proceed on the assumption that foreign forces are subject to the authority of the territorial state, since one of the main functions of these agreements is to define under what circumstances foreign personnel should be exempt from local adjudicative and enforcement jurisdiction. Given that the territorial principle therefore entitles the receiving state to exercise the full spectrum of its jurisdictional competences over visiting forces, it would seem unnecessary for the local authorities to rely on other bases of jurisdiction, such as the nationality principle, to assert their authority over foreign forces present in their territory.[85] Nevertheless, these other bases of jurisdiction may complement the territorial principle in specific cases.[86]

11.3.1.2 Sending states

Any exercise of jurisdiction by the sending state over its armed forces abroad will by definition be extra-territorial in nature. The sending state consequently cannot invoke the territorial principle in order to claim the right to exercise jurisdiction over its armed forces abroad, but must rely on alternative principles. However, none of the other traditional principles of jurisdiction, such as the nationality, the protective and the passive personality principle, provide sending states with a sufficient legal basis to regulate the activities of their military personnel abroad. The reach of these principles is too narrow. For example, the nationality principle cannot provide a sufficient justification for imposing service laws and regulations on members of the sending state's armed forces who do not

---

[84] See for example, Agreement between the European Union and the Gabonese Republic on the Status of the European Union-led Forces in the Gabonese Republic, 16 June 2006, Art. 2(1) [2006] OJ L187/43. However, the exact scope of this duty is subject to debate: see Aurel Sari, 'The EU Status of Forces Agreement: Continuity and Change in the Law of Visiting Forces' (2007) 46 *Military Law and the Law of War Review* 9 at 90–105.

[85] On these bases of jurisdiction, see Michael Akehurst, 'Jurisdiction in International Law' (1972–1973) 46 *British Yearbook of International Law* 145 at 156–66; Ryngaert, n. 81 above, 85–126.

[86] For example, pursuant to the nationality principle, a state may extend the reach of its criminal laws to its nationals serving in foreign armed forces: see Militärstrafgesetz vom 13 Juni 1927 (MStG) (Swiss Military Penal Code), art. 94, which penalizes Swiss nationals who enlist in foreign armed forces.

hold its nationality.[87] Moreover, the traditional bases of jurisdiction do not explain the sending state's competence to exercise extra-territorial adjudicative and enforcement jurisdiction over members of its armed forces. As the Permanent Court of International Justice (PCIJ) has pointed out in the *Lotus* case, a state 'may not exercise its power in any form in the territory of another state' without being entitled by a permissive rule of international law to do so.[88] Yet state practice shows that national service laws and regulations routinely entitle the competent military authorities to take disciplinary measures against members of their armed forces abroad.[89]

Given the inapplicability and limits of the traditional bases of jurisdiction, a sending state's competence to exercise prescriptive, adjudicative and enforcement jurisdiction over its armed forces outside its own territory is best explained with reference to what has been called the principle of organic jurisdiction.[90] International law recognizes the inalienable right of every state to freely organize itself and choose its own form of government.[91] Amongst other things, this includes the competence to establish organs and subdivisions at all levels of government, to transfer governmental functions to international organizations and to regulate and control its organs and officials. The term 'organic jurisdiction' describes this latter competence to exercise jurisdiction over organs and officials.[92] Most of the time, states exercise this competence within their own territory. In such cases, the principle of organic

[87] The protective and universal principle would not be applicable to minor infringements of discipline, while the passive personality principle would not cover crimes committed by a sending state's forces to the detriment, for example, of the local population.

[88] *SS Lotus (France v Turkey)* (1927) PCIJ Series A, No 10, at 18–19. See also *Re Bolton and another, ex parte Beane* (1987) 162 CLR 514 at 519, High Court of Australia.

[89] Rain Liivoja, *An Axiom of Military Law: Applicability of National Criminal Law to Military Personnel and Associated Civilians Abroad* (Dissertation, Helsinki, 2011), pp. 159–222; Frank Adaka, 'The Enforcement of Military Justice and Discipline in External Military Operations: Exploring the Fault Lines' (2008) 47 *Military Law and the Law of War Review* 253.

[90] Finn Seyersted, 'Jurisdiction over Organs and Officials of States, the Holy See and Intergovernmental Organisations' (1965) 14 *International and Comparative Law Quarterly* 31 (Part I) and 493 (Part II).

[91] Convention on Rights and Duties of States adopted by the Seventh International Conference of American States (Montevideo Convention), 16 December 1933, Art. 3, 165 LNTS 19; Friendly Relations Declaration, third principle.

[92] See Seyersted, n. 90 above, 33–43.

jurisdiction overlaps with, and is obscured by, the territorial principle.[93] Some commentators have therefore questioned whether organic jurisdiction really 'amounts to anything more than territorial or personal jurisdiction of the State'.[94] However, the consistent practice of states in regulating the conduct of their organs and officials outside their own territory suggests that organic jurisdiction does in fact represent a separate basis of jurisdiction in international law.[95]

National armed forces constitute an organ of the state to which they belong.[96] The right of each state to freely organize itself therefore extends to the organization and administration of its armed forces. Although the composition, administration and legal regulation of the armed forces differs greatly from one state to another,[97] all states aim to maximize the military effectiveness of their troops. Considerations of military effectiveness have therefore given rise to highly specialized systems of internal administration and, in many states, to the evolution of military law and justice as distinct strands of domestic law.[98] Logic dictates that military personnel must remain subject to their national service law at all times and irrespective of their location. Otherwise, sending them abroad on official duty would be tantamount to releasing them from active military service. Unsurprisingly, state practice confirms that national service laws and regulations continue to apply to the armed forces during their presence abroad.[99] Not only that, but state practice

---

[93] *Ibid.* 34.

[94] Hazel Fox, 'Employment Contracts as an Exception to State Immunity: Is All Public Service Immune?' (1995) 66 *British Yearbook of International Law* 97 at 120.

[95] For example, in *Cyprus v Turkey (Admissibility)* (1975) 2 DR 125, para. 8, ECommHR, the European Commission of Human Rights held that 'authorised agents of a State, including diplomatic or consular agents and armed forces', remain under jurisdiction of their sending states.

[96] *Transaero, Inc v La Fuerza Aerea Boliviana*, 30 F.3d 148, 153 (DC Cir. 1994); *Shooting Range Extension* (1984) 86 ILR 533 at 534, Verwaltungsgerichtshof of Kassel.

[97] Generally, see Georg Nolte (ed.), *European Military Law Systems* (Berlin, De Gruyter, 2003).

[98] Some of the reasons underpinning the development of military law and justice were set out with great clarity by the Canadian Supreme Court in *R v Généreux* (1992) 1 SCR 259 at 293–6.

[99] See n. 89 above. For example, in *A v United Kingdom* (1987) 9 EHRR CD 369 at 375, ECommHR, a case involving a soldier who deserted from the Indian army arrested in the United Kingdom, the European Commission of Human Rights accepted that 'a serving soldier is considered subject to the military law of the country he serves regardless of his whereabouts'.

also demonstrates, as Vattel and Chief Justice Marshall had long recognized, that sending states are entitled to exercise those powers which are reasonably necessary to ensure the continued functioning of their forces as an effective military unit in the territory of the receiving state.[100] Customary international law thus permits sending states to maintain discipline among their forces and to take measures which are necessary for their internal administration in the territory of receiving states.

11.3.1.3 Third states

Occasionally, third states may have an interest in exercising their jurisdiction over foreign armed forces and their members. For example, a third state may assist another state in apprehending a foreign deserter who is not normally stationed in its territory.[101] In the absence of more specific rules, for instance in the form of extradition treaties, the third state in question will have to rely on the general principles of state jurisdiction. The *Lozano* case illustrates the point.[102] On 4 March 2005, US troops shot and killed Nicola Calipari, an Italian military intelligence officer, at a roadblock in Iraq. The Italian authorities subsequently instituted proceedings against the US soldier responsible for firing the shots, Specialist Mario Lozano, to be tried *in absentia* for murder and attempted murder in Rome. The facts of this case presented the Italian authorities with something of a dilemma, since the proceedings concerned a situation where one sending state, Italy, sought to exercise its criminal jurisdiction over a member of the armed forces belonging to another sending state, the United States, for acts committed by the latter against its personnel and nationals in the territory of a receiving state, namely, Iraq. Since the applicable legal instruments regulated the status of the two foreign forces only *vis-à-vis* the receiving state, but not between each other, the Italian prosecutors justified their claim to exercise jurisdiction over Lozano with reference to the passive personality principle.[103]

---

[100] *Shooting Range Extension*, n. 96 above, 534.

[101] See for example, *A v United Kingdom*, n. 99 above.

[102] *Italy v Lozano* and *Lozano v Italy*, n. 52 above.

[103] *Lozano v Italy*, n. 52 above, 1228. See Eric Talbot Jensen, 'Exercising Passive Personality Jurisdiction over Combatants: A Theory in Need of a Political Solution' (2008) 42 *International Lawyer* 1107.

11.3.2 Limits to Territorial Sovereignty

The preceding section has shown that sending, receiving and third states may rely on a range of jurisdictional principles to assert their authority over their own and foreign forces. However, whether or not these states are entitled to exercise their jurisdiction in a particular case depends on other applicable rules of international law. Immunities from jurisdiction represent one set of such rules. Before turning to these, it is useful to briefly consider certain other limitations on territorial jurisdiction.

Classic formulations of the principle of territorial jurisdiction have often been framed in absolute terms. In *The Schooner Exchange*, Chief Justice Marshall boldly declared that the 'jurisdiction of the nation within its own territory is necessarily exclusive and absolute'.[104] More than a century later, Max Huber referred to the 'exclusive competence of the state in regard to its own territory' in the *Island of Palmas* case.[105] Statements to similar effect abound in the classical works on international law.[106] However, in reality, a receiving state's right to exercise jurisdiction over foreign forces pursuant to the territorial principle is neither exclusive nor absolute. It is not exclusive, since the principle of territorial sovereignty does not prevent the exercise of jurisdiction by sending states, or the performance of official acts by their personnel, in the territory of the receiving state pursuant to any applicable rules of customary international law or international agreements.[107] The territorial jurisdiction of the receiving state is not absolute either, because the principle of sovereign equality imposes certain limits *ratione materiae* on the exercise of authority by one state over another.[108] In particular, international law preserves a reserved domain of domestic jurisdiction within which states are free to act at their discretion to the extent that no applicable rules of international law govern their activities.[109]

---

104 *The Schooner Exchange*, n. 33 above, 136. See also *Church v Hubbart*, 6 U.S. 187, 234 (Sup. Ct 1804).

105 *Island of Palmas*, n. 83 above, 838 and 839.

106 See for example, Wheaton and Dana, n. 51 above, 111; Twiss, n. 46 above, 257; Hyde, n. 46 above, 346.

107 For examples of the performance of official acts within foreign territory, see Charles Rousseau, 'L'indépendance de l'État dans l'ordre international' (1948) 73-II *Recueil des Cours* 167 at 222–4.

108 As Max Huber noted in *Island of Palmas*, n. 83 above, 839, territorial sovereignty 'has as corollary a duty: the obligation to protect within the territory the rights of other States'.

109 *Nationality Decrees Issued in Tunis and Morocco*, Advisory Opinion (1923) PCIJ Series B, No. 4, 23–4. On the concept of a reserved domain, see

Two points follow from this. First, the very notion of a reserved domain implies that each state's jurisdictional competence within its own reserved domain is exclusive. Second, it follows that territorial sovereignty does not extend to matters falling within the exclusive domestic jurisdiction of another state. In the present context, there is ample support in international practice to suggest that sending states alone are competent to exercise their authority in matters relating to the discipline and internal administration of their armed forces.[110] Receiving states do not enjoy, nor do they claim to enjoy, a right to adopt disciplinary measures against members of foreign forces and to administer or control those forces. These matters fall within the exclusive jurisdiction of the sending state.

11.3.3 Jurisdiction in Times of Armed Conflict

The extent to which the law of armed conflict modifies these jurisdictional principles is unclear.[111] On the one hand, the principles in question are of general application and nothing indicates that they become inapplicable as such in times of armed conflict. On the other hand, the relationship between belligerent parties to an international armed conflict is very different compared to the relationship between states at peace. It is therefore reasonable to expect that the law of state jurisdiction may apply differently in times of war.

As far as the territorial state is concerned, any foreign armed forces present within its territory fall within the scope of its territorial jurisdiction. In principle, the territorial state may therefore exercise the full panoply of its jurisdictional competences over the armed forces of an invading state. In practice, however, invading forces typically adopt a position resembling the one described in the US *Operational Law Handbook*:

Quincy Wright, 'Domestic Jurisdiction as a Limit on National and Supra-National Action' (1961) 56 *Northwestern University Law Review* 11; Bin Cheng, 'Jurimetrics: The Meaning and Measurement of Legal Sovereignty and Domestic Jurisdiction' (1991) 1 *University of Miami Yearbook of International Law* 30; Kristen Walker, 'An Exploration of Article 2(7) of the United Nations Charter as an Embodiment of the Public/Private Distinction in International Law' (1993–1994) 26 *New York University Journal of International Law and Politics* 173. See also Institute of International Law, 'La détermination du domaine réservé et ses effets, 30 April 1954' (1954) 45 AIDI 292.

[110] Dissenting Opinion of Judge Fernandes in *Right of Passage over Indian Territory (Portugal v India) (Merits)* [1960] ICJ Rep. 6 at 125.

[111] The subject has not received much attention in the literature.

> When engaged in traditional armed conflict with another national power, military forces care little about the domestic law of that nation. For example, during the Persian Gulf War, the coalition invasion force did not bother to stop at Iraqi traffic lights in late February 1991. The domestic law of Iraq did not bind the invasion force. This exception is based on the classical application of the Law of the Flag theory.[112]

This raises the question whether or not invading forces are bound by the law of the territorial state. The notion that invading forces are exempt from the territorial jurisdiction of their adversary is difficult to reconcile with the fact that territoriality constitutes one of the axiomatic principles of the international legal order. An attempt to legally anchor this notion in the law of the flag doctrine is unconvincing. Not even the most generous formulations of the doctrine suggest that local law is completely *inapplicable* to foreign forces. The position taken in the *Operational Law Handbook* is also difficult to reconcile with the fact that the law of armed conflict recognizes that the territorial state may, indeed occasionally must, exercise criminal jurisdiction over members of the invading force following their capture.[113] An alternative view suggests that invading forces *are* subject to the jurisdiction of the territorial state, and consequently a duty to respect its laws, but as a matter of fact do not comply with that duty. One difficulty with this view is that it implies that the territorial state, or third parties who have suffered harm at the hands of the invading force, may bring claims against the invading state for violations of local law committed by its troops during the invasion. That may potentially expose invading forces to a flood of claims for breaches of ordinary law, such as traffic violations, unless such claims are barred by the law of state immunity or other exemptions from jurisdiction.[114]

As far as invading states are concerned, it is important to recall that the relationship between a state and its armed forces is an internal matter.[115] Consequently, the right of one state to regulate the conduct of its armed forces pursuant to the principle of organic jurisdiction does not depend on the consent of another state and, therefore, whether or not its forces

---

112 John Rawcliffe (ed.), *Operational Law Handbook*, Judge Advocate General's Legal Center and School (Charlottesville, VA, 2007), p. 68.

113 For example, Convention (III) Relative to the Treatment of Prisoners of War, 12 August 1949, 75 UNTS 135, Art. 85, recognizes that a Detaining Power may prosecute a prisoner of war for breaches of its law committed prior to capture, while Art. 129 imposes an obligation to penalize grave breaches and suppress other breaches of the Convention.

114 See 11.4.3 below.

115 See 11.3.2 above.

are present abroad with the territorial state's consent. There is some support for this position in the law of armed conflict, which requires belligerents to exercise responsible command over their troops.[116] This duty clearly implies that invading states are entitled to maintain discipline in the territory of their adversary.[117] While the matter is not necessarily settled, these considerations suggest that invading states may exercise prescriptive and enforcement jurisdiction in times of armed conflict in the territory of their adversary even without its consent.

11.4 STATE IMMUNITY AND FUNCTIONAL IMMUNITY

There can be no doubt that the principle of state immunity applies to national armed forces. It has been common ground at all times during the evolution of the law of state immunity that the term 'state' includes the organs of state government for the purposes of applying this body of law.[118] Given that national armed forces constitute organs of their respective states,[119] they clearly benefit from the principle of state immunity. The International Law Commission's (ILC) Commentary on the 1991 Draft Articles on the Jurisdictional Immunities of States and Their Property expressly referred to the armed forces as one of the autonomous state organs to which the law of state immunity applies.[120]

Even though the applicability of the principle of state immunity to foreign armed forces is not in doubt, it is not immediately clear whether the immunities of such forces are governed solely by the general rules of state immunity, including those codified in the UN Convention on State

---

[116] Cf. Geneva Convention (III), Art. 4(A)(2). See Jean-Marie Henckaerts and Louise Doswald Beck (eds), *Customary International Humanitarian Law* (Cambridge, Cambridge University Press, 2005), Rule 139.

[117] Cf. Geneva Convention (III), Art. 129. Henckaerts and Doswald-Beck, n. 116 above, Rule 157.

[118] United Nations Convention on Jurisdictional Immunities of States and Their Property, 2 December 2004, Art. 2(1)(b)(i), Annex to GA Res. 59/38 (2 December 2004) (2005) 44 ILM 801. Cf. Gerhard Hafner and Ulrike Köhler, 'The United Nations Convention on Jurisdictional Immunities of States and their Property' (2004) 35 *Netherlands Yearbook of International Law* 3 at 13–17.

[119] See n. 96 above.

[120] Draft Articles on the Jurisdictional Immunities of States and Their Property, with Commentaries, reproduced in (1991) II(2) *Yearbook of the International Law Commission* 13 at 15–16.

Immunity of 2004 (UNCSI),[121] or by special rules and principles of international law applicable only to the armed forces. This section will examine this question, before turning to discuss the functional immunities enjoyed by members of foreign armed forces.

11.4.1 Law of State Immunity

11.4.1.1 General rules of state immunity

Acts performed by or concerning the armed forces are frequently cited in sweeping terms as prime examples of sovereign or public acts to which immunity from foreign jurisdiction attaches,[122] including by proponents of the restrictive theory of state immunity.[123] Measures adopted in the internal administration of the armed forces undeniably belong to 'the core area of state sovereignty'.[124] However, it does not follow that *all* acts carried out by or relating to the armed forces are inevitably sovereign in character.[125] Just like any other organ of government, the armed forces too are capable of entering into private law transactions to which immunity may not apply under the restrictive theory of state immunity.[126] Consequently, whether or not acts undertaken by or in relation to the armed forces of one state are exempt from the adjudicative and enforcement jurisdiction of another state depends on whether any of

---

[121] United Nations Convention on Jurisdictional Immunities of States and Their Property, 2 December 2004, Annex to GA Res. 59/38 (2 December 2004) (2005) 44 ILM 801.

[122] *Victory Transport Inc. v Comisaria General*, 336 F.2d 354, 360 (2d Cir. 1964); *McElhinney v Williams and Secretary of State for Northern Ireland* [1995] 3 IR 382 at 402, Irish Supreme Court; C-292/05 *Lechouritou and others v Germany* [2007] ECR I-1519, ECJ, para. 37. See also *Ex Parte Pinochet Ugarte (No. 3)* [2000] 1 AC 147 at 269, HL.

[123] H. Lauterpacht, 'The Problem of Jurisdictional Immunities of Foreign States' (1951) 28 *British Yearbook of International Law* 220 at 238–9; Jean-Flavien Lalive, 'L'immunité de juridiction des états et des organisations internationales' (1953) 84-III *Recueil des Cours* 205 at 285–6.

[124] *McElhinney v Ireland*, Application No. 31253/96 (2002) 34 EHRR 322, ECtHR, para. 38.

[125] Cf. J. Craig Barker, 'State Immunity, Diplomatic Immunity and Act of State: A Triple Protection Against Legal Action?' (1998) 47 *International and Comparative Law Quarterly* 950 at 956.

[126] Cf. *Trendtex Trading Corp. v Central Bank of Nigeria* [1977] QB 529 at 558, CA. As Hoffmann LJ suggested in *Littrell v United States (No. 2)* [1995] 1 WLR 82 at 95, CA, there is no single test or 'bright line' by which sovereign military activities may be distinguished from non-sovereign transactions performed by the armed forces.

the exemptions recognized in the law of state immunity are applicable to them or not. This question must be answered in the light of the facts of each particular case.

The applicability of the principles of state immunity to foreign armed forces is well established in domestic and international case law. The following paragraphs give some examples of this jurisprudence. In *Littrell*,[127] a former member of the US Air Force stationed in the United Kingdom brought proceedings before the British courts against the US government to claim damages for personal injuries he sustained as a result of medical treatment he received in a US military hospital located in the United Kingdom. The US government claimed immunity from British jurisdiction. The Court of Appeal held that the NATO SOFA of 1951, to which both the United Kingdom and the United States were parties, had no bearing on the case, as the relevant provisions had not been enacted into domestic law.[128] Since the UK State Immunity Act (SIA) 1978[129] specifically excluded the immunities of visiting forces from its scope, the question had to be decided with reference to the common law rules on sovereign immunity, including any incorporated rules of customary international law.[130] Counsel for the plaintiff submitted that the British courts were competent under customary international law to exercise their jurisdiction, since doing so did not interfere with military matters or the right of the United States to maintain discipline among its troops. Lord Hoffmann rejected this argument on the ground that for 'an English court to allow visiting US servicemen to sue their government would clearly be an interference with this aspect of the relationship between the troops and their sovereign'.[131] The provision of medical services to members of visiting forces, including the standard of care provided to them by the sending state, was thus judged to be a matter falling within the internal administration of those forces and therefore an act to which immunity attaches.

The Supreme Court of Canada followed a similar line of reasoning in *Re Canada Labour Code*.[132] The case turned on the question whether labour relations at a military base maintained by the United States in

---

[127] *Littrell v United States (No. 2)*, n. 126 above.

[128] *Ibid.* 88.

[129] State Immunity Act 1978, reprinted in Andrew Dickinson, Rae Lindsay and James P. Loonam (eds), *State Immunity: Selected Materials and Commentary* (Oxford, Oxford University Press, 2004), p. 329.

[130] *Littrell v United States (No. 2)*, n. 126 above, 87.

[131] *Ibid.* 91.

[132] *Re Canada Labour Code* (1992) 2 SCR 50, Supreme Court of Canada.

Canada were covered by section 5 of the Canadian State Immunity Act 1982, which provides that a foreign state is not immune from the jurisdiction of the Canadian courts 'in any proceedings that relate to any commercial activity of the foreign state'.[133] According to the Supreme Court, employment at a foreign military base constitutes a multifaceted relationship involving both commercial and sovereign aspects. In determining whether or not the commercial activity exception in section 5 applied, labour relations at the base had to be considered in their entire context.[134] Relying on this approach, the Supreme Court upheld the immunity of the United States on the ground that the application of Canadian labour regulations could threaten the military mission of the base.[135]

The rules of state immunity were also central to the *McElhinney* case. On 4 March 1991, the plaintiff, John McElhinney, accidentally drove through a British checkpoint established at the border between Northern Ireland and Ireland, dragging one of the British soldiers manning the checkpoint into Irish territory with his car. The soldier fired several shots at the vehicle and later confronted McElhinney with his gun. McElhinney initiated proceedings before the Irish courts against both the soldier and the Secretary of State for Northern Ireland, claiming damages. The Irish High Court found that the principle of sovereign immunity applied to the case.[136] On appeal, the Irish Supreme Court affirmed that in carrying out his duties at the checkpoint, the soldier acted within the sphere of governmental or sovereign activity and that his acts were therefore covered, in principle, by the rule of sovereign immunity.[137] McElhinney subsequently brought a complaint against Ireland before the European Court of Human Rights (ECtHR), arguing that by applying the doctrine of sovereign immunity, the Irish courts denied his right to a judicial determination of his claim in contravention of Article 6(1) of the ECHR.[138] The ECtHR agreed that the application of the rules of sovereign immunity impacted the applicant's right of access to court under Article 6(1) of the ECHR. However, it denied that this limitation

---

[133] State Immunity Act, RS, 1985, c. S-18, reprinted in Dickinson, Lindsay and Loonam, n. 129 above, 488, 490.

[134] *Ibid.* para. 36.

[135] *Ibid.* paras 54–5.

[136] *McElhinney v Williams* [1995] IR 382 at 388–9, High Court of Ireland.

[137] *McElhinney v Williams and Secretary of State for Northern Ireland*, n. 122 above, 399.

[138] *McElhinney v Ireland*, n. 124 above.

constituted a breach of the ECHR, since it pursued a legitimate aim and was proportionate.[139]

In addition to upholding sending states' immunity from adjudicative jurisdiction, domestic courts have also confirmed their exemption from the enforcement jurisdiction of receiving states. In the *Shooting Range Extension* case,[140] for instance, a German citizen applied for an injunction to prevent the extension of a shooting range used by US armed forces stationed in Germany or, in the alternative, for an order requiring the US military authorities to comply with local building regulations. In its judgment, the Administrative Court of Kassel pointed out that visiting armed forces enjoy immunity from local jurisdiction and 'related matters' under customary international law.[141] Even though US forces deployed in Germany were required to respect local law and, more specifically, to respect German building regulations whilst carrying out military construction projects, this did not entitle the German courts to compel those forces to comply with the relevant German regulations as requested by the applicant.[142]

A number of states have also made express provisions for foreign armed forces in their domestic legislation on state immunity. UK SIA 1978, section 16(2), for example, provides that nothing contained in the first Part of the Act, which sets out the general rule of immunity and various exceptions to it, applies 'to proceedings relating to anything done by or in relation to the armed forces of a state while present in the United Kingdom and, in particular, has effect subject to the Visiting Forces Act 1952'.[143] The UK SIA 1978 thus accords priority to the more specialized rules contained in the Visiting Forces Act 1952 and, with regard to questions not addressed by the 1952 Act, to the relevant rules of common law.[144] A somewhat similar result is obtained by section 1604 of the US Foreign Sovereign Immunities Act (FSIA) 1976, which subjects the application of the Act to any 'existing international agreements to which

---

139 *Ibid.* paras 35 and 37.

140 *Shooting Range Extension*, n. 96 above.

141 *Ibid.* 534.

142 *Ibid.* 535.

143 Dickinson, Lindsay and Loonam, n. 129 above, 414. To similar effect, see Singapore State Immunity Act 1979, s. 19(2)(a), reprinted in Dickinson, Lindsay and Loonam, n. 129 above, 504, 512.

144 *Holland v Lampen-Wolfe* [2000] 1 WLR 1573 at 1584–5, HL. See Mizushima Tomonori, 'One immunity has gone … another …: *Holland v Lampen-Wolfe*' (2001) 64 *Modern Law Review* 472.

the United States is a party at the time of the enactment of this Act'.[145] The US courts have interpreted this clause as requiring them to give effect to the jurisdictional arrangements contained in the NATO SOFA over any conflicting provisions of the US FSIA 1976.[146] The state immunity acts of other states also contain special rules on foreign armed forces, such as provisions expressly excluding military property from the definition of commercial property.[147]

11.4.1.2 *Lex specialis* rules of state immunity

The question whether the jurisdictional immunities applicable to foreign armed forces differ from the general rules of state immunity, and if so in what way, has not been systematically addressed in international law. However, it is widely recognized that special considerations and principles do apply. In 1983, Professor Ian Brownlie prepared a questionnaire in his capacity as the Rapporteur of a Commission set up by the Institute of International Law to study the contemporary problems concerning the jurisdictional immunity of states.[148] In his questionnaire, Professor Brownlie requested the other members of the Commission to offer their views as to whether or not 'the subject "foreign armed forces" can be subsumed under existing legal categories and does not constitute a special legal category of its own'.[149] Three members answered the question in the affirmative without explaining their position in any detail.[150] Two members suggested that the jurisdictional immunities of visiting forces could be subsumed under the general law of state immunity, but added that these immunities were in some respects exceptional and deserved special attention.[151] One reply suggested that

---

[145] Foreign Sovereign Immunities Act 1976 (US), reprinted in Dickinson, Lindsay and Loonam, n. 129 above, 217, 238.

[146] See for example, *Moore v United Kingdom*, 384 F.3d 1079 (9th Cir. 2004).

[147] State Immunity Act 1985, s. 13 (Canada); Foreign States Immunities Act 1985 (No. 196), s. 32(3)(a) (Australia), reprinted in Dickinson, Lindsay and Loonam, n. 129 above, 469 at 482.

[148] Ian Brownlie, 'Contemporary Problems concerning the Jurisdictional Immunity of States, Preliminary Report' (1987) 62 *Annuaire de l'Institut de Droit International* 13 at 43.

[149] *Ibid.*

[150] Ian Brownlie, 'Definitive Report and Draft Set of Resolutions by Ian Brownlie, QC' (1987) 62 *Annuaire de l'Institut de Droit International* 45 at 126 (M. Bos), 129 (J. Crawford) and 138 (P. Francescakis).

[151] *Ibid.* 132 (M.D. de Velasco Vallejo) and 146 (S. Sucharitkul).

they may not necessarily be so subsumed,[152] while one member believed that the immunities of visiting forces could be regarded as a separate legal category in view of the special jurisdictional arrangements found in state practice.[153] Although hardly conclusive, these views demonstrate a broadly held understanding that the immunities of foreign forces are subject to special rules, and therefore merit separate discussion, but also an uncertainty as to their relationship with the general rules of state immunity.

Turning to international practice, there is considerable support for the notion that the jurisdictional immunities of visiting forces are governed by special rules of international law. Article 31 of the European Convention on State Immunity of 1972 (ECSI) thus declares that '[n]othing in this Convention shall affect any immunities or privileges enjoyed by a Contracting State in respect of anything done or omitted to be done by, or in relation to, its armed forces when on the territory of another Contracting State'.[154] According to the Explanatory Report on the Convention, the purpose of Article 31 is to recognize that the Convention cannot be invoked to resolve problems arising out of the stationing of forces, given that such problems are dealt with by special agreements, which operate as *lex specialis*.[155] The UN Convention on State Immunity (UNCSI) does not contain a provision similar to Article 31 of the ECSI, nor does it list the immunities of visiting forces among the privileges and immunities which remain unaffected by the Convention.[156] However, in a statement made in the Sixth Committee on 25 October 2004, the Chairman of the Ad Hoc Committee on Jurisdictional Immunities of States and Their Property, Professor Gerhard Haffner, pointed out that a 'general understanding had always prevailed' that military activities were not covered by the Convention.[157] According to Professor Haffner, the exclusion of military activities was:

> an example of the general approach of the Convention: it did not apply where there was a special immunity regime, including immunities *ratione personae*

[152] *Ibid.* 157 (Y. Takano).

[153] *Ibid.* 108–9 and 113–14 (M. Bedjaoui).

[154] European Convention on State Immunity, 16 May 1972, 1495 UNTS 182.

[155] Explanatory Report on the European Convention on State Immunity, reprinted in Dickinson, Lindsay and Loonam, n. 129 above, 36, 64. Note the reference to Art. 33 of the Convention.

[156] UN Convention on State Immunity, Art. 3.

[157] Summary Record of the 13th Meeting of the Sixth Committee, UN Doc. A/C.6/59/SR.13 (22 March 2005), para. 36. See also Hafner and Köhler, n. 118 above, 46–7.

> (*lex specialis*). Sometimes that was expressly stated in the text, sometimes not. Thus, for example, the express mention of heads of State in article 3 [of the UNCSI] should not be read as suggesting that the immunity *ratione personae* of other state officials was affected by the Convention.[158]

It has been shown elsewhere that neither the text nor the preparatory work of the UN Convention bear out the claim that military activities are excluded from its scope in their entirety.[159] However, what the records also reveal is an understanding that the activities of foreign armed forces raise distinct considerations and that their legal status demands special treatment. In his Second Report on Jurisdictional Immunities of States and Their Property submitted in 1981, Special Rapporteur Sompong Sucharitkul recommended that the Draft Articles under preparation were not meant to deal with the status of certain types of state organs or affect the extent of their jurisdictional immunities under international agreements and the prevailing rules of customary international law.[160] Despite expressly mentioning visiting armed forces as one of the organs which should remain outside the scope of the Draft Articles,[161] Sucharitkul did not incorporate a reference to them in the safeguard clause which later became Article 3 of the UNCSI. The United Kingdom subsequently sought to remedy this omission by suggesting that an additional paragraph should be added to the text[162] to provide that the Draft Articles were 'without prejudice to the question of the privileges and immunities enjoyed by the armed forces of one State while present in another State

---

158 *Ibid.* para. 37.

159 Andrew Dickinson, 'Status of Forces Under the UN Convention on State Immunity' (2006) 55 *International and Comparative Law Quarterly* 427 at 429–31; Roger O'Keefe, 'The "General Understandings"' in Roger O'Keefe, Christian J. Tams and Antonios Tzanakopoulos (eds), *The United Nations Convention on Jurisdictional Immunities of States and their Property: A Commentary* (1st edn, Oxford, Oxford University Press, 2013), p. 19 at 21–7.

160 Sompong Sucharitkul, Special Rapporteur, *Second Report on Jurisdictional Immunities of States and Their Property* , UN Doc. A/CN.4/331 and Add.1 (11 April and 30 June 1981), reproduced in (1980) II(1) *Yearbook of the International Law Commission* 199 at 212. See also Sompong Sucharitkul, 'Immunities of Foreign States Before National Authorities' (1976) 149-I *Recueil des Cours* 87 at 108.

161 *Ibid.*

162 Then Article 4 of the Draft Articles on Jurisdictional Immunities of States and Their Property, reproduced in (1988) II(1) *Yearbook of the International Law Commission* 47.

with the latter's consent'.[163] However, Sucharitkul's successor, Special Rapporteur Motoo Ogiso, denied the need for such a paragraph, since in his view the privileges and immunities of visiting forces 'are determined by agreement between the States concerned rather than by customary international law'.[164] Considering that the Convention already contained several safeguard clauses deferring to other applicable agreements, he considered it unnecessary to add the privileges and immunities of armed forces to the general savings clause under Article 3 of the Convention.[165]

The matter was raised again by Japan in a *note verbale* dated 30 September 1993.[166] After observing that status of forces agreements are concluded on the basis of a delicate balance of interests between their parties, Japan suggested that 'establishing unified multilateral rules on the matter of jurisdictional immunity of foreign armed forces from civil proceedings' might easily affect this balance and create a situation where the legal status of foreign troops does not correspond to the nature of the bilateral relationship between the sending state and the host state.[167] To avoid such a situation, Japan proposed that the jurisdictional immunities of armed forces stationed abroad should continue to be dealt with on a bilateral level and be excluded from the scope of the Draft Articles.

---

[163] Jurisdictional Immunities of States and their Property, Comments and Observations Received from Governments, UN Doc. A/CN.4/410 and Add.1-5, reproduced in (1988) II(1) *Yearbook of the International Law Commission* 45 at 85.

[164] Motoo Ogiso, Special Rapporteur, *Preliminary Report on Jurisdictional Immunities of States and Their Property*, UN Doc. A/CN.4/415 (20 May 1988), reproduced in (1988) II(1) *Yearbook of the International Law Commission* 96 at 103.

[165] Ogiso thus expressed his support for 'maintaining the phrase "Unless otherwise agreed" in [what is now UNCSI, Art. 12] in order to cover situations such as injury or damage caused by armed forces stationed in the territorial State with, of course, the latter's agreement. The usual practice was that proceedings initiated in relation to such injury or damage were covered by status-of-forces agreements, and it was desirable to avoid confusion between such agreements and the draft articles under consideration by maintaining the words in question'. See Summary Record of the 1768th Meeting, UN Doc. A/CN.4/SR.1768 (26 May 1983), reproduced in (1983) I *Yearbook of the International Law Commission* 81, para. 11.

[166] *Note verbale* dated 30 September 1993 from the Permanent Representative of Japan to the United Nations addressed to the Secretary-General, UN Doc. A/48/464 (1 October 1993), p. 4.

[167] *Ibid.*

Although no state expressed an objection to this proposal,[168] it was never incorporated into the text of the Convention. The published records do not reveal why. The most likely explanation is that the majority of states shared Special Rapporteur Ogiso's position that the Convention's safeguard clauses for international agreements eliminated the need to exclude foreign forces from its scope in express terms in Article 3 of the UNCSI.[169] The text and drafting history of the ECSI and the UNCSI thus demonstrate that these instruments defer, just like domestic legislation on state immunity, to the rules of any applicable status of forces agreements as well as any *lex specialis* rules of customary international law.

One example of such *lex specialis* rules concerns the inapplicability of the territorial tort exception to the activities of foreign forces. In *McElhinney*, the claimant relied on this exception to argue that the principle of state immunity was not available to shield torts committed by foreign state agents in the territory of the forum state from the jurisdiction of the local courts. The Irish courts and the European Court of Human Rights both rejected this argument.[170] According to the ECtHR, there appears to be:

> a trend in international and comparative law towards limiting State immunity in respect of personal injury caused by an act or omission within the forum State, but that this practice is by no means universal. Further, it appears ... that the trend may primarily refer to 'insurable' personal injury, that is incidents arising out of ordinary road traffic accidents, rather than matters relating to the core area of State sovereignty such as the acts of a soldier on foreign territory which, of their very nature, may involve sensitive issues affecting diplomatic relations between States and national security. Certainly, it cannot be said that Ireland is alone in holding that immunity attaches to suits in respect of such torts committed by *acta jure imperii* or that, in

---

[168] The absence of objections was specifically recalled by Japan and duly noted by the Chairman of the informal consultations held in the framework of the Sixth Committee on the Draft Articles, see Convention on the Jurisdictional Immunities of States and Their Property, Informal Consultations held Pursuant to General Assembly Decision 48/413, UN Doc. A/C.6/49/L.2 (4 October 1994), p. 5.

[169] It is worth noting in this context that Spain proposed the addition of a second clause to UNCSI, Art. 12 to accord priority to the claims settlement provisions found in relevant international agreements, including status of forces agreements, in more explicit terms. See Jurisdictional Immunities of States and Their Property, Comments and Observations Received from Governments, UN Doc. A/CN.4/410 and Add.1-5, reproduced in (1988) II(1) *Yearbook of the International Law Commission* 45 at 80.

[170] *Ibid.* 404. See also *Lozano v Italy*, n. 52 above, 1232.

> affording this immunity, Ireland falls outside any currently accepted international standards.[171]

The drafting history of Article 12 of the UNCSI, which codifies the territorial tort exception, confirms these findings. Although the precise scope of Article 12 has never been defined during the drafting process, the dominant understanding has always been that it is confined principally to insurable risks and as such 'is primarily concerned with accidents occurring routinely within the territory of the State of the forum'.[172] In the absence of a consensus on a more precise definition, the scope of Article 12 has thus been determined from two opposing angles. Injury and damage caused by traffic accidents and other injury and damage of a similarly isolated and insurable nature are included within its scope, even when caused in a sovereign capacity. However, incidents covered by special legal regimes, such as the law of diplomatic immunity and status of forces agreements,[173] and injury and damage caused on an altogether larger scale, for instance, in the context of an armed conflict,[174] are excluded. Since Article 12 is a 'residual rule',[175] it is subject to the arrangements made for the exercise of civil jurisdiction under any

---

[171] *McElhinney v Ireland*, n. 124 above, para. 38.

[172] Draft Articles on Jurisdictional Immunities of States and Their Property with Commentaries, n. 120 above, 45. The notion that Art. 12 is primarily limited to traffic accidents has been affirmed repeatedly: see for example, Summary Record of the 2191st Meeting, 11 July 1990, UN Doc. A/CN.4/SR.2191, reproduced in (1990) I *Yearbook of the International Law Commission* 306, para. 74. See also *Note verbale* dated 12 August 1993 from the Permanent Representative of Belgium to the United Nations addressed to the Secretary General, UN Doc. A/48/313 (13 August 1993), p. 5.

[173] See S. Sucharitkul, Special Rapporteur, *Fifth Report on Jurisdictional Immunities of States and Their Property*, UN Doc. A/CN.4/363, Corr.1 and Add.1 (22 March and 11 April 1983), reproduced in (1983) II(1) *Yearbook of the International Law Commission* 25, para. 75; Summary Record of the 1770th Meeting, UN Doc. A/CN.4/SR.1770 (30 May 1983), reproduced in (1983) I *Yearbook of the International Law Commission* 93, para. 32. See also Summary Record of the 2120th Meeting, UN Doc. A/CN.4/SR.2120 (16 June 1989), reproduced in (1989) I *Yearbook of the International Law Commission* 176, paras 11–12.

[174] Sixth Committee, Summary Record of the 18th Meeting, UN Doc. A/C.6/54/SR.18 (27 October 1999), para. 45; Sixth Committee, Summary Record of the 18th Meeting, UN Doc. A/C.6/57/SR.18 (22 October 2002), para. 28.

[175] Summary Record of the 1767th Meeting, UN Doc. A/CN.4/SR.1767 (25 May 1983), reproduced in (1983) I *Yearbook of the International Law Commission* 74, para. 24; Summary Record of the 1769th Meeting, UN Doc. A/CN.4/SR.1769 (27 May 1983), reproduced in (1983) I *Yearbook of the International*

applicable status of forces agreements. In cases where no status of forces agreements apply, Article 12 may be taken to suggest that insurable torts committed by foreign forces, such as traffic accidents, are not immune from local civil jurisdiction. However, the fact that status of forces agreements routinely exempt claims for damages caused in the conduct of official duty from local jurisdiction means that there is a distinct lack of state practice confirming that the territorial tort exception extends to foreign armed forces.[176] Therefore, the better view is that the territorial tort exception does not apply to the acts of foreign forces as a matter of customary international law at all.

11.4.2 Functional Immunity

It is a well-established principle of customary international law that state agents and officials enjoy immunity from the adjudicative and enforcement jurisdiction of another state for acts performed in their official capacity. The relationship of this principle with the law of state immunity is less certain. The prevailing view treats the functional immunity of state agents and officials as a corollary of state immunity:[177] suing them for their official conduct indirectly impleads their state and hence is caught by the principle of state immunity.[178] An alternative approach treats functional immunity as a distinct principle which is concerned with attribution of acts undertaken on behalf of a state.[179] As the International Criminal Tribunal for the former Yugoslavia explained in the *Blaškić* case:

> State officials acting in their official capacity … are mere instruments of a State and their official action can *only* be attributed to the State. They cannot be the subject of sanctions or penalties for conduct that is not private but

---

Law Commission 85, para. 45; Summary Record of the 1770th Meeting, n. 3 above, para. 41.

[176] See 11.5.1 and 11.5.2 below. This aspect of the matter is often overlooked: see Joanne Foakes and Roger O'Keefe, 'Article 12' in Roger O'Keefe, Christian J. Tams and Antonios Tzanakopoulos (eds), *The United Nations Convention on Jurisdictional Immunities of States and Their Property: A Commentary* (1st edn, Oxford, Oxford University Press, 2013), p. 209.

[177] Fox and Webb, n. 32 above, 361–9.

[178] See *Ex Parte Pinochet Ugarte (No. 3)* [2000] 1 AC 147 at 268–70 and 281, HL.

[179] Fox and Webb, n. 32 above, 365; Rosanne van Alebeek, *The Immunity of States and Their Officials in International Criminal Law and International Human Rights Law* (Oxford, Oxford University Press, 2008), pp. 103–57.

> undertaken on behalf of a State. In other words, State officials cannot suffer the consequences of wrongful acts which are not attributable to them personally but to the State on whose behalf they act: they enjoy so-called 'functional immunity'.[180]

For our purposes, it is not necessary to decide which of these approaches is preferable. Military personnel benefit from immunity for acts performed in an official capacity under both. In fact, the applicability of the principle of functional immunity is confirmed by a large body of international practice. The following provides some examples.

One of the earliest pertinent cases arose out of the famous *Caroline* incident.[181] During the Upper Canada Rebellion of 1837–38, a group of British militia members and soldiers crossed the Niagara River and destroyed *The Caroline*, an American steamboat aiding the Canadian rebels. Two American citizens lost their lives as a result. In 1840, the local authorities arrested Alexander McLeod and charged him with murder and arson in relation to the raid. The British government formally demanded his immediate release, asserting that the act for which McLeod was charged 'was a transaction of a public character'.[182] The British government declared that:

> [i]t would be contrary to the universal practice of civilized nations to fix individual responsibility upon persons who with the sanction or by the orders of the constituted authorities of a State engaged in military or naval enterprizes in their country's cause.[183]

The government of the United States shared this view. In his reply to the note demanding McLeod's release, the US Secretary of State confirmed that:

---

[180] *Prosecutor v Tihomir Blaskić (Judgment on the Request of Croatia for Review of the Decision of Trial Chamber II of 18 July 1997)* (1997) 110 ILR 607, ICTY Appeals Chamber, para. 38 (emphasis added).

[181] For the facts of the case, see *William Renwick Riddell, 'An International Murder Trial' (1919) 10 Journal of the American Institute of Criminal Law and Criminology* 176; R.Y. Jennings, 'The Caroline and McLeod Cases' (1938) 32 *American Journal of International Law* 82.

[182] Correspondence between Great Britain and the United States, respecting the Arrest and Imprisonment of Mr McLeod, for the Destruction of the Steamboat Caroline, March–April 1841, reproduced in (1857) 29 *BFSP*, 1840–1841, at 1126.

[183] *Ibid.*

> an individual forming part of a public force, and acting under the authority of his Government, is not to be held answerable, as a private trespasser or malefactor, is a principle of public law sanctioned by the usages of all civilized nations, and which the Government of The United States has no inclination to dispute.[184]

These principles have been affirmed in subsequent cases. In *Underhill v Hernandez*, the US Circuit Court for the Second Circuit held that military personnel 'are not in any case amenable to the civil or criminal laws of a foreign state, in respect to acts done in their capacity as agents, for which they would be punishable or civilly responsible if done in their private capacity'.[185] In *Amrane v John*, the Civil Tribunal of Alexandria dismissed an action brought against the Commander of the British Forces in Egypt to obtain compensation for injuries caused in a traffic accident involving a vehicle operated by a British soldier.[186] According to the Tribunal, members of the British Army in Egypt were exempt from local jurisdiction on the basis that the acts of a foreign sovereign are not justiciable before the courts of another sovereign, provided that those acts were performed in the exercise of public authority, rather than by public officials in their own private interests.[187] The Mixed Courts of Egypt have also accepted that members of friendly forces are immune from local jurisdiction whenever they commit an offence in the performance of their duties.[188] However, this did not prevent them from exercising their powers of judicial review to determine whether the defendants were in fact acting on official duty.[189] More recently, the Italian Court of Cassation confirmed in the *Lozano* case that the principle of functional immunity applies to foreign armed forces as a matter of customary international law.[190] In particular, the court noted that the principle had found widespread recognition in the literature and case law.[191] The court

---

184 *Ibid.* 1140.

185 *Underhill v Hernandez*, 65 F. 577, 581 (Cir. Ct of Appeals, 2d Cir. 1895).

186 *Amrane v John* (1932) 6 AD 174, 7 AD 187, 24 GTM 108, Civil Tribunal of Alexandria (Egypt).

187 *Ibid.* GTM 109.

188 *Ministère Public v Triandafilou* (1942) 11 AD 165, Court of Cassation of Egypt.

189 See for example, *Ministère Public v Tsoukharis* (1943) 12 AD 150, Mixed Court of Cassation of Egypt; *Manuel v Ministère Public*, n. 59 above.

190 *Lozano v Italy*, n. 52 above, 1230–32.

191 The Court of Cassation referred to several national and international decisions, including *Jones v Saudi Arabia* [2007] 1 AC 270, HL; *Al-Adsani v United Kingdom* (2002) 24 EHRR 11, ECtHR; *Kalogeropoulou and others v*

also saw it reflected in the provisions of the ECSI and the UNCSI and, as far as criminal proceedings are concerned, in Article 98 of the Statute of the International Criminal Court.[192]

In a handful of cases, the courts have taken a different line. In *Saorstat v de las Morenas*, which involved an action for damages brought against a Spanish colonel for breach of a contract he entered into in Ireland in the execution of his official duties, the Irish Supreme Court flatly denied the existence of functional immunity as a principle of international law.[193] While such an outright denial is exceptional, a minority of cases have qualified the application of the principle on two main grounds. First, in the *Caroline* affair, the Supreme Court of the State of New York held that the official character of the attack did not shield McLeod from the jurisdiction of the US courts, since the destruction of *The Caroline* was unlawful as a matter of international law.[194] In the *Rainbow Warrior* affair, a New Zealand court sentenced two French officers acting in an official capacity to lengthy prison terms without regard to the principle of functional immunity.[195] In *Lozano*, the Italian Court of Cassation consider whether functional immunity applied to acts carried out in violation of international law, such as acts constituting international crimes. The

---

Greece and Germany (2002) 129 ILR 537, ECtHR and *Case concerning the Arrest Warrant of 11 April 2000 (Democratic Republic of the Congo v Belgium)* [2002] ICJ Rep. 3.

[192] Rome Statute of the International Criminal Court, 17 July 1998, 2187 UNTS 90. Article 98 of the Statute requires the sending state's cooperation and consent by waiving the immunity attaching to members of its armed forces before the receiving state may surrender such foreign personnel to the International Criminal Court. See Dieter Fleck, 'Are Foreign Military Personnel Exempt from International Criminal Jurisdiction under Status of Forces Agreements?' (2003) 1 *Journal of International Criminal Justice* 651.

[193] *Saorstat and Continental Steamship Company Ltd v Rafael de las Morenas* [1945] IR 291, Irish Supreme Court.

[194] *The People v McLeod*, 25 Wend. 483, 588–9 (Sup. Ct Jud. New York 1841).

[195] *R v Mafart and Prieur* (1985) 74 ILR 241, 250, New Zealand High Court. It appears that the question of immunity was not raised before the domestic court. However, France did assert functional immunity at a later stage: see Memorandum of the Government of the French Republic to the Secretary-General of the United Nations, reproduced in (1990) 19 *Report of International Arbitral Awards* 207, 211. The fact that the UN Secretary-General did not uphold the French claim does not undermine the principle of functional immunity as a matter of law, since the Secretary-General explicitly based himself on equitable, not legal, considerations: see Ruling of 6 July 1986 by the Secretary-General of the United Nations, *ibid.* 212, 213.

court largely followed its reasoning in *Ferrini*,[196] arguing that any conflict between the principle of state immunity and fundamental human rights norms had to be resolved in favour of the latter. Second, in the case of *Papa Coli*, the District Court of Haifa declined to grant immunity to a member of the Senegalese contingent of the United Nations Interim Force in Lebanon who was accused of smuggling explosives into Israeli territory.[197] The court found that the defendant was not present in Israel with the consent and invitation of the Israeli authorities, and held that he was therefore not covered by the rule of immunity recognized in *The Schooner Exchange*.[198]

This line of cases does not cast doubt on the customary nature of the principle of functional immunity. The principle that foreign military personnel are exempt from local civil and criminal jurisdiction for acts performed in the course of their official duties finds overwhelming support in state practice, both in the majority of the case law and in the form of status of forces agreements.[199] Rather, these cases question, first, whether functional immunity extends to acts performed in violation of international law. While it is settled that functional immunity does not shield the perpetrators of international crimes from criminal jurisdiction before domestic or international tribunals,[200] the prevailing view is that immunity continues to apply at the domestic level in civil proceedings.[201] Second, they question whether functional immunity extends to personnel present abroad without the consent of the territorial state. Given the pivotal role of consent in Chief Justice Marshall's reasoning, *The Schooner Exchange* suggest that the answer is negative. However,

---

[196] *Ferrini v Germany*, No. 5044/04, Italian Court of Cassation, Judgment, 6 November 2003, 128 ILR 658. See Carlo Focarelli, 'Denying Foreign State Immunity for Commission of International Crimes: The *Ferrini* Decision' (2005) 54 *International and Comparative Law Quarterly* 951.

[197] *Israel v Papa Coli Ben Dista Saar* (1979) UNJYB 205, District Court of Haifa.

[198] *Ibid.* 206. However, note that the court also held, presumably as an alternative ground, that the accused's visit to Israel fell 'more into the category of personal visits' rather than an act performed in the conduct of official duty (*ibid.*).

[199] Almost without exception, status of forces agreements confer, as a minimum, immunity on foreign military personnel from local civil and criminal jurisdiction for on-duty acts.

[200] See Dapo Akande and Sangeeta Shah, 'Immunities of State Officials, International Crimes, and Foreign Domestic Courts' (2010) 21 *European Journal of International Law* 815.

[201] *Jones v Saudi Arabia*, n. 191 above, paras 24–7.

international law has evolved considerably since 1812 and immunity is now generally considered to derive from the nature of the act rather than from the territorial sovereign's consent. This suggests that functional immunity applies even to troops who are present abroad without the territorial state's consent.

11.4.3 Immunity in Times of Armed Conflict

The impact of the law of armed conflict on the application of the law of state immunity and the functional immunity of military personnel is uncertain. It is common ground that the law of state immunity applies to judicial proceedings instituted in times of peace before the courts of a former belligerent in relation to acts performed by the armed forces of its former adversary during an earlier armed conflict. This follows from the *Jurisdictional Immunities of the State* case, where the International Court of Justice found 'that customary international law continues to require that a state be accorded immunity in proceedings for torts allegedly committed on the territory of another State by its armed forces and other organs of State in the course of conducting an armed conflict'.[202] The law of state immunity thus distinguishes between the public and private acts of state organs even in times of war.[203]

While *Jurisdictional Immunities of the State* confirms that international law accords immunity to public acts in proceedings instituted between former belligerents in times of peace, it is not immediately clear to what extent state immunity also operates as a procedural bar to proceedings instituted between belligerents during active hostilities. For instance, the law of armed conflict permits the destruction and seizure of enemy property provided that such destruction or seizure is 'imperatively demanded by the necessities of war'.[204] Military necessity thus entitles one belligerent to destroy or confiscate the public property, including military property, of another belligerent, subject to the rules of the law of armed conflict and other relevant rules of international law.[205] To the

[202] *Jurisdictional Immunities of the State*, n. 76 above, para. 78.

[203] See for example, *Ministry of Foreign Affairs v Federici and Japanese State*, 65 ILR 275, Tribunal of Rome (Italy), 28 November 1968.

[204] Regulations respecting the Laws and Customs of War on Land, annexed to Convention No. IV Respecting the Laws and Customs of War on Land, Art. 23(g), 18 October 1907, 36 Stat. 2227, T.S. No. 539. See Henckaerts and Doswald-Beck, n. 116 above, Rule 50.

[205] See for example, Vienna Convention on Diplomatic Relations, Art. 45(a), 18 April 1961, 500 UNTS 95.

extent that such acts amount to measures of constraint, they run counter to the law of state immunity. This suggests that enforcement measures adopted against enemy property pursuant to the law of armed conflict either do not constitute measures of constraint within the meaning of the law of state immunity or that the law of armed conflict operates as the *lex specialis* to the extent that they do.

The application of the principle of functional immunity to enemy combatants raises similar difficulties. However, in practice, it seems that these difficulties are mitigated by the fact that members of the armed forces of a belligerent benefit from combatant privilege under the law of armed conflict, which shields them from the enforcement jurisdiction of the territorial state in respect of lawful acts of war.[206] The principle of combatant privilege thus provides members of foreign armed forces with a degree of immunity from local jurisdiction in times of war which broadly corresponds to the immunity they enjoy in times of peace pursuant to the principle of functional immunity.

11.5 STATUS OF FORCES AGREEMENTS

States have entered into international agreements to regulate the presence of foreign armed forces on their territory for centuries.[207] The first, still rudimentary, agreements drafted for the sole purpose of defining the legal position of friendly forces were concluded during the First World War.[208] In the inter-war period, status of forces agreements became more detailed

---

[206] *Trial of Wilhelm List and others (Hostages Trial)* (1946) 8 Law Reports of Trials of War Criminals 34 at 50, US Military Tribunal. See also *United States v Lindh*, 212 F.Supp.2d 541, 553–5 (ED Va. 2002). See Gary D. Solis, *The Law of Armed Conflict: International Humanitarian Law in War* (Cambridge, Cambridge University Press, 2010), pp. 41–2.

[207] See for example, Convention between Prussia and Russia for the Passage of Troops, 28 May 1815, 64 CTS 363.

[208] See for example, Agreement between Belgium and France for the Better Prosecution of Acts Prejudicial to the Armed Forces, 14 August 1914, 220 CTS 274; Declaration between France and Great Britain respecting Military Penal Jurisdiction, 15 December 1915, 221 CTS 225; Exchange of Notes between France and the United States respecting the Jurisdiction of Courts Martial, 14 January 1918, 223 CTS 39.

and sophisticated.[209] The Second World War saw to a sharp increase in treaty practice, as the Allied powers entered into a large number of status agreements with their co-belligerents.[210] Overall, state practice during this period reflects an understanding that the jurisdictional arrangements applicable to friendly forces must, as a general principle, respect the authority of the sending state in matters relating to the internal administration and discipline of its troops. It was likewise understood that this does not entitle the sending state to claim, as a right existing under general international law, absolute immunity for its armed forces from all forms of local jurisdiction, both civil and criminal. However, beyond these basic principles, state practice neither followed, nor gave rise to, a uniform legal approach as regards the exercise of jurisdiction over members of friendly forces. During the Cold War, a period of consolidation set in. The new strategic context compelled the Western Powers to conclude the first ever multilateral status of forces agreements. In addition, the development of peace-keeping prompted the United Nations and other international actors to enter into numerous agreements defining the legal position of peace operations. As a result, two highly influential jurisdictional regimes have emerged in the second half of the twentieth century based on the NATO SOFA of 1951 and the UN Model SOFA of 1990. This section provides an overview of the main features of these two regimes and offers some thoughts on their impact on the development of customary international law.

---

[209] See for example, Military Agreement between Great Britain and Iraq, 25 March 1924, 35 LNTS 103; Convention concerning the Immunities and Privileges to be Enjoyed by the British Forces in Egypt, 26 August 1936, 173 LNTS 433.

[210] See for example, Agreement between the United States and the United Kingdom relating to Jurisdiction over Criminal Offences, 27 July 1942, 117 UNTS 312; Agreement between the United Kingdom and the French National Committee on the Defence of the Island of Madagascar and its Dependencies and the Island of Reunion, 14 December 1942 (Cmd 6986); Exchange of Notes Constituting an Agreement between His Majesty's Government in the United Kingdom and the Belgian Government concerning Civil Administration and Jurisdiction in Belgian Territory Liberated by an Allied Expeditionary Force, 16 May 1944, 90 UNTS 284; Agreement between the United States of America and the Union of Soviet Socialist Republics relating to Prisoners of War and Civilians Liberated by Forces Operating under Soviet Command and Forces Operating under United States of America Command, 11 February 1945, 68 UNTS 180.

11.5.1 Military Alliances and the NATO SOFA

Following the end of the Second World War, foreign forces remained stationed abroad in large numbers. The first multilateral status of forces agreement drawn up to address the novel strategic questions presented by the Cold War was the Brussels Treaty SOFA, concluded on 21 December 1949 between Belgium, France, Luxembourg, the Netherlands and the United Kingdom.[211] It was agreed at the very beginning of the drafting process that the aim of the negotiations was to arrive at 'a general agreement between the Five Powers *on a basis of complete reciprocity*'.[212] Although the final text leaned heavily on earlier bilateral practice, the significance of the Brussels Treaty SOFA lay in the fact that it adapted these bilateral arrangements for a multilateral setting, in particular by laying down rules governing the exercise of jurisdiction over foreign personnel which were designed to balance the competing legal interests of sending states and receiving states in an equitable manner. The Brussels Treaty SOFA thus set up a system of concurrent jurisdiction under which conflicts of competence in criminal matters were to be resolved primarily by administrative action, while civil claims against foreign forces were to be settled by the receiving state on the basis of its own laws, with the costs of satisfying these claims to be distributed between the states parties. Although the Brussels Treaty SOFA never entered into force, it shaped modern treaty practice by serving as a basis for the NATO SOFA.[213]

Building on the Brussels Treaty SOFA, Article VII of the NATO SOFA allocates the right to exercise criminal jurisdiction over foreign forces between sending states and receiving states on a flexible basis. It upholds the principle of concurrent jurisdiction underlying the Brussels Treaty SOFA, but at the same time enables sending states to exercise their jurisdiction in those types of cases where their interests are most directly affected.[214] Article VII achieves this result in three main steps.[215] The

---

[211] Agreement Relative to the Status of Members of the Armed Forces of the Brussels Treaty Powers, 21 December 1949 (Cmd. 7868, 1950).

[212] *Report from the Military Committee*, DG/1/13/65 (15 June 1949), p. 19 (emphasis added). On file with the author.

[213] D–D(51) 23 (23 January 1951), reproduced in J.M. Snee, *NATO Agreements on Status: Travaux Préparatoires* (1966).

[214] MS(J)–R(51) 2 (8 February 1951), reproduced in *ibid.* paras 14–17.

[215] For more detailed accounts of Article VII, see Serge Lazareff, *Status of Military Forces under Current International Law* (Leiden, Sijthoff, 1971), pp. 268–362; Conderman, n. 71 above.

first paragraph of Article VII recognizes the authority of sending states and receiving states to exercise their jurisdiction over individuals falling within the scope of the NATO SOFA. The second paragraph of Article VII declares that each state benefits from an exclusive right to exercise its jurisdiction with respect of offences, including offences relating to its security, which are punishable by its own law, but not by the law of the other state. The third paragraph of Article VII provides that in cases where jurisdiction is concurrent, the sending state has a primary right to exercise its jurisdiction, first, in relation to offences committed by its personnel against each other or against their sending state and, second, in relation to offences arising out of any act or omission done in the performance of official duty. In all other cases, the primary right to exercise jurisdiction lies with the receiving state. Either state may waive its primary right on behalf of the other state.

As far as jurisdiction in civil proceedings is concerned, Article VIII of the NATO SOFA puts in place a rather complex arrangement based on three core principles.[216] First, the contracting parties agreed to the mutual waiver of claims for certain types of damages caused or suffered by their armed forces in the performance of their official functions. Second, Article VIII exempts foreign personnel from the jurisdiction of local courts in relation to non-contractual claims arising out of acts or omissions done in the performance of official duty as well as certain other claims. However, it enables individuals suffering such damages to bring their claims against the receiving state, which is bound to settle them in accordance with the laws and regulations applicable with respect to claims arising from the activities of its own armed forces. Third, members of foreign forces are subject to local civil jurisdiction in matters not related to their official duties. Article VIII thus preserves intact the principle of state immunity together with the functional immunity of foreign personnel, but at the same time provides claimants with an alternative remedy before the domestic courts of the receiving state.

The NATO SOFA has had a profound effect on state practice. Since 1951, its provisions have been applied or reproduced in a large number of bilateral and multilateral agreements either unchanged or subject to varying degrees of adjustments. The entire text of the NATO SOFA was adopted in the Partnership for Peace Status of Forces Agreement of 1995, which requires its 45 states parties to apply the NATO SOFA between

---

[216] For more detailed accounts of Article VIII, see Lazareff, n. 215 above, 268–362; Jody M. Prescott, 'Claims' in Dieter Fleck (ed.), *The Handbook of the Law of Visiting Forces* (Oxford, Oxford University Press, 2001), p. 159 at 163–8.

themselves as if they were parties to it.[217] The same technique of referring to the NATO SOFA or its individual provisions, in particular Article VII on criminal jurisdiction and Article VIII on civil jurisdiction, has been employed in many other instruments.[218] In addition, the jurisdictional provisions of the NATO SOFA have influenced the terms of countless other status agreements, including multilateral instruments such as the European Union Status of Forces Agreement of 2003.[219]

11.5.2 Peace Support Operations

International practice concerning the legal status of peace operations is surprisingly consistent. The main reason for this is that states and international organizations engaged in this field have for the most part followed the practice established by the United Nations. Since peace operations conducted under the command and control of the UN constitute subsidiary organs of either the Security Council or the General Assembly, they and their members are, in principle, covered by the Convention on the Privileges and Immunities of the UN of 1946.[220] However, in practice, the UN has declined to treat military members of national contingents participating in its peace operations as experts on

---

[217] Partnership for Peace Status of Forces Agreement, 19 June 1995, TIAS 12666.

[218] See for example, Agreement between Hungary, Romania, the Slovak Republic and Ukraine on the Multinational Engineer Battalion, 18 January 2002, Magyar Közlöny, 2003/33, 2347.

[219] Agreement between the Member States of the European Union concerning the status of military and civilian staff seconded to the institutions of the European Union, of the headquarters and forces which may be made available to the European Union in the context of the preparation and execution of the tasks referred to in Article 17(2) of the Treaty on European Union, including exercises, and of the military and civilian staff of the Member States put at the disposal of the European Union to act in this context (EU SOFA), 17 November 2003 [2003] OJ C321/6. For a detailed assessment, see Aurel Sari, 'The EU Status of Forces Agreement: Continuity and Change in the Law of Visiting Forces' (2007) 46 *Military Law and the Law of War Review* 9.

[220] 13 February 1946, 1 UNTS 15. See Regulations for UNEF, Art. 10, UN Doc. ST/SGB/UNEF/1 (20 February 1957), Annex II to Exchange of Letters Constituting an Agreement between the United Nations and Finland concerning the Service with the United Nations Emergency Force of National Contingent Provided by the Government of Finland, 27 June 1957, 271 UNTS 136. See Michael Bothe and Thomas Dörschel, 'The UN Peacekeeping Experience' in Dieter Fleck (ed.), *The Handbook of the Law of Visiting Forces* (Oxford, Oxford University Press, 2001), p. 487 at 496.

mission benefiting from the protection of the Convention. Beginning with the United Nations Emergency Force (UNEF) in Egypt, the UN has therefore entered into status agreements to define the legal position of its peace-keeping operations and their members in express terms.

The UNEF Status of Forces Agreement granted different privileges and immunities to different categories of personnel.[221] Members of national contingents remained subject to the exclusive jurisdiction of their contributing states in respect of any criminal offences committed by them in Egypt and were exempt from local civil jurisdiction and from other legal process in any matter relating to their official duties.[222] These jurisdictional arrangements were followed, with some variations, in subsequent peace-keeping operations conducted by the UN during the Cold War.[223] In 1990, this body of practice was codified in the UN Model SOFA.[224] Like the UNEF SOFA, the UN Model SOFA distinguishes between different categories of personnel. All members of UN peace-keeping operations, including military personnel, are 'immune from legal process in respect of words spoken or written and all acts performed by them in their official capacity'.[225] This immunity extends to both civil and criminal matters.[226] As regards the exercise of criminal jurisdiction, military members of a UN operation are subject to the exclusive jurisdiction of their respective contributing states in respect of any criminal offences committed by them in the territory of the receiving state. As regards the exercise of civil jurisdiction, proceedings instituted against members of a UN operation must be notified immediately to the Special Representative/Commander, and must be discontinued if the latter certifies that they relate to official duties.[227]

---

221 Exchange of Letters Constituting an Agreement concerning the Status of the United Nations Emergency Force in Egypt, 8 February 1957, 260 UNTS 62.

222 *Ibid.* paras 11 and 12.

223 See for example, Exchange of Letters Constituting an Agreement concerning the Status of the United Nations Peace-Keeping Force in Cyprus, 31 March 1964, 492 UNTS 58. See Robert C.R. Siekmann, *National Contingents in United Nations Peace-Keeping Forces* (Dordrecht, M. Nijhoff, 1991), pp. 120–54.

224 See n. 72 above.

225 UN Model SOFA, para. 46.

226 UN Model SOFA, para. 46 derives from UN Privileges and Immunities Convention, Art. 22, which provides in express terms that experts on mission for the UN have 'immunity from legal process of every kind' for acts performed on duty.

227 UN Model SOFA, para. 48.

Since 1990, the UN Model SOFA has served as the basis for a large number of status agreements concluded by the UN.[228] During the last decade, the Security Council has on several occasions decided that the UN Model SOFA should apply provisionally to UN operations pending the conclusion of a permanent SOFA between the UN and receiving states.[229] In addition, the jurisdictional arrangements developed by the UN have exerted a strong influence on international practice. In the majority of cases, peace operations conducted by states or other international organizations have followed the approach adopted by the UN, granting military personnel complete immunity from local jurisdiction in criminal matters as well as immunity from civil jurisdiction for acts committed in the performance of their official duties. Agreements to this effect include the instruments concluded for the Multinational Force of Observers,[230] the Implementation Force (IFOR) and Stabilization Force (SFOR) deployed by NATO in Bosnia and Herzegovina,[231] the Bougainville Truce Monitoring Group[232] and ISAF.[233] In some cases, military personnel deployed on peace operations benefit from broader privileges and immunities. Members of KFOR, for instance, are 'immune from jurisdiction before courts in Kosovo in respect of any administrative, civil or criminal act committed by them in the territory of Kosovo'.[234]

---

[228] See for example, Agreement between the United Nations and the Government of the Central African Republic on the Status of the United Nations Mission in the Central African Republic (MINURCA), 8 May 1998, 2015 UNTS 734; Agreement between Ethiopia and the United Nations concerning the Status of the United Nations Mission in Ethiopia and Eritrea, 23 March 2001, 2141 UNTS 24.

[229] See for example, Security Council Resolution 1590, UN Doc. S/RES/1590 (24 March 2005). This practice followed a recommendation to this effect by General Assembly Resolution 52/12B (19 December 1997), para. 7.

[230] Protocol relating to the Establishment and Maintenance of a Multinational Force and Observers, 3 August 1981, 1335 UNTS 328.

[231] See for example, Agreement between the Republic of Bosnia and Herzegovina and the North Atlantic Treaty Organisation (NATO) concerning the Status of NATO and its Personnel, 23 November 1995, Appendix B to Annex 1-A to the Dayton Agreement (1996) 35 ILM 102.

[232] Agreement between Australia, Papua New Guinea, New Zealand, Fiji and Vanuatu concerning the Neutral Truce Monitoring Group for Bougainville, 5 December 1997 [1997] ATS 30.

[233] Military Technical Agreement between the International Security Assistance Force (ISAF) and the Interim Administration of Afghanistan (Interim Administration), 4 January 2002 (2002) 41 ILM 1032.

[234] UNMIK Regulation No. 2000/47 on the Status, Privileges and Immunities of KFOR and UNMIK and Their Personnel in Kosovo, 18 August 2000, available

11.5.3 Impact of Status of Forces Agreements

It is important to emphasize that treaty practice in this area is not uniform.[235] States continue to send their armed forces abroad for a wide variety of reasons. Since the political and operational considerations vary dramatically from one deployment to another, legal arrangements adopted in one case may not be appropriate in others. For this reason, no single treaty regime has emerged to govern the status of all foreign military deployments with general effect. In addition to the jurisdictional arrangements reflected in the NATO SOFA and the UN Model SOFA, a range of other approaches remain in use. These include agreements conferring broader rights of exclusive jurisdiction outside the context of peace operations,[236] instruments relying on the provisions of the Vienna Convention on Diplomatic Relations[237] and agreements which for one reason or another are atypical.[238]

Different types of status of forces agreements offer different answers to the same basic question: how to reconcile the divergent legal interests of

---

at www.unmikonline.org/. See Ombudsperson Institution in Kosovo, *Special Report No. 1 on the Compatibility with Recognized International Standards of UNMIK Regulation No. 2000/47 on the Status, Privileges and Immunities of KFOR and UNMIK and Their Personnel in Kosovo (18 August 2000)* (26 April 2001), esp. pp. 21–8.

235 As one expert on the topic has noted, status of forces agreements 'come in a variety of sizes and flavours': Max S. Johnson, 'NATO SOFA: Enunciating Customary International Law or Just a Model, and What Does the Future Portend?' in Horst Fischer *et al.* (eds), *Krisensicherung und Humanitärer Schutz – Crisis Management and Humanitarian Protection: Festschrift für Dieter Fleck* (Berlin, 2004), p. 287 at 291.

236 See for example, Vereinbarung zwischen der Regierung der Bundesrepublik Deutschland und der Regierung der Vereinigten Republik Tansania über die Rechtsstellung der an der Übung 'TANZANITE 2002' beteiligten Streitkräfte der Bundeswehr in der Vereinigten Republik Tansania, 22 January 2002, BGBl (2002) II 621.

237 See for example, Agreement regarding the Status of United States Military and Civilian Personnel of the United States Department of Defense Who may be Present in Rwanda in connection with the Military Airlift of Rwandan Military Forces in Support of Operations in Darfur and Future Mutually Agreed Activities, 11 July 2005, KAV 7344. See also Aurel Sari, 'Status of Forces and Status of Mission Agreements under the ESDP: The EU's Evolving Practice' (2008) 19 *European Journal of International Law* 67.

238 Cf. Convention relating to the Conditions for French Technical Military Assistance in the Training, Organization and Equipment of the Comorian Forces and the Training of Comorian Soldiers at Military Schools and Instruction Centres in France, 4 August 1979, 1309 UNTS 178.

sending states and receiving states, in particular as regards the exercise of jurisdiction over military personnel present abroad. The fact that status of forces agreements do not provide a single answer to this question renders it more difficult to assess their impact on the development of rules of customary international law. There can be little doubt that status of forces agreements reflect pre-existing rules of custom, including the principles of territorial and organic jurisdiction and the principles of state and functional immunity discussed earlier. The more difficult question is whether the specific provisions of particular agreements have passed into customary international law.

There certainly exists a large and consistent body of state practice which could, in principle, count towards the development of rules of customary international law. However, proving the existence of corresponding *opinio juris* is more difficult. This is so not least because the existence of distinct jurisdictional regimes means that the relevant provisions of a particular type of status agreement could only have passed into custom with respect to the specific operational context for which they were designed. For example, the jurisdictional provisions of the NATO SOFA *may* have attained the status of customary rules in the context of structured military cooperation between political allies, but certainly not in other circumstances. However, since these contexts cannot be defined with great precision, the scope of application of any customary rules, and thus their very existence, remains uncertain. Nonetheless, when viewed as a whole, treaty practice in this area confirms four fundamental points. First, states prefer to regulate the legal position of friendly foreign forces by means of special agreements, rather than leave their status to be determined by general rules of international law. Second, treaty practice confirms that, as a minimum, foreign military personnel are exempt from local jurisdiction in civil and criminal proceedings for acts performed in the exercise of their official duties. Third, international practice also demonstrates that in certain circumstances operational considerations may warrant more extensive immunities. Finally, the additional privileges and exemptions commonly accorded in status of forces agreements, such as the right to wear uniform on duty,[239] confirm the customary principle that sending states are

---

[239] See for example, Exchange of Notes Constituting an Agreement relating to the United States Military and Civilian Personnel of the United States Department of Defense Who may be Temporarily Present in Ethiopia in connection with Humanitarian Relief, Joint Exercises and Training, and Other Agreed Activities, 27 February 2002, KAV 5992.

entitled to take those measures which are reasonably necessary for the internal administration of their force as an effective military unit.

11.6 CONCLUSION

No overarching legal framework has developed in international law to regulate the legal position of foreign armed forces in a comprehensive manner. The objectives pursued by foreign military deployments and their operational environments are too diverse. The legal framework governing the presence of foreign armed forces is therefore multifaceted and will remain so for the foreseeable future. Unsurprisingly, this creates uncertainty as to the position of customary international law in this area, reinforcing the preference of states and international organizations to define the status of foreign troops by way of tailor-made international agreements.

However, international practice recognizes that the unique composition, responsibilities and nature of the armed forces raise special legal and practical considerations. This is reflected both in customary international law and in international treaty practice. This point is frequently overlooked. On the one hand, foreign military personnel are not devoid of 'status' in the absence of an applicable status of forces agreement. They are not tourists, but representatives of their sending state, entitled to be treated as such as a matter of general international law. Even in the absence of an express agreement, sending states may take measures in the territory of another state which are reasonably necessary for the internal administration of their forces as effective military units. On the other hand, status of forces agreements constitute a very substantial source of state practice and *opinio juris* which must not be ignored in assessing the rules of general international law applicable in this area. This body of practice confirms many of the generally applicable principles, such as the principle of functional immunity, but also demonstrates the existence of special considerations, such as the legitimacy of more extensive exemptions from local jurisdiction in more demanding operational environments.

12. Immunity from execution

Xiaodong Yang

12.1 INTRODUCTION

It should not be assumed that, once a court has denied immunity to a defendant foreign state and decided that that foreign state lost the case, the claimant can simply go ahead and attach the assets of that foreign state to execute the judgment. Owing to historical reasons, particularly to the incremental nature of the process whereby the former absolute immunity doctrine was replaced by the now prevailing doctrine of restrictive immunity, there has been established in current law on state immunity a clear distinction between the issues related to the adjudicative process and those related to the process of enforcement and execution. To start with, three rules can be briefly noted here. First and foremost, a loss of immunity at the adjudicative stage does not automatically lead to a loss of immunity from enforcement and execution; second, enforcement or execution is permissible only with regard to property used for commercial or private purposes but not against property used for sovereign or public purposes; finally, certain categories of state property, such as diplomatic and military property, enjoy absolute immunity from execution.

Thus, even if a court may be competent to exercise jurisdiction in a particular case against a defendant foreign state, either because the foreign state has waived its immunity from adjudication or because its activities which form the subject matter of the case do not fall within those recognized by current law as protected by immunity, that does not necessarily mean that the court can authorize enforcement measures against any property of that state situated in the territory of the state of the forum, or against the state itself by way of injunction. Quite separate considerations and conditions are required. These considerations and conditions are the main concern of the present chapter.

In point of time the coercive measures at the disposal of a court fall into two broad timelines: before and after its judgment. The court may take certain measures, first at the start or during the litigation for the purposes of establishing its jurisdiction and/or ensuring the presence of the defending party and its assets within the jurisdiction in view of a final judgment, and secondly, following and in execution of the judgment. In other words, coercive measures can also potentially be taken by a court at a time when the court is still considering, or even before it starts considering, the merits of the case, and when, consequently, it will be premature to expect a final judgment in favour of the claimant against the defendant foreign state. These are commonly known as 'interlocutory' or 'provisional' or 'preventive' measures, which are taken at the start of or during the litigation but before the passing of judgment. These pre-judgment measures prepare for but do not prejudge the final outcome of the case. To the extent that the coercive measures at the disposal of a court extend beyond the execution of judgment in both time and scope, it will not be entirely accurate to refer to 'execution' and 'immunity from execution' alone. A broader term such as 'enforcement' will be needed, and will thus be used, alongside the term 'execution', in the present discussion to cover both pre- and post-judgment measures.

12.2 CONTEXT

If there is one phrase that best captures the essence of the question of immunity from execution, that phrase should be 'the last bastion of state immunity';[1] for the phrase signifies an array of defence mechanisms in space, and a sequence of events in time. Needless to say, the question of immunity from execution does not arise until after the question of immunity from adjudication has been decided in the negative, resulting in a judgment in the favour of the claimant and against the foreign state. What is of great interest is that, historically, even though many national courts moved from absolute to restrictive immunity in their hearing and deciding of cases against foreign states, they only addressed the question of execution many years later. The consequence of such a historical development was that the question of immunity from execution came to be decided separately from the question of immunity from adjudication and from this grew the whole legal regime concerning execution. National legislation in some countries, which served to consolidate initiatives in courts, further clarified and crystallized the distinction

[1] *Report of the International Law Commission on the Work of Its Forty-third Session*, A/46/10, ch II, 'Jurisdictional Immunities of States and Their Property' (containing Draft Articles on the Jurisdictional Immunities of States and Their Property and Commentaries thereto), reproduced in (1991) 2 *Yearbook of the International Law Commission* 12 at 56, commentary to Article 18, para. (2).

between immunity from adjudication and immunity from execution. With this in mind, the following points can be noted as constituting the context for the issue of immunity from execution:

(1) The question whether the property of a defendant foreign state should enjoy immunity from execution or enforcement was determined, as a matter of law, much later than the question of immunity from adjudication.
(2) Immunity from adjudication and immunity from execution are two distinct issues. The question of immunity from execution or enforcement must be decided separately from the question of immunity from adjudication, with either different conditions and requirements, or a separate application of the same conditions and requirements.
(3) Waiver/loss of immunity at the adjudicative stage does not lead automatically to waiver/loss of immunity at the execution stage, which requires separate considerations and decisions.
(4) Immunity is the rule and non-immunity the exception – a shift of the burden of proof.
(5) The rule of thumb is that property used for sovereign/public purposes is immune from execution unless the foreign state explicitly waives its immunity.
(6) There are also other requirements and conditions apart from the test of public/private purpose.
(7) The important issue of pre-judgment attachment should also be considered.
(8) The fact that property is owned by a separate entity is strong evidence that that property is not used for public purposes; however, the property of a separate entity cannot be executed against to satisfy a judgment against the foreign state itself, or vice versa.
(9) There exists residual absolute immunity for certain categories of state property, which are considered as inherently serving sovereign purposes.

One essential element of the context is the terminology used in the discussion of the issues related to enforcement and execution. It should be noted from the outset that current international law on state immunity does not contain a standard set of terms referring to the enforcement or execution measures that a court can take at different stages of the litigation, for the simple reason that what is called 'law' at the international level is but a common denominator of diverse judicial practices developed within various national courts that have had the occasion to consider and decide upon the question of jurisdictional immunities of foreign states and their property. As a result, a variety of terms are used by different jurisdictions to refer to enforcement measures. The US Foreign Sovereign Immunities Act (FSIA) 1976, for example, refers to 'attachment in aid of execution, or execution' and 'attachment prior to the entry of judgment' (s. 1610(a) and (d)). The UK State Immunity Act (SIA) 1978 speaks of enforcement measures in the following terms:

> relief shall not be given against a State by way of injunction or order for specific performance or for the recovery of land or other property; and the property of a State shall not be subject to any process for the enforcement of a judgment or arbitration award or, in an action *in rem*, for its arrest, detention or sale (s. 13(2)).[2]

Note the differentiation between 'relief' as against 'a state' and 'process for the enforcement of a judgment' as against 'the property of a state'. This is because, in English law, the injunctive relief operates against the defendant *in personam* and prevents the defendant from removing his assets from the jurisdiction of the court.[3] Moreover, the measures, such as 'arrest, detention or sale', which can be taken against the property of a foreign state in an 'action *in rem*', can potentially be taken at the start of or during the litigation, in other words, before the passing of judgment.[4]

The general distinction between the processes at pre- and post-judgment stages can be observed in all the current legal instruments on state immunity. Apart from the US and the UK statutes, the Japanese Act on Civil Jurisdiction over Foreign States (ACJFS) 2009, refers to 'provisional measures or enforcement of judgments' (article 17(1)), and the Israeli Foreign States Immunity Law (FSIL) 2008 (No. 5769-2008), somewhat less clearly, to 'proceedings for execution of a judgment or other decision of a court' (s. 15). At the international level, the 1972

2 For near-same provisions see State Immunity Act (SIA) 1979, s. 15(2) (Singapore); State Immunity Ordinance (SIO) 1981, s. 14(2) (Pakistan); Foreign Sovereign Immunity Act (FSIA) 1981 (South Africa), s. 14(1); State Immunity Act (SIA) 1982, ss. 11 and 12 (Canada). For somewhat varied provisions in the same spirit see Foreign States Immunities Act (FSIA) 1985, s. 30 (Australia).

3 See the celebrated case of *Trendtex Trading Corp. v Central Bank of Nigeria* [1977] QB 529, 64 ILR 111, CA (Civ. Div.), in which injunctive relief was granted against the Central Bank of Nigeria.

4 See for example, *The Philippine Admiral (Owners) v Wallem Shipping (Hong Kong) Ltd)* (1975) [1977] AC 373, 64 ILR 90, Judicial Committee of the Privy Council, and *I Congreso del Partido* (1981) [1983] 1 AC 244, 64 ILR 307, HL.

European Convention on State Immunity (ECSI) talks of 'measures of execution or preventive measures' (Article 23), and the 2004 United Nations Convention on Jurisdictional Immunities of States and Their Property[5] makes separate provisions for 'pre-judgment measures of constraint' (Article 18) and 'post-judgment measures of constraint' (Article 19).

The same diversity of terms which nonetheless broadly differentiate between pre- and post-judgment measures can also be observed in the case law of those states without national legislation on foreign state immunity, ranging from 'conservatory attachment/seizure/measures', 'safeguarding/protective measures' and 'interim protection', on the one hand, and measures of 'execution' or 'forced/forcible execution', on the other.[6]

12.3 LATER EVOLUTION OF IMMUNITY FROM EXECUTION

The question of execution of judgment against a foreign state, for reasons which may never be known, did not arise until long after the principle of restrictive immunity *from adjudication*, now misleadingly referred to as the principle of restrictive immunity, had been established as a principle of customary international law. Thus, while it was repeatedly held by the courts initiating and leading the trend of restrictive immunity that a foreign state could no longer claim immunity from (adjudicatory) jurisdiction, execution against foreign states was entertained as a possibility only at a much later stage, and it has remained until this day that execution against foreign state property is allowed reluctantly and subject

---

[5] Contained in UN General Assembly Resolution 59/38 of 2 December 2004, not yet in force.

[6] See for example, *Philippine Embassy Bank Account*, Case No. 2 BvM 1/76 (1977) BVerfGE 46, 342, 65 ILR 146, German Federal Constitutional Court; *National Iranian Oil Co. (Revenues from Oil Sales)*, Case No. 2 BvR 678, 679, 680, 681, 683/81 (1983) BVerfGE 64, 1, 65 ILR 215, German Federal Constitutional Court; *Popular Revolutionary Republic of Guinea v Atlantic Triton Co.* (1984), Court of Appeal of Rennes (Second Chamber); (1986) Court of Cassation (First Civil Chamber) (France) (1987) 114 *Journal du droit international* 125, 82 ILR 75; *Islamic Republic of Iran v Société Eurodif*, (1990) 79 *Revue critique de droit international privé* 346, (1989) 89 ILR 31, Court of Cassation (Civil Chamber) (France); *Rafidain Bank and Iraqi Ministry for Industry v Consarc Corp.* (1993) 106 ILR 274, Court of Appeal of Brussels (Eighth Chamber) (Belgium).

to stringent conditions. This fact led to the dichotomous treatment of the issue of adjudicative jurisdiction and that of executory jurisdiction, and consequently to the distinction between immunity from adjudication/suit and immunity from execution. Owing to the fact that the denial of immunity from execution developed at a much later stage, the rules and principles concerning immunity from execution were developed separately from those concerning immunity from adjudication.

The current law on state immunity is the result of a century-long evolution that started with a general, blanket and thus 'absolute' immunity of states from the jurisdiction of foreign national courts. By virtue of the doctrine and practice of absolute immunity, a state could not be subjected to the jurisdiction of a foreign domestic court without its consent. It should be noted, however, that 'not without its consent' naturally implies that it was, and still is, possible for a state to waive its immunity before a foreign national court. Additionally, even at the time of absolute immunity, courts still exercised undisputed jurisdiction in cases involving local immovable property pursuant to the ancient principle of *lex rei sitae*. Thus, up to this day, waiver of immunity and local immovable property remain among the cases in which immunity is not available to foreign states.[7] As that immunity was eroded gradually and incrementally through first national judicial decisions and then national statutes and international treaties, so that it became increasingly difficult for defendant foreign states to claim absolute immunity before national courts, it so happened that the immunity of foreign states from enforcement and execution was preserved for a long time after the predominant practice in the world had moved from absolute to restrictive immunity. Thus, even if in a growing number of situations the defendant foreign state was no longer immune from the adjudication of the local court with regard to commercial activities, it was not possible, over an extended period of time, to execute a successful judgment against it. Of course, there is no fundamental reason why a court should not be in a position to execute its decisions against a foreign state. Rather, the opposite ought to

[7] For examples of current national legislation see Foreign Sovereign Immunities (FSIA) Act 1976, s. 1605(a)(4) (US); State Immunity Act (SIA) 1978, s. 6(a) (UK); State Immunity Ordinance (SIO) 1982, s. 7(1) (Pakistan); State Immunity Act (SIA) 1979, s. 8(1) (Singapore); Foreign States Immunities Act (FSIA) 1981, s. 7(1) (South Africa); State Immunity Act (SIA) 1982, s. 12(c) (Canada); and Foreign States Immunities Act (FSIA) 1985, s. 14(1) (Australia). For international treaties see the 1972 European Convention on State Immunity (ECSI), Art. 9 and the 2004 UN Convention on Jurisdictional Immunities of States and Their Property, Art. 13(a).

be true. If anything, it would be surprising, in a case against a private individual, for example, to assert that, even if it has the power to adjudicate on the merits of the case and pass a judgment against the defendant, the court should, as a matter of principle, have no authority to execute that judgment. Yet this was precisely the case regarding defendant foreign states. Thus, either out of judicial restraint or because of executive intervention, it was not possible for a successful claimant to enforce the court's judgment against a foreign state during a long period in which national courts in a great number of countries were regularly asserting (adjudicative) jurisdiction over foreign states.

Thus, in Belgium and Italy, the two originators of the doctrine of restrictive immunity, even though the claim of absolute immunity from adjudication was rejected as early as the late nineteenth century, immunity from execution has persisted up to this day, though now in a reduced state. While denying immunity to foreign states with regard to the adjudicative process, the Belgian courts granted almost absolute immunity from execution, irrespective of the distinction between public and private acts of the defendant state at the adjudicative stage,[8] until half a century later, when exemption from execution was held no longer to be available with regard to commercial activities.[9] Similarly, in the Italian courts, if there had been any question as to whether execution should be allowed against the property of foreign states now that immunity was no longer available at the adjudicatory stage, that question was answered definitively in the negative by Royal Executive Order No. 1621 of 30 August 1925 (Measures of Execution Against the Property of Foreign States in the Kingdom of Italy), transformed into Law No. 1623 of 15 July 1926, which prohibited execution on foreign state property except by express authorization of the Minister of Justice.[10] This situation lasted

---

[8] See for example, *West Russian Steamship Co. v Captain Sucksdorff* (1920) 1 AD 152 at 153–4, Commercial Tribunal of Antwerp (Belgium); *State of Portugal v Sauvage* (1921) 1 AD 154 at 155, Court of Appeal of Brussels (Belgium); *Brasseur and Associates v Republic of Greece* (1932–33) 6 AD 164 at 167, Civil Tribunal of Antwerp and Court of Appeal of Brussels (Belgium).

[9] *Socobelge v Greek State* (1951) 18 ILR 3 at 6, Civil Tribunal of Brussels (Belgium). For more recent Belgian practice see Pierre d'Argent, 'Jurisprudence belge relative au droit international public (1993–2003): Immunités' (2003) 36 *Revue belge de droit international* 605.

[10] Law No. 1263 of 15 July 1926 was cited in, for example, *Prefect of Milan v Federici and Savoldi*, Case No. 3032 (1968) 65 ILR 270 at 271, Italian Court of Cassation; *Campione v Peti-Nitrogenmuvek NV and Hungarian Republic*, Case No. 3368 (1972) 65 ILR 287 at 293, Italian Court of Cassation (Joint Session); *Banamar-Capizzi v Embassy of the Popular Democratic Republic of Algeria*,

up until 1992, when the law was declared 'invalid under the Constitution' by the Italian Constitutional Court.[11] Of course, by that time, the Italian Court of Cassation had already accepted the 'general rule of customary international law forbidding the forum State from instituting execution proceedings on the assets of foreign States'.[12] However, the Law of 1926 was not the first time the Italian legislature placed a hold on enforcement measures against foreign state property. Under Decree-Law No. 63 of 28 April 2010, transformed into Law No. 98 of 23 June 2010, and Decree-Law No. 216 of 29 December 2011, enforcement measures against German state properties in Italy were suspended (albeit for a limited period of time) pending the decision of the International Court of Justice (ICJ) in a case brought by Germany against Italy.[13] This seems to have again run afoul of the view of the Italian Constitutional Court, which, in its Judgment No. 238, rendered on 22 October 2014, declared unconstitutional Article 3 of Law No. 5 of 14 January 2013, which required the Italian judges to deny jurisdiction in compliance with the Judgment of the ICJ.[14] On the other hand, it should also be noted that the position of the Italian Constitutional Court may not be so radical as it may first appear. For, at the same time that it held the Law of 1926 unconstitutional, the Constitutional Court actually envisaged that there could be property of a foreign state 'which, pursuant to the generally

---

Case No. 2085 (1989) 87 ILR 56 at 61, Italian Court of Cassation (Plenary Session); *Libyan Arab Socialist People's Jamahiriya v Rossbeton SRL*, Case No. 2502 (1989) 87 ILR 63 at 66–7, Italian Court of Cassation (Plenary Session).

[11] *Condor and Filvem v Minister of Justice*, Case No. 329 (1992) 101 ILR 394 at 406, Italian Constitutional Court. For a convenient introduction to Italian practice up to 1992 see Maurizio Ragazzi, 'Italy: Constitutional Court Judgment on Sovereign Immunity with regard to Measures of Constraint' (1994) 33 ILM 593. For developments after 1992 see discussion below.

[12] *Banamar-Capizzi v Embassy of the Popular Democratic Republic of Algeria*, Case No. 2085 (1989) 87 ILR 56 at 59, Italian Court of Cassation (Plenary Session).

[13] See *Jurisdictional Immunities of the State (Germany v Italy, Greece Intervening)* [2012] ICJ 99 at 116 and 146, paras 35 and 111. For a concise note on Law No. 98 of 23 June 2010 see Rachele Cera, 'Legislation: State Immunity from Italian Jurisdiction' (2010) 13 *Yearbook of International Humanitarian Law* 560.

[14] Judgment No. 238, 22 October 2014. See English translation of the judgment provided by the Italian Constitutional Court:, available at www.cortecostituzionale.it/documenti/download/doc/recent_judgments/S238_2013_en.pdf.

recognized rules of international law, cannot be subject to coercive measures'.[15]

The Greek courts have operated under a similar statute, namely, the Emergency Law No. 15/1938, which likewise prohibited execution against foreign state property without the prior authorization of the Minister of Justice.[16] The substance of this Law is now the subject of article 923 of the Greek Code of Civil Procedure, which remains in force to this day and featured prominently in the series of cases in the Greek courts involving acts in violation of the laws of war committed by the German occupation forces during the Second World War.[17]

In Austria, the possibility of enforcement measures against foreign state property was entertained[18] many years after the courts denied immunity to foreign states in adjudicative proceedings;[19] and such possibility was subject to a general rule set forth by the Supreme Court to the effect that:

> No execution may be levied on extraterritorial property. A freezing order or a garnishee order may only be granted against persons outside the jurisdiction, including foreign States, under the conditions stated in Article IX(2) of the Introductory Act to the Jurisdictional Statute.[20]

Article IX(2) of the Introductory Act to the Jurisdictional Statute (EGJN) provides:

> Persons who enjoy exterritoriality according to principles of public international law shall be subject to domestic jurisdiction if and insofar as they submit voluntarily to the jurisdiction of domestic courts, or if the litigation

---

15 *Condor and Filvem v Minister of Justice*, Case No. 329 (1992) 101 ILR 394 at 406, Italian Constitutional Court.

16 Cited in *Sale of British Embassy Building*, Judgment No. 460/1962 (1962) 65 ILR 247, Greek Court of Cassation (First Chamber).

17 See, especially, *Prefecture of Voiotia v Federal Republic of Germany*, Case No. 11/2000 (2000) 129 ILR 513, Greek Court of Cassation and *Kalogeropoulou v Greece and Germany*, Application No. 59021/00 (2002-X) ECHR Reports 421, (2002) 129 ILR 537, ECtHR (First Section), 12 December 2002.

18 *British Embassy Driver*, Case No. E 630/78 (1978) 65 ILR 20, Superior Provincial Court (Oberlandesgericht) of Vienna (Austria).

19 *Dralle v Republic of Czechoslovakia* (1950) 17 ILR 155, Austrian Supreme Court.

20 *Neustein v Republic of Indonesia*, Case No. 6 Ob 126/58 (1958) 65 ILR 3 at 9, Austrian Supreme Court.

concerned relates to their immovable assets located in Austria or to their vested rights in respect of domestic immovables belonging to other persons.[21]

Under this law, the only cases in which enforcement measures could be taken against the property of a foreign state are voluntary submission and immovable property, cases which, one must say, were the hallmarks of the absolute immunity doctrine. In other words, at a time when restrictive immunity from adjudicative proceedings was established with regard to commercial or other private-law activity, the standard of absolute immunity was retained for enforcement measures against foreign state property.

Similarly, in Germany, the question of enforcement was determined by the judicial authorities years after the establishment of restrictive immunity with regard to adjudication. Thus, while it was decided in the 1963 *Empire of Iran* case that a foreign state no longer enjoyed immunity from suit,[22] it took another 20 years for the decision to be reached that, after all, a foreign state could not enjoy immunity from enforcement with regard to property used by a separate legal entity and for private purposes.[23] At the same time, it was held that a waiver or loss of immunity at the adjudicative stage does not automatically lead to a waiver or loss of immunity at the execution stage, which should be treated separately.[24]

The same time lag is also found in the French and Spanish practice, in that absolute immunity from execution was rejected much later than absolute immunity from adjudication.[25]

---

[21] *Ibid.* 9, n. 3. For text see also *Leasing v Algeria* (1986) 116 ILR 526 at 530 (Austria); duplicate report *sub nom Republic of 'A' Embassy Bank Account* (1986) 77 ILR 488 at 491, n. 5 (Austria); I. Seidl-Hohenveldern, 'State Immunity' (1979) 10 *NYIL* 97.

[22] *Claim against Empire of Iran* (1963) BVerfGE 16, 27, 45 ILR 57 German Federal Constitutional Court.

[23] *Philippine Embassy Bank Account*, Case No. 2 BvM 1/76 (1977) BVerfGE 46, 342, 65 ILR 146, 150, 164, German Federal Constitutional Court; *National Iranian Oil Co. Revenues from Oil Sales*, Case No. 2 BvR 678, 679, 680, 681, 683/81 (1983) BVerfGE 64, 1, 65 ILR 215 at 226–9, German Federal Constitutional Court.

[24] *Philippine Embassy Bank Account*, n. 23 above, 65 ILR 146 at 160; *Kenyan Diplomatic Residence*, Case No. IXa ZB 19/03 (2003) 128 ILR 632 at 638–9, German Federal Supreme Court (BGH).

[25] See for example, *Administration des Chemins de Fer du Gouvernement Iranien v Société Levant Express Transport* (1969) 52 ILR 315, French Court of Cassation (restrictive immunity from suit); *Clerget v Banque Commerciale pour l'Europe du Nord* (1971) 65 ILR 54, French Court of Cassation (First Civil Chamber), (absolute immunity from execution); *Procureur de la République v SA*

The Swiss courts seem to be the only exception; for the earliest cases of restrictive immunity in Switzerland mostly concerned forcible measures against assets of foreign states.[26] This is not surprising, given the particular status of Switzerland as a hub of banking activities in the world. However, since the very beginning, the Swiss government has made clear its opposition to the taking of execution measures against foreign state property.[27] Besides, the Swiss courts have consistently observed a territorial connection requirement whereby they would assert jurisdiction only when the debt in question arose in Switzerland or is otherwise connected to the Swiss territory. Moreover, at present, Switzerland is a party to the 1972 ECSI which subjects enforcement against foreign state property to a number of strict conditions.

12.4 IMMUNITY FROM EXECUTION AS DISTINCT FROM IMMUNITY FROM ADJUDICATION

A defining feature of the current law on state immunity is the distinction between and the separate treatment of immunity from adjudication (in

---

Ipitrade International (1978) 65 ILR 75, Tribunal de grande instance of Paris (France) (same); *Emilio BM v Embassy of Equatorial Guinea*, Case No. 727 (1986) 86 ILR 508 at 511, Spanish Supreme Court (restrictive immunity from adjudication but government endorsement needed in a separate procedure for execution); *Diana A v Republic of South Africa*, Case No. 7231 (1986) 86 ILR 512 at 516, Spanish Supreme Court (same); *Abbott v Republic of South Africa*, Decision No. 107/92 (1992) 113 ILR 411 at 422, 425–6, Spanish Constitutional Court (Second Chamber), (accepting the judge's autonomy in deciding on execution).

[26] See *Oesterreich. Finanzministerium v Dreyfus* (1918) BGE 44 I 49, in which the Swiss Federal Tribunal upheld the validity of an attachment order against assets of Austria in regard to a claim for the return of Austrian state treasury notes circulated in Switzerland; *Greek Republic v Walder* (1930) BGE 56 I 237, 5 AD 121, Swiss Federal Tribunal (writ of attachment against Greece rejected); *Kingdom of Greece v Julius Bär & Co.* (1956) ATF 82 I 75, 23 ILR 195, Swiss Federal Tribunal (attachment against Greece rejected); *Soviet Republic (Immunity in Greece)* (1928) 4 AD 172, Court of Athens (Greece) (measure of distraint upon foreign state property confirmed).

[27] See the Swiss Government Ordinance of 12 July 1918 prohibiting arrest and execution against the property of foreign states, cited in *Greek Republic v Walder*, n. 26 above, 5 AD 121 at 122, n. 2; and the Swiss Federal Council Decree of 24 October 1939 subjecting execution to the consent of the Federal Council, noted in *State Immunity* (1939/1940) 10 AD 235 at 238–9 (Switzerland).

other words, the court's hearing a case and taking a decision on the merits) and immunity from enforcement or execution (in other words, the court's taking a forcible measure either before or during the adjudication, or following and in execution of a judgment), with the consequent principle that loss of immunity from adjudication, whether due to a waiver of immunity by the defendant foreign state or because of a denial of immunity by the court, does not entail loss of immunity from enforcement or execution. This should already be notable from the history of the doctrine and practice of restrictive immunity, as discussed above, in which immunity from execution was denied at a much later stage; but it is even more obvious in various legal instruments. With slight variations two different terms are used by the current legal instruments on state immunity and in case law to cover these two immunities. Somewhat confusingly, however, immunity from adjudication is often referred to as 'immunity from jurisdiction' ('*immunité de juridiction*' in the French language), though the latter term, together with the cognate expression 'jurisdictional immunity/immunities', is perfectly suited to cover both immunity from the adjudicative process and immunity from enforcement/execution, given that both the power to adjudge a case and the power to impose forcible measures are the necessary components of a court's judicial power and thus, broadly speaking, within its jurisdiction.

Under the US FSIA1976, the two immunities are dealt with in two separate groups of provisions. Section 1604, 'Immunity of a foreign state from jurisdiction', provides that:

> a foreign state shall be immune from the jurisdiction of the courts of the United States and of the States except as provided in sections 1605 to 1607.

Section 1609, 'Immunity from attachment and execution of property of a foreign state', provides that:

> the property in the United States of a foreign state shall be immune from attachment arrest and execution except as provided in sections 1610 and 1611.

Clearly, sections 1604–1607 deal with immunity from adjudication and its exceptions, and sections 1609–1611 deal with immunity from attachment and execution and its exceptions. Waivers of these two immunities are likewise addressed separately with respect to adjudication and execution. In fact, in the US FSIA1976 the requirement of waiver is repeated every time there might be some doubt:

> A foreign state shall not be immune from the jurisdiction of courts of the United States or of the States in any case in which the foreign state has waived its immunity either explicitly or by implication. (s. 1605(a)(1))

> The property in the United States of a foreign state … used for a commercial activity in the United States, shall not be immune from attachment in aid of execution, or from execution … if the foreign state has waived its immunity from attachment in aid of execution or from execution either explicitly or by implication. (s. 1610(a)(1))

> [a]ny property in the United States of an agency or instrumentality of a foreign state engaged in commercial activity in the United States shall not be immune from attachment in aid of execution, or from execution … if the agency or instrumentality has waived its immunity from attachment in aid of execution or from execution either explicitly or implicitly. (s. 1610(b)(1))

> The property of a foreign state … used for a commercial activity in the United States, shall not be immune from attachment prior to the entry of judgment … if the foreign state has explicitly waived its immunity from attachment prior to judgment. (s. 1610(d)(1))

As explained in the legislative report, the arrangements under the FSIA 1976:

> would remedy, *in part*, the present predicament of a plaintiff who has obtained a judgment against a foreign state. Under existing law, a foreign state in our courts enjoys absolute immunity from execution, even in ordinary commercial litigation where commercial assets are available for the satisfaction of a judgment. [The FSIA] seeks to restrict this broad immunity from execution … by *partially* lowering the barrier of immunity from execution.[28]

So the intention of the legislator was only partially to lift immunity from execution and never to lift it wholly and completely.[29] Thus, the existence of two immunities, as set forth in the FSIA 1976, has been regularly confirmed in case law, so that a court would:

---

[28] US House of Representatives, *Legislative History of the FSIA*, Report No. 94-1487 (1976), pp. 8 and 27; 1976 USCCAN 6604, 6606 and 6626 (emphasis added).

[29] See *Letelier v Republic of Chile and Linea Aerea Nacional-Chile*, 748 F.2d 790, 799 (2d Cir. 1984), 79 ILR 561, Court of Appeals for the Second Circuit (US); reversing *Letelier v Republic of Chile*, 567 F.Supp. 1490 (SDNY 1983), District Court for the Southern District of New York and *Letelier v Republic of Chile*, 575 F.Supp. 1217 (SDNY 1983), District Court for the Southern District of New York. See also *Connecticut Bank of Commerce v Republic of Congo (Af-Cap I)*, 309 F.3d 240, 252 (5th Cir. 2002), Court of Appeals for the Fifth Circuit (US).

> reject [the plaintiff's] argument [when] it conflates the considerations and effects attendant to commencement and/or notice of a suit seeking to execute upon the foreign sovereign's property with those attendant to deciding whether to authorize execution upon that property.[30]

Furthermore, though only implied in the above-quoted repetition of different waivers for different immunities, it is a long established principle in US jurisprudence that waiver of immunity from adjudication is separate from and does not automatically entail waiver of immunity from execution.[31]

The UK SIA 1978 also addresses the two immunities in two sets of provisions, though in a different manner. Part I of the SIA 1978, 'Proceedings in United Kingdom by or against Other States', is divided into four sections with the following headings:

- 'Immunity from jurisdiction' (s. 1);
- 'Exceptions from immunity' (ss. 2–11);
- 'Procedure' (ss. 12–13); and
- 'Supplementary provisions' (ss. 14–17).

Section 1 of the Act, 'General immunity from jurisdiction', provides:

> A State is immune from the jurisdiction of the courts of the United Kingdom except as provided in the following provisions of this Part [in other words, Part I] of this Act.

Next follow the provisions on 'Exceptions from immunity' (ss. 2–11), which, on closer inspection, deal with situations where a foreign state cannot claim immunity from the *adjudication* of the UK courts. Among these exceptions one finds 'submission to jurisdiction' in section 2, which provides:

> A State is not immune as respects proceedings in respect of which it has submitted to the jurisdiction of the courts of the United Kingdom.

After that, section 13(2), under 'Procedure', provides that:

---

30 *FG Hemisphere Associates, LLC v République du Congo*, 455 F.3d 575, 589 (5th Cir. 2006), Court of Appeals for the Fifth Circuit (US), quoting *Connecticut Bank of Commerce v Republic of Congo (Af-Cap I)*, n. 29 above.

31 *Ministry of Defense and Support for Armed Forces of Islamic Republic of Iran v Cubic Defense Systems, Inc.*, 385 F.3d 1206, 1219 (9th Cir. 2004), Court of Appeals for the Ninth Circuit (US).

(a) relief shall not be given against a State by way of injunction or order for specific performance or for the recovery of land or other property; and
(b) the property of a State shall not be subject to any process for the enforcement of a judgment or arbitration award or, in an action *in rem*, for its arrest, detention or sale.

Then follows the possibility of waiver of immunity from enforcement under section 13(3):

> Subsection (2) above does not prevent the giving of any relief or the issue of any process with the written consent of the State concerned; and any such consent (which may be contained in a prior agreement) may be expressed so as to apply to a limited extent or generally; *but a provision merely submitting to the jurisdiction of the courts is not to be regarded as a consent for the purposes of this subsection*.[32]

This last segment of the provision is in direct counterpoint to the submission to jurisdiction in section 2 quoted above, with the effect that a waiver of immunity from adjudication does not entail a waiver of immunity from execution in a UK court.

This distinction between immunity from adjudication and immunity from enforcement by means of two distinct groups of provisions has been duly noted by the judicial authorities. In the words of Lord Diplock:

> The [SIA] … draws a clear distinction between the adjudicative jurisdiction and the enforcement jurisdiction of courts of law in the United Kingdom. Sections 2 to 11 deal with adjudicative jurisdiction. Sections 12 to 14 deal with procedure and of these, sections 13(2) to (6) and 14(3) and (4) deal in particular with enforcement jurisdiction. Section 13(3) … makes it clear that such submission does not of itself imply any submission to the enforcement jurisdiction of the courts. Separate consent to that is needed.[33]

---

[32] Emphasis added. See similar arrangements in SIA 1979, ss. 3 and 15 (Singapore); 1981 SIO 1981, ss. 3 and 14 (Pakistan); FSIA 1981, ss. 2 and 14 (South Africa); SIA 1982, ss. 3, 11 and 12 (Canada); FSIA 1985, Part II ('Immunity from jurisdiction') and Part IV ('Enforcement'), see especially ss. 9, 30 and 31 (Australia); FSIL 2008, Chs 2 ('Immunity from jurisdiction') and 3 ('Immunity from Execution Proceedings'), see especially ss. 2, 15 and 17(c) (Israel); ACJFS 2009, Section 2 ('Cases where Foreign States are not Immune from the Proceedings on the Merits') and Section 3 ('Cases where Foreign States are not Immune from the Proceedings on Provisional Measures and Enforcement of Judgments against Their Property'), see especially art. 17 (Japan).

[33] *Alcom Ltd v Republic of Colombia* [1984] 1 AC 580 at 600, 74 ILR 170 at 183, HL. See also *Al-Adsani v Government of Kuwait* (1996) 107 ILR 536 at 542, 548, CA; *Svenska Petroleum Exploration AB v Government of the Republic*

The two-immunity scheme is also adopted on the international plane. The 1972 ECSI envisages two immunities: while providing that:

> A Contracting State shall be entitled to immunity from the jurisdiction of the courts of another Contracting State if the proceedings do not fall within Articles 1 to 14. (Article 15)

It also provides that:

> No measures of execution or preventive measures against the property of a Contracting State may be taken in the territory of another Contracting State except where and to the extent that the State has expressly consented thereto in writing in any particular case. (Article 23)

This general ban on measures of execution in the absence of consent was not adopted by the drafters of the 2004 UN Convention, which also provides for a limited number of situations in which the defendant foreign state cannot claim immunity from execution. What is significant for our purposes here is again the distinction between two immunities. The 2004 UN Convention starts with a general 'immunity from the jurisdiction of the courts of another State' in Article 5 in Part II, 'General principles', which is subject to the exceptions contained in Part III, 'Proceedings in which State immunity cannot be invoked'. Then, in Part IV, 'State immunity from measures of constraint in connection with proceedings before a court', one finds the following provisions:

> No pre-judgment measures of constraint, such as attachment or arrest, against property of a State may be taken in connection with a proceeding before a court of another State unless and except to the extent that the State has expressly consented to the taking of such measures. (Article 18(a))
>
> No post-judgment measures of constraint, such as attachment, arrest or execution, against property of a State may be taken in connection with a proceeding before a court of another State unless and except to the extent that the State has expressly consented to the taking of such measures. (Article 19(a))
>
> Where consent to the measures of constraint is required under articles 18 and 19, *consent to the exercise of jurisdiction under article 7* [consent to 'the

---

of Lithuania (No. 2) [2006] EWCA Civ 1529, [2007] QB 886 at 930, para. 135, CA; *ETI Euro Telecom International NV v Republic of Bolivia* [2008] EWCA Civ 880, [2009] 1 WLR 665 at 693, paras 127–8, CA; *Republic of Argentina v NML Capital Ltd* [2010] EWCA Civ 41, [2010] 3 WLR 874 at 886–7 and 899, paras 49, 51, 103, CA.

> exercise of jurisdiction'] *shall not imply consent to the taking of measures of constraint*. (Article 20, emphasis added)

In conclusion, the current law on state immunity draws a clear distinction between two immunities: immunity from adjudication and immunity from execution.[34] Thus, the issue of enforcement is considered to be distinct and separate from that of adjudication. Even if a court is satisfied that a defendant foreign state is not immune from the adjudicative process and, on considering the merits of the case, passes a judgment against that state, it is not an automatic process that the assets of the defendant foreign state can be attached straightaway to pay the judgment debt. A number of additional restrictions, conditions and qualifications must be fulfilled before execution can take place. It is to these restrictions, conditions and qualifications that we will turn in the rest of the chapter.

12.5 IMMUNITY FROM EXECUTION FOR PROPERTY USED FOR SOVEREIGN PURPOSES

One criterion that is universally applied in current state practice is that the property of a defendant foreign state that is used for sovereign or public or governmental purposes is immune from execution. This rule has been repeatedly confirmed by the highest judicial authorities in various countries. In the *Philippine Embassy* case, for instance, the German Constitutional Court found that:

---

[34] For scholarly opinion affirming the distinction see for example, Hazel Fox and Philippa Webb, *The Law of State Immunity* (3rd edn, Oxford University Press, 2013), ch. 16; Joe Verhoeven, *Le droit international des immunitiés: contestation ou consolidation?* (Brussels, De Boeck & Larcier, 2004), pp. 36–42; Isabelle Pingel-Lenuzza, *Les immunités des Etats en droit international* (Bruylant, 1997), pp. 339–76; Michel Cosnard, *La soumission des États aux tribunaux internes – Face à la théorie des immunités des États* (Paris, Éditions Pedone, 1996), pp. 95–142 at 143–202; Christoph H. Schreuer, *State Immunity: Some Recent Developments* (Cambridge, Grotius Publications, 1988), ch. 6; Gamal Moursi Badr, *State Immunity: An Analytical and Prognostic View* (The Hague/Boston/Lancaster, Martinus Nijhoff Publishers, 1984), pp. 115–27, 129–32; James Crawford, 'Execution of Judgments and Foreign Sovereign Immunity' (1981) 75 *American Journal of International Law* 820; Sir Ian Sinclair, 'The Law of Sovereign Immunity: Recent Developments' (1980-II) 167 *Recueil des Cours: Collected Courses of the Hague Academy of International Law* 113 at 242.

> There exists the following general rule of international law: Forced execution of judgment by the State of the forum under a writ of execution against a foreign State which has been issued in respect of non-sovereign acts (*acta iure gestionis*) of that State, on property of that State which is present or situated in the territory of the State of the forum is inadmissible without the consent of the foreign State if, at the time of the initiation of the measure of execution, such property serves sovereign purposes of the foreign State.[35]

The Austrian Supreme Court was so much in agreement that it quoted the above pronouncement word for word in its own judgment.[36]

In a similar vein, the Swiss Federal Tribunal declared:

> the levying of execution against the assets of a foreign State is only admissible in principle against those assets which are not allocated for the performance of sovereign functions. Having regard to the nature of the assets subjected to attachment, immunity under public international law can be claimed … so long as the assets have been allocated in a recognizable manner for an identifiable purpose related to the exercise of State sovereignty.[37]

Such was also the view of the Italian Court of Cassation:

---

[35] *Philippine Embassy Bank Account*, n. 23 above, 65 ILR 146 at 150; 164, Ground C; see also 65 ILR 146, 181, Ground C.I.6; 184, Ground C.II.1. See also *National Iranian Oil C. Revenues from Oil Sales*, n. 23 above, 65 ILR 215 at 226, Ground B.III.1; 241–2, Ground B.III.2(d); *Kenyan Diplomatic Residence*, Case No. IXa ZB 19/03 (2003) 128 ILR 632 at 636, Ground II.3b, German Federal Supreme Court (BGH).

[36] *Leasing West GmbH v People's Democratic Republic of Algeria*, Case No. 3 Ob 38/86 (1986) 116 ILR 526 at 528, Austrian Supreme Court (OGH); duplicate report *sub nom Republic of 'A' Embassy Bank Account*, Case No. 3 Ob 38/86 (1986) 77 ILR 488, Austrian Supreme Court. See also *Foreign State Bank Account* (1986) 86 ILR 570, note, Austrian Supreme Court; *Radiation Contamination Claim* (1988) 86 ILR 571 at 573, Austrian Supreme Court.

[37] *Z v Geneva Supervisory Authority for the Enforcement of Debts and Bankruptcy* (1990) 102 ILR 205 at 207, Ground 2b, Swiss Federal Tribunal. See also *Kingdom of Greece v Julius Bär & Co.* (1956) ATF 82 I 75, 23 ILR 195 at 198–9, Ground 10, Swiss Federal Tribunal; *United Arab Republic v Mrs X* (1960) ATF 86 I 23, 65 ILR 385 at 391, Ground 4; 392, Ground 5, Swiss Federal Tribunal; *Arab Republic of Egypt v Cinetelevision International Registered Trust* (1979) 65 ILR 425 at 430, Ground 4b, Swiss Federal Tribunal; *Griessen* (1982) ATF 108 III 107, 82 ILR 5 at 7, Ground 1, Swiss Federal Tribunal; *Libyan Arab Socialist People's Jamahiriya v Actimon SA* (1985) BGE 111 Ia 62, 82 ILR 30 at 35–6, Ground 7b, Swiss Federal Tribunal; *Kingdom of Spain v Company X SA* (1986) BGE 112 Ia 148, 82 ILR 38 at 41, Ground 4a; 44, Ground 5a, Swiss Federal Tribunal.

> the prevailing tendency is to consider the assets used for a public function or power, or indeed for sovereign purposes, as immune ... Execution against assets used for sovereign or public purposes is therefore forbidden.[38]

And of the Spanish Supreme Court:

> It is considered beyond dispute that a domestic court cannot take measures of execution (or preventive measures) against property held by a foreign State on the territory of the forum state where such property is intended for the purpose of supporting sovereign activities or activities carried on *jure imperii* ... international law bars forced execution on property of the foreign State used or intended to be used in activities of a sovereign or *de imperio* nature, permitting it only in respect of property intended for the purposes of economic activities.[39]

Conversely, in the opinion of the French Court of Cassation:

> Foreign States enjoy immunity from execution as a matter of principle. Nevertheless this immunity can be set aside in exceptional cases such as where the assets attached have been allocated for an economic or commercial activity of a private law nature, which has given rise to the claim at issue.[40] ...
>
> The assets of a foreign State are, in principle, not subject to seizure, subject to exceptions in particular where they have been allocated for an economic or commercial activity under private law which is at the origin of the title of the attaching debtor.[41]

It is therefore the unanimous position of various national courts that enforcement or execution can only be allowed against the property of a

---

[38] *Banamar-Capizzi v Embassy of the Popular Democratic Republic of Algeria*, Case No. 2085 (1989) 87 ILR 56 at 60, 62, Italian Court of Cassation (Plenary Session). See also *Libyan Arab Socialist People's Jamahiriya v Rossbeton SRL*, Case No. 2502 (1989) 87 ILR 63 at 66, 67, 68, Italian Court of Cassation (Plenary Session); *Condor and Filvem v Minister of Justice*, Case No. 329 (1992) 101 ILR 394 at 402, 403, 404, Italian Constitutional Court.

[39] *Abbott v Republic of South Africa*, Decision No. 107/92 (1992) 113 ILR 411 at 419–20, 423, Spanish Constitutional Court (Second Chamber).

[40] *Islamic Republic of Iran v Société Eurodif* (1984) 77 ILR 513 at 515, French Court of Cassation (First Civil Chamber). See also *Islamic Republic of Iran) v Société Eurodif*, (1989) 89 ILR 31 at 34–5, French Court of Cassation (Civil Chamber); *Ministry for Economic and Financial Affairs of the Islamic Republic of Iran v Société Framatome* (1990) 113 ILR 452 at 456, French Court of Cassation (First Civil Chamber).

[41] *Société Sonatrach v Migeon* (1985) 77 ILR 525 at 527, French Court of Cassation (First Civil Chamber).

foreign state used for commercial purposes, while property used for sovereign or public purposes is still protected by immunity. This is exactly the same rule that has been written into various legal instruments on immunity.

Section 1610(a) of the US FSIA 1976, in allowing attachment or execution against foreign state property under certain circumstances, refers to the use or purpose of the targeted property in several places:

> (a) The property in the United States of a foreign state … *used for* a commercial activity in the United States, shall not be immune from attachment in aid of execution, or from execution … if – …
>
> (2) the property is or was *used for* the commercial activity upon which the claim is based, or …
> (4) the execution relates to a judgment establishing rights in property –
>
> (A) which is acquired by succession or gift, or
>
> (B) which is immovable and situated in the United States.
>
> Provided, That such property is not *used for purposes of* maintaining a diplomatic or consular mission or the residence of the Chief of such mission. (emphasis added)

Thus, the wreck of a former navy vessel was immune from arrest, because it had not been engaged in a commercial activity when it sank in the year 1804.[42] Since 'used for' is the decisive test, much of the courts' attention in the United States has been devoted to the interpretation of the phrase 'used for'. In this respect 'used for a commercial activity' is usually contrasted with 'acquired through a commercial activity': what matters is what a particular piece of property has been used for, but not how the foreign state has come into possession of that property. If the property in question is used for non-commercial purposes, then it is immune from execution, even if the foreign state acquired that property through a commercial transaction. Thus, the residence of the head of a permanent mission to the United Nations should be immune from attachment, even though the property had been purchased by the sending

---

[42] *Odyssey Marine Exploration, Inc. v Unidentified Shipwrecked Vessel*, 657 F.3d 1159, 1177 (11th Cir. 2011), Court of Appeals for the Eleventh Circuit (US); affirming *Odyssey Marine Exploration, Inc. v Unidentified Shipwrecked Vessel*, 675 F.Supp.2d 1126, 1138 (M.D. Fla. 2009), District Court for the Middle District of Florida.

state in a commercial transaction as between a seller and a buyer.[43] In the words of the Court of Appeals for the Fifth Circuit:

> What matters under the statute is what the property is 'used for', not how it was generated or produced. If property in the United States is used for a commercial purpose here, that property is subject to attachment and execution even if it was purchased with tax revenues or some other noncommercial source of government income. Conversely, even if a foreign state's property has been generated by commercial activity in the United States, that property is not thereby subject to execution or attachment if it is not 'used for' a commercial activity within our borders ... To use property for a commercial activity, within the ordinary meaning of 'use', would be to put the property in the service of the commercial activity, to carry out the activity by means of the property.[44]

The totality of the circumstances should be considered in determining the use of the property:

> determining the commercial (or non-commercial) status of a property's use requires a more holistic approach. Specifically, we think that an analysis applied to such a question should examine the totality of the circumstances surrounding the property. This analysis should include an examination of the uses of the property in the past as well as all facts related to its present use, with an eye toward determining whether the commercial use of the property, if any, is so exceptional that it is 'an out of character' use for that particular property.[45]

The Court of Appeals for the Ninth Circuit agreed by holding that:

> property is 'used for a commercial activity in the United States' when the property in question is put into action, put into service, availed or employed *for* a commercial activity, not *in connection* with a commercial activity or *in relation* to a commercial activity. The FSIA does not contemplate a strained analysis of the words 'used for' and 'commercial activity', and neither do we. Rather, we anticipate that this determination will be made by considering the use of the property in question in a straight-forward manner, with a proper

---

[43] *City of Englewood v Socialist People's Libyan Arab Jamahiriya*, 773 F.2d 31, 36–7 (3rd Cir. 1985), Court of Appeals for the Third Circuit (US).

[44] *Connecticut Bank of Commerce v Republic of Congo (Af-Cap I)*, 309 F.3d 240, 251, 254 (5th Cir. 2002), Court of Appeals for the Fifth Circuit (US). See also *Walker International Holdings Ltd v Republic of Congo*, 395 F.3d 229, 235–6 (5th Cir. 2004), Court of Appeals for the Fifth Circuit (US); *Af-Cap, Inc. v Chevron Overseas (Congo) Ltd*, 475 F.3d 1080, 1084, 1087, 1091–5 (9th Cir. 2007), Court of Appeals for the Ninth Circuit (US).

[45] *Af-Cap, Inc. v Republic of Congo (Af-Cap II)*, 383 F.3d 361, 369–70 (5th Cir. 2004), Court of Appeals for the Fifth Circuit (US).

appreciation of the fact that the further removed the property is from the referenced commercial transaction, the less likely it is that the property was used *for* that transaction.[46]

Section 13(4) of the UK SIA 1978 provides that the property of a foreign state shall not be immune from execution if the property 'is for the time being in use or intended for use for commercial purposes'.[47] The SIA 1978 defines 'commercial purposes' as 'purposes of such transactions or activities as are mentioned in section 3(3)' (section 17(1)). In its turn, section 3(3) defines 'commercial transaction' as follows:

(a) any contract for the supply of goods or services;
(b) any loan or other transaction for the provision of finance and any guarantee or indemnity in respect of any such transaction or of any other financial obligation; and
(c) any other transaction or activity (whether of a commercial, industrial, financial, professional or other similar character) into which a State enters or in which it engages otherwise than in the exercise of sovereign authority.

This strongly suggests that the identification of a commercial transaction, with all its associated difficulties, will be conducted again at the execution stage, especially where the targeted property is used for a different commercial transaction from the one that is the subject of the litigation. Also, since the definition of 'commercial transaction' within the SIA 1978 itself serves as the test for enforcement measures, the scope of such enforcement measures is both defined and narrowed by the considerations and limitations associated with the definition of commercial transaction.

The special feature of the Australian FSIA 1985 is that it introduces the concept of 'commercial property', which is not immune from execution. 'Commercial property' is defined as 'property, other than diplomatic property or military property, that is in use by the foreign state concerned substantially for commercial purposes' (section 32(3)(a)). It

---

[46] *Af-Cap, Inc. v Chevron Overseas (Congo) Ltd*, 475 F.3d 1080, 1091, 1094 (9th Cir. 2007), Court of Appeals for the Ninth Circuit (emphasis in the original). This reasoning was repeated in *Ministry of Defense and Support for Armed Forces of Islamic Republic of Iran v Cubic Defense Systems, Inc.*, 495 F.3d 1024, 1036 (9th Cir. 2007), Court of Appeals for the Ninth Circuit (US).

[47] See similar provisions in the SIA 1979, s. 15(4) (Singapore); SIO 1981, s. 14(2)(b) (Pakistan); FSIA 1981, s. 14(3) (South Africa); SIS 1982, s. 12(1)(b) (Canada). The Japanese ACJFS 2009 provides that execution is allowed against 'property in use or intended for use for other than government non-commercial purposes'.

then provides a somewhat loose definition of 'commercial purposes' by stating that 'a reference in this Act to a commercial purpose includes a reference to a trading, a business, a professional and an industrial purpose' (section 3(5)). It also provides that 'property that is apparently vacant or apparently not in use shall be taken to be being used for commercial purposes' (section 32(3)(b)).

On the international plane, the 1972 ECSI provides a much narrower test by tying up the question of execution closely with that of adjudication, so that execution is only possible against the property used for the commercial activity which is the subject matter of the case:

> A judgment rendered against a Contracting State in proceedings relating to an industrial or commercial activity … may be enforced in the State of the forum against property of the State against which judgment has been given, used exclusively in connection with such an activity. (Article 26)

The 2004 UN Convention adds further conditions:

> the property is specifically in use or intended for use by the State for other than government non-commercial purposes and is in the territory of the State of the forum, provided that post-judgment measures of constraint may only be taken against property that has a connection with the entity against which the proceeding was directed. (Article 19(c))

The 'entity connection' will be discussed below.

12.6 OTHER CONDITIONS FOR EXECUTION

12.6.1 Waiver of Immunity from Execution

Given the high degree of caution on the part of national courts in their handling of attachment of property of foreign states, a waiver of immunity by the defendant foreign state would make it much easier to satisfy the judgment in favour of the claimant; thus waiver assumes a much more prominent role with regard to enforcement than at the adjudicative stage. In fact, in current legal instruments on jurisdictional immunities of foreign states and their property, be they national legislation or international treaties, waiver is treated as the primary condition for execution.[48] On a technical level, two important questions arise: first,

---

[48] See FSIA1976, s. 1610(a)(1) (US); SIA 1978, s. 13(3) (UK); SIA 1979, s. 15(3) (Singapore); SIO 1981, s. 14(3) (Pakistan); FSIA 1981, s. 14(2) (South

whether a waiver of immunity from adjudication entails a waiver of immunity from enforcement and execution; and, secondly, what acts on the part of the defendant foreign state should be regarded as constituting a waiver. As discussed above, it is now a generally established principle in the law of state immunity that a waiver of immunity from adjudication does not automatically contain or lead to a waiver of immunity from enforcement or execution, for which a separate waiver is necessary. This means that, in a typical lawsuit against a foreign state, the immunity of that state from the judicial process in the courts of the forum state must be waived twice, the first time to make it possible for the court to hear the case and pass a judgment on the merits, and the second time to allow enforcement or execution against the property of the defendant foreign state. If there happens to be one single act of waiving the immunity, it will be necessary for the defendant foreign state to state clearly and unambiguously that it intends to waive immunity from *both* the adjudication of the case *and* the taking of enforcement and execution measures. Indeed, in some legal instruments, explicit waiver is required for enforcement or execution. Article 23 of the ECSI, for example, provides that:

> No measures of execution or preventive measures against the property of a Contracting State may be taken in the territory of another Contracting State except where and to the extent that the State has expressly consented thereto in writing in any particular case.

The UK SIA1978, which gives effect to the ECSI in UK law, requires 'written consent of the State concerned' for both injunctive relief and execution (section 13(3)).[49]

Likewise, under Article 19(a) of the 2004 UN Convention:

> No post-judgment measures of constraint, such as attachment, arrest or execution, against property of a State may be taken in connection with a proceeding before a court of another State unless and except to the extent that the State has expressly consented to the taking of such measures.

Africa); SIA 1982, s. 12(1)(a) (Canada); FSIA 1985, s. 31(1) (Australia); FSIL 5769-2008, s. 17(a) (Israel); ACJFS 2009, art. 17(1) (Japan); 1972 ECSI, Art. 23; 2004 UN Convention, Art. 19(a).

[49] This requirement is reproduced in SIA 1979, s. 15(3) (Singapore); SIO 1981, s. 14(3) (Pakistan); and FSIA 1981, s. 14(2) (South Africa). Under the Israeli FSIL 5769-2008, 'Assets of a foreign state shall not benefit from immunity … if the foreign state has expressly waived such immunity in writing' (s. 17(a)). The Japanese ACJFS 2009 also provides that 'Foreign States shall not be immune from … enforcement of judgments against their property if they have expressly consented to the taking of such measures' (art. 17(1)).

Interestingly, the Australia FSIA 1985 simply provides that a foreign state 'may at any time by agreement' waive its immunity from execution (section 31(1)) without specifying whether the waiver should be explicit or implicit. The drafters of the legislation, however, made clear that there should be no misunderstanding:

> Unlike immunity from jurisdiction, there should be no scope for waiver of immunity from execution arising by implication. In particular it should not be implied from a waiver of immunity from jurisdiction that immunity from execution has thereby been waived.[50]

On the other hand, in some jurisdictions implicit waiver of immunity is also possible. Under the US FSIA1976, a defendant foreign state can waive its 'immunity from attachment in aid of execution or from execution either explicitly or by implication' (section 1610(a)(1)). Similarly, the Canadian SIA 1982 provides that the property of a foreign state located in Canada is immune from attachment and execution except where 'the state has, either explicitly or by implication, waived its immunity from attachment, execution, arrest, detention, seizure or forfeiture'.

12.6.2 Earmarking

Closely connected with waiver is the possibility that the defendant foreign state may earmark, or allocate, or designate certain property for the purposes of satisfying a particular claim brought against it. The idea originated with the 2004 UN Convention, Article 19(b) of which provides that:

> No post-judgment measures of constraint, such as attachment, arrest or execution, against property of a State may be taken in connection with a proceeding before a court of another State unless and except to the extent that the State has allocated or earmarked property for the satisfaction of the claim which is the object of that proceeding.

According to the UN International Law Commission, which drafted the UN Convention, such a provision 'should have the effect of preventing extraneous or unprotected claimants from frustrating the intention of the

---

[50] Australian Law Reform Commission, *Report No. 24, Foreign State Immunity* (1984), p. 72, para. 121.

State to satisfy *specific* claims or to make payment for an *admitted* liability'.[51]

This formula was adopted in the Japanese ACJFS 2009, but only with regard to provisional measures.[52]

The practical impact of such a formula remains to be seen in light of further practice. In any case, it is hard to imagine that a defendant foreign state which has allocated property to satisfy a specific claim has not waived its immunity with respect to that property and that claim. It should also be noted that such earmarking is restricted by the specificity of the property and the claim, and does not necessarily determine the question whether the earmarked property is adequate to satisfy the claim in full. At any rate, earmarking makes it easier for the claimant to apply for enforcement, as other issues, such as the purpose or use of the property, are in effect no longer relevant.

12.6.3 Targeted Property Must be Situated in the Territory of the Forum State

It is commonly understood that the property of a defendant foreign state targeted for enforcement or execution must be situated in the territory of the forum state. Indeed, it would be surprising, in the absence of a pre-agreed arrangement for mutual judicial assistance, if a court should actually attempt to issue an attachment order against a piece of property or a bank account in the territory of another state. Because, under international law, the jurisdiction of a state (and that of its courts) is largely territorial, an extra-territorial exercise of jurisdiction, unless firmly based on consent, would be rightfully regarded as an encroachment upon the territorial jurisdiction (and sovereignty) of the state affected by such exercise. Thus, section 1610(a)(1) of the US FSIA 1976 provides:

> The property *in the United States* of a foreign state … used for a commercial activity *in the United States*, shall not be immune from attachment in aid of execution, or from execution … if the foreign state has waived its immunity

---

[51] The Commission went on to admit that 'the question whether particular property has or has not been allocated for the satisfaction of a claim may in some situations be ambiguous and should be resolved by the court' (1991-II-2) *Yearbook of the International Law Commission* 12 at 58, commentary to Article 18(1)(b), para. 10 (emphasis added). Article 18 in the ILC report later became Article 19 in the UN Convention.

[52] Discussed in the context of pre-judgment measures.

> from attachment in aid of execution or from execution either explicitly or by implication.[53]

Clearly, even when a defendant foreign state has completely waived its immunity from execution, executionary measures can only be taken against its 'property in the United States' that is 'used for a commercial activity in the United States'.[54] For the purposes of execution, the property must be in the United States at the time of the taking of execution measures, which means that any property that was in US territory at the start of the litigation but was later moved out of the United States, so that it is now exclusively situated in a foreign country, is beyond the reach of the enforcement measures.[55]

12.6.4 Requirement of a Jurisdictional Link

The law in some countries requires a jurisdictional connection between the targeted foreign state property and the forum state. Section 1610(a)(2) of the US FSIA 1976 provides that execution is allowed if the foreign state property in question 'is or was used for the commercial activity upon which the claim is based'. This creates particular difficulties in cases involving non-commercial tort, namely. personal injury or death, and damage to or loss of property occurring in the United States, as envisaged by section 1605(a)(5) of the FSIA. To start with, causing physical personal injury is by definition not a commercial activity,[56]

---

[53] Emphasis added. See also SIA 1982, s. 12(1) (Canada) ('property of a foreign state that is located in Canada'); 2004 UN Convention on Jurisdictional Immunities of States and Their Property, Art. 19(c) ('the property is … in the territory of the State of the forum').

[54] See for example, *Af-Cap, Inc. v Republic of Congo*, 462 F.3d 417, 429, n. 10 (5th Cir. 2006), Court of Appeals for the Fifth Circuit; *Kensington International Ltd v Republic of Congo*, 461 F.3d 238, 243 (2d Cir. 2006), Court of Appeals for the Second Circuit; *FG Hemisphere Associates, LLC v République du Congo*, 455 F.3d 575, 585 (5th Cir. 2006), Court of Appeals for the Fifth Circuit; *Walker International Holdings Ltd v Republic of Congo*, 395 F.3d 229, 234 (5th Cir. 2004), Court of Appeals for the Fifth Circuit; *Af-Cap, Inc. v Republic of Congo (Af-Cap II)*, 383 F.3d 361, 367 (5th Cir. 2004), Court of Appeals for the Fifth Circuit; *Connecticut Bank of Commerce v Republic of Congo (Af-Cap I)*, 309 F.3d 240, 247, 251 (5th Cir. 2002), Court of Appeals for the Fifth Circuit.

[55] *FG Hemisphere Associates, LLC v République du Congo*, n. 54 above, 588–90.

[56] Under the US FSIA 1976, 'A "commercial activity" means either a regular course of commercial conduct or a particular commercial transaction or

which makes it impossible, strictly speaking, to carry out any execution in such a case, simply because there is no 'commercial activity' upon which the claim is based. Even if the word 'commercial' could be disregarded, it would be surprising if the claimant could identify a piece of property of the foreign state that was used for the tortious act and which could be executed upon. In *Letelier*, for example, even though the claimant successfully obtained a judgment against Chile with regard to the murder of a former Chilean Foreign Minister in Washington by Chilean secret service agents,[57] no property of the Chilean state could be identified which had a sufficient nexus with the assassination (disregarding the fact that an 'assassination' was not a 'commercial activity') to satisfy the jurisdictional link requirement for the execution of the judgment.[58]

In keeping with the requirement that the targeted property must be situated in the territory of the forum state, the Swiss case law requires a so-called 'domestic connection' (*Binnenbeziehung*) with the Swiss territory. The fact that a particular transaction has a commercial or private-law character is insufficient for the exercise of jurisdiction over the merits or for the taking of enforcement measures. There must also be a connection between the legal relationship giving rise to the claim and the Swiss territory. Attachment of the property of a foreign state will be permissible only when (1) the claim arose out of a commercial activity or a private-law transaction; (2) the activity or transaction has a connection with the Swiss territory; and (3) the property in question is not used by the foreign state for sovereign purposes. In the words of the Swiss Federal Tribunal:

> In order to consider the debt out of which arose the claims for attachment as one established in Swiss territory, it should have been either originated, concluded, or performed here by the debtor, or there should have been at least

act'. Commerciality, therefore, lies at the heart of the definition of a 'commercial activity' (s. 1603(d)).

[57] *Letelier v Chile*, 488 F.Supp. 665 (DDC 1980), 63 ILR 378, Court of Appeals for the DC Circuit.

[58] Thereby provoking the remark that the US FSIA created, in this respect, a 'right without a remedy'. *Letelier v Chile*, 748 F.2d 790, 798–9 (2d Cir. 1984), 79 ILR 561, Court of Appeals for the Second Circuit. It should also be noted that, in a number of situations this jurisdictional link requirement is explicitly ruled out by the US FSIA 1976. These situations include foreign expropriation measures against US citizens, succession or gift, immovable property, indemnity obligations, arbitral awards, acts of a 'State sponsor of terrorism', and an agency or instrumentality of a foreign state (s. 1610(a)(3)(4)(5)(6)(7) and (b)(2)).

> such acts performed by the debtor for which he must have designated a place of performance in Switzerland.[59]

This means that, where a territorial connection cannot be established, enforcement measures will be denied, and the Swiss case law even held that, in the absence of a territorial link, it was not necessary to determine whether the defendant foreign state had acted *jure gestionis* or had waived its immunity, since Swiss law did not permit proceedings against a foreign state unless there was a close connection between the subject matter and Switzerland (*Binnenbeziehung*).[60] Such a stringent territorial requirement, according to the Swiss Federal Tribunal, is calculated to safeguard the 'interests of Switzerland', because:

> to permit legal actions against foreign States if a somewhat intensive domestic relationship is lacking … could … easily cause political and other difficulties.[61]

---

[59] *Greek Republic v Walder*, (1930) BGE 56 I 237, 5 AD 121 at 123, Swiss Federal Tribunal. See also *Kingdom of Greece v Julius Bär & Co.*, (1956) ATF 82 I 75, 23 ILR 195 at 196–7, 200, Swiss Federal Tribunal.

[60] *Socialist Libyan Arab Popular Jamahiriya v Libyan American Oil Co.* (1980) BGE 106 Ia 142, 62 ILR 228 at 234, Ground 3b, Swiss Federal Supreme Court, First Public Law Department. See also *United Arab Republic v Mrs X* (1960) ATF 86 I 23, 65 ILR 385 at 389, Ground 2; 391, Grounds 3 and 4, Swiss Federal Tribunal; *Italian Republic, Italian Ministry of Transport and Italian State Railways v Beta Holding SA* (1966) 65 ILR 394 at 398–9, Ground 5; 401, Ground 7b, Swiss Federal Tribunal; *Banque Centrale de la République de Turquie v Weston Compagnie de Finance et d'Investissement SA* (1978) BGE 104 Ia 367, 65 ILR 417 at 419–20, Ground 2c; 423, Ground 4; 424–5, Ground 4d, Swiss Federal Tribunal; *Arab Republic of Egypt v Cinetelevision International Registered Trust* (1979) 65 ILR 425 at 430, Ground 4a; 432, Ground 5b, Swiss Federal Tribunal; *Banco de la Nacion Lima v Banco Cattolica del Veneto* (1984) BGE 110 Ia 43, 82 ILR 10, 11–12, Ground 4a, Swiss Federal Tribunal; *Libya (Libyan Arab Socialist People's Jamahiriya) v Actimon SA* (1985) BGE 111 Ia 62, 82 ILR 30 at 32–3, Ground 4; 34, Ground 5b, Swiss Federal Tribunal; *Swissair v X* (1985) 82 ILR 36 at 37, Swiss Federal Tribunal; *Kingdom of Spain v Company X SA* (1986) BGE 112 Ia 148, 82 ILR 38 at 40, Ground 3b, Swiss Federal Tribunal; *S v Socialist Republic of Romania* (1987) ATF 113 Ia 172, 82 ILR 45 at 48, Ground 2, Swiss Federal Tribunal.

[61] *Socialist Libyan Arab Popular Jamahiriya v Libyan American Oil Co.* (1980) BGE 106 Ia 142, (1980) BGE 106 Ia 142, 62 ILR 228 at 234, Ground 3b, Swiss Federal Supreme Court, First Public Law Department.

This can easily be understood when one appreciates the importance of Switzerland as a world banking centre.[62] Since many governments, institutions, including central banks, deposit their funds in Swiss banks, it would be undesirable for the Swiss judicial system to become the global clearing house for commercial and other disputes having no connection with the Swiss territory.

12.6.5 Property Owned by a Separate Entity

States regularly establish, in their own territories or in other states, entities that have a separate legal personality, can possess and dispose of property and are capable of suing and being sued. In most cases such entities engage in commercial activities, such as foreign trade, international transportation and investment. Since they are separate from their national states, courts have much less apprehension in attaching their property. In most jurisdictions, therefore, the rule is that separate entities do not enjoy immunity, either from adjudication or from execution, unless they are engaged in the exercise of sovereign authority.

The US FSIA 1976 draws a clear distinction between the property of a foreign state and the property of an agency or instrumentality of a foreign state in relation to post-judgment attachment. Section 1610(b) provides:

> any property in the United States of an agency or instrumentality of a foreign state engaged in commercial activity in the United States shall not be immune from attachment in aid of execution, or from execution … if – … (2) the judgment relates to a claim for which the agency or instrumentality is not immune … regardless of whether the property is or was involved in the act upon which the claim is based.

Thus, so long as 'the judgment relates to a claim for which the agency or instrumentality is not immune' under the FSIA, then execution can be carried out against 'any property, commercial and non-commercial, of the agency or instrumentality',[63] 'regardless of whether the property is or was involved in the act upon which the claim is based'. By contrast, execution against the property of the foreign state itself can only take place when 'the property is or was used for the commercial activity upon which the claim is based' (section 1610(a)(2)). In addition, whereas the

---

[62] See Schreuer, n. 34 above, 36; Peter D. Trooboff, 'Foreign State Immunity: Emerging Consensus on Principles' (1986-V) 200 *Recueil des Cours: Collected Courses of the Hague Academy of International Law* 235 at 388.

[63] US House of Representatives, *Legislative History of the FSIA*, Report No. 94-1487, n. 28 above, 29.

property of a foreign state can be targeted only if it is 'used for a commercial activity in the United States' (section 1610(a)), '*any* property of an agency or instrumentality of a foreign State' (emphasis added) can be attached, regardless of its use, provided that the separate entity is 'engaged in commercial activity in the United States'.

Under the UK SIA1978, a 'separate entity', namely, an entity 'which is distinct from the executive organs of the government of the State and capable of suing or being sued', is excluded from the definition of a 'State' (section 14(1)), so that the immunity of a foreign state is as a matter of principle not available to a separate entity, which is immune only with respect to 'anything done by it in the exercise of sovereign authority' (section 14(2)).[64] Thus, if a separate entity is not immune from adjudication, then its property will not be immune from enforcement measures either. This provision gives effect to the ECSI, which provides that 'the expression "Contracting State" shall not include any legal entity of a Contracting State which is distinct therefrom and is capable of suing or being sued, even if that entity has been entrusted with public functions' (Article 27(1)), and that a separate entity is immune only 'in respect of acts performed by the entity in the exercise of sovereign authority (*acta jure imperii*)' (Article 27(2)).

Of course, because of their separate legal personalities, the property of a separate entity cannot be attached to satisfy a judgment against the foreign state itself, and vice versa.[65]

---

[64] See similar provisions in SIA 1979, s. 16(1)(2) (Singapore); SIO 1981, s. 15(1)(2) (Pakistan); FSIA 1981, ss. 1(2) and 15(1) (South Africa); FSIA 1985, s. 35 (Australia). Under the Canadian SIA 1982, the term 'foreign state' includes 'any agency of the foreign state' that is 'an organ of the foreign state but that is separate from the foreign state' (s. 2); however, an 'agency of a foreign State' is, unlike the state itself, subject to injunctive relief (s. 11(3)), attachment, execution, arrest, detention, seizure and forteiture (s. 12(2)), and penalty or fine (s. 13(2)).

[65] *First National City Bank v Banco para el Comercio Exterior de Cuba*, 462 U.S. 611, 626–7 (1983), 80 ILR 566, 576–7, US Supreme Court; *Letelier v Republic of Chile and Linea Aerea Nacional-Chile*, 748 F.2d 790, 794–5 (2d Cir. 1984), 79 ILR 561, Court of Appeals for the Second Circuit (US); *Hercaire International, Inc. v Argentina*, 821 F.2d 559, 565 (11th Cir. 1987), 98 ILR 48, Court of Appeals for the Eleventh Circuit (US).

12.7 IMMUNITY FROM PRE-JUDGMENT MEASURES

As mentioned previously, pre-judgment measures are those taken before the judgment is rendered. That is, they may be taken at a time when the court has just denied immunity from adjudication to the defendant foreign state and proceeded to consider the merits of the case, or while the court is actively considering the issue of immunity from adjudication, or even at the very start of litigation, well before the court actually starts considering the issue of immunity from adjudication. The purpose of such measures is to ensure that the defendant has enough assets within the court's jurisdiction to satisfy an eventual judgment against him. Such measures may take the form of an injunction, in other words, an order that imposes some restrictions on the action of the defendant, such as preventing him from moving certain assets out of the jurisdiction, or of an attachment order, which freezes certain assets of the defendant so that they are no longer freely disposable by him. In short, such measures are taken at the start or during the litigation with a view to conserving the objective of that litigation so that the interests of a potentially successful claimant can be safeguarded. They are thus only of an 'interim' or 'provisional' nature and do not prejudge the outcome on the merits: a claimant may successfully obtain pre-judgment measures but later lose the case on the merits. Unsurprisingly, these measures are commonly referred to as 'interim relief', 'interim measures', 'provisional measures', 'interlocutory measures', 'preventive measures', 'conservatory measures' or 'safeguarding measures', and so on.

One can at once see that, apart from the particular timing of these measures, namely, any time *before* the judgment is rendered, they are little different to those measures that courts regularly take for the execution of their judgments. Such measures therefore constitute a use of the court's *enforcement* power for the purpose of securing a meaningful exercise of its *adjudicative* power: they are enforcement measures taken at the adjudicative stage. If, as discussed above, the prevailing rule is that immunity from adjudication and immunity from execution are regarded by current law as two separate issues requiring separate considerations, and that therefore loss of immunity from adjudication does not necessarily entail loss of immunity from enforcement, then to allow the taking of enforcement measures while the issue of immunity from enforcement lies in the relatively distant future marks a significant departure from that rule. Now, because pre-judgment measures are enforcement measures taken at the adjudicative stage, the court must at once be satisfied that the defendant foreign state is not immune from *adjudication* and that its property is not immune from *enforcement*. Even though called 'pre-judgment', these provisional measures nonetheless raise questions which are normally considered only at the post-judgment, in other words, execution, stage. Thus, the peculiar nature of pre-judgment measures makes the taking of such measures a particularly contentious issue. So it is important to know what conditions and standards are applied by the courts when they consider the issue of pre-judgment measures.

Different legal systems have developed different standards regarding pre-judgment attachment. The practice in the civil law countries, for example, is that the same conditions and requirements apply equally to pre- and post-judgment attachment. When these courts speak of enforcement measures against the property of a foreign state used for commercial purposes, they often mean both pre-judgment and post-judgment measures.

The Swiss courts, for instance, have long been applying the same test for both pre- and post-judgment measures provided there is a connection with the Swiss territory.[66]

The German Federal Constitutional Court declared that the 'purpose' test also applies to safeguarding (in other words, pre-judgment) measures:

> According to established general State practice supported by cogent legal arguments, assets of a foreign State situated or present within the State of the forum cannot be subjected to measures of enforcement *or even safeguarding measures* without the consent of the foreign State concerned, so long as they serve *sovereign purposes* of that State.[67]

In the opinion of the Austrian Supreme Court:

> assets of foreign States serving sovereign functions [are] not subject to domestic jurisdiction. Consequently a bank account of a foreign State could

---

[66] See *United Arab Republic v Mrs X* (1960) ATF 86 I 23, 65 ILR 385 at 391, Ground 4, Swiss Federal Tribunal; *Banque Centrale de la République de Turquie v Weston Compagnie de Finance et d'Investissement SA* (1978) BGE 104 Ia 367, 65 ILR 417 at 424–5, Ground 4d, Swiss Federal Tribunal.

[67] *National Iranian Oil Co. Revenues from Oil Sales*, Case No. 2 BvR 678, 679, 680, 681, 683/81 (1983) BVerfGE 64, 1, 65 ILR 215 at 242, Ground B.III.2(d), German Federal Constitutional Court (emphasis added). See also *Philippine Embassy Bank Account*, Case No. 2 BvM 1/76 (1977) BVerfGE 46, 342, 65 ILR 146 at 167, 181, Ground C.I.4 and 6; 185, Ground C.II.3, German Federal Constitutional Court.

> not be subjected to an interim attachment even where the claim against the foreign State was admissible.[68]

Such is also the view of the Italian Constitutional Court:

> If immunity from jurisdiction does not apply to activities *jure privatorum*, the same must be true for immunity from the execution of a judgment that has recognized a private claim, where the foreign State does not comply with that judgment … This argument applies also to provisional measures, which aim at preserving the guarantee of the debt'.[69]

And the Spanish Constitutional Court:

> It is considered beyond dispute that a domestic court cannot take measures of execution (or preventive measures) against property held by a foreign State on the territory of the forum state where such property is intended for the purpose of supporting sovereign activities or activities carried on *jure imperii*.[70]

In the French practice, the same test is applied equally to both pre- and post-judgment measures so that, in general, the word 'execution' is used to denote both conservatory or interim measures and the actual execution of judgments. Thus, when a French court says that 'the immunity from execution which applies to the property of a foreign State is not absolute and can be set aside in exceptional cases wherever the property seized is allocated, at the wishes of that State, for the performance of a purely commercial purpose'[71] it may very well mean, as it did in this case, immunity from provisional measures.

---

[68] *Leasing West GmbH v People's Democratic Republic of Algeria*, Case No. 3 Ob 38/86 (1986) 116 ILR 526 at 528, Austrian Supreme Court (OGH); duplicate report *sub nom Republic of 'A' Embassy Bank Account*, Case No. 3 Ob 38/86 (1986) 77 ILR 488, Austrian Supreme Court. See also *British Embassy Driver* (1978) 65 ILR 20 at 22 (Austria); *Foreign State Bank Account* (1986) 86 ILR 570, note (Austria); *Radiation Contamination Claim* (1988) 86 ILR 571 at 573 (Austria).

[69] *Condor and Filvem v Minister of Justice*, Case No. 329 (1992) 101 ILR 394 at 401 (Italian Constitutional Court).

[70] *Abbott v Republic of South Africa*, Decision No. 107/92 (1992) 113 ILR 411 at 419–20, 423, Spanish Constitutional Court (Second Chamber). See also 425 and 426.

[71] *Société Air Zaire v Gauthier and Van Impe* (1984) 77 ILR 510 at 511, Court of Appeal of Paris (First Chamber) (France). See also *Creighton Ltd v Minister of Finance of Qatar* (2000) 127 ILR 154 at 155, French Court of Cassation (First Civil Chamber).

The drafters of the 1972 ECSI succinctly summed up the position of the civil law jurisdictions:

> Where Article 26 [of the ECSI] permits execution against the property of a foreign State in the State of the forum conservatory measures may also be taken against such property with a view to ensuring eventual execution of the judgment.[72]

The Australia FSIA 1985 goes one step further by allowing a more generous approach to interim measures. It provides that 'a court may make any order (including an order for interim or final relief) against a foreign State that it may otherwise lawfully make' except for 'an order that a foreign State employ a person or re-instate a person in employment' (section 29).

In stark contrast, it is more difficult to obtain pre-judgment measures in the United States and the United Kingdom. Under the US FSIA1976, 'attachment in aid of execution' or 'execution' can be obtained if, among other things:

> (1) the foreign state has waived its immunity from attachment in aid of execution or from execution *either explicitly or by implication* … or
> (2) the property is or was used for the commercial activity upon which the claim is based.
>
> (section 1610(a), emphasis added)

However, 'attachment prior to the entry of judgment',[73] namely, pre-judgment attachment, can take place only if:

> (1) the foreign state has *explicitly* waived its immunity from attachment prior to judgment … and

---

[72] Council of Europe, *Explanatory Reports on the European Convention on State Immunity and the Additional Protocol* (1972), p. 36, para. 106, commentary to Article 26.

[73] The use of the word 'attachment' makes it debatable whether other types of measures are envisaged by the US FSIA 1976. In practice, an order holding the defendant foreign state in contempt of court has been issued: *Agudas Chasidei Chabad of United States v Russian Federation et al.*, 915 F.Supp.2d 148, 153–4 (DDC 2013), District Court for the District of Columbia (US). It has also been held that 'pre-judgment security' is an 'attachment' under the FSIA: *Pine Top Receivables of Illinois, LLC v Banco de Seguros del Estado*, 771 F.3d 980, 984 (7th Cir. 2014), Court of Appeals for the Seventh Circuit (US).

(2) the purpose of the attachment is to secure satisfaction of a judgment that has been or may ultimately be entered against the foreign state, and not to obtain jurisdiction. (section 1610(d), emphasis added)

Now the obvious difference is that immunity from pre-judgment attachment must be explicitly waived while immunity from execution can be waived either explicitly or by implication. Moreover, the possibility of effecting execution against property used for the commercial activity upon which the claim is based is simply not available for pre-judgment attachment.

Under the US FSIA 1976, the sole decisive factor for pre-judgment attachment is thus an explicit waiver, to which much judicial attention has been devoted. As the statutory language makes clear, the waiver must be explicit, and it must be a waiver specifically of 'immunity from attachment prior to judgment'. Not only must the waiver be explicit, that is, clear and unambiguous;[74] it must at the same time be specific enough to waive the immunity from pre-judgment attachment, even if it does not necessarily have to refer to 'pre-judgment attachment' in so many words.[75] Examples of an explicit waiver of immunity from pre-judgment attachment include a waiver of 'immunity from attachment prior to judgment',[76] a waiver of immunity 'with respect to any attachment',[77] or simply a waiver of immunity from 'attachment'.[78] On the other hand, a waiver clause which states that the defendant 'shall not claim or enjoy

[74] See for example, *Kensington International Ltd v Republic of Congo*, 461 F.3d 238, 243 (2d Cir. 2006), Court of Appeals for the Second Circuit (US); *Banco de Seguros del Estado v Mutual Marine Office, Inc.*, 344 F.3d 255, 261 (2d Cir. 2003), Court of Appeals for the Second Circuit (US).

[75] *Libra Bank Ltd v Banco Nacional de Costa Rica, SA*, 676 F.2d 47, 49–50 (2d Cir. 1982), 72 ILR 119, Court of Appeals for the Second Circuit (US). See also, for example, *S & S Machinery Co. v Masinexportimport and Romanian Bank for Foreign Trade*, 706 F.2d 411, 416, 418 (2d Cir. 1983), 72 ILR 183, Court of Appeals for the Second Circuit (US); *Venus Lines Agency v CVG Industria Venezolana de Aluminio, CA*, 210 F.3d 1309, 1312 (11th Cir. 2000), Court of Appeals for the Eleventh Circuit (US).

[76] *Kensington International Ltd v Republic of Congo*, 461 F.3d 238, 243, 243–4 (2d Cir. 2006), Court of Appeals for the Second Circuit (US); *Atwood Turnkey Drilling, Inc. v Petroleo Brasileiro, SA*, 875 F.2d 1174, 1177 (5th Cir. 1989), Court of Appeals for the Firth Circuit (US).

[77] *Sperry International Trade, Inc. v Government of Israel*, 532 F.Supp. 901, 908–9 (SDNY 1982), District Court for the Southern District of New York (US).

[78] *Venus Lines Agency v CVG Industria Venezolana de Aluminio, CA*, 210 F.3d 1309, 1312 (11th Cir. 2000), Court of Appeals for the Eleventh Circuit (US).

immunity from suit, execution of judgment, or other liability' does not constitute an explicit waiver of immunity from pre-judgment attachment.[79] Nor does a so-called 'reserves clause' in a reinsurance contract, which requires the contractor to deposit a certain amount of 'reserves' with the insurer.[80]

The UK SIA 1978 also draws a distinction between pre-judgment measures (in the form of injunction) and post-judgment execution, and stipulates a similar arrangement to that under the US FSIA 1976. Section 13 of the SIA 1978 provides:

> (2) Subject to subsections (3) and (4) below:
>
> (a) relief shall not be given against a State by way of injunction or order for specific performance or for the recovery of land or other property; and
> (b) the property of a State shall not be subject to any process for the enforcement of a judgment or arbitration award or, in an action *in rem*, for its arrest, detention or sale.
>
> (3) Subsection (2) above does not prevent the giving of any relief or the issue of any process with the written consent of the State concerned; and any such consent (which may be contained in a prior agreement) may be expressed so as to apply to a limited extent or generally; but a provision merely submitting to the jurisdiction of the courts is not to be regarded as a consent for the purposes of this subsection.
>
> (4) Subsection (2)(b) above does not prevent the issue of any process in respect of property which is for the time being in use or intended for use for commercial purposes.[81]

---

[79] *Reading & Bates Corp. v National Iranian Oil Co.*, 478 F.Supp. 724, 728–9 (SDNY 1979), 63 ILR 305, District Court for the Southern District of New York (US); *E-Systems, Inc. v Islamic Republic of Iran*, 491 F.Supp. 1294, 1300–2 (ND Tex. 1980), 63 ILR 424, District Court for the Northern District of Texas (US); *New England Merchants National Bank v Iran Power Generation and Transmission Co.*, 502 F.Supp. 120, 126–7 (SDNY 1980), 63 ILR 497, District Court for the Southern District of New York (US); *Chicago Bridge & Iron Co. v Islamic Republic of Iran*, 506 F.Supp. 981, 985 (ND Ill. 1980), 63 ILR 511, District Court for the Northern District of Illinois (US); *Security Pacific National Bank v Government and State of Iran*, 513 F.Supp. 864, 879–80 (CD Cal. 1981), District Court for the Central District of California (US).

[80] *Pine Top Receivables of Illinois, LLC v Banco de Seguros del Estado*, 771 F.3d 980, 985 (7th Cir. 2014), Court of Appeals for the Seventh Circuit (US).

[81] See identical or similar provisions in SIA 1979, s. 15(2), (3), (4) (Singapore); SIO 1981, s. 14(2), (3) (Pakistan); FSIA 1981, s. 14 (South Africa); and SIA 1982, ss. 11(1) and 12(1)(a) (Canada).

Thus, while execution can take place under other conditions, injunctive relief against a foreign state is only possible in the case of written consent.

Along the same lines, the 2004 UN Convention addresses pre-judgment measures and post-judgment measures in two separate articles. Article 18, 'State immunity from pre-judgment measures of constraint', provides:

> No pre-judgment measures of constraint, such as attachment or arrest, against property of a State may be taken in connection with a proceeding before a court of another State unless and except to the extent that:
>
> (a) the State has expressly consented to the taking of such measures … or
> (b) the State has allocated or earmarked property for the satisfaction of the claim which is the object of that proceeding.

Apart from express consent to pre-judgment measures, Article 18 adds the possibility of the foreign state earmarking the property for the satisfaction of the claim thereby achieving the objective of an interim protective measure through an alternative means. It should be noted, however, that once a foreign state actually took the decision to allocate or earmark certain property for the specific purpose of satisfying the claim under dispute, the state must be taken as having consented to the taking of pre-judgment measures. In this sense the provision on earmarking can be regarded as an extension of the provision on express consent.

Compare the above with the provisions of Article 19, 'State immunity from post-judgment measures of constraint', which provides one additional scenario for post-judgment measures:

> No post-judgment measures of constraint, such as attachment, arrest or execution, against property of a State may be taken in connection with a proceeding before a court of another State unless and except to the extent that:
>
> (a) the State has expressly consented to the taking of such measures … or
> (b) the State has allocated or earmarked property for the satisfaction of the claim which is the object of that proceeding; or
> (c) it has been established that the property is specifically in use or intended for use by the State for other than government non-commercial purposes and is in the territory of the State of the forum, provided that post-judgment measures of constraint may only be taken against property that has a connection with the entity against which the proceeding was directed.

12.8 RESIDUAL ABSOLUTE IMMUNITY: CERTAIN CATEGORIES OF PROPERTY IMMUNE FROM EXECUTION

Both by case law and by legislation, it has been established that certain categories of foreign state property enjoy special protection and cannot be subjected to execution without express, in other words, clear and unambiguous, consent of the defendant foreign state. It may not be entirely accurate to say, in a strict sense, that these categories are protected by absolute immunity from execution. This is mainly for two reasons. First, as a matter of legal principle, absolute immunity is no longer a valid norm in current international law: it has since been replaced by the principle of restrictive immunity, whereby immunity from both adjudication and execution must now be defended and justified by reference to a set of well-recognized rules. Thus the very notion of 'absolute immunity' might prove repugnant to many judges, practitioners and scholars alike. Secondly, as will be discussed later, some exceptions are still allowed, however limited such exceptions and their circumstances tend to be. Therefore, the expression 'residual absolute immunity' is used here more in a figurative sense, to indicate the high degree of protection which makes it extremely difficult, if not impossible, to seek enforcement measures against the categories of state property discussed below.

The first question is why these categories of property should enjoy such heavy protection. One may come up with a host of reasons, such as that they serve an inherently sovereign purpose, that they are the most essential and thus sensitive parts of the property of a state, or that enforcement measures against such property would never be regarded by the defendant state as a purely judicial matter but would instead be viewed as an unfriendly act at the state-to-state level and would therefore have serious diplomatic and political consequences. One may also wish to resort to Latin maxims, such as, for example, the principle of *ne impediatur legatio*, essential for diplomatic or consular missions in the unimpeded exercise of their functions. These, and many more that can be contemplated, are legitimate considerations[82] which must have, in their

---

[82] And the courts are aware of them too. See for example, *Leasing West GmbH v People's Democratic Republic of Algeria*, Case No. 3 Ob 38/86 (1986) 116 ILR 526 at 528, Austrian Supreme Court (OGH); duplicate report *sub nom Republic of 'A' Embassy Bank Account*, Case No. 3 Ob 38/86 (1986) 77 ILR 488, Austrian Supreme Court; *Radiation Contamination Claim*, (1988) 86 ILR 571 at

combined effect, contributed to the current rule affording special protection to such property. On the other hand, it should be noted that, as is so often the case in international law, it is not easy to draw a sharp distinction between the material considerations behind, and strictly legal bases of, certain practice, as there may not be a sharp distinction between 'law' and 'practice'. After all, in the words of the Statute of the International Court of Justice, 'a general practice' could be 'accepted as law'. Thus, for our purposes, once it is established in state practice that certain special categories of state property enjoy, as a matter of law, special protection, it will not be very profitable to question the legal basis of such protection. What matters then is not so much *why* such protection should be accorded but *how* such protection is in fact accorded. This is precisely what this part of the discussion sets out to examine: the requirements and conditions for granting special protection to particular categories of state property.

12.8.1 Diplomatic Premises and Bank Accounts

The term 'property' here covers both movable and immovable property, such as embassy premises and embassy bank accounts. By extension, similar protection will also be available to the property of any other type of special mission enjoying privileges and immunities pursuant to agreement between the sending and the receiving states. The legal basis for the protection of diplomatic property predates and exists separately from the regime of state immunity, in the treaties and customary international law relating to diplomatic immunities. Nonetheless, the law of state immunity further clarifies and thus extends the scope of that protection to items

---

573, Austrian Supreme Court; *Alcom Ltd v Republic of Colombia* [1984] 1 AC 580 at 597, 599, 603–4, 74 ILR 170 at 180, 182, 187, HL; *Philippine Embassy Bank Account*, Case No. 2 BvM 1/76 (1977) BVerfGE 46, 342, 65 ILR 146 at 185–6, 187–9, 190–91, German Federal Constitutional Court; *Kenyan Diplomatic Residence*, Case No. IXa ZB 19/03 (2003) 128 ILR 632 at 635, 636, 638, German Federal Supreme Court (BGH); *Abbott v Republic of South Africa*, Decision No. 107/92 (1992) 113 ILR 411 at 423–4, Spanish Constitutional Court (Second Chamber); *United Arab Republic v Mrs X* (1960) ATF 86 I 23, 65 ILR 385 at 392, Swiss Federal Tribunal; *Italian Republic, Italian Ministry of Transport and Italian State Railways v Beta Holding SA* (1966) 65 ILR 394 at 402, Swiss Federal Tribunal; *Griessen* (1982) ATF 108 III 107, 82 ILR 5 at 7, Swiss Federal Tribunal; *Kingdom of Spain v Company X SA* (1986) BGE 112 Ia 148, 82 ILR 38 at 41, Swiss Federal Tribunal.

such as embassy bank accounts, which are previously not specifically mentioned in, for instance, the 1961 Vienna Convention on Diplomatic Relations. It should also be noted that, in practice, such protection is also extended to consular premises and bank accounts.

The inviolability of diplomatic premises is a long-established principle in international law, longer, in fact that the law of state immunity itself. Article 22(3) of the 1961 Vienna Convention on Diplomatic Relations[83] provides:

> The premises of the mission, their furnishings and other property thereon and the means of transport of the mission shall be immune from search, requisition, attachment or execution.

Section 1610(a)(4)(B) of the US FSIA 1976 protects the immovable property of a foreign state situated in the United States which is 'used for purposes of maintaining a diplomatic or consular mission or the residence of the Chief of such mission'.[84] According to the legislators, such property includes 'embassies and related buildings'.[85] Thus, not only

---

[83] 500 UNTS 95; entry into force 24 April 1964.

[84] See for example, *New York v Permanent*, 446 F.3d 365, 370 (2d Cir. 2006), Court of Appeals for the Second Circuit (US) (citing s. 1610(a)(4)(B)); affirming *New York v Permanent*, 376 F.Supp.2d 429 (SDNY 2005), District Court for the Southern District of New York; *Af-Cap v Congo*, 326 F.Supp.2d 128, 130–31 (DDC 2004), District Court for the District of Columbia (US); *Hegna v Iran*, 287 F.Supp.2d 608, 610 (D Md. 2003), District Court for the District of Maryland (US); affirmed, *Hegna v Iran*, 376 F.3d 226 (4th Cir. 2004), Court of Appeals for the Fourth Circuit; *S & S v Masinexportimport*, 802 F.Supp. 1109, 1110–12 (SDNY 1992), 107 ILR 239, District Court for the Southern District of New York (US); *Gerritsen v Escobar*, 688 F.Supp. 556, 559 (CD Cal. 1988), District Court for the Central District of California (US). The US Terrorism Risk Insurance Act 2002, Public Law 107-297, enacted on 26 November 2002, Title II, s. 201(b)(2), 116 Stat. 2337, excludes from the scope of protection 'property subject to the Vienna Convention on Diplomatic Relations or the Vienna Convention on Consular Relations that has been used in the United States for any nondiplomatic purpose (including use as rental property), or the proceeds of such use; or the proceeds of any sale or transfer for value to a third party of any asset subject to the Vienna Convention on Diplomatic Relations or the Vienna Convention on Consular Relations'.

[85] US House of Representatives, *Legislative History of the FSIA*, Report No. 94-1487, n. 28 above, 29.

consulate buildings[86] but also living quarters of embassy staff members and their families[87] will be immune from execution.

Needless to say, in order for protection to continue to be available, the premises in question must continue to be used for diplomatic purposes.[88] No protection will be available for premises no longer used for such purposes.[89]

The UK SIA 1978 confirms immunity enjoyed by diplomatic missions under the Vienna Convention.[90] The Australian FSIA 1985 not only confirms such immunity in the same manner (section 6), but adds a further provision for good measure; that is, even in the case where a foreign state waived immunity from execution:

> A waiver does not apply in relation to property that is diplomatic property or military property unless a provision in the agreement expressly designates the property as property to which the waiver applies. (section 31(4))[91]

It also defines 'diplomatic property' as 'property that, at the relevant time, is in use predominantly for the purpose of establishing or maintaining a diplomatic or consular mission, or a visiting mission, of a foreign State to Australia' (section 3(1)).

Bank accounts of diplomatic missions are not mentioned in the Vienna Convention on Diplomatic Relations. Thus it becomes questionable if protection by virtue of the privileges and immunities under the Vienna Convention also applies to bank accounts of embassies and other missions enjoying diplomatic immunities. In practice, however, the

---

[86] *Gerritsen v Escobar y Cordova*, 688 F.Supp. 556, 559 (CD Cal. 1988), District Court, Central District of California (US); *S & S Machinery Co. v Masinexportimport*, 802 F.Supp. 1109, 1110–11 (SDNY 1992), 107 ILR 239, District Court, Southern District of New York (US).

[87] *United States v County of Arlington, Virginia*, 669 F.2d 925, 934 (4th Cir. 1982), 72 ILR 652 and 98 ILR 1, Court of Appeals of the Fourth Circuit (US); *United States v County of Arlington, Virginia*, 702 F.2d 485 (4th Cir. 1983), Court of Appeals of the Fourth Circuit (US).

[88] *Kenyan Diplomatic Residence*, Case No. IXa ZB 19/03 (2003) 128 ILR 632 at 635, 636, 638, German Federal Supreme Court (BGH).

[89] *Hungarian Embassy*, Case No. VZR 122/65 (1969) 65 ILR 110 at 112, German Federal Supreme Court; *Westminster City Council v Government of the Islamic Republic of Iran* [1986] 1 WLR 979, 108 ILR 557, High Court (Ch. Div.) (UK); *Lab Chrysotile Inc. v Rasheed Bank* [2003] 127 ACWS (3d) 757, Quebec Court of Appeal (Canada).

[90] UK SIA 1978, s. 16(1).

[91] See also s. 32(3)(a), which excludes diplomatic and military property from the definition of 'commercial property'.

question has been answered in the affirmative, and the rule has been simply taken for granted that embassy bank accounts enjoy absolute immunity from execution.

The general prohibition on execution measures against foreign embassy bank accounts was persuasively set out by the German Federal Constitutional Court in the following terms:

> Claims against a general current bank account of the embassy of a foreign State which exists in the State of the forum and the purpose of which is to cover the embassy's costs and expenses are not subject to forced execution by the State of the forum … preventive measures or measures of execution against a foreign State may not, under international law, be levied on property which at the relevant time was being used by its diplomatic mission for the performance of its official function. The principle of international law *ne impediatur legatio* precludes such measures where they might impair the exercise of diplomatic duties. Because of the difficulties of delimitation involved in judging whether that ability to function is endangered, and because of the potential for abuse, general international law makes the area of protection enjoyed by the foreign State very wide and refers to the typical abstract danger, but not to the specific threat to the ability of the diplomatic mission to function posed by measures on the part of the receiving State … Moreover, for the executing authorities of the receiving State to require the sending State, without its consent, to provide details concerning the existence or the past, present or future purposes of funds in such an account would constitute interference, contrary to international law, in matters within the exclusive competence of the sending State.[92] …
>
> The [defendant foreign state] is … not required to disclose details of its sovereign activity, in particular the exercise of official functions by its diplomatic service. The taking of evidence in that regard would lead to the disclosure of internal matters (for example, the frequency with which the residency was used by members of the mission or by delegations, the number of persons, precise details of the purpose of the meetings), knowledge and review of which would infringe the principle of non-intervention in the exercise of another State's sovereign powers (*ne impediatur legatio*).[93]

Furthermore, according to the supreme judicial authorities in the United Kingdom and Austria, a bank account of an embassy is one and indivisible and cannot be divided into those parts serving private and those serving public purposes, even though some parts of such an

---

[92] *Philippine Embassy Bank Account*, Case No. 2 BvM 1/76 (1977) BVerfGE 46, 342, 65 ILR 146 at 150, 164, 185–6, 189, German Federal Constitutional Court.

[93] *Kenyan Diplomatic Residence*, Case No. IXa ZB 19/03 (2003) 128 ILR 632 at 638, German Federal Supreme Court (BGH).

account may indeed be or have been devoted to commercial acts or transactions. Thus, unless it could be shown that the bank account in question has been earmarked by the foreign state solely for settling liabilities incurred in commercial transactions or otherwise serves exclusively private law purposes, an application for enforcement against such account must be rejected.[94]

In other words, when in doubt, grant immunity (*in dubio pro immunitate*). All the defendant foreign state has to do is assert an abstract danger that embassy functions might be impaired by the enforcement measures. Thus it is now fully established that all diplomatic property, movable and immovable, is immune from attachment, arrest, seizure or any other form of forcible execution. Article 21(1)(a) of the 2004 UN Convention summarizes the current rule by reference to the 'purpose' test:

> property, including any bank account, which is used or intended for use in the performance of the functions of the diplomatic mission of the State or its consular posts, special missions, missions to international organizations or delegations to organs of international organizations or to international conferences … shall not be considered as property specifically in use or intended for use by the State for other than government non-commercial purposes.

---

[94] *Alcom Ltd v Republic of Colombia* [1984] 1 AC 580 at 604, 74 ILR 170 at 187, per Lord Diplock, HL; *Leasing West GmbH v People's Democratic Republic of Algeria*, Case No. 3 Ob 38/86 (1986) 116 ILR 526 at 529, Austrian Supreme Court (OGH); duplicate report *sub nom Republic of 'A' Embassy Bank Account*, Case No. 3 Ob 38/86 (1986) 77 ILR 488, Austrian Supreme Court; *Banamar-Capizzi v Embassy of the Popular Democratic Republic of Algeria*, Case No. 2085 (1989) 87 ILR 56 at 60–61, Italian Court of Cassation (Plenary Session); *Abbott v Republic of South Africa*, Decision No. 107/92 (1992) 113 ILR 411 at 424, Spanish Constitutional Court (Second Chamber); *État C v Dame X* (1998) 8 *Revue suisse de droit international et de droit européen* 643, Cour d'Appel of Canton de Berne (Switzerland). For cases in the United States, see *In the Matter of the Application of Liberian Eastern Timber Corp. v Government of the Republic of Liberia*, 659 F.Supp. 606, 610 (D.D.C. 1987), 89 ILR 360, District Court for the District of Columbia; *Flatow v Islamic Republic of Iran*, 76 F.Supp.2d 16, 22–4 (DDC 1999), District Court for the District of Columbia; *Foxworth v Permanent Mission of the Republic of Uganda to the United Nations*, 796 F.Supp. 761, 763 (SDNY 1992), 99 ILR 138, District Court for the Southern District of New York; *In the Matter of the Application of Liberian Eastern Timber Corp. v Government of the Republic of Liberia*, 659 F.Supp. 606, 610–11 (DDC 1987), 89 ILR 360, District Court for the District of Columbia.

12.8.2 Foreign Central Banks' Accounts

In some jurisdictions, notably the United States and the United Kingdom, bank accounts kept by foreign central banks are placed under special protection. Section 1611(b)(1) of the US FSIA 1976 provides:

> [T]he property of a foreign state shall be immune from attachment and from execution, if the property is that of a foreign central bank or monetary authority held for its own account, unless such bank or authority, or its parent foreign government, has explicitly waived its immunity from attachment in aid of execution, or from execution.[95]

Since, under section 1611(b)(1), immunity is accorded to the 'property a foreign central bank held for its own account', the question arises as to the meaning of the phrase 'held for its own account'. According to the legislative report:

> Section 1611(b)(1) … applies to funds of a foreign central bank or monetary authority which are deposited in the United States and "held" for the bank's or authority's "own account" – in other words, funds used or held in connection with central banking activities, as distinguished from funds used solely to finance the commercial transactions of other entities or of foreign states. If execution could be levied on such funds without an explicit waiver, deposit of foreign funds in the United States might be discouraged. Moreover, execution against the reserves of foreign states could cause significant foreign relations problems.[96]

This does not definitively settle the matter, for then it may be asked what are or can be properly regarded as 'central banking activities'. Since neither the US FSIA 1976 nor the legislative report provides a model list of 'central banking activities', this issue still entails much discussion in the courts.[97]

---

[95] For US practice on foreign central bank accounts see especially Paul L. Lee, 'Central Banks and Sovereign Immunity' (2003) 41 *Columbia Journal of Transnational Law* 327 at 375–91; Joseph W. Dellapenna, *Suing Foreign Governments and Their Corporations* (2nd edn, New York, Transnational Publishers, 2003), pp. 756–60.

[96] US House of Representatives, *Legislative History of the FSIA*, Report No. 94-1487, n. 28 above, 31.

[97] See *Banco Nacional de Cuba v Chase Manhattan Bank*, 505 F.Supp. 412, 420 (SDNY 1980), District Court for the Southern District of New York (US); affirmed, *Banco Nacional de Cuba v Chase Manhattan Bank*, 658 F.2d 875 (2d Cir. 1981), Court of Appeals for the Second Circuit; *Banque Compafina v Banco de Guatemala*, 583 F.Supp. 320, 321, 323 (SDNY 1984), 92 ILR 399, District

The UK SIA 1978 also accords absolute immunity from execution to foreign central bank accounts, though in a different formula. Section 14(4) provides that:

> Property of a State's central bank or other monetary authority shall not be regarded … as in use or intended for use for commercial purposes; and where any such bank or authority is a separate entity [provisions on immunity from execution] shall apply to it as if references to a State were references to the bank or authority.[98]

Since the property of a foreign central bank, whether or not held for its own account, is statutorily prejudged not to be in use or intended for use for commercial purposes, then the property of a foreign central bank, as long as it remains the central bank of a foreign state, is immune from enforcement measures regardless of its actual uses; that is to say, even if the foreign central bank has been engaged in commercial activity and therefore has been denied immunity from adjudication, and even if its property may have been used or intended to be used for commercial activities, immunity from execution is still available, unless the foreign central bank in question waives that immunity.[99]

Court for the Southern District of New York (US); *Weston Compagnie de Finance et d'Investissement, SA v La Republica del Ecuador*, 823 F.Supp. 1106, 1113 (SDNY 1993), District Court for the Southern District of New York (US); *Bank of Credit and Commerce International (Overseas) Ltd v State Bank of Pakistan*, 46 F.Supp.2d 231, 239 (SDNY 1999), District Court for the Southern District of New York (US); *LNC Investments, Inc. v Republic of Nicaragua*, 115 F.Supp.2d 358, 364 (SDNY 2000), District Court for the Southern District of New York (US); affirmed, *LNC Investments, Inc. v Banco Central de Nicaragua*, 228 F.3d 423 (2d Cir. 2000), Court of Appeals for the Second Circuit (US); *Olympic Chartering SA v Ministry of Industry and Trade of Jordan*, 134 F.Supp.2d 528, 534, n. 3 (SDNY 2001), District Court for the Southern District of New York (US); *EM Ltd v Republic of Argentina*, 473 F.3d 463, 485, n. 22 (2d Cir. 2007), Court of Appeals for the Second Circuit (US).

[98] See also SIA 1979, s. 16(4) (Singapore); SIO 1981, s. 15(4) (Pakistan); FSIA 1981, s. 15(3) (South Africa); and 2004 UN Convention, Art. 21(1)(c).

[99] Hansard, Parliamentary Debates, Series 5, House of Commons Debates, 13 June 1978, vol. 951, col. 844; *Banca Carige SpA Cassa di Risparmio Genova e Imperia v Banco Nacional de Cuba* [2001] 1 WLR 2039 at 2044, para. 6; 2051, para. 23, 124 ILR 550 at 553, 561, Ch. Div. (Companies Ct); *AIC Ltd v Federal Government of Nigeria* [2003] EWHC 1357 (QB), (2003) 129 ILR 571 at 586, para. 47, High Court (QB); *AIG Capital Partners Inc v Republic of Kazakhstan (National Bank of Kazakhstan Intervening)* [2006] 1 WLR 1420 at 1435, para. 33;1441, para. 57, 129 ILR 589 at 607, 614–15, High Court (QB). See also

The protection afforded to foreign central banks can also be found in other jurisdictions.[100]

12.8.3 Warships

Section 1611(b)(2) of the US FSIA 1976 grants immunity from execution to the property of a foreign state that 'is, or is intended to be, used in connection with a military activity and (A) is of a military character, or (B) is under the control of a military authority or defence agency'.[101] The Australian FSIA 1985 provides for a general immunity for 'military property', which can only be waived expressly and specifically (sections 31(4) and 32(3)(a)), with a definition of 'military property' that covers:

> (a) a ship of war, a Government yacht, a patrol vessel, a police or customs vessel, a hospital ship, a defence force supply ship or an auxiliary vessel, being a ship or vessel that, at the relevant time, is operated by the foreign State concerned (whether pursuant to requisition or under a charter by demise or otherwise); or

---

William Blair, 'The Legal Status of Central Bank Investments under English Law' (1998) 57 *Cambridge Law Journal* 374, 380–81.

[100] Law of the People's Republic of China on Judicial Immunity from Compulsory Measures concerning the Property of Foreign Central Banks, promulgated in 2005, grants absolute immunity from pre-judgment attachment and execution to the property of foreign central banks. The Chinese text is available at www.gov.cn/flfg/2005-10/26/content_83865.htm. The official English version is available at www.npc.gov.cn/englishnpc/Law/2007-12/13/content_1384123.htm. For comment see Lijiang Zhu, 'State Immunity from Measures of Constraints for the Property of Foreign Central Banks: The Chinese Perspective' (2007) 6 *Chinese Journal of International Law* 67. For further comment on China's position see Dahai Qi, 'State Immunity, China and Its Shifting Position' (2008) 7 *Chinese Journal of International Law* 307. Under the 2009 Japanese Act on Civil Jurisdiction over Foreign States, a foreign central bank is regarded as a foreign state, and the property of a central bank should not be considered as in use or intended for use for other than government non-commercial purposes (art. 19), see (2010) 53 *Japanese Yearbook of International Law* 830. For comment see Takehiro Nobumori, 'Recent Sovereign Immunity Legislation in Japan from a Perspective of Central Banks' (2010) 53 *Japanese Yearbook of International Law* 275.

[101] For detailed explanation see US House of Representatives, *Legislative History of the FSIA*, Report No. 94-1487, n. 28 above, 31. See also *All American Trading Corp. v Cuartel General Fuerza Aerea Guardia Nacional de Nicaragua*, 818 F.Supp. 1552, 1556 (SD Fla. 1993), District Court for the Southern District of Florida (US). See also Canadian SIA 1982, s. 12(3) and 2004 UN Convention, Art. 21(1)(b).

(b) property (not being a ship or vessel) that is –
  (i) being used in connection with a military activity; or
  (ii) under the control of a military authority or defence agency for military or defence purposes. (section 3(1))[102]

These statutory provisions, however, remain to be tested in practice. At any rate, in current international law, the immunity of warships, for example, is a well-established principle.[103] In the *ARA Libertad* case, the Ghanaian maritime authorities detained a visiting Argentine Navy warship, anchored at a Ghanaian port during an official visit upon invitation of the government of Ghana, in implementation of a Ghanaian national court order issued during a private legal action involving defaulted Argentine sovereign bonds. The International Tribunal for the Law of the Sea prescribed provisional measures ordering that Ghana 'forthwith and unconditionally release the frigate *ARA Libertad*', on the grounds that:

> A warship is an expression of the sovereignty of the State whose flag it flies and enjoys immunity, including in internal waters. Any act which prevents by force a warship from discharging its mission and duties is a source of conflict that may endanger friendly relations among States. Actions taken by the Ghanaian authorities that prevent the *ARA Libertad*, a warship belonging to the Argentine Navy, from discharging its mission and duties, affect the immunity enjoyed by this warship under general international law.[104]

12.8.4 Cultural Property and Objects of Art?

Article 21(1) of the 2004 UN Convention provides:

> The following categories, in particular, of property of a State shall not be considered as property specifically in use or intended for use by the State for

---

[102] For explanation see the Australian Law Reform Commission, Report No. 24 (1984), p. 80, para. 130.

[103] See the 1926 International Convention for the Unification of Certain Rules relating to the Immunity of State-owned Vessels (Brussels Convention), Art. 3(1) 176 LNTS 199; 1958 Convention on the Territorial Sea and the Contiguous Zone, Arts 18–22, 516 UNTS 205; 1958 Convention on the High Seas, Arts 8–9, 450 UNTS 11; 1969 International Convention on Civil Liability for Oil Pollution Damage, Art. 11(1), 973 UNTS 3; 1973 International Convention for the Prevention of Pollution from Ships, Art. 3(3), 1340 UNTS 184; 1982 UN Convention on the Law of the Sea, Arts 29, 32, 95, 96, 236, 1833 UNTS 3.

[104] *ARA Libertad*, Case No. 20, International Tribunal for the Law of the Sea, Order of 15 December 2012, paras 94, 95, 97, 98. The text of the order is available on the Tribunal's official website at www.itlos.org.

> other than government non-commercial purposes under article 19, subparagraph (c): … (d) property forming part of the cultural heritage of the State or part of its archives and not placed or intended to be placed on sale; (e) property forming part of an exhibition of objects of scientific, cultural or historical interest and not placed or intended to be placed on sale.[105]

It is not yet clear in practice whether and to what extent cultural objects on loan enjoy immunity from execution.[106] In a case involving the attachment of three pieces of art loaned by the Czech Republic to the Belvedere Museum in Vienna for an exhibition, the Austrian Supreme Court denied immunity on the grounds that the Czech Republic had not obtained immunity from enforcement under the relevant federal law and that there was no indication that the art works served sovereign purposes.[107] By contrast, under the Japanese ACJFS 2009, 'cultural heritage pertaining to the Foreign State' and 'objects of exhibition which are of scientific, cultural or historical interest', 'which [are] not placed or intended to be placed on sale', 'shall not be considered to be included in the property' 'in use or intended for use by the Foreign State for other than government non-commercial purposes' (article 18).[108]

12.9 CONCLUSION

The current law on state immunity treats the issue of adjudication and that of enforcement or execution separately and requires separate and distinct considerations for them. Thus the question whether a defendant foreign state or its property should be subject to enforcement measures cannot be decided solely by reference to the question whether that state

---

105 See similar provisions in Japanese ACJFS 2009, art. 18(2)(iii)(a) and (c), which protect 'cultural heritage pertaining to the foreign State' and 'objects of exhibition which are of scientific, cultural or historical interest' from enforcement or execution, provided that such property is 'not placed or intended to be placed on sale', see (2010) 53 *Japanese Yearbook of International Law* 830.

106 For the status of cultural objects on loan in general see Nout van Woudenberg, *State Immunity and Cultural Objects on Loan* (Brill-Nijhoff, 2012).

107 Case No. 3 Ob 18/12m, Austrian Supreme Court, Judgment of 11 July 2012, Ground 3. The German text of the decision is available on the Austrian Government's official website at www.ris.bka.gv.at/default.aspx. However, for the decision in the High Court and scholarly commentary confirming immunity of cultural objects from execution see Helmut Tichy *et al.*, 'Recent Austrian Practice in the Field of International Law: Report for 2011' (2012) 67 *Zeitschrift für öffentliches Recht [Austrian Journal of Public and International Law]* 170.

108 (2010) 53 *Japanese Yearbook of International Law* 830.

should be immune from the adjudicative process. Even if the court is satisfied that it can exercise its jurisdiction over the foreign state, it must still conduct a separate determination of the issue of enforcement. Artificial as this may seem, current state practice is uniform in drawing a distinction between 'immunity from adjudication' (actually more commonly known as 'immunity from jurisdiction') and 'immunity from execution' (that is, immunity from all kinds of enforcement measures including execution), and in developing separate and independent (though naturally interconnected) standards and criteria for the two immunities. Loss of immunity with respect to the adjudicative process does not necessarily entail loss of immunity with respect to enforcement; and a waiver of immunity from jurisdiction does not automatically mean a waiver of immunity from enforcement, for which a separate waiver is necessary. Even though the defendant foreign state can waive both immunities in one act, there is still the requirement that the terms of the waiver be broad enough to cover both immunities. Conceptually, therefore, a clear distinction between the two immunities has been strictly adhered to in current state practice.

The universally accepted test for execution against foreign state property is that property used for sovereign or public purposes is immune from enforcement and execution, so enforcement measures can only be taken against property used for commercial activities. Of course, the actual application of this test varies from jurisdiction to jurisdiction as courts must consider the case and reach a decision pursuant to diverse procedural rules and case law in different forum states.

Some other conditions have also emerged from the judicial practice. Besides the requirement that the targeted property be located within the territory of the forum state, in some jurisdictions there is also the requirement that connection be established either between the targeted property and the claim or between the claim and the territory of the forum state.

Moreover, some residue of the previous absolute immunity has survived for certain categories of state property, such as the property of a diplomatic mission or that of the military. In any case, if the sovereign use or purpose of the property should be decisive in securing immunity, then diplomatic and military property, by serving archetypal sovereign purposes, should be immune from enforcement or execution.

Also worth noting is the practice, in some jurisdictions, of drawing a further distinction between enforcement measures taken at the preliminary or interlocutory stage and those in execution of a successful judgment. Again further considerations are required.

One can only speculate *why* such distinctions are necessary as a matter of law. What is important, however, is *how* such distinctions are applied by various national courts pursuant to their respective national procedural rules. The state practice at present cannot be described as uniform, owing in large part to these divergent procedural rules. On the other hand, the general trend of requiring a separate determination for enforcement measures and immunizing property serving sovereign purposes seems to have solidified enough to warrant the status of customary international law.

13. Torture, jurisdiction and immunity: theories and practices in search of one another

François Larocque

13.1 INTRODUCTION

That the prohibition of torture has attained the status of a peremptory norm of international law has been beyond question for some time.[1] The torture victim's right to civil redress is also generally uncontroversial and widely recognized in international law,[2] as well as in the domestic law of certain states, either through specific legislative schemes,[3] the general law of torts or obligations[4] and, in many civil law countries, through the normal operation of the criminal law.[5] More controversial, however, is the scope of the adjudicative jurisdiction of national courts with respect to civil claims for torture. It has been contended, at least since the 1990s, that national courts have the jurisdiction to adjudicate civil claims for torture, even in circumstances when the alleged torture has occurred in

[1] *Filártiga v Peña-Irala*, 630 F.2d 876 (2d Cir 1980); *Questions relating to the Obligation to Prosecute or Extradite (Belgium v Senegal)* [2012] ICJ Reports 422, ICJ, Judgment, para. 99.

[2] Convention Against Torture and Other Cruel, Inhuman or Degrading Treatment or Punishment (CAT), Art. 14, 1465 UNTS 85; Committee Against Torture, *General Comment No. 3: Implementation of Article 14 by State Parties*, CAT/C/GC/3 (13 December 2012); *Basic Principles and Guidelines on the Right to a Remedy and Reparation for Victims of Gross Violations of International Human Rights Law and Serious Violations of International Humanitarian Law*, GA Res/60/147, UN Doc. A/Res/60/147 (16 December 2005).

[3] Alien Tort Statute (ATS) and Torture Victim Protection Act (TVPA), 28 USC § 1350; Torture Prohibition Act, RSY 2002, c. 220.

[4] Beth Stevens *et al.*, *International Human Rights Litigation in US Courts* (2nd edn, Leiden, Martinus Nijhoff, 2008), pp. 120–27; François Larocque, 'The Tort of Torture' (2009) 17 *Tort Law Review* 158.

[5] *Sosa v Alvarez-Machain*, 542 U.S. 692, 762 (Breyer J); *Kiobel v Royal Dutch Petroleum*, 133 S. Ct 1659, 1676 (2013); *Prosecutor v Max Joseph Milde* (2008) 92 RDI 618 (Ct Cass. It.); *Ely Ould Dah v France* (2009) 48 ILM 884, ECtHR.

another country, that is to say, outside the territorial jurisdiction of the forum.[6] More specifically, it has been argued that the universal *criminal* jurisdiction to prosecute individual torturers entails the recognition of a corresponding principle of universal *civil* jurisdiction to hold states and their functionaries liable for torture.[7] A related question is whether this putative universal civil jurisdiction with respect to torture, like its criminal counterpart, is inimical to the application of immunities.[8]

The idea that the peremptory prohibition of torture has given rise to a type of universal civil jurisdiction has found some acceptance in the literature, but does not yet form part of the mainstream.[9] It might be that

---

[6] Harold Hongju Koh, 'Transnational Public Law Litigation' (1991) 100 Yale LJ 2347; Benedetto Conforti and Francesco Francioni (eds), *Enforcing International Human Rights in Domestic Courts* (The Hague, Kluwer International, 1997); Craig Scott (ed.), *Torture as Tort: Comparative Perspectives on the Development of Transnational Human Rights Litigation* (Oxford, Hart Publishing, 2001); François Larocque, *Civil Actions for Uncivilized Acts: The Adjudicative Jurisdiction of Common Law Courts in Transnational Human Rights Proceedings* (Toronto, Irwin Law, 2010).

[7] Kathryn Lee Boyd, 'Universal Jurisdiction and Structural Reasonableness' (2004) 40 *Texas Int'l LJ* 1; Jane Wright, 'Retribution But No Recompense: A Critique of the Torturer's Immunity from Civil Suit' (2010) 30 *Oxford J Leg. St* 143 at 151–62.

[8] Lorna MacGregor, 'State Immunity and Human Rights' (2013) 11 *JICJ* 125; Roger O'Keefe, 'State Immunity and Human Rights: Heads and Walls, Hearts and Minds' (2011) 44 *Vanderbilt J Transnt'l L* 999; Christopher Keith Hall, 'The Duty of States Parties to the Convention Against Torture to Provide Procedures Permitting Victims to Recover Reparations for Torture Committed Abroad' (2008) 18:5 *EJIL* 921; Craig Forcese, 'De-Immunizing Torture: Reconciling Human Rights and State Immunity' (2007) 52 *McGill LJ* 127; François Larocque, 'La Loi sur l'immunité des états canadienne et la torture' (2010) 55 *McGill LJ* 81.

[9] Jeffrey Blum and Ralph Steinhardt, 'Federal Jurisdiction over International Human Rights Claims: The Alien Tort Claims Act after *Filártiga v Peña-Irala*' (1981) 22 *Harv Int'l LJ* 53; *Restatement (Third) of the Foreign Relations Law of the United States* (St Paul, MN, ALI Publishers, 1987), s. 404; Brief of the *Amicus Curiae* European Commission in *Sosa v Alvarez-Machain*, 2004 WL 177036 ('European Commission Brief in *Sosa*'); Beth Van Schaack 'Justice Without Borders: Universal Civil Jurisdiction' (2005) 99 *ASIL Proceedings* 120; Donald Francis Donovan and Anthea Roberts, 'The Emerging Recognition of Universal Civil Jurisdiction' (2006) 100 *AJIL* 142; Lorna MacGregor, 'The Need to Resolve the Parodoxes of the Civil Dimension of Universal Jurisdiction' (2005) 99 *ASIL Proceedings* 125; Kate Parlett 'Universal Civil Jurisdiction for Torture' (2007) 4 *EHRLR* 385; see *contra* Menno T. Kamminga, 'Universal Civil Jurisdiction: Is it Legal? Is it Desirable?' (2005) 99 *ASIL*

the impetus to fully theorize a putative principle of universal civil jurisdiction has been stifled by a consistent stream of national court rulings since the 1990s, holding that the law of state immunity constitutes an absolute bar to civil claims for extra-territorial torture.[10] The implicit conceit of these decisions appears to be that, since acts of torture attract immunity, it is of little import whether national courts possess the adjudicative jurisdiction to entertain civil claims with respect to extra-territorial torture. It is noteworthy that almost[11] none of these national court decisions even attempted to address the logically prior question of jurisdiction before dismissing the plaintiffs' case on the basis of immunity. This line of jurisprudence was essentially confirmed by the International Court of Justice (ICJ) in the case on *Jurisdictional Immunities of the State*, which held that states enjoy immunity at international law in civil claims for violations of international humanitarian law committed by occupying military forces during war-time.[12]

There are lingering inconsistencies between the theories and practices surrounding torture, jurisdiction and immunity, which are perhaps symptomatic of a deeper problem. The community of nations is united in its unequivocal condemnation of torture, yet torture is regularly employed with impunity in prison cells, interrogation rooms and so-called 'black-sites' throughout the world. Torture survivors and victims' families are explicitly entitled to a range of civil remedies for pain, suffering and death, yet in the vast majority of cases, they are denied justice and access

---

Proceedings 123; Curtis A. Bradley, 'Universal Jurisdiction and US Law' (2001) *U Chi. Legal Forum* 323; Eugene Kontorovich, 'The Piracy Analogy: Modern Universal Jurisdiction's Hollow Foundation' (2004) 45 *Harv. Int'l LJ* 183.

10 *Al-Adsani v Kuwait* (1995) 103 ILR 420, QB, aff'd (1996) 107 ILR 536, CA; *Al-Adsani v United Kingdom* (2001) 34 EHRR 273; *Arar v Syrian Republic* [2005] OJ No. 752, SCJ; *Bouzari v Islamic Republic of Iran* [2002] OJ No. 1624, SCJ, aff'd (2004) 71 OR (3d) 675, CA; *Mitchell v Al-Dali*, Case No. A2 2004/0489, QB, aff'd *sub nom Jones v Saudi-Arabia* [2004] EWCA Civ 1394, varied [2006] UKHL 26; *Jones and others v United Kingdom*, Application Nos 34356/06 and 40528/06, ECtHR, 14 January 2014; *Fang and others v Jiang Zemin and others* (2007) NZAR 420, HC; *Steen v Islamic Republic of Iran* 2011 ONSC 6464 aff'd 2013 ONCA 30; *Kazemi (Estate of) v Islamic Republic of Iran* 2011 QCCS 196, varied *sub nom Islamic Republic of Iran v Hashemi* 2012 QCCA 1449, aff'd *sub nom Kazemi Estate v Islamic Republic of Iran* 2014 SCC 62.

11 *Bouzari*, n. 10 above, 2002; see also *Saleh v United Arab Emirates* (2003) 15 CCLT (3d) 231, SCJO (claim for extra-territorial torture dismissed for lack of real and substantial connection to Ontario without raising state immunity).

12 *Jurisdictional Immunities of the State (Germany v Italy: Greece Intervening)* [2012] ICJ Reports 99, ICJ.

to a court of law for the determination of their rights. The prohibition of torture at international law forms part of the theoretically inviolable and hierarchically superior *jus cogens*, yet its civil enforcement is routinely eschewed on the basis of ordinary and hierarchically inferior *jus dispositivum*, such as state immunity. The unhappy disconnect between the legal prohibition of torture (what *ought* to be done) and the real-world impunity surrounding torture (what is *actually* done) is a particularly troubling type of performative contradiction, because it not only risks invalidating the prescription itself, but also threatens the integrity of the international legal system as a whole. The enduring malaise of international law is its propensity to repudiate its own effectiveness.

Were the consequences of international law's self-denying tendencies are purely theoretical, they would matter a great deal more to academic lawyers than to anyone else. But the reality is quite another. By failing to walk its own talk in the area of human rights, the international law of human rights is failing the individuals it purports to protect: the tormented and battered men, women and children who have suffered or died from state sanctioned abuse. Instead of finding relief or vindication in the law, torture victims and survivors' families have been systemically turned away by an international legal system that prioritizes the impersonal dignity of sovereign states over the inherent dignity of the human person. Where torture, jurisdiction and immunity are concerned, international law is quite tragically a 'travesty'.[13] Indeed, as Philip Allott once lamented:

> Law constrains or it is a travesty to call it law. Law enters decisively into the willing of its subjects or it is a travesty to call it law. Law transcends the power of the powerful and transforms the situation of the weak or it is a travesty to call it law. A legal system which does its best to make sense of murder, theft, exploitation, oppression, abuse of power and injustice, perpetrated by public authorities in the public interest is a perversion of a legal system.[14]

This chapter will describe this sad state of affairs and propose possible paths through the gloom, with a view to resolving some inconsistencies between theories and practices surrounding torture, jurisdiction and immunity.

---

[13] *Al-Adsani v United Kingdom* (2001) 34 EHRR 273, Dissenting Opinion of Judge Loucaides, para. 1.

[14] Philip Allott, *Eunomia: New Order for a New World* (Oxford, Oxford University Press, 2001).

13.2 TORTURE

13.2.1 In Theory

It is hardly necessary to devote much time and space in this chapter to the demonstration of torture prohibition's special status at international law. It will suffice, for present purposes, to recall that the ban on torture has been incorporated in every important human rights declaration and treaty since the creation of the United Nations.[15] In 1986, the Special Rapporteur on Torture, Peter Kooijmans (as he then was) observed '[i]f ever a phenomenon was outlawed unreservedly and unequivocally it is torture'.[16] If any doubts lingered as to the strength of its international legal prohibition, these were surely jettisoned in 2012 when the International Court of Justice finally felt able to recognize the prohibition of torture as *jus cogens*.[17]

The decisions of national courts also consistently express the enhanced status of the legal norms prohibiting torture, and do so with the literary

---

[15] Universal Declaration on Human Rights, adopted 10 December 1948, UNGA Res 217 A(III), Art. 5; Geneva Conventions (I)–(IV), Common Art. 3 adopted 12 August 1949, entered into force 21 October 1950, (I) 75 UNTS 31; (II) 75 UNTS 85; (III) 75 UNTS 135; (IV) 75 UNTS 287; European Convention for the Protection of Human Rights and Fundamental Freedoms (ECHR), Art. 3, adopted 4 November 1950, entered into force 3 September 1953, ETS 5, 213 UNTS 221; International Covenant on Civil and Political Rights, Art. 7, adopted 16 December 1966, entered into force 23 March 1976, 999 UNTS 171; American Convention on Human Rights, Art. 5, adopted 21 November 1969, entered into force 18 July 1978, OAS Treaty Series No. 36, 1144 UNTS 123; Declaration on the Protection of All Persons from Being Subjected to Torture and Other Cruel, Inhuman or Degrading Treatment or Punishment, 30 UN GAOR Supp. (No. 34) at 91, UN Doc. A/10034 (1975); African Charter on Human and Peoples' Rights, Art. 5, adopted 27 June 1981, entered into force 21 October 1986, CAB/LEG/ 67/3 rev. 5, 21 ILM 58; Convention Against Torture and Other Cruel, Inhuman or Degrading Treatment or Punishment (CAT), Art. 14, adopted 10 December 1984, entered into force 26 June 1987, 1465 UNTS 85; Arab Charter on Human Rights, Art. 8, adopted 22 May 22 2004, entered into force 15 March 2008, (2005) 12 IHHR 893,; ASEAN Human Rights Declaration, Art. 14, adopted 18 November 2012, available at www.refworld.org/docid/50c9fea82.html.

[16] Peter Kooijmans, *Report of the Special Rapporteur on Torture and other Cruel, Inhumane or Degrading Treatment or Punishment*, E/CN.4/1986/15 (19 February 1986), p. 3.

[17] *Obligation to Prosecute or Extradite*, n. 1 above, para. 99.

gravitas that characterizes much of Western international legal writing.[18] Indeed, one of the striking features of the national jurisprudence in civil proceedings with respect to torture is the lyrical tone of the prose used to describe its unlawfulness. Consider, for example, Judge Kaufman's famous dictum that 'the torturer has become, like the pirate and the slave trader before him, *hostis humani generis*, an enemy of all mankind'.[19] In that sentence, one of many poetic crescendos in a self-consciously historic decision, Judge Kaufman equated torture to other forms of egregious abuses – piracy and slavery – in order to convey the normative weight and scope he understood the torture prohibition to possess.

Even in those cases where the immunity of the torturing state or state official is ultimately upheld and the plaintiff denied a remedy, judges couch their decisions in the lexicon of moral aversion, perhaps to express genuine sympathy with the claimants, but also to convey the symbolic importance of the international proscription of torture. For example, the decision of the Quebec Court of Appeal in Kazemi opens with a lapidary assertion: 'Torture of a human being is evil and abhorrent'.[20] The Supreme Court of Canada also referred to acts of torture suffered by Zahra Kazemi as 'a tragedy', 'horrific', 'atrocious' and 'shock[ing] the conscience'.[21]

These statements, however, pale in comparison with the House of Lords' positively epic characterizations of the torture prohibition at common law. In *A(FC) and others v Secretary of State for the Home Department (No. 2)*, a case on the admissibility in English courts of evidence obtained through torture, the Lords each expressed in their own words (though Lord Carswell found some inspiration in Tennyson) the nature of the common law's absolute revulsion of torture and of its poisoned fruits.[22] In a rare display of Blackstonian hubris, Lord Hoffman described the special nature of the torture prohibition in English law as follows:

> Just as the writ of *habeas corpus* is not only a special (and nowadays infrequent) remedy for challenging unlawful detention but also carries a symbolic significance as a touchstone of English liberty which influences the

---

[18] Philip Allott, 'Language, Method and the Nature of International Law' (1971) 45 *BYIL* 70.

[19] *Filártiga,* n. 1 above, 890.

[20] *Kazemi* (2012), n. 10 above, para. 7.

[21] *Kazemi* (2014), n. 10 above, paras, 1, 3 and 95.

[22] *A(FC) and others v Secretary of State for the Home Department (No. 2)* [2005] UKHL 71, paras 11–12 (Lord Bingham), paras 64–5 (Lord Nicholls), para. 100 (Lord Hope), para. 129 (Lord Rodger), para. 146–52 (Lord Carswell).

> rest of our law, so the rejection of torture by the common law has a special iconic importance as the touchstone of a humane and civilised legal system. Not only that: the abolition of torture, which was used by the state in Elizabethan and Jacobean times to obtain evidence admitted in trials before the court of Star Chamber, was achieved as part of the great constitutional struggle and civil war which made the government subject to the law. Its rejection has a constitutional resonance for the English people which cannot be overestimated.[23]

So it is that the torture prohibition at international and domestic law enjoys an 'iconic' and 'constitutional resonance'.[24] It is, *in theory*, one of the hallmarks of modernity and the basic expression of humanity's highest aspirations to live free from fear and violence.

Jeremy Waldron proposes that the prohibition of torture can be conceptualized as a 'legal archetype', not in the Lockean or Jungian sense, but in a manner more akin to a Dworkininan principle.[25] As a legal archetype, the prohibition of torture operates in the background and foreground of a given legal system, alongside other positive legal rules, epitomizing a fundamental policy that is emblematic of the entire *corpus juris*. Viewed in this light, the universal stance against torture can be understood as the normative distillation of a common understanding about the very nature of the rule of law, a deeply-felt intuition that law, not violence, is the surest way forward for humanity. Waldron puts it this way:

> Law is not brutal in its operation. Law is not savage. Law does not rule through abject fear and terror, or by breaking the will of those whom it confronts. If law is forceful or coercive, it gets its way by nonbrutal methods which respect rather than mutilate the dignity and agency of those who are its subjects. The idea is that even where law has to operate forcefully, there will not be the connection that has existed in other times or places between law and brutality. People may fear and be deterred by legal sanctions; they may dread lawsuits; they may even on occasion be forced by legal means or legally empowered officials to do things or go places against their will. But even when this happens, they will not be herded like cattle or broken like horses; they will not be beaten like dumb animals or treated as bodies to be

23 *Ibid.* para. 83 (Lord Hoffman).

24 *Ibid.* Indeed, many countries have included the torture prohibition in their constitutional bill of rights. See for example, Canadian Charter of Rights and Freedoms, s. 12; Constitution of the United States of America, Eighth Amendment; Constitution of the Islamic Republic of Iran, art. 38; South African Bill of Rights, art. 12.

25 Jeremy Waldron, 'Torture and Positive Law: Jurisprudence for the White House' (2005) 105 *Columbia Law Review* 1681 at 1718–28.

> manipulated. Instead, there will be an enduring connection between the spirit of law and respect for human dignity, respect for human dignity even in extremis, where law is at its most forceful and its subjects at their most vulnerable. I think the rule against torture functions as an archetype of this very general policy.

Like Lord Hoffman, Waldron compares the iconic significance of the ban on torture to the writ of habeas corpus,[26] and also (perhaps less convincingly) to the US Constitution's Second Amendment and to ground-breaking precedents like *Brown v Board of Education* and *Donoghue v Stephenson.*[27] One might add *Marbury v Madison* and *Edwards v Canada*[28] to the list of Anglo-North-American jurisprudential archetypes. As dominant features of the legal system, the effect of legal archetypes is to exert a gravitational force on every other rule, pulling them into their orbit and controlling their development. Or, to borrow Lord Hoffman's phrasing, the torture prohibition 'carries a symbolic significance … which influences the rest of our law'.[29]

13.2.2 Torture in Practice

Noting the universal abhorrence with which torture is viewed, Judge Kaufman commented in *Filártiga* that the 'prohibition of torture is often honoured in the breach'.[30] Shakespearean distortion aside,[31] His Honour's point is that, despite its international condemnation, torture is

---

[26] *Ibid.* 1724–6.

[27] *Brown v Board of Education*, 347 U.S. 483 (1954) (desegregating US schools and discrediting all legally sanctioned forms of racial discrimination); *Donoghue v Stephenson* [1932] AC 562, HL (establishing a general principle of duty of care in the private law of negligence).

[28] *Marbury v Madison*, 5 U.S. (Cranch.) 137 (1803) (establishing the judiciary's power to declare the law and interpret the Constitution); *Edwards v Canada* [1930] AC 124, PC (establishing the 'living tree' doctrine of constitutional interpretation for Canada and recognizing women as 'persons').

[29] *A(FC)*, n. 22 above.

[30] *Filártiga,* n. 1 above, 884, n. 15.

[31] Judge Kaufman's phrase was almost certainly inspired from a passage in *Hamlet* (Act 1, scene IV) in which the titular character laments his uncle's excessive drinking habits: 'But to my mind, though I am native here, and to the manner born, it is a custom more honor'd in the breach than the observance'. Hamlet means, with respect to a vile or bad custom, that it is more honourable to disregard the practice. Judge Kaufman used the sentence to mean the exact opposite, namely, that the torture prohibition is a honourable custom that is unfortunately often ignored.

routinely resorted to in every corner of the world, either to elicit statements and confessions or to punish and intimidate. Sometimes torture occurs on the zealous initiative of sadistic lower level officials, other times as a result of a direct order from high-ranking superiors. As Amnesty International acknowledges, 'a comprehensive and categorical statistical assessment of the global scale of torture is impossible'.[32] However, between January 2009 and May 2013, the organization received 'reports of torture and other ill-treatment committed by state officials in 141 countries, and from every world region', with most cases originating from countries that are party to the Convention Against Torture (CAT).[33]

This paradox is exacerbated by the fact that the practice of torture is by no means limited to the dark, damp dungeons of failed states and rogue regimes. Sadly, the use of torture has become a dishonourable stain on the constitutions of democratic states that, since 11 September 2001, regularly sacrifice fundamental human rights on the altar of national security. Waldron forcefully decried the 'dishonour' the United States brought upon itself in Abu Ghraib and Guantanamo, and further noted that 'the use of torture has in recent decades disfigured the security polices of France (in Algeria), Britain (in Northern Ireland), Israel (in the Occupied Territories), and now the United States (in Iraq, Afghanistan, and Cuba)'.[34]

It is a distinctively twenty-first century phenomenon that those states that use torture also adamantly deny it[35] or, more often, attempt to legally characterize their methods as amounting to something less than torture. This phenomenon is perhaps, as Koskenniemi warned, a consequence of international human rights law's post-war descent into the mainstream of

---

32 Amnesty International, *Torture in 2014: 30 Years of Broken Promises* (2014), p. 10. Report available at www.amnesty.org/en/documents/ACT40/004/2014/en/

33 *Ibid.*

34 Waldron, n. 25 above, 1681, 1684. In light of the actions of its peacekeeping force in Somalia, Canada can also claim its own place in this league. For an overview of the misconduct of Canadian soldiers in Somalia and of the subsequent enquiry and proceedings, see www.cbc.ca/archives/categories/war-conflict/peacekeeping/the-somalia-affair/topic-the-somalia-affair.html. Canada is also alleged to have facilitated the torture of prisoners in Afghanistan. See www.theglobeandmail.com/news/politics/canada-complicit-in-torture-of-innocent-afghans-diplomat-says/article1347481.

35 'That states engage in official torture cannot be doubted … all that engage in torture deny it': *Siderman de Blake v Republic of Argentina*, 965 F.2d 699, 717 (9th Cir. 1992).

positivism.[36] By codifying the prohibition of torture in treaties and statutes, and by providing definitions of what torture *is*, we have unwittingly opened the possibility of delineating what it is *not*. Human rights treaties and statutes, including those relating to torture, are inherently vulnerable to 'analytic distinctions whose one social function is the legitimation of oppressive practices through the strategy of the exception: once you define a right, you delimit it. And once you delimit it, you offer a formally valid argument for someone to deny that right'.[37]

The US government's war on terror has provided the perfect rhetorical ecosystem in which arguments defending the use of torture can emerge and flourish.[38] Notable jurists such as Professor John Yoo, then the Deputy Attorney General of the United States, advised the Bush administration that the Geneva Conventions' common Article 3 did not apply to the US military campaign against Al-Queda and the Taliban, and by extension to the treatment of its prisoners and detainees.[39] Similarly, federal Judge Jay Bybee, who served in the Office of Legal Counsel of the Department of Justice between 2001 and 2003, advised the Bush administration on the standards of conduct required under US federal laws and the CAT.[40] He concluded that only acts of an extreme nature specifically intended to inflict severe pain or suffering rise to the level of 'torture' within the meaning of the CAT, and that certain acts might be cruel, inhumane and degrading, but still 'not produce pain and suffering of the requisite intensity to fall within [the legal] proscription of torture'.[41] Official legal opinions such as these received academic support from Harvard law professor Alan Dershowitz who published entire books arguing that the use of non-lethal torture methods could be morally and

---

[36] Martti Kosekenniemi, 'The Pull of the Mainstream', Book review of Theodore Meron, *Human Rights and Humanitarian Law as Customary Norms* in (1990) 88(6) *Mich. L Rev.* 1946.

[37] *Ibid.* 1962.

[38] Karen Greenberg and Joshua Datel (eds), *The Torture Papers: The Road to Abu Ghraib* (Cambridge, Cambridge University Press, 2005); Karen Greenberg, *The Torture Debate in America* (Cambridge, Cambridge University Press, 2006).

[39] Memorandum from John Yoo, Deputy Assistant Attorney General and Robert J. Delahunty, Special Counsel, to William J. Haynes II, General Counsel, Department of Defence (9 January 2002), p. 1.

[40] Memorandum from Jay S. Bybee, Assistant Att'y Gen, Office of Legal Counsel, to Alberto R. Gonzales, Counsel to the President, Regarding Standards of Conduct for Interrogation under 18 USC §§ 2340–2340A (1 August 2002) (on file with author).

[41] *Ibid.* 1.

legally justifiable to extract information from so-called 'ticking bomb terrorists' in order to save lives.[42] Dershowitz further advised that the use of torture in such circumstances should be authorized by emergency court order,[43] a proposal that essentially revives the torture warrants that were historically obtained under the Crown prerogative in proceedings of the Star Chamber.[44] The last torture warrant in English legal history was issued in 1640.[45]

With respect to torture, ours is a time of great hypocrisy. Our theory of torture is not reflected in our practices. Our deeds do not match our declarations. We affect a false appearance of virtue, denouncing and banning torture in absolute terms, while dissimulating an authentic propensity to use it when it is convenient or believed to be necessary. It is a monumental failing, one that can perhaps be fatalistically forgiven on account that we are (all too) human. To paraphrase Romans, we know the law to be good, but we are unable to carry it out. We do not do the good we want, but the evil we do not want is what we keep doing.[46] In our darkest hour, we try to convince ourselves, like Yoo, Bybee and Dershowitz, that torture is the virtuous thing to do, espousing for duration of the argument, a near-sighted and exclusionary view of the collective good. One or dozens must suffer, we rationalize, so that thousands may live. Perhaps a more generous assessment is that humanity is hypocritical with respect to torture in the etymological sense of the word.[47] Perhaps, according to this more generous view, it is not that we

---

42 See Alan M. Dershowitz, *Why Terrorism Works: Understanding the Threat, Responding to the Challenge* (New Haven, CT, Yale University Press, 2002), pp. 132–64; Alan M. Dershowitz, *Shouting Fire: Civil Liberties in a Turbulent Age* (Boston, NJ, Little, Brown & Co, 2002), p. 470. See *contra* François Larocque, 'The Choice of Torture' (2003) 23(1) *Lawyer's Weekly* 4 (2 May 2003).

43 Dershowitz, n. 42 above.

44 Sir William Holdsworth, *A History of English Law* (3rd edn, London, Sweet & Maxwell, 1945), vol. 5, pp. 194–5. See also David Hope, 'Torture' (2004) 53 *ICLQ* 807 at 810–11; John H. Langbein, *Torture and the Law of Proof* (Chicago, IL, University of Chicago Press, 1977), pp. 3–69; A.L. Lowell, 'The Judicial Use of Torture' (1897) 11 *Harv. L Rev.* 220 at 233, 290–300.

45 *A(FC),* n 22 above, para. 12 (Lord Bingham). See also para. 64 (Lord Nicholls), para. 83 (Lord Hoffman), para. 147 (Lord Carswell) and para. 160 (Lord Brown).

46 Romans 7: 14–19.

47 The literal meaning of the Greek ὑπόκρισις is to *under* (hypo) + *decide, determine, judge* (crisis). See 'hypocrisy', *OED Online* (Oxford, Oxford University Press, March 2014).

are incapable of not resorting to torture, even in times of perceived urgency, but simply that we have not yet decided to live up to our own ideals. This possibility will be discussed further in the final section of this chapter.

13.3 JURISDICTION AND EXTRA-TERRITORIAL TORTURE

This section will examine an important inconsistency that persists with respect to jurisdiction and extra-territorial torture. It will be argued that in this area, too, international legal theories and practices needlessly diverge, leading to unsatisfactory results.

13.3.1 In Theory

Jurisdiction generally refers to the authority of the state to make and apply law within its own territory.[48] However, when torture survivors and victims' families initiate proceedings in the civil courts of one country with respect to acts of torture that occurred in another country, they are in effect asking the forum court to extend their jurisdiction to matters and persons situated outside their prima facie sphere of power. The appropriateness of such extra-territorial jurisdiction therefore arises.

In criminal matters, it is well established since *The Lotus* case that international law imposes very few restrictions on the exercise of extra-territorial jurisdiction.[49] Save for the clear interdiction on the exercise of state power within the boundaries of another state without the

---

[48] Michael Akehurst, 'Jurisdiction in International Law' (1972) 46 *BYIL* 146; Derek W. Bowett, 'Jurisdiction: Changing Patterns of Authority over Activities and Resources' (1983) 53 *BYIL* 26; Ian Brownlie, *Principles of Public International Law* (6th edn, Oxford, Oxford University Press, 2003), p. 297; Michael Byers, *Custom, Power and the Powers of Rules: International Relations and Customary International Law* (Cambridge, Cambridge University Press, 1999), p. 53; Patrick Capps, Malcolm Evans and Stratos Konstadinidis (eds), *Asserting Jurisdiction: International and European Legal Perspectives* (Oxford, Hart, 2003), p. xix; Edwin Dickinson (Rapp), 'Harvard Research on Jurisdiction with respect to Crime' (1935) 29 *AJIL Supp.* 429 at 467–632; Vaughan Lowe, 'Jurisdiction' in Malcolm Evans (ed.), *International Law* (Oxford, Oxford University Press, 2003), p. 336; Robert Jennings and Andrew Wattas (eds), *Oppenheim's International Law* (9th edn, London, Longman, 1992), p. 456.

[49] *The SS Lotus* (1927) PCIJ, Series A, No. 10, 18.

latter's consent,[50] each state may, as a function of their sovereignty, extend their criminal laws to extra-territorial matters or persons and they do so on a variety of rationales. Most international law textbooks identify five permissive principles under which states assert extra-territorial jurisdiction in criminal law matters:[51]

> These five general principles are: first, the *territorial principle*, determining jurisdiction by reference to the place where the offence is committed; second, the *nationality principle*, determining jurisdiction by reference to the nationality or national character of the person committing the offence; third, the *protective principle*, determining jurisdiction by the national interest injured by the offence; fourth, the *universality principle*, determining jurisdiction by the custody of the person committing the offence; and fifth, the *passive personality principle*, determining jurisdiction by reference to the nationality or national character of the person injured by the offence.[52]

The various principles of extra-territorial criminal jurisdiction form part of international law as 'general principles of law recognized by civilized nations'.[53] They are both normative and descriptive principles. They are normative in the sense that they permit the use of extra-territorial jurisdiction in appropriate circumstances.[54] They are descriptive in the sense that each principle represents an acceptable justification for the assertion of jurisdiction over foreign nationals in criminal matters, such that they can be taken as 'evidence of the reasonableness of the exercise of jurisdiction'.[55]

Since the coming into force of the CAT,[56] criminal jurisdiction over acts of extra-territorial torture is generally underwritten by the universality principle, though some have argued that international law permitted universal jurisdiction with respect to torture well before 1988.[57] Other

---

50 *Ibid.* 19; *R v Hape* [2007] 2 SCR 292, para. 60.

51 Akehurst, n. 48 above, 152–69; Brownlie, n. 48 above, ch. 15; Lowe, n. 48 above, 336–43; Antonio Cassese, *International Criminal Law* (Oxford, Oxford University Press, 2003), ch. 15; Malcolm Shaw, *International Law* (Cambridge, Cambridge University Press, 2003), ch. 12.

52 Dickinson, n. 48 above, 444–5 (emphasis added).

53 United Nations, Statute of the International Court of Justice, Art. 38(1)(c), 18 April 1946; Dickinson, n. 48 above.

54 Dickinson, n. 48 above, 444–5 ; *The SS Lotus*, n. 49 above, 20.

55 Brownlie, n. 48 above, 305.

56 See the CAT.

57 Most notably Lord Millett in *R v Bow Street Metropolitan Stipendiary Magistrate and others, ex parte Pinochet Ugarte (No. 3)* [2000] 1 AC 147 at 276, HL (*Pinochet (No. 3)*.

jurisdictional grounds, such as nationality or passive personality, might also come into play depending on the particular facts of a given case. The great innovation of the CAT is that it *obligates* state parties to exercise universal jurisdiction over any alleged torturer that is present on their territory.[58] The CAT also requires states parties to investigate and punish acts of torture occurring on their territory (territoriality principle) and at the hands of their own nationals (nationality principle).[59] By contrast, the CAT merely *allows* a state party ('if that State considers it appropriate') to assert jurisdiction in matters where the torture victim is a national (passive personality).[60]

Extra-territorial civil jurisdiction at international law is not nearly as well theorized as in the criminal sphere. This discrepancy is puzzling because, in general, international law views civil and criminal exercises of extra-territorial jurisdiction in the same light, since both types of adjudication amount in substance to the exercise of state power. As Brownlie put it, 'there is in principle no great difference between the problems created by the assertion of civil and criminal jurisdiction over aliens'.[61] Similarly, according to Jessup, '[f]rom the standpoint of considering transnational law there seems to be little reason for attempting to distinguish between civil and criminal cases in determining jurisdiction'.[62]

International law is certainly not indifferent to the exercise of extra-territorial jurisdiction in civil proceedings. For instance, there is widespread consensus that extra-territorial civil jurisdiction should only be asserted where the defendant attorns to the forum or where there is a meaningful nexus between the forum and the claim.[63] The relevant connecting factors are fundamentally territorial in nature, and include the convenience of the parties having regard to their place of domicile, the

---

58 CAT, Art. 5(2).

59 *Ibid.* Art. 5(1)(a) and (b).

60 *Ibid.* Art. 5(1)(c).

61 Brownlie, n. 48 above, 298; Francis A. Mann, 'The Doctrine of Jurisdiction in International Law' (1964-I) 111 *RC* 1 at 43–51; Luc Reydams, *Universal Jurisdiction: International and Municipal Legal Perspectives* (Oxford, Oxford University Press, 2003), pp. 2–3. But see Akehurst, n. 48 above, 170.

62 Philip Jessup, *Transnational Law* (New Haven, CT, Yale University Press, 1956), p. 64.

63 Council Regulation (EC) 44/2001 of 22 December 2000 on jurisdiction and the recognition and enforcement of judgments in civil and commercial matters [2000] OJ L12, 16 January 2001; *Spiliada Maritime Corp. v Cansulex Ltd* [1987] AC 460, HL; *Club Resorts Ltd v Van Breda* 2012 SCC 17; Lowe, n. 48 above, 336; Brownlie, n. 48 above, 297.

location of the evidence and of witnesses, and, crucially, the place where the wrongful acts took place. Clearly, in the context of civil proceedings for extra-territorial acts of torture, the assessment of such factors, in the vast majority of cases, will lead to the conclusion that the foreign country where the torture occurred is the most natural forum. As the Human Rights Committee of the ILA British Branch observed, in such cases, 'the forum with which the action has its closest and most real connection is the forum in which the acts complained of … took place. The relevant witnesses will (usually) be there; relevant documents (if any) will be there; and the governing law will almost certainly (applying English choice of law rules) be the law of the foreign forum'.[64] Accordingly, a flexible approach is needed in civil proceedings for extra-territorial torture, an approach that takes into account and gives appropriate weight to the particular subject matter of the proceedings and that does not insist on direct territorial connections in cases where none could ever exist.

Two related principles are emerging as viable alternatives to the traditional real and substantial connection requirement and could supply an appropriate jurisdictional basis in civil proceedings with respect to extra-territorial torture: the principles of necessity and universality.

13.3.1.1 Forum of necessity jurisdiction

Under the doctrine of forum of necessity, civil courts enjoy a residual discretion to assert personal jurisdiction over a defendant in exceptional circumstances, even in the absence of meaningful territorial connections between the claim and the forum. The objective of forum of necessity jurisdiction is to provide plaintiffs with access to a court in circumstances where it is impossible or unreasonable to expect them to commence proceedings elsewhere. It ensures access to justice in cases where it would otherwise be denied.

The idea of forum of necessity apparently first appeared in Switzerland with the adoption of the Loi fédérale du 18 décembre 1987 sur le droit international privé ('Swiss Act')[65] and it has since been adopted by other

[64] International Law Association, Committee on International Human Rights Law and Practice, *Report on Civil Actions in the English Courts for Serious Human Rights Violations Abroad*, reproduced in [2001] 2 EHRLR 129 at 146.

[65] Loi fédérale du 18 décembre 1987 sur le droit international privé, RS 291, s. 3 ('Swiss Act') ('3. Lorsque la présente loi ne prévoit aucun for en Suisse et qu'une procédure à l'étranger se révèle impossible ou qu'on ne peut raisonnablement exiger qu'elle y soit introduite, les autorités judiciaires ou administratives suisses du lieu avec lequel la cause présente un lien suffisant sont compétentes.'). ('3. If this Code does not provide for jurisdiction in Switzerland and if

countries, such as Canada.[66] During the drafting of the Swiss Act, Professor Vischer, one of the statute's principal authors, described the underlying policy objective of the doctrine as follows:

> A general forum of necessity in Switzerland is offered to foreigners when the absence of this forum has a totally inappropriate effect for the claimant, in the sense of an international denial of justice. The grant of this forum of necessity must be applied in a restrictive way, but its availability stems from the fact that there may always be situations not foreseen by the legislator making it absolutely imperative to provide access to our courts.[67]

In a subsequent commentary, Professor Vischer further emphasized that the doctrine's main international legal function was to prevent denials of justice by providing plaintiffs with access to national courts:

> The negative conflict can lead to a 'déni de justice' for the claimant, if he cannot obtain jurisdiction on the grounds that no State considers its courts competent. It is generally recognized that public international law demands that States should take the necessary precautions to provide respective jurisdiction or order to avoid denial of justice. The European Convention on Human Rights even confers on the prohibition of denial of justice the quality of being a human right (Art. 6§1).[68]

As will be discussed below, however, the right to access a court of law for the determination of one's rights, even fundamental rights, such as the right to remedy in cases of torture, is ultimately weighed against other concerns and considerations, such as international relations and immunities.[69]

---

proceedings abroad are impossible or cannot reasonably be required to be brought, the Swiss judicial or administrative authorities at the place with which the facts of the case are sufficiently connected shall have jurisdiction.' Private translation of the official text by UMBRICHT Attorneys, Switzerland, available at http://tinyurl.com/p76uyg9.)

[66] Quebec Civil Code, SQ 1991, c. 64, art. 3136; Court Jurisdiction and Proceedings Transfer Act, SBC 2003, c. 28, s. 6; Court Jurisdiction and Proceedings Transfer Act, SNS 2003, c. 2, s. 7; *Van Breda v Village Resorts Ltd* (2010) 98 OR (3rd) 721, 2010 ONCA 84, para. 100 (recognizing forum of necessity jurisdiction at common law).

[67] Frank Vischer, 'Drafting National Legislation on Conflict of Laws: The Swiss Experience' (1977) 41 *L and Contemp. Prob.* 131 at 136.

[68] Frank Vischer, 'General Course on Private International Law' (1992) 232 *RC* 9 at 204.

[69] See nn. 110 to 119 below and accompanying text.

While the outer limits of forum of necessity jurisdiction remain to be established, it is nevertheless possible to identify a range of cases in which its use is clearly appropriate. These include tort claims relating to egregious human rights violations instituted by plaintiffs who cannot return to the forum where the harm occurred without risking their lives or further injury. The Court of Appeal for Ontario pointed to the doctrine of forum of necessity 'as a possible basis for jurisdiction' in cases relating to extra-territorial torture, such as *Bouzari v Islamic Republic of Iran*.[70] Torture victims and their families are often unable to seek civil redress in the countries where the abuse occurred because they would be at risk of violence or death or because the judicial systems in those countries are unable or unwilling to process their claims. In those exceptional situations, commencing proceedings in the place where the violations took place is either a practical impossibility or an unreasonable expectation to place upon the plaintiff, or both.

In *Lamborghini*, the Quebec Court of Appeal held that the forum of necessity provision of the Quebec Civil Code applies to situations where proceedings cannot be commenced in the natural forum due to perilous circumstances for the plaintiffs:

> [Article 3136] represents a very narrow exception to the normal rules regarding jurisdiction. It does not allow the Québec Court to take jurisdiction that it would not otherwise have. It seeks to regulate certain problems regarding access to justice for a petitioner who finds himself in the territory of Québec when the foreign forum normally competent in the matter is not accessible for exceptional reasons, such as a legal or practical impossibility, which are almost absolute. In this regard, one could think that the results from the rupture of diplomatic or business relations with a foreign state or the need for protection of a political refugee, or the existence of serious physical danger if one initiated proceedings before a foreign court.[71]

While less-than-perilous circumstances may also justify the assertion of jurisdiction on the basis of necessity, the doctrine clearly applies in cases where survivors of human rights violations cannot sue in the place where the harm occurred without risk to life or limb. Indeed, the entire body of international human rights law, and particularly those conventional and customary norms that have attained the status of *jus cogens*, such as the

---

70 *Van Breda*, n. 48 above, para. 54.

71 Unofficial English translation taken from *Josephson (Litigation Guardian of) v Balfour Recreation Commission* 2010 BCSC 603, para. 89. For original French version see *Lamborghini (Canada) Inc. v Automobili Lamborghini SPA* [1996] QJ No. 4175, para. 44, CA.

prohibition against torture, would be made illusory if there were no court available to apply that law.

13.3.1.2 Universal civil jurisdiction and extra-territorial torture

The other emerging principle that is relevant to the present discussion is universal civil jurisdiction. While such a principle does not yet form part of the mainstream, it has generated an increasing amount of commentary from courts[72] and scholars.[73]

From the outset, it is important to define what is meant by 'universal jurisdiction' in order to avoid any misconceptions as to the scope of its underlying principle. For the purposes of the present discussion, universal jurisdiction is understood as the presence-based adjudicative authority of a state over persons who are alleged to have committed international crimes.[74] As Judges Higgins, Kooijmans and Buergenthal noted in the *Arrest Warrant* case, what by 'the loose use of language … has come to be referred to as "universal jurisdiction" … is really an obligatory territorial jurisdiction over persons, albeit in relation to acts committed elsewhere'.[75] To be sure, universal jurisdiction does not refer to unlimited judicial power over extra-territorial events and persons on the basis, for instance, that the wrongful conduct at issue is prohibited by a peremptory norm of international law. Aside from the discredited Belgian statute that purported to authorize *in absentia* jurisdiction over extra-territorial persons and grave violations of international humanitarian law,[76] there is

---

[72] *Arrest Warrant of 11 April 2000 (Congo v Belgium)* [2002] ICJ Reports 79, Separate Concurring Opinion of Judges Higgins, Kooijmans and Buergenthal, para. 48; *Sosa,* n. 5 above, 772; *Xuncax v Gramajo*, 886 F.Supp. 162, 182 (D Mass. 1995).

[73] See n. 9 above.

[74] Antonio Cassese, 'Is the Bell Tolling for Universality? A Plea for a Sensible Notion of Universal Jurisdiction' (2003) 1 *JICJ* 589; Roger O'Keefe, 'Universal Jurisdiction: Clarifying the Basic Concept' (2004) 2 *JICJ* 735.

[75] *Arrest Warrant,* n. 72 above, Separate Concurring Opinion of Judges Higgins, Kooijmans and Buergenthal, para. 41.

[76] See Loi du 16 juin 1993 relative à la répression des infractions graves aux Conventions internationales de Genève du 12 août 1949 et aux Protocoles I et 11 du 8 juin 1977, additionnels a ces Conventions, replaced by Loi du 10 février 1999 relative à la répression des violations graves du droit international humanitaire, (1999) 38 ILM 918, amended by Loi modifiant la loi du 16 juin 1993 relative à la répression des violations graves du droit international humanitaire et l'article 144e du Code judiciaire (23 April 2003) (2003) 42 ILM 749, replaced by Loi relative à la répression des violations graves du droit international humanitaire (5 August 2003) (2003) 42 ILM 1258.

little practice in support of so-called 'pure'[77] universal adjudicative jurisdiction. In cases where it applies, for example, on the basis of a treaty such as the CAT, the exercise of universal jurisdiction by national courts requires some link to the forum, usually in the form of the offender/defendant's presence in the territory.[78]

As Lowe observed, there appears to be two 'strands' of conduct that give rise to universal jurisdiction. The first consists of 'heinous crimes, such as genocide, crimes against humanity and serious war crimes'.[79] It is the particularly egregious nature of the acts that justify the exercise of universal jurisdiction. The second strand includes serious wrongs for which no redress or legal sanction is likely to be available, owing to the particular circumstances surrounding their perpetration.[80] Piracy and aircraft hijacking are said to fall into this category because they are committed outside the territorial jurisdiction of all states and can potentially involve the nationals of any state.[81] Systemic or social circumstances, such as war-time, civil unrest and governmental corruption, may also conspire to make redress or justice impossible and validate the exercise of universal jurisdiction.[82] Aside from piracy, international law recognizes the use of universal jurisdiction in criminal proceedings for torture,[83] genocide, war crimes and crimes against humanity.[84] Generally, universal jurisdiction appears to attach to crimes that have achieved the status of peremptory norms of international law (*jus cogens*). This comports with an understanding of peremptory norms as

---

77 *Ibid.* para. 45.

78 Institut de droit international, *Universal Criminal Jurisdiction with regard to the Crime of Genocide, Crimes Against Humanity and War Crimes*, Christian Tomuschat (Rapp.), 17th Commission, Warsaw Session (2005), Art. 3b. For a useful summary of national practice, see UN Secretary-General, *The Scope and Application of the Principle of Universal Jurisdiction*, Report of the Secretary-General prepared on the basis of comments and observations of Governments, UN GAOR, 65th Sess., UN Doc. A/65/181 (29 July 2010). See also *Ould Dah*, n. 5 above, 894.

79 Lowe, n. 48 above, 343; European Commission Brief, n. 9 above, 15.

80 Lowe, n. 48 above.

81 But see *Kiobel*, n. 48 above, 1672–5, in which Breyer J observed that piracy unavoidably involves the boarding of a ship at sea which 'falls within the [territorial] jurisdiction of the nation whose flag it flies'.

82 *United States v Yousef*, 327 F.3d 56, 105 (2d Cir. 2003); Willard B. Cowles, 'Universality of Jurisdiction Over War Crimes' (1945) 33 Cal. L Rev. 177, 194.

83 See n. 56–7 above and accompanying text.

84 Rome Statute of the International Criminal Court, 17 July 1998, UN Doc. A/CONF183/9, 2187 UNTS 90.

coextensive with and protective of world public order and of international security interests, the underlying rationale of universal jurisdiction.[85]

The various rationales that form the basis of universal criminal jurisdiction arguably produce equally credible and persuasive arguments in support of universal jurisdiction in civil proceedings. The justifications put forth in support of universal civil jurisdiction tend to follow two distinct yet interrelated lines of arguments. The first line addresses the international legal plausibility of universal civil jurisdiction. For instance, the American Law Institute adopts the view, predicated on *The Lotus* case, that universal civil jurisdiction is permissible at international law insofar as it is not prohibited. 'In general, jurisdiction on the basis of universal interests has been exercised in the form of criminal law, but international law does not preclude the application of non-criminal law on this basis, for example, by providing a remedy in tort or restitutions for victims of piracy.'[86] The second line of argument addresses the broad structural differences and commonalties between criminal punishment and civil redress. One such argument was put forth by Reydams for whom universal civil jurisdiction logically follows from its relevance in criminal matters. Because civil jurisdiction is considered less intrusive, he argued, it ought to apply *mutatis mutandis* in the same manner as criminal jurisdiction. 'The presumption is that if universal criminal jurisdiction is permissible under international law, universal civil jurisdiction is also permissible (*qui peut le plus peut le moins*, the greater includes the lesser).'[87]

The distinguished editors of the ninth edition of *Oppenheim's International Law* cite *Filártiga*[88] and point to the US Alien Tort Statute (ATS)[89] in support of the proposition that serious violations of human

---

[85] Alexander Orakhelashvili, 'State Immunity and International Public Order' (2002) 45 *GYIL* 227 at 255; see also generally, Alexander Orakhelashvili, *Peremptory Norms in International Law* (Oxford, Oxford University Press, 2006).

[86] *Restatement of the Law (Third) of Foreign Relations Law of the United States* (St Paul, MN, ALI Publishers, 1988) § 404 cmt b.

[87] Reydams, n. 61 above, 2–3. See, *contra*, Sir Franklin Berman, 'Jurisdiction: The State' in Patrick Capps, Malcolm Evans and Stratos Konstadinidis (eds), *Asserting Jurisdiction: International and European Legal Perspectives* (Oxford, Hart, 2003), p. 13.

[88] See n. 1 above.

[89] See n. 3 above.

rights, such as torture, are subject to universal civil jurisdiction.[90] While the jurisdiction exercised under the ATS has unquestionably been far-reaching,[91] there is reason to question whether the ATS is in fact predicated solely on the principle of universality. In their concurring opinion in the *Arrest Warrant* case, Judges Higgins, Kooijmans and Buergenthal described the ATS as 'the beginnings of a very broad form of extra-territorial jurisdiction'.[92] The judges stopped short of characterizing the ATS as granting universal jurisdiction, and noted moreover that the US model had 'not attracted the approbation of States generally'.[93] Indeed, the international response to ATS jurisdiction has been variegated.[94]

Moreover, in *Kiobel*, the United States Supreme Court held that claims brought under the ATS were subject to the presumption against extra-territoriality.[95] Under US law, it is presumed that 'legislation of Congress, unless a contrary intent appears, is meant to apply only within the territorial jurisdiction of the United States'.[96] Accordingly, plaintiffs

---

90 Sir Robert Jennings and Arthur Watts (eds), *Oppenheim's International Law* (9th edn, London, Longman, 1992), pp. 469–70.

91 Larocque, n. 6 above, ch. 2.

92 *Arrest Warrant of 11 April 2000 (Congo v Belgium)* [2002] ICJ Reports 79, Separate Concurring Opinion of Judges Higgins, Kooijmans and Buergenthal, para. 48.

93 *Ibid.*

94 For example, Ecuador initially approved of the ATS proceedings in *Aguinda v Texaco Inc.*, 1994 US Dist LEXIS 4718 (SDNY 1994), then later protested in *Jota v Texaco*, 157 F.3d 153 (2d Cir. 1998). Similarly, South Africa protested against US civil jurisdiction in *In Re South African Apartheid Litigation*, 238 F.Supp.2d 1379 (SDNY 2002) but supported broad based, justice-oriented civil jurisdiction in *Connelly v RTZ Corporation plc* [1998] AC 854, HL and *Lubbe v Cape plc* [2000] 1 WLR 1545, HL. See also *Doe v Exxon Mobile Corp.*, 654 F.3d 11, 64, n. 56 (CADC) for a list of foreign states who approved and later objected to ATS jurisdiction.

95 For analysis of *Kiobel* and its significance, see Austen Parrish, 'Kiobel, Unilateralism and Retreat from Extraterritoriality' (2013) 28 *Maryland J Int'l L* 208; Jordan J. Paust, 'Human Rights Through the ATS After *Kiobel*: Partial Extraterritoriality, Misconceptions and Elusive and Problematic Judicially-Created Criteria' (2014) 6 *Duke Forum for Law and Social Change* 31; Anthony Colangelo, '*Kiobel*: Muddling the Distinction Between Prescriptive and Adjudicative Jurisdiction' (2013) 28 *Maryland J Int'l L* 62.

96 *Morrison v National Australian Bank Ltd* (2010) 130 S. Ct 2869, 2877; *EEOC v Arabian American Oil Co.*, 499 U.S. 244, 248 (1991). See also William S. Dodge, 'Understanding the Presumption Against Extraterritoriality' (1998) 16 *Berkley J Int'l L* 85.

who wish to sue in the United States under the ATS must, since *Kiobel*, show that their 'claims touch and concern the territory of the United States, [and] do so with sufficient force to displace the presumption against extra-territorial application'.[97] While the Court was unanimous as to the disposition in *Kiobel*, i.e. that no jurisdiction lay under the ATS in that specific case where the corporate defendant had weak ties to the United States, the judges diverged (five to four) on the usefulness of the presumption against extra-territoriality. Rather than invoking the presumption, Justice Breyer would have limited ATS jurisdiction to cases where '(1) the alleged tort occurs on American soil, (2) the defendant is an American national, or (3) the defendant's conduct substantially and adversely affects an important American national interest, and that includes a distinct interest in preventing the United States from becoming a safe harbor (free of civil as well as criminal liability) for a torturer or other common enemy of mankind'.[98] Arguably, there is no great difference between the majority's 'touch and concern' standard and the minority's reliance on established principles of so-called 'foreign relations law', as both approaches ultimately hinge on showing some kind of nexus between ATS claims and the forum. In short, after *Kiobel*, ATS jurisdiction can no longer be touted as being universal (if it ever was). Rather more reasonably, ATS jurisdiction over extra-territorial violations of international law depends on the existence of meaningful connections between the claim and the territory of the United States. In this sense, the post-*Kiobel* ATS is more aligned with the generally accepted practice and principles that govern the exercise of extra-territorial civil jurisdiction.[99]

In *Sosa*, the European Commission argued that the ATS could defensibly be interpreted as providing for a type of universal civil jurisdiction over a limited set of offences, which included torture, but only if it is exercised consistently with international law and only when the ends of justice so require. The European Commission argued that, 'to the extent recognized, [universal civil jurisdiction] should apply only to a narrow category of conduct and should be exercised only when the claimant would otherwise be subject to a denial of justice'.[100] Under this

[97] *Kiobel*, n. 5 above, 1669 (per Roberts CJ).

[98] *Ibid.* 1671 (per Breyer J).

[99] Eugene Kontorovich, '*Kiobel* Surprise: Unexpected by Scholars but Consistent with International Trends' (2014) 89 *Notre Dame L Rev.* 1671.

[100] European Commission Brief, n. 9 above, 26–7.

view, universal civil jurisdiction could serve a similar function to the doctrine of forum of necessity: while the former is predicated on the importance of enforcing a specific category of international norms, the latter is focused on preventing denials of justice in analogous cases. European support for a cautious, justice-oriented version of universal civil jurisdiction is not surprising given Europe's leading role in the work of the Hague Conference on Private International Law where a version of universal civil jurisdiction was once on the agenda. In its Preliminary Draft Convention on Jurisdiction and Foreign Judgments in Civil and Commercial Matters, the Conference had proposed the right of states to assert broad extra-territorial civil jurisdiction over a core category of violations of international law, subject to the ability of the forum to properly assert personal jurisdiction over the defendant.[101] This proposal ultimately proved too contentious and was eventually set aside,[102] but the favoured approach was in line with the European Commission's submissions in *Sosa*, namely, that universal jurisdiction should be exercised in respect of violations of peremptory norms of international law, in circumstances where the claimant faces the prospect of being denied justice and the claim presents a sufficient nexus to the forum.

The availability of monetary damages in certain countries in the context of criminal prosecutions further supports the recognition of universal civil jurisdiction. Indeed, in many civil law countries, victims of crime are permitted to join criminal proceedings as a 'partie civile' and obtain damages as part of the court's sentence.[103] In his concurrent opinion in *Sosa*, Justice Breyer explained the significance of such remedies in relation to universal civil jurisdiction:

---

[101] Hague Conference on Private International Law, Preliminary Draft Convention on Jurisdiction and Foreign Judgments in Civil and Commercial Matters, 30 October 1999, Preliminary Doc. No. 11. For analysis of the drafting history of the Preliminary Draft Convention, see Beth Van Schaack, 'In Defense of Civil Redress: The Domestic Enforcement of Human Rights Norms in the Context of Proposed Hague Judgments Convention' (2001) 42 *Harv. J Int'l L* 141.

[102] Donovan and Roberts, n. 9 above, 151–2.

[103] Such civil actions are possible in Austria, Belgium, Denmark, Finland, France, Germany, Greece, Italy, Luxembourg, the Netherlands, Portugal, Spain and Sweden. European Commission Brief, n. 9 above, n. 48; Van Schaack, n. 101 above, 143. Canadian courts can also award damages upon sentencing in certain circumstances: Canadian Criminal Code, RSC 1985, c. C-48, s. 738.

> The fact this procedural consensus exists [viz. a consensus that 'universal jurisdiction exists to prosecute a subset' of certain universally condemned behaviour which includes torture] suggests that recognition of universal jurisdiction in respect of a limited set of norms is consistent with principles of international comity. That is, allowing every nation's courts to adjudicate foreign conduct involving foreign parties in such cases will not significantly threaten the practical harmony that comity principles seek to protect. That consensus concerns criminal jurisdiction, but consensus as to universal criminal jurisdiction itself suggests that universal tort jurisdiction would be no more threatening. Cf. Restatement para. 404, Comment b. That is because the criminal courts of many nations combine civil and criminal proceedings, allowing those injured by criminal conduct to be represented and to recover damages in the criminal proceedings itself.[104]

The fact that certain states allow under their laws the award of damages in relation to crimes, including crimes of universal competence, lends credence to the proposition that civil jurisdiction over the same wrongful conduct does not require a huge leap of faith. While the criminal sentence that orders the offender to pay compensation or make restitution is not the same as an award for damages at the outcome of a civil trial, this overlap of remedies reflects the broader point, made by the European Commission in *Sosa*, that 'criminal punishment and civil liability operate with different intensity to vindicate important standards of conduct and deter future wrongdoing'.[105]

13.3.2 In Practice

The assertion of adjudicative jurisdiction by national courts over foreign nationals with respect to extra-territorial violations of peremptory norms of international law is a relatively new phenomenon. Starting in the second half of the twentieth century, a handful of *causes célèbres* stand out.[106] The coming into force of the Rome Statute and the establishment of the International Criminal Court (ICC), which operates on basis of

---

[104] *Sosa*, n. 5 above, 762 (per Breyer J). See also *Kiobel,* n. 5 above, 1676, where Breyer J echoes this point. See also *Prosecutor v Furundzija*, IT-95-17/1-T, ICTY, Judgment of 10 December 1998, para. 155, where the possibility was raised of initiating civil proceedings for crimes of universal competence.

[105] European Commission Brief, n. 9 above, 22.

[106] *Israel (AG) v Adolf Eichmann* (1961) 36 ILR 5, Israel Dst Ct, confirmed (1962) 36 ILR 277, Israel Sup. Ct ; *R v Finta* [1994] 1 SCR 701; *Pinochet (No. 3)*, n. 57 above.

complementarity,[107] have given rise to a further handful of national prosecutions for core crimes.[108]

The idea of civil jurisdiction over non-nationals with respect to extra-territorial violations of international law is still in its early phase of development, and for the moment, mostly limited to the United States.[109]

---

107 Rome Statute of the International Criminal Court, 17 July 1998, UN Doc. A/CONF.183/9, 2187 UNTS 90. Under the Rome Statute, national courts have primary jurisdiction over international crimes (Preamble, Art. 1). The ICC has complementary jurisdiction and may only exercise it if national courts are unwilling or unable to carry out criminal investigations and prosecutions. The subsidiary nature of the ICC's jurisdiction rests on two rationales. First, to avoid inundating the ICC with cases from all over the world, it was decided that states should have the first opportunity to prosecute international criminals, given that it is in fact their duty to do so. Second, the ICC's complementary jurisdiction is respectful of each state's sovereignty. If a state is willing and able to conduct a fair trial under one of the usual jurisdictional grounds (for example, territoriality, nationality or universality) the ICC should not usurp that state's jurisdiction in a given case. In short, complementarity is about deference to a given state's power and duty to put its national laws and judicial system to the service of the international community by prosecuting and punishing acts that threaten world public order. See also Antonio Cassese *et al.*, *The Rome Statute of the International Criminal Court: A Commentary* (Oxford, Oxford University Press, 2002), para. 18.1; Jann K. Kleffner, *Complementarity in the Rome Statute and National Criminal Jurisdictions* (Oxford, Oxford University Press, 2008), ch. 6.

108 See for example, *R v Munyaneza* 2009 QCSC 2201, confirmed 2014 QCCA 96 (accused found guilty in Canada of genocide, crimes against humanity and war crimes committed in Rwanda); *General Prosecutor v François Bazaramba*, Eastern Uusimaa District Court, 11 June 2010, confirmed Helsinki Court of Appeal, 30 March 2012 (accused found guilty in Finland of genocide committed in Rwanda); *Public Prosecutor v Sadi Budingo*, Oslo District Court, 14 February 2013, confirmed Norwegian Borgarting Court of Appeal, 16 January 2015 (accused found guilty in Norway of genocide committed in Rwanda); *Prosecutor v Onesphore Rwabukombe*, *Oberlandesgericht*, Frankfurt am Main, 18 February 2014 (accused found guilty in Germany for genocide committed in Rwanda); *Affaire Pascal Simbikangwa*, Cour d'Assise de Paris, 14 March 2014 (accused found guilty in France of crimes against humanity and genocide in Rwanda). See also *Affaire Ely Ould Dah*, Cour d'Assise du Gard, 1 July 2005 (on the basis of the CAT and national universal jurisdiction legislation, the accused was found guilty *in absentia* in France of torture committed in Mauritania). For a survey of slightly less recent European activity in this area, see Wolfgang Kaleck, 'From Pinochet to Rumsfeld: Universal Jurisdiction in Europe 1998–2008' (2009) 30 *Mich. J Int'l L* 937.

109 See generally Stevens *et al.*, n. 4 above.

Even though the First US Congress enacted the ATS in 1789,[110] lawsuits for extra-territorial human rights violations did not begin until after the 1980 ground-breaking decision in *Filártiga*. Outside of the United States, tort claims for extra-territorial human rights violations remain few and far between.[111]

Despite there being, according to Brownlie, 'no great difference between the problems created by the assertion of civil and criminal jurisdiction over aliens',[112] the guarded treatment civil claims for extra-territorial human rights violations continue to receive suggests that, at least in the minds of certain judges and commentators, there is indeed a difference between civil and criminal jurisdiction. Common objections are raised to the assertion of civil jurisdiction over extra-territorial human rights abuses.[113] For example, the broad jurisdiction exercised by US federal courts since *Filártiga* has been likened to a type of legal 'hegemony or imperialism'[114] where courts appoint themselves as 'the *custos morum* of the whole world'.[115] It is also sometimes argued that such litigation might cause embarrassment to the executive branch and

---

110 William Casto, 'The Federal Court's Protective Jurisdiction over Torts Committed in Violation of the Law of Nations' (1986) 18 *Conn. L Rev.* 467; Anne-Marie Burley, 'The Alien Tort Statute and the Judiciary Act of 1789: A Badge of Honor' (1989) 83 *AJIL* 461; William Dodge, 'The Historical Origins of the Alien Tort Statute: A Response to the Originalists' (1996) 19 *Hastings Int'l and Comp. L Rev.* 221.

111 See nn. 10 and 11 above. See also *Bouzari v Bahramani* 2013 ONSC 6337 (in a fresh claim for the same acts at issue in *Bouzari*, n. 10 above, defendant moved to have Ontario proceedings dismissed on the basis that England was the most appropriate forum).

112 Brownlie, n. 48 above, 298.

113 See generally Jan Klabbers, 'Doing the Right Thing? Foreign Tort Law and Human Rights' in Craig Scott (ed.), *Torture as Tort: Comparative Perspectives on the Development of Transnational Human Rights Litigation* (Oxford, Hart Publishing, 2001), p. 562; Curtis Bradley, 'The Cost of International Human Rights Litigation' (2001) 2 *Chi. J Int'l L* 457; O'Keefe, n. 48 above; Larocque, n. 6 above, 306–13.

114 Hazel Fox, 'Approaches of Domestic Court to the Assertion of International Jurisdiction' in Patrick Capps, Malcolm Evans and Stratos Konstadinidis (eds), *Asserting Jurisdiction: International and European Legal Perspectives* (Oxford, Hart, 2003), p. 187.

115 *Kiobel*, n. 5 above, 1674.

have a chilling effect on international relations.[116] Finally, some commentators argue that even if jurisdiction were asserted, a successful judgment would prove too difficult to enforce.[117] Of course, such arguments can and have been made with respect to universal criminal jurisdiction,[118] but they do not necessarily lead to the conclusion that national courts cannot enforce those international norms that entitle victims of egregious human rights abuses to civil redress, such as torture. Arguably, those considerations, important as they are, point to the need for heightened judicial forbearance, not categorical abstention.

The 2013 decision in *Kiobel* is illustrative. After more than three decades of litigation under the ATS, the Supreme Court has ruled that ATS claims (not the statute itself) are subject to the presumption against extra-territoriality.[119] This in turn has already and quite predictably had the effect of reducing the volume of ATS cases by causing the dismissal of matters deemed to be insufficiently connected to the United States.[120] This novel application of the presumption against extra-territoriality as a limit on adjudicative jurisdiction is perhaps difficult to explain in an increasingly connected world, where people, capital and information cross borders with increasing ease and frequency, but it is a defensible judicial policy that properly leaves the door ajar to the assertion of civil jurisdiction over allegation of serious violations of international human rights. In his terse concurring opinion in *Kiobel*, Justice Kennedy emphasized that, 'in those disputes, the proper implementation of the presumption against extra-territorial application may require some further elaboration and explanation'.[121]

---

116 Curtis A. Bradley, 'The Cost of International Human Rights Litigation' (2001) 2 *Chi. J Int'l L* 457, 461; *Sosa*, n. 5 above, 727–8 ; *Kiobel*, n. 5 above, 1664.

117 Hazel Fox, 'Private Law Damages as a Method of State Accountability: The Tort Exception to State Immunity' (1993) *Third World Legal Stud.* 107 at 118.

118 See for example, Henry Kissinger, 'The Pitfalls of Universal Jurisdiction' (2001) 80(4) *Foreign Affairs* (July/August).

119 *Kiobel,* n. 5 above, 1664–5.

120 See for example, *Balintulo v Daimler AG et al.*, 727 F.3d 174 (2d Cir. 2014); *Al Shimari v CACI International Inc.*, 727 F.3d 174 (EDVA 2013), overturned 758 F.3d 516 (4th Cir. 2014); *Giraldo v Drummond Co.*, 2013 US Dist LEXIS 103981 (EDAL 2013), affirmed 2015 US App LEXIS 4863 (11th Cir. 2015). See also Ralph Steinhardt, 'The ATS after Kiobel', *ASIL Unbound*, 31 January 2014, available at http://shar.es/1gsEnb.

121 *Kiobel,* n. 5 above, 1669.

The exercise of civil jurisdiction over extra-territorial acts of torture is mandated at international law, at least for the 153 states parties to the CAT. In 2012, the Committee against Torture issued its General Comment on Article 14 of the CAT.[122] That Article codifies, *inter alia*, the obligation of each state party to 'ensure in its legal system that the victim of an act of torture obtains redress and has an enforceable right to fair and adequate compensation, including the means for as full rehabilitation as possible'.[123] There lingered a debate in the case law[124] and literature[125] as to whether Article 14 obligated states parties to provide civil redress to victims that were tortured in the forum (territoriality principle) or whether it established an obligation to assert jurisdiction over acts of extra-territorial torture as well (universality principle). It is now clear, in the authoritative view of the Committee, that:

> the application of article 14 is not limited to victims who were harmed in the territory of the State party or by or against nationals of the State party. The Committee has commended the efforts of States parties for providing civil remedies for victims who were subjected to torture or ill-treatment outside their territory. This is particularly important when a victim is unable to exercise the rights guaranteed under article 14 in the territory where the violation took place. Indeed, article 14 requires States parties to ensure that all victims of torture and ill-treatment are able to access remedy and obtain redress.[126]

Despite the absence of any territorial language in Article 14, the Committee against Torture has taken the view that the CAT requires states parties to provide 'all' victims of torture with a remedy through their civil jurisdiction, irrespective of where the torture occurred. It can

---

[122] Committee Against Torture, *General Comment No. 3: Implementation of Article 14 by States Parties*, CAT/C/GC/3 (13 December 2012).

[123] CAT, Art. 14.

[124] See for example, *Bouzari* (2002), n. 10 above, paras 44–55; *Bouzari* (2004), n. 10 above, paras 76–83; *Jones* (2006), n. 10 above, para. 25 (per Lord Bingham) and para. 46 (per Lord Hoffman); *Kazemi* (2014), n. 10 above, paras 140–50 (per LeBel J) and 214–26 (per Abella J).

[125] See for example, Manfred Nowak and Elizabeth McArthur, *The United Nations Convention Against Torture: A Commentary* (Oxford, Oxford University Press, 2008), pp. 492 and 502; Andrew Byrnes, 'Civil Remedies for Torture Committed Abroad: An Obligation under the Convention against Torture?' in Craig Scott (ed.), *Torture as Tort: Comparative Perspectives on the Development of Transnational Human Rights Litigation* (Oxford, Hart Publishing, 2001), pp. 546 and 548; Larocque, n. 6 above, 260–66.

[126] *General Comment No. 3*, n. 122 above, para. 22.

now be argued that Article 14 mandates a broad civil extra-territorial jurisdiction equivalent to the criminal jurisdiction provided for under Article 5, though the Committee could have been more explicit on that point. It is also worth pointing out that the Committee buttressed its interpretation of Article 14 with the underlying policy objective of the doctrine of forum of necessity,[127] stating that a broad approach to civil jurisdiction was 'particularly important when a victim is unable to exercise the rights guaranteed under article 14 in the territory where the violation took place'.[128]

Unfortunately, national courts routinely disregard the views of the Committee against Torture. In *Jones*, which was admittedly released before the publication of the Committee's General Comment on Article 14, the House of Lords was blatantly dismissive of the treaty body's interpretations of the CAT. Lord Bingham characterized the weight of the Committee's recommendations as being 'slight', while Lord Hoffman regarded 'it as having no value'.[129] This aspect of the Lord's decision has been justly criticized.[130] The Supreme Court of Canada took a more conciliatory view of the Committee's work in *Kazemi*, recognizing the Committee's commentaries and recommendations as 'importan[t]', 'useful' and forming 'part of a dialogue within the international community'.[131] Nevertheless, in the Court's view, the Committee's interpretations should not be given more weight than the 'pronouncements of State parties and judicial authorities' and ultimately 'do not overrule adjudicative interpretations of the articles in the CAT'.[132] This last statement is unexceptionable as a matter of Canadian law, but it unhappily undermines the object and framework of the CAT. National courts should adopt the Committee's commentaries and recommendations, not as evidence of some widespread international practice, but rather as persuasive authority regarding the evolving scope of the states parties' obligations under the CAT, with a view of furthering that treaty's

---

[127] See nn. 67–8 above and accompanying text.

[128] *General Comment No. 3*, n. 122 above, para. 22.

[129] *Jones* (2006), n. 10 above, para. 23 (per Lord Bingham) and para. 57 (per Lord Hoffman).

[130] Nowak and McArthur, n. 125 above, 500; Larocque, n. 6 above, 264–6; Alexander Orakhelashvili, 'State Immunity and Hierarchy of Norms: Why the House of Lords Got It Wrong' (2008) 18(5) *EJIL* 955 at 963.

[131] *Kazemi* (2014), n. 10 above, paras 147–8 (per LeBel J) and paras 224–6 (per Abella J).

[132] *Ibid.* paras 147–8.

purpose 'to make more effective the struggle against torture'.[133] The gravitational pull of the torture prohibition at both international law and national law commands as much.

As long as national courts remain unwilling to take direction from the Committee on the proper interpretation of the CAT, the assertion of jurisdiction over acts of extra-territorial torture will be governed by a patchwork of asymmetrical rules that will vary with the nature of the proceedings and the legal tradition of the forum. For instance, if an alleged torturer travels to a civil law state party, like France, he may be both criminally prosecuted and civilly sued under the CAT for his wrongdoing.[134] If, however, he opts to visit London or Toronto, he need only fear a criminal indictment since the courts of those countries will not take civil jurisdiction over him unless the plaintiffs can establish a territorial link between their civil claim and the forum[135] or show some form of legal or practical necessity.[136] With great respect to Lord Bingham, the untenable distinction between criminal proceedings (which are subject to universal jurisdiction) and civil proceedings (which are not) can be 'wished away'.[137] The interpretation of Article 14 advanced by the Committee profitably harmonizes the panoply of possible international responses to torture by applying the same jurisdictional principle to both civil and criminal proceedings, thereby reinforcing the CAT's overarching purpose and policy.

Wishful thinking aside, it may be that the development of a cogent principle of universal civil jurisdiction for torture has been stifled by the nearly unanimous chain of national court decisions since the 1990s, holding that the law of state immunity constitutes an absolute bar to civil claims for extra-territorial torture.[138] The implicit conceit of these decisions appears to be that, since acts of torture attract immunity, it is of little import whether national courts possess the adjudicative jurisdiction to entertain civil claims with respect to extra-territorial torture. That issue will be examined in the final section of this chapter.

---

[133] CAT, Preamble.
[134] See *Ould Dah*, n. 5 above.
[135] See *Saleh*, n. 11 above.
[136] See *Bahramani*, n. 111 above.
[137] *Jones* (2006), n. 10 above, para. 32.
[138] See n. 5 above.

13.4 STATE IMMUNITY AND TORTURE

This section highlights some problems that arise between the peremptory prohibition of torture at international law and the doctrine of state immunity.

13.4.1 In Theory

The law of state immunity can be stated easily enough and the underlying principles are relatively straightforward. Simply put, in its modern form, state immunity is a procedural rule that operates to prevent the national courts of one state from exercising its adjudicative jurisdiction over the sovereign conduct of another state. This broad definition warrants a number of qualifications.

First, it is essential to emphasize that state immunity is a doctrine of judicial restraint that operates as an exception to the primary rules of territorial jurisdiction of the forum. As the ICJ stated in the *Arrest Warrant* case, 'it is only where a state has jurisdiction under international law in relation to a particular matter that there can be any question of immunities in regard of the exercise of that jurisdiction'.[139] More recently, in the *Jurisdictional Immunities* case, the ICJ characterized state immunity as 'a departure from the principle of territorial sovereignty and the jurisdiction which flows from it'.[140] Higgins described the relationship between jurisdiction and immunity as follows:

> It is very easy to elevate sovereign immunity into a superior principle of international law and to lose sight of the essential reality that it is an exception to the normal doctrine of jurisdiction. It is a derogation from the normal rule of territorial sovereignty. It is sovereign immunity which is the exception to jurisdiction and not jurisdiction which is the exception to a basic rule of immunity. An exception to the normal rules of jurisdiction should only be granted when international law requires – that is to say, when it is consonant with justice and with the equitable protection of the parties. It is not to be granted 'as of right'.[141]

---

[139] *Arrest Warrant Case*, n. 72 above, para. 46.

[140] *Jurisdictional Immunities*, n. 12 above, para. 57.

[141] Rosalyn Higgins, 'Certain Unresolved Aspects of the Law of State Immunity' (1982) 29 *Neth. Int'l L Rev.* 265 at 271. See also Lee M. Caplan, 'State Immunity, Human Rights, and Jus Cogens: A Critique of the Normative Hierarchy Theory' (2003) 97 *AJIL* 741 at 744 ('as a fundamental matter, state immunity operates as an exception to the principle of adjudicatory jurisdiction');

As with most questions, it matters where one begins when reasoning about state immunity. As Keitner has argued, by starting from a 'baseline' of immunity, rather than jurisdiction, national courts run the risk of overextending the doctrine beyond what is required at international law.[142] Unfortunately, as illustrated by Lord Bingham's comments in *Jones*, the normative and logical priority of jurisdiction over immunity is not always well understood by national courts.[143] *Ex falso sequitur quodlibet.*

Second, contrary to diplomatic or head-of-state immunity, which are immunities *ratione personae* that inure to certain individuals while they exercise specific government functions, state immunity is a subject matter immunity that applies *ratione materiae* to particular state acts or conduct.[144] The doctrine was once believed to be absolute, mostly by common law courts,[145] but that paradigm has been replaced by the modern restrictive doctrine under which only official or sovereign acts of state (acts *jure imperii*) attract immunity, that is, acts performed in a public capacity by or on behalf of the state. Under the restrictive doctrine, therefore, the characterization of state acts as being sovereign or

---

Lorna MacGregor, 'Torture and State Immunity: Deflecting Impunity, Distorting Sovereignty' (2007) 18 *EJIL* 903 at 912.

[142] Chimène Keitner, 'Foreign Official Immunity and the "Baseline" Problem' (2011) 80 *Fordham L Rev.* 605 at 621. See also *Jurisdictional Immunities*, n. 12 above, para. 55 ('States sometimes decide to accord an immunity more extensive than that required by international law').

[143] See for example, Lord Bingham's misstatement of the law in *Jones* (2006), n. 10 above, para. 14 ('the rule of international law is not that a state should not exercise over another state a jurisdiction which it has but that (save in cases recognised by international law) a state has no jurisdiction over another state. I do not understand how a state can be said to deny access to its court if it has no access to give').

[144] *Pinochet (No. 3),* n. 57 above, 269; *Holland v Lampen-Wolfe* [2000] 1 WLR 1573 at 1583, HL; *Verlinden BV v Central Bank of Nigeria,* 461 U.S. 480, 493 (1983).

[145] *The Cristina* [1938] AC 485 at 490, HL; *Ex parte Republic of Peru*, 318 U.S. 578 (1943); *Dessaules v Republic of Poland* [1944] SCR 275; Hazel Fox and Philippa Webb, *The Law of State Immunity* (3rd edn, Oxford, Oxford University Press, 2013), p. 26. On the history of state immunity, see Sir Ian Sinclair, 'The Law of Sovereign Immunity: Recent Developments' (1980-II) 167 *RC* 113 at 198; Hersh Lauterpacht, 'The Problem of Jurisdictional Immunities of Foreign States' (1951) 28 *BYIL* 220 at 228; Sompong Sucharitkul, 'Immunities of Foreign States before National Authorities' (1976-I) 149 *RC* 89; Peter D. Trooboff, 'Foreign State Immunity: Emerging Consensus on Principles' (1986-V) 200 *RC* 245.

non-sovereign becomes the decisive issue.[146] The proper methodology entails a case-by-case assessment of 'whether the act, by its nature or purpose, has contributed to the exercise of the foreign State's sovereignty'.[147] As will be seen below, the question of whether a state act that violates a peremptory norm of international law, such as the prohibition of torture, can be considered *jure imperii* has been recently settled, albeit on the basis of reasoning that strains both logic and credibility.

Third, the non-justiciability of official state acts derives from the principle of state equality at international law, traditionally expressed by the maxim *par in parem non habet imperium.*[148] Immunity was historically extended as a matter of courtesy and reciprocity among sovereigns and is still understood as 'play[ing] a large role in international relations'.[149] Despite state immunity's 'messy' origins and character (to borrow Peters' evocative phrasing)[150] it is important to recall that the doctrine was first administered and developed by national courts[151] and only later recognized as a rule of customary international law.[152] As Lord Denning MR summed up the situation in 1977:

> Each country delimits for itself the bounds of sovereign immunity. Each creates for itself the exceptions from it. It is, I think, for the courts of this country to define the rule as best they can, seeking guidance from the decisions of the courts of other countries, from the jurists who have studied the problem, from treaties and conventions and, above all, defining the rule in terms which are consonant with justice rather than adverse to it.[153]

---

146 James Crawford, 'International Law and Foreign Sovereigns: Distinguishing Immune Transactions' (1983) 54 *BYIL* 75; Lauterpacht, n. 145 above, 222–6.

147 *Sabeh El Leil v France,* Application No. 34869/05, EctHR, 29 June 2011, para. 24.

148 *Jurisdictional Immunities* n. 12 above, para. 57; *Kazemi* (2014), n. 10 above, para. 35.

149 *Kazemi* (2014), n. 10 above, 38 ; *Jurisdictional Immunities*, n. 10 above; *Jones* (2006), n. 10 above, para. 18 ; *Al-Adsani* (2001), n. 10 above, para. 54.

150 Anne Peters, 'Immune Against Constitutionalisation?' in Anne Peters, Evelyne Lagrange *et al.* (eds), *Immunities in the Age of Global Constitutionalism* (Leiden, Brill Nijhoff, 2015), p. 1.

151 *Trendtex Trading Corp. v Central Bank of Nigeria* [1977] 2 WLR 456, CA; *The Philippine Admiral* [1976] 2 WLR 214 at 232–3, PC; *Jaffe v Miller* (1993) 13 OR (3d) 745 at 752, CA.

152 *Jurisdictional Immunities*, n. 12 above, paras 54, 58; *Kazemi* (2014), n. 10 above.

153 *Trendtex,* n. 151 above, 364.

In the late twentieth century, many countries of the Anglo-American legal world adopted legislation codifying the doctrine of restrictive immunity,[154] while other countries continued to develop the rule as a matter of common law.[155] Interestingly, the courts in many civil law countries, which traditionally favour legislation over judge-made law, continue to administer the restrictive theory of immunity without the benefit of legislation, on the basis of customary international law and their respective constitutions.[156] The US, UK and Canadian codifications[157] were intended to uniformly implement the restrictive principle and to depoliticize the adjudication of civil claims.[158] Unfortunately, the US, UK and Canadian statutes appear to have caused the national courts of those countries to abdicate their traditional law-making function in the area of state immunity.[159] In those countries, being dualist legal systems with respect to the domestic reception of international norms, the law of state immunity has been statutorily frozen in its dishevelled 1970s form and, in the absence of legislative amendment, rendered impermeable to modern-day developments at international law. Accordingly, if any change to customary international law of state immunity is to occur, it must necessarily emanate from the national legislatures or from the less fettered courts of civil law countries.[160]

---

[154] See for example, Australia, Canada, Malaysia, Pakistan, the United Kingdom and the United States.

[155] See for example, Kenya, Ireland, New Zealand, Nigeria and Zimbabwe.

[156] For a dramatic recent example, see Italian Constitutional Court, Decision No. 238/2014, 23 October 2014, where the Italian Constitutional Court struck down legislation intended to implement the ICJ's judgment in the *Jurisdictional Immunities* case (n. 12 above) and to ratify the UNCSI (n. 163 below), on the basis that the statutes conflicted with basic tenets of the Italian constitutional order, including the right to access justice to protect fundamental human rights. The English translation of the Corte Costituzionale's Decision No. 238/2014 is available on the Court's website at www.cortecostituzionale.it/ActionPagina_1240.do.

[157] Foreign Sovereign Immunities Act, 28 USC § 1330 (1976); State Immunity Act 1978, c. 33 (UK); State Immunity Act, RSC 1985, c. S-18.

[158] Larocque, n. 6 above, 243–4.

[159] *Amerada Hess Shipping Corp. v Republic of Argentina*, 488 U.S. 428, 434 (1989); *Kazemi* (2014), n. 10 above, paras 54–6; *Jones* (2006), n. 10 above. It has been argued, at least with respect to the Canadian statute, that Parliament never intended to occupy the field and extinguish the pre-existing common law of state immunity. See Larocque, n. 8 above; Larocque, n. 6 above, 273–5.

[160] Decision No. 238/2014, n. 156 above, is evidence that the law of state immunity remains in flux.

Finally, while the restrictive doctrine of state immunity undoubtedly forms part of customary international law, it is not regarded as *jus cogens*, and its footing in the law of treaties remains precarious. Aside from an early convention relating to immunity of state-owned vessels,[161] the first multilateral convention on the general topic of state immunity was the European Convention on State Immunity,[162] which remains unpopular, having been ratified by only eight European states since coming into force in 1976.[163] The newer United Nations Convention on the Jurisdictional Immunities of States and their Property (UNCSI), which opened for signature in 2004, is not faring much better.[164] Not only has the UNCSI not yet come into force, at the time of writing, only 17 states have ratified it.[165] Moreover, several states parties have filed declarations noting the UNCSI's silence on the right of victims to civil redress for extra-territorial human rights violations and holding the UNCSI as being without prejudice to any future international legal development concerning the protection of human rights.[166] Consequently, the binding sources of international law on state immunity remain largely unwritten.

13.4.2 In Practice

While the basic principle of state immunity can be rather easily summarized, the doctrine's practical application has proven much more difficult to manage, particularly in the context of civil claims for violations of fundamental human rights, such as torture. The practical challenges posed by immunity in such cases stem in part from conflicting views on the doctrine's scope and purpose, as well as from its relationship to other norms of international public order.

Initially an expression of political courtesy and reciprocity extended among sovereigns and governments, state immunity gradually became a

[161] Brussels Convention for the Unification of Certain Rules relating to the Immunity of State Owned Vessels, 10 April 1926 (1926) 176 LNTS 199.

[162] European Convention on State Immunity, ETS No. 074 (1972).

[163] At the time of writing, the European Convention on State Immunity has been ratified or acceded to by Austria, Belgium, Cyprus, Germany, Luxemburg, the Netherlands, Switzerland and the United Kingdom.

[164] United Nations Convention on the Jurisdictional Immunities of States and their Property, 2 December 2004, A/RES/59/38 (UNCSI).

[165] Pursuant to Art. 30, the UNCSI will come into force on the 30th day following the deposit of the 30th instrument of ratification.

[166] See declarations of Finland, Italy, Norway, Sweden and Switzerland, available at http://tiny.cc/anz8wx.

question of law to be administered by the judiciary. However, as stated above, the adoption of state immunity legislation in the United States, the United Kingdom and Canada has caused the courts of those countries to divest themselves of their historical creative function in this area, thus leaving emerging problems and phenomena to be resolved on the basis of stultified statutes. The Anglo-Canadian torture cases are illustrative. The courts in *Bouzari*, *Jones* and *Kazemi* were all asked to interpret their respective state immunity statutes consistently with evolving international norms respecting torture and the rights of victims to civil redress.[167] While the wording of the statutes admittedly do not leave much room for judicial innovation,[168] it was arguably still open to the courts to find an interpretive solution, either by reading-in a new exception for torture (which would have entailed a finding that such an exception existed at international law or was mandated by the domestic constitution) or, in the alternative, by excluding torture from the ambit of the immunity conferred by the statutes.[169] Under this second approach, which starts from a baseline of jurisdiction, the statutes are characterized as narrow codifications of the restrictive principle of state immunity, where the exceptional immunity granted by Parliament attaches only to true sovereign acts of foreign states. To succeed in a case like *Bouzari, Jones* and *Kazemi*, this argument requires the court to find that torture cannot be, for immunity purposes, an official or sovereign act of state. Of course, such a finding has become immeasurably more difficult to make after the *Jurisdictional Immunities* case.[170]

Ultimately, the courts in *Bouzari*, *Jones* and *Kazemi* all found that the denial of immunity with respect to torture was not required under constitutional or international law, and perhaps as significantly, that such a development was foreclosed in any event by the words of the state immunity statutes. Justice LeBel summed up the situation in *Kazemi*:

---

167 See n. 10 above.

168 The UK State Immunity Act 1978, s. 1(1) provides: 'A State is immune from the jurisdiction of the courts of the United Kingdom except as provided in the following provisions of this Part of this Act'. Similarly, the Canadian State Immunity Act, RSC 1985, s. 3(1) provides: 'Except as provided by this Act, a foreign state is immune from the jurisdiction of any court in Canada'.

169 *Ibid.*

170 *Jurisdictional Immunities,* n. 12 above, para. 60 (holding that state acts that breach peremptory norms of international law can still be acts *jure imperii* for immunity purposes).

> With regard to exceptions to state immunity, Professor H.H. Koh famously asked, 'if contracts, why not torture?' The answer is simple. Parliament has decided as much.
>
> State immunity is a complex doctrine that is shaped by constantly evolving international relations. Determining the exceptions to immunity requires a thorough knowledge of diplomacy and international politics and a careful weighing of national interests. Since the introduction of the SIA, such a task belongs to Parliament or the government, though decisions and laws pertaining to international affairs may be subject to constitutional scrutiny under the Charter … It is not, however, this Court's task to intervene in delicate international policy making.
>
> Parliament has the power and the capacity to decide whether Canadian courts should exercise civil jurisdiction. Parliament has the ability to change the current state of the law on exceptions to state immunity … and allow those in situations like Mr. Hashemi and his mother's estate to seek redress in Canadian courts. Parliament has simply chosen not to do it yet.[171]

In deciding that Canada's State Immunity Act barred civil claims for torture, the Supreme Court of Canada emphasized state immunity's role in 'diplomacy and international politics' and shored up this characterization in strong Diceyan terms, noting that it was up to Parliament, and no longer the courts, to affect change in the law of state immunity.

It is an unfortunate turn of events that legislation explicitly enacted to introduce the principle of restrictive immunity in jurisdictions that had hitherto adhered to an absolutist paradigm has been decisively interpreted as barring any further judicial development of the law. It was not what Parliament intended.[172] While legislatures can and indeed must take the lead in defining the broad principles that govern immunities, national courts should be able to develop those principles, as Lord Denning suggested in *Trendtex*, in light of evolving international law and 'in terms

---

[171] *Kazemi* (2014), n. 12 above, paras 168–70 (citations omitted).

[172] When the Bill that became the State Immunity Act was being studied in parliamentary committee, the principal drafter of the Act emphasized that courts were expected to interpret the statute in light of changing international law. See Senate of Canada, Minutes of the Permanent Committee on Justice and Legal Affairs (February 1982), pp. 59:17 and 60:17 ('Well, we did not intend to have this [Act] come back on a periodic review. Not that it would stand for perhaps a thousand years but we hope that the courts would be able to have that flexibility to interpret it in the light of new factual situations, new transactions … Therefore, it is imperative to have a reasonably flexible and supple bill, one that will allow Canadian courts to reflect changing international norms in this area.'). See generally, Larocque, n. 8 above.

which are consonant with justice rather than adverse to it'.[173] Unfortunately, state immunity's political origins and its continuing role in modern day international relations have compromised the doctrine's ontological and axiological status as *law*. Consider for instance the US and Canadian legislative amendments establishing a terrorism exception in their respective state immunity legislation. In the United States, the 1996 Antiterrorism and Effective Death Penalty Act,[174] codified as part of the Foreign Sovereign Immunities Act (FSIA) at 28 USC § 1605(a)(7), allows US citizens to bring a claim for compensatory and punitive damages against certain designated foreign states[175] for death or personal injury arising from an act of torture, extra-judicial killing, aircraft sabotage, hostage taking or for supporting such activities, provided the plaintiff gave the foreign state a reasonable opportunity to resolve the matter through arbitration. Similarly, Canada's 2012 Justice for Victims of Terrorism Act (JVTA),[176] permits Canadian citizens and permanent residents to sue certain designated foreign states[177] for loss or injuries arising from terrorism related activities, provided the plaintiff afforded the foreign state with a reasonable opportunity to arbitrate the claim. The US terrorism exception has been widely criticized[178] and the Canadian model is probably as problematic, as both statutes ultimately grant or

[173] *Trendtex,* n. 151 above, 364.

[174] Antiterrorism and Effective Death Penalty Act, Pub. L 104–132, §221, 221 Stat. 1214 (24 April 1996).

[175] The designation is made pursuant to Export Administration Act of 1979, s. 6(j), 50 USC App. 2405(j) and Foreign Assistance Act of 1961, s. 620A, 22 USC 2371. At the time of writing Cuba, Iran, Sudan and Syria are designated state sponsors of terrorism for immunity purposes. In April 2015, in line with government efforts to normalize relations with Cuba, the US State Department recommend the rescission of that country's designation. See US State Department, State Sponsors of Terrorism, available at http://go.usa.gov/32VHW.

[176] Justice for Victims of Terrorism Act (JVTA), SC 2012, c. 1, s. 4.

[177] The designation is made pursuant to State Immunity Act, RSC 1985, s. 6.1(2). At the time of writing, Iran and Syria are designated for immunity purposes. See Canada News Release, 'Canada Lists Both Iran and Syria as State Supporters of Terrorism' (7 September 2012), available at http://tiny.cc/ucz8wx.

[178] Ronald Bettauer, 'Germany Sues Italy at the International Court of Justice on Foreign Sovereign Immunity: Legal Underpinnings and Implications for U.S. Law' (2009) 13(22) *ASIL Insight* 1 at 5: 'Fox sees the U.S. legislation as "partisan" and not a satisfactory precedent for other states to adopt. Gattini calls the U.S. approach "of dubious value" because of its "unilateral nature and political overtones". Bankas called subsection (a)(7) and the pre-2008 amendments to it "draconian in many respects and therefore may be vigorously contested by defendant states". Professor van Alabeek says that "the terrorist

deny immunity by executive fiat, and not through a principled assessment of the impugned state act's legal character, as customarily required under the restrictive doctrine.

It is interesting to note, nevertheless, that both the US and Canadian statutes provide for the selective denial of immunity, in part at least, on the basis of terrorism's international unlawfulness. The JVTA recalls 'that terrorism is a matter of national concern that affects the security of the nation' and that 'United Nations Security Council Resolution 1373 (2001) reaffirms that acts of international terrorism constitute a threat to international peace and security, and reaffirms the need to combat by all means, in accordance with the Charter of the United Nations, threats to international peace and security caused by acts of terrorism'.[179] One wonders if it might be inferred, therefore, that Canada and the United States, as a matter of *opinio juris,* both consider the denial of immunity for terrorism as being justified in light of that particular act's international criminality. If so, then the politically driven US and Canadian amendments might be partly redeemed as codifying the kind of qualitative assessment of state conduct that the restrictive principle of state immunity requires. Moreover, the US and Canadian enactments can arguably be taken to stand for the notion that state immunity is a privilege that can be lost or removed in appropriate circumstances ('when it is consonant with justice and with the equitable protection of the parties'),[180] rather than an automatic and absolute attribute of sovereignty.

Of course, such a conception of state immunity runs counter to the orthodox view, namely, that 'States generally proceed on the basis that there is a right to immunity under international law',[181] even when the impugned state conduct violates international law. The ICJ held in the *Jurisdictional Immunities* case that the international illegality of the impugned state act has no bearing on its characterization as *jure imperii* for the purposes of determining immunity.[182] That case, it will be recalled, concerned war crimes and crimes against humanity perpetrated by the Third Reich during the Second World War. It is an unusual feature of the case that both parties agreed that the acts at issue – the murder of civilian populations in occupied territories and the forced deportation of

state exception to the FSIA causes the United States to violate its obligations under international law"'. (References omitted).

179 JVTA, Preamble.

180 Higgins, n. 141 above, 271.

181 *Jurisdictional Immunities,* n. 12 above, para 56.

182 *Ibid.* para. 60.

civilian inhabitants as well as prisoners of war to slave labour – were prohibited by peremptory norms of international law yet nevertheless constituted acts *jure imperii.*[183] With this unfortunate concession, Italy's only remaining rhetorical avenue was to argue that Germany's unlawful actions did not attract immunity because at least some of them occurred on Italian territory or, in the alternative because 'those acts involved the most serious violations of rules of international law of a peremptory character for which no alternative means of redress was available'.[184] This chapter will not address the Court's response to the first argument,[185] but will focus instead on the Court's endorsement of the view espoused by the various national courts in civil claims for torture,[186] viz. state immunity applies to conduct that contravenes international *jus cogens*.

Flagging the US Antiterrorism and Effective Death Penalty Act as an outlier,[187] the Court held 'that, under customary international law as it presently stands, a State is not deprived of immunity by reason of the fact that it is accused of serious violations of international human rights law or the international law of armed conflict'.[188] Then, turning to the *jus cogens* argument, the Court found that there existed no conflict between the substantive peremptory prohibition of war crimes and crimes against humanity and the hierarchically inferior procedural rule of state immunity. The ICJ held that:

> the two sets of rules address different matters. The rules of State immunity are procedural in character and are confined to determining whether or not the courts of one State may exercise jurisdiction in respect of another State. They do not bear upon the question whether or not the conduct in respect of which the proceedings are brought was lawful or unlawful.[189]

---

183 *Ibid.* The Court noted 'that Italy, in response to a question posed by a member of the Court, recognized that those acts had to be characterized as *acta jure imperii*, notwithstanding that they were unlawful'. This was an unfortunate concession on the part of Italy. As it will be argued below, state conduct that violates peremptory norms of international law should not, for the purposes of immunity, be characterized as valid or legitimate acts *jure imperii*.

184 *Ibid.* para. 61.

185 *Ibid.* paras 62–79.

186 *Ibid.* para. 85. See also n. 10 above.

187 *Ibid.* para. 88. The ICJ's decision was issued three weeks before the Canadian JVTA came into force. See nn. 174 to 179 above and accompanying text.

188 *Ibid.* para. 91.

189 *Jurisdictional Immunities,* n. 12 above, para. 93.

In this holding the ICJ adopted the line of reasoning famously advanced by Fox and endorsed by House of Lords in *Jones* and the Supreme Court of Canada in *Kazemi*, namely, that:

> State immunity is a procedural rule going to the jurisdiction of a national court. It does not go to substantive law; it does not contradict a prohibition contained in a *jus cogens* norm but merely diverts any breach of it to a different method of settlement. Arguably, then, there is no substantive content in the procedural plea of State immunity upon which a *jus cogens* mandate can bite.[190]

This reasoning warrants a few observations. First, Lord Bingham's easy acceptance of the proposition that a procedural rule (state immunity) remains unaffected by its interaction with peremptory substantive rule (the torture prohibition) should be contrasted with his Lordships' own indignation, a mere few months earlier, at the suggestion that a procedural rule (on the admissibility of evidence) could survive its interaction with a substantive peremptory norm of international and constitutional law (the torture prohibition). In *A(FC)*, Lord Bingham stated:

> But the English common law has regarded torture and its fruits with abhorrence for over 500 years, and that abhorrence is now shared by over 140 countries which have acceded to the Torture Convention. I am startled, even a little dismayed, at the suggestion (and the acceptance by the Court of Appeal majority) that this deeply-rooted tradition and an international obligation solemnly and explicitly undertaken can be overridden by a statute and a procedural rule which make no mention of torture at all.[191]

One wonders why or how the *jus cogens* character of the torture prohibition at international law and the constitutional resonance it carries at common law should imperatively be honoured in the law of evidence, but not in the law of state immunity.

Second, as Orakhelashvili correctly pointed out, 'international law knows of no straightforward distinction between "substantive" and "procedural" norms. All international norms derive from the agreement of states or acceptance by the international community as a whole, and there are neither established criteria nor a recognized agency to split them into such categories'.[192] A norm forms part of *jus cogens* or it does not. Once

---

[190] Fox and Webb, n. 145 above, 21; *Jones* (2006), n. 10 above, para. 24 (per Lord Bingham) and para. 44 (per Lord Hoffman); *Kazemi* (2014), n. 10 above, para. 161.

[191] *A(FC)*, n. 22 above, para. 51.

[192] Orakhelashvili, n. 130 above, 968.

the international community recognizes the peremptory character of a given norm, such as torture, all other norms of international law must be interpreted and applied consistently with that characterization. Courts should strive to avoid inconsistencies by giving full effect to the peremptoriness of the international norms they apply, irrespective of the substantive or procedural nature of that effect, subject only to specific and contrary direction from national legislature. As the Supreme Court of Canada stated in *R v Hape*, 'Parliamentary sovereignty dictates that a legislature may violate international law, but that it must do so expressly. Absent an express derogation, the courts may look to prohibitive rules of customary international law to aid in the interpretation of Canadian law and the development of the common law'.[193] In other words, it is the entire body of domestic law, be it substantive or procedural, statutory or common law, that must be interpreted and developed consistently with international law.

Another related question is the apparent inconsistency in the law of state immunity with respect to criminal and civil proceedings. The House of Lords held in *Jones* and *Pinochet (No. 3)* that the universal criminal jurisdiction over torture 'implies' the removal of immunity *ratione materiae* in criminal matters, but not in civil proceedings,[194] presumably because the concept of universal civil jurisdiction was not well established at international law. Accordingly, if such a notion were to become part of general international law, it too, 'by necessary implication' would cause the removal of immunity *ratione materiae* in civil proceedings.[195] But in *Jones* Lord Bingham went on to state that 'the distinction between criminal proceedings (which were the subject of universal jurisdiction under the Torture Convention) and civil proceedings (which were not) was fundamental to [the *Pinochet (No. 3)*] decision. This is not a distinction which can be wished away'.[196] With respect, Lord Bingham's account of *Pinochet (No. 3)* is incomplete. While the universal criminal jurisdiction mandated under the CAT was unquestionably central to the denial of immunity in that case, some of their Lordships also shored up their conclusion on the basis of the overriding effect of peremptory norms with respect to conflicting immunities.[197] It is thus unclear why

---

193 *Hape,* n. 50 above, para. 39.

194 *Jones* (2006), n. 10 above, para. 89 (per Lord Hoffman); *Pinochet (No. 3)*, n. 57 above, 205 (per Lord Browne-Wilkinson) and 264 (per Lord Hutton).

195 *Jones* (2006), n. 10 above, para. 71 (per Lord Hoffman).

196 *Ibid.* para. 32 (per Lord Bingham).

197 See for example, *Pinochet (No. 3)*, n. 57 above, 247 (per Lord Hutton), 278 (per Lord Millet) and 289 (per Lord Phillips).

peremptory norms could not have the same overriding effect in civil proceedings.

13.5 CONCLUSION: FINDING A WAY THROUGH TO TOMORROW

This chapter sought to highlight some of the problems and inconsistencies that have marked the debates and decisions involving issues of torture, jurisdiction and state immunity. The latest decisions to grapple with these problems, the European Court of Human Rights in *Jones* and Supreme Court of Canada in *Kazemi*, will almost certainly not be the last. But, as Webb has remarked, those decisions leave us in a 'strange situation'[198] in which state immunity is routinely lifted in banal commercial cases, maritime cases *in rem*, local torts, but not in matters involving the most fundamental norms of international law. This untenable situation is maintained by anachronistic thinking about sovereignty and the state. As Webb put it, the formalistic 'distinctions being drawn in immunities cases – civil/criminal, procedural/substantive, employment/human rights – are hard to reconcile with broader movements for accountability at the international level'.[199]

Many of the cases discussed in this chapter contain the hopeful evocation of a future world where such untenable distinctions no longer exist, where the CAT is fully implemented and civil redress finally made available to all victims of torture.[200] But that world, the courts have melancholically concluded, is not 'yet'[201] ours. Accordingly, one may ask, with dissenting Judge Ferrari Bravo, '*Quousque tandem*'?[202] The unashamedly optimistic answer – which the author believes to be the

---

198 Philippa Webb, '*Jones v UK*: The Re-integration of State and Official Immunity?', *EJIL Talk!*, 14 January 2014, available at http://tinyurl.com/pa6lggg.

199 *Ibid.*

200 See for example, *Bouzari* (2004), n. 10 above, para. 95 ('In the future, perhaps as the international human rights movement gathers greater force, this balance may change'); *Kazemi* (2012), n. 10 above, para. 56 ('The Committee points to a 'possible or even hoped for future' of conventional international law').

201 *Jurisdictional Immunities*, n. 12 above, para. 91; *Al-Adsani* (2001), n. 10 above, para. 66; *Jones* (2014), n. 10 above, para. 198; *Kazemi* (2014), n. 10 above, para. 148; *Kalogeropoulou and others v Greece and Germany* [2002-X] ECHR Reports 417, ECtHR, 12 December 2002.

202 *Al-Adsani* (2001), n. 10 above, Dissenting Opinion of Judge Ferrari Bravo.

correct one – is: no longer than a 'thought-instant'.[203] It takes no more than a single 'thought-instant to transform one's idea of international society from a state-centered to a human-centered mental universe. In the very next moment, one has a wholly new world-view, with wholly new values, wholly new possibilities, and wholly new purposes'.[204] It takes no more than a thought-instant to decide that states that breach peremptory norms of international law should not benefit from the protection of that law.

As Judges Higgins, Kooijmans and Buergenthal stated in their Joint Separate Opinion in the *Arrest Warrant* case, the notion of *acta jure imperii* is continually evolving, 'reflecting the changing priorities of society'.[205] In this connection, given the growing salience of peremptory norms and human rights, it seems, despite the ICJ's view in the *Jurisdictional Immunities* case, that the peremptory illegality of torture should somehow be factored into its characterization as a sovereign or non-sovereign act and in the ultimate grant or denial of immunity. In proposing a path forward, it is helpful to refer to some theory of the state and of the power it wields, as well as to some theory of international law as a whole, and both will be normative, not merely descriptive. Under the view that states are the ultimate embodiment of social power, including the power to make and break laws, torture – that is, extraordinary state-directed violence against an individual – can be conceived as the sovereign act par excellence. Under this world-view, described by Marshall CJ in *The Schooner Exchange*,[206] the planet is inhabited by equal and independent sovereigns, owing nothing to each other but that which they politely concede. However, through constant and deliberate practice, in their mutual interest and for that of their citizens, states have outlawed torture, imbuing that prohibition with the full force of their combined sovereignties, elevating it amongst those rules that govern the formation of all others. Arguably, in so restricting their respective sovereignties, states have permanently excluded torture from the panoply of possible policies that they may pursue, *ipso facto* gaining in protection what they have lost in prerogative. In other words, the sovereign discretion to commit the violence of torture has been reallocated to the empowerment of its peremptory prohibition. Thus, every time and

[203] Philip Allott, *Eunomia: New Order for a New World* (Oxford, Oxford University Press, 2001), p. xxxii.

[204] *Ibid*. pp. xxxii–xxxiii.

[205] *Arrest Warrant,* n. 72 above, Separate Opinion of Judges Higgins, Kooijmans and Buergenthal, para. 72.

[206] *The Schooner Exchange v McFaddon,* 11 U.S. 116 (1812).

everywhere torture is ordered, it is never an exercise of social power but simply the utterance of words, just words, not law, mere *flatus vocis*, not *acta jure imperii*. Following this conception of things, the *jus cogens* illegality of torture becomes a decisive component of the contextual characterization of state acts resulting in its *ab initio* removal from the ambit of immunity.

Put differently, we must conceive of a new world where state sovereignty and power serve humanity's highest aspirations of peace and freedom from fear and violence. State acts that breach these tenets of world public order are *ultra vires* and must not be countenanced by any court of law. This is hardly a new idea. One of its most eloquent articulations is owed to the learned judge of the Court of First Instance of Leivadia in *Prefecture of Voiotia v Federal Republic of Germany*, who stated that the 'acts of a state that violate *jus cogens* norms do not have the character of sovereign acts. In such cases it is considered that the accused state did not act within the ambit of its capacity as a sovereign. Acts contrary to *jus cogens* norms are null and void, and cannot constitute a source of legal rights or privileges, such as the claim to immunity'.[207] To hold up a qualified conception of state sovereignty and international society is not to simultaneously repudiate the principle of equality of states, but merely to recognize that while states are equal, they are not above the law that they themselves have created and that sustains their very existence.

---

[207] *Prefecture of Voiotia v Federal Republic of Germany*, No. 137/1997, 30 October 1997, as cited in Jordan J. Paust, 'Genocide in Rwanda, State Responsibility to Prosecute or Extradite, and Nonimmunity for Heads of State and Other Public Officials' (2011) 34(1) *Houston J Int'l L* 57 at 73, n. 63.

14. Immunities and international criminal tribunals

Robert Cryer

14.1 INTRODUCTION

Immunities for international crimes, and the state of international criminal justice more generally, are often seen as bellwethers for the state of development of international law.[1] Furthermore, it is true that while state action is not a *sine qua non* for all international crimes,[2] such activity remains the paradigmatic example of such cases[3] (and, for the crime of aggression, it is a definitional element of the offence).[4] As a result, it is

[1] See for example, Bruce Broomhall, *International Justice and the International Criminal Court: Between Sovereignty and the Rule of Law* (Oxford, Oxford University Press, 2003), ch. 7; Leila Nadya Sadat, *The International Criminal Court and The Transformation of International Law: Justice for the New Millennium* (New York, Transnational, 2002).

[2] Which, for these purposes are defined as those crimes directly criminalized under international law, as understood in the Nuremberg statement that 'crimes against international law are committed by men, not abstract entities, and only by punishing individuals who commit such crimes can the provisions of international law be enforced … individuals have international duties which transcend the national obligations of obedience imposed by the individual state' ('Nuremberg IMT: Judgment and Sentences' (1947) 41 *American Journal of International Law* 171 at 221. See generally on the definitional aspects Robert Cryer, Håkan Friman, Darryl Robinson and Elizabeth Wilmshurst, *An Introduction to International Criminal Law and Procedure* (3rd edn, Cambridge, Cambridge University Press, 2014), ch. 1.

[3] See for example, William Schabas, 'State Policy as an Element of International Crimes' (2008) 98 *Journal of Criminal Law and Criminology* 953; John Cerone, 'The Vanishing Relevance of State Affiliation in International Criminal Law: Private Security Contractors and Other Non-State Actors' in Bartram Brown (ed.), *Research Handbook on International Criminal Law* (Cheltenham, Edward Elgar, 2011), p. 17 and, importantly, Dapo Akande and Shangeeta Shah, 'Immunities of State Officials, International Crimes, and Foreign Domestic Courts' (2011) 21 *European Journal of International Law* 815.

[4] See Article 8*bis* of the Rome Statute, and Carrie McDougall, *The Crime of Aggression under the Rome Statute of the International Criminal Court*

often the case that state officials are putative defendants before international criminal courts.[5] This is one reason why immunities have proved so controversial. State officials, particularly high ranking officials, who are meant to be the target of prosecutions before international criminal courts,[6] are very effective about getting their (often personal) concerns foregrounded in international affairs.[7] A notable example of this, which is directly relevant to immunities for international crimes, is the action of the African Union in relation to the International Criminal Court (ICC), in which the charge against the ICC was led, in large part, by high ranking indictees, or similar figures who were appearing before the Court.[8]

However, immunities have also been controversial as they raise tensions between values that different aspects of international law seek to further. International criminal law seeks to limit impunity, albeit not at all costs; immunities, on the other hand, prioritize stability in international relations.[9] These sometimes competing interests are in a state of balance which, as Judges Higgins, Kooijmans and Buergenthal made clear in the

---

(Cambridge, Cambridge University Press, 2013), pp. 167–85; Mark Drumbl, 'The Push to Criminalize Aggression: Something Lost Among the Gains?' (2009) 41 *Case Western Reserve Journal of International Law* 291.

[5] As we will see, there are complex definitional issues that arise with respect to exactly what is an international criminal court.

[6] See Robert Cryer, 'Prosecuting the Leaders: Promises, Politics and Pragmatics' (2009) 1 *Göttingen Journal of International Law* 45.

[7] It is a well-known argument amongst for example, TWAIL scholars that powerful states are successful about getting their way in international law (see for example, Anton Anghie, *Imperialism, Sovereignty and the History of International Law* (Cambridge, Cambridge University Press, 2005), but as feminist international lawyers, and Marxists before them, have noted, international law also reflects the interests of the powerful within states, see for example, Hilary Charlesworth and Christine Chinkin, *The Boundaries of International Law: A Feminist Analysis* (Manchester, Manchester University Press, 2000); Vladimir Kartashkin, 'The Marxist-Leninist Approach: The Theory of Class Struggle and Contemporary International Law' in Ronald St. John MacDonald and Douglas M. Johnson, *The Structure and Processes of International Law* (Dordrecht, Martinus Nijhoff, 1986), p. 79.

[8] Kai Ambos, 'Expanding the Focus of the "African Criminal Court"' in William Schabas, Yvonne McDermott and Niamh Hayes (eds), *The Ashgate Research Companion to International Criminal Law* (Aldershot, Ashgate, 2012), p. 499.

[9] See for example, Cryer, Friman, Robinson and Wilmshurst, n. 2 above, 545–6.

Yerodia case, is not immutable.[10] As such, clashes over the appropriate weights to be given to those considerations are practically inevitable.

It is the purpose of this chapter to investigate how the law currently draws the line on this matter, with specific reference to how this applies with reference to international criminal courts, and the rationales that have been given for the position as it stands. As a result of its focus, it will involve discussion of the position before foreign domestic courts,[11] as it can be relevant to the position before international tribunals. This is the case in the first type of immunities that fall for consideration, functional immunity, where, for international crimes, the position is largely settled (that there is no such immunity for international crimes), albeit for reasons that are not universally agreed. As we will see, however, there are certain crimes, which relate to the administration of international criminal justice before international criminal courts and tribunals that do not amount to international crimes, therefore this chapter will discuss the rather overlooked question of whether or not there is, or can be, functional immunity before such courts.

From there the chapter will look at the more controversial issue of personal immunities. Here the position is different between national and international courts, but also between such international courts, as their bases and powers are not all the same, and this impacts upon the question of immunities. Therefore the question arises of what an international criminal court is, and what their different natures entails. The chapter will discuss this at the conceptual level, as well as by reference to the jurisprudence of the various tribunals. To finish, the chapter will look into the question of whether or not the position is likely to change in the future, or whether we can foresee a period of stasis, and whether, normatively, any developments would be desirable. It ought to be said at the outset that this chapter cannot be a comprehensive evaluation of all areas of this vast area of law, but seeks to bring some thoughts to the area.

---

[10] *Case concerning the Arrest Warrant of 11 April 2001 (DRC v Belgium)* ('*Yerodia* case') [2001] ICJ Rep. 3, Separate Opinion of Judges Higgins, Kooijmans and Buergenthal, para. 75.

[11] On which see for example, Akande and Shah, n. 3 above.

14.2 TYPES OF IMMUNITY: CIVIL, CRIMINAL, FUNCTIONAL AND PERSONAL

To begin, however, it is necessary to engage in a little conceptual ground clearing. The first is that there is a fundamental split in the law relating to immunities between civil and criminal jurisdiction. The considerations that apply to one may not always be applicable to the other. So, analogies made between the two need to be treated with caution, although not all are entirely inapposite. Some commentators have sought to argue that since civil law is, in the end, enforced by criminal law, there are strong links between the two (at least with respect to the existence of jurisdiction).[12] This is far from the accepted position, and the ICJ has recently quite firmly re-stated the position that civil and criminal law are, for the purposes of immunities, different. This occurred in the *Jurisdictional Immunities* case, which related to attempts by Italian courts to enforce judgments of Greek courts asserting that Germany was not immune from their jurisdiction for massacres in Greece in the Second World War. In addition to holding that Germany was entitled to state Immunity before Greek courts, even though the acts involved were found to be international crimes,[13] the ICJ specifically rejected any reliance on the famous (UK) *Pinochet* case, on the basis that it 'concerned the immunity of a former Head of State from the criminal jurisdiction of another State, not the immunity of the State itself in proceedings designed to establish its liability to damages'.[14] Indeed, in the *Croatia/Serbia* case the ICJ was very stern on the separation between state and individual responsibility, asserting that:

> State responsibility and individual criminal responsibility are governed by different legal régimes and pursue different aims. The former concerns the consequences of the breach by a State of the obligations imposed upon it by international law, whereas the latter is concerned with the responsibility of an

[12] Ian Brownlie, *Principles of International Law* (7th edn, Oxford, Oxford University Press, 2008), p. 300. See also Bernard H. Oxman, 'Jurisdiction of States' in Rüdiger Wolfrum (ed.), *The Max Planck Encyclopaedia of Public International Law* (Oxford, Oxford University Press, 2012), vol. VI, p. 546 at 547.

[13] *Jurisdictional Immunities of the State* (*Germany v Italy*) [2012] ICJ Rep. 99, para. 81. For an excellent overview of the ICJ's role in developing the law of immunities see Roger O'Keefe, 'Jurisdictional Immunities' in Christian Tams and James Sloan (eds), *The Development of International Law by the International Court of Justice* (Oxford, Oxford University Press, 2013), p. 107.

[14] *Ibid.* para. 87.

> individual as established under the rules of international and domestic criminal law, and the resultant sanctions to be imposed upon that person.[15]

Although speaking here of responsibility rather than immunity, given the deep connections between the two, the judgment is telling. This is also in accordance with the vast majority of state practice on this point,[16] and given that the jurisdiction of international criminal tribunals is criminal, not civil in its nature, and excludes questions directly determining state responsibility in damages,[17] the subject need not be further investigated here.

The second distinction that needs to be engaged with in a little more detail is the distinction between functional and personal immunities. Again, although they may (or may not) have similar underlying rationales, as we will see the law on this point is different between the two areas, although there are those who maintain that the same arguments for removing one set of immunities apply equally to the other. These arguments will be discussed below, where they are relevant, but it ought to be said that they have fallen on stony ground with states.

Turning first to functional immunities, these inhere in sovereign conduct. States, naturally, have to act through human functionaries, such as diplomats, police, members of the armed forces (and indeed all of those whose conduct is attributable to the state pursuant to the relevant

---

[15] *Case concerning Application of the Convention on the Prevention and Punishment of Genocide (Croatia v Serbia)* ICJ, Judgment, 3 February 2015, para. 129.

[16] *Jurisdictional Immunities*, n. 13 above, paras 83–6.

[17] See for example, ICC Statute, Art. 25(4) and W.A. Schabas, *The International Criminal Court: A Commentary on the Rome Statute* (Oxford, Oxford University Press, 2010), pp. 440–41. The ICJ has also indicated the separate nature of individual and state responsibility in this regard in *Case concerning the Application of the Convention on the Prevention and Punishment of the Crime of Genocide (Bosnia and Herzegovina v Serbia and Montenegro)* ('*Bosnian Genocide* case'), ICJ, Judgment, 26 February 2007, para. 173; Pierre-Marie Dupuy, 'International Criminal Responsibility of the Individual and International Responsibility of the State' in Antonio Cassese, Paola Gaeta and J.R.W.D. Jones (eds), *The Rome Statute of the International Criminal Court: A Commentary* (Oxford, Oxford University Press, 2002), p. 1085; André Nollkaemper, 'Concurrence Between Individual Responsibility and State Responsibility in International Law' (2003) 52 *ICLQ* 615; Beatrice I. Bonafé, *The Relationship Between State and Individual Responsibility for International Crimes* (Leiden, Martinus Nijhoff, 2009).

rules of state responsibility).[18] They are not removed by the passage of time or the change of identity of such officials, as such conduct is (simply) not conduct for which the individual is responsible. As a result, an individual pleading such immunity is engaging in two different arguments: the first is that the conduct is not theirs; the second is that to attempt to bring them to account for their activities would be to indirectly implead the state, and therefore violate the principle of *par in parem non habet imperium* (equals do not have authority over each other). It is for both of these reasons that functional immunity only extends to 'official' conduct. This makes sense because neither of the above rationales have any relationship to private activities which are not those of the state, and it is not to indirectly implead the state in such circumstances to subject someone to criminal process.

The other types of immunity are personal immunities.[19] These are different in nature and scope to functional immunities. These immunities apply to the person, rather than their conduct. Certain high level representatives of the state are automatically entitled to such personal immunity, often on the ground that to subject them to legal process would be detrimental to the dignity of the foreign state. Rightly or wrongly, this would certainly apply to the head of state, and arguably also the head of government (who tend to be assimilated in this regard).[20]

However, certain other high ranking members of government, and other officials, also have this personal immunity on the utilitarian grounds that without such immunity their roles would be difficult to perform. This has always been the basis of diplomatic immunity (diplomats and certain others having personal immunity in the states to which

---

[18] On which see ILC Articles on State Responsibility, Chapter II, and James Crawford, *State Responsibility: The General Part* (Cambridge, Cambridge University Press, 2013), chs 4–6.

[19] As O'Keefe rightly notes, the term is apt to mislead, as the immunities are of the state, rather than the person, Roger O'Keefe, *International Criminal Law* (Oxford, Oxford University Press, 2015), para. 10.9.

[20] See generally Sir Arthur Watts 'The Legal Position in International Law of Heads of States, Heads of Government and Foreign Ministers' (1994) 247 *RdC* 9. DRC Cooperation Decision (al-Bashir, 9 April 2014) para. 25, asserted that 'it is not disputed that under international law a sitting Head of State enjoys personal immunities from criminal jurisdiction and inviolability before national courts of foreign States even when suspected of having committed one or more of the crimes that fall within the jurisdiction of the Court'.

they are accredited),[21] but this was, controversially, expanded by the ICJ in the *Yerodia* case to include Foreign Ministers even at home.[22] Although it was not really consistent with previous practice on point (which was for it to be granted by consent on an ad hoc basis rather than as of right), the position for Foreign Ministers now seems to have become settled along the lines the ICJ has suggested.[23] Where there is controversy, though, is as to which other state officials obtain similar immunities as of right.[24] Outside of this, it bears remembering that states are entitled to grant immunities to other people under general international law,[25] although this possibility may have a tense relationship with certain other obligations of the state (such as to exercise jurisdiction over transnational crimes, or those obligations a state has undertaken with respect to cooperation with the ICC or the international courts).[26]

The two types of immunity run during the period of office of the official, in tandem, creating a double bar to proceedings.[27] However, once an official steps down from their post, they cease to benefit from their personal immunities. But the nature of their conduct, as being that of the state, does not alter, and therefore the functional immunity remains.[28] It

---

[21] Vienna Convention on Diplomatic Relations 1961, Arts 29–36. A very useful guide can be found in Sir Ivor Roberts (ed.), *Satow's Diplomatic Practice* (Oxford, Oxford University Press, 2009), ch. 9.

[22] See n. 10 above. There are also similar issues relating to officials of international organizations, see Chanaka Wickemasinghe, 'Immunities Enjoyed by Officials of States and International Organizations' in Malcolm Evans (ed.), *International Law* (4th edn, Oxford, Oxford University Press, 2014), p. 379 at pp. 399–40.

[23] O'Keefe, n. 13 above, 115–20.

[24] *Re Mofaz* (2004) 128 ILR 709; *Re Bo Xilai* (2005) 128 ILR 713.

[25] The existence of Status of Forces Agreements is based on this fact. See also Rain Liivoja, *An Axiom of Military Law: Applicability of National Criminal Law to Military Personnel and Associated Civilians Abroad* (Ph.D Thesis, University of Helsinki, 2011), pp. 122–32 (on file with author).

[26] Natalia Perova, *The United Nations, Member States, and Individuals Sharing Responsibility for Violations of International Law Committed During Peace Support Operations* (Unpublished Ph.D Thesis, 2014, ch. 5 (on file with author); Gerhard Werle and Florian Jessberger, *Principles of International Criminal Law* (3rd edn, Oxford, Oxford University Press, 2014), pp. 278–9. But see O'Keefe, n. 13 above, pp. 122–3 and O'Keefe, n. 19 above, para. 10.40 ff.

[27] See J. Craig Barker, 'State Immunity, Diplomatic Immunity and Act of State: A Triple Protection Against Legal Action' (1998) 47 *International and Comparative Law Quarterly* 950.

[28] Werle and Jessberger, n. 26 above, pp. 271–2, although their assertion that functional immunity is more than procedural is questionable; see the review of

is still important to note that both types of immunities are not fundamentally rights of the individuals they protect, they are those of the state. Hence, such immunities are waivable by the home state largely at will.[29]

14.3 FUNCTIONAL IMMUNITIES

It is fair to say that, when it comes to the extent to which foreign state officials enjoy the protection of international law before foreign domestic counts, the matter is complex. Various courts and thinkers have looked at the matter, but the majority view has been, for different reasons, that when issues of international crimes are at issue, they do not enjoy immunity before domestic or (at times for different reasons) international courts.[30] It is true that this view is not unchallenged today, but it remains the predominant one.[31]

14.3.1 National Courts

Although not the primary focus of this chapter, as it is dealt with elsewhere in this volume, the arguments for immunities before domestic courts need to be (briefly) canvassed since, as we will see, they impact on the powers of international courts. There are arguments of pure normativity, the structure of the international legal order, practice and the nature of international crimes. Of the first type of such arguments, perhaps the baldest statement of such a view was made by Sir Arthur Watts, who has said that 'for international conduct which is so serious as to be tainted with criminality to be regarded as attributable only to the impersonal state and not to the individuals who order or perpetrate it is both unrealistic and offensive to common notions of justice'.[32] In a similar manner, Paola Gaeta has argued that the nature of the prohibitions on violations of human rights mean that immunity should not stand in the

---

ICJ jurisprudence on point in O'Keefe, n. 13 above, pp. 109–11 and O'Keefe, n. 19 above, para. 10.7.

[29] James Crawford, *Brownlie's Principles of Public International Law* (8th edn, Oxford, Oxford University Press, 2012), p. 501; Hazel Fox, 'International Law and Restraints on the Exercise of Jurisdiction by National Courts of States' in Malcolm Evans (ed.), *International Law* (4th edn, Oxford, Oxford University Press, 2014), p. 336 at 346–7; O'Keefe, n. 19 above, para. 10.5–6.

[30] See for example, Akande and Shah, n. 3 above.

[31] Cryer, Friman, Robinson and Wilmshurst, n. 2 above, ch. 21.

[32] Sir Arthur Watts 'The Legal Position in International Law of Heads of States, Heads of Government and Foreign Ministers' (1994) 247 *RdC* 9 at 82.

way of accountability.[33] These arguments are, at one level, attractive, and have recently received strong defence.[34] Patrick Capps, for example, has argued that:

> the isolation strategy which is at the heart of the Autonomy Thesis, must be rejected if international law is to fulfil its coordinator role successfully. Instead we should adopt an integrated version of the Autonomy Thesis, which means that the international legal order should be consistent with underlying principles of public practical reasonableness in its constitutive, substantive and procedural form. These principles are the fundamental moral principles by which human beings can flourish, have independence, and not be dominated by others or by the state institutions that govern them.[35]

The difficulty with such arguments is that their structure is inherently naturalist, and therefore subject to critiques both traditional, like that of Georg Schwarzenberger,[36] but also more by modern strands of critical thought, such as feminist,[37] and TWAIL[38] approaches, which note natural law's exclusionary nature. On the traditional front, of value scepticism, those speaking in favour of immunities' coordinating role in international

---

[33] Paola Gaeta, 'Immunity of States and State Officials: A Major Stumbling Block to Judicial Scrutiny?' in Antonio Cassese (ed.), *Realizing Utopia: The Future of International Law* (Oxford, Oxford University Press, 2010), p. 227; see *contra* Bing Bing Jia, 'The Immunity of State Officials for International Crimes Revisited' (2012) 10 *Journal of International Criminal Justice* 1203 (arguing that sovereign equality remains the dominant principle in international society).

[34] See for example, Donald E. Childress III (ed.), *The Role of Ethics In International Law* (Cambridge, Cambridge University Press, 2012).

[35] Patrick Capps, 'International Legal Positivism and Modern Natural Law' in Jörg Kammerhoffer and Jean D'Aspremont (eds), *International Legal Positivism in a Post-Modern World* Cambridge, Cambridge University Press, (2014), p. 213 at 240.

[36] '[I]n a doubting, if not faithless age, natural law is hardly any longer a universal or generally acceptable ethical foundation of law. We are also too conscious of the fact that "*le droit naturel suppose une tênon pas critique … mais speculative*". Thus, lawyers who, in our time, draw upon natural law as an article of faith cannot expect more than the tolerance due to any metaphysical belief.' Georg Schwarzenberger, *The Frontiers of International Law* (London, Stevens, 1962), p. 66.

[37] Hilary Charlesworth and Christine Chinkin, *The Boundaries of International Law: A Feminist Analysis* (Manchester, Manchester University Press, 2000), pp. 25–6.

[38] Third World Approaches to International Law (TWAIL). See for example, Anthony Anghie, *Imperialism, Sovereignty and the Making of International Law* (Cambridge, Cambridge University Press, 2005), ch. 1.

affairs claim that this is as important, or even more important, than preventing impunity, and without an agreed upon meta principle, the discussion may simply be a dialogue of the deaf. In terms of more modern approaches, Third World scholars[39] and states have argued that they were not included in the process of removing immunities, which is a Western development that has been used against poorer countries.[40] Furthermore, states (on the whole) do not use natural law reasoning, and are rarely convinced by it, on the basis that it could easily be turned against them too.[41] Hence such arguments cannot, in themselves, convince.

The next set of arguments relate to nature of the international legal order or, more specifically, the idea that the prohibited conduct in international criminal law is banned by rules having the status of *jus cogens*. In a nutshell, the argument is that the principle of immunity is not *jus cogens* (if nothing else, immunities may be waived, and that is inconsistent with any such status), and it must be trumped by international crimes, as the superior norm.[42] There is a great deal of logical sense in such a claim. However, not all international crimes are contrary to *jus cogens* norms,[43] and that status, with few exceptions,[44] tends not to

---

[39] See n. 38 above, with reference to the African Union.

[40] This was the basis, for example, of much of the DRC's claim in relation to immunities in the *Yerodia* case.

[41] Although it must be said that although Sir Arthur Watts was the Legal Adviser to the UK Foreign and Commonwealth Office when he made his remarks, they were made, of course, in a personal capacity.

[42] The most notable of which are Alexander Orakhelashvili, 'State Immunity and International Public Order' (2002) 45 *German Yearbook of International Law* 227; Alexander Orakhelashvili, 'State Immunity and International Public Order Revisited' (2006) 49 *German Yearbook of International Law* 327; Alexander Orakhelashvili, *Peremptory Norms in International Law* (Oxford, Oxford University Press, 2006), ch. 10. See also Yasmin Q. Naqvi, *Impediments to Exercising Jurisdiction over International Crimes* (The Hague, TMC Asser Press, 2010), pp. 268–74.

[43] See for example, Rafaël Nieto-Navia, 'International Peremptory Norms (Jus Cogens) and International Humanitarian Law' in Lal Chand Vohrah *et al.* (eds), *Man's Inhumanity to Man, Essays in Honour of Antonio Cassese* (The Hague, Kluwer, 2003), p. 595.

[44] *Ferrini v Federal Republic of Germany*, Decision No. 5044/2004 (2004) 87 *Rivista di diritto internazionale* 539; (2004) 128 ILR 658; *Prefecture of Voiotia v Federal Republic of Germany*, Case No. 11/2000 [2000] 129 ILR 513.

hold sway in national courts.[45] The ICJ has also, in the civil context, proved deeply sceptical (to say the least) of the idea that the *jus cogens* nature of a prohibition, in the context of international crimes, trumps immunity. In the *Jurisdictional Immunities* case, the ICJ was abundantly clear on this point, saying that although the relevant crimes were contrary to *jus cogens* norms, that did not alter the position in relation to immunities:

> This argument therefore depends upon the existence of a conflict between a rule, or rules, of *jus cogens*, and the rule of customary law which requires one State to accord immunity to another. In the opinion of the Court, however, no such conflict exists. Assuming for this purpose that the rules of the law of armed conflict which prohibit the murder of civilians in occupied territory, the deportation of civilian inhabitants to slave labour and the deportation of prisoners of war to slave labour are rules of *jus cogens*, there is no conflict between those rules and the rules on State immunity. The two sets of rules address different matters. The rules of State immunity are procedural in character and are confined to determining whether or not the courts of one State may exercise jurisdiction in respect of another State. They do not bear upon the question whether or not the conduct in respect of which the proceedings are brought was lawful or unlawful … A *jus cogens* rule is one from which no derogation is permitted but the rules which determine the scope and extent of jurisdiction and when that jurisdiction may be exercised do not derogate from those substantive rules which possess *jus cogens* status, nor is there anything inherent in the concept of *jus cogens* which would require their modification or would displace their application.[46]

Hence, in spite of the logical case that has been made on this point, it has only made limited inroads into state practice; the area of practice where it may have had some purchase has, at least in the civil field, been the subject of an emphatic rebuff from the ICJ.

Thus, we need to turn now to state practice. Recently, the practice on this point (especially in cases such as *Pinochet*) has been subject to significant critique, on the basis that it is far more ambiguous than has traditionally been thought,[47] or that it is not sufficiently broad to displace

---

[45] *Jones v Saudi Arabia* [2006] UKHL 26, HL. This decision was upheld by the European Court of Human Rights in *Jones v United Kingdom*, ECtHR, Judgment, 14 January 2014.

[46] *Jurisdictional Immunities of the State (Germany v Italy, Greece Intervening)*, ICJ, Judgment, 3 February 2012, paras 92, 95. See also the discussion of practice in para. 96.

[47] Ingrid Wuerth, '*Pinochet's* Legacy Reassessed' (2012) 106 *American Journal of International Law* 731.

immunity.[48] These arguments, though, understate the simple fact that war criminals, who have tended (at least until recently) to act on behalf of states, have been prosecuted for (quite literally) hundreds of years.[49] This point is rightly emphasized by Dapo Akande and Sangeeta Shah, who note that the nature of international crimes has evolved to include (although is not limited to) activities that have traditionally been state based. Therefore, as soon as extra-territorial jurisdiction is accepted to exist in international law, then immunity cannot coexist with such a principle.[50] As will be seen, this could be important for the role of the International Criminal Court.

14.3.2 International Courts and Tribunals

In many ways, when it comes to international courts, the scene was set (perhaps unsurprisingly) by the Nuremberg International Military Tribunal (IMT), with its strong statement that:

> crimes against international law are committed by men, not abstract entities, and only by punishing individuals who commit such crimes can the provisions of international law be enforced He who violates the law of war cannot obtain immunity while acting in pursuance of the authority of the State if the State in authorising the action moves outside of its competence in international law … individuals have international duties which transcend the national obligations of obedience imposed by the individual state.[51]

This statement was made in response to the argument made on behalf of the defendants that all of their conduct was official conduct of Germany, and therefore solely attributable to that state, and thus the individuals involved were immune owing to state immunity. As the ICJ made clear in

---

[48] Crawford, n. 29 above, p. 500. For an overview of the relevant practice see O'Keefe, n. 13 above, pp. 127–31.

[49] See for example, Timothy L.H. McCormack 'From Sun Tzu to the Sixth Committee: The Evolution of an International Criminal Law Regime' in Gerry Simpson and Timothy L.H. McCormack (eds), *The Law of War Crimes: National and International Approaches* (The Hague, Kluwer, 1997), p. 31.

[50] Akande and Shah, n. 3 above. See also, Alexander Orakhelashvii, 'Immunities of State Officials, International Crimes and Foreign Courts: A Reply to Akande and Shah' (2011) 22 *European Journal of International Law* 849. The difference is, though, one of reasoning rather than result.

[51] Nuremberg IMT, Judgment and Sentences (1947) 41 *AJIL* 172 at 221. The Tribunal's strong statement was agreed with wholeheartedly by its Tokyo counterpart (see Tokyo IMT, Transcript 48, pp. 437–40).

Bosnian Genocide, that is not the case.[52] Liability can be divided without being diminished.

It has been thought that the Nuremberg IMT's comment could be explained on the basis that there was no German state to invoke immunity, but the simple text of the judgment makes a different argument, that when international criminality is involved, the state simply cannot immunize its officials. Similarly, although in the Tokyo IMT, it could be argued that Japan's unconditional surrender (or acceptance of the Potsdam Declaration, which accepted the prosecution of war criminals) was sufficient for jurisdiction,[53] the Tokyo Tribunal's reasoning adopted the broader approach taken by the Nuremberg Tribunal,[54] which, it bears remembering, was accepted as being reflective of customary law in UN General Assembly Resolution 95. For more than 50 years this seemed to be the accepted position.

However, this consensus was somewhat undermined by the ICJ's rather Delphic and (in)famous pronouncement in the *Yerodia* case, that immunity before domestic courts does not, *per se*, amount to impunity, owing to the fact that:

> First, such persons enjoy no criminal immunity under international law in their own countries, and may thus be tried by those countries' courts in accordance with the relevant rules of domestic law. Secondly, they will cease to enjoy immunity from foreign jurisdiction if the State which they represent or have represented decides to waive that immunity. Thirdly, after a person ceases to hold the office of Minister for Foreign Affairs, he or she will no longer enjoy all of the immunities accorded by international law in other States. Provided that it has jurisdiction under international law, a court of one State may try a former Minister for Foreign Affairs of another State in respect of acts committed prior or subsequent to his or her period of office, as well as in respect of acts committed during that period of office in a private capacity. Fourthly, an incumbent or former Minister for Foreign Affairs may be subject to criminal proceedings before certain international criminal courts, where they have jurisdiction. Examples include the International Criminal Tribunal for the former Yugoslavia (ICTY), and the International Criminal Tribunal for Rwanda (ICTR), established pursuant to Security Council Resolutions under Chapter VII of the United Nations Charter, and the future International Criminal Court created by the 1998 Rome Convention. The latter's Statute expressly provides, in Article 27, paragraph 2, that '[i]mmunities or special procedural rules which may attach to the official

52 *Bosnian Genocide* case, n. 17 above, para. 172.

53 See Neil Boister and Robert Cryer, *The Tokyo International Military Tribunal: A Reappraisal* (Oxford, Oxford University Press, 2008), p. 31.

54 Tokyo IMT, Transcript 48, pp. 437–49.

capacity of a person, whether under national or international law, shall not bar the Court from exercising its jurisdiction over such a person'.[55]

There are, or ought to be, limits to what this can mean, not least as this statement was *obiter dictum*.[56] The first argument has little relevance to international law. The second is trite. The third begs the question of what immunities remain after a state official has left office, in particular what amounts to private activity, which is in itself a strong course of contestation.[57]

The most pertinent for this chapter's purposes is the fourth argument. Irrespective of the question of the legality of immunities before domestic courts, for the International Criminal Tribunal for the former Yugoslavia and the International Criminal Tribunal for Rwanda, both as a matter of personal and substantive immunities, the question is relatively settled. Article 103 of the UN Charter provides that: 'In the event of a conflict between the obligations of the Members of the United Nations under the present Charter and their obligations under any other international agreement, their obligations under the present Charter shall prevail'. The practice of those tribunals in indicting current or former heads of state for international crimes can be explained in the light of this provision.[58]

14.3.3 Collateral Crimes

The above seems to apply to international crimes, but not necessarily to collateral offences tried before international tribunals. Interestingly, in the seminal *Blaškić* Appeal on a purported subpoena, the Trial Chamber wished to send for a Croatian state archivist to explain the absence of certain documents. The Appeals Chamber denied this, holding that:

> The Appeals Chamber dismisses the possibility of the International Tribunal addressing subpoenas to State officials acting in their official capacity. Such

---

55 *Yerodia,* n. 10 above, para. 61.

56 Chanaka Wickremasinghe, 'Arrest Warrant of 11 April 2003 (Democratic Republic of Congo v Belgium) Preliminary Objections and Merits' (2003) 52 *International and Comparative Law Quarterly* 775 at 781.

57 Hazel Fox, 'Some Aspects of Immunity from Criminal Jurisdiction of the State and its Officials' in Lal Chand Vohrah *et al.* (eds), *Man's Inhumanity to Man, Essays in Honour of Antonio Cassese* (The Hague, Kluwer, 2003), pp. 305–7.

58 On which see Andreas Paulus, 'Article 103' in Bruno Simma (ed.), *The Charter of the United Nations: A Commentary* (3rd edn, Oxford, Oxford University Press, 2012), p. 2110.

> officials are mere instruments of a State and their official action can only be attributed to the State. They cannot be the subject of sanctions or penalties for conduct that is not private but undertaken on behalf of a State. In other words, State officials cannot suffer the consequences of wrongful acts which are not attributable to them personally but to the State on whose behalf they act: they enjoy so-called 'functional immunity'.[59]

This statement could be explained by suggesting that the Appeals Chamber in *Blaškić* was fundamentally opposed to subpoenas, preferring to issue 'binding orders'. However, when discussing such binding orders, the Chamber came to the same conclusion, albeit on different reasons, the most important of which from our perspective being that the relevant addressee of the Security Council's obligation to cooperate was the state, rather than the individual, so that the state was the relevant international person bound by such an order.[60]

Outside of this decision, which rather mixed together the question of the issue of a subpoena and immunity from it, there is the question of offences against the administration of justice. These, in the ad hoc Tribunals, are roughly speaking contempt of court and the giving of false testimony.[61] The Tribunals treat these offences as a matter of their inherent powers[62] (although provisions regarding them have also been set out in the Rules of Procedure and Evidence). The arguments about international crimes being different to 'normal' crimes seems hardly applicable here. On the basis of *Blaškić,* the reasoning adopted there does not seem to apply, so a state official who commits contempt of one of the ad hoc Tribunals is in an interesting position. It could be argued that by providing false testimony before the court, the official has waived the immunity international law offers. However, the immunity here (functional immunity) is not theirs to waive, as it serves the function of preventing the state being indirectly impleaded. Thus, if the state does not waive the immunity (and there are strong reputational reasons why

---

59 *Prosecutor v Blaškić*, IT-95-14-AR 108bis, ICTY, Judgment on the Request of the Republic of Croatia for review of the Decision of Trial Chamber II of 18 July 1997, 29 October 1997, para. 38.

60 *Ibid.* paras 39–44.

61 William Shabas, *The International Criminal Court, Commentary on the Rome Statute* (Oxford, Oxford University Press, 2010) p. 853.

62 *Prosecutor v Tadić*, IT94-1-AR77, ICTY, Judgment on allegations of contempt against prior counsel, Milan Vujin, 31 January 2000, para. 13. The position is different before the Residual Mechanism, see Residual Mechanism Statute, Art. 1(4).

they might not wish to do so) it might be that the official is immune, which would be an unhappy situation.

The issue of interference with witnesses is similar, but not quite the same, insofar as there is no oath to the court to break, and the *Blaškić* argument might apply. It is also notable that, with respect to the International Committee of the Red Cross (ICRC), the ICTY has been very solicitous of claims of immunity[63] (albeit that it is a different institution not directly bound by the Statute, and the issue was immunity from giving testimony, not perjury or other offences against the administration of justice). Immunity here would be similarly unfortunate. Although there certainly has been interference with witnesses by some state officials,[64] there have been no prosecutions to date, and none are expected. Probably due to this, the UN Charter, Article 103 argument does not seem to have had much effect in the ICTY and ICTR.

The International Criminal Court (ICC) is different from the ICTY and ICTR, as provisions regarding offences against the administration of justice are contained in the ICC Statute itself. Article 70 provides:

> 1. The Court shall have jurisdiction over the following offences against its administration of justice when committed intentionally:
>
> (a) Giving false testimony when under an obligation pursuant to article 69, paragraph 1, to tell the truth;
> (b) Presenting evidence that the party knows is false or forged;
> (c) Corruptly influencing a witness, obstructing or interfering with the attendance or testimony of a witness, retaliating against a witness for giving testimony or destroying, tampering with or interfering with the collection of evidence;
> (d) Impeding, intimidating or corruptly influencing an official of the Court for the purpose of forcing or persuading the official not to perform, or to perform improperly, his or her duties;
> (e) Retaliating against an official of the Court on account of duties performed by that or another official;
> (f) Soliciting or accepting a bribe as an official of the Court in connection with his or her official duties.[65]

---

[63] *Prosecutor v Simic et al.*, IT-95-9-PT, ICTY, Decision on the prosecution motion under Rule 73 for a ruling concerning the testimony of a witness, 27 July 1999. The Chamber here controversially recognized a customary immunity for giving testimony of ICRC officials.

[64] See Robert Cryer, 'Witness Tampering and International Criminal Tribunals' (2014) 27 *Leiden Journal of International Law* 191 at 193–5.

[65] See generally Schabas, n. 17 above.

In relation to states parties, a similar argument can be made to the one to be made below with respect to personal immunities, that states parties, by ratifying the Statute of an international court, have waived any immunities. It might be a stretch, but is certainly plausible. However, non-states parties cannot be taken to have made such a waiver, and the same arguments on immunity would apply as for the ad hoc Tribunals (including the possible use of UN Charter, Article 103). Again, there have been no prosecutions of state officials for such offences (in particular witness intimidation), but there have been widespread allegations of such activity, especially (but not only) in Kenya, which the Prosecutor claimed led to the collapse of the case against President Kenyatta.[66]

14.4 PERSONAL IMMUNITIES

In national law, the issue of personal immunity is fairly clear, as discussed above. The ICJ in *Yerodia* refused to draw a distinction between domestic crimes and international crimes for the purposes of personal immunities. These immunities have caused comparatively little difficulties for the Tribunals themselves, at least at the theoretical level (in practice it has made cooperation difficult, not least owing to the hostility of many African states to the assertion of jurisdiction over the Presidents of Sudan and Kenya). With regard to the status of immunities we need to distinguish diplomatic immunities and head of state/ government and other high officials, and we also need to distinguish between the different international courts, and their personal jurisdiction and cooperation regimes. As will be recalled in the *Yerodia* case, the ICJ said that high ranking officials are not immune from the jurisdiction of 'certain' international courts, although unfortunately it did not deign to say which ones they were.

14.4.1 Nuremberg IMT

So, let us start at the beginning. In Nuremberg, the Allies simply decided to legislate away any immunities that existed. Hence, Article 7 of the Nuremberg IMT Statute read: 'The official position of defendants, whether as Heads of State or responsible officials in Government Departments, shall not be considered as freeing them from responsibility or mitigating punishment'. Hence the Allies can be said to have taken a

---

[66] *Prosecutor v Kenyatta,* ICC-01/09-02/11, ICJ, Notice of withdrawal of charges against Uhuru Muigai Kenyatta, 5 December 2014.

stern line. Although Admiral Dönitz, pursuant to Hitler's will, was meant to take over as Führer, it was never accepted by any other state that he was, in fact, head of state. As we saw above, the defendants attempted to rely on defence of act of state, but this was dismissed. In truth, there was no real Germany left upon which to rely in relation to personal immunities. The defendants were on their own, and personal immunity played little role in the proceedings.

14.4.2 Tokyo IMT

The provisions on this point in the Tokyo IMT's Statute are similar, although not quite identical to its Nuremberg cousin. Article 6 read:

> Responsibility of Accused. Neither the official position, at any time, of an accused, nor the fact that an accused acted pursuant to order of his government or of a superior shall, of itself, be sufficient to free such accused from responsibility for any crime with which he is charged, but such circumstances may be considered in mitigation of punishment if the Tribunal determines that justice so requires.

An interesting issue arose as to whether this running together of the provisions on immunity and superior orders permitted the Tribunal, unlike Nuremberg, to take the position that this permitted them to mitigate the sentences on this basis. There is no evidence this was the intention of the drafters of the Statute, and in practical terms, no mitigation was given on the basis of official position.

There was a claim before the Tokyo IMT of immunity from jurisdiction. This was from the previous Ambassador to Germany, Hiroshi Oshima.[67] The Tokyo IMT rejected this claim, on the basis that as it was an international tribunal for international crimes, there was no immunity.[68] For diplomats, this makes sense. Diplomats only obtain immunity from jurisdiction in the state in which they are accredited, and whilst on the way to, and back from, that post. The prosecution pointed out that, as the Tokyo IMT was clearly not a German court, the defendant was not immune from its proceedings.[69]

There was, of course, the matter of the position of the Emperor, the head of state and, at the time, a hugely influential government official.

---

[67] For discussion, see Tokyo IMT, Judgment, pp. 40541, 47107 ff.

[68] *Ibid.* 49824.

[69] *Ibid.* 48394–6. See Georg Schwazenberger, *International Law as Applied by International Courts and Tribunals*, vol. II, *The Law of Armed Conflict* (London, Stevens, 1968), pp. 508–9.

He was not prosecuted before the Tokyo IMT, indeed he was very deliberately kept out of the indictment proceedings and, to the most extent, the judgment. However, this had nothing to do with the provisions of Article 7, and everything to do with General MacArthur's decision that the occupation of Japan would run more smoothly if he remained in place.[70] The closest thing this had to an effect on proceedings was that the President, Sir William Webb, said that he would have sentenced the other defendants to lower sentences owing to the fact that the Emperor had not been tried,[71] but this was also not based on Article 7.

14.4.3 Ad Hoc Security Council Tribunals

The next international courts came nearly 50 years later, when the United Nations created the ICTY and ICTR (the Cold War having stymied any developments in the interim).[72] The provisions of the ICTY Statute were quite heavily modelled in places on those of the Nuremberg IMT Statute. The provision on immunity is one of them. Article 7(2) of the ICTY Statute (to which Article 6(2) essentially conforms) provides (briefly): 'The official position of any accused person, whether as Head of State or Government or as a responsible Government official, shall not relieve such person of criminal responsibility nor mitigate punishment'. Both the ICTY and ICTR have (strictly speaking) prosecuted ex-heads of state, Slobodan Milošević in the case of the ICTY, and Jean Kambanda in the case of the ICTR.[73] The difficulties involved in the case of Milošević were more to do with obtaining custody of him from Serbia than his liability under the Statute. He did claim before the ICTY that he was the head of state of Serbia, but this fell on deaf ears at the ICTY.[74] In any case, both Tribunals were created by the UN Security Council, and the Article 103 argument canvassed above with respect to functional immunity, in an interesting reversal (in that functional immunity was tended to

---

[70] Boister, and Cryer, n. 53 above, pp. 65–9; Yoriko Otomo, 'The Decision Not to Prosecute the Emperor' in Yuki Tanaka, Tim McCormck and Gerry Simpson (eds), *Beyond Victor's Justice? The Tokyo War Crimes Trial Revisited* (Leiden, Martinus Nijhoff, 2011), p. 63.

[71] Separate Opinion of the President, p. 6.

[72] Robert Cryer, *Prosecuting International Crimes: Selectivity and the International Criminal Law Regime* (Cambridge, Cambridge University Press, 2005), pp. 48–51.

[73] *Prosecutor v Milošević*, Case No. IT-02-54.

[74] See generally, Michael P. Scharf, 'The Legacy of the Nuremberg Trial' (2003) 37 *New England Law Review* 915.

be more limited than personal immunity in international criminal law), seems to have had more traction here.[75]

14.4.4 Special Court for Sierra Leone

The next 'international' tribunal is the Special Court for Sierra Leone (SCSL). According to the Secretary-General, the Special Court, which was created by an agreement between himself and the government of Sierra Leone, was a 'treaty-based *sui generis* court of mixed jurisdiction and composition'.[76] This seemed to be the generally accepted view.[77]

Its approach to immunity is (interestingly) a little more like the Tokyo IMT's in that it accepts (this time expressly) that mitigation may be at issue: Article 6(4) of its Statute provides: 'The fact that an accused person acted pursuant to an order of a Government or of a superior shall not relieve him or her of criminal responsibility, but may be considered in mitigation of punishment if the Special Court determines that justice so requires.'

This became a live issue when, in 2003, the Special Court indicted Charles Taylor, at the time the incumbent head of state in Liberia, who was accused of running a vicious proxy war in Sierra Leone. The arrest warrant was passed to Ghana, who did not enforce it. However, his counsel at the SCSL submitted a request that the indictment be withdrawn. This was decided upon in late May 2004, by which time Taylor was no longer in his role in Liberia, and had headed into exile in Nigeria.

Picking up on *Yerodia*, his defence team argued, *inter alia*, that as head of state he had absolute immunity before foreign domestic courts, absent some form of Chapter VII Security Council action (in other words, setting up a Tribunal under Chapter VII of the Charter). They argued that the Special Court was not such a body, hence its orders had only the binding force of a national court.[78] In truth, the points had some force (although others not important here were fairly clearly spurious). In

---

[75] That said, the status of Yugoslavia as a UN member at the time was (shall we say) complex, see Cryer, Friman, Robinson and Wilmshurst, n. 2 above, 557.

[76] *Report of the Secretary-General*, UN Doc. S/2000/915 (4 October 2000), para. 9.

[77] It was certainly this author's view, see Robert Cryer, 'A Special Court for Sierra Leone?' (2001) 50 *International and Comparative Law Quarterly* 435 at 437. See also, Zsuzanna Deed Racsmány, '*Prosecutor v Taylor*: The Status of the Special Court for Sierra Leone and its Implications for Immunity' (2005) 18 *Leiden Journal of International Law* 299 at 308.

[78] *Prosecutor v Taylor*, SCSL 2003-1-I, Decision on Immunity from Jurisdiction, 31 May 2004, para. 6. The decision is very ably critiqued by Deen

response, the prosecution made a number of arguments, the most relevant here being that the SCSL was an international court and therefore, by simple dint of that fact, personal immunities were irrelevant.[79] This argument was picked up on by the Appeals Chamber to reject the defence request.

First, the prosecution argued that the involvement of the Security Council meant the SCSL was an expression of the will of the international community, and an agreement between Sierra Leone and all UN member states.[80] Two points might be taken in objection.[81] First, the Security Council deliberately chose not to act itself, but by the Secretary-General, and not invoke its Chapter VII powers;[82] secondly, in that case, all UN member states might have wanted to be involved in the drafting of such a treaty, as that was, after all, the process used for creating the ICC. The prosecution's second argument was that the Preamble to Resolution 1315 (by which the Secretary-General was asked to negotiate the treaty with Sierra Leone) spoke of making every effort to bring those accountable to justice, thus establishing that the Special Court was part of the machinery of international justice.[83] This was perhaps arguable, although national courts are part of the 'machinery of international justice', but immunity remains. Also, the question then arose as to what powers such courts have?[84] And the answer to that comes not only from their Statutes, but the underlying authority for them, and here it was a treaty between a (duly authorized) UN official and Sierra Leone, not between every state in the world.[85] And it is worth remembering that the ICJ had said that 'certain' international courts do not have to respect immunities, thus implying that some do.[86] By far the easiest way to have proceeded was for the Special Court to declare the issue moot, as Taylor was simply no longer head of state, hence all that would have needed to be done if they had cancelled the warrant would be for the Prosecutor to reissue it that day.[87]

Racsmány, n. 77 above. See also Cryer, Firman, Robinson and Wilmshurst, n. 2 above, 561–4.

[79] *Ibid.* para. 7.

[80] *Ibid.* para. 38.

[81] In addition see Deen Racsmány, n. 77 above, 311–13.

[82] See *ibid.* 308–9.

[83] *Taylor*, n. 78 above, para. 39.

[84] See the discussion in Deen Racsmány, n. 77 above, 313–14.

[85] See also *ibid.* 312.

[86] *Ibid.* 317.

[87] *Taylor*, n. 78 above, para. 59; see also Deen Racsmány, n. 77 above, 321.

14.4.5 International Criminal Court

The establishment of the ICC was the first time a treaty on an international criminal tribunal was drafted.[88] As such, one might expect that immunities would be dealt with in a fairly comprehensive way.[89] States like to assert their immunities, but many states also accepted that immunities provided a significant obstacle to international justice. Hence, a compromise was found, which involved splitting off the question of immunity before the Court itself, from the obligations of states to cooperate with the Court. In relation to the former the position is contained in Article 27 of the ICC Statute:

> (1) This Statute shall apply equally to all persons without any distinction based on official capacity. In particular, official capacity as a Head of State or Government, a member of a Government or parliament, an elected representative or a government official shall in no case exempt a person from criminal responsibility under this Statute, nor shall it, in and of itself, constitute a ground for reduction of sentence.
>
> (2) Immunities or special procedural rules which may attach to the official capacity of a person, whether under national or international law, shall not bar the Court from exercising its jurisdiction over such a person.

As can be seen, the ICC Statute takes the pretty strong Nuremberg line of no immunity and no mitigation. The legality of this will be discussed below. With respect to cooperation, Article 98 – in a manner that seems inconsistent – provides that:

> (1) The Court may not proceed with a request for surrender or assistance which would require the requested State to act inconsistently with its obligations under international law with respect to the State or diplomatic

---

[88] On the drafting process see Phillipe Kirsch and John T. Holmes, 'The Rome Conference on an International Criminal Court: The Negotiating Process' (1999) 93 *American Journal of International Law* 2; M. Cherif Bassiouni, 'Negotiating the Treaty of Rome on the Establishment of an International Criminal Court' (1999) 32 *Cornell International Law Journal* 443.

[89] The standard work remains Dapo Akande, 'International Law Immunities and the International Criminal Court' (2004) 98 *American Journal of International Law* 407; see also Roger O'Keefe, 'The United States and the ICC: The Force and Farce of the Legal Arguments' (2011) 24 *Cambridge Review of International Affairs* 335; Bruce Broomhall, *International Justice and the International Court: Between Sovereignty and the International Criminal Court* (Oxford, Oxford University Press, 2003), ch. 7.

> immunity of a person or property of a third State, unless the Court can first obtain the cooperation of that third State for the waiver of the immunity.[90]

In spite of the apparent contradiction, the two provisions are in fact reconcilable, in that one relates to the Court's activity, the other to that of states Thus, more timid states could ensure that they would not have to ignore the immunity of foreign state officials, and the Court would probably not have to face the question of Article 27, due to the fact that it would not gain jurisdiction over anyone to whom it applied directly (i.e. those with personal immunities).[91] That said, unless the view is taken that international courts are just different (discussed to some extent above and to some extent below), the legality of the two stands or falls together.

In relation to states parties to the ICC Statute, the issue is fairly simple. The parties to the Statute can be taken to have waived their immunities.[92] There may be other bases, discussed below, but for our purposes (and with Occam's razor in mind), this can be taken as the least controversial approach to the provisions.

However, for non-parties this is not the case. Non-parties have not ratified the Statute, and the *pacta tertiis* principle means that they cannot be taken to have done so through the fact that other states have. So, if the provisions quoted above are to be lawful, another basis must be found. The first of these has been canvassed above, which is that there just is no immunity before international criminal tribunals. That was the view of the SCSL in the *Taylor* case which, in part, did rely on the ICC Statute. It was also a view taken, at one point, by the ICC itself.[93] In relation to the failure of Malawi and Chad to arrest al-Bashir, and in response to their assertion that this was due to his immunity, the Court suggested

---

[90] This chapter will not deal with the issue of Status of Forces Agreements and the like, covered by Article 98(2), as they are not strictly immunities, although they are analogous.

[91] See Akande, n. 89 above, 419–26.

[92] Crawford, n. 29 above, 501.

[93] *Prosecutor v Al-Bashir,* ICC-02/05-01/09, ICJ, Decision pursuant to Article 87(7) of the Rome Statute on the failure by the Republic of Malawi to comply with the cooperation requests issued by the Court with respect to the arrest and surrender of Omar Hassan Ahmad Al-Bashir, 12 December 2011('Malawi Decision'); *Prosecutor v Al-Bashir*, ICC-02/05-01/09, ICJ, Décision rendue en application de l'article 87-7 du Statut de Rome concernant le refus de la République du Tchad d'accéder aux demandes de cooperation dé livrées par la Cour concernant l'arrestation et la remise d'Omar Hassan Ahmad Al Bashir, 13 December 2011.

that, following the Second World War, prosecutions of heads of state, such as Slobodan Milošević and Charles Taylor, alongside the broad ratification of the ICC Statute, meant that custom had developed to the extent that there was no immunity in international courts,[94] arguing in addition (and not really consistently with the text of Article 98) that this includes cooperation.[95] With respect, the reasoning is rather thin; the 'precedents' cited are not directly on point, as they do not concern cooperation by domestic authorities, but rather the question of immunity as a defence when someone is already before the relevant court.[96] This is not to say that the ICC's judgment was wrong in its result, but its 'working out' was flawed.[97]

The next argument would be the *jus cogens* argument canvassed in relation to domestic courts. If the argument stands in respect of domestic courts, it could either be argued that it must apply equally to international courts, or that, by virtue of the *nemo dat quod non habet* principle, states had passed on that absence of immunity to the courts.

It might, though, even be possible to go further than that, and question whether the *nemo dat* principle actually applies to the law of international organizations, and as such states could create an organ that had powers that they did not have.[98] The most notable example of such a possibility would be the United Nations. It is possible to argue that Chapter VII of the UN Charter, in particular the right to use force against threats to international peace and security in Articles 39 and 42, are rights that states did not have prior to the Charter.[99] Hence, it could be argued that states may confer powers on organizations that they do not themselves have, doing collectively what they could not do individually.[100]

---

94 *Ibid.* paras 37–43.

95 *Ibid.* para. 44.

96 Dire Tladi, 'The ICC Decisions on Chad and Malawi: On Cooperation, Immunities and Article 98' (2013) 11 *Journal of International Criminal Justice* 199 at 206.

97 This paragraph draws on Robert Cryer, 'The International Criminal Court and its Relationship to Non-Party States' in Carsten Stahn, *The Practice of the International Criminal Court* (Oxford, Oxford University Press, 2015).

98 Having discussed this matter with Dr Antonios Tzanakopoulos, it would seem we have both separately been thinking similarly on this point, and I am grateful for the discussions I have had with him.

99 And there is much to be said for this view, see for example, Ian Brownlie, *International Law and the Use of Force by States* (Oxford, Oxford University Press, 1963), ch. V.

100 See Danesh Sarooshi, 'The Peace and Justice Paradox: The International Criminal Court and the Security Council' in Dominick McGoldrick, Peter Rowe

The applicability of the principle in international law cannot simply be assumed.[101] There could be an answer to this, that UN member states have consented to such use of force in advance. That argument runs into problems when it applies to states,[102] and as such might be the basis of an argument that international organizations (such as the ICC) can have different powers.

14.4.6 Curious Case of Security Council Referrals

Where the Security Council[103] has referred a situation to the ICC, the issue of immunities has arisen, especially with respect to heads of non-states parties. This issue has been at the centre of a bitter battle over the obligations of states parties to the ICC Statute to implement the arrest warrant issued against Omar al-Bashir, the President of Sudan. Should states recognize his immunity?[104] Sudan is not a party to the ICC Statute, but in 2005 the Security Council referred the situation in Darfur to the ICC in Resolution 1593.[105] Operative paragraph 2 of that Resolution required Sudan (although not other non-party states) to 'fully cooperate'

---

and Eric Donnelly, *The Permanent International Criminal Court: Legal and Policy Issues* (Oxford, Hart, 2004), p. 95 at 106–8; Nigel White and Robert Cryer, 'The ICC and the Security Council: An Uncomfortable Relationship' in José Doria, Hans-Peter Gasser and M. Cherif Bassiouni (eds), *The Legal Regime of the International Criminal Court* (Leiden, Martinus Nijhoff, 2009), p. 455 at 459.

[101] There is nothing about it in Hersch Lauterpacht's *Private Law Sources and Analogies of International Law* (London, Longmans, 1927); Bin Cheng, *General Principles of Law as Applied by International Courts and Tribunals* (London, Stevens, 1953) or in Robert Jennings and Arthur Watts, *Oppenheim's International Law* (19th edn, London, Longman, 1992).

[102] The ability of a state to consent to violation of a *jus cogens* rule must be, to say the least, questionable.

[103] This section draws on Cryer, n. 97 above.

[104] For states parties, ratification of the ICC Statute has been taken as a waiver of such immunities. On the al-Bashir indictment see Andrew T. Cayley, 'The Prosecutor's Strategy in Seeking the Arrest of Sudanese President Al Bashir on Charges of Genocide' (2008) 6 *Journal of International Criminal Justice* 829; Christopher Gosnell, 'The Request for an Arrest Warrant in *Al Bashir*: Idealistic Posturing or Calculated Plan?' (2008) 6 *Journal of International Criminal Justice* 841.

[105] On the referral see Robert Cryer, 'Sudan, Resolution 1593 and International Criminal Justice' (2006) 19 *Leiden Journal of International Law* 195.

with the ICC.[106] As the ICC has noted, this means that other non-states parties, in spite of the Security Council referral, are not obliged to cooperate with the Court (although they are 'urged' to do so), so may respect President al-Bashir's immunity.[107] Were the Council to require cooperation by non-states parties, the basis of the obligation to cooperate would be the relevant Security Council Resolution (and the UN Charter) rather than the ICC Statute *per se*.[108] In this situation, the basis for removal of immunity would be very similar to that used by the ad hoc criminal tribunals, i.e. UN Charter, Article 103 trumping immunity, and the matter would end there. The problem is, the Security Council did not do so.

Soon after the passage of Security Council Resolution 1593, differing views were expressed about whether Sudan's obligations under that Resolution meant that President al-Bashir's immunities as head of state were abrogated, such that (Article 98(1) notwithstanding) other states (whether parties to the ICC Statute or not) could arrest and transfer him to the ICC. Paula Gaeta took the view that in spite of Resolution 1593, and the fact that the ICC, as an international court, could lawfully try al-Bashir, his immunity before domestic jurisdictions was retained, and thus Article 98(1) remains applicable.[109] This follows, for Gaeta, from the fact that the ICC has to abide by its Statute, and has not obtained a waiver of immunity from Sudan, which (Resolution 1593 notwithstanding) remains a non-state party to the Statute.[110] In addition, unlike the Resolutions setting up the ICTY and ICTR (Resolutions 827 and 955, respectively), non-states parties to the ICC Statute are not required to cooperate with the Court, but are merely urged to do so. Hence, for Gaeta, Article 103 of the UN Charter does not 'bite' so as to give those states a defence that trumps immunity.[111] Dapo Akande has responded to

---

[106] Göran Sluiter, 'Obtaining Co-operation from Sudan: Where is the Law?' (2008) 6 *Journal of International Criminal Justice* 871 at 877–8 queries the nature of this obligation, but as he notes, the ICC has taken it to mean that Part 9 of the ICC Statute is applicable. See further Dapo Akande, 'The Effect of Security Council Resolutions and Domestic Proceedings on State Obligations to Cooperate with the ICC' (2012) 10 *Journal of International Criminal Justice* 299. The cognate paragraph of Resolution 1970 that referred the situation in Libya is similarly framed.

[107] See for example, *al-Bashir*, Kuwait Decision, para. 9.

[108] *Al-Bashir*, US Decision, para. 10.

[109] Paola Gaeta, 'Does President Al Bashir Enjoy Immunity from Arrest?' (2009) 7 *Journal of International Criminal Justice* 315.

[110] *Ibid.* 327–30.

[111] *Ibid.* 330–31.

this, arguing that Resolution 1593 renders Sudan functionally a party to the ICC Statute, therefore can be taken as having given up its immunities, due to the applicability of Article 27 to national authorities involved in cooperation as well as before the ICC.[112] This is because the Court must function in accordance with its Statute, which includes Article 27, and any other interpretation would render Article 27 practically redundant.[113]

The result Akande has argued for has prevailed in the jurisprudence of the ICC (although African states have not, in spite of his visits, arrested al-Bashir, and the African Union has insisted on the continued applicability of Article 98),[114] albeit not generally on the basis of Akande's reasoning. In the early decisions on non-cooperation by states (Malawi and Chad), the relevant ICC Pre-Trial Chamber determined that those states had violated their obligation to arrest al-Bashir.[115] It did so on the basis that, in the Chamber's view, heads of state have no immunity before international courts, a view discussed above.[116]

When the ICC returned to the issue of states not cooperating in arresting al-Bashir, in 2014, in the context of the Democratic Republic of Congo (DRC)'s failure to arrest al-Bashir, it changed tack somewhat:[117]

> the DRC claims that by issuing the 26 February 2014 Decision the Court placed the DRC in a situation where it was called upon to act inconsistently with its international obligations arising from the decision of the African Union 'to respect the immunities that come with [Omar al-Bashir's] position of Head of State … The Chamber does not consider that such inconsistency arises in the present case. This is so because by issuing Resolution 1593(2005) the SC *decided* that the 'Government of Sudan … *shall* cooperate fully with and provide any necessary assistance to the Court and the

---

[112] Dapo Akande, 'The Legal Nature of Security Council Referrals to the ICC and its Impact on Al-Bashir's Immunities' (2009) 7 *Journal of International Criminal Justice* 333. Tladi criticizes this on the basis that it does not explain why the Security Council thought it necessary to include a duty to cooperate on Sudan in Resolution 1593 (Tladi, n. 96 above, 212), however, this probably imputes too much subtlety to a negotiated text coming from a political body like the Security Council.

[113] Akande, n. 112 above, 340–42.

[114] See Carsten Stahn, 'Libya, the International Criminal Court and Complementarity: A Test for "Shared Responsibility"' (2012) 10 *JICJ* 325 at 331; Tladi, n. 96 above, 201–4.

[115] *Prosecutor v Al-Bashir*, Malawi Decision, n. 93 above.

[116] *Ibid.* para. 36.

[117] *Prosecutor* v *Al Bashir*, ICC-02/056-01/09, ICJ, Decision on the cooperation of the Democratic Republic of the Congo regarding Omar Al Bashir's arrest and surrender to the Court, 9 April 2014.

> Prosecutor pursuant to this resolution'. Since immunities attached to Omar al-Bashir are a procedural bar from prosecution before the Court, the cooperation envisaged in said resolution was meant to eliminate any impediment to the proceedings before the Court, including the lifting of immunities. Any other interpretation would render the SC decision requiring that Sudan 'cooperate fully' and 'provide any necessary assistance to the Court' senseless. Accordingly, the '*cooperation* of that third State [Sudan] for the waiver of the immunity', as required under the last sentence of article 98(1) of the Statute, was already ensured by the language used in paragraph 2 of SC Resolution 1593(2005). By virtue of said paragraph, the SC implicitly waived the immunities granted to Omar al-Bashir under international law and attached to his position as a Head of State. Consequently, there also exists no impediment at the horizontal level between the DRC and Sudan as regards the execution of the 2009 and 2010 Requests.[118]

Turning to the DRC's obligations to invoke Article 98(1) as a member of the African Union, the Chamber responded that under UN Charter, Article 103, the implicit waiver contained in Resolution 1593 trumped any obligations the DRC had by virtue of its membership of the African Union.[119] Whether this is considered convincing depends on whether it is thought that the nature of Resolution 1593 renders Sudan (*pace* Akande) essentially a party to the ICC Statute or whether it is necessary for the ICC to ask Sudan to waive al-Bashir's immunity. General principles, such as the duty not to evade treaty obligations[120] (here under the UN Charter) and the principle *ex injuria jus non oritur*[121] militate in favour of the absence of immunity here. Analogously it could also be argued that Sudan is estopped from claiming immunity by the principle *ex delicto non oritur actio*.[122] The ICC has not, to date, adopted such an approach, although its assertive jurisprudence here is consistent with that of a Court which, in this circumstance, has compulsory rather than optional jurisdiction.[123]

---

118 *Ibid.* paras 28–9.

119 *Ibid.* para. 31.

120 See Cheng, n. 101 above: 'International law prohibits the evasion of a treaty obligation under the guise of an alleged exercise of a right'.

121 *Ibid.* 187.

122 *Ibid.* 155–8.

123 On this see Hersch Lauterpacht, *The Development of International Law by the International Court of Justice* (London, Stevens, 1958), ch. 6.

14.5 CONCLUSION

To go back to the start, the law of immunities involves a balance, and like proportionality in humanitarian law, where civilian casualties have to be balanced against military advantage, different people, particularly those in different roles, will often take a divergent view on where that balance should lie. As the ICTY Prosecutor's report on Kosovo said with respect to proportionality: 'most applications of the principle are not so clear cut … because the comparison is often between unlike quantities and values … The answers to these questions are not simple. It may be necessary to resolve them on a case by case basis, and the answers may differ depending on the background and values of the decision maker. It is unlikely that a human rights lawyer and an experienced combat commander would assign the same relative values to military advantage and to injury to noncombatants'.[124] Here the analogy is between high state officials (or indeed, any state official) and non-state actors. State actors, particularly high state officials, can be expected to argue in favour of greater immunities, whereas non-state actors, who won't be able to claim immunity anyway, can expected to argue the opposite. In many ways this is true, as the practice of the African Union has shown, whilst non-governmental organizations tend to decry immunity as impunity, a point not convincingly put to rest by the ICJ's pronouncement in *Yerodia*. Even so, as this chapter has shown, there has been an erosion of immunities, perhaps more than could have been expected. On the other hand, there is a general sense that international criminal law is going through a period of retrenchment, with the heady days of 1998 and 1999 with the Rome Statute and the *Pinochet* case seeming rather far away.[125] Developments here are unlikely to come quickly, as the ICJ in the *Jurisdictional Immunities* case showed. As a non-state actor, I'm disappointed.

---

[124] *Final Report to the Prosecutor by the Committee Established to Review the NATO Bombing Campaign Against the Federal Republic of Yugoslavia* (13 June 2000), paras 48–50.

[125] David Luban, 'After the Honeymoon: Reflections on the Current State of International Criminal Justice' (2013) 11 *Journal of International Criminal Justice* 505; 'Symposium' (2008) 6 *Journal of International Criminal Justice* 899.

15. Jurisdictional immunity of international organizations: from abstract functionality to absolute immunity

Alexander Orakhelashvili

15.1 GENERAL ASPECTS

The reasons and basis for limiting, or not limiting, the national jurisdiction of the state in favour of an international organization could be complex. The problem is analytically similar to state immunity, in that it is about why the jurisdiction of one entity should be replaced to the benefit of another entity, or replaced by that other entity's jurisdiction, within the system of international law that always requires positive legal reasons to be advanced for justifying such outcomes. But rationales for or against immunities of international organizations are rather different from those that apply to states, because international organizations are structurally different from states, and their purposes and functions are not identical with those of states either.

The international organization's immunity restricts the sovereign territorial jurisdiction of the state just as much as any other immunity does. A clear legal basis for such immunity is thus required, in each and every case, to see why the host state should decline exercising its sovereign jurisdiction. It was noted in the early literature that, unlike the older absolute immunity doctrine applicable to states and derived from their sovereignty, international organizations would not enjoy immunity merely because of their status. Instead, further reasons should be furnished as to how indispensable particular immunities are for the organization's working.[1] As was also convincingly argued by Gaillard and Pingel-Lenuzza, protection through immunity would be permissible 'so

[1] E.H. Fedder, 'The Functional Basis of International Privileges and Immunities: A New Concept in International Law and Organization' (1960) 9 *American University Law Review* 60 at 64; the same factor is more reluctantly acknowledged by J. Kunz, 'Privileges and Immunities of International Organizations' (1947) 41 *AJIL* 828 at 847.

long as the applicable rules (whether contained in a constitutive instrument, headquarters agreement, or an ad hoc treaty) provide for the equitable resolution of disputes by means other than recourse to national courts' and guarantee access to justice for private persons.[2]

In practice, organizations need privileges for a broad range of aims as they face multiple concerns. Nevertheless, any applicable doctrine of immunity can be valid only if derived from the agreed rules of international law. Amerasinghe is quite sceptical that the doctrine of the immunity of organizations could be part of customary law, for it is a relatively recent phenomenon.[3] It is indeed difficult to identify a general, uniform and durable practice involving both states and international organizations which manifests the requisite *opinio juris*. After the establishment of the United Nations, state practice has not developed so as to elaborate on the special customary rule on organizational immunity, but has led to the conclusion of agreements between the organizations and their host states.[4] The regime established by the 1946 General Convention came into play early enough to enable the customary law to develop independently. And then, as Gaja has observed, the immunity of organizations hardly ever arises in courts of states that are not bound by any treaty on that subject matter.[5] Examining the range of doctrinal opinions, Singer also doubts that customary law prohibits states from asserting domestic jurisdiction over employment-related disputes between individuals and international organizations.[6] Bekker similarly thinks that customary law, due to its uncertainty in this area, is unlikely to provide any clear-cut answers to gaps left by conventional law.[7]

---

[2] E. Gaillard and I. Pingel-Lenuzza, 'International Organizations and Immunity from Jurisdiction: To Restrict or to Bypass' (2002) 51 *ICLQ* 1 at 3–4.

[3] C. Amerasinghe, *Principles of the Institutional Law of International Organisations* (2005), pp. 315 at 322, 345; he also allows some room for the 1946 Convention to be reflective of customary law, but does not suggest any uniformly applicable conclusion (at 346–7).

[4] For an overview of this practice see H. Aufricht, 'The Expansion of the Concept of Sovereign Immunity, with Special reference to International Organizations' (1952) 46 *ASIL Proceedings* 85 at 90–91.

[5] G. Gaja, 'Note on Jurisdictional Immunity of International Organisations' (2006) *ILC Yearbook* 27, para. 3.

[6] M. Singer, 'Jurisdictional Immunity of International Organizations: Human Rights and Functional Necessity Concerns' (1995–1996) 36 *VaJIL* 53 at 99.

[7] P.H.F. Bekker, *The Legal Position of Intergovernmental Organisations* (Nijhof 1994), p. 151.

As there is no customary law on the immunities of international organizations, there is no duty for states to grant immunity to organizations, in the absence of conventional obligations, in relation to any act of an international organization. Therefore, the rest of this analysis will be devoted to the clarification of standards of immunity under the relevant treaties.

15.2 VARYING RATIONALE OF IMMUNITIES

Given that the doctrine of the international organizations' immunity is relatively new (compared to state immunity), there is less coherence in the understanding of its conceptual basis. In doctrine and practice, various justifications of the functional doctrine have been suggested. There is no authoritative definition of functionality and thus some underlying idea must be identified to inform its meaning. That idea cannot be derived from common-sense reasoning, but must be in accordance with the legal framework generally applicable to international organizations. Some constituent instruments are silent on immunities and it is not clear at all that the relevant organizations are subject to any doctrine of functionality in the first place.

One justification for organizational immunities is to frame it as a 'jurisdictional' issue in relation to matters that fall within the international organization's jurisdiction. The reasoning here would be that jurisdiction over the particular matter, for instance, the employment of the organization's officials, should be deemed to be transferred to the organization's internal legal order and exempted from the host state's domestic law. For instance, Brower endorses the view that there is 'a broad consensus for the proposition that the internal laws of international organizations govern their employment relations to the exclusion of municipal law'. Brower contends that this position is also endorsed under customary international law, the sole evidence invoked to justify this position, however, being the US Restatement (Third).[8]

---

[8] C. Brower, 'International Immunities: Some Dissident Views on Municipal Courts' (2000–2001) 41 *VaJIL* 1 at 66–7; then transferring this to the functionality dimension, contending that 'member states must understand that the civil services of international organizations do not operate within the value systems of particular member states, but reflect common values. To achieve these goals, the internal laws of international organizations must constitute the exclusive source of rules for their employment relations', *ibid.* 69.

It seems that the validity of such a blanket and far-reaching state of affairs cannot be assumed in the absence of the express rules of international law to the same effect. Moreover, against such position is the rule, exemplified by Article 104 of the United Nations Charter, that an international organization should enjoy legal personality under the local state law in which it has headquarters, representation or otherwise conducts its activities. If so, then the organization should also operate under that local law in relation to the matters ordinarily governed by that local law. The least this factor does is to enhance the presumption against the validity of the jurisdictional exemption argument.

Amerasinghe refers to the functional derivation of immunities from the organization's personality.[9] But the organization's personality can at most lead to the exercise of particular capacities by the relevant organization, not to the establishment of particular substantive obligations of states in relation to that organization, such as the obligation to restrict the states' own national jurisdiction by granting immunity. The personality-driven view is unsustainable also because it could only generate absolute immunity: any immunity derived from mere status is bound to be absolute.

Another approach taken in jurisprudence, culminating with the European Court of Human Rights (ECtHR) decision in *Srebrenica Mothers Foundation*, is that '[t]he attribution of privileges and immunities to international organisations is an essential means of ensuring the proper functioning of such organisations free from unilateral interference by individual governments'.[10] But this statement does little to clarify the actual scope of immunity, or whether the reference is made to the same purpose-related necessity featured in UN Charter, Article 105. For the actual scope of immunity, we need to bear in mind the policy consideration described by Gaillard and Pingel-Lenuzza, to the effect that:

> Generally, no organisation could fulfil its mission if it was submitted to the jurisdiction of national courts for all of its activities. It is however difficult to see why respect for the functional autonomy of an international organisation should necessarily entail the exclusion of the jurisdiction of national courts, irrespective of the nature of the acts of that organisation. While it is important that disputes that might affect the exercise of an international organisation's

9 Amerasinghe, n. 3 above, 347.

10 *Stichting Mothers of Srebrenica and others v The Netherlands*, Application No. 65542/12, ECtHR, Judgment of 27 June 2013, para. 139 ('*Srebrenica Mothers*').

> essential prerogatives remain outside the reach of national courts, this is not the case for all disputes involving these organisations.[11]

Therefore, enabling international organizations to carry out and fulfil their tasks is not the same as exempting them from the domestic legal process. Legal systems, national or international, subject to law any entity, whether an individual, corporation, government or international organization, which is not the same as obstructing their existence and functioning. Furthermore, the organizations' institutional or functional necessity should be distinguished from the convenience of the organization's bureaucracy. As Singer observes:

> it is important to stress that functional necessity doctrine entitles an international organization to precisely the jurisdictional immunities that it strictly needs to enable it to pursue its purposes without undue interference. The courts should not enlarge this privilege to guarantee every international organization a quiet life, and certainly not a charmed life, set apart from the bustle and travails of the world. States have learned that the right to conduct their affairs without undue interference from other states does not entail the privilege of never having to defend a lawsuit. There is no *a priori* reason why international organizations should have qualitatively different requirements.[12]

It is an analytical commonplace to say that organizations should enjoy immunities when functionally necessary for their activities. This also is an indication that the organizational immunities are not solely procedural, but instead their determination and grant is premised on ascertaining the rightful scope of legitimate activities of the relevant organization. A thing being 'functionally necessary' for the organization's activities is, therefore, in essence a right thing for that organization to do.

The functional immunity doctrine is the most generally accepted and predominant explanation of the immunity of international organizations, but its general scope is far from being certain. It is true, as Reinisch suggests, that the non-interference with organizations' affairs certainly relieves them of external pressure.[13] But, as such, as we can see, the 'interference' point clarifies nothing regarding the actual scope of immunities. To illustrate, in relation to states, both absolute and restrictive

---

[11] Gaillard and Pingel-Lenuzza, n. 2 above, 4–5.

[12] Singer, n. 6 above, 128.

[13] A. Reinisch, 'Privileges and Immunities' in J. Klabbers and A. Wallendahl, *Research Handbook on the Law of International Organisations* (2011), pp. 134, 136–7.

doctrines of immunity could be premised on some notion of non-interference. The range of acts in relation to which no interference is warranted would be different depending on each particular doctrine. Moreover, the 'interference' point works better with regard to the organization's premises, detention of officials, archives or means of communication. But it is not as obvious with the jurisdictional immunity proper, unless it concerns the core of its institution-specific activities. There is no reason why requiring an organization to pay damages in contract or tort could prevent that organization from functioning independently. Their working order would not be disrupted. And, moreover, the immunity rule could not be rationally premised on the thesis that unless the organization is able to carry on assuming debts without repaying them, it could not properly function as an independent entity. The non-interference approach therefore lacks any coherent rational foundation as an independent test. Organizational immunity requires further guiding criteria to be substantiated.

15.3 ORGANIZATIONAL IMMUNITIES UNDER CONSTITUENT INSTRUMENTS

Constituent instruments of various international organizations adopt diverging solutions on immunity. Some instruments opt for absolute, and others for a more restricted, version of organizational immunities. As an example of endorsing absolute immunity, Article IX(3) of the Articles of Agreement establishing the International Monetary Fund (1944) provides that 'The Fund, its property and its assets, wherever located and by whomsoever held, shall enjoy immunity from every form of judicial process except to the extent that it expressly waives its immunity for the purpose of any proceedings or by the terms of any contract'.

A more 'functional' and limited approach is taken in Article VII(1) of the Articles of Agreement establishing the International Bank for the Reconstruction and Development, which states: 'To enable the Bank to fulfil the functions with which it is entrusted, the status, immunities and privileges set forth in this Article shall be accorded to the Bank in the territories of each member'.

It is stipulated in Article VIII(3) that:

> Actions may be brought against the Bank only in a court of competent jurisdiction in the territories of a member in which the Bank has an office, has appointed an agent for the purpose of accepting service or notice of process, or has issued or guaranteed securities. No actions shall, however, be brought

> by members or persons acting for or deriving claims from members. The property and assets of the Bank shall, wheresoever located and by whomsoever held, be immune from all forms of seizure, attachment or execution before the delivery of final judgment against the Bank.

Regarding the Bank's officials, Article VIII(8) adopts a more absolute approach, providing that 'All governors, executive directors, alternates, officers and employees of the Bank (i) shall be immune from legal process with respect to acts performed by them in their official capacity except when the Bank waives this immunity'.

Overall, it has been clarified that the reason for exposing the international financial institutions (IFIs) to national legal proceedings is to avoid giving them unfair advantage in their financial and commercial transactions in which they engage as private persons, such as sale and purchase of bonds, goods and services.[14] There is thus a general understanding that private activities should not be covered by immunities. But the legal position in the case of IFIs is due to whatever has been specified by states parties in the constituent instrument, rather than to the inherent merit of any particular version of organizational immunity.

Moving to the immunity of the United Nations, Article 105(1) of the UN Charter provides that the United Nations 'shall enjoy in the territory of each of its Members such privileges and immunities as are necessary for the fulfilment of its purposes'. The only obvious feature of the Article 105 standard clear on its face is that it does not endorse absolute immunity. Anything that lays down an additional criterion to be considered, be it functional necessity or something else, cannot, by definition, be absolute. The essence of functional immunity, as reflected in Article 105, is premised on the 'as are necessary' requirement. There is no *a priori* circumscribed, let alone absolutely guaranteed, immunity. The assessment of 'necessity' is required in every specific case considering the nature of the relevant acts and of the organization's functions. Some acts would thus be immune and others would not. At the same time, as Kelsen observes, the 'interpretation of the phrase "such privileges and immunities as are necessary" is not authentic, and the Charter does not answer the question as to who is competent to decide what is "necessary"'.[15]

What is, therefore, the meaning of the word 'necessary' in this context? In *Handyside v United Kingdom*, the ECtHR has described the normative side of the concept of 'necessity' in the context of the margin of

---

[14] Bekker, n. 7 above, 128.

[15] H. Kelsen, *The Law of the United Nations* (1952), p. 342.

appreciation available to states in relation to freedom of expression under Article 10(2) of the European Convention on Human Rights (ECHR), stressing that:

> whilst the adjective 'necessary', within the meaning of Article 10(2), is not synonymous with 'indispensable' (cf. in Articles 2(2) and 6(1), the words 'absolutely necessary' and 'strictly necessary' and, in Article 15(1), the phrase 'to the extent strictly required by the exigencies of the situation'), neither has it the flexibility of such expressions as 'admissible', 'ordinary', 'useful', 'reasonable' or 'desirable'. Nevertheless, it is for the national authorities to make the initial assessment of the reality of the pressing social need implied by the notion of 'necessity' in this context.[16]

It seems that such understanding of the term 'necessary', even if initially elaborated upon within a different legal framework, is appropriate to be used in the context of the UN Charter as well, given that respect for fundamental human rights constitutes one of the fundamental purposes of the United Nations under Article 1 of the Charter, against which background the provisions of the Charter, such as its Article 105, should be interpreted.[17] UN Charter, Article 105, could then be seen to be endorsing such functionality in relation to immunities as are in accordance with the organization's purposes. As human rights violations are not functionally necessary for the organization's activities, they should be deemed to be outside the scope of its functional immunities.

Moreover, in the Advisory Opinion in *Effect of Awards*, the International Court of Justice (ICJ) has observed that what is specified in the Charter as the organization's purpose was seen as internally applicable in employment disputes as between the UN and its staff members. The establishment of the UN Administrative Tribunal to do justice with respect to the employment claims of UN personnel was required by broader UN purposes to promote justice and individual rights.[18] This reasoning confirms that if an organization aims at higher objectives of justice, it has to guarantee that the same standards are observed in the process of its everyday work. There is no reason why the same equation

---

[16] *Handyside v United Kingdom*, Application No. 5493/72, ECtHR, Judgment of 7 December 1976, para. 48; see also *Silver v United Kingdom*, Application Nos 5947/72, 6205/73, 7052/75, Judgment of 25 March 1983, para. 97.

[17] This also accords with the requirement under 1969 Vienna Convention on the Law of Treaties, Art. 31(1) that a treaty provision should be interpreted in accordance with the object and purpose of that treaty.

[18] [1954] ICJ Reports 57.

should not apply to the organization's relationship to external entities. The extension of the overall relevance of the organization's purposes (in any event an interpretative factor relevant for the interpretation of all provisions of the UN Charter) is also necessary and justified, given that the organization's purposes are a legally relevant interpretative factor that can shed light on issues that are otherwise bound to remain relative, debatable and obscure.

15.4 REGIME OF IMMUNITIES UNDER THE 1946 GENERAL CONVENTION

Article II(2) of the 1946 Convention on the Privileges and Immunities of the United Nations provides, on broader terms, that the United Nations 'shall enjoy immunity from every form of legal process except insofar as in any particular case it has expressly waived its immunity'. Section 22(b) of the 1946 Convention provides that the experts on the UN mission enjoy immunity 'in respect of words spoken or written and acts done by them in the course of the performance of their mission, immunity from legal process of every kind'.

The standards under the UN Charter and the Convention are substantially different. One refers to functional immunity and the other accords absolute immunity to the UN. There is some relationship between the two instruments. The 1946 Convention contains a reference to UN Charter, Article 105 and its functional approach. In its turn, Article 105(3) provides for the possibility that particular treaties elaborate the approach taken under paragraphs (1) and (2) of the same Article. Still, on its face, the absolute immunity standard under the 1946 Convention purports to displace the functional immunity under the Charter, not elaborate it. All this also highlights the possibility of a normative conflict between the two treaties, with the potential to engage UN Charter, Article 103.

The cardinal difference between these two standards is confirmed in practice. The Dutch Supreme Court judgment in the *Srebrenica* case emphasized that the Court of Appeal should have granted immunity to the UN without examining any balance of underlying interests, as the ECtHR had done in *Waite and Kennedy*. The Supreme Court then upheld the absolute immunity of the United Nations,[19] leaving open the issue of

[19] *Mothers of Srebrenica v State of the Netherlands*, Supreme Court, First Division 10/04437 EV/AS, 13 April 2012, paras 4.3.5 and 4.3.6.

the precise impact of Article 105 on its own, and then via Article 103. On the doctrinal plane, and similarly, Amerasinghe does not share the view that the difference between *acta jure imperii* and *acta jure gestionis* could be imported into the 1946 Convention, because the Convention is not shaped around that distinction.[20] Quite simply, a harmonious reading of the two instruments does not work.[21]

There are also some provisions in the 1946 Convention that are unworkable. According to UN Charter, Article 23, the Secretary-General can waive immunity if that would impede the course of justice and the UN's interests would not be jeopardized.[22] Apart from the vagueness of the test that should inform the Secretary-General's judgment in such cases, Article 23 is faulty also because an impediment to the course of justice is the aim of any invocation of immunity. Conversely, any waiver of immunity implies some compromising on the underlying interest of the UN that would be satisfied if immunity was to be upheld.

Brower attempts to read the 1946 Convention immunity standard as reflective of the position taken under the UN Charter, suggesting that:

> one can appreciate concerns that the General Convention implements the functional necessity doctrine through provisions that resemble the doctrine of absolute state immunity. While such claims enjoy a superficial plausibility, they do not reflect a complete understanding of the General Convention. Specifically, they do not account for the countervailing role played by the duty of waiver, which reincorporates the functional necessity doctrine by requiring the Secretary-General to waive unnecessary immunities.[23]

It seems that Brower's position here is flawed. For, waiver operates only as a matter of grace and, therefore, it does not impact or pre-determine the scope of immunities the relevant organization could insist on having as a matter of right and entitlement. Consequently, and purely as a matter of the UN's entitlement, absolute immunity becomes no less absolute just because the entity enjoying it has the right to waive it in some cases, should it please to do so.

---

[20] Amerasinghe, n. 3 above, 322.

[21] One is therefore bound to disagree with Reinisch, n. 13 above, 136–7, that specific applicable instruments must be scrutinized to identify the scope of the functional doctrine.

[22] The pertinent part of Article 23 suggests that 'The Secretary-General shall have the right and the duty to waive the immunity of any expert in any case where, in his opinion, the immunity would impede the course of justice and it can be waived without prejudice to the interests of the United Nations'.

[23] Brower, n. 8 above, 27.

As to the merit of the waiver of immunities under the 1946 Convention, Brower contends that, '[s]tructurally speaking, the General Convention requires the United Nations to waive any immunity that would interrupt the normal judicial processes of member states *unless* it can justify the assertion of immunity on functional necessity grounds'.[24] But if that is true, then the 1946 Convention does not, after all, endorse absolute immunity, and that would indeed be an Article 105-compatible interpretation of the 1946 Convention. However, that interpretation can hold ground only if there is some intelligible standard by reference to which we could identify the meaning of 'functional necessity' shared both by states and the UN. Otherwise, the position will obtain that the UN can auto-determine the meaning of functionality and succeed in having absolute immunity. And also, most importantly, the text of the 1946 Convention, namely its Article 23, does not validate Brower's suggestion that the organization is under a certain duty to waive the immunities available to it under that Convention. The presence in Article 23 of the words 'in his opinion' is essentially a statutory endorsement of the auto-interpretation power of the Secretary-General. There is no jurisprudence to verify the legality of the Secretary-General's Article 23 determinations (or of the lack of making them) against the good faith requirement, although the possibility of that is there.

Last but not least, Article 29(a) of the 1946 Convention provides for the establishment of special mechanisms to resolve 'disputes arising out of contracts or other disputes of a private law character to which the United Nations is a party'.[25] Such alternative mechanism has never been established. This demonstrates that the original conditions on which absolute immunity was granted to the UN have not been genuinely observed, and the original balance of rights and obligations under the 1946 Convention has not been maintained. This factor should not be without implications in terms of the relationship of the 1946 Convention to Article 105 of the UN Charter, as discussed above.

---

24 *Ibid.*72 (emphasis in original).

25 In para. 53 of its submissions in *Cumaraswamy*, the UN conceded that, in principle at least, this requirement matters in the equation, and the Court reiterated (at 89) the same thesis.

15.5 IMMUNITY OF THE ORGANIZATION'S OFFICIALS

Article 18 of the 1946 Convention provides, in its pertinent parts, that 'Officials of the United Nations shall: (a) be immune from legal process in respect of words spoken or written and all acts performed by them in their official capacity'. As the UN Secretary-General's report has clarified, 'the term 'official' in the context of the relevant Conventions includes all members of staff, with the exception of those who are both recruited locally and paid at hourly rates.[26]

The substance of the officials' immunity calls for clarification of the scope of immunity and the yardstick against which it would be measured, as well as of the decision-making authority under, or pursuant to, the 1946 Convention that mentions that term. As Brower suggests, 'the Convention creates immunity only for *official* acts and only permits the Secretary-General to waive immunity for *official* acts, [therefore] the allocation of decision-making authority to municipal courts would pose a serious threat to the independence of international organizations'.[27]

But this confuses two matters that are separate from each other. The interpretation of the 1946 Convention as a treaty requires, in the first place, that an effort should be made to identify what 'official' and 'official capacity' mean. The meaning of these terms is also important for the broader context of immunities, to determine whether the 1946 Convention endorses absolute or functional immunity in relation to UN officials. The problems, indeed 'serious threat' to the organization's interests, would arise if a coherent meaning of these terms could not be identified, or if the practice of auto-determination of the relevant treaty provisions by the UN were to be endorsed.[28] Such auto-interpretation could in principle be carried out both by the UN and by its member-states. Unlike other treaties where organs of the UN appear as impartial supervisory organs (as the UN Human Rights Committee does in relation to the International Covenant on Civil and Political Rights (ICCPR)), the UN Secretary-General here is a party to the controversy arising before

---

26 *Personnel Questions: Respect for the Privileges and Immunities of Officials of the United Nations and the Specialised Agencies and Related Organisations, Report of the Secretary-General*, UN Doc. A.C.5/44/1 (2 November 1989), para. 8.

27 Brower, n. 8 above, 49 (footnotes omitted, emphasis in original).

28 Brower indeed endorses the auto-determination thesis by suggesting that the Secretary-General's waiver practice is an indication of how the functional doctrine works, *ibid.* 70.

national courts. The organization as a deliberative, or adjudicative, framework and the organization as a directly affected entity and party to the dispute, are not one and the same thing.

Brower suggests that 'international officials are not likely to commit intentional violations of municipal tort law in the absence of a colourable claim that they have a right to do so under international law'.[29] But it is difficult to agree that cases ranging from traffic accidents to physical abuse, all met with in the organization's practice, could reasonably be thought of as involving acts authorized by international law. In some cases, moreover, as Brower suggests:

> international officials are likely to commit intentional torts in an official capacity. These cases do not involve mistakes; they involve purposeful activities that international organizations have determined to be part of their *official* work. In other words, intentional tort claims usually involve circumstances in which organizations conclude that they have a right under international law to perform acts that would otherwise be actionable under municipal law.[30]

This line of reasoning is precisely an incidence of the auto-determination approach, in the sense that no discrete meaning accrues to the word 'official' in the 1946 Convention and, instead, the matter could exclusively turn on the officials' self-judging view as to the nature of their own activities. Another, similar, possibility is that, in the real world, in such situations the organizations' officials may think that an act is official, but they might well take a 'procedural' view of it, and do it whatever the merit of the act, assuming that no judicial proceedings will follow.

15.6 FUNCTIONAL DOCTRINE IN JUDICIAL PRACTICE: THE CUMARASWAMY CASE

The examination of the treaty-based functional immunities in the ICJ's jurisprudence[31] has been incomplete, and fallen short of doing justice to the entirety of the distinction between factual and normative dimensions

[29] *Ibid.* 65.

[30] *Ibid.* 64 (emphasis in original).

[31] *Applicability of Article VI, Section 22 of the Convention on the Privileges and Immunities of the United Nations*, Advisory Opinion [1989] ICJ Reports 177; *Difference relating to Immunity from Legal Process of a Special Rapporteur of the Commission on Human Rights*, Advisory Opinion [1999] ICJ Reports 62 (28 April 1999).

of the problem. To illustrate, in the *Cumaraswamy* Opinion, the Court has set out a general thesis that 'The determination whether an agent of the Organization has acted in the course of the performance of his mission depends upon the facts of a particular case'.[32] It is, however, unclear whether 'the facts of a particular case' means that the agent is in fact on the UN mission, or that whatever the agent does while on mission in fact falls within that mission's terms. To illustrate, the Special Rapporteur on the independence of the judiciary could, while on his mission, make statements that either do or do not bear the colour of his mission.

The ICJ in *Cumaraswamy* offered no objective examination of the terms and conditions under Article 22(b) of the 1946 Convention. As the Court's reasoning developed in the text of the Advisory Opinion, the notion of 'the course of the performance of their mission' under Article 22(b) to which the initial reference was made, then became that of the 'capacity as Special Rapporteur' in which, pursuant to the UN Secretary-General's view, the Special Rapporteur was acting;[33] but which notion did not figure in Article 22(b), unlike Article 18 of the 1946 Convention which deals with the UN officials as opposed to its experts. It is not plainly obvious that the two are invariably the same.[34] The Rapporteur may act in the specified role or position, yet in a manner that does not correspond to the aims and tasks of that position. Even if the two notions may overlap to some extent, identity between the two can hardly be maintained across the board in multiple cases involving different contexts. A statement that the standards of impartiality of the judiciary in a particular country is below the desired level, or a statement claiming that an official is a paedophile and therefore should not occupy a particular office, could both be made while the Rapporteur is on his mission. Yet the first statement would, but the second one would not necessarily, be under the colour of his mission.

The Advisory Opinion's treatment of the next issue, the Secretary-General's role, is no less problematic. The Court's initial premise was that:

---

[32] [1999] ICJ Reports 85.

[33] See UN Submissions, paras 17–18, 22, 44; and [1999] ICJ Reports 85, para. 52.

[34] Capacity means 'ability or power to do something' and 'a specified role or position', see *Compact Oxford English Dictionary* (3rd edn, 2005), p. 139; 'mission' refers to assignment, aim or task, see *ibid.* 651.

> In the process of determining whether a particular expert on mission is entitled, in the prevailing circumstances, to the immunity provided for in Section 22(b), the Secretary-General of the United Nations has a *pivotal role* to play. The Secretary-General, as the chief administrative officer of the Organization, has the authority and the responsibility to exercise the necessary protection where required.[35]

But the Court speaks here of the diplomatic protection of the organization's agent and the immunity of that agent as if the former was coextensive and coterminous with the latter. The correct position instead is that the Secretary-General is required to protect the agent, as part of his broader diplomatic protection authority, once it is clear that the agent is properly immune under Article 22(b); not that the Secretary-General can himself auto-determine whether immunities apply or should be asserted and then exercise protection. Otherwise, the Secretary-General would rank as the master of the Convention, and the agent whose immunities are protected by the Convention would be left at the Secretary-General's mercy, in terms of whether that protection could be enjoyed. The outcome would depend on what the UN says, not what the treaty requires. Some greater clarity is therefore required as to whether the Secretary-General's determination is constitutive of the agent's entitlements under the Convention.

In its statement to the ICJ, the UN has indeed relied on the Secretary-General's exclusive authority 'in matters of assertion and waiver of immunity',[36] as a matter of the UN's unilateral and exclusive determination of what the Convention's terms or other applicable standards mean.[37] This does endorse the auto-interpretation approach and the Court does not do much to dispel this impression. The Court adopts a hands-off approach in relation to the position that the Secretary-General and other UN organs may take to individual cases. This is problematic, given that the United Nations is prevailingly in the mood of asserting absolute immunity and, quite apart from whether the *Cumaraswamy* outcome is right or wrong, it is not difficult to figure out where the Secretary-General's broad discretion is likely to lead. The *Cumaraswamy* Opinion has not provided any viable safeguards against such risks.

---

35 [1999] ICJ Reports 84–5 (emphasis added).

36 UN Submissions in *Cumaraswamy*, para. 38 ff.

37 *Ibid*. para. 46: 'It is the long-lasting and uncontested practice of the United Nations that the authority to determine what constitutes an "official" or "unofficial" act is vested exclusively in the Secretary-General and that the question of whether the acts concerned were official acts, cannot consistently with the Convention, be determined by a national court'.

15.7 ORGANIZATION-SPECIFIC RESTRICTIVE DOCTRINE OF IMMUNITIES

15.7.1 Two Possible Tests

It is true that the organization's activities are not governmental in the same sense as those of states.[38] Still, there is ample room for distinguishing between activities that the organization needs to perform as an organization and those which, albeit ultimately serving the purpose of the organization's overall efficiency and success, could still be performed by any private person or entity. After all, with regard to states, it cannot be reasonably contested that the bulk of commercial and economic activities that are obviously outside the scope of any sovereign immunities are those that serve the purpose of the relevant state's prosperity and development.

Immunity is supposed to focus on the nature of the act, not its purpose. Even with state immunities, the genuine separation of sovereign (official) or non-sovereign (non-official) acts, and the requisite avoidance of the degeneration of the restrictive into the absolute doctrine of immunity, is possible only if the focus is maintained only on the properly sovereign nature of the act which cannot be performed by a private person or entity.

Admittedly, thus, the question of whether an act is performed under the colour of public authority of an entity is different from whether it is necessary for the purposes of that entity. But there is one important difference between states and organizations. The purposes of the state may not invariably be supported by the legal framework within which that state operates. However, with organizations which rely on the framework of state delegation of power and competence, purposes are part of the authority – indeed the product of that delegated authority. The organization may not legitimately have any purpose that does not derive from the law that applies to its activities. Given that the organization's immunities also refer to its purposes, their scope is bound to be different from the immunity available to states under the restrictive doctrine, and possibly cover a broader range of acts. Organizations could, arguably, be immune in respect of some acts for which the state would not be

---

[38] Bekker, n. 7 above, 158; also citing, at *ibid.* 154, the UN position that organizational immunities 'are functional and thus reflect their needs, which require complete protection from national jurisdiction', UN Doc. ST/LEG/SER.C/18.

immune. But how far the exact difference between the two standards could go depends on what exactly the relevant organization's 'purposes' are.

15.7.2 Relevance and Ambit of the Organization's Purposes

It is a methodological bottom-line that any coherent purposive functional doctrine of immunity has to refer to a coherent pre-existing standard, as opposed to the organization considering that, then and there, the relevant assertion of immunity is necessary for its purposes. The antecedent purposes should enable the organization to assert immunity, rather than the organization determining, through the assertion of immunity, what these purposes are.

On some interpretations, the 'purposive' approach could only be half a step away from the absolute immunity doctrine. The early doctrinal view was that the distinction between sovereign and commercial activities did not apply to an international organization which is not a sovereign. The General Convention instead provided for the organization's absolute immunity.[39] Along similar lines, Bekker submits that the organization's functions may require the performance of commercial activities that will thereby remain within the organization's official activities and will be covered by its immunity.[40] That amounts precisely to the concession of absolute immunity to organizations, and contradicts Bekker's suggestion that institutional immunities are neither absolute nor restrictive.[41] Reinisch also re-interprets the functional immunity into the absolute one.[42]

Some commercial activities could presumably be sustained by the purposes of organizations, such as entering into contracts.[43] But whether the same could be said for a breach of contract or a tort is doubtful. After

---

[39] A. Ehrenfeld, 'United Nations Immunity Distinguished from Sovereign Immunity' (1958) 52 *ASIL Proceedings* 88 at 92; see also G.H. Glenn, M.M. Kearney and D.J. Padilla, 'Immunities of International Organizations' (1981–82) 22 *Virginia Journal of International Law* 247 at 266–7.

[40] Bekker, n. 7 above, 158.

[41] *Ibid.* 156.

[42] Reinisch, n. 13 above, 139.

[43] In some cases activities of a commercial nature could be determined to be the organization's purpose if member states delegate such purpose to the organization via the constituent instrument or a comparable process. Regarding IFIs, see generally J.H. Glazer, 'A Functional Approach to the International Finance Corporation' (1957) 57 *Columbia Law Review* 1089 at 1097–8.

all, no particular purpose could viably be served both by the entering into a contract and by its abrogation.

Klabbers has got it generally right in suggesting that the broader version of 'purposes' of organizations, such as salvation of mankind, places the doctrine on a dubious footing.[44] However, if we opt for a narrower version of 'purposes', focusing on the purposes and functions of each specific organization, then the doctrine of functional necessity could be more suitably grounded in the framework of positive law, as opposed to the broader, and in essence naturalistic, perspective propagating the higher mission of organizations.

Where do the 'purposes' derive from? It is all too frequently pointed out in the immunities-related discourse that organizations need to function independently as separate persons. What is frequently overlooked is that organizations must function as separate persons strictly on terms of the delegation of institutional powers to organizations by states, through the organizations' constituent instruments. It would be absurd to suggest that an act can be one that is functionally necessary for the organization's operation if it is an act that falls outside that organization's delegated powers and therefore is not one that states parties to the constituent instrument have willed to be an act that the organization in question should be performing in the first place.

It stands to reason to consider that the organization's purposes refer to legitimate purposes as derived from positive law, not those that may be opportunistically identified *in casu* to protect the bureaucracy from any possible interference. The ordinary scope of powers of an organizations should therefore be factored into any viable notion of 'functional necessity'. Purposes of the organizations can justify attributing to them implied powers; these purposes within the meaning of the *Certain Expenses* case, namely, 'the stated purposes of the United Nations'[45] and those under Article 105 of the UN Charter, albeit relating to different areas, refer to the same concept: the purposes inferable from the terms of delegation under the constituent instrument. That could apply to the organization's implied powers as well, for these are necessary for the fulfilment of its express statutory purposes, provided that they do not involve any action contrary to the rules stated in the constituent instrument or any other rule that binds the relevant organization.

---

[44] J. Klabbers, *Introduction to International Institutional Law* (2nd edn, Cambridge University Press, 2009), p. 33.

[45] [1962] ICJ Reports 167.

The rationale for the immunities could thus be that by giving consent to the organization's constituent instrument, states parties must be deemed to have decided to internationalize those matters validly included in the relevant authority of organization and, therefore, as far as that authority goes, they must exempt those matters from their own national jurisdiction.[46] Moreover, as the ECtHR observed in *Al-Jedda v United Kingdom*, the purposes and principles of the United Nations, and hence the object and purpose of the UN Charter, include human rights principles which serve as a limitation on the UN's institutional authority.[47] On this view, the domestic jurisdiction would be limited accordingly, but not in relation to human rights claims.

Reinisch suggests that there is no grey area between the valid exercise of the delegated authority and *ultra vires* activities, for organizations can only act within the limits of their delegated authority.[48] On this approach, either *ultra vires* acts would not be the organization's own acts; or, alternatively, anything the organization would do as a matter of fact would rank as an *intra vires* conduct and then attract immunity. Both options fail to capture the essence of the *ultra vires* doctrine that refers to normative standards to judge the lawfulness of the factual conduct.

An organization can act *ultra vires*, as Article 8 of the Draft Articles on the Responsibility of International Organizations (DARIO) confirms to be the case, and *ultra vires* acts are still organizations' acts if factually performed by the organization or its agent, and thus attributable to the organization.[49] But even if performed in an 'official capacity', the *ultra vires* acts cannot, quite simply, be acts necessary for the achievement of organizational purposes and fall within the functional immunity doctrine. Otherwise, the attribution of an act to the organization would be equated to the organization's immunity for that act, whereupon absolute immunity would obtain, and the rationale for the purposive approach would disappear. The confusion in doctrine regarding this factor may be due to the fact that, while addressing *ultra vires* activities as a matter of DARIO, Article 8, the International Labour Commission (ILC) did not sufficiently

---

46 This is one area in which Brower's above argument could possibly work, and be placed on a recognizable basis under positive law.

47 *Al-Jedda v United Kingdom*, Application No. 27021/08, ECtHR (General Court), Judgment of 7 July 2011.

48 Reinisch, n. 13 above, 139, by reference to Seidl-Hohenveldern's unpublished report to the International Law Association.

49 Draft Articles on the Responsibility of International Organizations (DARIO), A/66/10 [2011] ILC Reports 52.

illustrate the essence and meaning of the distinctly organizational authority of international organizations that neither states nor private entities possess. This authority does not refer to what the organization wants to do or is actually doing, but queries whether whatever the organization does is covered by its authority. The essence of authority is the same for the purposes of both responsibility and immunities and, while responsibility includes conduct of the organization's that exceeds authority, for the purposes of immunity such conduct cannot feasibly be covered by any purposive or functional immunity approach which applies to the same organization, as purposes and functions rely on authority both in terms of their origin and meaning.

The 'procedural' nature of acts covered by immunity cannot, therefore, be so easily be disentangled from the aspects of its substantive legality under the framework of the delegation of powers. Those acts are only functionally necessary which the organization has expressly or impliedly been authorized to do. Serious violations of international law could not be among these, as neither the constituent instruments of organizations nor the mandates of peace-keeping forces contain any authorization of such conduct.

15.7.3 Uniquely Institutional Acts

Another possibility for identifying the essence of the functional test, borrowed from the restrictive state immunity doctrine, could envisage the category of uniquely institutional acts that private entities cannot perform. As the House of Lords held in *I Congreso*, the conduct of a state is not a sovereign act and attracts no immunity if it is an act which could be performed by any private actor, and a state invokes no governmental authority, even if the situation had to do with a highly contingent political context.[50]

The doctrinal contributions have not, so far, provided for a proper mutual comparison of the competing tests. As Singer suggests:

> The fact that an international organization may perform an act in furtherance of its purposes, or within its competence, does not imply that it requires jurisdictional immunity for that act. The two concerns should not be confused. Rather, the municipal courts should look to the two important policy considerations that justify granting jurisdictional immunity to international organizations. First, the organization has a functional need for autonomy in decision making in certain areas. Second, the organization has a functional

[50] *I Congreso* [1983] 1 AC 268, HL.

> need for some level of protection from divergent judgments in municipal courts.[51]

But this is, essentially, to reject the purposive approach and then to revert to the absolute immunity of organizations that follows from the recognition of its autonomy as a category with self-explanatory implications in the area of immunities.

In a way, Singer is right[52] to suggest that organization's immunities cannot be exhaustively stated from the functional or restrictive point of view. For, state immunities cannot be exhaustively listed under the restrictive doctrine either. Yet, in relation to states, that has never been a valid ground for not applying the restrictive doctrine in relation to assessing the nature of particular acts and transactions. There is nothing in the international legal system that makes the same approach categorically unsuitable in relation to international organizations.

Thus, if the restrictive doctrine were to be applied, it would not cover all acts of organizations performed in an 'official capacity' and on duty, but only those which are also uniquely institutional. This would prominently include policy and operational decisions that private entities cannot make, and that consequently are unlikely, as such, to involve a breach of contract, a tort or a crime.

As an illustration, a similar approach was upheld by the ECtHR in relation to state immunity, distinguishing between the organizational policy underlying the arrangement of a foreign embassy that falls within the area of sovereignty and may attract sovereign immunity, and the more specific issue of the embassy's compliance with the employee's contractual rights, which may not.[53] If the *Fogarty* equation were to be applied to organizations, it would protect the genuinely operational dimension intrinsically affiliated with the sphere of uniquely institutional acts and leave the rest of the activities aside. More specifically, there are things that only the organization and peace forces it deploys can do as part of their authority in the area of their deployment: the enactment of regulations and rules of engagement; maintaining cease-fires; monitoring border and disengagement zones; maintaining law and order; enforcing disarmament or demilitarization; or performing the tasks of maintaining the mission as such. Such doctrine of restrictive immunity would not cover human rights and humanitarian law violations, as these would not

[51] Singer, n. 6 above, 163–4.

[52] Singer, n. 6 above, 135.

[53] *Fogarty v United Kingdom*, Application No. 37112/97, ECtHR, 21 November 2001, paras 22, 30, 38.

be uniquely institutional. With state immunity, that distinction is obvious, especially in the jurisprudence of English courts which have kept sovereign immunity narrow to encompass only acts covered by armed forces that have purely sovereign and operational nature.[54]

15.7.4 Relationship Between the Two Tests

The question now is whether the delegation doctrine could rationalize the scope of uniquely institutional acts and thus lead to the convergence between the two above proposed tests. Indirectly, there is such possibility, because uniquely institutional are unique to the operation of organizations with delegated powers. Conversely, it is unlikely that anything covered by the organization's immunity shaped pursuant to the restrictive doctrine in the form of *I Congreso*, *Fogarty*, *Lampen-Wolfe* or *Littrell*, would be either *ultra vires* or not functionally necessary for the operation of an organization.

To such extent, the two tests do overlap. Nevertheless, they are not the same, because the purposive immunity could encompass acts of commercial and private nature that are not uniquely institutional, yet necessary for the organization's legitimate purposes. To illustrate, the lending activities and related financial operations of IFIs, even though otherwise wholly commercial, non-public and non-sovereign, could fall within the statutory competence of the organization. If the applicable standard is functionality and not the absolute doctrine along the above lines, then the organization could not be sued for those lending operations or development projects as such (but could be sued for the action/omission in that process that involves torts of various kinds or human rights violations). Needless to say, none of these two tests could, on any such version, provide immunity for violations of human rights and humanitarian law, whether in terms of prevention obligations or actual deeds.

In relation to international organizations, the difference between the two tests would further emphasize the activities that are not required for uniquely institutional purposes, but are nonetheless ones in which the organization engages due to the legal personality it enjoys as a private law entity under national legal systems. Thus, the organization acts just like any private person, not just in relation to matters that are functionally necessary for it to fulfil its purpose, for instance, hiring office space and staff, but also engaging in profit-related commercial activities. Those

---

[54] *Holland v Lampen-Wolfe* [2000] 3 All ER 845; *Littrell v United States* [1995] 1 WLR 182.

activities necessary for the organization's ordinary administration could not possibly be institutionally unique to the relevant international organization; yet they could be presented as ones functionally necessary for the fulfilment of its purposes, especially given that the requirement of their legal personality, on a domestic plane, follows from UN Charter, Article 104. But such version of immunity could in practice, again, be liable to be turned into the absolute immunity. In any case, the existence of legal personality on a domestic plane does not imply the relevant entity's exemption from the domestic legal process.

Another specific instance in relation to which the two tests may diverge relates to institutional decisions under DARIO, Article 17, adopted through the use of the organization's unique institutional delegated authority.[55] Such decisions are different from mere acts, and it is here that we can see how cross-cutting and mutually reinforcing are the concepts of authority with which the law of responsibility and law of immunities each operate. If such decision were to violate the relevant international law, the purposive test would lead to denying immunity to the organization, because an *ultra vires* decision would not be necessary for the functioning of an organization as a mechanism with delegated powers. The uniquely institutional acts test, on the other hand, would require the grant of immunity specifically for such decisions which, unlike particular acts such as torture or a commercial transaction capable of being performed by states, organizations or private persons alike, are activities that the organization solely and uniquely could perform. For, it is only the organization, not states or private entities, which has such decision-making powers.

In practice, the divergence of the two immunity-related tests in relation to Article 17 decisions is unlikely to be in any acute or urgent need of resolution. It is highly unlikely that the United Nations would be sued domestically for its Chapter VII decisions as such, separate from particular violations of international law that are carried out under the cover of those decisions. But conceptually and normatively, the separation between those framework decisions and particular acts carried out within those frameworks provides an important conceptual and normative flipside to precisely discern and understand where the organization's genuine

[55] DARIO, Art. 17 provides that 'An international organization incurs international responsibility if it circumvents one of its international obligations by adopting a decision binding member States or international organizations to commit an act that would be internationally wrongful if committed by the former organization'.

authority to serve its purposes and functions begins and ends. Consequently, the specific acts performed under the cover of the organization's decision need not always be seen as acts necessary for the organization's purposes and therefore ones for which the organization should be immune.

In relation to UN operations conducted under Chapter VII of the UN Charter, Brower states a peculiar view that:

> when the Security Council supervises military enforcement actions in accordance with Chapter VII of the United Nations Charter, members of the participating forces should not be exposed to municipal court jurisdiction for claims of personal injury and property damage that might otherwise lie under municipal law.[56]

Thus, Brower essentially endorses the same approach as was endorsed in the decision of the ECtHR in *Behrami*, in which the responsibility for acts perpetrated by UNMIK and KFOR were attributed to the United Nations who mandated their presence in Kosovo, not to member states who actually ran these missions' operations and had effective control over what they did.[57]

Note also that Brower speaks of activities *supervised*, not perpetrated by the UN. His argument is thus very far-reaching in the sense of proposing to re-allocate the responsibility of states that would arise under the ordinary principles of attribution of internationally wrongful acts to states pursuant to the ILC's Articles on State Responsibility (which approach professedly diverges from *Behrami*),[58] and then use this as a premise for projecting a consequent legal position that, due to that projected shift in responsibility relations, member states should be protected from domestic adjudication alongside the protection that the UN should enjoy from the domestic legal process. This shows, from the reverse side, the organic connection in the responsibility-related reasoning and immunity-related reasoning. A court pronouncing on one may, even if subconsciously, be pronouncing on the other. And in terms of immunities, one entity would be immune solely because the immunity would be available to the other entity. The soundness of such a position is difficult to substantiate as a matter of positive international law.

---

56 As in Brower, n. 8 above, 64.

57 *Behrami and Saramati v France*, Application Nos 71412/01 and 78166/01, ECtHR, Admissibility Decision of 2 May 2007.

58 See DARIO, n. 49 above. See especially the ILC's Commentary to Draft Article 7, and the negative position it took on *Behrami*.

Brower's position here is too far-reaching to be reconcilable with the governing legal framework, either as a matter of the UN Charter, or of the rules on responsibility. Moreover, in the area relating to human rights violations or other violations of international law, the bulk of cases will be about state activities carried out under an international organization's mandate, as was the case in *Behrami*, unless *Behrami* is still (and counter-factually) presented as being good law. A more recent decision of the ECtHR, in *Jaloud v The Netherlands*, has held that the Dutch military contingent independently engaged the responsibility of the Netherlands under the ECHR, even if the authority and direction of the contingent and its overall presence in Iraq operated on the basis of UN Security Council Resolution 1483(2003), and it was, to some extent, under the operational control of the UK command.[59] This is hardly reconcilable with *Behrami*.

The same approach could broadly apply, for instance, to the World Bank's responsibility for violations associated with the operation of the Bank's development projects. Much of the time, it is the recipient state who perpetrates the relevant violations in the first place, the organization's role being accessory, to be identified by reference to the criteria of foresight and contribution. The primary and most obvious respondent in national proceedings should be the state that perpetrates the relevant violation, rather than the organization under whose mandate, or in collaboration with which, that state acts, the mandate itself being unlikely to authorize those violations.

On balance, a 'no immunity' outcome with regard to organizations under general international law seems to be more plausible than any version of immunities, whether absolute or functional. The functional doctrine enjoys as little inherent authority in international law as does the autonomy-driven version of absolute immunity. But in terms of treaty-based immunities, there is ample room for rationalizing the functional doctrine differently from the absolute immunity, and then for applying in practice such limited immunity even in defiance of the standard suggested in Article II of the 1946 Convention. This latter standard should not be taken at its absolute face value, given that the original contractual balance under the 1946 Convention has never been properly observed.

59 *Jaloud v The Netherlands*, Application No. 47708/08, ECtHR, 20 November 2014, paras 143–51.

15.8 ORGANIZATIONAL IMMUNITIES AND THE EUROPEAN CONVENTION ON HUMAN RIGHTS

The above analysis has established that absolute immunity rests on dubious foundations, not least because 1946 Convention's alternative remedies system has not been established; limited functional immunity is available under UN Charter, Article 105, but not directly under general international law. It is also obvious from all relevant frameworks that if there were a coherent functional theory, it would not be viably supported by the international legal system unless it referred either to *intra vires* acts or to uniquely institutional acts.

The next step of analysis is more complex, and refers to the ECHR's 'equivalent protection' thesis that articulates some elements on which the 'putative' restrictive doctrine may legitimately be premised, such as non-interference with the organization's affairs, the balance of competing interests, the relevance of the individual's position, and the proportionality of interference with individual rights. To illustrate, in the key case of *Waite and Kennedy*, the ECtHR held that the European Space Agency (ESA) was entitled to immunity before German courts and that the limitation of the rights of the applicants under ECHR, Article 6 was thus legitimate. Under the approach articulated in *Waite and Kennedy*, an alternative remedy (such as the ESA Appeals Board in that case) has to be available to aggrieved individuals, before the organization can validly assert its immunity before national courts.[60] Therefore, immunity does not trump the Convention rights, but can be accommodated with these rights to the extent allowed by the doctrine of the margin of appreciation. Similarly, as Gaja has illustrated, national courts have emphasized that immunity of an organization persists if the latter secures jurisdictional protection 'of the same rights and interests in front of an independent and impartial court'.[61]

As is the case with the rest of the 'equivalent protection' area, here too the ECHR's primacy over other international obligations is the underlying rationale.[62] However, in immunity cases, the ECtHR also applies

---

60 *Waite and Kennedy v Germany*, Application No. 28934/95, ECtHR, Judgment of 18 February 1999.

61 *Pistelli*, Italian Court of Cassation, cited in G. Gaja, 'Note on Jurisdictional Immunity of International Organisations' (2006) *ILC Yearbook* 27.

62 See, for confirmation of this approach, *M & Co. v Federal Republic of Germany*, Application No. 13258/87, ECtHR, Judgment of 9 February 1990 (1990) 33 *YB ECHR* 51; *Waite and Kennedy v Germany*, n. 60 above, para. 67; *Matthews v United Kingdom*, Application No. 24833/94, ECtHR, Judgment of 18

the approach that the Convention must be interpreted in harmony with other international obligations. This was illustrated in the *Srebrenica Mothers Foundation* case, in which it was claimed that the UN should not enjoy immunity for its breach of prevention obligations in relation to the crisis in the Balkans. As the Court put it, in terms similar to several previous cases, '[w]hen creating new international obligations, States are assumed not to derogate from their previous obligations'.[63] The Court supported this position by reference to Article 31(3)(c) of the 1969 Vienna Convention on the Law of Treaties (VCLT), as although it 'postdates the United Nations Charter, the General Convention on Privileges and Immunities of the United Nations and the Convention, and is therefore not directly applicable (see Article 4 of the Vienna Convention), the Court must have regard to its provisions in so far as they codify pre-existing international law'.[64]

However, even though VCLT, Article 31(3)(c) requires the Court to take into account the relevant rules of international law in the process of the interpretation of the ECHR – to ascertain what the ECHR provisions on their own mean – it does not mandate the Court to subordinate the ECHR's own requirements to other rules of international law. In other words, if the ECHR requires a particular outcome, and the 1946 Convention requires the opposite outcome, subordinating the former to the latter would not be an interpretation of the ECHR, but the resolution of a normative conflict in favour of the 1946 Convention. Moreover, it is a cardinal requirement under the VCLT that the provisions of the ECHR have to be interpreted effectively, as providing effective protection to individuals, before the issue of the legitimate scope of application of Article 31(3)(c) could be considered. For the rule requiring interpretation according to the ordinary meaning and the object and purpose of the Convention, under Article 31(1), is a priority rule.[65]

February 1999, paras 26–35; *Bosphorus Hava Yolları Turizm v Ireland*, Application No. 45036/98, ECtHR, Judgment of 30 June 2005, paras 155–6; *Soering v United Kingdom*, Application No. 14038/88, ECtHR, Judgment of 7 July 1989; *Al-Saadoon and Mufdhi v United Kingdom*, Application No. 61498/08, ECtHR (Fourth Chamber), Judgment of 2 March 2010; *Capital Bank v Bulgaria*, Application No. 49429/99, ECtHR, Judgment of 24 November 2005, paras 38, 43, 110–11.

[63] *Srebrenica Mothers*, n. 10 above, para. 139(g).

[64] *Ibid.* para. 144.

[65] As the ILC has observed at the drafting stage of what is now VCLT, Art. 31, 'when a treaty is open to two interpretations one of which does and the other does not enable the treaty to have appropriate effects, good faith and the objects

All this obviously becomes more imperative if the 'equivalent protection' requirement is borne in mind. The Court has mentioned previous cases from that category, yet found that:

> The present case is different from all those mentioned. At its root is a dispute between the applicants and the United Nations based on the use by the Security Council of its powers under Chapter VII of the United Nations Charter.

Moreover:

> since operations established by United Nations Security Council resolutions under Chapter VII of the United Nations Charter are fundamental to the mission of the United Nations to secure international peace and security, the Convention cannot be interpreted in a manner which would subject the acts and omissions of the Security Council to domestic jurisdiction without the accord of the United Nations. To bring such operations within the scope of domestic jurisdiction would be to allow individual States, through their courts, to interfere with the fulfilment of the key mission of the United Nations in this field, including with the effective conduct of its operations.[66]

In addition, the Court stated that it saw:

> no reason to reach a different finding as regards the immunity enjoyed by the United Nations in the present case, especially since – unlike the acts impugned in the *Jurisdictional Immunities* case – the matters imputed to the United Nations in the present case, however they may have to be judged, ultimately derived from resolutions of the Security Council acting under Chapter VII of the United Nations Charter and *therefore had a basis in international law* (emphasis added).

An adverse inference from this reasoning could be that it is actually not the immunity of international organizations (or any immunity at all) that makes the difference in this case, but the additional factor of Chapter VII's involvement. But the Court's broader handling of the relationship between the ECHR and the UN Charter, including Resolutions adopted on the basis of the latter, is no less problematic. To say the least, the 'matters' for which immunity of the United Nations was approved did not derive from the Security Council Resolutions. The Court engaged in no meaningful interpretation of any Security Council Resolution to see

---

and purposes of the treaty demand that the former interpretation should be adopted', (1966) II *YB ILC* 219.

[66] *Srebrenica Mothers*, n. 10 above, paras 152–4.

whether it authorized the acts that were complained of against the Netherlands.

The issue of the reality (or the lack of it) of the Security Council's support for underlying acts should, no doubt, count in the equation as to which competing interests have to be weighed up and balanced in terms of the ECHR-specific assessment of necessity and proportionality. Needless to say, the UN's abandonment of victims in Srebrenica could not reasonably be presented as 'the key mission of the United Nations in this field', or conduct that the UN had either mandated or foreseen. In the absence of demonstrating collusion between the UN and the Dutch government in relation to what was done in Srebrenica, the role of the UN is entirely separate from that of the Netherlands. Consequently, there was no reason to conceptualize this situation as one relating to the UN's immunity for the Dutchbat's specific conduct; unless, of course, the UN, rather than the Dutch government, is liable for that specific conduct, which possibility indeed follows from *Behrami*, but has correctly and convincingly been rejected both by the ILC and by Dutch courts. The interdependence between the law of responsibility and law of immunities is borne out by this dimension as well.

The next issue relates to the requirement under the ECHR that the individual's position and interest should be properly considered in 'equivalent protection' cases as a necessary part of any balance being drawn. As the ECtHR's other cases indicate, this may require addressing the precise intention of the Security Council, the actual application of its relevant Resolution, or even declining to give effect to its Resolutions when the fundamental guarantees under the ECHR are at stake. Moreover, and pursuant to *Al-Jedda v United Kingdom*, the ECHR rights can be read into the purposes and principles of the UN to see whether the proper interpretation of UN Charter, Article 105 will lead to such immunities as prevent litigation to vindicate fundamental human rights.

Yet another issue relates to the ECtHR's handling of the issue of alternative remedies. While the Court in *Srebrenica* acknowledged the requirements under *Waite and Kennedy*, it also referred to the ICJ's decision in *Germany v Italy*, where the immunity of Germany were upheld for war crimes even if no alternative forum was made available to victims to obtain justice. The ECtHR has preferred the ICJ's approach and added that, 'As regards international organisations, this Court's judgments in *Waite and Kennedy* and *Beer and Regan* cannot be interpreted in such absolute terms either'.[67] This begs the question as to

[67] *Ibid.* paras 164–5.

what in reality remains of the 'equivalent protection' standard under ECHR, Article 6.

The same query could be raised in relation to the relevance of Article 29 of the 1946 Convention. According to the ICJ:

> the United Nations has not, until now, made provision for 'modes of settlement' appropriate to the dispute here in issue. Regardless of whether Article VIII, section 29 of the Convention on the Privileges and Immunities of the United Nations can be construed so as to require a dispute settlement body to be set up in the present case, this state of affairs is not imputable to the Netherlands.

But such a non-imputation thesis is questionable, because Article 29 is precisely about the conditions on which the Netherlands is bound to comply with the 1946 Convention, and whether it complies with it compatibly with ECHR, Article 6 and the 'equivalent protection' imperative.

There is no reason to regard the 1946 UN Convention as exempted from supervision under the ECHR standard on 'equivalent protection', if the UN Charter itself is not, as several cases have demonstrated. The opposite approach would inevitably be premised on the position that the ECHR standard of protection gives way to the requirements under another treaty, and the ECHR would be normatively deferred to the 1946 Convention. The proper application of the 'equivalent protection' thesis would have led the ECtHR to the conclusion that the UN has failed to introduce the alternative protection mechanism, whereby it would have turned the conditional immunity accorded to it under the 1946 Convention into absolute immunity, and therefore its system of dealing with the issues at hand was manifestly deficient. The matter would then, immunities-wise, revert to UN Charter, Article 105, under which the immunity is functional in any event and can more easily be factored into the proportionality equation under the relevant ECHR provisions. Depending on the circumstances, immunity under that standard would be granted or denied.

One pertinent circumstance in the case at hand was that the responsibility of the Netherlands for the same events had been accepted by the Dutch court, and the victims therefore were not left without any possible remedy. The Court could have factored that into the application of the *Waite and Kennedy* test of proportionality and possibly upheld the UN's immunity on those grounds, instead of distancing from it on blanket terms, and thereby compromising on the 'equivalent protection' requirement, with the outcome that ECHR, Article 6 has been deferred to the organization's absolute immunity resting on dubious normative foundations. Had the Court, instead of blindly following the far-reaching *Behrami* paradigm, properly separated the particular acts of the state from the overall UN framework within which those acts were performed, it would have been able to base its reasoning more on the categories related to attribution, and less on those related to immunity. In this way, a similar result could have been arrived at without ruining much of what the decades-long ECHR practice had been building on in terms of protecting individuals who do not find adequate protection within the framework of international organizations.

15.9 CONCLUSION

It is an irony that, despite so much practice and doctrinal reasoning, there may be no commonly shared grounds as to on what grounds and for what acts international organizations should enjoy immunity from national jurisdictions. As a common-sense matter, this may result in uncertainty; as a matter of positivist legal reasoning, this is merely the absence of the organizations' entitlement to immunity under general international law. The problem, incidental to this, is that the unresolved rationales of general principles, and of individual decisions, in the area of immunities leave room for poorly reasoned judicial decisions, focusing more on the need to handle situations then and there, rather than maintaining the coherence of the legal system of which international tribunals are constituent elements. The upholding of immunities of international organizations in the absence of alternative proceedings, for instance as required under Article 29 of the General Convention, is yet another incidence of the functionality doctrine effectively degenerating, in practice, into the organizations' absolute immunity from domestic legal proceedings.

Index